T0251313

Big Data Computing

Big Data Computing

Edited by
Rajendra Akerkar
Western Norway Research Institute
Sogndal, Norway

CRC Press
Taylor & Francis Group
Boca Raton London New York

CRC Press is an imprint of the
Taylor & Francis Group, an **informa** business

A CHAPMAN & HALL BOOK

CRC Press
Taylor & Francis Group
6000 Broken Sound Parkway NW, Suite 300
Boca Raton, FL 33487-2742

© 2014 by Taylor & Francis Group, LLC
CRC Press is an imprint of Taylor & Francis Group, an Informa business

No claim to original U.S. Government works

Version Date: 20130916

International Standard Book Number-13: 978-1-4665-7837-1 (Hardback)

Library of Congress Cataloging-in-Publication Data

Big data computing / editor, Rajendra Akerkar.
    pages cm
  Includes bibliographical references and index.
  ISBN 978-1-4665-7837-1 (hardback)
  1. Database management. 2. Data mining. 3. Big data. I. Akerkar, Rajendra.

QA76.9.D3B52796 2014
006.3'12--dc23
                              2013037013

Visit the Taylor & Francis Web site at
http://www.taylorandfrancis.com

and the CRC Press Web site at
http://www.crcpress.com

To

All the visionary minds who have helped create a modern data science profession

Contents

Section I Introduction

Section II Semantic Technologies and Big Data

Section III Big Data Processing

Section IV Big Data and Business

Section V Big Data Applications

Preface

In the international marketplace, businesses, suppliers, and customers create and consume vast amounts of information. Gartner* predicts that enterprise data in all forms will grow up to 650% over the next five years. According to IDC,† the world's volume of data doubles every 18 months. Digital information is doubling every 1.5 years and will exceed 1000 exabytes next year according to the MIT Centre for Digital Research. In 2011, medical centers held almost 1 billion terabytes of data. That is almost 2000 billion file cabinets' worth of information. This deluge of data, often referred to as *Big Data*, obviously creates a challenge to the business community and data scientists.

The term *Big Data* refers to data sets the size of which is beyond the capabilities of current database technology. It is an emerging field where innovative technology offers alternatives in resolving the inherent problems that appear when working with massive data, offering new ways to reuse and extract value from information.

Businesses and government agencies aggregate data from numerous private and/or public data sources. *Private data* is information that any organization exclusively stores that is available only to that organization, such as employee data, customer data, and machine data (e.g., user transactions and customer behavior). *Public data* is information that is available to the public for a fee or at no charge, such as credit ratings, social media content (e.g., LinkedIn, Facebook, and Twitter). Big Data has now reached every sector in the world economy. It is transforming competitive opportunities in every industry sector including banking, healthcare, insurance, manufacturing, retail, wholesale, transportation, communications, construction, education, and utilities. It also plays key roles in trade operations such as marketing, operations, supply chain, and new business models. It is becoming rather evident that enterprises that fail to use their data efficiently are at a large competitive disadvantage from those that can analyze and act on their data. The possibilities of Big Data continue to evolve swiftly, driven by innovation in the underlying technologies, platforms, and analytical capabilities for handling data, as well as the evolution of behavior among its users as increasingly humans live digital lives.

It is interesting to know that Big Data is different from the conventional data models (e.g., relational databases and data models, or conventional governance models). Thus, it is triggering organizations' concern as they try to separate information nuggets from the data heap. The conventional models of structured, engineered data do not adequately reveal the realities of Big

---

* http://www.gartner.com/it/content/1258400/1258425/january_6_techtrends_rpaquet.pdf
† http://www.idc.com/

Data. The key to leveraging Big Data is to realize these differences before expediting its use. The most noteworthy difference is that data are typically governed in a centralized manner, but Big Data is self-governing. Big Data is created either by a rapidly expanding universe of machines or by users of highly varying expertise. As a result, the composition of traditional data will naturally vary considerably from Big Data. The composition of data serves a specific purpose and must be more durable and structured, whereas Big Data will cover many topics, but not all topics will yield useful information for the business, and thus they will be sparse in relevancy and structure.

The technology required for Big Data computing is developing at a satisfactory rate due to market forces and technological evolution. The ever-growing enormous amount of data, along with advanced tools of exploratory data analysis, data mining/machine learning, and data visualization, offers a whole new way of understanding the world.

Another interesting fact about Big Data is that not everything that is considered "Big Data" is in fact Big Data. One needs to explore deep into the scientific aspects, such as analyzing, processing, and storing huge volumes of data. That is the only way of using tools effectively. Data developers/scientists need to know about analytical processes, statistics, and machine learning. They also need to know how to use specific data to program algorithms. The core is the analytical side, but they also need the scientific background and *in-depth* technical knowledge of the tools they work with in order to gain control of huge volumes of data. There is no one tool that offers this *per se.*

As a result, the main challenge for Big Data computing is to find a novel solution, keeping in mind the fact that data sizes are always growing. This solution should be applicable for a long period of time. This means that the key condition a solution has to satisfy is *scalability*. Scalability is the ability of a system to accept increased input volume without impacting the profits; that is, the gains from the input increment should be proportional to the increment itself. For a system to be totally scalable, the size of its input should not be a design parameter. Pushing the system designer to consider all possible deployment sizes to cope with different input sizes leads to a scalable architecture without primary bottlenecks. Yet, apart from scalability, there are other requisites for a Big Data–intensive computing system.

Although *Big Data* is an emerging field in data science, there are very few books available in the market. This book provides authoritative insights and highlights valuable lessons learnt by authors—with experience.

Some universities in North America and Europe are doing their part to feed the need for analytics skills in this era of Big Data. In recent years, they have introduced master of science degrees in Big Data analytics, data science, and business analytics. Some contributing authors have been involved in developing a course curriculum in their respective institution and country. The number of courses on "Big Data" will increase worldwide because it is becoming a key basis of competition, underpinning new waves of productivity growth, innovation, and consumer surplus, according to a research by *MGI and McKinsey's Business Technology Office.*[*]

The main features of this book can be summarized as

1. It describes the contemporary state of the art in a new field of Big Data computing.
2. It presents the latest developments, services, and main players in this explosive field.
3. Contributors to the book are prominent researchers from academia and practitioners from industry.

Organization

This book comprises five sections, each of which covers one aspect of Big Data computing. Section I focuses on what Big Data is, why it is important, and how it can be used. Section II focuses on semantic technologies and Big Data. Section III focuses on Big Data processing—tools, technologies, and methods essential to analyze Big Data efficiently. Section IV deals with business and economic perspectives. Finally, Section V focuses on various stimulating Big Data applications. Below is a brief outline with more details on what each chapter is about.

Section I: Introduction

Chapter 1 provides an approach to address the problem of "understanding" Big Data in an effective and efficient way. The idea is to make adequately grained and expressive knowledge representations and fact collections that evolve naturally, triggered by new tokens of relevant data coming along. The chapter also presents primary considerations on assessing fitness in an evolving knowledge ecosystem.

Chapter 2 then gives an overview of the main features that can characterize architectures for solving a Big Data problem, depending on the source of data, on the type of processing required, and on the application context in which it should be operated.

---

[*] http://www.mckinsey.com/Insights/MGI/Research/Technology_and_Innovation/Big_data_The_next_frontier_for_innovation

Chapter 3 discusses Big Data from three different standpoints: the business, the technological, and the social. This chapter lists some relevant initiatives and selected thoughts on Big Data.

Section II: Semantic Technologies and Big Data

Chapter 4 presents foundations of Big Semantic Data management. The chapter sketches a route from the current data deluge, the concept of Big Data, and the need of machine-processable semantics on the Web. Further, this chapter justifies different management problems arising in Big Semantic Data by characterizing their main stakeholders by role and nature.

A number of challenges arising in the context of Linked Data in Enterprise Integration are covered in Chapter 5. A key prerequisite for addressing these challenges is the establishment of efficient and effective link discovery and data integration techniques, which scale to large-scale data scenarios found in the enterprise. This chapter also presents the transformation step of Linked Data Integration by two algorithms.

Chapter 6 proposes steps toward the solution of the data access problem that end-users usually face when dealing with Big Data. The chapter discusses the state of the art in ontology-based data access (OBDA) and explains why OBDA is the superior approach to the data access challenge posed by Big Data. It also explains why the field of OBDA is currently not yet sufficiently complete to deal satisfactorily with these problems, and it finally presents thoughts on escalating OBDA to a level where it can be well deployed to Big Data.

Chapter 7 addresses large-scale semantic interoperability problems of data in the domain of public sector administration and proposes practical solutions to these problems by using semantic technologies in the context of Web services and open data. This chapter also presents a case of the Estonian semantic interoperability framework of state information systems and related data interoperability solutions.

Section III: Big Data Processing

Chapter 8 presents a new way of query processing for Big Data where data exploration becomes a first-class citizen. Data exploration is desirable when new big chunks of data arrive speedily and one needs to react quickly. This chapter focuses on database systems technology, which for several years has been the prime data-processing tool.

Chapter 9 explores the MapReduce model, a programming model used to develop largely parallel applications that process and generate large amounts of data. This chapter also discusses how MapReduce is implemented in Hadoop and provides an overview of its architecture.

A particular class of stream-based joins, namely, a join of a single stream with a traditional relational table, is discussed in Chapter 10. Two available stream-based join algorithms are investigated in this chapter.

Section IV: Big Data and Business

Chapter 11 provides the economic value of Big Data from a macro- and a microeconomic perspective. The chapter illustrates how technology and new skills can nurture opportunities to derive benefits from large, constantly growing, dispersed data sets and how semantic interoperability and new licensing strategies will contribute to the uptake of Big Data as a business enabler and a source of value creation.

Nowadays businesses are enhancing their business intelligence practices to include predictive analytics and data mining. This combines the best of strategic reporting and basic forecasting with advanced operational intelligence and decision-making functions. Chapter 12 discusses how Big Data technologies, advanced analytics, and business intelligence (BI) are interrelated. This chapter also presents various areas of advanced analytic technologies.

Section V: Big Data Applications

The final section of the book covers application topics, starting in Chapter 13 with novel concept-level approaches to opinion mining and sentiment analysis that allow a more efficient passage from (unstructured) textual information to (structured) machine-processable data, in potentially any domain.

Chapter 14 introduces the *spChains* framework, a modular approach to support mastering of complex event processing (CEP) queries in an abridged, but effective, manner based on stream processing block composition. The approach aims at unleashing the power of CEP systems for teams having reduced insights into CEP systems.

Real-time electricity metering operated at subsecond data rates in a grid with 20 million nodes originates more than 5 petabytes daily. The requested decision-making timeframe in SCADA systems operating load shedding might be lower than 100 milliseconds. Chapter 15 discusses the real-life optimization task and the data management approach permitting a solution to the issue.

Chapter 16 presents an innovative outlook to the scaling of geographical space using large street networks involving both cities and countryside. Given a street network of an entire country, the chapter proposes to decompose the street network into individual blocks, each of which forms a minimum ring or cycle such as city blocks and field blocks. The chapter further elaborates the power of the block perspective in reflecting the patterns of geographical space.

Chapter 17 presents the influence of recent advances in natural language processing on business knowledge life cycles and processes of knowledge management. The chapter also sketches envisaged developments and market impacts related to the integration of semantic technology and knowledge management.

Intended Audience

The aim of this book is to be accessible to researchers, graduate students, and to application-driven practitioners who work in *data science* and related fields. This edited book requires no previous exposure to large-scale data analysis or NoSQL tools. Acquaintance with traditional databases is an added advantage.

This book provides the reader with a broad range of Big Data concepts, tools, and techniques. A wide range of research in Big Data is covered, and comparisons between state-of-the-art approaches are provided. This book can thus help researchers from related fields (such as databases, data science, data mining, machine learning, knowledge engineering, information retrieval, information systems), as well as students who are interested in entering this field of research, to become familiar with recent research developments and identify open research challenges on Big Data. This book can help practitioners to better understand the current state of the art in Big Data techniques, concepts, and applications.

The technical level of this book also makes it accessible to students taking advanced undergraduate level courses on Big Data or Data Science. Although such courses are currently rare, with the ongoing challenges that the areas of intelligent information/data management pose in many organizations in both the public and private sectors, there is a demand worldwide for graduates with skills and expertise in these areas. It is hoped that this book helps address this demand.

In addition, the goal is to help policy-makers, developers and engineers, data scientists, as well as individuals, navigate the new Big Data landscape.

I believe it can trigger some new ideas for practical Big Data applications.

Acknowledgments

The organization and the contents of this edited book have benefited from our outstanding contributors. I am very proud and happy that these researchers agreed to join this project and prepare a chapter for this book. I am also very pleased to see this materialize in the way I originally envisioned. I hope this book will be a source of inspiration to the readers. I especially wish to express my sincere gratitude to all the authors for their contribution to this project.

I thank the anonymous reviewers who provided valuable feedback and helpful suggestions.

I also thank Aastha Sharma, David Fausel, Rachel Holt, and the staff at CRC Press (Taylor & Francis Group), who supported this book project right from the start.

Last, but not least, a very big thanks to my colleagues at Western Norway Research Institute (Vestlandsforsking, Norway) for their constant encouragement and understanding.

I wish all readers a fruitful time reading this book, and hope that they experience the same excitement as I did—and still do—when dealing with *Data*.

Rajendra Akerkar

Editor

Rajendra Akerkar is professor and senior researcher at Western Norway Research Institute (Vestlandsforsking), Norway, where his main domain of research is semantic technologies with the aim of combining theoretical results with high-impact real-world solutions. He also holds visiting academic assignments in India and abroad. In 1997, he founded and chaired the Technomathematics Research Foundation (TMRF) in India.

His research and teaching experience spans over 23 years in academia including different universities in Asia, Europe, and North America. His research interests include ontologies, semantic technologies, knowledge systems, large-scale data mining, and intelligent systems.

He received DAAD fellowship in 1990 and is also a recipient of the prestigious BOYSCASTS Young Scientist award of the Department of Science and Technology, Government of India, in 1997. From 1998 to 2001, he was a UNESCO-TWAS associate member at the Hanoi Institute of Mathematics, Vietnam. He was also a DAAD visiting professor at Universität des Saarlandes and University of Bonn, Germany, in 2000 and 2007, respectively.

Dr. Akerkar serves as editor-in-chief of the *International Journal of Computer Science & Applications* (*IJCSA*) and as an associate editor of the *International Journal of Metadata, Semantics, and Ontologies* (*IJMSO*). He is co-organizer of several workshops and program chair of the international conferences ISACA, ISAI, ICAAI, and WIMS. He has co-authored 13 books, approximately 100 research papers, co-edited 2 e-books, and edited 5 volumes of international conferences. He is also actively involved in several international ICT initiatives and research & development projects and has been for more than 16 years.

Contributors

Rajendra Akerkar
Western Norway Research Institute
Sogndal, Norway

Mario Arias
Digital Enterprise Research Institute
National University of Ireland
Galway, Ireland

Sören Auer
Enterprise Information Systems
    Department
Institute of Computer Science III
Rheinische Friedrich-Wilhelms-
    Universität Bonn
Bonn, Germany

Pierfrancesco Bellini
Distributed Systems and Internet
    Technology
Department of Systems and
    Informatics
University of Florence
Firenze, Italy

Dario Bonino
Department of Control and
    Computer Engineering
Polytechnic University of Turin
Turin, Italy

Diego Calvanese
Department of Computer Science
Free University of Bozen-Bolzano
Bolzano, Italy

Erik Cambria
Department of Computer Science
National University of Singapore
Singapore

Giuseppe Caragnano
Advanced Computing and
    Electromagnetic Unit
Istituto Superiore Mario Boella
Torino, Italy

Michael Cochez
Faculty of Information
    Technology
University of Jyväskylä
Jyväskylä, Finland

Fulvio Corno
Department of Control and
    Computer Engineering
Polytechnic University of Turin
Turin, Italy

Dipankar Das
Department of Computer
    Science
National University of Singapore
Singapore

Luigi De Russis
Department of Control and
    Computer Engineering
Polytechnic University of Turin
Turin, Italy

Mariano di Claudio
Department of Systems
    and Informatics
University of Florence
Firenze, Italy

Gillian Dobbie
Department of Computer Science
The University of Auckland
Auckland, New Zealand

Vadim Ermolayev
Zaporozhye National University
Zaporozhye, Ukraine

Javier D. Fernández
Department of Computer Science
University of Valladolid
Valladolid, Spain

Philipp Frischmuth
Department of Computer Science
University of Leipzig
Leipzig, Germany

Martin Giese
Department of Computer Science
University of Oslo
Oslo, Norway

Claudio Gutiérrez
Department of Computer
    Science
University of Chile
Santiago, Chile

Peter Haase
Fluid Operations AG
Walldorf, Germany

Hele-Mai Haav
Institute of Cybernetics
Tallinn University of
    Technology
Tallinn, Estonia

Ian Horrocks
Department of Computer Science
Oxford University
Oxford, United Kingdom

Stratos Idreos
Dutch National Research Center
    for Mathematics and Computer
    Science (CWI)
Amsterdam, the Netherlands

Yannis Ioannidis
Department of Computer Science
National and Kapodistrian
    University of Athens
Athens, Greece

Bin Jiang
Department of Technology
    and Built Environment
University of Gävle
Gävle, Sweden

Monika Jungemann-Dorner
Senior International Project
    Manager
Verband der Verein
    Creditreform eV
Neuss, Germany

Jakub Klimek
Department of Computer
    Science
University of Leipzig
Leipzig, Germany

Herald Kllapi
Department of Computer Science
National and Kapodistrian
    University of Athens
Athens, Greece

Manolis Koubarakis
Department of Computer
    Science
National and Kapodistrian
    University of Athens
Athens, Greece

Peep Küngas
Institute of Computer Science
University of Tartu
Tartu, Estonia

Maurizio Lenzerini
Department of Computer
  Science
Sapienza University of Rome
Rome, Italy

Xintao Liu
Department of Technology
  and Built Environment
University of Gävle
Gävle, Sweden

Miguel A. Martínez-Prieto
Department of Computer
  Science
University of Valladolid
Valladolid, Spain

Ralf Möller
Department of Computer
  Science
TU Hamburg-Harburg
Hamburg, Germany

Lorenzo Mossucca
Istituto Superiore Mario Boella
Torino, Italy

Mariano Rodriguez Muro
Department of Computer Science
Free University of Bozen-Bolzano
Bolzano, Italy

M. Asif Naeem
Department of Computer Science
The University of Auckland
Auckland, New Zealand

Paolo Nesi
Department of Systems
  and Informatics
Distributed Systems and Internet
  Technology
University of Florence
Firenze, Italy

Axel-Cyrille Ngonga Ngomo
Department of Computer Science
University of Leipzig
Leipzig, Germany

Daniel Olsher
Department of Computer Science
National University of Singapore
Singapore

Özgür Özçep
Department of Computer Science
TU Hamburg-Harburg
Hamburg, Germany

Tassilo Pellegrin
Semantic Web Company
Vienna, Austria

Jordà Polo
Barcelona Supercomputing Center
  (BSC)
Technical University of Catalonia
  (UPC)
Barcelona, Spain

Dheeraj Rajagopal
Department of Computer Science
National University of Singapore
Singapore

Nadia Rauch
Department of Systems
  and Informatics
University of Florence
Firenze, Italy

Riccardo Rosati
Department of Computer Science
Sapienza University of Rome
Rome, Italy

Pietro Ruiu
Istituto Superiore Mario Boella
Torino, Italy

Rudolf Schlatte
Department of Computer
    Science
University of Oslo
Oslo, Norway

Michael Schmidt
Fluid Operations AG
Walldorf, Germany

Mikhail Simonov
Advanced Computing and
    Electromagnetics Unit
Istituto Superiore Mario Boella
Torino, Italy

Ahmet Soylu
Department of Computer
    Science
University of Oslo
Oslo, Norway

Marcus Spies
Ludwig-Maximilians University
Munich, Germany

Vagan Terziyan
Department of Mathematical
    Information Technology
University of Jyväskylä
Jyväskylä, Finland

Olivier Terzo
Advanced Computing and
    Electromagnetics Unit
Istituto Superiore Mario Boella
Torino, Italy

Arild Waaler
Department of Computer Science
University of Oslo
Oslo, Norway

Gerald Weber
Department of Computer Science
The University of Auckland
Auckland, New Zealand

Roberto V. Zicari
Department of Computer Science
Goethe University
Frankfurt, Germany

Section I

Introduction

1

Toward Evolving Knowledge Ecosystems for Big Data Understanding

Vadim Ermolayev, Rajendra Akerkar, Vagan Terziyan,
and Michael Cochez

CONTENTS

Introduction

Big Data is a phenomenon that leaves a rare information professional negligent these days. Remarkably, application demands and developments in the context of related disciplines resulted in technologies that boosted data generation and storage at unprecedented scales in terms of volumes and rates. To mention just a few facts reported by Manyika et al. (2011): a disk drive capable of storing all the world's music could be purchased for about US $600; 30 billion of content pieces are shared monthly only at Facebook (facebook.com). Exponential growth of data volumes is accelerated by a dramatic increase in social networking applications that allow nonspecialist users create a huge amount of content easily and freely. Equipped with rapidly evolving mobile devices, a user is becoming a nomadic gateway boosting the generation of additional real-time sensor data. The emerging Internet of Things makes every thing a data or content, adding billions of additional artificial and autonomic sources of data to the overall picture. Smart spaces, where people, devices, and their infrastructure are all loosely connected, also generate data of unprecedented volumes and with velocities rarely observed before. An expectation is that valuable information will be extracted out of all these data to help improve the quality of life and make our world a better place.

Society is, however, left bewildered about how to use all these data efficiently and effectively. For example, a topical estimate for the number of a need for data-savvy managers to take full advantage of Big Data in the United States is 1.5 million (Manyika et al. 2011). A major challenge would be finding a balance between the two evident facets of the whole Big Data adventure: (a) the more data we have, the more potentially useful patterns it may include and (b) the more data we have, the less the hope is that any machine-learning algorithm is capable of discovering these patterns in an acceptable time frame. Perhaps because of this intrinsic conflict, many experts consider that this Big Data not only brings one of the biggest challenges, but also a most exciting opportunity in the recent 10 years (cf. Fan et al. 2012b)

The avalanche of Big Data causes a conceptual divide in minds and opinions. Enthusiasts claim that, faced with massive data, a scientific approach "... hypothesize, model, test—is becoming obsolete. ... Petabytes allow us to say: 'Correlation is enough.' We can stop looking for models. We can analyze the data without hypotheses about what it might show. We can throw the numbers into the biggest computing clusters the world has ever seen and let statistical algorithms find patterns ..." (Anderson 2008). Pessimists, however, point out that Big Data provides "... destabilising amounts of knowledge and information that lack the regulating force of philosophy" (Berry 2011). Indeed, being abnormally big does not yet mean being healthy and wealthy and should be treated appropriately (Figure 1.1): a diet, exercise, medication, or even surgery (philosophy). Those data sets, for which systematic health treatment is ignored in favor of correlations, will die sooner—as useless. There is a hope, however, that holistic integration of evolving algorithms, machines, and people reinforced by research effort across many domains will guarantee required fitness of Big Data, assuring proper quality at right time (Joseph 2012).

Mined correlations, though very useful, may hint about an answer to a "what," but not "why" kind of questions. For example, if Big Data about Royal guards and their habits had been collected in the 1700s' France, one could mine today that all musketeers who used to have red Burgundy regularly for dinners have not survived till now. Pity, red Burgundy was only one of many and a very minor problem. A scientific approach is needed to infer real reasons—the work currently done predominantly by human analysts.

Effectiveness and efficiency are the evident keys in Big Data analysis. Cradling the gems of knowledge extracted out of Big Data would only be effective if: (i) not a single important fact is left in the burden—which means completeness and (ii) these facts are faceted adequately for further inference—which means expressiveness and granularity. Efficiency may be interpreted as the ratio of spent effort to the utility of result. In Big Data analytics, it could be straightforwardly mapped to timeliness. If a result is not timely, its utility (Ermolayev et al. 2004) may go down to zero or even far below in seconds to milliseconds for some important industrial applications such as technological process or air traffic control.

Notably, increasing effectiveness means increasing the effort or making the analysis computationally more complex, which negatively affects efficiency.

FIGURE 1.1
Evolution of data collections—dimensions (see also Figure 1.3) have to be treated with care. (Courtesy of Vladimir Ermolayev.)

Finding a balanced solution with a sufficient degree of automation is the challenge that is not yet fully addressed by the research community.

One derivative problem concerns knowledge extracted out of Big Data as the result of some analytical processing. In many cases, it may be expected that the knowledge mechanistically extracted out of Big Data will also be big. Therefore, taking care of Big Knowledge (which has more value than the source data) would be at least of the same importance as resolving challenges associated with Big Data processing. Uplifting the problem to the level of knowledge is inevitable and brings additional complications such as resolving contradictory and changing opinions of everyone on everything. Here, an adequate approach in managing the authority and reputation of "experts" will play an important role (Weinberger 2012).

This chapter offers a possible approach in addressing the problem of "understanding" Big Data in an effective and efficient way. The idea is making adequately grained and expressive knowledge representations and fact collections evolve naturally, triggered by new tokens of relevant data coming along. Pursuing this way would also imply conceptual changes in the Big Data Processing stack. A refined semantic layer has to be added to it for providing adequate interfaces to interlink horizontal layers and enable knowledge-related functionality coordinated in top-down and bottom-up directions.

The remainder of the chapter is structured as follows. The "Motivation and Unsolved Issues" section offers an illustrative example and the analysis of the demand for understanding Big Data. The "State of Technology, Research, and Development in Big Data Computing" section reviews the relevant research on using semantic and related technologies for Big Data processing and outlines our approach to refine the processing stack. The "Scaling with a Traditional Database" section focuses on how the basic data storage and management layer could be refined in terms of scalability, which is necessary for improving efficiency/effectiveness. The "Knowledge Self-Management and Refinement through Evolution" section presents our approach, inspired by the mechanisms of natural evolution studied in evolutionary biology. We focus on a means of arranging the evolution of knowledge, using knowledge organisms, their species, and populations with the aim of balancing efficiency and effectiveness of processing Big Data and its semantics. We also provide our preliminary considerations on assessing fitness in an evolving knowledge ecosystem. Our conclusions are drawn in the "Some Conclusions" section.

Motivation and Unsolved Issues

Practitioners, including systems engineers, Information Technology architects, Chief Information and Technology Officers, and data scientists, use the phenomenon of Big Data in their dialog over means of improving sense-making. The phenomenon remains a constructive way of introducing others, including nontechnologists, to new approaches such as the Apache Hadoop (hadoop.apache.org) framework. Apparently, Big Data is collected to be analyzed. "Fundamentally, big data analytics is a workflow that distills terabytes of low-value data down to, in some cases, a single bit of high-value data. . . . The goal is to see the big picture from the minutia of our digital lives" (cf. Fisher et al. 2012). Evidently, "seeing the big picture" in its entirety is the key and requires making Big Data healthy and understandable in terms of effectiveness and efficiency for analytics.

In this section, the motivation for understanding the Big Data that improves the performance of analytics is presented and analyzed. It begins with presenting a simple example which is further used throughout the chapter. It continues with the analysis of industrial demand for Big Data analytics. In this context, the major problems as perceived by industries are analyzed and informally mapped to unsolved technological issues.

Illustrative Example

Imagine a stock market analytics workflow inferring trends in share price changes. One possible way of doing this is to extrapolate on stock price data. However, a more robust approach could be extracting these trends from market news. Hence, the incoming data for analysis would very likely be several streams of news feeds resulting in a vast amount of tokens per day. An illustrative example of such a news token is:

Posted: Tue, 03 Jul 2012 05:01:10-04:00

LONDON (Reuters)

U.S. planemaker Boeing hiked its 20-year market forecast, predicting demand for 34,000 new aircraft worth $4.5 trillion, on growth in emerging regions and as airlines seek efficient new planes to counter high fuel costs.[*]

Provided that an adequate technology is available,[†] one may extract the knowledge pictured as thick-bounded and gray-shaded elements in Figure 1.2.

This portion of extracted knowledge is quite shallow, as it simply interprets the source text in a structured and logical way. Unfortunately, it does

---

[*] topix.com/aircraft/airbus-a380/2012/07/boeing-hikes-20-year-market-forecast (accessed July 5, 2012).

[†] The technologies for this are under intensive development currently, for example, wit.istc.cnr.it/stlab-tools/fred/ (accessed October 8, 2012).

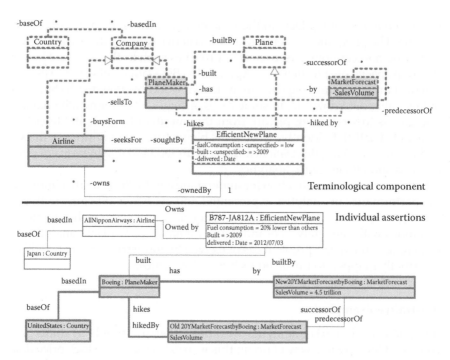

FIGURE 1.2
Semantics associated with a news data token.

not answer several important questions for revealing the motives for Boeing to hike their market forecast:

Q1. What is an efficient new plane? How is efficiency related to high fuel costs to be countered?

Q2. Which airlines seek for efficient new planes? What are the emerging regions? How could their growth be assessed?

Q3. How are plane makers, airlines, and efficient new planes related to each other?

In an attempt to answering these questions, a human analyst will exploit his commonsense knowledge and look around the context for additional relevant evidence. He will likely find out that Q1 and Q3 could be answered using commonsense statements acquired from a foundational ontology, for example, CYC (Lenat 1995), as shown by dotted line bounded items in Figure 1.2.

Answering Q2, however, requires looking for additional information like: the fleet list of All Nippon Airways* who was the first to buy B787 airplanes

---

* For example, at airfleets.net/flottecie/All%20Nippon%20Airways-active-b787.htm (accessed July 5, 2012).

from Boeing (the rest of Figure 1.2); and a relevant list of emerging regions and growth factors (not shown in Figure 1.2). The challenge for a human analyst in performing the task is low speed of data analysis. The available time slot for providing his recommendation is too small, given the effort to be spent per one news token for deep knowledge extraction. This is one good reason for growing demand for industrial strength technologies to assist in analytical work on Big Data, increase quality, and reduce related efforts.

Demand in Industry

Turning available Big Data assets into action and performance is considered a deciding factor by today's business analytics. For example, the report by Capgemini (2012) concludes, based on a survey of the interviews with more than 600 business executives, that Big Data use is highly demanded in industries. Interviewees firmly believe that their companies' competitiveness and performance strongly depend on the effective and efficient use of Big Data. In particular, on average,

- Big Data is already used for decision support 58% of the time, and 29% of the time for decision automation
- It is believed that the use of Big Data will improve organizational performance by 41% over the next three years

The report by Capgemini (2012) also summarizes that the following are the perceived benefits of harnessing Big Data for decision-making:

- More complete understanding of market conditions and evolving business trends
- Better business investment decisions
- More accurate and precise responses to customer needs
- Consistency of decision-making and greater group participation in shared decisions
- Focusing resources more efficiently for optimal returns
- Faster business growth
- Competitive advantage (new data-driven services)
- Common basis for evaluation (one true starting point)
- Better risk management

Problems in Industry

Though the majority of business executives firmly believe in the utility of Big Data and analytics, doubts still persist about its proper use and the availability of appropriate technologies. As a consequence, "We no longer speak of the Knowledge Economy or the Information Society. It's all data now: Data Economy and Data Society. This is a confession that we are no longer in control of the knowledge contained in the data our systems collect" (Greller 2012).

Capgemini (2012) outlines the following problems reported by their interviewees:

- *Unstructured data are hard to process at scale.* Forty-two percent of respondents state that unstructured content is too difficult to interpret. Forty percent of respondents believe that they have too much unstructured data to support decision-making.
- *Fragmentation is a substantial obstacle.* Fifty-six percent of respondents across all sectors consider organizational silos the biggest impediment to effective decision-making using Big Data.
- *Effectiveness needs to be balanced with efficiency in "cooking" Big Data.* Eighty-five percent of respondents say the major problem is the lack of effective ability to analyze and act on data in real time.

The last conclusion by Capgemini is also supported by Bowker (2005, pp. 183–184) who suggests that "raw data is both an oxymoron and a bad idea; to the contrary, data should be cooked with care." This argument is further detailed by Bollier (2010, p. 13) who stresses that Big Data is a huge "mass of raw information." It needs to be added that this "huge mass" may change in time with varying velocity, is also noisy, and cannot be considered as self-explanatory. Hence, an answer to the question whether Big Data indeed represent a "ground truth" becomes very important—opening pathways to all sorts of philosophical and pragmatic discussions. One aspect of particular importance is interpretation that defines the ways of cleaning Big Data. Those ways are straightforwardly biased because any interpretation is subjective.

As observed, old problems of data processing that are well known for decades in industry are made even sharper when data becomes Big. Boyd and Crawford (2012) point out several aspects to pay attention to while "cooking" Big Data, hinting that industrial strength technologies for that are not yet in place:

- *Big Data changes the way knowledge is acquired and even defined.* As already mentioned above (cf. Anderson 2008), correlations mined from Big Data may hint about model changes and knowledge representation updates and refinements. This may require conceptually novel solutions for evolving knowledge representation, reasoning, and management.
- *Having Big Data does not yet imply objectivity, or accuracy, on time.* Here, the clinch between efficiency and effectiveness of Big Data interpretation and processing is one of the important factors. Selecting

a sample of an appropriate size for being effective may bring bias, harm correctness, and accuracy. Otherwise, analyzing Big Data in source volumes will definitely distort timeliness.

- Therefore, *Big Data is not always the best option*. A question that requires research effort in this context is about the appropriate sample, size, and granularity to best answer the question of a data analyst.

- Consequently, *taken off-context Big Data is meaningless in interpretation*. Indeed, choosing an appropriate sample and granularity may be seen as contextualization—circumscribing (Ermolayev et al. 2010) the part of data which is potentially the best-fitted sample for the analytical query. Managing context and contextualization for Big Data at scale is a typical problem and is perceived as one of the research and development challenges.

One more aspect having indirect relevance to technology, but important in terms of socio-psychological perceptions and impact on industries, is *ethics* and *Big Data divide*. Ethics is concerned with legal regulations and constraints of allowing a Big Data collector interpreting personal or company information without informing the subjects about it. Ethical issues become sharper when used for competition and lead to the emergence of and separation to Big Data rich and poor implied by accessibility to data sources at required scale.

Major Issues

Applying Big Data analytics faces different issues related with the characteristics of data, analysis process, and also social concerns. Privacy is a very sensitive issue and has conceptual, legal, and technological implications. This concern increases its importance in the context of big data. Privacy is defined by the International Telecommunications Union as the "right of individuals to control or influence what information related to them may be disclosed" (Gordon 2005). Personal records of individuals are increasingly being collected by several government and corporate organizations. These records usually used for the purpose of data analytics. To facilitate data analytics, such organizations publish "appropriately private" views over the collected data. However, privacy is a double-edged sword—there should be enough privacy to ensure that sensitive information about the individuals is not disclosed and at the same time there should be enough data to perform the data analysis. Thus, privacy is a primary concern that has widespread implications for someone desiring to explore the use of Big Data for development in terms of data acquisition, storage, preservation, presentation, and use.

Another concern is the access and sharing of information. Usually private organizations and other institutions are reluctant to share data about their clients and users, as well as about their own operations. Barriers may include legal considerations, a need to protect their competitiveness, a culture of confidentiality, and, largely, the lack of the right incentive and information structures. There are also institutional and technical issues, when data are stored in places and ways that make them difficult to be accessed and transferred.

One significant issue is to rethink security for information sharing in Big Data use cases. Several online services allow us to share private information (i.e., facebook.com, geni.com, linkedin.com, etc.), but outside record-level access control we do not comprehend what it means to share data and how the shared data can be linked.

Managing large and rapidly increasing volumes of data has been a challenging issue. Earlier, this issue was mitigated by processors getting faster, which provide us with the resources needed to cope with increasing volumes of data. However, there is a fundamental shift underway considering that data volume is scaling faster than computer resources. Consequently, extracting sense of data at required scale is far beyond human capability. So, we, the humans, increasingly "... require the help of automated systems to make sense of the data produced by other (automated) systems" (Greller 2012). These instruments produce new data at comparable scale—kick-starting a new iteration in this endless cycle.

In general, given a large data set, it is often necessary to find elements in it that meet a certain criterion which likely occurs repeatedly. Scanning the entire data set to find suitable elements is obviously impractical. Instead, index structures are created in advance to permit finding the qualifying elements quickly.

Moreover, dealing with new data sources brings a significant number of analytical issues. The relevance of these issues will vary depending on the type of analysis being conducted and on the type of decisions that the data might ultimately inform. The big core issue is to analyze what the data are really telling us in an entirely transparent manner.

State of Technology, Research, and Development in Big Data Computing

After giving an overview of the influence of Big Data on industries and society as a phenomenon and outlining the problems in Big Data computing context as perceived by technology consumers, we now proceed with the analysis of the state of development of those technologies. We begin with presenting the overall Big Data Processing technology stack and point out how different dimensions of Big Data affect the requirements to technologies, having understanding—in particular, semantics-based processing—as a primary focus. We continue with presenting a selection of Big Data research and development projects and focus on what they do in advancing the state-of-the-art in semantic technologies for Big Data processing. Further, we summarize the analysis by pointing out the observed complications and overheads in processing Big Data semantics. Finally, we outline a high-level proposal for the refinement of the Big Data semantics layer in the technology stack.

Big Data Processing—Technology Stack and Dimensions

At a high level of detail, Driscoll (2011) describes the Big Data processing technology stack comprising three major layers: foundational, analytics, and applications (upper part of Figure 1.3).

The foundational layer provides the infrastructure for storage, access, and management of Big Data. Depending on the nature of data, stream processing solutions (Abadi et al. 2003; Golab and Tamer Ozsu 2003; Salehi 2010), distributed persistent storage (Chang et al. 2008; Roy et al. 2009; Shvachko et al. 2010), cloud infrastructures (Rimal et al. 2009; Tsangaris et al. 2009; Cusumano 2010), or a reasonable combination of these (Gu and Grossman 2009; He et al. 2010; Sakr et al. 2011) may be used for storing and accessing data in response to the upper-layer requests and requirements.

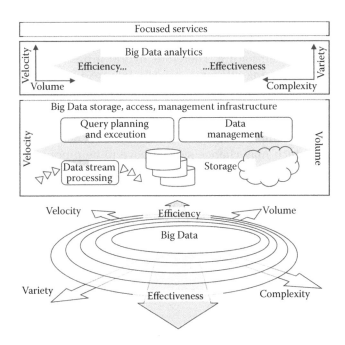

FIGURE 1.3
Processing stack, based on Driscoll (2011), and the four dimensions of Big Data, based on Beyer et al. (2011), influencing efficiency and effectiveness of analytics.

The middle layer of the stack is responsible for analytics. Here data warehousing technologies (e.g., Nemani and Konda 2009; Ponniah 2010; Thusoo et al. 2010) are currently exploited for extracting correlations and features (e.g., Ishai et al. 2009) from data and feeding classification and prediction algorithms (e.g., Mills 2011).

Focused applications or services are at the top of the stack. Their functionality is based on the use of more generic lower-layer technologies and exposed to end users as Big Data products.

Example of a startup offering focused services is BillGuard (billguard. com). It monitors customers' credit card statements for dubious charges and even leverages the collective behavior of users to improve its fraud predictions. Another company called Klout (klout.com/home) provides a genuine data service that uses social media activity to measure online influence. LinkedIn's *People you may know* feature is also a kind of focused service. This service is presumably based on graph theory, starting exploration of the graph of your relations from your node and filtering those relations according to what is called "homophily." The greater the homophily between two nodes, the more likely two nodes will be connected.

According to its purpose, the foundational layer is concerned about being capable of processing as much as possible data (*volume*) and as soon as possible. In particular, if streaming data are used, the faster the stream is (*velocity*), the more difficult it is to process the data in a stream window. Currently available technologies and tools for the foundational level are not equally well coping with volume and velocity dimensions which are, so to say, anticorrelated due to their nature. Therefore, hybrid infrastructures are in use for balancing processing efficiency aspects (Figure 1.3)—comprising solutions focused on taking care of volumes, and, separately, of velocity. Some examples are given in "Big Data in European Research" section.

For the analytics layer (Figure 1.3), *volume* and *velocity* dimensions (Beyer et al. 2011) are also important and constitute the facet of efficiency—big volumes of data which may change swiftly have to be processed in a timely fashion. However, two more dimensions of Big Data become important—*complexity* and *variety*—which form the facet of effectiveness. *Complexity* is clearly about the adequacy of data representations and descriptions for analysis. *Variety* describes a degree of syntactic and semantic heterogeneity in distributed modules of data that need to be integrated or harmonized for analysis. A major conceptual complication for analytics is that efficiency is anticorrelated to effectiveness.

Big Data in European Research

Due to its huge demand, Big Data Computing is currently on the hype as a field of research and development, producing a vast domain of work. To keep the size of this review observable for a reader, we focus on the batch of the running 7th Framework Programme (FP7) Information and Communication

Technology (ICT; cordis.europa.eu/fp7/ict/) projects within this vibrant field. Big Data processing, including semantics, is addressed by the strategic objective of Intelligent Information Management (IIM; cordis.europa.eu/fp7/ict/content-knowledge/projects_en.html). IIM projects funded in frame of FP7 ICT Call 5 are listed in Table 1.1 and further analyzed below.

SmartVortex [Integrating Project (IP); smartvortex.eu] develops a technological infrastructure—a comprehensive suite of interoperable tools, services, and methods—for intelligent management and analysis of massive data streams. The goal is to achieving better collaboration and decision-making in large-scale collaborative projects concerning industrial innovation engineering.

Legend: AEP, action extraction and prediction; DLi, data linking; DM, data mining; DS, diversity in semantics; DV, domain vocabulary; FCA, formal concept analysis; IE, information extraction; Int, integration; KD, knowledge discovery; M-LS, multi-lingual search; MT, machine translation; O, ontology; OM, opinion mining; QL, query language; R, reasoning; SBI, business intelligence over semantic data; SDW, semantic data warehouse (triple store); SUM, summarization.

LOD2 (IP; lod2.eu) claims delivering: industrial strength tools and methodologies for exposing and managing very large amounts of structured information; a bootstrap network of multidomain and multilingual ontologies from sources such as Wikipedia (wikipedia.org) and OpenStreetMap (openstreetmap.org); machine learning algorithms for enriching, repairing, interlinking, and fusing data from Web resources; standards and methods for tracking provenance, ensuring privacy and data security, assessing information quality; adaptive tools for searching, browsing, and authoring Linked Data.

Tridec (IP; tridec-online.eu) develops a service platform accompanied with the next-generation work environments supporting human experts in decision processes for managing and mitigating emergency situations triggered by the earth (observation) system in complex and time-critical settings. The platform enables "smart" management of collected sensor data and facts inferred from these data with respect to crisis situations.

First [Small Targeted Research Project (STREP); project-first.eu] develops an information extraction, integration, and decision-making infrastructure for financial domain with extremely large, dynamic, and heterogeneous sources of information.

iProd (STREP; iprod-project.eu) investigates approaches of reducing product development costs by efficient use of large amounts of data comprising the development of a software framework to support complex information management. Key aspects addressed by the project are handling heterogeneous information and semantic diversity using semantic technologies including knowledge bases and reasoning.

Teleios (STREP; earthobservatory.eu) focuses on elaborating a data model and query language for Earth Observation (EO) images. Based on

TABLE 1.1

FP7 ICT Call 5 Projects and their Contributions to Big Data Processing and Understanding

Acronym	IIM Cluster[a]			Domain(s)/Industry(ies)	Contribution to Coping with Big Data dimensions[b]				Contribution to Big Data Processing Stack Layers[c]			Contribution to Big Data Understanding
	Online Content, Interactive and Social Media	Reasoning and Information Exploitation	Knowledge Discovery and Management		Volume	Velocity	Variety	Complexity	i. Fast Access to/Management of Data at Scale	ii. Fast Analytics of Data at Scale	iii. Focused Services	
SmartVortex	X	X	X	Industrial innovation engineering	X	X			X	X		
LOD2	X	X	X	Media and publishing, corporate data intranets, eGovernment	X	X	X	X	X	X		O, ML
Tridec		X	X	Crisis/emergency response, government, oil and gas	X	X		X	X	X		R
First		X	X	Market surveillance, investment management, online retail banking and brokerage	X	X	X		X	X		IE
iProd		X	X	Manufacturing: aerospace, automotive, and home appliances	X		X	X	X	X		R, Int
Teleios		X	X	Civil defense, environmental agencies. Use cases: a virtual observatory for TerraSAR-X data; real-time fire monitoring	X		X	X	X	X		DM, QL, KD

Project	Application domain									Big Data Stack contributions[c]
Khresmoi	Medical imaging in healthcare, biomedicine	X			X	X		X	X	IE, DLi, M-LS, MT
Robust	Online communities (internet, extranet and intranet) addressing; customer support; knowledge sharing; hosting services	X	X		X					AEP
Digital.me	Personal sphere	X		X	X					
Fish4Knowledge	Marine sciences, environment	X		X	X		X			DV (fish), SUM
Render	Information management (wiki), news aggregation (search engine), customer relationship management (telecommunications)	X		X	X		X			DS
PlanetData	Cross-domain			X	X					
LATC	Government			X	X			X		
Advance	Logistics	X	X		X		X			
Cubist	Market intelligence, computational biology, control centre operations			X	X		X	X		SDW, SBI, FCA
Promise	Cross-domain			X	X	X	X			
Dicode	Clinico-genomic research, healthcare, marketing	X		X	X	X	X			DM, OM

a IIM clustering information has been taken from the Commission's source cordis.europa.eu/fp7/ict/content-knowledge/projects_en.html.

b As per the Gartner report on extreme information management (Gartner 2011).

c The contributions of the projects to the developments in the Big Data Stack layers have been assessed based on their public deliverables.

these, a scalable and adaptive environment for knowledge discovery from EO images and geospatial data sets, and a query processing and optimization technique for queries over multidimensional arrays and EO image annotations are developed and implemented on top of the MonetDB (monetdb.org) system.

Khresmoi (IP; khresmoi.eu) develops an advanced multilingual and multimodal search and access system for biomedical information and documents. The advancements of the Khresmoi comprise: an automated information extraction from biomedical documents reinforced by using crowd sourcing, active learning, automated estimation of trust level, and target user expertise; automated analysis and indexing for 2-, 3-, 4D medical images; linking information extracted from unstructured or semistructured biomedical texts and images to structured information in knowledge bases; multilingual search including multiple languages in queries and machine-translated pertinent excerpts; visual user interfaces to assist in formulating queries and displaying search results.

Robust (IP; robust-project.eu) investigates models and methods for describing, understanding, and managing the users, groups, behaviors, and needs of online communities. The project develops a scalable cloud and stream-based data management infrastructure for handling the real-time analysis of large volumes of community data. Understanding and prediction of actions is envisioned using simulation and visualization services. All the developed tools are combined under the umbrella of the risk management framework, resulting in the methodology for the detection, tracking, and management of opportunities and threats to online community prosperity.

Digital.me (STREP; dime-project.eu) integrates all personal data in a personal sphere at a single user-controlled point of access—a user-controlled personal service for intelligent personal information management. The software is targeted on integrating social web systems and communities and implements decentralized communication to avoid external data storage and undesired data disclosure.

Fish4Knowledge (STREP; homepages.inf.ed.ac.uk/rbf/Fish4Knowledge/) develops methods for information abstraction and storage that reduce the amount of video data at a rate of 10×10^{15} pixels to 10×10^{12} units of information. The project also develops machine- and human-accessible vocabularies for describing fish. The framework also comprises flexible data-processing architecture and a specialized query system tailored to the domain. To achieve these, the project exploits a combination of computer vision, video summarization, database storage, scientific workflow, and human–computer interaction methods.

Render (STREP; render-project.eu) is focused on investigating the aspect of diversity of Big Data semantics. It investigates methods and techniques, develops software, and collects data sets that will leverage diversity as a source of innovation and creativity. The project also claims providing enhanced support for feasibly managing data on a very large scale and for designing novel algorithms that reflect diversity in the ways information is selected, ranked, aggregated, presented, and used.

PlanetData [Network of Excellence (NoE); planet-data.eu] works toward establishing a sustainable European community of researchers that supports organizations in exposing their data in new and useful ways and develops technologies that are able to handle data purposefully at scale. The network also facilitates researchers' exchange, training, and mentoring, and event organization based substantially on an open partnership scheme.

LATC (Support Action; latc-project.eu) creates an in-depth test-bed for data-intensive applications by publishing data sets produced by the European Commission, the European Parliament, and other European institutions as Linked Data on the Web and by interlinking them with other governmental data.

Advance (STREP; advance-logistics.eu) develops a decision support platform for improving strategies in logistics operations. The platform is based on the refinement of predictive analysis techniques to process massive data sets for long-term planning and cope with huge amounts of new data in real time.

Cubist (STREP; cubist-project.eu) elaborates methodologies and implements a platform that brings together several essential features of Semantic Technologies and Business Intelligence (BI): support for the federation of data coming from unstructured and structured sources; a BI-enabled triple store as a data persistency layer; data volume reduction and preprocessing using data semantics; enabling BI operations over semantic data; a semantic data warehouse implementing FCA; applying visual analytics for rendering, navigating, and querying data.

Promise (NoE; promise-noe.eu) establishes a virtual laboratory for conducting participative research and experimentation to carry out, advance, and bring automation into the evaluation and benchmarking of multilingual and multimedia information systems. The project offers the infrastructure for access, curation, preservation, re-use, analysis, visualization, and mining of the collected experimental data.

Dicode (STREP; dicode-project.eu) develops a workbench of interoperable services, in particular, for: (i) scalable text and opinion mining; (ii) collaboration support; and (iii) decision-making support. The workbench is designed to reduce data intensiveness and complexity overload at critical decision points to a manageable level. It is envisioned that the use of the workbench will help stakeholders to be more productive and concentrate on creative activities.

In summary, the contributions to Big Data understanding of all the projects mentioned above result in the provision of different functionality for a semantic layer—an interface between the Data and Analytics layers of the Big Data processing stack—as pictured in Figure 1.4.

However, these advancements remain somewhat insufficient in terms of reaching a desired balance between efficiency and effectiveness, as outlined

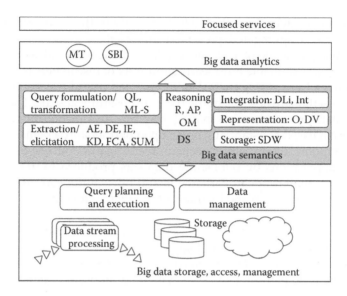

FIGURE 1.4
Contribution of the selection of FP7 ICT projects to technologies for Big Data understanding. Abbreviations are explained in the legend to Table 1.1.

in the introduction of this chapter. Analysis of Table 1.1 reveals that no one of the reviewed projects addresses all four dimensions of Big Data in a balanced manner. In particular, only two projects—*Trydec* and *First*—claim contributions addressing Big Data velocity and variety-complexity. This fact points out that the clinch between efficiency and effectiveness in Big Data processing still remains a challenge.

Complications and Overheads in Understanding Big Data

As observed, the mankind collects and stores data through generations, without a clear account of the utility of these data. Out of data at hand, each generation extracts a relatively small proportion of knowledge for their everyday needs. The knowledge is produced by a generation for their needs—to an extent they have to satisfy their "nutrition" requirement for supporting decision-making. Hence, knowledge is "food" for data analytics. An optimistic assumption usually made here is that the next generation will succeed in advancing tools for data mining, knowledge discovery, and extraction. So the data which the current generation cannot process effectively and efficiently is left as a legacy for the next generation in a hope that the ancestors cope better. The truth, however, is that the developments of data and knowledge-processing tools fail to keep pace with the explosive growth of data in all four dimensions mentioned above. Suspending understanding Big Data until an advanced next-generation capability is at hand is therefore an illusion of a solution.

Do today's state-of-the-art technologies allow us to understand Big Data with an attempt to balance effectiveness and efficiency?—probably not. Our brief analysis reveals that Big Data computing is currently developed toward more effective versus efficient use of semantics. It is done by adding the semantics layer to the processing stack (cf. Figures 1.3 and 1.4) with an objective of processing all the available data and using all the generated knowledge. Perhaps, the major issue is the attempt to eat all we have on the table. Following the metaphor of "nutrition," it has to be noted that the "food" needs to be "healthy" in terms of all the discussed dimensions of Big Data.

Our perceptions of the consequences of being not selective with respect to consuming data for understanding are as follows.

The major problem is the introduction of a new interface *per se* and in an improper way. The advent of semantic technologies aimed at breaking down data silos and simultaneously enabling efficient knowledge management at scale. Assuming that databases describe data using multiple heterogeneous labels, one might expect that annotating these labels using ontology elements as semantic tags enables virtual integration and provides immediate benefits for search, retrieval, reasoning, etc. without a need to modify existing code, or data. Unfortunately, as noticed by Smith (2012), it is now too easy to create "ontologies." As a consequence, myriads of them are being created in *ad hoc* ways and with no respect to compatibility, which implies the creation of new semantic silos and, further bringing something like a "Big Ontology" challenge to the agenda. According to Smith (2012), the big reason is the lack of a rational (monetary) incentive for investing in reuse. Therefore, it is often accepted that a new "ontology" is developed for a new project. Harmonization is left for someone else's work—in the next generation. Therefore, the more semantic technology simplifying ontology creation is successful, the more we fail to achieve our goals for interoperability and integration (Smith 2012).

It is worth noting here that there is still a way to start doing things correctly which, according to Smith (2012), would be "to create an incremental, evolutionary process, where what is good survives, and what is bad fails; create a scenario in which people will find it profitable to reuse ontologies, terminologies and coding systems which have been tried and tested; silo effects will be avoided and results of investment in Semantic Technology will cumulate effectively."

A good example of a collaborative effort going in this correct direction is the approach used by the Gene Ontology initiative (geneontology.org) which follows the principles of the OBO Foundry (obofoundry.org). The Gene Ontology project is a major bioinformatics initiative with the aim of standardizing the representation of gene and gene product attributes across species and databases. The project provides a controlled vocabulary of terms for describing gene product characteristics and gene product annotation data, as well as tools to access and process this data. The mission of OBO Foundry is to support community members in developing and publishing fully interoperable ontologies in the biomedical domain following common evolving design philosophy and implementation and ensuring a gradual improvement of the quality of ontologies.

Furthermore, adding a data semantics layer facilitates increasing effectiveness in understanding Big Data, but also substantially increases the computational overhead for processing the representations of knowledge—decreasing efficiency. A solution is needed that harmonically and rationally balances between the increase in the adequacy and the completeness of Big Data semantics, on the one hand, and the increase in computational complexity, on the other hand. A straightforward approach is using scalable infrastructures for processing knowledge representations. A vast body of related work focuses on elaborating this approach (e.g., Broekstra et al. 2002; Wielemaker et al. 2003; Cai and Frank 2004; DeCandia et al. 2007).

The reasons to qualifying this approach only as a mechanistic solution are

- Using distributed scalable infrastructures, such as clouds or grids, implies new implementation problems and computational overheads.
- Typical tasks for processing knowledge representations, such as reasoning, alignment, query formulation and transformation, etc., scale hardly (e.g., Oren et al. 2009; Urbani et al. 2009; Hogan et al. 2011)—more expressiveness implies harder problems in decoupling the fragments for distribution. Nontrivial optimization, approximation, or load-balancing techniques are required.

Another effective approach to balance complexity and timeliness is maintaining history or learning from the past. A simple but topical example in data processing is the use of previously acquired information for saving approximately 50% of comparison operations in sorting by selection (Knuth 1998, p. 141). In Distributed Artificial Intelligence software, agent architectures maintaining their states or history for more efficient and effective deliberation have also been developed (cf. Dickinson and Wooldridge 2003). In Knowledge Representation and Reasoning, maintaining history is often implemented as inference or query result materialization (cf. Kontchakov et al. 2010; McGlothlin and Khan 2010), which also do not scale well up to the volumes characterizing real Big Data.

Yet another way to find a proper balance is exploiting incomplete or approximate methods. These methods yield results of acceptable quality much faster than approaches aiming at building fully complete or exact, that is, ideal results. Good examples of technologies for incomplete or partial reasoning and approximate query answering (Fensel et al. 2008) are elaborated in the FP7 LarKC project (larkc.eu). Remarkably, some of the approximate querying techniques, for example, Guéret et al. (2008), are based on evolutionary computing.

Refining Big Data Semantics Layer for Balancing Efficiency Effectiveness

As one may notice, the developments in the Big Data semantics layer are mainly focused on posing and appropriately transforming the semantics of queries all the way down to the available data, using networked ontologies.

At least two shortcomings of this, in fact, unidirectional* approach need to be identified:

1. *Scalability overhead implies insufficient efficiency.* Indeed, executing queries at the data layer implies processing volumes at the scale of stored data. Additional overhead is caused by the query transformation, distribution, and planning interfaces. Lifting up the stack and fusing the results of these queries also imply similar computational overheads. A possible solution for this problem may be sought following a supposition that the volume of knowledge describing data adequately for further analyses is substantially smaller than the volume of this data. Hence, down-lifting queries for execution need to be stopped at the layer of knowledge storage for better efficiency. However, the knowledge should be consistent enough with the data so that it can fulfill completeness and correctness requirements specified in the contract of the query engine.

2. *Having ontologies inconsistent with data implies effectiveness problems.* Indeed, in the vast majority of cases, the ontologies containing knowledge about data are not updated consistently with the changes in data. At best, these knowledge representations are revised in a sequence of discrete versions. So, they are not consistent with the data at an arbitrary point in time. This shortcoming may be overcome only if ontologies in a knowledge repository evolve continuously in response to data change. Ontology evolution will have a substantially lower overhead because the volume of changes is always significantly lower than the volume of data, though depends on data velocity (Figure 1.3).

To sum up, relaxing the consequences of the two outlined shortcomings and, hence, balancing efficiency and effectiveness may be achievable if a bidirectional processing approach is followed. Top-down query answering has to be complemented by a bottom-up ontology evolution process, which meet at the knowledge representation layer. In addition to a balance between efficiency and effectiveness, such an approach of processing huge data sets may help us "... find and see dynamically changing ontologies without hav-

---

* Technologies for information and knowledge extraction are also developed and need to be regarded as bottom-up. However, these technologies are designed to work off-line for updating the existing ontologies in a discrete manner. Their execution is not coordinated with the top-down query processing and data changes. So, the shortcomings outlined below persist.

ing to try to prescribe them in advance.* Taxonomies and ontologies are things that you might discover by observation, and watch evolve over time" (cf. Bollier 2010).

Further, we focus on outlining a complementary bottom-up path in the overall processing stack which facilitates existing top-down query answering frameworks by providing knowledge evolution in line with data change—as pictured in Figure 1.5. In a nutshell, the proposed bottom-up path is characterized by:

- Efficiently performing simple scalable queries on vast volumes of data or in a stream window for extracting facts and decreasing volumes (more details could be found in the "Scaling with a Traditional Database" section)
- Adding extracted facts to a highly expressive persistent knowledge base allowing evolution of knowledge (more details on that could be seen in Knowledge Self-Management and Refinement through Evolution)
- Assessing fitness of knowledge organisms and knowledge representations in the evolving knowledge ecosystem (our approach to that is also outlined in the "Knowledge Self-Management and Refinement through Evolution" section)

This will enable reducing the overheads of the top-down path by performing refined inference using highly expressive and complex queries over

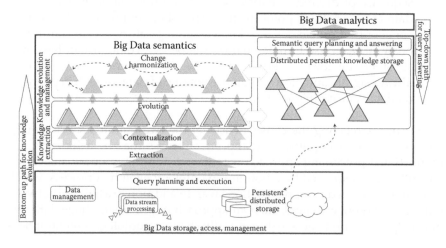

FIGURE 1.5
Refining Big Data semantics layer for balancing efficiency and effectiveness.

---

* Underlined by the authors of this chapter.

evolving (i.e., consistent with data) and linked (i.e., harmonized), but reasonably small fragments of knowledge. Query results may also be materialized for further decreasing computational effort.

After outlining the abstract architecture and the bottom-up approach, we will now explain at a high level how Big Data needs to be treated along the way. A condensed formula for this high-level approach is "3F + 3Co" which is unfolded as

3F: Focusing-Filtering-Forgetting

3Co: Contextualizing-Compressing-Connecting

Notably, both 3F and 3Co are not novel and used in parts extensively in many domains and in different interpretations. For example, an interesting interpretation of 3F is offered by Dean and Webb (2011) who suggest this formula as a "treatment" for senior executives (CEOs) to deal with information overload and multitasking. Executives are offered to cope with the problem by focusing (doing one thing at a time), filtering (delegating so that they do not take on too many tasks or too much information), and forgetting (taking breaks and clearing their minds).

Focusing

Following our Boeing example, let us imagine a data analyst extracting knowledge tokens from a business news stream and putting these tokens as missing bits in the mosaic of his mental picture of the world. A tricky part of his work, guided by intuition or experience in practice, is choosing the order in which the facts are picked up from the token. Order of focusing is very important as it influences the formation and saturation of different fragments in the overall canvas. Even if the same input tokens are given, different curves of focusing may result in different knowledge representations and analysis outcomes.

A similar aspect of proper focusing is of importance also for automated processing of Big Data or its semantics. One could speculate whether a processing engine should select data tokens or assertions in the order of their appearance, in a reversed order, or anyhow else. If data or assertions are processed in a stream window and in real time, the order of focusing is of lesser relevance. However, if all the data or knowledge tokens are in a persistent storage, having some intelligence for optimal focusing may improve processing efficiency substantially. With smart focusing at hand, a useful token can be found or a hidden pattern extracted much faster and without making a complete scan of the source data. A complication for smart focusing is that the nodes on the focusing curve have to be decided upon on-the-fly because generally the locations of important tokens cannot be known in advance. Therefore, the processing of a current focal point should not only yield what is intended directly of this portion of data, but also hint about the next point on the curve.

A weak point in such a "problem-solving" approach is that some potentially valid alternatives are inevitably lost after each choice made on the decision path. So, only a suboptimal solution is practically achievable. The evolutionary approach detailed further in section "Knowledge Self-Management and Refinement through Evolution" follows, in fact, a similar approach of smart focusing, but uses a population of autonomous problem-solvers operating concurrently. Hence, it leaves a much smaller part of a solution space without attention, reduces the bias of each choice, and likely provides better results.

Filtering

A data analyst who receives dozens of news posts at once has to focus on the most valuable of them and filter out the rest which, according to his informed guess, do not bring anything important additionally to those in his focus. Moreover, it might also be very helpful to filter out noise, that is, irrelevant tokens, irrelevant dimensions of data, or those bits of data that are unreadable or corrupted in any other sense. In fact, an answer to the question about what to trash and what to process needs to be sought based on the understanding of the objective (e.g., was the reason for Boeing to hike their market forecast valid?) and the choice of the proper context (e.g., should we look into the airline fleets or the economic situation in developing countries?).

A reasonable selection of features for processing or otherwise a rational choice of the features that may be filtered out may essentially reduce the volume as well as the variety/complexity of data which result in higher efficiency balanced with effectiveness.

Quite similar to focusing, a complication here is that for big heterogeneous data it is not feasible to expect a one-size-fits-all filter in advance. Even more, for deciding about an appropriate filtering technique and the structure of a filter to be applied, a focused prescan of data may be required, which implies a decrease in efficiency. The major concern is again how to filter in a smart way and so as to balance the intentions to reduce processing effort (efficiency) and keep the quality of results within acceptable bounds (effectiveness).

Our evolutionary approach presented in the section "Knowledge Self-Management and Refinement through Evolution" uses a system of environmental contexts for smart filtering. These contexts are not fixed but may be adjusted by several independent evolutionary mechanisms. For example, a context may become more or less "popular" among the knowledge organisms that harvest knowledge tokens in them because these organisms may migrate freely between contexts in search for better, more appropriate, healthier knowledge to collect. Another useful property we propose for knowledge organisms is their resistance to sporadic mutagenic factors, which may be helpful for filtering out noise.

Forgetting

A professional data analyst always keeps a record of data he used in his work and the knowledge he created in his previous analyses. The storage for all these gems of expertise is, however, limited, so it has to be cleaned periodically. Such a cleaning implies trashing potentially valuable things, though never or very rarely used, but causing doubts and further regrets about the lost. Similar thing happens when Big Data storage is overflown—some parts of it have to be trashed and so "forgotten." A question in this respect is about which part of a potentially useful collection may be sacrificed. Is forgetting the oldest records reasonable?—perhaps not. Shall we forget the features that have been previously filtered out?—negative again. There is always a chance that an unusual task for analysis pops up and requires the features never exploited before. Are the records with minimal potential utility the best candidates for trashing?—could be a rational way to go, but how would their potential value be assessed?

Practices in Big Data management confirm that forgetting following straightforward policies like fixed lifetime for keeping records causes regret almost inevitably. For example, the Climate Research Unit (one of the leading institutions that study natural and anthropogenic climate change and collect climate data) admits that they threw away the key data to be used in global warming calculations (Joseph 2012).

A better policy for forgetting might be to extract as much as possible knowledge out of data before deleting these data. It cannot be guaranteed, however, that future knowledge mining and extraction algorithms will not be capable of discovering more knowledge to preserve. Another potentially viable approach could be "forgetting before storing," that is, there should be a pragmatic reason to store anything. The approach we suggest in the section "Knowledge Self-Management and Refinement through Evolution" follows exactly this way. Though knowledge tokens are extracted from all the incoming data tokens, not all of them are consumed by knowledge organisms, but only those assertions that match to their knowledge genome to a sufficient extent. This similarity is considered a good reason for remembering a fact. The rest remains in the environment and dies out naturally after the lifetime comes to end as explained in "Knowledge Self-Management and Refinement through Evolution".

Contextualizing

Our reflection of the world is often polysemic, so a pragmatic choice of a context is often needed for proper understanding. For example, "taking a mountain hike" or "hiking a market forecast" are different actions though the same lexical root is used in the words. An indication of a context: recreation or business in this example would be necessary for making the statement explicit. To put it even broader, not only the sense of statements, but also judgments, assessments, attitudes, and sentiments about the same data or knowledge token may well differ in different contexts. When it goes about data, it might be useful to know:

1. The "context of origin"—the information about the source; who organized and performed the action; what were the objects; what features have been measured; what were the reasons or motives for collecting these data (transparent or hidden); when and where the data were collected; who were the owners; what were the license, price, etc.

2. The "context of processing"—formats, encryption keys, used preprocessing tools, predicted performance of various data mining algorithms, etc.; and

3. The "context of use"—potential domains, potential or known applications, which may use the data or the knowledge extracted from it, potential customers, markets, etc.

Having circumscribed these three different facets of context, we may say now that data contextualization is a transformation process which decontextualizes the data from the context of origin and recontextualizes it into the context of use (Thomason 1998), if the latter is known. This transformation is performed via smart management of the context of processing.

Known data mining methods are capable of automatically separating the so-called "predictive" and "contextual" features of data instances (e.g., Terziyan 2007). A predictive feature stands for a feature that directly influences the result of applying to data a knowledge extraction instrument—knowledge discovery, prediction, classification, diagnostics, recognition, etc.

RESULT = INSTRUMENT(Predictive Features).

Contextual features could be regarded as arguments to a meta-function that influences the choice of appropriate (based on predicted quality/performance) instrument to be applied to a particular fragment of data:

INSTRUMENT = CONTEXTUALIZATION(Contextual Features).

Hence, a correct way to process each data token and benefit of contextualization would be: (i) decide, based on contextual features, which would be an appropriate instrument to process the token; and then (ii) process it using the chosen instrument that takes the predictive features as an input. This approach to contextualization is not novel and is known in data mining and knowledge discovery as a "dynamic" integration, classification, selection, etc. Puuronen et al. (1999) and Terziyan (2001) proved that the use of dynamic contextualization in knowledge discovery yields essential quality improvement compared to "static" approaches.

Compressing

In the context of Big Data, having data in a compact form is very important for saving storage space or reducing communication overheads. Compressing is a process of data transformation toward making data more compact in terms of required storage space, but still preserving either fully (lossless compression) or partly (lossy compression) the essential features of these data—those potentially required for further processing or use.

Compression, in general, and Big Data compression, in particular, are effectively possible due to a high probability of the presence of repetitive, periodical, or quasi-periodical data fractions or visible trends within data. Similar to contextualization, it is reasonable to select an appropriate data compression technique individually for different data fragments (clusters), also in a dynamic manner and using contextualization. Lossy compression may be applied if it is known how data will be used, at least potentially. So that some data fractions may be sacrificed without losing the facets of semantics and the overall quality of data required for known ways of its use. A relevant example of a lossy compression technique for data having quasi-periodical features and based on a kind of "meta-statistics" was reported by Terziyan et al. (1998).

Connecting

It is known that nutrition is healthy and balanced if it provides all the necessary components that are further used as building blocks in a human body. These components become parts of a body and are tightly connected to the rest of it. Big Data could evidently be regarded as nutrition for knowledge economy as discussed in "Motivation and Unsolved Issues". A challenge is to make this nutrition healthy and balanced for building an adequate mental representation of the world, which is Big Data understanding. Following the allusion of human body morphogenesis, understanding could be simplistically interpreted as connecting or linking new portions of data to the data that is already stored and understood. This immediately brings us about the concept of linked data (Bizer et al. 2009), where "linked" is interpreted as a sublimate of "understood." We have written "a sublimate" because having data linked is not yet sufficient, though necessary for further, more intelligent phase of building knowledge out of data. After data have been linked, data and knowledge mining, knowledge discovery, pattern recognition, diagnostics, prediction, etc. could be done more effectively and efficiently. For example, Terziyan and Kaykova (2012) demonstrated that executing business intelligence services on top of linked data is noticeably more efficient than without using linked data. Consequently, knowledge generated out of linked data could also be linked using the same approach, resulting in the linked knowledge. It is clear from the Linking Open Data Cloud Diagram by Richard Cyganiak and Anja Jentzsch (lod-cloud.net) that knowledge (e.g., RDF or OWL modules) represented as a linked data can be relatively easily linked to different public data sets, which creates a cloud of linked open semantic data.

Mitchell and Wilson (2012) argue that the key to extract value from Big Data lies in exploiting the concept of linked. They believe that linked data potentially creates ample opportunities from numerous data sources. For example, using links between data as a "broker" brings more possibilities of extracting new data from the old, creating insights that were previously unachievable, and facilitating exciting new scenarios for data processing.

For developing an appropriate connection technology, the results are relevant from numerous research and development efforts, for example, Linking Open Data (LOD; w3.org/wiki/SweoIG/TaskForces/CommunityProjects/ LinkingOpenData) project, DBpedia (dbpedia.org), OpenCyc (opencyc.org), FOAF (foaf-project.org), CKAN (ckan.org), Freebase (freebase.com), Factual (factual.com), and INSEMTIVES (insemtives.eu/index.php). These projects create structured and interlinked semantic content, in fact, mashing up the features from Social and Semantic Web (Ankolekar et al. 2007). One strength of their approach is that collaborative content development effort is propagated up the level of the data-processing stack which allows creating semantic representations collaboratively and in an evolutionary manner.

Autonomic Big Data Computing

The treatment offered in the "Refining Big Data Semantics Layer for Balancing Efficiency-Effectiveness" section requires a paradigm shift in Big Data computing. In seeking for a suitable approach to building processing infrastructures, a look into Autonomic Computing might be helpful. Started by International Business Machines (IBM) in 2001, Autonomic Computing refers to the characteristics of complex computing systems allowing them to manage themselves without direct human intervention. A human, in fact, defines only general policies that constrain self-management process. According to IBM,* the four major functional areas of autonomic computing are: (i) *self-configuration*—automatic configuration of system components; (ii) *self-optimization*—automatic monitoring and ensuring the optimal functioning of the system within defined requirements; (iii) *self-protection*—automatic identification and protection from security threats; and (iv) *self-healing*— automatic fault discovery and correction. Other important capabilities of autonomic systems are: *self-identity* in a sense of being capable of knowing itself, its parts, and resources; *situatedness and self-adaptation*—sensing the influences from its environment and acting accordingly to what happens in the observed environment and a particular context; being *non-proprietary* in a sense of not constraining itself to a closed world but being capable of functioning in a heterogeneous word of open standards; and *anticipatory* in

---

* research.ibm.com/autonomic/overview/elements.html (accessed October 10, 2012).

a sense of being able to automatically anticipate needed resources and seamlessly bridging user tasks to their technological implementations hiding complexity.

However, having an autonomic system for processing Big Data semantics might not be sufficient. Indeed, even such a sophisticated entity system may once face circumstances which it would not be capable of reacting to by reconfiguration. So, the design objectives will not be met by such a system and it should qualify itself as not useful for further exploitation and die. A next-generation software system will then be designed and implemented (by humans) which may inherit some valid features from the ancestor system but shall also have some principally new features. Therefore, it needs to be admitted that it is not always possible for even an autonomic system to adapt itself to a change within its lifetime. Consequently, self-management capability may not be sufficient for the system to survive autonomously—humans are required for giving birth to ancestors. Hence, we are coming to the necessity of a self-improvement feature which is very close to evolution. In that we may seek for inspiration in bio-social systems. Nature offers an automatic tool for adapting biological species across generations named genetic evolution. An evolutionary process could be denoted as the process of proactive change of the features in the populations of (natural or artificial) life forms over successive generations providing diversity at every level of life organization. Darwin (1859) put the following principles in the core of his theory:

- Principle of variation (variations of configuration and behavioral features);
- Principle of heredity (a child inherits some features from its parents);
- Principle of natural selection (some features make some individuals more competitive than others in getting needed for survival resources).

These principles may remain valid for evolving software systems, in particular, for Big Data computing. Processing knowledge originating from Big Data may, however, imply more complexity due to its intrinsic social features.

Knowledge is a product that needs to be shared within a group so that survivability and quality of life of the group members will be higher than those of any individual alone. Sharing knowledge facilitates collaboration and improves individual and group performance. Knowledge is actively consumed and also left as a major inheritance for future generations, for example, in the form of ontologies. As a collaborative and social substance, knowledge and cognition evolve in a more complex way for which additional facets have to be taken into account such as social or group focus of attention, bias, interpretation, explicitation, expressiveness, inconsistency, etc.

In summary, it may be admitted that Big Data is collected and supervised by different communities following different cultures, standards, objectives, etc. Big Data semantics is processed using naturally different ontologies. All these loosely coupled data and knowledge fractions in fact "live their own lives" based on very complex processes, that is, evolve following the evolution of these cultures, their cognition mechanisms, standards, objectives, ontologies, etc. An infrastructure for managing and understanding such data straightforwardly needs to be regarded as an ecosystem of evolving processing entities. Below we propose treating ontologies (a key for understanding Big Data) as genomes and bodies of those knowledge processing entities. For this, basic principles by Darwin are applied to their evolution aiming to get optimal or quasi-optimal (according to evolving definition of the quality) populations of knowledge species. These populations represent the evolving understanding of the respective islands of Big Data in their dynamics. This approach to knowledge evolution will require interpretation and implementation of concepts like "birth," "death," "morphogenesis," "mutation," "reproduction," etc., applied to knowledge organisms, their groups, and environments.

Scaling with a Traditional Database

In some sense, "Big data" is a term that is increasingly being used to describe very large volumes of unstructured and structured content—usually in amounts measured in terabytes or petabytes—that enterprises want to harness and analyze.

Traditional *relational* database management technologies, which use indexing for speedy data retrieval and complex query support, have been hard pressed to keep up with the data insertion speeds required for big data analytics. Once a database gets bigger than about half a terabyte, some database products' ability to rapidly accept new data start [start is to database products] to decrease.

There are two kinds of scalability, namely vertical and horizontal. Vertical scaling is just adding more capacity to a single machine. Fundamentally, every database product is vertically scalable to the extent that they can make good use of more central processing unit cores, random access memory, and disk space. With a horizontally scalable system, it is possible to add capacity by adding more machines. Beyond doubt, most database products are *not* horizontally scalable.

When an application needs more write capacity than they can get out of a single machine, they are required to shard (partition) their data across multiple database servers. This is how companies like Facebook (facebook.com) or Twitter (twitter.com) have scaled their MySQL installations to massive proportions. This is the closest to what one can get into horizontal scalability with database products.

Sharding is a client-side affair, that is, the database server does not do it for user. In this kind of environment, when someone accesses data, the data access layer uses consistent hashing to determine which machine in the cluster a precise data should be written to (or read from). Enhancing capacity to a sharded system is a process of *manually* rebalancing the data across the cluster. The database system itself takes care of rebalancing the data and guaranteeing that it is adequately replicated across the cluster. This is what it means for a database to be horizontally scalable.

In many cases, constructing Big Data systems on premise provides better data flow performance, but requires a greater capital investment. Moreover, one has to consider the growth of the data. While many model linear growth curves, interestingly the patterns of data growth within Big Data systems are more exponential. Therefore, model both technology and costs to match up with sensible growth of the database so that the growth of the data flows.

Structured data transformation is the traditional approach of changing the structure of the data found within the source system to the structure of the target system, for instance, a Big Data system. The advantage of most Big Data systems is that deep structure is not a requirement; without doubt, structure can typically be layered in after the data arrive at the goal. However, it is a best practice to form the data within the goal. It should be a good abstraction of the source operational databases in a structure that allows those who analyze the data within the Big Data system to effectively and efficiently find the data required. The issue to consider with scaling is the amount of latency that transformations cause as data moves from the source(s) to the goal, and the data are changed in both structure and content. However, one should avoid complex transformations as data migrations for operational sources to the analytical goals. Once the data are contained within a Big Data system, the distributed nature of the architecture allows for the gathering of the proper result set. So, transformations that cause less latency are more suitable within Big Data domain.

Large Scale Data Processing Workflows

Overall infrastructure for many Internet companies can be represented as a pipeline with three layers: Ingestion, Storage & Processing, and Serving. The most vital among the three is the Storage & Processing layer. This layer can be represented as a multisub-layer stack with a scalable file system such as Google File System (Ghemawat et al. 2003) at the bottom, a framework for distributed sorting and hashing, for example, Map-Reduce (Dean and Ghemawat 2008) over the file system layer, a dataflow programming framework over the map-reduce layer, and a workflow manager at the top.

Debugging large-scale data, in the Internet firms, is crucial because data passes through many subsystems, each having different query interface, different metadata representation, different underlying models (some have files, some have records, some have workflows), etc. Thus, it is hard to maintain consistency and it is essential to factor out the debugging from the subsystems. There should be a self-governing system that takes care of all the metadata management. All data-processing subsystems can dispatch their metadata to such system which absorbs all the metadata, integrates them, and exposes a query interface for all metadata queries. This can provide a uniform view to users, factors out the metadata management code, and decouples metadata lifetime from data/subsystem lifetime.

Another stimulating problem is to deal with different data and process granularity. Data granularity can vary from a web page, to a table, to a row, to a cell. Process granularity can vary from a workflow, to a map-reduce program, to a map-reduce task. It is very hard to make an inference when the given relationship is in one granularity and the query is in other granularity and therefore it is vital to capture provenance data across the workflow. While there is no one-size-fits-all solution, a good methodology could be to use the best granularity at all levels. However, this may cause a lot of overhead and thus some smart domain-specific techniques need to be implemented (Lin and Dyer 2010; Olston 2012).

Knowledge Self-Management and Refinement through Evolution

World changes—so do the beliefs and reflections about it. Those beliefs and reflections are the knowledge humans have about their environments. However, the nature of those changes is different. The world just changes in events. Observation or sensing (Ermolayev et al. 2008) of events invokes generation of data—often in huge volumes and with high velocities. Humans evolve—adapt themselves to become better fitted to the habitat.

Knowledge is definitely a product of some processes carried out by conscious living beings (for example, humans). Following Darwin's (1859) approach and terminology to some extent, it may be stated that knowledge, both in terms of scope and quality, makes some individuals more competitive than others in getting vital resources or at least for improving their quality of life. The major role of knowledge as a required feature for survival is decision-making support. Humans differ in fortune and fate because they make different choices in similar situations, which is largely due to their possession of different knowledge. So, the evolution of conscious beings noticeably depends on the knowledge they possess. On the other hand, making a choice in turn triggers the production of knowledge by a human. Therefore, it is natural to assume that knowledge evolves triggered by the evolution of conscious beings, their decision-making needs and taken decisions, quality standards, etc. To put both halves in one whole, knowledge evolves in support of and to support the proactive needs of the owners more effectively, for example, to better interpret or explain the data generated when observing events, corresponding to the diversity and complexity of these data. This observation leads us to a hypothesis about the way knowledge evolves:

> The mechanisms of knowledge evolution are very similar to the mechanisms of biological evolution. Hence, the methods and mechanisms for the evolution of knowledge could be spotted from the ones enabling the evolution of living beings.

In particular, investigating the analogies and developing the mechanisms for the evolution of formal knowledge representations—specified as ontologies—is of interest for the Big Data semantics layer (Figure 1.5). The triggers for ontology evolution in the networked and interlinked environments could be external influences coming bottom-up from external and heterogeneous information streams.

Recently, the role of ontologies as formal and consensual knowledge representations has become established in different domains where the use of knowledge representations and reasoning is an essential requirement. Examples of these domains range from heterogeneous sensor network data processing through the Web of Things to Linked Open Data management and use. In all these domains, distributed information artifacts change sporadically and intensively in reflection of the changes in the world. However, the descriptions of the knowledge about these artifacts do not evolve in line with these changes.

Typically, ontologies are changed semiautomatically or even manually and are available in a sequence of discrete revisions. This fact points out a serious disadvantage of ontologies built using state-of-the-art knowledge engineering and management frameworks and methodologies: expanding and amplified distortion between the world and its reflection in knowledge. It is also one of the major obstacles for a wider acceptance of semantic technologies in industries (see also Hepp 2007; Tatarintseva et al. 2011).

The diversity of domain ontologies is an additional complication for proper and efficient use of dynamically changing knowledge and information artifacts for processing Big Data semantics. Currently, the selection of the best suiting one for a given set of requirements is carried out by a knowledge engineer using his/her subjective preferences. A more natural evolutionary approach for selecting the best-fitting knowledge representations promises enhancing robustness and transparency, and seems to be more technologically attractive.

Further, we elaborate a vision of a knowledge evolution ecosystem where agent-based software entities carry their knowledge genomes in the form of ontology schemas and evolve in response to the influences percieved from their environments. These influences are thought of as the tokens of Big Data (like news tokens in the "Illustrative Example" section) coming into the species' environments. Evolution implies natural changes in the ontologies which reflect the change in the world snap-shotted by Big Data tokens. Inspiration and analogies are taken from evolutionary biology.

Knowledge Organisms, their Environments, and Features

Evolving software entities are further referred to as individual *Knowledge Organisms* (KO). It is envisioned (Figure 1.6) that a KO:

1. Is *situated in its environment* as described in "Environment, Perception (Nutrition), and Mutagens"

2. Carries its individual *knowledge genome* represented as a schema or Terminological Box (TBox; Nardi and Brachman 2007) of the respective ontology (see "Knowledge Genome and Knowledge Body")

3. Has its individual *knowledge body* represented as an assertional component (ABox; Nardi and Brachman 2007) of the respective ontology (see "Knowledge Genome and Knowledge Body")

4. Is capable of *perceiving* the influences from the environment in the form of knowledge tokens (see "Environment, Perception (Nutrition), and Mutagens") that may cause the changes in the genome (see "Mutation") and body (see "Morphogenesis")—the *mutagens*

5. Is capable of *deliberating* about the *affected parts* of its genome and body (see "Morphogenesis" and "Mutation")

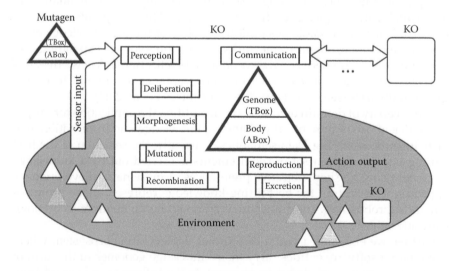

FIGURE 1.6
A Knowledge Organism: functionality and environment. Small triangles of different transparency represent knowledge tokens in the environment—consumed and produced by KOs. These knowledge tokens may also referred to as mutagens as they may trigger mutations.

6. Is capable of consuming some parts of a mutagen for: (a) *morphogenesis* changing only the body (see "Morphogenesis"); (b) *mutation* changing both the genome and body (see "Mutation"); or (c) *recombination*—a mutual enrichment of several genomes in a group of KO which may trigger *reproduction*—recombination of body replicas giving "birth" to a new KO (see "Recombination and Reproduction")

7. Is capable of *excreting* the unused parts of mutagens or the "dead" parts of the body to the environment

The results of mainstream research in distributed artificial intelligence and semantic technologies suggest the following basic building blocks for developing a KO. The features of situatedness (Jennings 2000) and deliberation (Wooldridge and Jennings 1995) are characteristic to intelligent software agents, while the rest of the required functionality could be developed using the achievments in Ontology Alignment (Euzenat and Shvaiko 2007). Recombination involving a group of KOs could be thought of based on the known mechanisms for multiissue negotiations on semantic contexts (e.g., Ermolayev et al. 2005) among software agents—the members of a reproduction group.

Environment, Perception (Nutrition), and Mutagens

An environmental context for a KO could be thought of as an arial of its habitat. Such a context needs to be able to provide nutrition that is "healthy" for particular KO species, that is, matching their genome noticeably. The food for nutrition is provided by Knowledge Extraction and Contextualization functionality (Figure 1.7) in a form of knowledge tokens. Hence, several

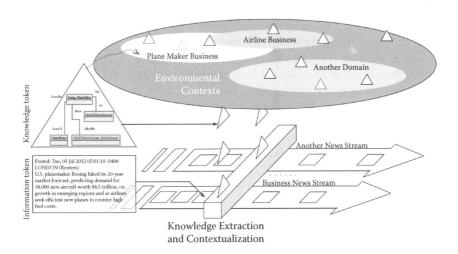

FIGURE 1.7
Environmental contexts, knowledge tokens, knowledge extraction, and contextualization.

and possibly overlapping environmental contexts need to be regarded in a hierarchy which corresponds to several subject domains of intetrest and a foundational knowledge layer. By saying this, we subsume that there is a single domain or foundational ontology module schema per environmental context. Different environmental contexts corresponding to different subject domais of interest are pictured as ellipses in Figure 1.7.

Environmental contexts are sowed with knowledge tokens that correspond to their subject domains. It might be useful to limit the lifetime of a knowledge token in an environment—those which are not consumed dissolve finally when their lifetime ends. Fresh and older knowledge tokens are pictured with different transparency in Figure 1.7.

KOs inhabit one or several overlapping environmental contexts based on the nutritional healthiness of knowledge tokens sowed there, that is, the degree to which these knowledge tokens match to the genome of a particular KO. KOs use their perceptive ability to find and consume knowledge tokens for nutrition. A KO may decide to migrate from one environment to another based on the availability of healthy food there. Knowledge tokens that only partially match KOs' genome may cause both KO body and genome changes and are thought of as mutagens. Mutagens, in fact, deliver the information about the changes in the world to the environments of KOs.

Knowledge tokens are extracted from the information tokens either in a stream window or from the updates of the persistent data storage and further sawn in the appropriate environmental context. The context for placing a newly coming KO is chosen by the contextualization functionality (Figure 1.7) based on the match ratio to the ontology schema characterizing the context in the environment. Those knowledge tokens that are not mapped well to any of the ontology schemas are sown in the environment without attributing them to any particular context.

For this, existing shallow knowledge extraction techniques could be exploited, for example, Fan et al. (2012a). The choice of appropriate techniques depends on the nature and modality of data. Such a technique would extract several interrelated assertions from an information token and provide these as a knowledge token coded in a knowledge representation language of an appropriate expressiveness, for example, in a tractable subset of the Web Ontology Language (OWL) 2.0 (W3C 2009). Information and knowledge* tokens for the news item of our Boeing example are pictured in Figure 1.7.

---

* Unified Modeling Language (UML) notation is used for picturing the knowledge token in Figure 1.7 because it is more illustrative. Though not shown in Figure 1.7, it can be straightforwardly coded in OWL, following, for example, Kendall et al. (2009).

Knowledge Genome and Knowledge Body

Two important aspects in contextualized knowledge representation for an outlined knowledge evolution ecosystem have to be considered with care (Figure 1.8):

- A knowledge genome etalon for a population of KOs belonging to one species
- An individual knowledge genome and body for a particular KO

A knowledge genome etalon may be regarded as the schema (TBox) of a distinct ontology module which represents an outstanding context in a subject domain. In our proposal, the etalon genome is carried by a dedicated Etalon KO (EKO; Figure 1.8) to enable alignments with individual genomes and other etalons in a uniform way. The individual assertions (ABox) of this ontology module are spread over the individual KOs belonging to the corresponding species—forming their individual bodies.

The individual genomes of those KOs are the recombined genomes of the KOs who gave birth to this particular KO. At the beginning of times, the individual genomes may be replicas of the etalon genome. Anyhow, they evolve independently in *mutations* or because of *morphogenesis* of an individual KO, or because of *recombinations* in reproductive groups.

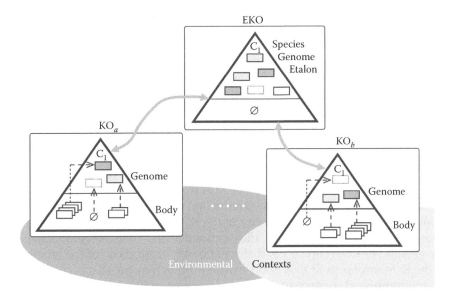

FIGURE 1.8
Knowledge genomes and bodies. Different groups of assertions in a KO body are attributed to different elements of its genome, as shown by dashed arrows. The more assertions relate to a genome element, the more dominant this element is as shown by shades of gray.

Different elements (concepts, properties, axioms) in a knowledge genome may possess different strengths, that is, be dominant or recessive. For example (Figure 1.8) concept C_1 in the genome of KO_a is quite strong because it is reinforced by a significant number of individual assertions attributed to this concept, that is, dominant. On the contrary, C_1 in the genome of KO_b is very weak—that is, recessive—as it is not supported by individual assertions in the body of KO_b. Recessivness or dominance values may be set and altered using techniques like spreading activation (Quillian 1967, 1969; Collins and Loftus 1975) which also appropriately affect the structural contexts (Ermolayev et al. 2005, 2010) of the elements in focus.

Recessive elements may be kept in the genome as parts of the genetic memory, but until they do not contradict any dominant elements. For example, if a dominant property of the *PlaneMaker* concept in a particular period of time is *PlaneMaker–hikes–MarketForecast*, then a recessive property *PlaneMaker–lessens–MarketForecast* may die out soon with high probability, as contradictory to the corresponding dominant property.

The etalone genome of a species evolves in line with the evolution of the individual genomes. The difference, however, is that EKO has no direct relationship (situatedness) to any environmental context. So, all evolution influences are provided to EKO by the individual KOs belonging to the corresponding species via communication. If an EKO and KOs are implemented as agent-based software entities, the techniques like agent-based ontology alignment are of relevance for evolving etalon genomes. In particular, the alignment settings are similar to a Structural Dynamic Uni-directional Distributed (SDUD) ontology alignment problem (Ermolayev and Davidovsky 2012). The problem could be solved using multiissue negotiations on semantic contexts, for example, following the approach of Ermolayev et al. (2005) and Davidovsky et al. (2012). For assuring the consistency in the updated ontology modules after alignment, several approaches are applicable: incremental updates for atomic decompositions of ontology modules (Klinov et al. 2012); checking correctness of ontology contexts using ontology design patterns approach (Gangemi and Presutti 2009); evaluating formal correctness using formal (meta-) properties (Guarino and Welty 2001).

An interesting case would be if an individual genome of a particular KO evolves very differently to the rest of KOs in the species. This may happen if such a KO is situated in an environmental context substantially different from the context where the majority of the KOs of this species are collecting knowledge tokens. For example, the dominancy and recessiveness values in the genome of KO_b (Figure 1.8) differ noticeably from those of the genomes of the KOs similar to KO_a. A good reason for this may be: KO_b is situated in an environmental context different to the context of KO_a—so the knowledge tokens KO_b may consume are different to the food collected by KO_a. Hence, the changes to the individual genome of KO_b will be noticeably different to those of KO_a after some period of time. Such a *genetic drift* may cause that the structural difference in individual genomes goes beyond a threshold within which recombination gives ontologically viable posterity. A new knowledge genome etalon may, therefore, emerge if the group of the KOs with genomes drifted in a similar direction reaches a critical mass—giving birth to a new species.

The following are the features required to extend an ontology representation language for to cope with the mentioned evolutionary mechanisms:

- A temporal extension that allows representing and reasoning about the lifetime and temporal intervals of validity of the elements in knowledge genomes and bodies. One relevant extension and reasoning technique is OWL-MET (Keberle 2009).
- An extension that allows assigning meta-properties to ontological elements for verifying formal correctness or adherence to relevant design patterns. Relevant formalisms may be sought following Guarino and Welty (2001) or Gangemi and Presutti (2009).

Morphogenesis

Morphogenesis in a KO could be seen as a process of developing the shape of a KO body. In fact, such a development is done by adding new assertions to the body and attributing them to the correct parts of the genome. This process could be implemented using ontology instance migration technique (Davidovsky et al. 2011); however, the objective of morphogenesis differs from that of ontology instance migration. The task of the latter is to ensure correctness and completeness, that is, that, ideally, all the assertions are properly aligned with and added to the target ontology ABox. Morphogenesis requires that only the assertions that fit well to the TBox of the target ontology are consumed for shaping it out. Those below the fitness threshold are excreted. If, for example, a mutagen perceived by a KO is the one of our Boeing example presented in Figures 1.2 or 1.7, then the set of individual assertions will be[*]

{AllNipponAirways:Airline, B787-JA812A:EfficientNewPlane, Japan:Country, **Boeing:PlaneMaker**, New20YMarketForecastbyBoeing:MarketForecast, United States:Country, Old20YMarketForecastbyBoeing:MarketForecast}.   (1.1)

Let us now assume that the genome (TBox) of the KO contains only the concepts represented in Figure 1.2 as grey-shaded classes—{Airline, PlaneMaker, MarketForecast} and thick-line relationships—{seeksFor–soughtBy}. Then only the bolded assertions from (1.1) could be consumed for morphogenesis by this KO and the rest have to be excreted back to the environment. Interestingly, the ratio of mutagen ABox consumption may be used as a good

---

[*] The syntax for representing individual assertions is similar to the syntax in UML for compatibility with Figure 1.2: ⟨assertion-name⟩:⟨concept-name⟩.

metric for a KO in deliberations about: its resistance to mutations; desire to migrate to a different environmental context, or to start seeking for reproduction partners.

Another important case in a morphogenesis process is detecting a contradiction between a newly coming mutagenic assertion and the assertion that is in the body of the KO. For example, let us assume that the body already comprises the property *SalesVolume* of the assertion named *New20YMarketForecastbyBoeing* with the value of 2.1 million. The value of the same property coming with the mutagen equals to 4.5 million. So, the KO has to resolve this contradiction by: either (i) deciding to reshape its body by accepting the new assertion and excreting the old one; or (ii) resisting and declining the change. Another possible behavior would be collecting and keeping at hand the incoming assertions until their dominance is not proved by the quantity. Dominance may be assessed using different metrics. For example, a relevant technique is offered by the Strength Value-Based Argumentation Framework (Isaac et al. 2008).

Mutation

Mutation of a KO could be understood as the change of its genome caused by the environmental influences (mutagenic factors) coming with the consumed knowledge tokens. Similar to the biological evolution, a KO and its genome are resistent to mutagenic factors and do not change at once because of any incoming influence, but only because of those which could not be ignored because of their strength. Different genome elements may be differently resistant. Let us illustrate different aspects of mutation and resistance using our Boeing example. As depicted in Figure 1.9, the change of the *AirPlaneMaker* concept name (to *PlaneMaker*) in the genome did not happen though a new assertion had been added to the body as a result of morphogenesis (*Boeing*: (*PlaneMaker*) *AirPlaneMaker**). The reason *AirPlaneMaker* concept resisted this mutation was that the assertions attributed to the concept of *PlaneMaker* were in the minority—so, the mutagenic factor has not yet been strong enough. This mutation will have a better chance to occur if similar mutagenic factors continue to come in and the old assertions in the body of the KO die out because their lifetime periods come to end. More generally, the more individual assertions are attributed to a genome element at a given point in time—the more strong this genome element is to mutations.

In contrast to the *AirPlaneMaker* case, the mutations brought by *hikes—hikedBy* and *successorOf—predecessorOf* object properties did happen (Figure 1.9) because the KO did not possess any (strong) argument to resist

---

* UML syntax is used as basic. The name of the class from the knowledge token is added in brackets before the name of the class to which the assertion is attributed in the KO body. This is done for keeping the information about the occurrences of a different name in the incoming knowledge tokens. This historical data may further be used for evaluating the strength of the mutagenic factor.

them. Indeed, there were no contradictory properties both in the genome and the body of the KO before it accepted the grey-shaded assertions as a result of morphogenesis.

Not all the elements of an incoming knowledge token could be consumed by a KO. In our example (Figure 1.9), some of the structural elements (*AirLine, EfficientNewPlane, seeks—soughtBy*) were

- Too different to the genome of this particular KO, so the similarity factor was too low and the KO did not find any match to its TBox. Hence, the KO was not able to generate any replacement hypotheses also called propositional substitutions (Ermolayev et al. 2005).
- Too isolated from the elements of the genome—having no properties relating them to the genome elements. Hence, the KO was not able to generate any merge hypotheses.

These unused elements are excreted (Figure 1.9) back to the environment as a knowledge token. This token may further be consumed by another

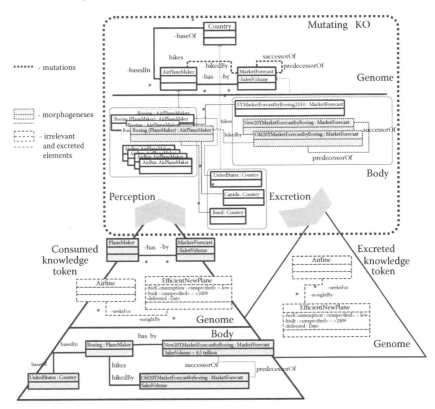

FIGURE 1.9
Mutation in an individual KO illustrated by our Boeing example.

KO with different genome comprising matching elements. Such a KO may migrate from a different environmental context (e.g., Airlines Business).

Similar to morphogenesis, mutation may be regarded as a subproblem of ontology alignment. The focus is, however, a little bit different. In contrast to morphogenesis which was interpreted as a specific ontology instance migration problem, mutation affects the TBox and is therefore structural ontology alignment (Ermolayev and Davidovsky 2012). There is a solid body of related work in structural ontology alignment. Agent-based approaches relevant to our context are surveyed, for example, in Ermolayev and Davidovsky (2012).

In addition to the requirements already mentioned above, the following features extending an ontology representation language are essential for coping with the mechanisms of mutation:

- The information of the attribution of a consumed assertion to a particular structural element in the knowledge token needs to be preserved for future use in possible mutations. An example is given
  in Figure 1.8—*Boeing: (PlaneMaker) AirPlaneMaker*. The name of the
  concept in the knowledge token (*PlaneMaker*) is preserved and the
  assertion is attributed to the *AirPlaneMaker* concept in the genome.

Recombination and Reproduction

As mutation, recombination is a mechanism of adapting KOs to environmental changes. Recombination involves a group of KOs belonging to one or several similar species with partially matching genomes. In contrast to mutation, recombination is triggered and performed differently. Mutation is invoked by external influences coming from the environment in the form of mutagens. Recombination is triggered by a conscious intention of a KO to make its genome more resistant and therefore better adapted to the environment in its current state. Conscious in this context means that a KO first analyzes the strength and adaptation of its genome, detects weak elements, and then reasons about the necessity of acquiring external reinforcements for these weak elements. Weaknesses may be detected by:

- Looking at the proportion of consumed and excreted parts in the
  perceived knowledge tokens—reasoning about how healthy is the
  food in its current environmental context. If not, then new elements
  extending the genome for increasing consumption and decreasing
  excretion may be desired to be acquired.
- Looking at the resistance of the elements in the genome to mutations. If weaknesses are detected, then it may be concluded that the
  assertions required for making these structural elements stronger
  are either nonexistent in the environmental context or are not consumed. In the latter case, a structural reinforcement by acquiring

new genome elements through recombination may be useful. In the former case (nonexistence), the KO may decide to move to a different environmental context.

Recombination of KOs as a mechanism may be implemented using several available technologies. Firstly, a KO needs to reason about the strengths and weaknesses of the elements in its genome. For this, in addition to the extra knowledge representation language features mentioned above, it needs a simple reasoning functionality (pictured in Figure 1.6 as Deliberation). Secondly, a KO requires a means for getting in contact with the other KOs and checking if they have similar intentions to recombine their genomes. For this, the available mechanisms for communication (e.g., Labrou et al. 1999; Labrou 2006), meaning negotiation (e.g., Davidovsky et al. 2012), and coalition formation (e.g., Rahwan 2007) could be relevant.

Reproduction is based on recombination mechanism and results and goes further by combining the replicas of the bodies of those KOs who take part in the recombination group resulting in the production of a new KO. A KO may intend to reproduce itself because his lifetime period comes to an end or because of the other individual or group stimuli that have to be researched.

Populations of Knowledge Organisms

KOs may belong to different *species*—the groups of KOs that have similar genomes based on the same etalon carried by the EKO. KOs that share the same areal of habitat (environmental context) form the *population* which may comprise the representatives of several species. Environmental contexts may also overlap. So, the KOs of different species have possibilities to interact. With respect to species and populations, the mechanisms of (i) *migration*, (ii) *genetic drift*, (iii) *speciation*, and (iv) *breeding* for evolving knowledge representations are of interest.

Migration is the movement of KOs from one environmental context to another context because of different reasons mentioned in the "Knowledge Organisms, their Environments, and Features" section. Genetic drift is the change of genomes to a degree beyond the species tolerance (similarity) threshold caused by cumulative efffect of a series of mutations as explained in the "Knowledge Genome and Knowledge Body" section. Speciation effect occurs if genetic drift results in a distinct group of KOs capable of reproducing themselves with their recombined genomes.

If knowledge evolves in a way similar to biological evolution, the outcome of this process would best-fit KOs desires of environmental mimicry, but perhaps not the requirements of ontology users. Therefore, for ensuring human stakeholders' commitment to the ontology, it might be useful to keep the evolution process under control. For this, constraints, or restrictions in another form, may be introduced for relevant environmental contexts and fitness measurement functions so as to guide the evolution toward a desired goal. This artificial way of control over the natural evolutionary order of things may be regarded as breeding—a controlled process of sequencing desired mutations that causes the emergence of a species with the required genome features.

Fitness of Knowledge Organisms and Related Ontologies

It has been repeatedly stated in the discussion of the features of KOs in "Knowledge Organisms, their Environments, and Features" that they exhibit proactive behavior. One topical case is that a KO would rather migrate away from the current environmental context instead of continuing consuming knowledge tokens which are not healthy for it in terms of structural similarity to its genome. It has also been mentioned that a KO may cooperate with other KOs to fulfill its evolutionary intentions. For instance, KOs may form cooperative groups for recombination or reproduction. They also interact with their EKOs for improving the etalon genome of the species. Another valid case, though not mentioned in "Knowledge Organisms, their Environments, and Features", would be if a certain knowledge token is available in the environment and two or more KOs approach it concurrently with an intention to consume. If those KOs are cooperative, the token will be consumed by the one which needs it most—so that the overall "strength" of the species is increased. Otherwise, if the KOs are competitive, as it often happens in nature, the strongest KO will get the token. All these cases require a quantification of the strength, or fitness, of KOs and knowledge tokens. Fitness is, in fact, a complex metric having several important facets.

Firstly, we summarize what fitness of a KO means. We outline that their fitness is inseparable from (in fact, symmetric to) the fitness of the knowledge tokens that KOs consume from and excrete back to their environmental contexts. Then, we describe several factors which contribute to fitness. Finally, we discuss how several dimensions of fitness could be used to compare different KOs.

To start our deliberations about fitness, we have to map the high-level understanding of this metric to the requirements of Big Data processing as presented in the "Motivation and Unsolved Issues" and "State of Technology, Research, and Development in Big Data Computing" sections in the form of the processing stack (Figures 1.3 through 1.5). The grand objective of a Big Data computing system or infrastructure is providing a capability for data analysis with balanced effectiveness and efficiency. In particular, this capability subsumes facilitating decision-making and classification, providing adequate inputs to software applications, etc. An evolving knowledge ecosystem, comprising environmental contexts populated with Kos, is introduced in the semantics processing layer of the overall processing stack. The aim of introducing the ecosystem is to ensure seamless and balanced connection between a user who operates the system at the upper layers and the lower layers that provide data.

Ontologies are the "blood and flesh" of the KOs and the whole ecosystem as they are both the code registering a desired evolutionary change and the result of this evolution. From the data-processing viewpoint, the ontologies are consensual knowledge representations that facilitate improving data integration, transformation, and interoperability between the processing nodes in the infrastructure. A seamless connection through the layers of the processing stack is facilitated by the way ontologies are created and changed. As already mentioned above in the introduction of the "Knowledge Self-Management and Refinement through Evolution" section, ontologies are traditionally designed beforehand and further populated by assertions taken from the source data. In our evolving ecosystem, ontologies evolve in parallel to data processing. Moreover, the changes in ontologies are caused by the mutagens brought by the incoming data. Knowledge extraction subsystem (Figure 1.7) transforms units of data to knowledge tokens. These in turn are sown in a corresponding environmental context by a contextualization subsystem and further consumed by KOs. KOs may change their body or even mutate due to the changes brought by consumed mutagenic knowledge tokens. The changes in the KOs are in fact the changes in the ontologies they carry. So, ontologies change seamlessly and naturally in a way to best suite the substance brought in by data. For assessing this change, the judgments about the value and appropriateness of ontologies in time are important. Those should, however, be formulated accounting for the fact that an ontology is able to self-evolve.

A degree to which an ontology is reused is one more important characteristic to be taken into account. Reuse means that data in multiple places refers to this ontology and when combined with interoperability it implies that data about similar things is described using the same ontological fragments. When looking at an evolving KO, having a perfect ontology would mean that if new knowledge tokens appear in the environmental contexts of an organism, the organism can integrate all assertions in the tokens, that is, without a need to excrete some parts of the consumed knowledge tokens back to the environment. That is to say, the ontology which was internal to the KO before the token was consumed was already prepared for the integration of the new token. Now, one could turn the viewpoint by saying that the information described in the token was already described in the ontology which the KO had and thus that the ontology was reused in one more place. This increases the value, that is, the fitness of the ontology maintained by the KO.

Using similar argumentation, we can conclude that if a KO needs to excrete a consumed knowledge token, the ontology fits worse to describing the fragment of data to which the excreted token is attributed. Thus, in conclusion, we could say that the fitness of a KO is directly dependent on the proportion between the parts of knowledge tokens which it: (a) is able to consume for morphogenesis and possibly mutation; versus (b) needs to excrete back to the environment. Additionally, the age of the assertions which build up the current knowledge body of a KO influences its quality. If the proportion of very young assertions in the body is high, the KO might be not resistant to stochastic changes, which is not healthy. Otherwise, if only long-living assertions form the body, it means that the KO is either in a wrong context or too resistant to mutagens. Both are bad as no new information is added, the KO ignores changes, and hence the ontology it carries may become irrelevant. Therefore, a good mix of young and old assertions in the body of a KO indicates high fitness—KO's knowledge is overall valid and evolves appropriately.

Of course stating that fitness depends only on the numbers of used and excreted assertions is an oversimplification. Indeed, incoming knowledge tokens that carry assertions may be very different. For instance, the knowledge token in our Boeing example contains several concepts and properties in its TBox: a Plane, a PlaneMaker, a MarketForecast, an Airline, a Country, SalesVolume, seeksFor—soughtBy, etc. Also, some individuals attributed to these TBox elements are given in the ABox: UnitedStates, Boeing, New20YMarketForecastByBoeing, 4.5 trillion, etc. One can imagine a less complex knowledge token which contains less information. In addition to size and complexity, a token has also other properties which are important to consider. One is the source where the token originates from. A token can be produced by knowledge extraction from a given channel or can be excreted by a KO. When the token is extracted from a channel, its value depends on the quality of the channel, relative to the quality of other channels in the system (see also the context of origin in the "Contextualizing" section). The quality of knowledge extraction is important as well, though random errors could be mitigated by statistical means. Further, a token could be attributed to a number of environmental contexts. A context is important, that is, adds more value to a token in the context if there are a lot of knowledge tokens in that context or more precisely there have appeared many tokens in the context recently. Consequently, a token becomes less valuable along its lifetime in the environment.

Till now, we have been looking at different fitness, value, and quality factors in insulation. The problem is, however, that there is no straightforward way to integrate these different factors. For this, an approach to address the problem of assessing the quality of an ontology as a dynamic optimization problem (Cochez and Terziyan 2012) may be relevant.

Some Conclusions

For all those who use or process Big Data a good mental picture of the world, dissolved in data tokens, may be worth of petabytes of raw information and save weeks of analytic work. Data emerge reflecting a change in the world. Hence, Big Data is a fine-grained reflection of the changes around us. Knowledge extracted from these data in an appropriate and timely way is an essence of adequate understanding of the change in the world. In this chapter, we provided the evidence that numerous challenges stand on the way of understanding the sense, the trends dissolved in the petabytes of Big Data—extracting its semantics for further use in analytics. Among those challenges, we have chosen the problem of balancing between effectiveness and efficiency in understanding Big Data as our focus. For better explaining our motivation and giving a reader the key that helps follow how our premises are transformed into conclusions, we offered a simple walkthrough example of a news token.

We began the analysis of Big Data Computing by looking at how the phenomenon influences and changes industrial landscapes. This overview helped us figure out that the demand in industries for effective and efficient use of Big Data, if properly understood, is enormous. However, this demand is not yet fully satisfied by the state-of-the-art technologies and methodologies. We then looked at current trends in research and development in order to narrow the gaps between the actual demand and the state of the art. The analysis of the current state of research activities resulted in pointing out the shortcomings and offering an approach that may help understand Big Data in a way that balances effectiveness and efficiency.

The major recommendations we elaborated for achieving the balance are: (i) devise approaches that intelligently combine top-down and bottom-up processing of data semantics by exploiting "3F + 3Co" in dynamics, at run time; (ii) use a natural incremental and evolutionary way of processing Big Data and its semantics instead of following a mechanistic approach to scalability.

Inspired by the harmony and beauty of biological evolution, we further presented our vision of how these high-level recommendations may be approached. The "Scaling with a Traditional Database" section offered a review of possible ways to solve scalability problem at data processing level. The "Knowledge Self-Management and Refinement through Evolution" section presented a conceptual level framework for building an evolving ecosystem of environmental contexts with knowledge tokens and different species of KOs that populate environmental contexts and collect knowledge tokens for nutrition. The genomes and bodies of these KOs are ontologies describing corresponding environmental contexts. These ontologies evolve in line with the evolution of KOs. Hence they reflect the evolution of our understanding of Big Data by collecting the refinements of our mental picture of the change in the world. Finally, we found out that such an evolutionary approach to building knowledge representations will naturally allow assuring fitness of knowledge representations—as the fitness of the corresponding KOs to the environmental contexts they inhabit.

We also found out that the major technological components for building such evolving knowledge ecosystems are already in place and could be effectively used, if refined and combined as outlined in the "Knowledge Self-Management and Refinement through Evolution" section.

Acknowledgments

This work was supported in part by the "Cloud Software Program" managed by TiViT Oy and the Finnish Funding Agency for Technology and Innovation (TEKES).

References

Abadi, D. J., D. Carney, U. Cetintemel, M. Cherniack, C. Convey, S. Lee, M. Stonebraker, N. Tatbul, and S. Zdonik. 2003. Aurora: A new model and architecture for data stream management. *VLDB Journal* 12(2): 120–139.

Anderson, C. 2008. The end of theory: The data deluge makes the scientific method obsolete. Wired Magazine 16:07 (June 23). http://www.wired.com/science/discoveries/magazine/16–07/pb_theory.

Ankolekar, A., M. Krotzsch, T. Tran, and D. Vrandecic. 2007. The two cultures: Mashing up Web 2.0 and the Semantic Web. In *Proc Sixteenth Int Conf on World Wide Web (WWW'07)*, 825–834. New York: ACM.

Berry, D. 2011. The computational turn: Thinking about the digital humanities. Culture Machine 12 (July 11). http://www.culturemachine.net/index.php/cm/article/view/440/470.

Beyer, M. A., A. Lapkin, N. Gall, D. Feinberg, and V. T. Sribar. 2011. 'Big Data' is only the beginning of extreme information management. Gartner Inc. (April). http://www.gartner.com/id=1622715 (accessed August 30, 2012).

Bizer, C., T. Heath, and T. Berners-Lee. 2009. Linked data—The story so far. *International Journal on Semantic Web and Information Systems* 5(3): 1–22.

Bollier, D. 2010. The promise and peril of big data. Report, Eighteenth Annual Aspen Institute Roundtable on Information Technology, the Aspen Institute. http://www.aspeninstitute.org/sites/default/files/content/docs/pubs/The_Promise_and_Peril_of_Big_Data.pdf (accessed August 30, 2012).

Bowker, G. C. 2005. *Memory Practices in the Sciences*. Cambridge, MA: MIT Press.

Boyd, D. and K. Crawford. 2012. Critical questions for big data. *Information, Communication & Society* 15(5): 662–679.

Broekstra, J., A. Kampman, and F. van Harmelen. 2002. Sesame: A generic architecture for storing and querying RDF and RDF schema. In *The Semantic Web—ISWC 2002*, eds. I. Horrocks and J. Hendler, 54–68. Berlin, Heidelberg: Springer-Verlag, LNCS 2342.

Cai, M. and M. Frank. 2004. RDFPeers: A scalable distributed RDF repository based on a structured peer-to-peer network. In Proc Thirteenth Int Conf World Wide Web (WWW'04), 650–657. New York: ACM.

Capgemini. 2012. The deciding factor: Big data & decision making. Report. http://www.capgemini.com/services-and-solutions/technology/business-information-management/the-deciding-factor/ (accessed August 30, 2012).

Chang, F., J. Dean, S. Ghemawat, W. C. Hsieh, D. A. Wallach, M. Burrows, T. Chandra, A. Fikes, and R. E. Gruber. 2008. Bigtable: A distributed storage system for structured data. *ACM Transactions on Computer Systems* 26(2): article 4.

Cochez, M. and V. Terziyan. 2012. Quality of an ontology as a dynamic optimisation problem. In *Proc Eighth Int Conf ICTERI 2012*, eds. V. Ermolayev et al., 249–256. CEUR-WS vol. 848. http://ceur-ws.org/Vol-848/ICTERI-2012-CEUR-WS-DEIS-paper-1-p-249-256.pdf.

Collins, A. M. and E. F. Loftus. 1975. A spreading-activation theory of semantic processing. *Psychological Review* 82(6): 407–428.

Cusumano, M. 2010. Cloud computing and SaaS as new computing platforms. *Communications of the ACM* 53(4): 27–29.

Darwin, C. 1859. *On the Origin of Species by Means of Natural Selection, or the Preservation of Favoured Races in the Struggle for Life*. London: John Murrey.

Davidovsky, M., V. Ermolayev, and V. Tolok. 2011. Instance migration between ontologies having structural differences. *International Journal on Artificial Intelligence Tools* 20(6): 1127–1156.

Davidovsky, M., V. Ermolayev, and V. Tolok. 2012. Agent-based implementation for the discovery of structural difference in OWL DL ontologies. In *Proc. Fourth Int United Information Systems Conf (UNISCON 2012)*, eds. H. C. Mayr, A. Ginige, and S. Liddle, Berlin, Heidelberg: Springer-Verlag, LNBIP 137.

Dean, J. and S. Ghemawat. 2008. MapReduce: Simplified data processing on large clusters. *Communications of the ACM* 51(1): 107–113.

Dean, D. and C. Webb. 2011. Recovering from information overload. *McKinsey Quarterly*. http://www.mckinseyquarterly.com/Recovering_from_information_overload_2735 (accessed October 8, 2012).

DeCandia, G., D. Hastorun, M. Jampani, G. Kakulapati, A. Lakshman, A. Pilchin, S. Sivasubramanian, P. Vosshall, and W. Vogels. 2007. Dynamo: Amazon's highly available key-value store. In *21st ACM Symposium on Operating Systems Principles*, eds. T. C. Bressoud and M. Frans Kaashoek, 205–220. New York: ACM.

Dickinson, I. and M. Wooldridge. 2003. Towards practical reasoning agents for the semantic web. In *Proc. of the Second International Joint Conference on Autonomous Agents and Multiagent Systems*, 827–834. New York: ACM.

Driscoll, M. 2011. Building data startups: Fast, big, and focused. *O'Reilly Radar* (9). http://radar.oreilly.com/2011/08/building-data-startups.html (accessed October 8, 2012).

Ermolayev, V. and M. Davidovsky. 2012. Agent-based ontology alignment: Basics, applications, theoretical foundations, and demonstration. In *Proc. Int Conf on Web Intelligence, Mining and Semantics (WIMS 2012)*, eds. D. Dan Burdescu, R. Akerkar, and C. Badica, 11–22. New York: ACM.

Ermolayev, V., N. Keberle, O. Kononenko, S. Plaksin, and V. Terziyan. 2004. Towards a framework for agent-enabled semantic web service composition. *International Journal of Web Services Research* 1(3): 63–87.

Ermolayev, V., N. Keberle, W.-E. Matzke, and V. Vladimirov. 2005. A strategy for automated meaning negotiation in distributed information retrieval. In *Proc 4th Int Semantic Web Conference (ISWC'05)*, eds. Y. Gil et al., 201–215. Berlin, Heidelberg: Springer-Verlag, LNCS 3729.

Ermolayev, V., N. Keberle, and W.-E. Matzke. 2008. An ontology of environments, events, and happenings, computer software and applications, 2008. *COMPSAC '08. 32nd Annual IEEE International*, pp. 539, 546, July 28, 2008–Aug. 1, 2008. doi: 10.1109/COMPSAC.2008.141

Ermolayev, V., C. Ruiz, M. Tilly, E. Jentzsch, J.-M. Gomez-Perez, and W.-E. Matzke. 2010. A context model for knowledge workers. In *Proc Second Workshop on Content, Information, and Ontologies (CIAO 2010)*, eds. V. Ermolayev, J.-M. Gomez-Perez, P. Haase, and P. Warren, CEUR-WS, vol. 626. http://ceur-ws.org/Vol-626/regular2.pdf (online).

Euzenat, J. and P. Shvaiko. 2007. *Ontology Matching*. Berlin, Heidelberg: Springer-Verlag.

Fan, W., A. Bifet, Q. Yang, and P. Yu. 2012a. Foreword. In *Proc First Int Workshop on Big Data, Streams, and Heterogeneous Source Mining: Algorithms, Systems, Programming Models and Applications*, eds. W. Fan, A. Bifet, Q. Yang, and P. Yu, New York: ACM.

Fan, J., A. Kalyanpur, D. C. Gondek, and D. A. Ferrucci. 2012b. Automatic knowledge extraction from documents. *IBM Journal of Research and Development* 56(3.4): 5:1–5:10.

Fensel, D., F. van Harmelen, B. Andersson, P. Brennan, H. Cunningham, E. Della Valle, F. Fischer et al. 2008. Towards LarKC: A platform for web-scale reasoning, *Semantic Computing, 2008 IEEE International Conference on*, pp. 524, 529, 4–7 Aug. 2008. doi: 10.1109/ICSC.2008.41.

Fisher, D., R. DeLine, M. Czerwinski, and S. Drucker. 2012. Interactions with big data analytics. *Interactions* 19(3):50–59.

Gangemi, A. and V. Presutti. 2009. Ontology design patterns. In *Handbook on Ontologies*, eds. S. Staab and R. Studer, 221–243. Berlin, Heidelberg: Springer-Verlag, International Handbooks on Information Systems.

Ghemawat, S., H. Gobioff, and S.-T. Leung. 2003. The Google file system. *In Proc Nineteenth ACM Symposium on Operating Systems Principles (SOSP'03)*, 29–43. New York: ACM.

Golab, L. and M. Tamer Ozsu. 2003. Issues in data stream management. *SIGMOD Record* 32(2): 5–14.

Gordon, A. 2005. Privacy and ubiquitous network societies. In *Workshop on ITU Ubiquitous Network Societies*, 6–15.

Greller, W. 2012. Reflections on the knowledge society. http://wgreller.wordpress.com/2010/11/03/big-data-isnt-big-knowledge-its-big-business/ (accessed August 20, 2012).

Gu, Y. and R. L. Grossman. 2009. Sector and sphere: The design and implementation of a high-performance data cloud. *Philosophical Transactions of the Royal Society* 367(1897): 2429–2445.

Guarino, N. and C. Welty. 2001. Supporting ontological analysis of taxonomic relationships. *Data and Knowledge Engineering* 39(1): 51–74.

Guéret, C., E. Oren, S. Schlobach, and M. Schut. 2008. An evolutionary perspective on approximate RDF query answering. In *Proc Int Conf on Scalable Uncertainty Management*, eds. S. Greco and T. Lukasiewicz, 215–228. Berlin, Heidelberg: Springer-Verlag, LNAI 5291.

He, B., M. Yang, Z. Guo, R. Chen, B. Su, W. Lin, and L. Zhou. 2010. Comet: Batched stream processing for data intensive distributed computing, In *Proc First ACM symposium on Cloud Computing (SoCC'10)*, 63–74. New York: ACM.

Hepp, M. 2007. Possible ontologies: How reality constrains the development of relevant ontologies. *IEEE Internet Computing* 11(1): 90–96.

Hogan, A., J. Z. Pan, A. Polleres, and Y. Ren. 2011. Scalable OWL 2 reasoning for linked data. In Lecture Notes for the Reasoning Web Summer School, Galway, Ireland (August). http://aidanhogan.com/docs/rw_2011.pdf (accessed October 18, 2012).

Isaac, A., C. Trojahn, S. Wang, and P. Quaresma. 2008. Using quantitative aspects of alignment generation for argumentation on mappings. In *Proc ISWC'08 Workshop on Ontology Matching*, ed. P. Shvaiko, J. Euzenat, F. Giunchiglia, and H. Stuckenschmidt, CEUR-WS Vol-431. http://ceur-ws.org/Vol-431/om2008_Tpaper5.pdf (online).

Ishai, Y., E. Kushilevitz, R. Ostrovsky, and A. Sahai. 2009. Extracting correlations, *Foundations of Computer Science, 2009. FOCS '09. 50th Annual IEEE Symposium on*, pp. 261, 270, 25–27 Oct. 2009. doi: 10.1109/FOCS.2009.56.

Joseph, A. 2012. A Berkeley view of big data. Closing keynote of Eduserv Symposium 2012: Big Data, Big Deal? http://www.eduserv.org.uk/newsandevents/events/2012/symposium/closing-keynote (accessed October 8, 2012).

Keberle, N. 2009. Temporal classes and OWL. In *Proc Sixth Int Workshop on OWL: Experiences and Directions (OWLED 2009)*, eds. R. Hoekstra and P. F. Patel-Schneider, CEUR-WS, vol 529. http://ceur-ws.org/Vol-529/owled2009_submission_27.pdf (online).

Kendall, E., R. Bell, R. Burkhart, M. Dutra, and E. Wallace. 2009. Towards a graphical notation for OWL 2. In *Proc Sixth Int Workshop on OWL: Experiences and Directions (OWLED 2009)*, eds. R. Hoekstra and P. F. Patel-Schneider, CEUR-WS, vol 529. http://ceur-ws.org/Vol-529/owled2009_submission_47.pdf (online).

Klinov, P., C. del Vescovo, and T. Schneider. 2012. Incrementally updateable and persistent decomposition of OWL ontologies. In *Proc OWL: Experiences and Directions Workshop*, ed. P. Klinov and M. Horridge, CEUR-WS, vol 849. http://ceur-ws.org/Vol-849/paper_7.pdf (online).

Kontchakov, R., C. Lutz, D. Toman, F. Wolter, and M. Zakharyaschev. 2010. The combined approach to query answering in DL-Lite. In *Proc Twelfth Int Conf on the Principles of Knowledge Representation and Reasoning (KR 2010)*, eds. F. Lin and U. Sattler, 247–257. North America: AAAI.

Knuth, D. E. 1998. *The Art of Computer Programming. Volume 3: Sorting and Searching.* Second Edition, Reading, MA: Addison-Wesley.

Labrou, Y. 2006. Standardizing agent communication. In *Multi-Agent Systems and Applications*, eds. M. Luck, V. Marik, O. Stepankova, and R. Trappl, 74–97. Berlin, Heidelberg: Springer-Verlag, LNCS 2086.

Labrou, Y., T. Finin, and Y. Peng. 1999. Agent communication languages: The current landscape. *IEEE Intelligent Systems* 14(2): 45–52.

Lenat, D. B. 1995. CYC: A large-scale investment in knowledge infrastructure. *Communications of the ACM* 38(11): 33–38.

Lin, J. and C. Dyer. 2010. Data-Intensive Text Processing with MapReduce. Morgan & Claypool Synthesis Lectures on Human Language Technologies. http://lintool.github.com/MapReduceAlgorithms/MapReduce-book-final.pdf.

Manyika, J., M. Chui, B. Brown, J. Bughin, R. Dobbs, C. Roxburgh, and A. Hung Byers. 2011. Big data: The next frontier for innovation, competition, and productivity. McKinsey Global Institute (May). http://www.mckinsey.com/insights/mgi/research/technology_and_innovation/big_data_the_next_frontier_for_innovation (accessed October 8, 2012).

McGlothlin, J. P. and L. Khan. 2010. Materializing inferred and uncertain knowledge in RDF datasets. In *Proc Twenty-Fourth AAAI Conference on Artificial Intelligence (AAAI-10)*, 1951–1952. North America: AAAI.

Mills, P. 2011. Efficient statistical classification of satellite measurements. *International Journal of Remote Sensing* 32(21): 6109–6132.

Mitchell, I. and M. Wilson. 2012. Linked Data. Connecting and Exploiting Big Data. Fujitsu White Paper (March). http://www.fujitsu.com/uk/Images/Linked-data-connecting-and-exploiting-big-data-(v1.0).pdf.

Nardi, D. and R. J. Brachman. 2007. An introduction to description logics. In *The Description Logic Handbook*, eds. F. Baader, D. Calvanese, D. L. McGuinness, D. Nardi, and P. F. Patel-Schneider. New York: Cambridge University Press.

Nemani, R. R. and R. Konda. 2009. A framework for data quality in data warehousing. In *Information Systems: Modeling, Development, and Integration*, eds. J. Yang, A. Ginige, H. C. Mayr, and R.-D. Kutsche, 292–297. Berlin, Heidelberg: Springer-Verlag, LNBIP 20.

Olston, C. 2012. Programming and debugging large scale data processing workflows. In *First Int Workshop on Hot Topics in Cloud Data Processing (HotCDP'12)*, Switzerland.

Oren, E., S. Kotoulas, G. Anadiotis, R. Siebes, A. ten Teije, and F. van Harmelen. 2009. Marvin: Distributed reasoning over large-scale Semantic Web data. *Journal of Web Semantics* 7(4): 305–316.

Ponniah, P. 2010. *Data Warehousing Fundamentals for IT Professionals*. Hoboken, NJ: John Wiley & Sons.

Puuronen, S., V. Terziyan, and A. Tsymbal. 1999. A dynamic integration algorithm for an ensemble of classifiers. In *Foundations of Intelligent Systems: Eleventh Int Symposium ISMIS'99*, eds. Z.W. Ras and A. Skowron, 592–600. Berlin, Heidelberg: Springer-Verlag, LNAI 1609.

Quillian, M. R. 1967. Word concepts: A theory and simulation of some basic semantic capabilities. *Behavioral Science* 12(5): 410–430.

Quillian, M. R. 1969. The teachable language comprehender: A simulation program and theory of language. *Communications of the ACM* 12(8): 459–476.

Rahwan, T. 2007. Algorithms for coalition formation in multi-agent systems. PhD diss., University of Southampton. http://users.ecs.soton.ac.uk/nrj/download-files/lesser-award/rahwan-thesis.pdf (accessed October 8, 2012).

Rimal, B. P., C. Eunmi, and I. Lumb. 2009. A taxonomy and survey of cloud computing systems. In *Proc Fifth Int Joint Conf on INC, IMS and IDC*, 44–51. Washington, DC: IEEE CS Press.

Roy, G., L. Hyunyoung, J. L. Welch, Z. Yuan, V. Pandey, and D. Thurston. 2009. A distributed pool architecture for genetic algorithms, *Evolutionary Computation, 2009. CEC '09. IEEE Congress on*, pp. 1177, 1184, 18–21 May 2009. doi: 10.1109/CEC.2009.4983079

Sakr, S., A. Liu, D.M. Batista, and M. Alomari. 2011. A survey of large scale data management approaches in cloud environments. *IEEE Communications Society Surveys & Tutorials* 13(3): 311–336.

Salehi, A. 2010. *Low Latency, High Performance Data Stream Processing: Systems Architecture. Algorithms and Implementation*. Saarbrücken: VDM Verlag.

Shvachko, K., K. Hairong, S. Radia, R. Chansler. 2010. The Hadoop distributed file system, *Mass Storage Systems and Technologies (MSST), 2010 IEEE 26th Symposium on*, pp.1,10, 3–7 May 2010. doi: 10.1109/MSST.2010.5496972.

Smith, B. 2012. Big data that might benefit from ontology technology, but why this usually fails. In *Ontology Summit 2012, Track 3 Challenge: Ontology and Big Data*. http://ontolog.cim3.net/file/work/OntologySummit2012/2012-02-09_BigDataChallenge-I-II/Ontology-for-Big-Data—BarrySmith_20120209.pdf (accessed October 8, 2012).

Tatarintseva, O., V. Ermolayev, and A. Fensel. 2011. Is your Ontology a burden or a Gem?—Towards Xtreme Ontology engineering. In *Proc Seventh Int Conf ICTERI 2011*, eds. V. Ermolayev et al., 65–81. CEUR-WS, vol. 716. http://ceur-ws.org/Vol-716/ICTERI-2011-CEUR-WS-paper-4-p-65–81.pdf (online).

Terziyan, V. 2001. Dynamic integration of virtual predictors. In *Proc Int ICSC Congress on Computational Intelligence: Methods and Applications (CIMA'2001)*, eds. L. I. Kuncheva et al., 463–469. Canada: ICSC Academic Press.

Terziyan, V. 2007. Predictive and contextual feature separation for Bayesian meta-networks. In *Proc KES-2007/WIRN-2007*, ed. B. Apolloni et al., 634–644. Berlin, Heidelberg: Springer-Verlag, LNAI 4694.

Terziyan, V. and O. Kaykova. 2012. From linked data and business intelligence to executable reality. *International Journal on Advances in Intelligent Systems* 5(1–2): 194–208.

Terziyan, V., A. Tsymbal, and S. Puuronen. 1998. The decision support system for tele-medicine based on multiple expertise. *International Journal of Medical Informatics* 49(2): 217–229.

Thomason, R. H. 1998. Representing and reasoning with context. In *Proc Int Conf on Artificial Intelligence and Symbolic Computation (AISC 1998)*, eds. J. Calmet and J. Plaza, 29–41. Berlin, Heidelberg: Springer-Verlag, LNAI 1476.

Thusoo, A., Z. Shao, S. Anthony, D. Borthakur, N. Jain, J. S. Sarma, R. Murthy, and H. Liu. 2010. Data warehousing and analytics infrastructure at Facebook. In *Proc 2010 ACM SIGMOD Int Conf on Management of Data*, 1013–1020. New York: ACM.

Tsangaris, M. M., G. Kakaletris, H. Kllapi, G. Papanikos, F. Pentaris, P. Polydoras, E. Sitaridi, V. Stoumpos, and Y. E. Ioannidis. 2009. Dataflow processing and optimization on grid and cloud infrastructures. *IEEE Data Engineering Bulletin* 32(1): 67–74.

Urbani, J., S. Kotoulas, E. Oren, and F. van Harmelen. 2009. Scalable distributed reasoning using MapReduce. In Proc Eighth Int Semantic Web Conf (ISWC'09), eds. A. Bernstein, D. R. Karger, T. Heath, L. Feigenbaum, D. Maynard, E. Motta, and K. Thirunarayan, 634–649. Berlin, Heidelberg: Springer-Verlag.

W3C. 2009. OWL 2 web ontology language profiles. W3C Recommendation (October). http://www.w3.org/TR/owl2-profiles/.

Weinberger, D. 2012. *Too Big to know. Rethinking Knowledge now that the Facts aren't the Facts, Experts are Everywhere, and the Smartest Person in the Room is the Room*. First Edition. New York, NY: Basic Books.

Wielemaker, J., G. Schreiber, and B. Wielinga. 2003. Prolog-based infrastructure for RDF: Scalability and performance. In *The Semantic Web—ISWC 2003*, eds. D. Fensel, K. Sycara, and J. Mylopoulos, 644–658. Berlin, Heidelberg: Springer-Verlag, LNCS 2870.

Wooldridge, M. and N. R. Jennings. 1995. Intelligent agents: Theory and practice. *The Knowledge Engineering Review* 10(2): 115–152.

2

Tassonomy and Review of Big Data Solutions Navigation

Pierfrancesco Bellini, Mariano di Claudio, Paolo Nesi, and Nadia Rauch

CONTENTS

Introduction

Although the management of huge and growing volumes of data is a challenge for the past many years, no long-term solutions have been found so far. The term "Big Data" initially referred to huge volumes of data that have the size beyond the capabilities of current database technologies, consequently for "Big Data" problems one referred to the problems that present a combination of large volume of data to be treated in short time. When one establishes that data have to be collected and stored at an impressive rate, it is clear that the biggest challenge is not only about the storage and management, their analysis, and the extraction of meaningful values, but also deductions and actions in reality is the main challenge. Big Data problems were mostly related to the presence of unstructured data, that is, information that either do not have a default schema/template or that do not adapt well to relational tables; it is therefore necessary to turn to analysis techniques for unstructured data, to address these problems.

Recently, the Big Data problems are characterized by a combination of the so-called 3Vs: *volume, velocity,* and *variety;* and then a fourth V too has been added: *variability.* In essence, every day a large *volume* of information is produced and these data need a sustainable access, process, and preservation according to the *velocity* of their arrival, and therefore, the management of large volume of data is not the only problem. Moreover, the *variety* of data, metadata, access rights and associating computing, formats, semantics, and software tools for visualization, and the *variability* in structure and data models significantly increase the level of complexity of these problems. The first V, *volume,* describes the large amount of data generated by individuals, groups, and organizations. The volume of data being stored today is exploding. For example, in the year 2000 about 800,000 petabytes of data in the world were generated and stored (Eaton et al., 2012) and experts estimated that in the year 2020, about 35 zettabyte of data will be produced. The second V, *velocity,* refers to speed at which Big Data are collected, processed, and elaborated, may handle a constant flow of massive data, which are impossible to be processed with traditional solutions. For this reason, it is not only important to consider "where" the data are stored, but also "how" they are stored. The third V, *variety,* is concerned with the proliferation of data types from social, mobile sources, machine-to-machine, and traditional data that are part of it. With the explosion of social networks, smart devices, and sensors, data have become complex, because they include raw, semistructured, and unstructured data from log files, web pages, search indexes, cross media, emails, documents, forums, and so on. *Variety* represents all types of data and usually the enterprises must be able to analyze all of them, if they want to gain advantage. Finally, *variability*, the last V, refers to data unpredictability and to how these may change in the years, following the implementation of the architecture. Moreover, the concept of variability can be attributed to assigning a variable interpretation to the data and to the confusions created in Big Data analysis, referring, for example, to different meanings in Natural Language that some data may have. These four properties can be considered orthogonal aspects of data storage, processing, and analysis and it is also interesting that increasing variety and variability also increases the attractiveness of data and their potentiality in providing hidden and unexpected information/meanings.

Especially in science, the need of new *"infrastructures for global research data"* that can achieve interoperability to overcome the limitations related to language, methodology, and guidelines (policy) would be needed in short time. To cope with these types of complexities, several different techniques and tools may be needed, they have to be composed and new specific algorithms and solutions may also have to be defined and implemented. The wide range of problems and the specifics needs make almost impossible to identify unique architectures and solutions adaptable to all possible applicative areas. Moreover, not only the number of application areas so different from each other, but also the different channels through which data are daily collected increases the difficulties of companies and developers to identify which is the right way to achieve relevant results from the accessible data. Therefore, this chapter can be a useful tool for supporting the researchers and technicians in making decisions about setting up some Big Data infrastructure and solutions. To this end, it is very helpful to have an overview about Big Data techniques; it can be used as a sort of guidelines to better understand possible differences and relevant best features among the many needed and proposed by the product as the key aspects of Big Data solutions. These can be regarded as requirements and needs according to which the different solutions can be compared and assessed, in accordance with the case study and/or application domain.

To this end, and to better understand the impact of Big Data science and solutions, in the following, a number of examples describing major applicative domains taking advantage from the Big Data technologies and solutions are reported: education and training, cultural heritage, social media and social networking, health care, research on brain, financial and business, marketing and social marketing, security, smart cities and mobility, etc.

Big Data technologies have the potential to revolutionize education. *Educational data* such as students' performance, mechanics of learning, and answers to different pedagogical strategies can provide an improved understanding of students' knowledge and accurate assessments of their progress.

These data can also help identify clusters of students with similar learning style or difficulties, thus defining a new form of customized education based on sharing resources and supported by computational models. The proposed new models of teaching in Woolf et al. (2010) are trying to take into account student profile and performance, pedagogical and psychological and learning mechanisms, to define personalized instruction courses and activities that meet the different needs of different individual students and/or groups. In fact, in the educational sector, the approach to collect, mine, and analyze large data sets has been consolidated, in order to provide new tools and information to the key stakeholders. This data analysis can provide an increasing understanding of students' knowledge, improve the assessments of their progress, and help focus questions in education and psychology, such as the method of learning or how different students respond to different pedagogical strategies. The collected data can also be used to define models to understand what students actually know and understand how to enrich this knowledge, and assess which of the adopted techniques can be effective in whose cases, and finally produce a case-by-case action plan. In terms of Big Data, a large variety and variability of data is presented to take into account all events in the students' career; the data volume is also an additional factor. Another sector of interest, in this field, is the e-learning domain, where two main kinds of users are defined: the learners and the learning providers (Hanna, 2004). All personal details of learners and the online learning providers' information are stored in specific database, so applying data mining with e-learning can enable one to realize teaching programs targeted to particular interests and needs through an efficient decision making.

For the management of large amounts of *cultural heritage* information data, Europeana has been created with over 20 millions of content indexed that can be retrieved in real time. Earlier, each of them was modeled with a simple metadata model, ESE, while a new and more complete models called EDM (Europeana Data Model) with a set of semantic relationships is going to be adopted in the 2013 [Europeana]. A number of projects and activities are connected to Europeana network to aggregate content and tools. Among them ECLAP is a best practice network that collected not only content metadata for Europeana, but also real content files from over 35 different institutions having different metadata sets and over 500 file formats. A total of more than 1 million of cross media items is going to be collected with an average of some hundreds of metadata each, thus resulting in billions of information elements and multiple relationships among them to be queried, navigated, and accessed in real time by a large community of users [ECLAP] (Bellini et al., 2012a).

The volume of data generated by *social network* is huge and with a high variability in the data flow over time and space, due to human factor; for example, Facebook receives 3 billion uploads per month, which corresponds to approximately 3600 TB/year. Search engine companies such as Google and Yahoo! collect every day trillions of bytes of data, around which real new business is developed, offering useful services to its users and companies in real time (Mislove et al., 2006). From these large amounts of data collected through social networks (e.g., Facebook, Twitter, MySpace), social media and Big Data solutions may estimate the user-collective profiles and behavior, analyze product acceptance, evaluate the market trend, keep trace of user movements, extract unexpected correlations, evaluate the models of influence, and perform different kinds of predictions (Domingos, 2005). Social media data can be exploited by considering geo-referenced information and Natural Language Processing for analyzing and interpreting urban living: massive folk movements, activities of the different communities in the city, movements due to large public events, assessment of the city infrastructures, etc. (Iaconesi and Persico, 2012). In a broader sense, by this information it is possible to extract knowledge and data relationships, by improving the activity of query answering.

For example, in *Healthcare/Medical field* large amount of information about patients' medical histories, symptomatology, diagnoses, and responses to treatments and therapies is collected. Data mining techniques might be implemented to derive knowledge from this data in order to either identify new interesting patterns in infection control data or to examine reporting practices (Obenshain, 2004). Moreover, predictive models can be used as detection tools exploiting *Electronic Patient Record* (EPR) accumulated for each person of the area, and taking into account the statistical data. Similar solutions can be adopted as decision support for specific triage and diagnosis or to produce effective plans for chronic disease management, enhancing the quality of healthcare and lowering its cost. This activity may allow detecting the inception of critical conditions for the observed people over the whole population. In Mans et al. (2009), techniques to the fast access and extraction of information from event's log from medical processes, to produce easily interpretable models, using partitioning, clustering, and preprocessing techniques have been investigated. In medical field, especially hospital, run time data are used to support the analysis of existing processes. Moreover, taking into account genomic aspects and EPR for millions of patients leads to cope with Big Data problems. For genome sequencing activities (HTS, high-throughput sequencing) that produce several hundreds of millions of small sequences, a new data structure for indexing called Gkarrays (Rivals et al., 2012) has been proposed, with the aim of improving classical indexing system such as hash table. The adoption of sparse hash tables is not enough to index huge collections of k-mer (subword of a given length k in a DNA sequence, which represents the minimum unit accessed). Therefore, new data structure has been proposed based on three arrays: the first for storing the start position of each k-mer, the second as an inverted array allows finding any k-mer from a position in a read, and the last records the interval of position of each distinct k-mer, in sorted order. This structure allowed obtaining in constant time, the number of reads that contain a k-mer. A project of the University of Salzburg with the National Institute of sick of Salzburg studies how to apply machine learning techniques to the evaluation of large amounts of tomographic images generated by computer (Zinterhof, 2012). The idea is to apply proven techniques of machine learning for image segmentation, in the field of computer tomography.

In several areas of *science and research* such as astronomy (automated sky survey), sociology (web log analysis of behavioral data), and neuroscience (genetic and neuroimaging data analysis), the aim of Big Data analysis is to extract meaning from data and determine what actions take. To cope with the large amount of experimental data produced by research experiments, the University Montpellier started the ZENITH project [Zenith] that adopts a hybrid architecture p2p/cloud (Valduriez and Pacitti, 2005). The idea of Zenith is to exploit p2p to facilitate the collaborative nature of scientific data, centralized control, and use the potentialities of computing, storage, and network resources in the Cloud model, to manage and analyze this large amount of data. The storage infrastructure used in De Witt et al. (2012) is called CASTOR and allows for the management of metadata related to scientific files of experiments at CERN. For example, the database of RAL (Rutherford Appleton Laboratory) uses a single table for storing 20 GB (which reproduces the hierarchical structure of the file) that runs about 500 transactions per second on 6 clusters. With the increasing number of digital scientific data, one of the most important challenges is the digital preservation and for this purpose is in progress the SCAPE (SCAlable Preservation Environment) project [SCAPE Project]. The platform provides an extensible infrastructure to achieve the conservation of workflow information of large volume of data. The AzureBrain project (Antoniu et al., 2010) aims to explore cloud computing techniques for the analysis of data from genetic and neuroimaging domains, both characterized by a large number of variables. The Projectome project, connected with the *Human Brain* Project, HBP, aims to set up a high-performance infrastructure for processing and visualizing neuroanatomical information obtained by using confocal ultramicroscopy techniques (Silvestri et al., 2012), the solution is connected with the modeling of knowledge of and information related to rat brains. Here, the single image scan of a mouse is more than 1 Tbyte and it is 1000 times smaller than a human brain.

The task of finding patterns in *business data* is not new; nowadays it is getting a larger relevance because enterprises are collecting and producing a huge amount of data including massive contextual information, thus taking into account a larger number of variables. Using data to understand and improve business operations, profitability, and growth is a great opportunity and a challenge in evolving. The continuous collection of large amounts of data (business transaction, sales transaction, user behavior), widespread use of networking technologies and computers, and design of Big Data warehouse and data mart have created enormously valuable assets. An interesting possibility to extract meaningful information from these data could be the use of machine learning techniques in the context of mining business data (Bose and Mahapatra, 2001), or also to use an alternative approach of structured data mining to model classes of customers in client databases using fuzzy clustering and fuzzy decision making (Setnes et al., 2001). These data can be analyzed in order to define prediction about the behavior of users, to identify buying pattern of individual/group customers, and to provide new custom services (Bose and Mahapatra, 2001). Moreover, in recent years, the major market analysts conduct their business investigations with data that are not stored within the classic RDBMS (Relational DataBase Management System), due to the increase of various and new types of information. Analysis of web users' behavior, customer loyalty programs, the technology of remote sensors, comments into blogs, and opinions shared on the network are contributing to create a new business model called *social media marketing* and the companies must properly manage these information, with the corresponding potential for new understanding, to maximize the business value of the data (Domingos, 2005). In financial field, instead, investment and business plans may be created thanks to predictive models derived using techniques of reasoning and used to discover meaningful and interesting patterns in business data.

Big Data technologies have been adopted to find solutions to *logistic and mobility management* and optimization of multimodal transport networks in the context of Smart Cities. A data-centric approach can also help for enhancing the efficiency and the dependability of a transportation system. In fact, through the analysis and visualization of detailed road network data and the use of a predictive model, it is possible to achieve an intelligent transportation environment. Furthermore, through the merging of high-fidelity geographical stored data and real-time sensor networks scattered data, it can be made an efficient urban planning system that mix public and private transportation, offering people more flexible solutions. This new way of traveling has interesting implications for energy and environment. The analysis of the huge amount of data collected from the metropolitan multimodal transportation infrastructure, augmented with data coming from sensors, GPS positions, etc., can be used to facilitate the movements of people via local public transportation solutions and private vehicles (Liu et al., 2009). The idea is to provide intelligent real-time information to improve traveler experience and operational efficiencies (see, for example, the solutions for the cities of Amsterdam, Berlin, Copenhagen, and Ghent). In this way, in fact, it is possible in order to use the Big Data both as historical and real-time data for the applications of machine learning algorithms aimed to traffic state estimation/planning and also to detect unpredicted phenomena in a sufficiently accurate way to support near real-time decisions.

In security field, *Intelligence, Surveillance, and Reconnaissance* (ISR) define topics that are well suited for data-centric computational analyses. Using analysis tools for video and image retrieval, it is possible to establish alert for activity and event of interest. Moreover, intelligence services can use these data to detect and combine special patterns and trends, in order to recognize threats and to assess the capabilities and vulnerabilities with the aim to increase the security level of a nation (Bryant et al., 2010).

In the field of *energy resources optimization and environmental monitoring,* the data related to the consumption of electricity are very important. The analysis of a set of load profiles and geo-referenced information, with appropriate data mining techniques (Figueireido et al., 2005), and the construction of predictive models from that data, could define intelligent distribution strategies in order to lower costs and improve the quality of life in this field, and another possible solution is an approach that provides for the adoption of a conceptual model for a smart grid data management based on the main features of a cloud computing platform, such as collection and real-time management of distributed data, parallel processing for research and interpretation of information, multiple and ubiquitous access (Rusitschka et al., 2010).

In the above overview about some of the application domains for Big Data technologies, it is evident that to cope with those problems several different kinds of solutions and specific products have been developed. Moreover, the complexity and the variability of the problems have been addressed with a combination of different open source or proprietary solutions, since presently there is not an ultimate solution to the Big Data problem that includes in an integrated manner data gathering, mining, analysis, processing, accessing, publication, and rendering. It would therefore be extremely useful if a "map" of the hot spots to be taken into account, during the design process and the creation of these architectures, which helps the technical staff to orient themselves in the wide range of products accessible on the Internet and/or offered by the market. To this aim, we have tried to identify the main features that can characterize architectures for solving a Big Data problem, depending on the source of data, on the type of processing required, and on the application context in which should be to operate.

The paper is organized as follows. In the "Main Requirements and Features of Big Data Solutions" section, the main requirements and features for Big Data solutions are presented by taking into account infrastructural and architectural aspects, data management, and data analytics aspects. Section "Overview of Big Data Solutions" reports a brief overview of existing solutions for Big Data and their main application fields. In the "Comparison and Analysis of Architectural Features" section, a comparison and analysis of the architectural features is presented. The analysis has permitted to put in evidence the most relevant features and different among the different solution. Section "Application Domains Comparison" is characterized by the description of the main application domains of the Big Data technologies and includes our assessment of these applicative domains in terms of the identified features reported in the "Overview of Big Data Solutions" section. Therefore, this section can be very useful to identify which are the major challenges of each domain and the most important aspects to be taken into account for each domain. This analysis allowed us to perform some comparison and consideration about the most commonly adopted tools in the different domains. Also in the same session, the identified application domains are crossed with the solutions analyzed in "Overview of Big Data Solutions" section, thus providing a shortcut to determine whose products have already been applied to a specific field of application, that is, a hint for the development of future applications. Finally, in the "Conclusions" section, conclusions are drawn.

Main Requirements and Features of Big Data Solutions

In this section, according to the above-reported short overview of Big Data problems, we have identified a small number of main aspects that should be addressed by architectures for management of Big Data problems. These aspects can be regarded as a collection of major requirements to cope with most of the issues related to the Big Data problems. We have divided the identified main aspects in three main categories which, respectively, concern with the infrastructure and the architecture of the systems that should cope with Big Data; with the management of the large amount of data and characteristics related to the type of physical storage; and with the accesses to data and techniques of data analytics, such as ingestion, log analysis, and everything else is pertinent to post-production phase of data processing. In some cases, the features are provided and/or inherited by the operating system or by the cloud/virtual infrastructure. Therefore, the specific Big Data solutions and techniques have to be capable of taking advantage from the underlining operating system and the infrastructure.

Infrastructral and Architectural Aspects

The typical Big Data solutions are deployed on cloud exploiting the flexibility of the infrastructure. As a result, some of the features of Big Data solutions may depend on the architecture and infrastructure facilities from which the solution inherits/exploits the capabilities. Moreover, specific tool for data gathering, processing, rendering, etc. may be capable or incapable of exploiting a different range of cloud-based architectural aspects. For example, not all databases can be distributed on multiple servers, not all algorithms can be profitable remapped on a parallel architecture, not all data access or rendering solutions may exploit multilayered caches, etc. To this end, in the following paragraphs, a set of main features are discussed, among them are the: scalability, multitiered memory, availability, parallel and distributed process management, workflow, self-healing, and data security, and privacy. A summary map is reported in the "Overview of Big Data Solutions" section.

Scalability

This feature may impact on the several aspects of the Big Data solution (e.g., data storage, data processing, rendering, computation, connection, etc.) and has to cope with the capability of maintaining acceptable performances coping from small-to-large problems. In most cases, the scalability is obtained by using distributed and/or parallel architectures, which may be allocated on cloud. Both computing and storage resources can be located over a network to create a distribute system where managing also the distribution of workload.

As regards the *computational scalability*, processing a very huge data set is important to optimize the workload, for example, with a parallel architecture, as proposed in Zenith project [Zenith], which may perform several operations simultaneously (on an appropriate number of tasks), or providing a dynamic allocation of computation resources (i.e., a process releases a resource as soon as it is no more needed, and thus it can be assigned to another process) technique used in the ConPaas platform (Pierre et al., 2011). Usually, the traditional computational algorithms are not scalable and thus specific restructuring of the algorithms have to be defined and adopted. On the other hand, not all the algorithms can take advantage by parallel and/or distributed architectures for computing; specific algorithms have to be defined, provided that an efficient parallel and/or distributed solution exists. The evolution to distributed and parallel processing is just the first step, since processes have to be allocated and managed in some parallel architecture, which can be developed *ad hoc* or generally setup. Semantic grid and parallel architectures can be used to the problem (Bellini et al., 2012b) [BlueGene].

Each system for Big Data may provide a *scalable storage* solution. In fact, the main problem could be to understand in which measure a storage solution has to be scalable to satisfy the worst operative cases or the most common cases (and, in general, the most expensive cases). Moreover, for large experiments, the data collection and processing may be not predictable with high precision in the long term, for example, for the storage size and cost. For example, it is not clear how much storage would be needed to collect genomic information and EHR (Electronic Healthcare Records) for a unified European health system in 5 or 10 years. In any case because EHR contains a large amount of data, an interesting approach for their management could be the use of a solution based on HBase that builds a system distributed, fault-tolerant, and scalable database on clouds, built on top of the HDFS, with random real-time read/write access to big data, overcoming the design limits of traditional RDBMS (Yang et al., 2011). Furthermore, to focus on this problem, a predictive model to understand how will increase the need for storage space should be made, while complexities and costs of this model are high. In most cases, it is preferable to have a pragmatic approach, first guess and work with the present problems by using cheap hardware and if necessary, increase the storage on demand. This approach obviously cannot be considered completely scalable, scalability is not just about the storage size, and then remains the need to associate the solution presented, with a system capable of scaling operationally (Snell, 2011).

A good solution to optimize the reaction time and to obtain a scalable solution at limited costs is the adoption of a *multitiered storage* system, including cache levels, where data pass from one level to another along the hierarchy of storage media having different response times and costs. In fact, a multitier approach to storage, utilizing arrays of disks for all backup with a primary storage and the adoption of an efficient file systems, allows us to both provide backups and restores to online storage in a timely manner, as well as to scale up the storage when primary storage grows. Obviously, each specific solution does not have to implement all layers of the memory hierarchy because their needs depend on the single specific case, together with the amount of information to be accessed per second, the deepness of the cache memories, binning in classes of different types of data based on their availability and recoverability, or the choice to use a middleware to connect separate layers. The structure of the multitiered storage can be designed on the basis of a compromise from access velocity to general storage cost. The multiple storages create as counterpart a large amount of maintenance costs.

Scalability may take advantage from the recent cloud solutions that implements techniques for dynamic and bursting on cloud storage and processes from private to public clouds and among the latter. Private cloud computing has recently gained much traction from both commercial and open-source interests (Microsoft, 2012). For example, tools such as OpenStack [OpenStack Project] can simplify the process of managing virtual machine resources. In most cases, for small-to-medium enterprises, there is a trend to migrate multitier applications into public cloud infrastructures (e.g., Amazon), which are delegated to cope with scalability via elastic cloud solutions. A deep discussion on cloud is out of the scope of this chapter.

High Availability

The high availability of a service (e.g., it may be referred to general service, to storage, process, and network) is a key requirement in an architecture that can affect the simultaneous use of a large number of users and/or computational nodes located in different geographical locations (Cao et al., 2009). Availability refers to the ability of the community of users to access a system exploiting its services. A high availability leads to increased difficulties in guarantee data updates, preservations, and consistency in real time, and it is fundamental that a user perceives, during his session, the actual and proper reactivity of the system. To cope with these features, the design should be fault-tolerant, as in redundant solution for data and computational capabilities to make them highly available despite the failure of some hardware and software elements of the infrastructure. The availability of a system is usually expressed as a percentage of time (the nines method) that a system is up over a given period of time, usually a year. In cloud systems, for instance, the level of 5 nines (99.999% of time means HA, high availability) is typically related to the service at hardware level, and it indicates a downtime per year of approximately 5 min, but it is important to note that time does not always have the same value but it depends on the organization referred to by the critical system. The present solutions obtain the HA score by using a range of techniques of cloud architectures as *fault-tolerant* capabilities for virtual machines, redundant storage for distributed database and balancing for the front end, and the dynamic move of virtual machines.

Computational Process Management

The computational activities on Big Data may take a long time and may be distributed on multiple computational computers/nodes on some parallel architecture, in connection with some networking systems. Therefore, one of the main characteristics of most of the Big Data solutions has to cope with the needs of *controlling computational processes* by means of: allocating them on a *distributed system*, putting them in execution on demand or periodically, killing them, recovering processing from failure, returning eventual errors, scheduling them over time, etc. Sometimes, the infrastructure that allows to put in execution parallel computational processes can work as a service, thus it has to be accessible for multiple users and/or other multitier architecture and servers. This means that sophisticated solutions for parallel processing and scheduling are needed, including the definition of Service Level Agreement (SLA) and in classical grid solutions. Example of solutions to cope with these aspects are solutions for computational grid, media grid, semantic computing, distributed processing such as AXCP media grid (Bellini et al., 2012c) and general grid (Foster et al., 2002). The solution for parallel data processing has to be capable of dynamically exploiting the computational power of the underlining infrastructure, since most of the Big Data problems may be computationally intensive for limited time slots. Cloud solutions may help one to cope with the concepts of elastic cloud for implementing dynamic computational solutions.

Workflow Automation

Big Data processes are typically formalized in the form of process workflows from data acquisition to results production. In some cases, the workflow is programed by using simple XML (Extensible Markup Language) formalization or effective programing languages, for example, in Java, JavaScript, etc. Related data may strongly vary in terms of dimensions and data flow (i.e., variability): an architecture that handles well with both limited and large volumes of data, must be able to full support creation, organization, and transfer of these workflows, in single cast or broadcast mode. To implement this type of architectures, sophisticated automation systems are used. These systems work on different layers of the architecture through applications, APIs (Application Program Interface), visual process design environment, etc. Traditional Workflow Management Systems (WfMS) may not be suitable for processing a huge amount of data in real time, formalizing the stream processing, etc. In some Big Data applications, the high data flow and timing requirements (soft real time) have made inadequate the traditional paradigm *"store-then-process,"* so that the complex event processing (CEP) paradigms are proposed (Gulisano et al., 2012): a system that processes a continuous stream of data (event) on the fly, without any storage. In fact, the CEP can be regarded as an event-driven architecture (EDA), dealing with the detection and production of reaction to events, that specifically has the task of filtering, match and aggregate low-level events in high-level events. Furthermore, creating a parallel-distributed CEP, where data are partitioned across processing nodes, it is possible to realize an elastic system capable of adapting the processing resources to the actual workload reaching the high performance of parallel solutions and overcoming the limits of scalability.

An interesting application example is the Large Hadron Collider (LHC), the most powerful particle accelerator in the world, that is estimated to produce 15 million gigabytes of data every year [LHC], then made available to physicists around the world thanks to the infrastructure support *"worldwide LHC computing grid"* (WLCG). The WLCG connects more than 140 computing centers in 34 countries with the main objective to support the collection and storage of data and processing tools, simulation, and visualization. The idea behind the operation requires that the LHC experimental data are recorded on tape at CERN before being distributed to 11 large computer centers (centers called *"Tier 1"*) in Canada, France, Germany, Italy, the Netherlands, Scandinavia, Spain, Taiwan, the UK, and the USA. From these sites, the data are made available to more than 120 *"Tier-2"* centers, where you can conduct specific analyses. Individual researchers can then access the information using computer clusters or even their own personal computer.

Cloud Computing

The cloud capability allows one to obtain seemingly unlimited storage space and computing power that it is the reason for which cloud paradigm is considered a very desirable feature in each Big Data solution (Bryant et al., 2008). It is a new business where companies and users can rent by using the "as a service" paradigm infrastructure, software, product, processes, etc., Amazon [Amazon AWS], Microsoft [Microsoft Azure], Google [Google Drive]. Unfortunately, these public systems are not enough to extensive computations on large volumes of data, due to the low bandwidth; ideally a cloud computing system for Big Data should be geographically dispersed, in order to reduce its vulnerability in the case of natural disasters, but should also have a high level of interoperability and data mobility. In fact, there are systems that are moving in this direction, such as the OpenCirrus project [Opencirrus Project], an international test bed that allows experiments on interlinked cluster systems.

Self-Healing

This feature refers to the capability of a system to autonomously solve the failure problems, for example, in the computational process, in the database and storage, and in the architecture. For example, when a server or a node fails, it is important to have the capability of automatically solve the problem to avoid repercussions on the entire architecture. Thus, an automated recovery from failure solution that may be implemented by means of fault-tolerant solutions, balancing, hot spare, etc., and some intelligence is needed. Therefore, it is an important feature for Big Data architectures, which should be capable of autonomously bypassing the problem. Then, once informed about the problems and the performed action to solve it, the administrator may perform an intervention. This is possible, for example, through techniques that automatically redirected to other resources, the work that was planned to be carried out by failed machine, which has to be automatically put offline. To this end, there are commercial products which allow setting up distributed and balanced architecture where data are replicated and stored in clusters geographically dispersed, and when a node/storage fails, the cluster can self-heal by recreating the missing data from the damage node, in its free space, thus reconstructing the full capability of recovering from the next problem. On the contrary, the breakdown results and capacity may decrease in the degraded conditions until the storage, processor, resource is replaced (Ghosh et al., 2007).

Data Management Aspects

In the context of data management, a number of aspects characterize the Big Data solutions, among them: the maximum size of the database, the data models, the capability of setting up distributed and clustered data management solutions, the sustainable rate for the data flow, the capability of partitioning the data storage to make it more robust and increase performance, the query model adopted, the structure of the database (relational, RDF (resource description framework), reticular, etc.), etc. Considering data structures for Big Data, there is a trend to find a solution using the so-called *NoSQL databases* (NoSQL, Simple Query Language), even if there are good solutions that still use relational database (Dykstra, 2012). In the market and from open source solutions, there are several different types of NoSQL databases and rational reasons to use them in different situations, for different kinds of data. There are many methods and techniques for dealing with Big Data, and in order to be capable of identifying the best choice in each case, a number of aspects have to be taken into account in terms of architecture and hardware solutions, because different choices can also greatly affect the performance of the overall system to be built. Related to the database performance and data size, there is the so-called CAP Theorem that plays a relevant role (Brewer, 2001, 2012). The *CAP theorem* states that any distributed storage system for sharing data can provide only two of the three main features: *consistency, availability,* and *partition tolerance* (Fox and Brewer, 1999). Property of consistency states that a data model after an operation is still in a consistent state providing the same data to all its clients. The property of availability means that the solution is robust with respect to some internal failure, that is, the service is still available. Partition tolerance means that the system is going to continue to provide service even when it is divided in disconnected subsets, for example, a part of the storage cannot be reached. To cope with CAP theorem, Big Data solutions try to find a trade-off between continuing to issue the service despite of problems of partitioning and at the same time attempting to reduce the inconsistencies, thus supporting the so-called eventual consistency.

Furthermore, in the context of relational database, the ACID (Atomicity, Consistency, Isolation and Durability) properties describe the reliability of database transactions. This paradigm does not apply to NoSQL database where, in contrast to ACID definition, the data state provides the so-called BASE property: Basic Available, Soft state, and Eventual consistent. Therefore, it is typically hard to guaranteed an architecture for Big Data management in a fault-tolerant BASE way, since, as the Brewer's CAP theorem says, there is no other choice to make a compromise if you want to scale up. In the following, some of the above aspects are discussed and better explained.

Database Size

In Big Data problems, the database size may easily reach magnitudes like hundreds of Tera Byte (TB), Peta Byte (PB), or Exa Byte (EB). The evolution of Big Data solutions has seen an increment of the amounts of data that can be managed. In order to exploit these huge volumes of data and to improve the productivity of scientific, new technologies, new techniques are needed. The real challenge of database size are related to the indexing and to access at the data. These aspects are treated in the following.

Data Model

To cope with huge data sets, a number of different data models are available such as Relational Model, Object DB, XML DB, or Multidimensional Array model that extend database functionality as described in Baumann et al. (1998). Systems like Db4o (Norrie et al., 2008) or RDF 3X (Schramm, 2012) propose different solutions for data storage can handle structured information or less and the relationships among them. The data model represents the main factor that *influences* the performance of the data management. In fact, the performance of indexing represents in most cases the bottleneck of the elaboration. Alternatives may be solutions that belong to the so-called category of NoSQL databases, such as ArrayDBMS (Cattel, 2010), MongoDB [mongoDB], CouchDB [Couchbase], and HBase [Apache HBase], which provide higher speeds with respect to traditional RDBMS (relational database management systems). Within the broad category of NoSQL database, large NoSQL families can be identified, which differ from each other for storage and indexing strategy:

- *Key-value stores:* high scalable solution, which allows one to obtain good speed in the presence of large lists of elements, such as stock quotes; examples are Amazon Dynamo [Amazon Dynamo] and Oracle Berkeley [Oracle Berkeley].
- *Wide column stores (big tables):* are databases in which the columns are grouped, where keys and values can be composed (as HBase [Apache HBase], Cassandra [Apache Cassandra]). Very effective to cope with time series and with data coming from multiple sources, sensors, device, and website, needing high speed. Consequently, they provide good performance in reading and writing operations, while are less suitable for data sets where the data have the same importance of the data relationships.
- *Document stores:* are aligned with the object-oriented programing, from clustering to data access, and have the same behavior of key-value stores, where the value is the document content. They are useful when data are hardly representable with a relational model due to high complexity; therefore, are used with medical records or to cope with data coming from social networks. Examples are MongoDB [mongoDB] and CouchDB [Couchbase].
- *Graph databases:* they are suitable to model relationships among data. The access model is typically transactional and therefore suitable for applications that need transactions. They are used in fields such as geospatial, bioinformatics, network analysis, and recommendation engines. The execution of traditional SQL queries is not simple. Examples are: Neo4J [Neo4j], GraphBase [GraphBase], and AllegroGraph [AllegroGraph].

Other NoSQL database categories are: object databases, XML databases, multivalue databases, multimodel databases, multidimensional database, etc. [NoSQL DB].

It is therefore important to choose the right NoSQL storage type during the design phase of the architecture to be implemented, considering the different features that characterize the different databases. In other words, it is very important to use the right tool for each specific project, because each storage type has its own weaknesses and strengths.

Resources

The main performance bottlenecks for NoSQL data stores correspond to main computer resources: network, disk and memory performance, and the computational capabilities of the associated CPUs. Typically, the Big Data stores are based on clustering solutions in which the whole data set is partitioned in *clusters* comprising a number of nodes, *cluster size*. The number of nodes in each cluster affects the completion times of each job, because a greater number of nodes in a cluster corresponds to a lower completion time of the job. In this sense, also the memory size and the *computational capabilities* of each node influence the node performance (De Witt et al., 2008). Most of the NoSQL databases use persistent socket connections; while disk is always the slowest component for the inherent latency of non-volatile storages. Thus, any high-performance database needs to have some form of memory caching or memory-based storage to optimize the *memory performance*. Another key point is related to the *memory size* and usage of the solution selected. Some solutions, such as HBase [Apache HBase], are considered memory-intensive, and in these cases a sufficient amount of memory on each server/node has to be guaranteed to cover the needs of the cluster that are located in its region of interest. When the amount of memory is insufficient, the overall performance of the system would drastically decrease (Jacobs, 2009). The *network* capability is an important factor that affects the final performance of the entire Big Data management. In fact, network connections among clusters make extensive use during read and write operations, but there are also algorithms like Map-Reduce, that in shuffle step make up a high-level network usage. It is therefore important to have a highly available and resiliency network, which is also able to provide the necessary redundancy and that could scale well, that is, it allows the growth of the number of clusters.

Data Organization

The data organization impacts on storage, access, and indexing performance of data (Jagadish et al., 1997). In most cases, a great part of data accumulated are not relevant for estimating results and thus they could be filtered out and/or stored in compressed size, as well as moved into slower memory along the multitier architecture. To this end, a challenge is to define *rules for arranging and filtering data* in order to avoid/reduce the loss of useful information preserving performances and saving costs (Olston et al., 2003). The distribution of data in different remote tables may be the cause of inconsistencies when connection is lost and the storage is partitioned for some fault. In general, it is not always possible to ensure *locally available data* on the node that would process them. It is evident that if this condition is generally achieved, the best performance would be obtained. Otherwise, it would be needed to retrieve the missed data blocks, to transfer them and process them in order to produce the results with a high consumption of resources on the node requested them and on the node that owns them, and thus on the entire network; therefore, the time of completion would be significantly higher.

Data Access for Rendering

The activity of data rendering is related to the access of data for representing them to the users, and in some cases by performing some prerendering processing. The presentation of original or produced data results may be a relevant challenge when the data size is so huge that their processing for producing a representation can be highly computational-intensive, and most of the single data would not be relevant for the final presentation to the user. For example, representing at a glance the distribution of 1 billion of economical transactions on a single image would be in any way limited to some thousands of points; the presentation of the distribution of people flows in the large city would be based on the analysis of several hundreds of millions of movements, while their representation would be limited on presenting a map on an image of some Mbytes. A query on a huge data set may produce enormous set of results. Therefore, it is important to know in advance their size and to be capable of analyzing Big Data results with scalable display tools that should be capable of producing a clear vision in a range of cases, from small-to-huge set of results. For example, the node-link representation of the RDF graph does not provide a clear view of the overall RDF structure: one possible solution to this problem is the use of a 3D adjacency matrix as an alternate visualization method for RDF (Gallego et al., 2011). Thanks to some graph display tools, it is possible to highlight specific data aspects. Furthermore, it should be possible to guarantee efficient access, perhaps with the definition of standard interfaces especially in business and medical applications on multichannel and multidevice delivering of results without decreasing data availability. An additional interesting feature for data access can be the save of user experience in data access and navigation (parameters and steps for accessing and filtering them). The adoption of semantic queries in RDF databases is essential for many applications that need to produce heterogeneous results and thus in those cases the data rendering is very important for presenting them and their relationships. Other solutions for data access are based on the production of specific indexes, such as Solr [Apache Solr] or in NoSQL databases. An example are the production of faceted results, in which the query results are divided into multiple categories on which the user can further restrict the search results, by composing by using "and"/"or" different facets/filters. This important feature is present in solutions such as RDF-HDT Library, eXist project (Meier, 2003).

Data Security and Privacy

The problem of data security is very relevant in the case of Big Data solutions. The data to be processed may contain sensitive information such as EPR, bank data, general personal information as profiles, and content under IPR (intellectual property rights) and thus under some licensing model. Therefore, sensitive data cannot be transmitted, stored, or processed in clear, and thus have to be managed in some coded protected format, for example, with some encryption. Solutions based on conditional access, channel protection, and authentication may still have sensible data stored in clear into the storage. They are called Conditional Access Systems (CAS) and are used to manage and control the user access to services and data (normal users, administrator, etc.) without protecting each single data element via encryption. Most Big Data installations are based on web services models, with few facilities for countering web threats, whereas it is essential that data are protected from theft and unauthorized accesses. While, most of the present Big Data solutions present only conditional access methods based on credentials only for accessing the data information and not to protect them with encrypted packages. On the other hand, content protection technologies are sometimes supported by Digital Rights Management (DRM), solutions that allow to define and execute licenses that formalize the rights that can be exploited on a given content element, who can exploit that rights and at which condition (e.g., time, location, number of times, etc.). The control of the user access rights is *per se* a Big Data problem (Bellini et al., 2013). The DRM solutions use authorization, authentication, and encryption technologies to manage and enable the exploitation of rights at different types of users; logical control of some users with respect to each single pieces of the huge quantities of data. The same technology can be used to provide contribution to safeguard the data privacy allowing keeping the encrypted data until they are effectively used by authorized and authenticated tools and users. Therefore, the access to data outside permitted rights and content would be forbidden. Data security is a key aspect of architecture for the management of such big quantities of data and is excellent to define who can access to what. This is a fundamental feature in some areas such as health/medicine, banking, media distribution, and e-commerce. In order to enforce data protection, some frameworks are available to implement DRM and/or CAS solutions exploiting different encryption and technical protection techniques (e.g., MPEG-21 [MPEG-21], AXMEDIS (Bellini et al., 2007), ODRL (Iannella, 2002)). In the specific case of EPR, several millions of patients with hundreds of elements have to be managed; where for each of them some tens of rights should to be controlled, thus resulting in billions of accesses and thus of authentications per day.

Data Analytics Aspects

Data analysis aspects have to do with a large range of different algorithms for data processing. The analysis and review of the different data analytic algorithms for Big Data processing is not in the focus of this chapter that aims at analyzing the architectural differences and the most important features of Big Data solutions. On the other hand, the data analytic algorithms may range on data: ingestion, crawling, verification, validation, mining, processing, transcoding, rendering, distribution, compression, etc., and also for

the estimation of relevant results such as the detection of unexpected correlations, detection of patterns and trends (for example, of events), estimation
of collective intelligence, estimation of the inception of new trends, prediction of new events and trends, analysis of the crowd sourcing data for senti-
ment/affective computing with respects to market products or personalities,
identification of people and folk trajectories, estimation of similarities for
producing suggestion and recommendations, etc. In most of these cases, the
data analytic algorithms have to take into account of user profiles, content
descriptors, contextual data, collective profiles, etc.

The major problems of Big Data are related to how their "meanings" are
discovered; usually this research occurs through complex modeling and analytics processes: hypotheses are formulated, statistical, visual, and semantic
models are implemented to validate them, and then new hypotheses are formulated again to take deductions, find unexpected correlations, and produce
optimizations. Also, in several of these cases, the specific data analytic algorithms are based on statistical data analysis; semantic modeling, reasoning,
and queries; traditional queries; stream and signal processing; optimization
algorithms; pattern recognition; natural language processing; data clustering; similarity estimation; etc.

In the following, key aspects are discussed and better explained.

Data Mining/Ingestion

Aspects are two key features in the field of Big Data solutions; in fact, in
most cases there is a trade-off between the speed of data ingestion, the ability to answer queries quickly, and the quality of the data in terms of update,
coherence, and consistency. This compromise impacts the design of the storage system (i.e., OLTP vs OLAP, On-Line Transaction Processing vs On-Line
Analytical Processing), that has to be capable of storing and index the new
data at the same rate at which they reach the system, also taking into account
that a part of the received data could not be relevant for the production of
requested results. Moreover, some storage and file systems are optimized to
read and others for writing; while workloads generally involve a mix of both
these operations. An interesting solution is GATE, a framework and graphical
development environment to develop applications and engineering components for language processing tasks, especially for data mining and information extraction (Cunningham et al., 2002). Furthermore, the data mining
process can be strengthened and completed by the usage of *crawling techniques*,
now consolidated in the extraction of meaningful data from web pages richer
information, also including complex structures and tags. The processing of a
large amount of data can be very expensive in terms of resources used and
computation time. For these reasons, it may be helpful to use a distributed
approach of crawlers (with additional functionality) who works as distributed system under, with a central control unit which manages the allocation
of tasks between the active computers in the network (Thelwall, 2001).

Another important feature is the ability to get advanced *faceted* results from queries on the large volumes of available data: this type of queries allows the user to access the information in the store, along multiple explicit dimensions, and after the application of multiple filters. This interaction paradigm is used in mining applications and allows to analyze and browse data across multiple dimensions; the faceted queries are especially useful in e-commerce websites (Ben-Yitzhak et al., 2008). In addition to the features already seen, it is important to take into account the ability to *process data in real time*: today, in fact, especially in business, we are in a phase of rapid transition; there is also the need to faster reactions, to be able to detect patterns and trends in a short time, in order to reduce the response time to customer requests. This increases the need to evaluate information as soon as an event occurs, that is, the company must be able to answer questions on the fly according to real-time data.

Data Access for Computing

The most important enabling technologies are related to the data modeling and to the data indexing. Both these aspects should be focused on fast access/retrieve data in a suitable format to guarantee high performance in the execution of the computational algorithms to be used for producing results. The *type of indexing* may influence the speed of data retrieval operations at only cost of an increased storage space. Couchbase [Couchbase] offers an incremental indexing system that allows an efficient access to data at multiple points. Another interesting method is the use of Hfile (Aiyer et al., 2012) and the already mentioned Bloom filters (Borthakur et al., 2011). It consists of an index-organized data file created periodically and stored on disk. However, in Big Data context, there is the need to manage often irregular data, with a heterogeneous structure and do not follow any predefined schema. For these reasons could be interesting the application of an alternative indexing technique suitable for semistructured or unstructured data as proposed in McHugh et al. (1998). On the other hand, where data come from different sources, to establish relationships among datasets, allows data integration and can lead to determine additional knowledge and deductions. Therefore, the modeling and management of data relationships may become more important than the data, especially where relationships play a very strong role (social networks, customer management). This is the case of new data types for social media that are formalized as highly interrelated content for which the management of multi-dimensional relationships in real time is needed. A possible solution is to store relationships in specific data structures that ensure good ability to access and extraction in order to adequately support predictive analytics tools. In most cases, in order to guarantee the demanded performance in the rendering and production of data results, a set of precomputed partial results and/or indexes can be estimated. These precomputed partial results should be stored into high-speed *caches stores*, as *temporary data*. Some kinds of data analytic algorithms create enormous amounts of temporary data that must be opportunely managed to avoid memory problems and to save time for the successive computations. In other cases, however, in order to make some statistics on the information that is accessed more frequently, it is possible to use techniques to create well-defined cache system or temporary files to optimize the computational process. With the same aim, some *incremental and/or hierarchical algorithms* are adopted in combination of the above-mentioned techniques, for example, the hierarchical clustering *k*-means and *k*-medoid for recommendation (Everitt et al., 2001; Xui and Wunsch, 2009; Bellini et al., 2012c). A key element of Big Data access for data analysis is the presence of *metadata as data descriptors*, that is, additional information associated with the main data, which help to recover and understand their meaning with the context. In the financial sector, for example, metadata are used to better understand customers, date, competitors, and to identify impactful market trends; it is therefore easy to understand that having an architecture that allows the storage of metadata also represents a benefit for the following operations of data analysis. Structured metadata and organized information help to create a system with more easily identifiable and accessible information, and also facilitate the knowledge identification process, through the analysis of available data and metadata. A variety of attributes can be applied to the data, which may thus acquire greater relevance for users. For example, keyword, temporal, and geospatial information, pricing, contact details, and anything else that improves the quality of the information that has been requested. In most cases, the production of suitable data descriptors could be the way to save time in recovering the real full data, since the matching and the further computational algorithms are based on those descriptors rather than on the original data. For example, the identification duplicated documents could be performed by comparing the document descriptors, the production of user recommendations can be performed on the basis of collective user descriptors or on the basis of the descriptors representing the centre of the clusters.

Overview of Big Data Solutions

In this section, a selection of representative products for the implementation of different Big Data systems and architectures has been analyzed and organized in a comparative table on the basis of the main features identified in the previous sections. To this end, the following paragraphs provide a brief overview of these considered solutions as reported in Table 2.1, described in the next section.

The *ArrayDBMS* extends database services with query support and a multi-dimensional array modeling, because Big Data queries often involve a high number of operations, each of which is applied to a large number of elements in the array. In these conditions, the execution time with traditional database would be unacceptable. In the literature, and from the real applications, a large number of examples are available that use various types of ArrayDBMS, and among them, we can recall a solution that is based on ArrayDBMS Rasdaman (Baumann et al., 1998): different from the other types, Rasdaman ArrayDBMS provides support for domain-independent arrays of arbitrary size and it uses a general-purpose declarative query language, that is also associated with an optimized internal execution, transfer, and storage. The conceptual model consists of arrays of any size, measures, and types of cells, which are stored in tables named collections that contain an OID (object ID) column and an array column. The RaSQL language offers expressions in terms of multi-dimensional arrays of content objects. Following the standard paradigm *Select-from-where*, firstly the query process gathers collections inspected, then the *"where"* clause filters the array corresponding to the predicate, and finally, the *"Select"* prepares the matrices derived from initial query. Internally, Rasdaman decomposes each object array in *"tiles"* that form the memory access units, the querying units and the processing units. These parts are stored as BLOBs (Binary Large Object) in a relational database. The formal model of algebra for Rasdaman arrays offers a high potential for query optimization. In many cases, where phenomena are sampled or simulated, the results are data that can be stored, searched, and submitted as an array. Typically, the data arrays are outlined by metadata that describe them; for example, geographically referenced images may contain their position and the reference system in which they are expressed.

Couchbase

[Couchbase] is designed for real-time applications and does not support SQL queries. Its incremental indexing system is realized to be native to JSON (JavaScript Object Notation) storage format. Thus, JavaScript code can be used to verify the document and select which data are used as index key. Couchbase Server is an elastic and open-source NoSQL database that automatically distributes data across commodity servers or virtual machines and can easily accommodate changing data management requirements, thanks to the absence of a schema to manage. Couchbase is also based on Memcached which is responsible for the optimization of network protocols and hardware, and allows obtaining good performance at the network level. Memcached [Memcached] is an open-source distributed caching system based on main memory, which is specially used in high trafficked websites and high-performance demand web applications. Moreover, thanks to Memcached, CouchBase can improve its online users experience maintaining low latency and good ability to scale up to a large number of users. CouchBase Server allows managing in a simple way system updates, which can be performed without sending offline the entire system. It also allows

TABLE 2.1

Main Features of Reviewed Big Data Solutions

	ArrayDBMS	CouchBase	Db4o	eXist	Google MapReduce	Hadoop
Infrastructural and Architectural Aspects						
Distributed	Y	Y	Y	A	Y	Y
High availability	A	Y	Y	Y	Y	Y
Process management	Computation-insensitive	Auto distribution	NA	So high for update of entire files	Configurable	Configurable
Cloud	A	Y	A	Y/A	Y	Y
Parallelism	Y	Y	Transactional	Y	Y	Y
Data Management Aspects						
Data dimension	100 PB	PB	254 GB	2^{31}doc.	10 PB	10 PB
Traditional/not traditional	NoSQL	NoSQL	NoSQL	NoSQL	NoSQL	NoSQL
SQL interoperability	Good	SQL-like language	A	A	A	Low
Data organization	Blob	Blob 20 MB	Blob	NA	Blob	Chunk
Data model	Multidim. array	1 document/concept (document store)	object DB + B-tree for index	XML-DB + index tree	Big table (CF, KV, OBJ, DOC)	Big table (column family)
Memory footprint	Reduces	Documents + bidimensional index	Objects + index	Documents + index	NA	NA
Users access type	Web interface	Multiple point	Remote user interface	Web interface, REST interface	Many types of interface	API, common line interface or HDFS-UI web app
Data access performance	Much higher if metadata are stored in DBMS	Speed up access to a document by automatically caching	Various techniques for optimal data access performance	NA	NA	NA
Data Analitycs Aspects						
Type of indexing	Multidimensional index	Y (incremental)	B-Tree field indexes	B+-tree (XISS)	Distributed multilevel tree indexing	HDFS
Data relationships	Y	NA	Y	Y	Y	A
Visual rendering and visualization	Y (rView)	NA	Y	NA	P	A
Faceted query	NA	A	P	Y	A (Lucene)	A (Lucene)
Statistical analysis tools	Y	Y/A	A (optional library)	A (JMXClient)	A	Y
Log analysis	NA	Y	NA	NA	Y	Y
Semantic query	P	A (elastic search)	P	A	A	P (index for semantic search)
Indexing speed	More than RDBMS	Non-optimal performance	5–10 times more than SQL	High speed with B+Tree	Y/A	A
Real-time processing	NA	Indexing + creating view on the fly	More suitable for real-time processing of events	NA	A	A (streambased, Hstreaming)

Note: Y, supported; N, no info; P, partially supported; A, available but supported by means a plug-in or external extension; NA, not available.

HBase	Hive	MonetDB	MongoDB	Objectivity	OpenQM	RdfHdt Library	RDF 3X
Y	Y	Y	Y	Y	NA	A	Y
Y	Y	P	Y	Y	Y	A	A
Write-intensive		Read-dominated (or rapidly change)	Read-dominated	More Possibility	Divided among more processes	NA	Optimized
Y	Y	A	Y	Y	NA	A	A
Y	Y	Y	Y	Y	NA	NA	Y
PB	PB	TB	PB	TB	16 TB	100 mil Triples (TB)	50 mil Triples
NoSQL	NoSQL	SQL	NoSQL	XML/SQL++	NoSQL	NoSQL	NoSQL
A	Y	Y	JOIN not support	Y (SQL++)	NA	Y	Y
A	Bucket	Blob	Chunk 16 MB	Blob	Chunk 32 KB	NA	Blob
Big table (column family)	Table—partitions—Bucket (column family)	BAT (Ext SQL)	1 Table for each collection (document DB)	Classic Table in which define + models (GraphDB)	1 file/table (data + dictionary) (MultivalueDB)	3 structures, RDF graph for Header (RDF store)	1 Table + permutations (RDF store)
Optimized use	NA	Efficient use	Document + Metadata	Like RDBMS	No compression	–50% data set	Less than data set
Jython or scala interface, rest or thrift gateway	HiveQL queries	Full SQL interfaces	Command Line, Web Interface	Multiple access from different query application, AMS	Console or web application	Access on demand	Web interface (SPARQL)
NA	Accelerate queries with bitmap indices	Fast data access (MonetDB/XQuery is among the fastest and mostscalable)	Over 50 GB, 10 times faster than MySQL	Not provide any optimization for accessing replicas	NA	NA	NA
h-files	Bitmap indexing	Hash index	Index RDBMS like	Y (function e objectivity/SQL++ interfaces)	B-tree based	RDF-graph	Y (efficient triple indexes)
Y	NA	Y	Y	Y	Y	Y	Y
NA	NA	NA	A	A (PerSay)	Y	Y	P
A (filter)	NA	NA	NA	Y (Objectivity PQE)	NA	Y	NA
Y	y	A (SciQL)	Y (network traffic)	Y	A	A	Y
P	Y	NA	A	Y	NA	Y	Y
Y	NA	NA	NA	NA	NA	Y	Y
Y	NA	More than RDBMS	High speed if DB dimension doesnot exceed memory	High speed	Increased speed with alternate key	15 times faster than RDF	Aerodynamic
A (HBaseHUT library)	A (Flume + Hive indexes our data and can be queried in real-time)	NA	Y	Y (release 8)	NA	NA	NA

realizing a reliable and highly available storage architecture, thanks to the multiple copies of the data stored within each cluster.

The *db4o* is an object-based database (Norrie et al., 2008) which provides a support to make application objects persistent. It also supports various forms of querying over these objects such as query expression trees and iterator query methods, query-by-example mechanisms to retrieve objects. Its advantages are the simplicity, speed, and small memory footprint.

eXist

eXist (Meier, 2003) is grounded on an open-source project to develop a native XML database system that can be integrated into a variety of possible applications and scenarios, ranging from web-based applications to documentation systems. The eXist database is completely written in Java and maybe deployed in different ways, either running inside a servlet-engine as a stand-alone server process, or directly embedded into an application. eXist provides schema-less storage of XML documents in hierarchical collections. It is possible to query a distinct part of collection hierarchy, using an extended XPath syntax, or the documents contained in the database. The eXist's query engine implements efficient, index-based query processing. According to path join algorithms, a large range of queries are processed using index information. This database is an available solution for applications that deal with both large and small collections of XML documents and frequent updates of them. eXist also provides a set of extensions that allow to search by keyword, by proximity to the search terms, and by regular expressions.

Google Map-Reduce

Google Map-Reduce (Yang et al., 2007) is the programing model for processing Big Data used by Google. Users specify the computation in terms of a map and a reduction function. The underlying system parallelizes the computation across large-scale clusters of machines and is also responsible for the failures, to maintain effective communication and the problem of performance. The Map function in the master node takes the inputs, partitioning them into smaller subproblems, and distributes them to operational nodes. Each operational node could perform this again, creating a multilevel tree structure. The operational node processes the smaller problems and returns the response to its parent node. In the Reduce function, the root node takes the answers from the subproblems and combine them to produce the answer at the global problem is trying to solve. The advantage of Map-Reduce consists in the fact that it is intrinsically parallel and thus it allows to distribute processes of mapping operations and reduction. The operations of Map are independent of each other, and can be performed in parallel (with limitations given from the data source and/or the number of CPU/cores near to that data); in the same way, a series of Reduce can perform the reduction step. This results in running queries or other highly distributable algorithms potentially in real time, that is a very important feature in some work environments.

Hadoop

[Hadoop Apache Project] is a framework that allows managing distributed processing of Big Data across clusters of computers using simple programing models. It is designed to scale up from single servers to thousands of machines, each of them offering local computation and storage. The Hadoop library is designed to detect and handle failures at the application layer, so delivering a highly available service on top of a cluster of computers, each of which may be prone to failures. Hadoop was inspired from Google's Map-Reduce and Google File System, GFS, and in practice it has been realized to be adopted in a wide range of cases. Hadoop is designed to scan large data set to produce results through a distributed and highly scalable batch processing systems. It is composed of the Hadoop Distribute File System (HDFS) and of the programing paradigm Map-Reduce (Karloff et al., 2010); thus, it is capable of exploiting the redundancy built into the environment. The programing model is capable of detecting failures and solving them automatically by running specific programs on various servers in the cluster. In fact, redundancy provides fault tolerance and capability to self-healing of the Hadoop Cluster. HDFS allows applications to be run across multiple servers, which have usually a set of inexpensive internal disk drives; the possibility of the usage of common hardware is another advantage of Hadoop. A similar and interesting solution is HadoopDB, proposed by a group of researchers at Yale. HadoopDB was conceived with the idea of creating a hybrid system that combines the main features of two technological solutions: parallel databases in performance and efficiency, and Map-Reduce-based system for scalability, fault tolerance, and flexibility. The basic idea behind HadoopDB is to use Map-Reduce as the communication layer above multiple nodes running single-node DBMS instances. Queries are expressed in SQL and then translated into Map-Reduce. In particular, the solution implemented involves the use of PostgreSQL as database layer, Hadoop as a communication layer, and Hive as the translation layer (Abouzeid et al., 2009).

Hbase

Hbase (Aiyer et al., 2012) is a large-scale distributed database build on top of the HDFS, mentioned above. It is a nonrelational database developed by means of an open source project. Many traditional RDBMSs use a single mutating B-tree for each index stored on disk. On the other hand, Hbase uses a Log Structured Merge Tree approach: first collects all updates into a special data structure on memory and then, periodically, flush this memory on disk, creating a new index-organized data file, the called also Hfile. These indices are immutable over time, while the several indices created on the disk are periodically merged. Therefore, by using this approach, the writing to the disk is sequentially performed. HBase's performance is satisfactory in most cases and may be further improved by using Bloom filters (Borthakur et al., 2011). Both HBase and HDFS systems have been developed by considering elasticity as fundamental principle, and the use of low cost disks has been one of the main goals of HBase. Therefore, to scale the system results is easy and cheap, even if it has to maintain a certain fault tolerance capability in the individual nodes.

Hive

[Apache Hive] is an open-source data warehousing solution based on top of Hadoop. Hive has been designed with the aim of analyzing large amounts of data more productively, improving the query capabilities of Hadoop. Hive supports queries expressed in an SQL-like declarative language—HiveQL— to extract data from sources such as HDFS or HBase. The architecture is divided into: Map-Reduce paradigm for computation (with the ability for users to enrich the queries with custom Map-Reduce scripts), metadata information for a data storage, and a processing part that receives a query from user or applications for execution. The core in/out libraries can be expanded to analyze customized data formats. Hive is also characterized by the presence of a system catalog (Metastore) containing schemas and statistics, which is useful in operations such as data exploration, query optimization, and query compilation. In Facebook, the Hive warehouse contains tens of thousands of tables and stores over 700 TB of data and is being used extensively for both reporting and *ad-hoc* analyses by more than 200 users per month (Thusoo et al., 2010).

MonetDB

MonetDB (Zhang et al., 2012) is an open-source DBMS for data mining applications. It has been designed for applications with large databases and queries, in the field of Business Intelligence and Decision Support. MonetDB has been built around the concept of bulk processing: simple operations applied to large volumes of data by using efficient hardware, for large-scale data processing. At present, two versions of MonetDB are available and are working with different types of databases: MonetDB/SQL with relational database, and MonetDB/XML with an XML database. In addition, a third version is under development to introduce RDF and SPARQL (SPARQL Protocol and RDF Query Language) supports. MonetDB provides a full SQL interface and does not allow a high-volume transaction processing with its multilevel ACID properties. The MonetDB allows performance improvement in terms of speed for both relational and XML databases thanks to innovations introduced at DBMS level, a storage model based on vertical fragmentation, run-time query optimization, and on modular software architecture. MonetDB is designed to take advantage of the large amount of main memory and implements new techniques for an efficient support of workloads. MonetDB represents relational tables using the vertical fragmentation (column-stores), storing each column in a separate table, called BAT (Binary Association Table). The left column, usually the OID (object-id), is called the head and the right column, which usually contains the actual attribute values, is called the tail.

MongoDB

[MongoDB] is a document-oriented database that memorizes document data in BSON, a binary JSON format. Its basic idea consists in the usage of a more flexible model, like the *"document,"* to replace the classic concept of a *"row."* In fact, with the document-oriented approach, it is possible to represent complex hierarchical relationships with a single record, thanks to embedded documents and arrays. MongoDB is open-source and it is schema-free—that is, there is no fixed or predefined document's keys—and allows defining indices based on specific fields of the documents. In order to retrieve data, *ad-hoc* queries based on these indices can be used. Queries are created as BSON objects to make them more efficient and are similar to SQL queries. MongoDB supports MapReduce queries and atomic operations on individual fields within the document. It allows realizing redundant and fault-tolerant systems that can easily horizontally scaled, thanks to the sharing based on the document keys and the support of asynchronous and master–slave replications. A relevant advantage of MongoDB are the opportunities of creating data structures to easily store polymorphic data, and the possibility of making elastic cloud systems given its scale-out design, which increases ease of use and developer flexibility. Moreover, server costs are significantly low because MongoDB deployment can use commodity and inexpensive hardware, and their horizontal scale-out architecture can also reduce storage costs.

Objectivity

[Objectivity Platform] is a distributed OODBMS (Object-Oriented Database Management System) for applications that require complex data models. It supports a large number of simultaneous queries and transactions and provides high-performance access to large volumes of physically distributed data. Objectivity manages data in a transparent way and uses a distributed database architecture that allows good performance and scalability. The main reasons for using a database of this type include the presence of complex relationships that suggest tree structures or graphs, and the presence of complex data, that is, when there are components of variable length and in particular multi-dimensional arrays. Other reasons are related to the presence of a database that must be geographically distributed, and which is accessed via a processor grid, or the use of more than one language or platform, and the use of workplace objects. Objectivity has an architecture consisting of a single distributed database, a choice that allows achieving high performance in relation to the amount of data stored and the number of users. This architecture distributes tasks for computation and data storage in a transparent way through the different machines and it is also scalable and has a great availability.

OpenQM

[OpenQM Database] is a DBMS that allows developing and run applications that includes a wide range of tools and advanced features for complex applications. Its database model belongs to the family of Multivalue and therefore has many aspects in common with databases Pick-descended and is transactional. The development of applications Multivalue is often faster than using other types of database and this therefore implies lower development costs and easier maintenance. This instrument has a high degree of compatibility with other types of systems with database Multivalue as UniVerse [UniVerse], PI/open, D3, and others.

The *RDF-HDT* (Header-Dictionary-Triples) [RDF-HDT Library] is a new representation format that modularizes data and uses structures of large RDF graphs to get a big storage space and is based on three main components: Header, Dictionary, and a set of triples. Header includes logical and physical data that describes the RDF data set, and it is the entry point to the data set. The Dictionary organizes all the identifiers in an RDF graph and provides a catalog of the amount of information in RDF graph with a high level of compression. The set of Triples, finally, includes the pure structure of the underlying RDF graph and avoids the noise produced by long labels and repetitions. This design gains in modularity and compactness, and addresses other important characteristics: allows access addressed on-demand to the RDF graph and is used to design specific compression techniques RDF (HDT-compress) able to outperform universal compressors. RDF-HDT introduces several advantages like compactness and compression of stored data, using small amount of memory space, communication bandwidth, and time. RDF-HDT uses a low storage space, thanks to the asymmetric structure of large RDF graph and its representation format consists of two primary modules, Dictionary and Triple. Dictionary contains mapping between elements and unique IDs, without repetition, thanks to which achieves a high compression rate and speed in searches. Triple corresponds to the initial RDF graph in a compacted form where elements are replaced with corresponding IDs. Thanks to the two processes, HDT can be also generated from RDF (HDT encoder) and can manage separate logins to run queries, to access full RDF or to carry out management operations (HDT decoder)

RDF-3X

RDF-3X (Schramm, 2012) is an RDF store that implements SPARQL [SPARQL] that achieves excellent performance making an RISC (Reduced Instruction

Set Computer) architecture with efficient indexing and query processing. The design of RDF-3X solution completely eliminates the process of tuning indices thanks to an exhaustive index of all permutations of subject–predicate–object triples and their projections unary and binary, resulting in highly compressed indices and in a query processor that can provide data results with excellent performance. The query optimizer can choose the optimal join orders also for complex queries and a cost model that includes statistical synopses for entire join paths. RDF-3X is able to provide good support for efficient online updates, thanks to an architecture staging.

Comparison and Analysis of Architectural Features

A large number of products and solutions have been reviewed for analyzing the most interested products for the readers and for the market, while a selection of solutions and products has been proposed in this paper with the aim of representing all of them. The analysis performed has been very complex since a multidisciplinary team has been involved in assessing the several aspects in multiple solutions including correlated issues in the case of tools depending on other solutions (as reported in Table 2.1). This is due to the fact that features of Big Data solutions are strongly intercorrelated and thus it was impossible to identify orthogonal aspects to provide a simple and easy to read taxonomical representation. Table 2.1 can be used to compare different solutions in terms of: infrastructure and the architecture of the systems that should cope with Big Data; data management aspects; and of data analytics aspects, such as ingestion, log analysis, and everything else is pertinent to post-production phase of data processing. Some of the information related to specific features of products and tools have not been clearly identified. In those cases, we preferred to report that the information was not available.

Application Domains Comparison

Nowadays, as reported in the introduction, Big Data solutions and technologies are currently used in many application domains with remarkable results and excellent future prospects to fully deal with the main challenges like data modeling, organization, retrieval, and data analytics. A major investment in Big Data solutions can lay the foundations for the next generations of advances in medicine, science, research, education, and e-learning, business and financial, healthcare, smart city, security, info mobility, social media, and networking.

In order to assess different fields and solutions, a number of factors have been identified. In Table 2.2, the relevance of the main features of Big

TABLE 2.2

Relevance of the Main Features of Big Data Solutions with Respect to the Most Interesting Applicative Domains

	Data Analysis Scientific Research (biomedical)	Educational and Cultural Heritage	Energy/ Transportation	Financial/ Business	Healthcare	Security	Smart Cities and mobility	Social Media Marketing	Social Network Internet Service Web Data
Infrastructural and Architectural Aspects									
Distributed management	H	M	H	H	H	H	M	H	H
High availability	H	M	H	H	H	H	H	M	H
Internal parallelism (related to velocity)	H	M	H	M	H	H	H	M	M
Data Management Aspects									
Data dimension (data volume)	H	M	M	H	M	H+	H+	H+	H+
Data replication	H	L	M	H	H	H	H	H	M
Data organization	Chuncks, Blob	Blob	Cluster, Blob	Cluster, Chuncks	Blob, Chuncks	Blob	Blob	Chuncks (16 MB), Blob	Chunks, Bucket
Data relationships	H	M	L	H	H	M	H	H	H
SQL interoperability	M	M	L	H	H	L	H	H	M
Data variety	H	M	M	M	M	H	H	H	H
Data variability	H	H	M	H	H	H	H	H	H
Data Access Aspects									
Data access performance	H	H	L	M	H	L	H	L	H

Data access type	AQL (SQL array version), full SQL interfaces, specific API	Standard interfaces, remote user interfaces	Remote user interface, get API, multiple access query	HDFS-UI web app, API, common line interfaces, AMS	API, common line interfaces, concurrency access	Remote user interfaces, multiple access from different query application	Interfaces for on-demand access, ad-hoc SQL interfaces	API and customized interfaces, command Line, web interfaces, AMS	Open ad-hoc SQL access (es. HiveQL), Web interfaces, REST interfaces
Visual rendering and visualization	H	M	M	H	H	L	H	M	M
Faceted Query results	L	H	L	H	H	L	L	H	H
Graph relationships navigation	L	M	M	H	M	L	H	H	H
Data Analytics Aspects									
Type of indexing	Array multi-dimensional, hash index	Ontologies, index RDBMS like,	Key index distributed, B-tree field indexes	HDFS, index, RDBMS like, B-tree index	Multi-dimensional index, HDFS, index, RDBMS like	Distributed multi-level tree indexing, HDFS, index, RDBMS like	Hash index, HDFS, RDF-graph	Distributed index, RDBMS like	Inverted index, MinHash, B+-tree, HDFS, RDF graph
Indexing speed	L	L	L	H	M	H	H	M	H
Semantic query	H	M	M	M	H	L	L	M	H
Statistical analysis tools in queries	H	H	H	H	H	L	M	H	H
CEP (active query)	H	L	M	H	H	M	H	L	H
Log analysis	L	M	L	H	H	H	H	H	H
Streaming processing	M	L	M	H	M	H	H	M	H (network monitoring)

Data solutions with respect to the most interesting applicative domains is reported. When possible, each feature has been expressed for that applicative domain in terms of relevance by expressing: high, medium, and low relevance/impact. For some features, the assessment of the grading was not possible, and thus a comment including commonly adopted specific solutions and/or technologies has been provided.

The main features are strongly similar to those adopted in Table 2.1 (the features those not presented relevant differences in the different domains have been removed to make the table more readable). Table 2.2 could be considered a key lecture to compare Big Data solutions on the basis of the relevant differences. The assessment has been performed according to the state-of-the-art analysis of several Big Data applications in the domains and corresponding solutions proposed. The application domains should be considered as macro-areas rather than specific scenarios. Despite the fact that the state of the art of this matter is in continuous evolution, the authors think that the work presented in this chapter can be used as the first step to understand which are the key factors for the identification of the suitable solutions to cope with a specific new domain. This means that the considerations have to be taken as examples and generalization of the analyzed cases.

Table 2.2 can be read line by line. For example, considering the infrastructural aspect of supporting distributed architectures "Distributed management," at the first glance, one could state that this feature is relevant for all the applicative domains. On the other hand, a lower degree of relevance has been notified for the educational domain. For example, the student profile analysis for the purpose of the personalized courses are typically locally based and are accumulating a lower number of information with respect to global market analysis, security, social media, etc. The latter cases are typically deployed as multisite geographical distributed databases at the worldwide level, while educational applications are usually confined at regional and local levels. For instance, in high educational domains, a moderate number of information is available and their use is often confined at local level for the students of the institute. This makes the advantage of geographically distributed services less important and interesting. While social networking applications typically needs highly distributed architectures since also their users are geographically distributed. Similar considerations can be applied for the demand of database consistency and may be about the high availability that could be less relevant for educational and social media with respect to the demands of safety critical situations of energy management and of transportation. Moreover, the internal parallelism of the solution can be an interesting feature that can be fully exploited only in specific cases depending on the data analytic algorithms adopted and when the problems can take advantage from a parallel implementation of the algorithm. This feature is strongly related to the reaction time, for example, in most of the social media solution, the estimation of suggestions and thus of clustering user profiles and content is something that is performed offline updating values periodically but not in real time.

As regards the data management aspects, the amount of data involved is considerably huge in almost all the application domains (in the order of several petabytes and exabyte). On the other hand, this is not always true for the size of individual files (with the exception of satellite images, medical images, or other multimedia files that can also be several gigabytes in size). The two aspects (number of elements to be indexed and accessed, and typical data size) are quite different and, in general, the former (number of elements) creates major problems, for processing and accessing them. For this reason, security, social media, and smart cities have been considered the applicative domains with higher demand of Big Data solutions in terms of volume. Moreover, in many cases, the main problem is not their size, rather the management and the preservation of the relationships among the various elements; they represent the effective semantic value of data set (the data model of Table 2.1 may help in comparing the solutions). For example, for the user profile (human relationships), traffic localization (service relationships, time relationships), patients' medical records (events and data relationships), etc. Data relationships, often stored in dedicated structures, and making specific queries and reasoning can be very important for some applications such as social media and networking. Therefore, for this aspect, the most challenging domains are again smart cities, social networks, and health care. In this regard, in these last two application domains, the use of graph relationship navigation constitutes a particularly useful support to improve the representation, research, and understanding of information and meanings explicitly not evident in the data itself.

In almost all domains, the usage and the interoperability of both SQL and NoSQL database are very relevant, and some differences can be detected in the data organization. In particular, the interoperability with former SQL is a very important feature in application contexts such as healthcare, social media marketing, business, and smart cities, to the widespread use of traditional RDBMS, rather than in application domains such as research scientific, social networks, and web data, security, and energy, mainly characterized by unstructured or semistructured data. Some of the applicative domains intrinsically present a large variety and variability of data, while others present more standardized and regular information. A few of these domains present both variety and variability of data such as the scientific research, security, and social media which may involve content-based analysis, video processing, etc.

Furthermore, the problems of data access is of particular importance in terms of performances and for the provided features related to the rendering, representation, and/or navigation of produced results as visual rendering tools, presentation of results by using faceted facilities, etc. Most of the domains are characterized by the needs of different custom interfaces for the data rendering (built *ad hoc* on the main features) that provide safe and consistent data access. For example, in health and scientific research, it is important to take account of issues related to the concurrent access and thus data consistency, while in social media and smart cities it is important to provide on-demand and multidevice access to information, graphs, real-time conditions, etc. A flexible visual rendering (distributions, pies, histograms, trends, etc.) may be a strongly desirable features to be provided, for many scientific and research applications, as well as for financial data and health care (e.g., for reconstruction, trend analysis, etc.). Faceted query results can be very interesting for navigating in mainly text-based Big Data as for educational and cultural heritage application domains. Graph navigation among resulted relationships can be an avoidable solution to represent the resulted data in smart cities and social media, and for presenting related implications and facts in financial and business applications. Moreover, in certain specific contexts, the data rendering has to be compliant with standards, for example, in the health care.

In terms of data analytic aspects, several different features could be of interest in the different domains. The most relevant feature in this area is the type of indexing, which in turn characterizes the indexing performance. The indexing performance are very relevant in the domains in which a huge amount of small data have to be collected and need to be accessed and elaborated in the short time, such as in finance, health care, security, and mobility. Otherwise, if the aim of the Big Data solution is mainly on the access and data processing, then fast indexing can be less relevant. For example, the use of HDFS may be suitable in contexts requiring complex and deep data processing, such as the evaluation on the evolution of a particular disease in the medical field, or the definition of a specific business models. This approach, in fact, runs the process function on a reduced data set, thus achieving scalability and availability required for processing Big Data. In education, instead, the usage of ontologies and thus of RDF databases and graphs provides a rich semantic structure better than any other method of knowledge representation, improving the precision of search and access for educational contents, including the possibility of enforcing inference in the semantic data structure.

The possibility of supporting statistical and logical analyses on data via specific queries and reasoning can be very important for some applications such as social media and networking. If this feature is structurally supported, it is possible to realize direct operations on the data, or define and store specific queries to perform direct and fast statistical analysis: for example, for estimating recommendations, firing conditions, etc.

In other contexts, however, it is very important to the continuous processing of data streams, for example, to respond quickly to requests for information and services by the citizens of a "smart city," real-time monitoring of the performance of financial stocks, or report to medical staff unexpected changes in health status of patients under observation. As can be seen from the table, in these contexts, a particularly significant feature is the use of the approach CEP (complex event processing), based on active query, which

TABLE 2.3

Relevance of the Main Features of Big Data Solutions with Respect to the Most Interesting Applicative Domains

	ArrayDBMS	CouchBase	Db4o	eXist	Google MapReduce	Hadoop	HBase	Hive	MonetDB	MongoDB	Objectivity	OpenQM	RdfHdt Library	RDF 3X
Data analysis scientific research (biomedical)	X		X	X	X				X	X	X	X	X	X
Education and cultural heritage					X	X		X		X				
Energy/transportation		X	X	X					X		X			
Financial/business	X	X				X		X	X	X	X			
Healthcare	X		X		X	X	X		X	X	X	X		
Security			X	X							X	Y		
Smart mobility, smart cities		X	X	X					X	X	X			
Social marketing	X	X				X	X	X	X	X			X	X
Social media	X	X				X	X	X	X	X	X		X	X

Note: Y = frequently adopted.

improves the user experience with a considerable increase in the speed of analysis; on the contrary, in the field of education, scientific research and transport speed of analysis is not a feature of primary importance, since in these contexts, the most important thing is the storage of data to keep track of the results of experiments or phenomena or situations occurred in a specific time interval, then the analysis is a passage that can be realized at a later time.

Lastly, it is possible to observe Table 2.3 in which the considered application domains are shown in relation to the products examined in the previous session and to the reviewed scenarios. Among all the products reviewed, MonetDB and MongoDB are among the most flexible and adaptable to different situations and contexts of applications. It is also interesting to note that RDF-based solutions have been used mainly on social media and networking applications.

Shown below are the most effective features of each product analyzed and the main application domains in which their use is commonly suggested.

HBase over HDFS provides an elastic and fault-tolerant storage solution and provides a strong consistency. Both HBase and HDFS are grounded on the fundamental design principle of elasticity. Facebook messages (Aiyer et al., 2012) exploit the potential of HBase to combine services such as messages, emails, and chat in a real-time conversation, which leads to manage approximately 14 TB of messages and 11 TB of chats, each month. For these reasons, it is successfully used in the field of social media Internet services as well as on social media marketing.

RDF-3X is considered as one of the fastest RDF representations and it provides an advantage with handling of the small data. The physical design of RDF-3X completely eliminates the need for index tuning, thanks to highly compressed indices for all permutations of triples and their binary and unary projections. Moreover, RDF-3X is optimized for queries and provides a suitable support for efficient online updates by means of a staging architecture.

MonetDB achieves a significant speed improvement for both relational/SQL and XML/XQuery databases over other open-source systems; it introduces innovations at all layers of a DBMS: a storage model based on vertical fragmentation (column store), a modern CPU-tuned query execution architecture, automatic, and self-tuning indexes, a run-time query optimization, and a modular software architecture. MonetDB is primarily used for the management of the large amount of images, for example, in astronomy, seismology, and earth observations. These relevant features collocate MonetDB as on the best tools in the field of scientific research and scientific data analysis, thus defining an interesting technology on which to develop scientific applications and create interdisciplinary platform for the exchange of data in the world community of researchers.

HDT has been proved by experiments to be a good tool for compacting data set. It allows to be compacted more than 15 times with respect to standard RDF representations; thus, improving parsing and processing, while maintaining a consistent publication scheme. Thus, RDF-HDT allows to improve compactness and compression, using much less space, thus saving storing space and communication bandwidth. For these reasons, this solution is especially suited to share data on the web, but also in those contexts that require operations such as data analysis and visualization of results, thanks to the support of 3D visualization of the RDF Adjacency matrix of the RDF Graph.

eXist's query engine implements efficient index structure to collect data for scientific and academic research, educational assessments, and for consumption in the energy sector, and its index-based query processing is needed to efficiently perform queries on large document collections. Experiments have, moreover, demonstrated the linear scalability of eXist's indexing, storage, and querying architecture. In general, the search expressions using full text index perform better with eXist, than that with the corresponding queries based on XPath.

In scientific/technical applications, ArrayDBMS is often used in combination with complex queries, and therefore, the optimization results are fundamental. ArrayDBMS may be used with both hardware and software parallelisms, which make possible the realization of efficient systems in many fields, such as geology, oceanography, atmospheric sciences, gene data, etc.

Objectivity/DB guarantees a complete support for ACID and can be replicated to multiple locations. Objectivity/DB is highly reliable and thanks to the possibility of schema evolution, it provides advantages over other technologies that had a difficult time with change/update a field. Thus, it has been typically used for making data-insensitive systems or real-time applications, which manipulate the large volumes of complex data. Precisely because of these features, the main application fields are the healthcare and financial services, respectively, for the real-time management of electronic health records and for the analysis of products with higher consumption, with also the monitoring of sensitive information to support intelligence services.

OpenQM enables the system development with reliability and also provides efficiency and stability. The choice of using OpenQM is usually related to the need for speed, security, and reliability and also related to the ability of easily built excellent GUI interfaces into the database.

Couchbase is a high-performance and scalable data solution supporting high availability, fault tolerance, and data security. Couchbase may provide extremely fast response time. It is particularly suggested for applications developed to support the citizens in the new model of smart urban cities (smart mobility, energy consumption, etc.). Thanks to its low latency, Couchbase is mainly used in the development of gaming online, and, in applications where obtaining a significant performance improvements is very important, or where the extraction of meaningful information from the large amount of data constantly exchanged is mandatory. For example, in social networks such as Twitter, Facebook, Flickr, etc.

The main advantage of Hadoop is its ability to analyze huge data sets to quickly spot trends. In fact, most customers use Hadoop together with other types of software such as HDFS. The adoption of Google MapReduce provides several benefits: the indexing code is simpler, smaller, and easier to understand, and it guarantees fault tolerance and parallelization. Both Hadoop and Google MapReduce are preferably used in applications requiring large distributed computation. The New York Times, for example, uses Hadoop to process row images and turn them into a pdf format in an acceptable time (about 24 h each 4 TB of images). Other big companies exploit the potential of these products: Ebay, Amazon, Twitter, and Google itself that uses MapReduce to regenerate the Google's Index, to update indices and to run various types of analyses. Furthermore, this technology can be used in medical fields to perform large-scale data analysis with the aim of improving treatments and prevention of disease.

Hive significantly reduces the effort required for a migration to Hadoop, which makes it perfect for data warehousing and also it has the ability to create *ad-hoc* queries, using a jargon similar to SQL. These features make Hive excellent for the analysis of large data sets especially in social media marketing and web application business.

MongoDB provides relevant flexibility and simplicity, which may reduce development and data modeling time. It is typically used in applications requiring insertion and updating in real time, in addition to real-time query processing. It allows one to define the consistency level that is directly related to the achievable performance. If high performance is not a necessity, it is possible to obtain maximum consistency, waiting until the new element has been replicated to all nodes. MongoDB uses internal memory to store the working set, thus allowing faster access of data. Thanks to its characteristics, MongoDB is easily usable in business and in social marketing fields and, it is actually successfully used in Gaming environment, thanks to its high performance for small operations of read/write. As many other Big Data solutions, it is well suited for applications that handled high volumes of data where traditional DBMS might be too expensive.

Db4o does not need a mapping function between the representation in memory and what actually is stored on disk, because the application schema corresponds with the data schema. This advantage allows one to obtain better performance and good user experience. Db4o also permits one to database access by using simple programing language (Java, .NET, etc.), and thanks to its type safety, it does not need to hold in check query against code injection. Db4o supports the paradigm CEP (see Table 2.2) and is therefore very suitable for medical applications, scientific research, analysis of financial and real-time data streams, in which the demand for this feature is very high.

Conclusions

We have entered an era of Big Data. There is the potential for making faster advances in many scientific disciplines through better analysis of these large volumes of data and also for improving the profitability of many enterprises. The need for these new-generation data management tools is being driven by the explosion of Big Data and by the rapidly growing volumes and variety of data that are collecting today from alternative sources such as social networks like Twitter and Facebook.

NoSQL Database Management Systems represents a possible solution to these problems; unfortunately they are not a definitive solutions: these tools have a wide range of features that can be further developed to create new products more adaptable to this huge stream of data constantly growing and to its open challenge such as error handling, privacy, unexpected correlation detection, trend analysis and prediction, timeliness analysis, and visualization. Considering this latter challenge, it is clear that, in a fast-growing market for maps, charts, and other ways to visually sort using data, these larger volumes of data and analytical capabilities become the new coveted features; today, in fact in the "Big Data world," static bar charts and pie charts just do not make more sense, and more and more companies are demanding more dynamic, interactive tools, and methods for line-of-business managers and information workers for viewing, understanding, and operating on the analysis of big data.

Each product compared in this review presents different features that may be needed in different situations with which we are dealing. In fact, there is still no definitive ultimate solution for the management of Big Data. The best way to determine on which product to base the development of your system may consist in analyzing the available data sets carefully and determine what are the requirements to which you cannot give up. Then, an analysis of the existing products is needed to determine the pros and cons, also considering other nonfunctional features such as the programing language, the integration aspects, the legacy constraints, etc.

References

Abouzeid A., Bajda-Pawlikowski C., Abadi D., Silberschatz A., Rasin A., HadoopDB: An architectural hybrid of MapReduce and DBMS technologies for analytical workloads. *Proceedings of the VLDB Endowment*, 2(1), 922–933, 2009.

Aiyer A., Bautin M., Jerry Chen G., Damania P., Khemani P., Muthukkaruppan K., Ranganathan K., Spiegelberg N., Tang L., Vaidya M., Storage infrastructure behind Facebook messages using HBase at scale. *Bulletin of the IEEE Computer Society Technical Committee on Data Engineering*, 35(2), 4–13, 2012.

AllegroGraph, http://www.franz.com/agraph/allegrograph/

Amazon AWS, http://aws.amazon.com/

Amazon Dynamo, http://aws.amazon.com/dynamodb/

Antoniu G., Bougè L., Thirion B., Poline J.B., AzureBrain: *Large-scale Joint Genetic and Neuroimaging Data Analysis on Azure Clouds*, Microsoft Research Inria Joint Centre, Palaiseau, France, September 2010. http://www.irisa.fr/kerdata/lib/exe/fetch.php?media=pdf:inria-microsoft.pdf

Apache Cassandra, http://cassandra.apache.org/

Apache HBase, http://hbase.apache.org/

Apache Hive, http://hive.apache.org/

Apache Solr, http://lucene.apache.org/solr/

Baumann P., Dehmel A., Furtado P., Ritsch R., The multidimensional database system RasDaMan. *SIGMOD'98 Proceedings of the 1998 ACM SIGMOD International Conference on Management of Data*, Seattle, Washington, pp. 575–577, 1998, ISBN: 0-89791-995-5.

Bellini P., Cenni D., Nesi P., On the effectiveness and optimization of information retrieval for cross media content, *Proceedings of the KDIR 2012 is Part of IC3K 2012, International Joint Conference on Knowledge Discovery*, Knowledge Engineering and Knowledge Management, Barcelona, Spain, 2012a.

Bellini P., Bruno, I., Cenni, D., Fuzier, A., Nesi, P., Paolucci, M., Mobile medicine: Semantic computing management for health care applications on desktop and mobile devices. *Multimedia Tools and Applications, Springer*, 58(1), 41–79, 2012b.

DOI 10.1007/s11042-010-0684-y. http://link.springer.com/article/10.1007/s11042-010-0684-y

Bellini P., Bruno I., Cenni D., Nesi P., Micro grids for scalable media computing and intelligence in distributed scenarios. *IEEE MultiMedia*, 19(2), 69–79, 2012c.

Bellini P., Bruno I., Nesi P., Rogai D., Architectural solution for interoperable content and DRM on multichannel distribution, *Proc. of the International Conference on Distributed Multimedia Systems, DMS 2007*, Organised by Knowledge Systems Institute, San Francisco Bay, USA, 2007.

Bellini P., Nesi P., Pazzaglia F., Exploiting P2P scalability for grant authorization digital rights management solutions, *Multimedia Tools and Applications, Multimedia Tools and Applications Journal*, Springer, April 2013.

Ben-Yitzhak O., Golbandi N., Har'El N., Lempel R., Neumann A., Ofek-Koifman S., Sheinwald D., Shekita E., Sznajder B., Yogev S., Beyond basic faceted search, *Proc. of the 2008 International Conference on Web Search and Data Mining*, pp. 33–44, 2008.

BlueGene IBM project, http://www.research.ibm.com/bluegene/index.html

Borthakur D., Muthukkaruppan K., Ranganathan K., Rash S., SenSarma J., Spielberg N., Molkov D. et al., Apache Hadoop goes realtime at Facebook, *Proceedings of the 2011 International Conference on Management of Data*, Athens, Greece, 2011.

Bose I., Mahapatra R.K., Business data mining—a machine learning perspective. *Information & Management*, 39(3), 211–225, 2001.

Brewer E., CAP twelve years later: How the rules have changed. *IEEE Computer*, 45(2), 23–29, 2012.

Brewer E., Lesson from giant-scale services. *IEEE Internet Computing*, 5(4), 46–55, 2001.

Bryant R., Katz R.H., Lazowska E.D., Big-data computing: Creating revolutionary breakthroughs in commerce, science and society, *In Computing Research Initiatives for the 21st Century, Computing Research Association, Ver.8*, 2008. http://www.cra.org/ccc/files/docs/init/Big_Data.pdf

Bryant R.E., Carbonell J.G., Mitchell T., From data to knowledge to action: Enabling advanced intelligence and decision-making for America's security, *Computing Community Consortium*, Version 6, July 28, 2010.

Cao L., Wang Y., Xiong J., Building highly available cluster file system based on replication, *International Conference on Parallel and Distributed Computing, Applications and Technologies*, Higashi Hiroshima, Japan, pp. 94–101, December 2009.

Cattel R., Scalable SQL and NoSQL data stores. *ACM SIGMOND Record*, 39(4), 12–27, 2010.

Couchbase, http://www.couchbase.com/

Cunningham H., Maynard D., Bontcheva K., Tablan V., GATE: A framework and graphical development environment for robust NLP tools and applications, *Proceedings of the 40th Anniversary Meeting of the Association for Computational Linguistics*, Philadelphia, July 2002.

De Witt D.J., Paulson E., Robinson E., Naugton J., Royalty J., Shankar S., Krioukov A., Clustera: an integrated computation and data management system. *Proceedings of the VLDB Endowment*, 1(1), 28–41, 2008.

De Witt S., Sinclair R., Sansum A., Wilson M., Managing large data volumes from scientific facilities. *ERCIM News* 89, 15, 2012.

Domingos P., Mining social networks for viral marketing. *IEEE Intelligent Systems*, 20(1), 80–82, 2005.

Dykstra D., Comparison of the frontier distributed database caching system to NoSQL databases, *Computing in High Energy and Nuclear Physics (CHEP) Conference*, New York, May 2012.

Eaton C., Deroos D., Deutsch T., Lapis G., *Understanding Big Data: Analytics for Enterprise Class Hadoop and Streaming Data*, McGraw Hill Professional, McGraw Hill, New York, 2012, ISBN: 978-0071790536.

ECLAP, http://www.eclap.eu

Europeana Portal, http://www.europeana.eu/portal/

Everitt B., Landau S., Leese M., *Cluster Analysis*, 4th edition, Arnold, London, 2001.

Figueireido V., Rodrigues F., Vale Z., An electric energy consumer characterization framework based on data mining techniques. *IEEE Transactions on Power Systems*, 20(2), 596–602, 2005.

Foster I., Jeffrey M., and Tuecke S. Grid services for distributed system integration, *IEEE Computer*, 5(6), 37–46, 2002.

Fox A., Brewer E.A., Harvest, yield, and scalable tolerant systems, *Proceedings of the Seventh Workshop on Hot Topics in Operating Systems*, Rio Rico, Arizona, pp. 174–178, 1999.

Gallego M.A., Fernandez J.D., Martinez-Prieto M.A., De La Fuente P., RDF visualization using a three-dimensional adjacency matrix, *4th International Semantic Search Workshop (SemSearch)*, Hyderabad, India, 2011.

Ghosh D., Sharman R., Rao H.R., Upadhyaya S., Self-healing systems—Survey and synthesis, *Decision Support Systems*, 42(4), 2164–2185, 2007.

Google Drive, http://drive.google.com

GraphBase, http://graphbase.net/

Gulisano V., Jimenez-Peris R., Patino-Martinez M., Soriente C., Valduriez P., A big data platform for large scale event processing, *ERCIM News*, 89, 32–33, 2012.

Hadoop Apache Project, http://hadoop.apache.org/

Hanna M., Data mining in the e-learning domain. *Campus-Wide Information Systems*, 21(1), 29–34, 2004.

Iaconesi S., Persico O., The co-creation of the city, re-programming cities using real-time user generated content, *1st Conference on Information Technologies for Performing Arts, Media Access and Entertainment*, Florence, Italy, 2012.

Iannella R., Open digital rights language (ODRL), Version 1.1 W3C Note, 2002, http://www.w3.org/TR/odrl

Jacobs A., The pathologies of big data. *Communications of the ACM—A Blind Person's Interaction with Technology*, 52(8), 36–44, 2009.

Jagadish H.V., Narayan P.P.S., Seshadri S., Kanneganti R., Sudarshan S., Incremental organization for data recording and warehousing, *Proceedings of the 23rd International Conference on Very Large Data Bases*, Athens, Greece, pp. 16–25, 1997.

Karloff H., Suri S., Vassilvitskii S., A model of computation for MapReduce. *Proceedings of the Twenty-First Annual ACM-SIAM Symposium on Discrete Algorithms*, pp. 938–948, 2010.

LHC, http://public.web.cern.ch/public/en/LHC/LHC-en.html

Liu L., Biderman A., Ratti C., Urban mobility landscape: Real time monitoring of urban mobility patterns, *Proceedings of the 11th International Conference on Computers in Urban Planning and Urban Management*, Hong Kong, June 2009.

Mans R.S., Schonenberg M.H., Song M., Van der Aalst W.M.P., Bakker P.J.M., Application of process mining in healthcare—A case study in a Dutch hospital. *Biomedical Engineering Systems and Technologies, Communications in Computer and Information Science*, 25(4), 425–438, 2009.

McHugh J., Widom J., Abiteboul S., Luo Q., Rajaraman A., Indexing semistructured data, Technical report, Stanford University, California, 1998.

Meier W., eXist: An open source native XML database. *Web, Web-Services, and Database Systems—Lecture Notes in Computer Science*, 2593, 169–183, 2003.

Memcached, http://memcached.org/

Microsoft Azure, http://www.windowsazure.com/it-it/

Microsoft, *Microsoft private cloud*. Tech. rep., 2012.

Mislove A., Gummandi K.P., Druschel P., Exploiting social networks for Internet search, *Record of the Fifth Workshop on Hot Topics in Networks: HotNets V, Irvine, CA*, pp. 79–84, November 2006.

MongoDB, http://www.mongodb.org/

MPEG-21, http://mpeg.chiariglione.org/standards/mpeg-21/mpeg-21.htm

Neo4J, http://neo4j.org/

Norrie M.C., Grossniklaus M., Decurins C., Semantic data management for db4o, *Proceedings of 1st International Conference on Object Databases (ICOODB 2008)*, Frankfurt/Main, Germany, pp. 21–38, 2008.

NoSQL DB, http://nosql-database.org/

Obenshain M.K., Application of data mining techniques to healthcare data, *Infection Control and Hospital Epidemiology*, 25(8), 690–695, 2004.

Objectivity Platform, http://www.objectivity.com

Olston C., Jiang J., Widom J., Adaptive filters for continuous queries over distributed data streams, *Proceedings of the 2003 ACM SIGMOD International Conference on Management of Data*, pp. 563–574, 2003.

OpenCirrus Project, https://opencirrus.org/

OpenQM Database, http://www.openqm.org/docs/

OpenStack Project, http://www.openstack.org

Oracle Berkeley, http://www.oracle.com/technetwork/products/berkeleydb/

Pierre G., El Helw I., Stratan C., Oprescu A., Kielmann T., Schuett T., Stender J., Artac M., Cernivec A., ConPaaS: An integrated runtime environment for elastic cloud applications, *ACM/IFIP/USENIX 12th International Middleware Conference*, Lisboa, Portugal, December 2011.

RDF-HDT Library, http://www.rdfhdt.org

Rivals E., Philippe N., Salson M., Léonard M., Commes T., Lecroq T., A scalable indexing solution to mine huge genomic sequence collections. *ERCIM News*, 89, 20–21, 2012.

Rusitschka S., Eger K., Gerdes C., Smart grid data cloud: A model for utilizing cloud computing in the smart grid domain, *1st IEEE International Conference of Smart Grid Communications*, Gaithersburg, MD, 2010.

Setnes M., Kaymak U., Fuzzy modeling of client preference from large data sets: An application to target selection in direct marketing. *IEEE Transactions on Fuzzy Systems*, 9(1), February 2001.

SCAPE Project, http://scape-project.eu/

Schramm M., Performance of RDF representations, *16th TSConIT*, 2012.

Silvestri Ludovico (LENS), Alessandro Bria (UCBM), Leonardo Sacconi (LENS), Anna Letizia Allegra Mascaro (LENS), Maria Chiara Pettenati (ICON), SanzioBassini

(CINECA), Carlo Cavazzoni (CINECA), Giovanni Erbacci (CINECA), Roberta Turra (CINECA), Giuseppe Fiameni (CINECA), Valeria Ruggiero (UNIFE), Paolo Frasconi (DSI-UNIFI), Simone Marinai (DSI-UNIFI), Marco Gori (DiSI-UNISI), Paolo Nesi (DSI-UNIFI), Renato Corradetti (Neuroscience-UNIFI), GiulioIannello (UCBM), Francesco SaverioPavone (ICON, LENS), Projectome: Set up and testing of a high performance computational infrastructure for processing and visualizing neuro-anatomical information obtained using confocal ultra-microscopy techniques, *Neuroinformatics 2012 5th INCF Congress*, Munich, Germany, September 2012.

Snell A., Solving big data problems with private cloud storage, *White paper,* October 2011.

SPARQL at W3C, http://www.w3.org/TR/rdf-sparql-query/

Thelwall M., A web crawler design for data mining. *Journal of Information Science*, 27(1), 319–325, 2001.

Thusoo A., Sarma J.S., Jain N., Zheng Shao, Chakka P., Ning Zhang, Antony S., Hao Liu, Murthy R., Hive—A petabyte scale data warehouse using Hadoop, *IEEE 26th International Conference on Data Engineering (ICDE)*, pp. 996–1005, Long Beach, CA, March 2010.

UniVerse, http://u2.rocketsoftware.com/products/u2-universe

Valduriez P., Pacitti E., Data management in large-scale P2P systems. High Performance Computing for Computational Science Vecpar 2004—*Lecture Notes in Computer Science*, 3402, 104–118, 2005.

Woolf B.P., Baker R., Gianchandani E.P., *From Data to Knowledge to Action: Enabling Personalized Education.* Computing Community Consortium, Version 9, Computing Research Association, Washington DC, 2 September 2010. http://www.cra.org/ccc/files/docs/init/Enabling_Personalized_Education.pdf

Xui R., Wunsch D.C. II, *Clustering*, John Wiley and Sons, USA, 2009.

Yang H., Dasdan A., Hsiao R.L., Parker D.S., Map-reduce-merge: simplified relational data processing on large clusters, *SIGMOD'07 Proceedings of the 2007 ACM SIGMOD International Conference on Management of Data*, Beijing, China, pp. 1029–1040, June 2007, ISBN: 978-1-59593-686-8.

Yang J., Tang D., Zhou Y., A distributed storage model for EHR based on HBase, *International Conference on Information Management, Innovation Management and Industrial Engineering*, Shenzhen, China, 2011.

Zenith, http://www-sop.inria.fr/teams/zenith/

Zhang Y., Kersten M., Ivanova M., Pirk H., Manegold S., An implementation of ad-hoc array queries on top of MonetDB, *TELEIOS FP7-257662 Deliverable D5.1*, February 2012.

Zinterhof P., Computer-aided diagnostics. *ERCIM News*, 89, 46, 2012.

3

Big Data: Challenges and Opportunities

Roberto V. Zicari

CONTENTS

Introduction

"Big Data is the new gold" (Open Data Initiative)

Every day, 2.5 quintillion bytes of data are created. These data come from digital pictures, videos, posts to social media sites, intelligent sensors, purchase transaction records, cell phone GPS signals, to name a few. This is known as Big Data.

There is no doubt that Big Data and especially *what we do with it* has the potential to become a driving force for innovation and value creation. In this chapter, we will look at Big Data from three different perspectives: the business perspective, the technological perspective, and the social good perspective.

The Story as it is Told from the Business Perspective

Now let us define the term *Big Data.* I have selected a definition, given by McKinsey Global Institute (MGI) [1]:

"Big Data" refers to datasets whose size is beyond the ability of typical database software tools to capture, store, manage and analyze.

This definition is quite general and open ended, and well captures the rapid growth of available data, and also shows the need of technology to "catch up" with it. This definition is not defined in terms of data size; in fact, data sets will increase in the future! It also obviously varies by sectors, ranging from a few dozen terabytes to multiple petabytes (1 petabyte is 1000 terabytes).

(Big) Data is in every industry and business function and is an important factor for production. MGI estimated that 7 exabytes of new data enterprises globally were stored in 2010. Interestingly, more than 50% of IP traffic is non-human, and M2M will become increasingly important. *So what is Big Data supposed to create?* Value. But what "value" exactly? Big Data *per se* does not produce any value.

David Gorbet of MarkLogic explains [2]: "the increase in data complexity is the biggest challenge that every IT department and CIO must address. Businesses across industries have to not only store the data but also be able to leverage it quickly and effectively to derive business value."

Value comes only from what we infer from it. That is why we need *Big Data Analytics*.

Werner Vogels, CTO of Amazon.com, describes Big Data Analytics as follows [3]: "in the old world of data analysis you knew exactly which questions you wanted to asked, which drove a very predictable collection and storage model. In the new world of data analysis your questions are going to evolve and changeover time and as such you need to be able to collect, store and analyze data without being constrained by resources."

According to MGI, the "value" that can be derived by analyzing Big Data can be spelled out as follows:

- Creating transparencies;
- Discovering needs, exposing variability, and improving performance;
- Segmenting customers; and
- Replacing/supporting human decision-making with automated algorithms—Innovating new business models, products, and services.

"The most impactful Big Data Applications will be industry- or even organization-specific, leveraging the data that the organization consumes and generates in the course of doing business. There is no single set formula for extracting value from this data; it will depend on the application" explains David Gorbet.

"There are many applications where simply being able to comb through large volumes of complex data from multiple sources via interactive queries can give organizations new insights about their products, customers, services, etc. Being able to combine these interactive data explorations with some analytics and visualization can produce new insights that would otherwise be hidden. We call this Big Data Search" says David Gorbet.

Gorbet's concept of "Big Data Search" implies the following:

- There is no single set formula for extracting value from Big Data; it will depend on the application.
- There are many applications where simply being able to comb through large volumes of complex data from multiple sources via

interactive queries can give organizations new insights about their products, customers, services, etc.

- Being able to combine these interactive data explorations with some analytics and visualization can produce new insights that would otherwise be hidden.

Gorbet gives an example of the result of such Big Data Search: "it was analysis of social media that revealed that Gatorade is closely associated with flu and fever, and our ability to drill seamlessly from high-level aggregate data into the actual source social media posts shows that many people actually take Gatorade to treat flu symptoms. Geographic visualization shows that this phenomenon may be regional. Our ability to sift through all this data in real time, using fresh data gathered from multiple sources, both internal and external to the organization helps our customers identify new actionable insights."

Where Big Data will be used? According to MGI, Big Data can generate financial value across sectors. They identified the following key sectors:

- Health care (this is a very sensitive area, since patient records and, in general, information related to health are very critical)
- Public sector administration (e.g., in Europe, the Open Data Initiative—a European Commission initiative which aims at opening up Public Sector Information)
- Global personal location data (this is very relevant given the rise of mobile devices)
- Retail (this is the most obvious, since the existence of large Web retail shops such as eBay and Amazon)
- Manufacturing

I would add to the list two additional areas

- Social personal/professional data (e.g., Facebook, Twitter, and the like)

What are examples of *Big Data Use Cases?* The following is a sample list:

- Log analytics
- Fraud detection
- Social media and sentiment analysis
- Risk modeling and management
- Energy sector

Currently, the key *limitations* in exploiting *Big Data*, according to MGI, are

- Shortage of talent necessary for organizations to take advantage of Big Data
- Shortage of knowledge in statistics, machine learning, and data mining

Both limitations reflect the fact that the current underlying technology is quite difficult to use and understand. As every new technology, Big Data Analytics technology will take time before it will reach a level of maturity and easiness to use for the enterprises at large. All the above-mentioned examples of values generated by analyzing Big Data, however, do not take into account the possibility that such derived "values" are *negative*.

In fact, the analysis of Big Data if improperly used poses also *issues*, specifically in the following areas:

- Access to data
- Data policies
- Industry structure
- Technology and techniques

This is outside the scope of this chapter, but it is for sure one of the most important nontechnical challenges that Big Data poses.

The Story as it is Told from the Technology Perspective

The above are the business "promises" about Big Data. But what is the reality today? Big data problems have several characteristics that make them *technically challenging*.

We can group the challenges when dealing with Big Data in three dimensions: *data, process, and management*. Let us look at each of them in some detail:

Data Challenges

Volume

The volume of data, especially machine-generated data, is exploding, how fast that data is growing every year, with new sources of data that are emerging. For example, in the year 2000, 800,000 petabytes (PB) of data were stored in the world, and it is expected to reach 35 zettabytes (ZB) by 2020 (according to IBM).

Social media plays a key role: Twitter generates 7+ terabytes (TB) of data every day. Facebook, 10 TB. Mobile devices play a key role as well, as there were estimated 6 billion mobile phones in 2011.

The challenge is how to deal with the size of Big Data.

Variety, Combining Multiple Data Sets

More than 80% of today's information is unstructured and it is typically too big to manage effectively. What does it mean?
David Gorbet explains [2]:

It used to be the case that all the data an organization needed to run its operations effectively was structured data that was generated within the organization. Things like customer transaction data, ERP data, etc. Today, companies are looking to leverage a lot more data from a wider variety of sources both inside and outside the organization. Things like documents, contracts, machine data, sensor data, social media, health records, emails, etc. The list is endless really.

A lot of this data is unstructured, or has a complex structure that's hard to represent in rows and columns. And organizations want to be able to combine all this data and analyze it together in new ways.

For example, we have more than one customer in different industries whose applications combine geospatial vessel location data with weather and news data to make real-time mission-critical decisions.

Data come from sensors, smart devices, and social collaboration technologies. Data are not only structured, but raw, semistructured, unstructured data from web pages, web log files (click stream data), search indexes, e-mails, documents, sensor data, etc.

Semistructured Web data such as A/B testing, sessionization, bot detection, and pathing analysis all require powerful analytics on many petabytes of semistructured Web data.

The challenge is how to handle multiplicity of types, sources, and formats.

Velocity

Shilpa Lawande of Vertica defines this challenge nicely [4]: "as businesses get more value out of analytics, it creates a success problem—they want the data available faster, or in other words, want real-time analytics.

And they want more people to have access to it, or in other words, high user volumes."

One of the key challenges is how to react to the flood of information in the time required by the application.

Veracity, Data Quality, Data Availability

Who told you that the data you analyzed is good or complete? Paul Miller [5] mentions that "a good process will, typically, make bad decisions if based upon bad data. E.g. what are the implications in, for example, a Tsunami that affects several Pacific Rim countries? If data is of high quality in one country, and poorer in another, does the Aid response skew 'unfairly' toward the well-surveyed country or toward the educated guesses being made for the poorly surveyed one?"

There are several challenges:

How can we cope with uncertainty, imprecision, missing values, misstatements or untruths?

How good is the data? How broad is the coverage?

How fine is the sampling resolution? How timely are the readings?

How well understood are the sampling biases?

Is there data available, at all?

Data Discovery

This is a huge challenge: how to find high-quality data from the vast collections of data that are out there on the Web.

Quality and Relevance

The challenge is determining the quality of data sets and relevance to particular issues (i.e., the data set making some underlying assumption that renders it biased or not informative for a particular question).

Data Comprehensiveness

Are there areas without coverage? What are the implications?

Personally Identifiable Information

Much of this information is about people. Partly, this calls for effective industrial practices. "Partly, it calls for effective oversight by Government. Partly—perhaps mostly—it requires a realistic reconsideration of what privacy really means". (Paul Miller [5])

Can we extract enough information to help people without extracting so much as to compromise their privacy?

Data Dogmatism

Analysis of Big Data can offer quite remarkable insights, but we must be wary of becoming too beholden to the numbers. Domain experts—and common sense—must continue to play a role.

For example, "It would be worrying if the healthcare sector only responded to flu outbreaks when Google Flu Trends told them to." (Paul Miller [5])

Scalability

Shilpa Lawande explains [4]: "techniques like social graph analysis, for instance leveraging the influencers in a social network to create better user experience are hard problems to solve at scale. All of these problems combined create a perfect storm of challenges and opportunities to create faster, cheaper and better solutions for Big Data analytics than traditional approaches can solve."

Process Challenges

"It can take significant exploration to find the right model for analysis, and the ability to iterate very quickly and 'fail fast' through many (possible throw away) models—at scale—is critical." (Shilpa Lawande)

According to Laura Haas (IBM Research), process challenges with deriving insights include [5]:

- Capturing data
- Aligning data from different sources (e.g., resolving when two objects are the same)
- Transforming the data into a form suitable for analysis
- Modeling it, whether mathematically, or through some form of simulation
- Understanding the output, visualizing and sharing the results, think for a second how to display complex analytics on a iPhone or a mobile device

Management Challenges

"Many data warehouses contain sensitive data such as personal data. There are legal and ethical concerns with accessing such data.

So the data must be secured and access controlled as well as logged for audits." (Michael Blaha)

The main management challenges are

- Data privacy
- Security

- Governance
- Ethical

The challenges are: Ensuring that data are used correctly (abiding by its intended uses and relevant laws), tracking how the data are used, transformed, derived, etc., and managing its lifecycle.

Big Data Platforms Technology: Current State of the Art

The industry is still in an immature state, experiencing an explosion of different technological solutions. Many of the technologies are far from robust or enterprise ready, often requiring significant technical skills to support the software even before analysis is attempted. At the same time, there is a clear shortage of analytical experience to take advantage of the new data. Nevertheless, the potential value is becoming increasingly clear.

In the past years, the motto was "rethinking the architecture": scale and performance requirements strain conventional databases.

> "The problems are a matter of the underlying architecture. If not built for scale from the ground-up a database will ultimately hit the wall—this is what makes it so difficult for the established vendors to play in this space because you cannot simply retrofit a 20+year-old architecture to become a distributed MPP database over night," says Florian Waas of EMC/Greenplum [6].
>
> "In the Big Data era the old paradigm of shipping data to the application isn't working any more. Rather, the application logic must 'come' to the data or else things will break: this is counter to conventional wisdom and the established notion of strata within the database stack. With terabytes, things are actually pretty simple—most conventional databases scale to terabytes these days. However, try to scale to petabytes and it's a whole different ball game." (Florian Waas)

This confirms Gray's Laws of Data Engineering, adapted here to Big Data:

Take the Analysis to the Data!

In order to analyze Big Data, the current state of the art is a parallel database or NoSQL data store, with a Hadoop connector. *Hadoop* is used for processing the *unstructured* Big Data. Hadoop is becoming the standard platform for doing large-scale processing of data in the enterprise. Its rate of growth far exceeds any other "Big Data" processing platform.

What Is Apache Hadoop?

Hadoop provides a new open source platform to analyze and process Big Data. It was inspired by Google's MapReduce and Google File System (GFS) papers. It is really an ecosystems of projects, including:

Higher-level declarative languages for writing queries and data analysis pipelines, such as:

- Pig (Yahoo!)—relational-like algebra—(used in ca. 60% of Yahoo! MapReduce use cases)
- PigLatin
- Hive (used by Facebook) also inspired by SQL—(used in ca. 90% of Facebook MapReduce use cases)
- Jaql (IBM)
- Several other modules that include Load, Transform, Dump and store, Flume Zookeeper Hbase Oozie Lucene Avro, etc.

Who Are the Hadoop Users?

A simple classification:

- Advanced users of Hadoop.

  They are often PhDs from top universities with high expertise in analytics, databases, and data mining. They are looking to go beyond batch uses of Hadoop to support real-time streaming of content. Product recommendations, ad placements, customer churn, patient outcome predictions, fraud detection, and sentiment analysis are just a few examples that improve with real-time information.

  How many of such advanced users currently exist?

  "There are only a few Facebook-sized IT organizations that can have 60 Stanford PhDs on staff to run their Hadoop infrastructure. The others need it to be easier to develop Hadoop applications, deploy them and run them in a production environment." (JohnSchroeder [7])

  So, not that many apparently.
- New users of Hadoop

  They need Hadoop to become easier. Need it to be easier to develop Hadoop applications, deploy them, and run them in a production environment.

  Organizations are also looking to expand Hadoop use cases to include business critical, secure applications that easily integrate with file-based applications and products.

  With mainstream adoption comes, the need for tools that do not require specialized skills and programers. New Hadoop developments must be simple for users to operate and to get data in and out. This includes direct access with standard protocols using existing tools and applications.

Is there a real need for it? See also Big Data Myth later.

An Example of an Advanced User: Amazon

"We chose Hadoop for several reasons. First, it is the only available framework that could scale to process 100s or even 1000s of terabytes of data and scale to installations of up to 4000 nodes. Second, Hadoop is open source and we can innovate on top of the framework and inside it to help our customers develop more performant applications quicker.

Third, we recognized that Hadoop was gaining substantial popularity in the industry with multiple customers using Hadoop and many vendors innovating on top of Hadoop. Three years later we believe we made the right choice. We also see that existing BI vendors such as Microstrategy are willing to work with us and integrate their solutions on top of Elastic. MapReduce." (Werner Vogels, VP and CTO Amazon [3])

Big Data in Data Warehouse or in Hadoop?

Roughly speaking we have:

- *Data warehouse*: structured data, data "trusted"
- *Hadoop*: semistructured and unstructured data. Data "not trusted"

An interesting historical perspective of the development of Big Data comes from Michael J. Carey [8]. He distinguishes between:

Big Data in the Database World (Early 1980s Till Now)

- Parallel Databases. Shared-nothing architecture, declarative set-oriented nature of relational queries, divide and conquer parallelism (e.g., Teradata). Later phase re-implementation of relational databases (e.g., HP/Vertica, IBM/Netezza, Teradata/Aster Data, EMC/Greenplum, Hadapt)

and

Big Data in the Systems World (Late 1990s Till Now)

- Apache Hadoop (inspired by Google GFS, MapReduce), contributed by large Web companies. For example, Yahoo!, Facebook, Google BigTable, Amazon Dynamo

The Parallel database software stack (Michael J. Carey) comprises

- SQL $\rightarrow$ SQL Compiler
- *Relational Dataflow Layer* (runs the query plans, orchestrate the local storage managers, deliver partitioned, shared-nothing storage services for large relational tables)
- *Row/Column Storage Manager* (record-oriented: made up of a set of row-oriented or column-oriented storage managers per machine in a cluster)

Note: no open-source parallel database exists! SQL is the only way into the system architecture. Systems are monolithic: Cannot safely cut into them to access inner functionalities.

The Hadoop software stack comprises (Michael J. Carey):

- HiveQL. PigLatin, Jaql script $\rightarrow$ HiveQL/Pig/Jaql (High-level languages)
- Hadoop M/R job $\rightarrow$ Hadoop MapReduce Dataflow Layer/
- (for batch analytics, applies Map ops to the data in partitions of an HDFS file, sorts, and redistributes the results based on key values in the output data, then performs reduce on the groups of output data items with matching keys from the map phase of the job).
- Get/Put ops $\rightarrow$ Hbase Key-value Store (accessed directly by client app or via Hadoop for analytics needs)
- Hadoop Distributed File System (byte oriented file abstraction—files appears as a very large contiguous and randomly addressable sequence of bytes

Note: all tools are open-source! No SQL. Systems are not monolithic: Can safely cut into them to access inner functionalities.

A key requirement when handling Big Data is *scalability.*

Scalability has three aspects

- data volume
- hardware size
- concurrency

What is the trade-off between *scaling out* and *scaling up*? What does it mean in practice for an application domain?

Chris Anderson of Couchdb explains [11]: "scaling up is easier from a software perspective. It's essentially the Moore's Law approach to scaling—buy a bigger box. Well, eventually you run out of bigger boxes to buy, and then you've run off the edge of a cliff. You've got to pray Moore keeps up.

Scaling out means being able to add independent nodes to a system. This is the real business case for NoSQL. Instead of being hostage to Moore's Law, you can grow as fast as your data. Another advantage to adding independent nodes is you have more options when it comes to matching your workload. You have more flexibility when you are running on commodity hardware—you can run on SSDs or high-compute instances, in the cloud, or inside your firewall."

Enterprise Search

Enterprise Search implies being able to search multiple types of data generated by an enterprise. There are two alternatives: Apache Solr or implementing a proprietary full-text search engine.

There is an ecosystem of open source tools that build on Apache Solr.

Big Data "Dichotomy"

The prevalent architecture that people use to analyze structured and unstructured data is a two-system configuration, where *Hadoop* is used for processing the unstructured data and a relational database system or an NoSQL data store is used for the structured data as a front end.

NoSQL data stores were born when Developers of very large-scale user-facing Web sites implemented key-value stores:

- Google Big Table
- Amazon Dynamo
- Apache Hbase (open source BigTable clone)
- Apache Cassandra, Riak (open source Dynamo clones), etc.

There are concerns about performance issues that arise along with the transfer of large amounts of data between the two systems. The use of connectors could introduce delays and data silos, and increase Total Cost of Ownership (TCO).

Daniel Abadi of Hadapt says [10]: "this is a highly undesirable architecture, since now you have two systems to maintain, two systems where data may be stored, and if you want to do analysis involving data in both systems, you end up having to send data over the network which can be a major bottleneck."

Big Data is not (only) Hadoop.

"Some people even think that 'Hadoop' and 'Big Data' are synonymous (though this is an over-characterization). Unfortunately, Hadoop was designed based on a paper by Google in 2004 which was focused on use cases involving unstructured data (e.g., extracting words and phrases from Web pages in order to create Google's Web index). Since it was not originally designed to leverage the structure in relational data in order to take short-cuts in query processing, its performance for processing relational data is therefore suboptimal" says Daniel Abadi of Hadapt.

Duncan Ross of Teradata confirms this: "the biggest technical challenge is actually the separation of the technology from the business use! Too often people are making the assumption that Big Data is synonymous with *Hadoop,* and any time that technology leads business things become difficult. Part of this is the difficulty of use that comes with this.

It's reminiscent of the command line technologies of the 70s—it wasn't until the GUI became popular that computing could take off."

Hadoop and the Cloud

Amazon has a significant web-services business around Hadoop.

But in general, people are concerned with the protection and security of their data. *What about traditional enterprises?*

Here is an attempt to list the *pros* and *cons* of Hadoop.

Hadoop Pros

- Open source.
- Nonmonolithic support for access to file-based external data.
- Support for automatic and incremental forward-recovery of jobs with failed task.
- Ability to schedule very large jobs in smaller chunks.
- Automatic data placement and rebalancing as data grows and machines come and go.
- Support for replication and machine fail-over without operation intervention.
- The combination of scale, ability to process unstructured data along with the availability of machine learning algorithms, and recommendation engines create the opportunity to build new game changing applications.
- Does not require a schema first.
- Provides a great tool for exploratory analysis of the data, as long as you have the software development expertise to write MapReduce programs.

Hadoop Cons

- Hadoop is difficult to use.
- Can give powerful analysis, but it is fundamentally a batch-oriented paradigm. The missing piece of the Hadoop puzzle is accounting for real-time changes.

- Hadoop file system (HDS) has a centralized metadata store (NameNode), which represents a single point of failure without availability. When the NameNode is recovered, it can take a long time to get the Hadoop cluster running again.
- Hadoop assumes that the workload it runs will belong running, so it makes heavy use of checkpointing at intermediate stages. This means parts of a job can fail, be restarted, and eventually complete successfully—there are no transactional guarantees.

Current Hadoop distributions challenges

- Getting data in and out of Hadoop. Some Hadoop distributions are limited by the append-only nature of the Hadoop Distributed File System (HDFS) that requires programs to batch load and unload data into a cluster.
- The lack of reliability of current Hadoop software platforms is a major impediment for expansion.
- Protecting data against application and user errors.
- Hadoop has no backup and restore capabilities. Users have to contend with data loss or resort to very expensive solutions that reside outside the actual Hadoop cluster.

There is work in progress to fix this from vendors of commercial Hadoop distributions (e.g., MapR, etc.) by reimplementing Hadoop components. It would be desirable to have seamless integration.

> "Instead of stand-alone products for ETL,BI/reporting and analytics we have to think about seamless integration: in what ways can we open up a data processing platform to enable applications to get closer? What language interfaces, but also what resource management facilities can we offer? And so on." (Florian Waas)

Daniel Abadi: "A lot of people are using Hadoop as a sort of data refinery. Data starts off unstructured, and Hadoop jobs are run to clean, transform, and structure the data. Once the data is structured, it is shipped to SQL databases where it can be subsequently analyzed. This leads to the raw data being left in Hadoop and the refined data in the SQL databases. But it's basically the same data—one is just a cleaned (and potentially aggregated) version of the other. Having multiple copies of the data can lead to all kinds of problems. For example, let's say you want to update the data in one of the two locations—it does not get automatically propagated to the copy in the other silo. Furthermore, let's say you are doing some analysis in the SQL database and you see something interesting and want to drill down to the raw data—if the raw data is located on a different system, such a drill down becomes highly nontrivial. Furthermore, data provenance is a total nightmare. It's just a really ugly architecture to have these two systems with a connector between them."

Michael J. Carey adds that is:

- Questionable to layer a record-oriented data abstraction on top of a giant globally sequenced byte-stream file abstraction.

(E.g., HDFS is unaware of record boundaries. "Broken records" instead of fixed-length file splits, i.e., a record with some of its bytes in one split and some in the next)

- Questionable building a parallel data runtime on top of a unary operator model (map, reduce, combine). E.g., performing joins with MapReduce.
- Questionable building a key-value store layer with a remote query access at the next layer. Pushing queries down to data is likely to outperform pulling data up to queries.
- Lack of schema information, today is flexible, but a recipe for future difficulties. E.g., future maintainers of applications will likely have problems in fixing bugs related to changes or assumptions about the structure of data files in HDFS. (This was one of the very early lessons in the DB world).
- Not addressed single system performance, focusing solely on scale-out.

Technological Solutions for Big Data Analytics

There are several technological solutions available in the market for Big Data Analytics. Here are some examples:

An NoSQL Data Store (CouchBase, Riak, Cassandra, MongoDB, etc.) Connected to Hadoop

With this solution, an NoSQL data store is used as a front end to process selected data in real time data, and having Hadoop in the back end processing Big Data in batch mode.

> "In my opinion the primary interface will be via the real time store, and the Hadoop layer will become a commodity. That is why there is so much competition for the NoSQL brass ring right now" says J. Chris Anderson of Couchbase (an NoSQL datastore).

In some applications, for example, Couchbase (NoSQL) is used to enhance the batch-based Hadoop analysis with real-time information, giving the effect of a continuous process. Hot data live in Couchbase in RAM.

The process consists of essentially moving the data out of Couchbase into Hadoop when it cools off. CouchDB supplies a connector to Apache Sqoop (a Top-Level Apache project since March of 2012), a tool designed for efficiently transferring bulk data between Hadoop and relational databases.

An NewSQL Data Store for Analytics (HP/Vertica) Instead of Hadoop

Another approach is to use a NewSQL data store designed for Big Data Analytics, such as HP/Vertica. Quoting Shilpa Lawande [4] "Vertica was designed from the ground up for analytics." Vertica is a columnar database engine including sorted columnar storage, a query optimizer, and an execution engine, providing standard ACID transaction semantics on loads and queries.

With sorted columnar storage, there are two methods that drastically reduce the I/O bandwidth requirements for such Big Data analytics workloads. The first is that Vertica only reads the columns that queries need. Second, Vertica compresses the data significantly better than anyone else. Vertica's execution engine is optimized for modern multicore processors and we ensure that data stays compressed as much as possible through the query execution, thereby reducing the CPU cycles to process the query. Additionally, we have a scale-out MPP architecture, which means you can add more nodes to Vertica.

All of these elements are extremely critical to handle the data volume challenge. With Vertica, customers can load several terabytes of data quickly (per hour in fact) and query their data within minutes of it being loaded—that is real-time analytics on Big Data for you.

There is a myth that columnar databases are slow to load. This may have been true with older generation column stores, but in Vertica, we have a hybrid in-memory/disk load architecture that rapidly ingests incoming data into a write-optimized row store and then converts that to read-optimized sorted columnar storage in the background. This is entirely transparent to the user because queries can access data in both locations seamlessly. We have a very lightweight transaction implementation with snapshot isolation queries can always run without any locks.

And we have no auxiliary data structures, like indices or materialized views, which need to be maintained postload. Last, but not least, we designed the system for "always on," with built-in high availability features. Operations that translate into downtime in traditional databases are online in Vertica, including adding or upgrading nodes, adding or modifying database objects, etc. With Vertica, we have removed many of the barriers to monetizing Big Data and hope to continue to do so.

"Vertica and Hadoop are both systems that can store and analyze large amounts of data on commodity hardware. The main differences are how the data get in and out, how fast the system can perform, and what transaction guarantees are provided. Also, from the standpoint of data access, Vertica's interface is SQL and data must be designed and loaded into an SQL schema for analysis. With Hadoop, data is loaded AS IS into a distributed file system and accessed programmatically by writing Map-Reduce programs." (Shilpa Lawande [4])

A NewSQL Data Store for OLTP (VoltDB) Connected with Hadoop or a Data Warehouse

With this solution, a fast NewSQL data store designed for OLTP (VoltDB) is connected to either a conventional data warehouse or Hadoop.

"We identified 4 sources of significant OLTP overhead (concurrency control, write-ahead logging, latching and buffer pool management).

Unless you make a big dent in ALL FOUR of these sources, you will not run dramatically faster than current disk-based RDBMSs. To the best of my knowledge, VoltDB is the only system that eliminates or drastically reduces all four of these overhead components. For example, TimesTen uses conventional record level locking, an Aries-style write ahead log and conventional multi-threading, leading to substantial need for latching. Hence, they eliminate only one of the four sources.

VoltDB is not focused on analytics. We believe they should be run on a companion data warehouse. Most of the warehouse customers I talk to want to keep increasing large amounts of increasingly diverse history to run their analytics over. The major data warehouse players are routinely being asked to manage petabyte-sized data warehouses. VoltDB is intended for the OLTP portion, and some customers wish to run Hadoop as a data warehouse platform. To facilitate this architecture, VoltDB offers a Hadoop connector.

VoltDB supports standard SQL. Complex joins should be run on a companion data warehouse. After all, the only way to interleave 'big reads' with 'small writes' in a legacy RDBMS is to use snapshot isolation or run with a reduced level of consistency. You either get an out-of-date, but consistent answer or an up-to-date, but inconsistent answer. Directing big reads to a companion DW, gives you the same result as snapshot isolation. Hence, I do not see any disadvantage to doing big reads on a companion system.

Concerning larger amounts of data, our experience is that OLTP problems with more than a few Tbyte of data are quite rare. Hence, these can easily fit in main memory, using a VoltDB architecture.

In addition, we are planning extensions of the VoltDB architecture to handle larger-than-main-memory data sets." (Mike Stonebraker [13])

A NewSQL for Analytics (Hadapt) Complementing Hadoop

An alternative solution is to use a NewSQL designed for analytics (Hadapt) which complements Hadoop.

Daniel Abadi explains "at Hadapt, we're bringing 3 decades of relational database research to Hadoop. We have added features like indexing, co-partitioned joins, broadcast joins, and SQL access (with interactive query response times) to Hadoop, in order to both accelerate its performance for queries over relational data and also provide an interface that third party data processing and business intelligence tools are familiar with.

Therefore, we have taken Hadoop, which used to be just a tool for super-smart data scientists, and brought it to the mainstream by providing a high performance SQL interface that business analysts and data analysis tools already know how to use. However, we've gone a step further and made it possible to include both relational data and non-relational data in the same query; so what we've got now is a platform that people can use to do really new and innovative types of analytics involving both unstructured data like tweets or blog posts and structured data such as traditional transactional data that usually sits in relational databases.

What is special about the Hadapt architecture is that we are bringing database technology to Hadoop, so that Hadapt customers only need to deploy a single cluster—a normal Hadoop cluster—that is optimized for both structured and unstructured data, and is capable of pushing the envelope on the type of analytics that can be run over Big Data." [10]

A Combinations of Data Stores: A Parallel Database (Teradata) and Hadoop

An example of this solution is the architecture for Complex Analytics at eBay (Tom Fastner [12])

The use of analytics at Ebay is rapidly changing, and analytics is driving many key initiatives like buyer experience, search optimization, buyer protection, or mobile commerce. EBay is investing heavily in new technologies and approaches to leverage new data sources to drive innovation.

EBay uses three different platforms for analytics:

1. *"EDW"*: dual systems for transactional (*structured data*); Teradata 6690 with 9.5 PB spinning disk and 588 TB SSD
   - The largest mixed storage Teradata system worldwide; with spool, some dictionary tables and user data automatically managed by access frequency to stay on SSD.10+ years experience; very high concurrency; good accessibility; hundreds of applications.
2. *"Singularity"*: deep Teradata system for *semistructured data*; 36 PB spinning disk;
   - Lower concurrency that EDW, but can store more data; biggest use case is User Behavior Analysis; largest table is 1.2 PB with ~3 Trillion rows.

3. *Hadoop*: for *unstructured/complex data*; ~40 PB spinning disk;
   - Text analytics, machine learning, has the user behavior data and selected EDW tables; lower concurrency and utilization.

The main technical challenges for Big Data analytics at eBay are

- *I/O bandwidth*: limited due to configuration of the nodes.
- *Concurrency/workload management*: Workload management tools usually manage the limited resource. For many years, EDW systems bottleneck on the CPU; big systems are configured with ample CPU making I/O the bottleneck. Vendors are starting to put mechanisms in place to manage I/O, but it will take sometime to get to the same level of sophistication.
- *Data movement (loads, initial loads, backup/restores)*: As new platforms are emerging you need to make data available on more systems challenging networks, movement tools, and support to ensure scalable operations that maintain data consistency.

Scalability and Performance at eBay

- *EDW*: models for the unknown (close to third NF) to provide a solid physical data model suitable for many applications, which limits the number of physical copies needed to satisfy specific application requirements.

A lot of scalability and performance is built into the database, but as any shared resource it does require an excellent operations team to fully leverage the capabilities of the platform

- *Singularity*: The platform is identical to EDW, the only exception are limitations in the workload management due to configuration choices.

But since they are leveraging the latest database release, they are exploring ways to adopt new storage and processing patterns. Some new data sources are stored in a denormalized form significantly simplifying data modeling and ETL. On top they developed functions to support the analysis of the semistructured data. It also enables more sophisticated algorithms that would be very hard, inefficient, or impossible to implement with pure SQL.

One example is the pathing of user sessions. However, the size of the data requires them to focus more on best practices (develop on small subsets, use 1% sample; process by day).

- *Hadoop*: The emphasis on Hadoop is on optimizing for access. There usability of data structures (besides "raw" data) is very low

Unstructured Data

Unstructured data are handled on Hadoop only. The data are copied from the source systems into HDFS for further processing. They do not store any of that on the Singularity (Teradata) system.

Use of Data management technologies:

- *ETL*: AbInitio, home-grown parallel Ingest system
- *Scheduling*: UC4
- *Repositories*: Teradata EDW; Teradata Deep system; Hadoop
- *BI*: Microstrategy, SAS, Tableau, Excel
- *Data Modeling*: Power Designer
- *Ad hoc*: Teradata SQL Assistant; Hadoop Pig and Hive
- *Content Management*: Joomla-based

Cloud Computing and Open Source

"We do leverage internal cloud functions for Hadoop; no cloud for Teradata. Open source: committers for Hadoop and Joomla; strong commitment to improve those technologies." (Tom Fastner, Principal Architect at eBay)

Big Data Myth

It is interesting to report here what Marc Geall, a research analyst at Deutsche Bank AG/in London, writes about the "Big Data Myth," and predicts [9]:

"We believe that in-memory/NewSQL is likely to be the prevalent database model rather than NoSQL due to three key reasons:

1. The limited need of petabyte-scale data today even among the NoSQL deployment base,
2. Very low proportion of databases in corporate deployment which requires more than tens of TB of data to be handles,
3. Lack of availability and high cost of highly skilled operators (often post-doctoral) to operate highly scalable NoSQL clusters."

Time will tell us whether this prediction is accurate or not.

Main Research Challenges and Business Challenges

We conclude this part of the chapter by looking at three elements: data, platform, and analysis with two quotes:

Werner Vogels: "I think that sharing is another important aspect to the mix. Collaborating during the whole process of collecting data, storing it, organizing it and analyzing it is essential. Whether it's scientists in a research field or doctors at different hospitals collaborating on drug trials, they can use the cloud to easily share results and work on common datasets."

Daniel Abadi: "Here are a few that I think are interesting:

1. *Scalability of non-SQL analytics.* How do you parallelize clustering, classification, statistical, and algebraic functions that are not 'embarrassingly parallel' (that have traditionally been performed on a single server in main memory) over a large cluster of shared-nothing servers.

2. Reducing the cognitive complexity of 'Big Data' so that it can fit in the working set of the brain of a single analyst who is wrangling with the data.

3. Incorporating graph data sets and graph algorithms into database management systems.

4. Enabling platform support for probabilistic data and probabilistic query processing."

Big Data for the Common Good

"As more data become less costly and technology breaks barrier to acquisition and analysis, the opportunity to deliver actionable information for civic purposed grow. This might be termed the 'common good' challenge for Big Data." (Jake Porway, DataKind)

Very few people seem to look at how Big Data can be used for solving social problems. Most of the work in fact is not in this direction.

Why this? What can be done in the international research/development community to make sure that some of the most brilliant ideas do have an impact also for social issues?

In the following, I will list some relevant initiatives and selected thoughts for Big Data for the Common Good.

World Economic Forum, the United Nations Global Pulse Initiative

The United Nations Global Pulse initiative is one example. Earlier this year at the 2012 Annual Meeting in Davos, the World Economic Forum published a white paper entitled "Big Data, Big Impact: New Possibilities for International Development." The WEF paper lays out several of the ideas which fundamentally drive the Global Pulse initiative and presents in concrete terms the opportunity presented by the explosion of data in our world today, and how researchers and policy-makers are beginning to realize the potential for leveraging Big Data to extract insights that can be used for Good, in particular, for the benefit of low-income populations.

"A flood of data is created every day by the interactions of billions of people using computers, GPS devices, cell phones, and medical devices. Many of these interactions occur through the use of mobile devices being used by people in the developing world, people whose needs and habits have been poorly understood until now.

Researchers and policymakers are beginning to realize the potential for channeling these torrents of data into actionable information that can be used to identify needs, provide services, and predict and prevent crises for the benefit of low-income populations. Concerted action is needed by governments, development organizations, and companies to ensure that this data helps the individuals and communities who create it."

Three examples are cited in WEF paper:

- *UN Global Pulse*: an innovation initiative of the UN Secretary General, harnessing today's new world of digital data and real-time analytics to gain better understanding of changes in human well-being (www.unglobalpulse.orgGlobal).
- *Viral Forecasting*: a not-for-profit whose mission is to promote understanding, exploration, and stewardship of the microbial world (www.gvfi.orgUshadi).
- *SwiftRiver Platform*: a non-profit tech company that specializes in developing free and open source software for information collection, visualization, and interactive mapping (http://ushahidi.com).

What Are the Main Difficulties, Barriers Hindering Our Community to Work on Social Capital Projects?

I have listed below some extracts from [5]:

- Alon Havely (Google Research): "I don't think there are particular barriers from a technical perspective. Perhaps the main barrier is ideas of how to actually take this technology and make social impact. These ideas typically don't come from the technical community, so we need more inspiration from activists."
- Laura Haas: (IBM Research): "Funding and availability of data are two big issues here. Much funding for social capital projects comes from governments—and as we know, are but a small fraction of the overall budget. Further, the market for new tools and so on that might be created in these spaces is relatively limited, so it is not always attractive to private companies to invest. While there is a lot of publicly available data today, often key pieces are missing, or

privately held, or cannot be obtained for legal reasons, such as the privacy of individuals, or a country's national interests. While this is clearly an issue for most medical investigations, it crops up as well even with such apparently innocent topics as disaster management (some data about, e.g., coastal structures, may be classified as part of the national defense)."

- Paul Miller (Consultant): "Perceived lack of easy access to data that's unencumbered by legal and privacy issues? The large-scale and long term nature of most of the problems? It's not as 'cool' as something else? A perception (whether real or otherwise) that academic funding opportunities push researchers in other directions? Honestly, I'm not sure that there are significant insurmountable difficulties or barriers, if people want to do it enough. As Tim O'Reilly said in 2009 (and many times since), developers should 'Work on stuff that matters.' The same is true of researchers."

- Roger Barga (Microsot Research): "The greatest barrier may be social. Such projects require community awareness to bring people to take action and often a champion to frame the technical challenges in a way that is approachable by the community. These projects will likely require close collaboration between the technical community and those familiar with the problem."

What Could We Do to Help Supporting Initiatives for Big Data for Good?

I have listed below some extracts from [5]:

- Alon Havely (Google Research): "Building a collection of high quality data that is widely available and can serve as the backbone for many specific data projects. For example, datasets that include boundaries of countries/counties and other administrative regions, data sets with up-to-date demographic data. It's very common that when a particular data story arises, these data sets serve to enrich it."

- Laura Haas (IBM Research): "Increasingly, we see consortiums of institutions banding together to work on some of these problems. These Centers may provide data and platforms for data-intensive work, alleviating some of the challenges mentioned above by acquiring and managing data, setting up an environment and tools, bringing in expertise in a given topic, or in data, or in analytics, providing tools for governance, etc.

  My own group is creating just such a platform, with the goal of facilitating such collaborative ventures. Of course, lobbying our governments for support of such initiatives wouldn't hurt!"

- Paul Miller (Consultant): "Match domains with a need to researchers/companies with a skill/product. Activities such as the recent Big Data Week Hackathons might be one route to follow—encourage the organisers (and companies like Kaggle, which do this every day) to run Hackathons and competitions that are explicitly targeted at a 'social' problem of some sort. Continue to encourage the Open Data release of key public data sets. Talk to the agencies that are working in areas of interest, and understand the problems that they face. Find ways to help them do what they already want to do, and build trust and rapport that way."

- Roger Barga (Microsot Research): "Provide tools and resources to empower the long tail of research. Today, only a fraction of scientists and engineers enjoy regular access to high performance and data-intensive computing resources to process and analyze massive amounts of data and run models and simulations quickly. The reality for most of the scientific community is that's peed to discovery is often hampered as they have to either queue up for access to limited resources or pare down the scope of research to accommodate available processing power. This problem is particularly acute at the smaller research institutes which represent the long tail of the research community. Tier 1 and some tier 2 universities have sufficient funding and infrastructure to secure and support computing resources while the smaller research programs struggle. Our funding agencies and corporations must provide resources to support researchers, in particular those who do not have access to sufficient resources."

Conclusions: The Search for Meaning Behind Our Activities

I would like to conclude this chapter with this quote below which I find inspiring.

"All our activities in our lives can be looked at from different perspectives and within various contexts: our individual view, the view of our families and friends, the view of our company and finally the view of society—the view of the world. Which perspective means what to us is not always clear, and it can also change over the course of time. This might be one of the reasons why our life sometimes seems unbalanced. We often talk about work-life balance, but maybe it is rather an imbalance between the amount of energy we invest into different elements of our life and their meaning to us."

—Eran Davidson, CEO Hasso Plattner Ventures

Acknowledgments

I would like to thank Michael Blaha, Rick Cattell, Michael Carey, Akmal Chaudhri, Tom Fastner, Laura Haas, Alon Halevy, Volker Markl, Dave Thomas, Duncan Ross, Cindy Saracco, Justin Sheehy, Mike OSullivan, Martin Verlage, and Steve Vinoski for their feedback on an earlier draft of this chapter.
  But all errors and missing information are mine.

References

1. McKinsey Global Institute (MGI), Big Data: The next frontier for innovation, competition, and productivity, Report, June, 2012.
2. Managing Big Data. An interview with David Gorbet ODBMS Industry Watch, July 2, 2012. http://www.odbms.org/blog/2012/07/managing-big-data-an-interview-with-david-gorbet/
3. On Big Data: Interview with Dr. Werner Vogels, CTO and VP of Amazon. com. *ODBMS Industry Watch*, November 2, 2011. http://www.odbms.org/blog/2011/11/on-big-data-interview-with-dr-werner-vogels-cto-and-vp-of-amazon-com/
4. On Big Data: Interview with Shilpa Lawande, VP of Engineering at Vertica. *ODBMs Industry Watch*, November 16, 2011.
5. "Big Data for Good", Roger Barca, Laura Haas, Alon Halevy, Paul Miller, Roberto V. Zicari. *ODBMS Industry Watch*, June 5, 2012.
6. On Big Data Analytics: Interview with Florian Waas, EMC/Greenplum. *ODBMS Industry Watch*, February 1, 2012.
7. Next generation Hadoop—interview with John Schroeder. *ODBMS Industry Watch*, September 7, 2012.
8. Michael J. Carey, EDBT keynote 2012, Berlin.
9. Marc Geall, "Big Data Myth", Deutsche Bank Report 2012.
10. On Big Data, Analytics and Hadoop. Interview with Daniel Abadi. *ODBMS Industry Watch*, December 5, 2012.
11. Hadoop and NoSQL: Interview with J. Chris Anderson. *ODBMS Industry Watch*, September 19, 2012.
12. Analytics at eBay. An interview with Tom Fastner. *ODBMS Industry Watch*, October 6, 2011.
13. Interview with Mike Stonebraker. *ODBMS Industry Watch*, May 2, 2012.

Links:

ODBMS.org www.odbms.org
ODBMS Industry Watch, www.odbms.org/blog

Section II

Semantic Technologies and Big Data

4

Management of Big Semantic Data

Javier D. Fernández, Mario Arias, Miguel A. Martínez-Prieto,
and Claudio Gutiérrez

CONTENTS

In 2007, Jim Gray preached about the effects of the *Data deluge* in the sciences
(Hey et al. 2009). While experimental and theoretical paradigms originally
led science, some natural phenomena were not easily addressed by analytical models. In this scenario, computational simulation arose as a new paradigm enabling scientists to deal with these complex phenomena. Simulation
produced increasing amounts of data, particularly from the use of advanced
exploration instruments (large-scale telescopes, particle colliders, etc.) In this
scenario, scientists were no longer interacting directly with the phenomena,

but used powerful computational configurations to analyze the data gathered from simulations or captured by instruments. Sky maps built from the Sloan Digital Sky Survey observations, or the evidences found about the Higgs Boson are just two successful stories of just another paradigm, what Gray called the fourth paradigm: the eScience.

eScience sets the basis for scientific data exploration and identifies the common problems that arise when dealing with data at large scale. It deals with the complexities of the whole scientific data workflow, from the data creation and capture, through the *organization* and *sharing* of these data with other scientists, to the final processing and analysis of such data. Gray linked these problems to the way in which data are encoded "because the only way that scientists are going to be able to understand that information is if their software can understand the information." In this way, *data representation* emerges as one of the key factors in the process of storing, organizing, filtering, analyzing, and visualizing data at large scale, but also for sharing and exchanging them in the distributed scientific environment.

Despite its origins in science, the data deluge effects apply to many other fields. It is easy to find real cases of massive data sources, many of them are part of our everyday lives. Common activities, such as adding new friends on social networks, sharing photographs, buying something electronically, or clicking in any result returned from a search engine, are continuously recorded in increasingly large data sets. *Data is the new "raw material of business"*.

Although business is one of the major contributors to the data deluge, there are many other players that should not go unnoticed. The Open Government movement, around the world, is also converting public administrations in massive data generators. In recent years, they have released large data sets containing educational, political, economic, criminal, census information, among many others. Besides, we are surrounded by multitude of sensors which continuously report information about temperature, pollution, energy consumption, the state of the traffic, the presence or absence of a fire, etc. Any information anywhere and in anytime is recorded in big and constantly evolving heterogeneous data sets that take part in the data deluge. If we add the scientific contributions, the data sets released by traditional and digital libraries, geographical data or collections from mass media, we can see that the data deluge is definitely an ubiquitous revolution.

From the original eScience has evolved what has been called *data science* (Loukides 2012), a discipline that cope with this ubiquity, and basically refers to the science of transforming data in knowledge. The acquisition of this knowledge strongly depends on the existence of an effective data linkage, which enables computers for integrating data from heterogeneous data sets. We bump again with the question of how information is encoded for different kinds of automatic processing.

Definitively, data and information standards are at the ground of this revolution, and due to its size, semiautomatic processing of them is essential.

An algorithmic (and standardized) data encoding is crucial to enable computer exchange and understanding; for instance, this data representation must allow computers to resolve what a gene is or what a galaxy is, or what a temperature measurement is (Hey et al. 2009). Nowadays, the use of graph-oriented representations and rich semantic vocabularies are gaining momentum. On the one hand, graphs are flexible models for integrating data not only with different degrees of structure, but also enable these heterogeneous data to be linked in a uniform way. On the other hand, vocabularies describe what data mean. The most practical trend, in this line, suggests the use of the Resource Description Framework: RDF (Manola and Miller 2004), a standard model for data encoding and semantic technologies for publication, exchange, and consumption of this *Big Semantic Data* at universal scale.

This chapter takes a guided tour to the challenges of Big Semantic Data management and the role that it plays in the emergent *Web of Data*. Section "Big Data" provides a brief overview of Big Data and its dimensions. Section "What is Semantic Data?" summarizes the semantic web foundations and introduces the main technologies used for describing and querying semantic data. These basics set the minimal background for understanding the notion of web of data. It is presented in section "The Web of (Linked) Data" along with the Linked Data project and its open realization within the Linked Open Data movement. Section "Stakeholders and Processes in Big Semantic Data" characterizes the stakeholders and the main data flows performed in this web of Data: *publication, exchange*, and *consumption*, defines them and delves not only into their potential for data interoperability, but also in the scalability drawbacks arising when Big Semantic Data must be processed and queried. Innovative compression techniques are introduced in section "An Integrated Solution for Managing Big Semantic Data," showing how the three Big Data dimensions (volume, velocity, and variety) can be successfully addressed through an integrated solution, called *HDT* (*Header-Dictionary-Triples*). Section "Experimental Results" comprises our experimental results, showing that HDT allows scalability improvements to be achieved for storage, exchange, and query answering of such emerging data. Finally, section "Conclusions and Next Steps" concludes and devises the potential of HDT for its progressive adoption in Big Semantic Data management.

Big Data

Much has been said and written these days about *Big Data*. News in relevant magazines (Cukier 2010; Dumbill 2012b; Lohr 2012), technical reports (Selg 2012) and white papers from leading enterprises (Dijcks 2012), some emergent research works in newly established conferences,[*] disclosure books (Dumbill 2012a), and more applied ones (Marz and Warren 2013) are flooding us with numerous definitions, problems, and solutions related to Big Data. It is, obviously, a trending topic in technological scenarios, but it also is producing political, economical, and scientific impact.

We will adopt in this article a simple Big Data characterization. We refer to Big Data as "the data that exceed the processing capacity of conventional database systems" (Dumbill 2012b). Thus, any of these huge data sets generated in the data deluge may be considered Big Data. It is clear that they are too big, they move too fast, and they do not fit, generally, the relational model strictures (Dumbill 2012b). Under these considerations, Big Data result in the convergence of the following three V's:

Volume is the most obvious dimension because of a large amount of data continuously gathered and stored in massive data sets exposed for different uses and purposes. *Scalability* is the main challenge related to Big Data volume by considering that effective storage mechanisms are the first requirement in this scenario. It is worth noting that storage decisions influence data retrieval, the ultimate goal for the user, that expects it to be performed as fast as possible, especially in real-time systems.

Velocity describes how data flow, at high rates, in an increasingly distributed scenario. Nowadays, velocity increases in a similar way than volume. *Streaming data processing* is the main challenge related to this dimension because selective storage is mandatory for practical volume management, but also for real-time response.

Variety refers to various degrees of structure (or lack thereof) within the source data (Halfon 2012). This is mainly due to Big Data may come from multiple origins (e.g., sciences, politics, economy, social networks, or web server logs, among others) and each one describes its own semantics, hence data follow a specific structural modeling. The main challenge of Big Data variety is to achieve an effective mechanism for linking diverse classes of data differing in the inner structure.

While volume and velocity address physical concerns, variety refers to a logical question mainly related to the way in which data are modeled for enabling effective integration. It is worth noting that the more data are integrated, the more interesting knowledge may be generated, increasing the resulting data set value. Under these considerations, one of the main objectives in Big Data processing is to increase data value as much as possible by directly addressing the Big Data variety. As mentioned, the use of semantic

---

[*] Big Data conferences: http://lanyrd.com/topics/big-data/

technologies seems to be ahead in this scenario, leading to the publication of big semantic data sets.

What Is Semantic Data?

Semantic data have been traditionally related to the concept of Semantic Web. The *Semantic Web* enhances the current WWW by incorporating machine-processable semantics to their information objects (pages, services, data sources, etc.). Its goals are summarized as follows:

1. *To give semantics to information on the WWW.* The difference between the approach of information retrieval techniques (that currently dominate WWW information processing) and database ones is that in the latter data are structured via schemas that are essentially *metadata*. Metadata gives the meaning (the semantics) to data, allowing structured query, that is, querying data with logical meaning and precision.

2. *To make semantic data on the WWW machine-processable.* Currently, on the WWW the semantics of the data is given by humans (either directly during manual browsing and searching, or indirectly via information retrieval algorithms which use human feedback entered via static links or logs of interactions). Although it is currently successful, this process has known limitations (Quesada 2008). For Big Data, it is crucial to automatize the process of "understanding" (giving meaning to) data on the WWW. This amounts to develop machine-processable semantics.

To fulfill these goals, the Semantic Web community and the World Wide Consortium (W3C)* have developed (i) models and languages for representing the semantics and (ii) protocols and languages for querying it. We will briefly describe them in the next items.

Describing Semantic Data

Two families of languages sufficiently flexible, distributively extensible, and machine-processable have been developed for describing semantic data.

1. *The Resource Description Framework (RDF)* (Manola and Miller 2004). It was designed to have a simple data model, with a formal semantics, with an extensible URI-based vocabulary, and which allows

---

* http://www.w3.org

anyone to distributedly make statements about any resource on the Web. In this regard, an RDF description turns out to be a set of URI triples, with the standard intended meaning. It follows the ideas of semantic networks and graph data specifications, based on universal identifiers. It gives basic tools for linking data, plus a lightweight machinery for coding basic meanings. It has two levels:

a. *Plain RDF* is the basic data model for resources and relations between them. It is based on a basic vocabulary: a set of properties, technically binary predicates. Formally, it consists of triples of the form (s,p,o) (subject–predicate–object), where s,p,o are URIs that use distributed vocabularies. Descriptions are statements in the subject–predicate–object structure, where predicate and object are resources or strings. Both subject and object can be anonymous entities (blank nodes). Essentially, RDF builds graphs labeled with meaning.

b. *RDFS* adds over RDF a built-in vocabulary with a normative semantics, the RDF Schema (Brickley 2004). This vocabulary deals with inheritance of classes and properties, as well as typing, among other features. It can be thought of as a lightweight ontology.

2. *The Web Ontology Language (OWL)* (McGuinness and van Harmelen 2004). It is a version of logic languages adapted to cope with the Web requirements, composed of basic logic operators plus a mechanism for defining meaning in a distributed fashion.

From a metadata point of view, OWL can be considered a rich vocabulary with high expressive power (classes, properties, relations, cardinality, equality, constraints, etc.). It comes in many flavors, but this gain in expressive power is at the cost of scalability (complexity of evaluation and processing). In fact, using the semantics of OWL amounts to introduce logical reasoning among pieces of data, thus exploiting in complexity terms.

Querying Semantic Data

If one has scalability in mind, due to complexity arguments, the expressive power of the semantics should stay at a basic level of metadata, that is, *plain RDF*. This follows from the W3C design principles of interoperability, extensibility, evolution, and decentralization.

As stated, RDF can be seen as a graph labeled with meaning, in which each triple (s,p,o) is represented as a direct edge-labeled graph $s \xrightarrow{p} o$. The data model RDF has a corresponding query language, called SPARQL. SPARQL (Prud'hommeaux and Seaborne 2008) is the W3C standard for querying RDF. It is essentially a graph-pattern matching query language, composed of three parts:

a. The *pattern matching part,* which includes the most basic features of graph pattern matching, such as optional parts, union of patterns, nesting, filtering values of possible matchings, and the possibility of choosing the data source to be matched by a pattern.

b. The *solution modifiers* which, once the output of the pattern has been computed (in the form of a table of values of variables), allow to modify these values applying standard classical operators such as projection, distinct, order, and limit.

c. Finally, the *output* of an SPARQL query comes in tree forms. (1) May be: yes/no queries (ASK queries); (2) selections of values of the variables matching the patterns (SELECT queries), and (3) construction of new RDF data from these values, and descriptions of resources (CONSTRUCT queries).

An SPARQL query Q comprises head and body. The body is a complex RDF graph pattern expression comprising *triple patterns* (e.g., RDF triples in which each subject, predicate, or object may be a variable) with conjunctions, disjunctions, optional parts, and constraints over the values of the variables. The head is an expression that indicates how to construct the answer for Q. The evaluation of Q against an RDF graph G is done in two steps: (i) the body of Q is matched against G to obtain a set of bindings for the variables in the body and then (ii) using the information on the head, these bindings are processed applying classical relational operators (projection, distinct, etc.) to produce the answer Q.

Web of (Linked) Data

The WWW has enabled the creation of a global space comprising linked documents (Heath and Bizer 2011) that express information in a human-readable way. All agree that the WWW has revolutionized the way we consume information, but its document-oriented model prevents machines and automatic agents for directly accessing to the raw data underlying to any web page content. The main reason is that documents are the atoms in the WWW model and data lack of an identity within them. This is not a new story: an "universal database," in which all data can be identified at world scale, is a cherished dream in Computer Science.

The Web of Data (Bizer et al. 2009) emerges under all previous considerations in order to convert raw data into first class citizens of the WWW. It materializes the Semantic Web foundations and enables raw data, from diverse fields, to be interconnected within a cloud of data-to-data hyperlinks. It achieves a ubiquitous and seamless data integration to the lowest level of granularity over the WWW infrastructure. It is worth noting that this idea does not break with the WWW as we know. It only enhances the WWW with additional standards that enable data and documents to coexist in a common space. The Web of Data grows progressively according to the Linked Data principles.

Linked Data

The Linked Data project[*] originated in leveraging the practice of linking data to the semantic level, following the ideas of Berners-Lee (2006). Its authors state that:

> Linked Data is about using the WWW to connect related data that wasn't previously linked, or using the WWW to lower the barriers to linking data currently linked using other methods. More specifically, Wikipedia defines Linked Data as "a term used to describe a recommended best practice for exposing, sharing, and connecting pieces of data, information, and knowledge on the Semantic Web using URIs (Uniform Resource Identifiers) and RDF."

The idea is to leverage the WWW infrastructure to produce, publish, and consume data (not only documents in the form of web pages). These processes are done by different stakeholders, with different goals, in different forms and formats, in different places. One of the main challenges is the meaningful interlinking of this universe of data (Hausenblas and Karnstedt 2010). It relies on the following four rules:

1. *Use URIs as names for things.* This rule enables each possible real-world entity or its relationships to be unequivocally identified at universal scale. This simple decision guarantees that any raw data has its own identity in the global space of the Web of Data.
2. *Use HTTP URIs so that people can look up those names.* This decision leverages HTTP to retrieve all data related to a given URI.
3. *When someone looks up a URI, provide useful information, using standards.* It standardizes processes in the Web of Data and pacts the languages spoken by stakeholders. RDF and SPARQL, together with semantic technologies described in the previous section, defines the standards mainly used in the Web of Data.
4. *Include links to other URIs.* It materializes the aim of data integration by simply adding new RDF triples which link data from two different data sets. This inter-data set linkage enables the automatic browsing.

---

[*] http://www.linkeddata.org

These four rules provide the basics for publishing and integrating Big Semantic Data into the global space of the Web of Data. They enable raw data to be simply encoded by combining the RDF model and URI-based identification, both for entities and for their relationships adequately labeled over rich semantic vocabularies. Berners-Lee (2002) expresses the Linked Data relevance as follows:

Linked Data allows different things in different data sets of all kinds to be connected. The added value of putting data on the WWW is given by the way it can be queried in combination with other data you might not even be aware of. People will be connecting scientific data, community data, social web data, enterprise data, and government data from other agencies and organizations, and other countries, to ask questions not asked before.

Linked data is decentralized. Each agency can source its own data without a big cumbersome centralized system. The data can be stitched together at the edges, more as one builds a quilt than the way one builds a nuclear power station.

A virtuous circle. There are many organizations and companies which will be motivated by the presence of the data to provide all kinds of human access to this data, for specific communities, to answer specific questions, often in connection with data from different sites.

The project and further information about linked data can be found in Bizer et al. (2009) and Heath and Bizer (2011).

Linked Open Data

Although Linked Data do not prevent its application in closed environments (private institutional networks on any class of intranet), the most visible example of adoption and application of its principles runs openly. The Linked Open Data (LOD) movement set semantic data to be released under open licenses which do not impede data reuse for free. Tim Berners-Lee also devised a "five-star" test to measure how these Open Data implements the Linked Data principles:

1. Make your stuff available on the web (whatever format).
2. Make it available as structured data (e.g., excel instead of image scan of a table).
3. Use nonproprietary format (e.g., CSV instead of excel).
4. Use URLs to identify things, so that people can point at your stuff.
5. Link your data to other people's data to provide context.

The LOD cloud has grown significantly since its origins in May 2007.[*] The first report pointed that 12 data sets were part of this cloud, 45 were acknowledged in September 2008, 95 data sets in 2009, 203 in 2010, and 295 different data sets

---

[*] http://richard.cyganiak.de/2007/10/lod/

in the last estimation (September 2011). These last statistics* point out that more than 31 billion triples are currently published and more than 500 million links establish cross-relations between data sets. Government data are predominant in LOD, but other fields such as geography, life sciences, media, or publications are also strongly represented. It is worth emphasizing the existence of many cross-domain data sets comprising data from some diverse fields. These tend to be hubs because providing data that may be linked from and to the vast majority of specific data sets. DBpedia† is considered the nucleus for the LOD cloud (Auer et al. 2007). In short, DBpedia gathers raw data underlying to the Wikipedia web pages and exposes the resulting representation following the Linked Data rules. It is an interesting example of Big Semantic Data, and its management is considered within our experiments.

Stakeholders and Processes in Big Semantic Data

Although we identify data scientists as one of the main actors in the management of Big Semantic Data, we also unveil potential "traditional" users when moving from a Web of documents to a Web of data, or, in this context, to a Web of Big Semantic Data. The scalability problems arising for data experts and general users cannot be the same, as these are supposed to manage the information under different perspectives. A data scientist can make strong efforts to create novel semantic data or to analyze huge volumes of data created by third parties. She can make use of data-intensive computing, distributed machines, and algorithms, to spend several hours performing a closure of a graph is perfectly accepted. In contrast, a common user retrieving, for instance, all the movies shot in New York in a given year, expects not an immediate answer, but a reasonable response time. Although one could establish a strong frontier between data (and their problems) of these worlds, we cannot forget that establishing and discovering links between diverse data is beneficial for all parties. For instance, in life sciences it is important to have links between the bibliographic data of publications and the concrete genes studied in each publication, thus another researcher can look up previous findings of the genes they are currently studying.

The concern here is to address specific management problems while remaining in a general open representation and publication infrastructure in order to leverage the full potential of Big Semantic Data. Under this premise, a first characterization of the involved roles and processes would allow researchers and practitioners to clearly focus their efforts on a particular area. This section provides an approach toward this characterization. We

---

* http://www4.wiwiss.fu-berlin.de/lodcloud/state/
† http://dbpedia.org

first establish a simple set of stakeholders in Big Semantic Data, from where we define a common data workflow in order to better understand the main processes performed in the Web of Data.

Participants and Witnesses

One of the main breakthroughs after the creation of the Web was the consideration of the common citizen as the main stakeholder, that is, a part involved not only in the consumption, but also in the creation of content. To emphasize this fact, the notion of Web 2.0 was coined, and its implications such as blogging, tagging, or social networking became one of the roots of our current sociability.

The Web of Data can be considered as a complementary dimension to this successful idea, which addresses the data set problems of the Web. It focused on representing knowledge through machine-readable descriptions (i.e., RDF), using specific languages and rules for knowledge extraction and reasoning. How this could be achieved by the general audience, and exploited for the general market, will determine its chances to success beyond the scientific community.

To date, neither the creation of self-described semantic content nor the linkage to other sources is a simple task for a common user. There exist several initiatives to bring semantic data creation to a wider audience, being the most feasible use of RDFa (Adida et al. 2012). Vocabulary and link discovery can also be mitigated through searching and recommendation tools (Volz et al. 2009; Hogan et al. 2011). However, in general terms, one could argue that the creation of semantic data is still almost as narrow as the original content creation in Web 1.0. In the LOD statistics, previously reported, only 0.42% of the total data is user generated. It means that public organizations (governments, universities, digital libraries, etc.), researchers, and innovative enterprises are the main creators, whereas citizens are, at this point, just witnesses of a hidden increasingly reality.

This reality shows that these few creators are able to produce huge volumes of RDF data, yet we will argue, in the next section, about the quality of these publication schemes (in agreement with empirical surveys; Hogan et al. 2012). In what follows, we characterize a minimum set of stakeholders interacting with this huge graph of knowledge with such an enormous potential. Figure 4.1 illustrates the main identified stakeholders within Big Semantic Data. Three main roles are present: *creators, publishers,* and *consumers,* with an internal subdivision by creation method or intended use. In parallel, we distinguish between *automatic stakeholders, supervised processes,* and *human stakeholders.* We define below each stakeholder, assuming that (i) this classification may not be complete as it is intended to cover the minimum foundations to understand the managing processes in Big Semantic Data and (ii) categories are not disjoint; an actor could participate with several roles in a real-world scenario.

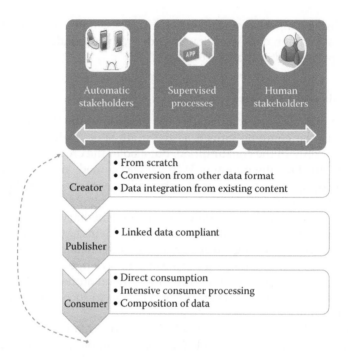

FIGURE 4.1
Stakeholder classification in Big Semantic Data management.

Creator: one that generates a new RDF data set by, at least, one of these processes:

- *Creation from scratch*: the novel data set is not based on a previous model. Even if the data exist beforehand, the data modeling process is unbiased from the previous data format. RDF authoring tools* are traditionally used.

- *Conversion from other data format*: the creation phase is highly determined by the conversion of the original data source; potential mappings between source and target data could be used; for example, from relational databases (Arenas et al. 2012), as well as (semi-)automatic conversion tools.†

- *Data integration from existing content*: the focus moves to an efficient integration of vocabularies and the validation of shared entities (Knoblock et al. 2012).

Several tasks are shared among all three processes. Some examples of this commonalities are the identification of the entities to be modeled (but this

---

* A list of RDF authoring tools can be found at http://www.w3.org/wiki/AuthoringToolsForRDF
† A list of RDF converters can be found at http://www.w3.org/wiki/ConverterToRdf

task is more important in the creation from scratch, as no prior identification has been done) or the vocabulary reuse (crucial in data integration in which different ontologies could be aligned). A complete description of the creation process is out of the scope of this work (the reader can find a guide for Linked Data creation in Heath and Bizer 2011).

Publisher: one that makes RDF data publicly available for different purposes and users. From now on, let us suppose that the publisher follows the Linked Data principles. We distinguish creators from publishers as, in many cases, the roles can strongly differ. Publishers do not have to create RDF content but they are responsible of the published information, the availability of the offered services (such as querying), and the correct adaptation to Linked Data principles. For instance, a creator could be a set of sensors giving the temperature in a given area in RDF (Atemezing et al. 2013), while the publisher is an entity who publish this information and provide entry points to this information.

Consumer: one that makes use of published RDF data:

- *Direct consumption*: a process whose computation task mainly involves the publisher, without intensive processing at the consumer. Downloads of the total data set (or subparts), online querying, information retrieval, visualization, or summarization are simple examples in which the computation is focused on the publisher.

- *Intensive consumer processing*: processes with a nonnegligible consumer computation, such as offline analysis, data mining, or reasoning over the full data set or a subpart (live views; Tummarello et al. 2010).

- *Composition of data*: those processes integrating different data sources or services, such as federated services over the Web of Data (Schwarte et al. 2011; Taheriyan et al. 2012) and RDF snippets in search engines (Haas et al. 2011).

As stated, we make an orthogonal classification of the stakeholders attending the nature of creators, publishers, and consumers. For instance, a sensor could directly create RDF data, but it could also consume RDF data.

Automatic stakeholders, such as sensors, Web processes (crawlers, search engines, recommender systems), RFID labels, smart phones, etc. Automatic RDF streaming, for instance, would become a hot topic, especially within the development of smart cities (De et al. 2012). Note that, although each piece of information could be particularly small, the whole system can be seen also as a big semantic data set.

Supervised processes, that is, processes with human supervision, as semantic tagging and folksonomies within social networks (García-Silva et al. 2012).

Human stakeholders, who perform most of the task for creating, publishing, or consuming RDF data.

The following running example provides a practical review of this classification. Nowadays, an RFID tag could document a user context through RDF metadata descriptions (Foulonneau 2011). We devise a system in which RFID tags provide data about temperature and position. Thus, we have thousands of sensors providing RDF excerpts modeling the temperature in distinct parts of a city. Users can visualize and query online this information, establishing some relationships, for example, with special events (such as a live concert or sport matches). In addition, the RDF can be consumed by a monitoring system, for example, to alert the population in case of extreme temperatures.

Following the classification, each sensor is an automatic creator, conforming altogether a potentially huge volume of RDF data. While a sensor should be designed to take care of RDF description (e.g., to follow a set of vocabularies and description rules and to minimize the size of descriptions), it cannot address publishing facilities (query endpoints, services to user, etc.). Alternatively, intermediate hubs would collect the data and the authoritative organization will be responsible of its publication, and applications and services over these data. This publication authority would be considered as a supervised process solving scalability issues of huge RDF data streams for collecting the information, filtering it (e.g., eliminating redundancy), and finally complying with Linked Data standards. Although these processes could be automatic, let us suppose that human intervention is needed to define links between data, for instance, linking positions to information about city events. Note also that intermediate hubs could be seen as supervised consumers of the sensors, yet the information coming from the sensors is not openly published but streamed to the appropriate hub. Finally, the consumers are humans, in the case of the online users (concerned of query resolution, visualization, summarization, etc.) or an automatic (or semiautomatic) process, in the case of monitoring (doing potential complex inference or reasoning).

Workflow of Publication-Exchange-Consumption

The previous RFID network example shows the enormous diversity of processes and different concerns for each type of stakeholder. In what follows, we will consider the creation step out of the scope of this work, because our approach relies on the existence of big RDF data sets (without belittling those ones which can be created hereinafter). We focus on tasks involving large-scale management; for instance, scalability issues of visual authoring a big RDF data set are comparable to RDF visualization by consumers, or the performance of RDF data integration from existing content depends on efficient access to the data and thus existing indexes, a crucial issue also for query response.

Management processes for publishers and consumers are diverse and complex to generalize. However, it is worth characterizing a common workflow present in almost every application in the Web of Data in order to place

FIGURE 4.2
Publication-Exchange-Consumption workflow in the Web of Data.

scalability issues in context. Figure 4.2 illustrates the identified workflow of Publication-Exchange-Consumption.

Publication refers to the process of making RDF data publicly available for diverse purposes and users, following the Linked Data principles. Strictly, the only obligatory "service" in these principles is to provide dereference-able URIs, that is, related information of an entity. In practice, publishers complete this basic functionality exposing their data through public APIs, mainly via SPARQL endpoints, a service which interprets the SPARQL query language. They also provide RDF dumps, files to fully or partly download the RDF data set.

Exchange is the process of information exchange between publishers and consumers. Although the information is represented in RDF, note that con-sumers could obtain different "views" and hence formats, and some of them not necessarily in RDF. For instance, the result of an SPARQL query could be provided in a CSV file or the consumer would request a summary with statistics of the data set in an XML file. As we are issuing manage-ment of semantic data sets, we restrict exchange to RDF interchange. Thus, we rephrase exchange as the process of RDF exchange between publishers and consumers after an RDF dump request, an SPARQL query resolution or another request or service provided by the publisher.

Consumption can involve, as stated, a wide range of processes, from direct consumption to intensive processing and composition of data sources. Let us simply define the consumption as the use of potentially large RDF data for diverse purposes.

A final remark must be done. The workflow definition seems to restrict the management to large RDF data sets. However, we would like to open scalability issues to a wider range of publishers and consumers with more limited resources. For instance, similar scalability problems arise when managing RDF in mobile devices; although the amount of information could be potentially smaller, these devices have more restrictive requirements for transmission costs/latency, and for postprocessing due to their inherent memory and CPU constraints (Le-Phuoc et al. 2010). In the following, when-ever we provide approaches for managing these processes in large RDF data sets, we ask the lecture to take into consideration this appreciation.

State of the Art for Publication-Exchange-Consumption

This section summarizes some of the current trends to address publication, exchange, and consumption at large scale.

Publication schemes: the straightforward publication, following Linked Data principles, presents several problems in large data sets (Fernández et al. 2010); a previous analysis of published RDF data sets reveals several undesirable features; the provenance and metadata about contents are barely present, and their information is neither complete nor systematic. Furthermore, the RDF dump files have neither internal structure nor a summary of their content. A massive empirical study of Linked Open Data sets in Hogan et al. (2012) draws similar conclusions; few providers attach human readable metadata to their resources or licensing information. Same features can be applied to SPARQL endpoints, in which a consumer knows almost nothing about the content she is going to query beforehand. In general terms, except for the general Linked Data recommendations (Heath and Bizer 2011), few works address the publication of RDF at large scale.

The Vocabulary of Interlinked Data sets: VoiD (Alexander et al. 2009) is the nearest approximation to the discovery problem, providing a bridge between publishers and consumers. Publishers make use of a specific vocabulary to add metadata to their data sets, for example, to point to the associated SPARQL endpoint and RDF dump, to describe the total number of triples, and to connect to linked data sets. Thus, consumers can look up this metadata to discover data sets or to reduce the set of interesting data sets in federated queries over the Web of Data (Akar et al. 2012). Semantic Sitemaps (Cyganiak et al. 2008) extend the traditional Sitemap Protocol for describing RDF data. They include new XML tags so that crawling tools (such as Sindice*) can discover and consume the data sets.

As a last remark, note that deferenceable URIs can be done in a straightforward way, publishing one document per URI or set of URIs. However, the publisher commonly materializes the output by querying the data set at URI resolution time. This moves the problem to the underneath RDF store, which has also to deal with scalability problems (see "Efficient RDF Consumption" below). The empirical study in Hogan et al. (2012) also confirmed that publishers often do not provide locally known inlinks in the dereferenced response, which must be taken into account by consumers.

RDF Serialization Formats: as we previously stated, we focus on exchanging large-scale RDF data (or smaller volumes in limited resources stakeholders). Under this consideration, the RDF serialization format directly determines the transmission costs and latency for consumption. Unfortunately, data sets are currently serialized in plain and verbose formats such as RDF/XML (Beckett 2004) or Notation3: N3 (Berners-Lee 1998), a more compact and readable alternative. Turtle (Beckett and Berners-Lee 2008) inherits N3 compact

---

* http://sindice.com/

ability adding interesting extra features, for example, abbreviated RDF data sets. RDF/JSON (Alexander 2008) has the advantage of being coded in a language easier to parse and more widely accepted in the programing world. Although all these formats present features to "abbreviate" constructions, they are still dominated by a document-centric and human-readable view which adds an unnecessary overhead to the final data set representation.

In order to reduce exchange costs and delays on the network, universal compressors (e.g., gzip) are commonly used over these plain formats. In addition, specific interchange oriented representations may also be used. For instance, the Efficient XML Interchange Format: EXI (Schneider and Kamiya 2011) may be used for representing any valid RDF/XML data set.

Efficient RDF Consumption: the aforementioned variety of consumer tasks hinders to achieve a one-size-fits-all technique. However, some general concerns can be outlined. In most scenarios, the performance is influenced by (i) the serialization format, due to the overall data exchange time, and (ii) the RDF indexing/querying structure. In the first case, if a compressed RDF has been exchanged, a previous decompression must be done. In this sense, the serialization format affects the consumption through the transmission cost, but also with the easiness of parsing. The latter factor affects the consumption process in different ways:

- For SPARQL endpoints and dereferenceable URIs materialization, the response time depends on the efficiency of the underlying RDF indexes at the publisher.

- Once the consumer has the data set, the most likely scenario is indexing it in order to operate with the RDF graph, for example, for intensive operation of inference, integration, etc.

Although the indexing at consumption could be performed once, the amount of resources required for it may be prohibitive for many potential consumers (especially for mobile devices comprising a limited computational configuration). In both cases, for publishers and consumers, an RDF store indexing the data sets is the main actor for efficient consumption.

Diverse techniques provide efficient RDF indexing, but there are still workloads for scalable indexing and querying optimization (Sidirourgos et al. 2008; Schmidt et al. 2010). On the one hand, some RDF stores are built over relational databases and perform SPARQL queries through SQL, for example, Virtuoso.[*] The most successful relational-based approach performs a vertical partitioning, grouping triples by predicates, and storing them in independent 2-column tables (S,O) (Sidirourgos et al. 2008; Abadi et al. 2009). On the other hand, some stores: Hexastore (Weiss et al. 2008) or RDF-3X (Neumann and Weikum 2010) build indices for all possible combinations of elements in RDF (SPO, SOP, PSO, POS, OPS, OSP), allowing (i) all triple patterns to

---

[*] http://www.openlinksw.com/dataspace/dav/wiki/Main/VOSRDF

be directly resolved in the corresponding index and (ii) the first join step to be resolved through fast merge-join. Although it achieves a global competitive performance, the index replication largely increases spatial requirements. Other solutions take advantage of structural properties of the data model (Tran et al. 2012), introduce specific graph compression techniques (Atre et al. 2010; Álvarez-García et al. 2011), or use distributed nodes within a MapReduce infrastructure (Urbani et al. 2010).

An Integrated Solution for Managing Big Semantic Data

When dealing with Big Semantic Data, each step in the workflow must be designed to address the three Big Data dimensions. While variety is managed through semantic technologies, this decision determines the way volume and velocity are addressed. As previously discussed, data serialization has a big impact on the workflow, as traditional RDF serialization formats are designed to be human readable instead of machine processable. They may fit smaller scenarios in which volume or velocity are not an issue, but under the presented premises, it clearly becomes a bottleneck of the whole process. We present, in the following, the main requirements for an RDF serialization format of Big Semantic Data.

- *It must be generated efficiently from another RDF input format.* For instance, a data creator having the data set in a semantic database must be able to dump it efficiently into an optimized exchange format.

- *It must be space efficient.* The generated dump should be as small as possible, introducing compression for space savings. Bear in mind that big semantic data sets are shared on the Web of Data and they may be transferred through the network infrastructure to hundreds or even thousands of clients. Reducing size will not only minimize the bandwidth costs of the server, but also the waiting time of consumers who are retrieving the data set for any class of consumption.

- *It must be ready to post process.* A typical case is performing a sequential triple-to-triple scanning for any post-processing task. This can seem trivial, but is clearly time-consuming when Big Semantic Data is postprocessed by the consumer. As shown in our experiments, just parsing a data set of 640 million triples, serialized in NTriples and gzip-compressed, wastes more than 40 min on a modern computational configuration.

- *It must be easy to convert to other representations.* The most usual scenario at consumption involves loading the data set into an RDF

Store. Most of the solutions reviewed in the previous section use disk-resident variants of B-Trees, which keep a subset of the pages in the main memory. For instance, if data are already sorted, this process is more efficient than doing it on unsorted elements. Therefore, having the data pre-sorted can be a step ahead in these cases. Also, many stores keep several indices for the different triples orderings (SPO, OPS, PSO, etc.). If the serialization format enables data traversing to be performed in different orders, the multi-index generation process can be completed more efficiently.

- *It should be able to locate pieces of data within the whole data set.* It is desirable to avoid a full scan over the data set just to locate a particular piece of data. Note that this scan is a highly time-consuming process in Big Semantic Data. Thus, the serialization format must retain all possible clues, enabling direct access to any piece of data in the data set. As explained in the SPARQL query language, a basic way of specifying which triples to fetch is specifying a triple pattern where each component is either a constant or a variable. A desirable format should be ready to solve most of the combinations of triple patterns (possible combinations of constants or variables in subject, predicates, and objects). For instance, a typical triple pattern is to provide a subject, leaving the predicate and object as variables (and therefore the expected result). In such cases, we pretend to locate all the triples that talk about a specific subject. In other words, this requirement contains a succinct intention; data must be encoded in such a way that "the data are the index."

Encoding Big Semantic Data: HDT

Our approach, *HDT: Header–Dictionary–Triples* (Fernández et al. 2010), considers all of the previous requirements, addressing a machine-processable RDF serialization format which enables Big Semantic Data to be efficiently managed within the common workflows of the Web of Data. The format formalizes a compact binary serialization optimized for storage or transmission over a network. It is worth noting that HDT is described and proposed for standardization as W3C Member Submission (Fernández et al. 2011). In addition, a succinct data structure has been proposed (Martínez-Prieto et al. 2012a) to browse HDT-encoded data sets. This structure holds the compactness of such representation and provides direct access to any piece of data as described below.

HDT organizes Big Semantic Data in three logical components (*Header, Dictionary,* and *Triples*) carefully described to address not only RDF peculiarities, but also considering how these data are actually used in the Publication-Exchange-Consumption workflow.

Header. The Header holds, in plain RDF format, metadata describing a big semantic data set encoded in HDT. It acts as an entry point for a consumer, who can peek on certain key properties of the data set to have an idea of its content, even before retrieving the whole data set. It enhances the VoID Vocabulary (Alexander et al. 2009) to provide a standardized binary data set description in which some additional HDT-specific properties are appended.[*] The Header component comprises four distinct sections:

- *Publication Metadata* provides information about the publication act, for instance, when was the data set generated, when was it made public, who is the publisher, where is the associated SPARQL endpoint, etc. Many properties of this type are described using the popular Dublin Core Vocabulary.[†]

- *Statistical Metadata* provides statistical information about the data set, such as the number of triples, the number of different subjects, predicates, objects, or even histograms. For instance, this class of metadata is very valuable or visualization software or federated query evaluation engines.

- *Format Metadata* describes how Dictionary and Triples components are encoded. This allows one to have different implementations or representations of the same data in different ways. For instance, one could prefer to have the triples in SPO order, whereas other applications might need it in OPS. Also the dictionary could apply a very aggressive compression technique to minimize the size as much as possible, whereas other implementation could be focused on query speed and even include a full-text index to accelerate text searches. These metadata enable the consumer for checking how an HDT-encoded data set can be accessed in the data structure.

- *Additional Metadata.* Since the Header contains plain RDF, the publisher can enhance it using any vocabulary. It allows specific data set/application metadata to be described. For instance, in life sciences a publisher might want to describe, in the Header, that the data set describes a specific class of proteins.

Since RDF enables data integration at any level, the Header component ensures that HDT-encoded data sets are not isolated and can be interconnected. For instance, it is a great tool for query syndication. A syndicated query engine could maintain a catalog composed by the Headers of different HDT-encoded data sets from many publishers and use it to know where to find more data about a specific subject. Then, at query time, the syndicated query engine can either use the remote SPARQL endpoint to query directly the third-party server or even download the whole data set and save it in a local cache. Thanks to the compact size of HDT-encoded data sets, both the transmission and storage costs are highly reduced.

---

[*] http://www.w3.org/Submission/2011/SUBM-HDT-Extending-VoID-20110330/
[†] http://dublincore.org/

Dictionary. The Dictionary is a catalog comprising all the different terms used in the data set, such as URIs, literals, and blank nodes. A unique identifier (ID) is assigned to each term, enabling triples to be represented as tuples of three IDs which, respectively, reference the corresponding terms in the dictionary. This is the first step toward compression, since it avoids long terms to be repeatedly represented. This way, each term occurrence is now replaced by its corresponding ID, whose encoding requires less bits in the vast majority of the cases. Furthermore, the catalog of terms within the dictionary may be encoded in many advanced ways focused on boosting querying or reducing size. A typical example is to use any kind of differential compression for encoding terms sharing long prefixes, for example, URIs.

The dictionary is divided into sections depending on whether the term plays subject, predicate, or object roles. Nevertheless, in semantic data, it is quite common that a URI appears both as a subject in one triple and as object on another. To avoid repeating those terms twice in the subjects and in the objects sections, we can extract them into a fourth section called *shared Subject-Object*.

Figure 4.3 depicts the 4-section dictionary organization and how IDs are assigned to the corresponding terms. Each section is sorted lexicographically and then correlative IDs are assigned to each term from 1 to n. It is worth noting that, for subjects and objects, the shared Subject–Object section uses the lower range of IDs; for example, if there are m terms playing interchangeably as subject and object, all x IDs such that $x < m$ belong to this shared section.

HDT allows one to use different techniques of dictionary representation. Each one can handle its catalog of terms in different ways, but must always implement these basic operations

- *Locate (term)*: finds the term and returns its ID
- *Extract (id)*: extracts the term associated to the ID
- *NumElements ()*: returns the number of elements of the section

More advanced techniques might also provide these optional operations

- *Prefix (p)*: finds all terms starting with the prefix p
- *Suffix (s)*: finds all terms ending with the suffix s

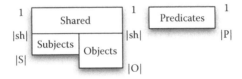

FIGURE 4.3
HDT dictionary organization into four sections.

- *Substring (s)*: finds all the terms containing the substring s
- *Regex (e)*: finds all strings matching the specified regular expression e

For instance, these advanced operations are very convenient when serving query suggestions to the user, or when evaluating SPARQL queries that include REGEX filters.

We suggest a Front-Coding (Witten et al. 1999) based representation as the most simple way of dictionary encoding. It has been successfully used in many WWW-based applications involving URL management. It is a very simple yet effective technique based on differential compression. This technique applies to lexicographically sorted dictionaries by dividing them into buckets of *b* terms. By tweaking this bucket size, different space/time trade-offs can be achieved. The first term in the bucket is explicitly stored and the remaining *b* − 1 ones are encoded with respect to their precedent: the common prefix length is first encoded and the remaining suffix is appended. More technical details about these dictionaries are available in Brisaboa et al. (2011).

The work of Martínez-Prieto et al. (2012b) surveys the problem of encoding compact RDF dictionaries. It reports that Front-Coding achieves a good performance for a general scenario, but more advanced techniques can achieve better compression ratios and/or handle directly complex operations. In any case, HDT is flexible enough to support any of these techniques, allowing stakeholders to decide which configuration is better for their specific purposes.

Triples. As stated, the Dictionary component allows spatial savings to be achieved, but it also enables RDF triples to be compactly encoded, representing tuples of three IDs referring the corresponding terms in the Dictionary. Thus, our original RDF graph is now transformed into a graph of IDs which encoding can be carried out in a more optimized way.

We devise a Triples encoding that organizes internally the information in a way that exploits graph redundancy to keep data compact. Moreover, this encoding can be easily mapped into a data structure that allows basic retrieval operations to be performed efficiently.

Triple patterns are the SPARQL query atoms for basic RDF retrieval. That is, all triples matching a template (*s, p, o*) (where *s, p,* and *o* may be variables) must be directly retrieved from the Triples encoding. For instance, in the geographic data set Geonames,[*] the triple pattern below searches all the subjects whose feature code (the predicate) is "P" (the object), a shortcode for "country." In other words, it asks about all the URIs representing countries:

> ? <http://www.geonames.org/ontology#featureCode>
>   <http://www.geonames.org/ontology#P>

Thus, the Triples component must be able to retrieve the subject of all those triples matching this pair of predicate and object.

---

[*] http://www.geonames.org

HDT proposes a Triples encoding named *BitmapTriples* (BT). This technique needs the triples to be previously sorted in a specific order, such as subject–predicate–object (SPO). BT is able to handle all possible triple orderings, but we only describe the intuitive SPO order for explanation purposes.

Basically, BT transforms the graph into a forest containing as many trees as different subjects are used in the data set, and these trees are then ordered by subject ID. This way, the first tree represents all triples rooted by the subject identified as 1, the second tree represents all triples rooted by the subject identified as 2, and so on. Each tree comprises three levels: the root represents the subject, the second level lists all predicates related to the subject, and finally the leaves organize all objects for each pair (*subject, predicate*). Predicate and object levels are also sorted.

- All predicates related to the subject are sorted in an increasing way. As Figure 4.4 shows predicates are sorted as {5, 6, 7} for the second subject.
- Objects follow an increasing order for each path in the tree. That is, objects are internally ordered for each pair (*subject, predicate*). As Figure 4.4 shows the object 5 is listed first (because it is related to the pair (2, 5)), then 1,3 (by considering that these are related to the pair (2, 6)), and 4 is the last object because of its relation to (2, 7).

Each triple in the data set is now represented as a full path root-to-leave in the corresponding tree. This simple reorganization reveals many interesting features.

- The subject can be implicitly encoded given that the trees are sorted by subject and we know the total number of trees. Thus, BT does not perform a triples encoding, but it represents pairs (predicate, object). This is an obvious spatial saving.
- Predicates are sorted within each tree. This is very similar to a well-known problem: posting list encoding for Information Retrieval (Witten et al. 1999; Baeza-Yates and Ribeiro-Neto 2011). This allows applying many existing and optimized techniques to our problem.

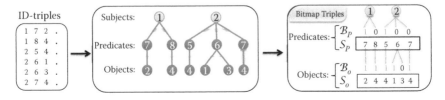

FIGURE 4.4
Description of Bitmap Triples.

Besides, efficient search within predicate lists is enabled by assuming that the elements follow a known ordering.

- Objects are sorted within each path in the tree, so (i) these can be effectively encoded and (ii) these can also be efficiently searched.

BT encodes the Triples component level by level. That is, predicate and object levels are encoded in isolation. Two structures are used for predicates: (i) an ID sequence (S_p) concatenates predicate lists following the tree ordering; (ii) a bitsequence (B_p) uses one bit per element in S_p: 1 bits mean that this predicate is the first one for a given tree, whereas 0 bits are used for the remaining predicates. Object encoding is performed in a similar way: S_o concatenates object lists, and B_o tags each position in such way that 1 bits represent the first object in a path, and 0 bits the remaining ones. The right part of Figure 4.4 illustrates all these sequences for the given example.

Querying HDT-Encoded Data Sets: HDT-FoQ

An HDT-encode data set can be directly accessed once its components are loaded into the memory hierarchy of any computational system. Nevertheless, this can be tuned carefully by considering the volume of the data sets and the retrieval velocity needed by specific applications. Thus, we require a data structure that keeps the compactness of the encoding to load data at the higher levels of the memory hierarchy. Data in faster memory always means faster retrieval operations. We call this solution *HDT-FoQ: HDT Focused on Querying*.

Dictionary. The dictionary component must be able to be directly mapped from the encoding to the computer because it must embed enough information to resolve the basic operations previously described. Thus, this component follows the idea of "the data are the index." We invite interested readers to review the paper of Brisaboa et al. (2011) for a more detailed description on how dictionaries provide indexing capabilities.

Triples. The previously described BitmapTriples approach is easy to map due to the simplicity of its encoding. Sequences S_p and S_o are loaded into two integer arrays using, respectively, $\log(|P|)$ and $\log(|O|)$ bits per element. Bit sequences can also be mapped directly, but in this case they are enhanced with an additional small structure (González et al. 2005) that ensures constant time resolution for some basic bit operations.

This simple idea enables efficient traversal of the Triples component. All these algorithms are described in Martínez-Prieto et al. (2012a), but we review them in practice over the example in Figure 4.4. Let us suppose that we ask for the existence of the triple (2, 6, 1). It implies that the retrieval operation is performed over the second tree:

1. We retrieve the corresponding predicate list. It is the 2nd one in S_p and it is found by simply locating where is the second 1 bit in B_p. In this case $P_2 = 3$, so the predicate list comprises all elements from $S_p[2]$

until the end (because no more this is the last 1 bit in $\mathcal{B}_p$). Thus, the predicate list is {5, 6, 7}.

2. The predicate 6 is searched in the list. We binary search it and find that it is the second element in the list. Thus, it is at position $P_2 + 2 - 1 = 3 + 2 - 1 = 4$ in $\mathcal{S}_p$ so we are traversing the 4th path of the forest.

3. We retrieve the corresponding object list. It is the 4th one in $\mathcal{S}_o$. We obtain it as before: firstly locate the fourth 1 bit in $\mathcal{B}_o$:$O_4 = 4$ and then retrieve all objects until the next 1 bit. That is, the list comprises the objects {1, 3}.

4. Finally, the object list is binary searched and locates the object 3 in its first position. Thus, we are sure that the triple (2, 6, 1) exists in the data set.

All triple patterns providing the subjects are efficiently resolved on variants of this process. Thus, the data structure directly mapped from the encoding provides fast subject-based retrieval, but makes difficult accessing by predicate and object. Both can easily be accomplished with a limited overhead on the space used by the original encoding. All fine-grain details about the following decisions are also explained in Martínez-Prieto et al. (2012a).

Enabling access by predicate. This retrieval operation demands direct access to the second level of the tree, so it means efficient access to the sequence $\mathcal{S}_p$. However, the elements of $\mathcal{S}_p$ are sorted by subject, so locating all predicate occurrences demands a full scanning of this sequence and this result in a poor response time.

Although accesses by predicate are uncommon in general (Arias et al. 2011), some applications could require them (e.g., extracting all the information described with a set of given predicates). Thus, we must address it by considering the need of another data structure for mapping $\mathcal{S}_p$. It must enable efficient predicate locating but without degrading basic access because it is used in all operations by subject. We choose a structure called wavelet tree.

The *wavelet tree* (Grossi et al. 2003) is a succinct structure which reorganizes a sequence of integers, in a range $[1, n]$, to provide some access operations to the data in logarithmic time. Thus, the original $\mathcal{S}_p$ is now loaded as a wavelet tree, not as an array. It means a limited additional cost (in space) which holds HDT scalability for managing Big Semantic Data. In return, we can locate all predicate occurrences in logarithmic time with the number of different predicates used for modeling in the data set. In practice, this number is small and it means efficient occurrence location within our access operations. It is worth noting that to access to any position in the wavelet tree has also now a logarithmic cost.

Therefore, access by predicate is implemented by firstly performing an occurrence-to-occurrence location, and for each one traversing the tree by following comparable steps to than explained in the previous example.

Enabling access by object. The data structure designed for loading HDT-encoded data sets, considering a subject-based order, is not suitable for doing accesses by object. All the occurrence of an object are scattered throughout the sequence S_o and we are not able to locate them unless we do sequential scan. Furthermore, in this case a structure like the Wavelet Tree becomes inefficient; RDF data sets usually have few predicates, but they contain many different objects and logarithmic costs result in very expensive operation.

We enhance HDT-FoQ with an additional index (called O-Index), that is responsible for solving accesses by object. This index basically gathers the positions in where each object appears in the original S_o. Please note that each leave is associated to a different triple, so given the index of an element in the lower level, we can guess the predicate and subject associated by traversing the tree upwards processing the bit sequences in a similar way than that used for subject-based access.

In relative terms, this O-Index has a significant impact in the final HDT-FoQ requirements because it takes considerable space in comparison to the other data structures used for modeling the Triples component. However, in absolute terms, the total size required by HDT-FoQ is very small in comparison to that required by the other competitive solutions in the state of the art. All these results are analyzed in the next section.

Joining Basic Triple Patterns. All this infrastructure enables basic triple patterns to be resolved, in compressed space, at higher levels of the hierarchy of memory. As we show below, it guarantees efficient triple pattern resolution. Although this kind of queries are massively used in practice (Arias et al. 2011), the SPARQL core is defined around the concept of Basic Graph Pattern (BGP) and its semantics to build conjunctions, disjunctions, and optional parts involving more than a single triple pattern. Thus, HDT-FoQ must provide more advanced query resolution to reach a full SPARQL coverage. At this moment, it is able to resolve conjunctive queries by using specific implementations of the well-known *merge* and *index* join algorithms (Ramakrishnan and Gehrke 2000).

Experimental Results

This section analyzes the impact of HDT for encoding Big Semantic Data within the Publication-Exchange-Consumption workflow described in the Web of Data. We characterize the publisher and consumer stakeholders of our experiments as follows:

- The *publisher* is devised as an efficient agent implementing a powerful computational configuration. It runs on an Intel Xeon E5645@2.4 GHz, hexa-core (6cores-12siblings: 2 thread per core), 96 GB DDR3@1066 Mhz.

- The *consumer* is designed on a conventional configuration because it plays the role of any agent consuming RDF within the Web of Data. It runs on an AMD-PhenomTM-II X4 955@3.2 GHz, quad-core (4cores-4siblings: 1thread per core), 8 GB DDR2@800 MHz.

The *network* is regarded as an ideal communication channel: free of errors and any other external interferences. We assume a transmission speed of 2 Mbyte/s.

All our experiments are carried out over an heterogeneous data configuration of many colors and flavors. We choose a variety of real-world semantic data sets of different sizes and from different application domains (see Table 4.1). In addition, we join together the three bigger data sets into a large mash-up of more than 1 billion triples to analyze performance issues in an integrated data set.

The prototype running these experiments is developed in C ++ using the HDT library publicly available at the official RDF/HDT website.[*]

Publication Performance

As explained, RDF data sets are usually released in plain-text form (NTriples, Turtle, or RDF-XML), and their big volume is simply reduced using any traditional compressor. This way, volume directly affects the publication process because the publisher must, at least, process the data set to convert it to a suitable format for exchange. Attending to the current practices, we set gzip compression as the baseline and we also include lzma because of its effectiveness. We compare their results against HDT, in plain and also in conjunction with the same compressors. That is, HDT plain implements the encoding described in section "Encoding Big Semantic Data: HDT", and HDT + X stands for the result of compressing HDT plain with the compressor X.

TABLE 4.1

Statistics of the Real-World Data sets Used in the Experimentation

Data set	Plain Ntriples	Size (GB)	Available at
LinkedMDB	6,148,121	0,85	http://queens.db.toronto.edu/~oktie/linkedmdb
DBLP	73,226,756	11,16	http://DBLP.l3s.de/DBLP++.php
Geonames	119,316,724	13,79	http://download.Geonames.org/all-Geonames-rdf.zip
DBpedia	296,907,301	48,62	http://wiki.dbpedia.org/Downloads37
Freebase	639,078,932	84,76	http://download.freebase.com/datadumps/[a]
Mashup	1,055,302,957	140,46	Mashup of Geonames + Freebase + DBPedia

[a] Dump on 2012-07-26 converted to RDF using http://code.google.com/p/freebase-quad-rdfize/.

[*] http://www.rdfhdt.org

Figure 4.5 shows compression ratios for all the considered techniques. In general, HDT plain requires more space than traditional compressors. It is an expected result because both Dictionary and Triples use very basic approaches. Advanced techniques for each component enable significant improvements in space. For instance, our preliminary results using the technique proposed in Martínez-Prieto et al. (2012b) for dictionary encoding show a significant improvement in space. Nevertheless, if we apply traditional compression over the HDT-encoded data sets, the spatial requirements are largely diminished. As shown in Figure 4.5, the comparison changes when the HDT-encoded data sets are compressed with gzip and lzma. These results show that HDT + lzma achieves the most compressed representations, largely improving the effectiveness reported by traditional approaches. For instance, HDT + lzma only uses 2.56% of the original mash-up size, whereas compressors require 5.23% (lzma) and 7.92% (gzip).

Thus, encoding the original Big Semantic Data with HDT and then applying compression reports the best numbers for publication. It means that publishers using our approach require 2–3 times less storage space and bandwidth than using traditional compression. These savings are achieved at the price of spending some time to obtain the corresponding representations. Note that traditional compression basically requires compressing the data set, whereas our approach firstly transforms the data set into its HDT encoding and then compresses it. These *publication times* (in minutes) are depicted in Table 4.2.

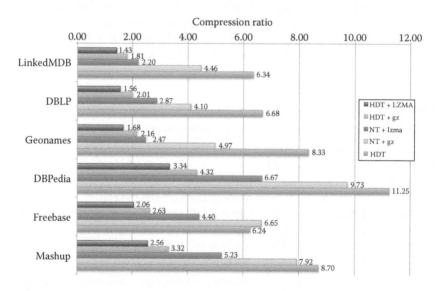

FIGURE 4.5
Dataset compression (expressed as percent of the original size in NTriples).

TABLE 4.2

Publication Times (Minutes)

Data set	gzip	lzma	HDT+ gzip	HDT+ lzma
LinkedMDB	**0.19**	14.71	1.09	1.52
DBLP	**2.72**	103.53	13.48	21.99
Geonames	**3.28**	244.72	26.42	38.96
DBPedia	**18.90**	664.54	84.61	174.12
Freebase	**24.08**	1154.02	235.83	315.34
Mash-up	**47.23**	2081.07	861.87	1033.0

Note: Bold values emphasize the best compression times.

As can be seen, direct publication, based on gzip compression, is up to 20 times faster than HDT + gzip. The difference is slightly higher compared to HDT + lzma, but this choice largely outperforms direct lzma compression. However, this comparison must be carefully analyzed because publication is a batch process and it is performed only once per data set, whereas exchange and postprocessing costs are paid each time that any consumer retrieves the data set. Thus, in practical terms, publishers will prioritize compression versus publication time because: (i) storage and bandwidth savings and (ii) the overall time that consumers wait when they retrieve the data set.

Exchange Performance

In the ideal network regarded in our experiments, exchange performance is uniquely determined by the data size. Thus, our approach also appears as the most efficient because of its excellent compression ratios. Table 4.3 organizes processing times for all data sets and each task involved in the workflow. Column exchange lists exchanging times required when lzma (in the baseline) and HDT + lzma are used for encoding.

For instance, the mash-up exchange takes roughly half an hour for HDT + lzma and slightly more than 1 h for lzma. Thus, our approach reduces by the half exchange time and also saves bandwidth in the same proportion for the mash-up.

Consumption Performance

In the current evaluation, consumption performance is analyzed from two complementary perspectives. First, we consider a *postprocessing* stage in which the consumer decompresses the downloaded data set and then indexes it for local consumption. Every consumption task directly relies on efficient query resolution, and thus, our second evaluation focuses on *query evaluation* performance.

TABLE 4.3

Overall Client Times (Seconds)

Data set	Config.	Exchange	Decomp.	Index	Total
LinkedMDB	Baseline	9.61	5.11	111.08	125.80
	HDT	**6.25**	**1.05**	**1.91**	**9.21**
DBLP	Baseline	164.09	70.86	1387.29	1622.24
	HDT	**89.35**	**14.82**	**16.79**	**120.96**
Geonames	Baseline	174.46	87.51	2691.66	2953.63
	HDT	**118.29**	**19.91**	**44.98**	**183.18**
DBPedia	Baseline	1659.95	553.43	7904.73	10118.11
	HDT	**832.35**	**197.62**	**129.46**	**1159.43**
Freebase	Baseline	1910.86	681.12	58080.09	60672.07
	HDT	**891.90**	**227.47**	**286.25**	**1405.62**
Mashup	Baseline	3757.92	1238.36	>24 h	>24 h
	HDT	**1839.61**	**424.32**	**473.64**	**2737.57**

Note: Bold values highlight the best times for each activity in the workflow. Baseline means that the file is downloaded in NTriples format, compressed using lzma, and indexed using RDF-3X. HDT means that the file is downloaded in HDT, compressed with lzma, and indexed using HDT-FoQ.

Both postprocessing and querying tasks require an RDF store enabling indexing and efficient SPARQL resolution. We choose three well-known stores for fair comparison with respect to HDT-FoQ:

- *RDF3X*[*] was recently reported as the fastest RDF store (Huang et al. 2011).
- *Virtuoso*[†] is a popular store performing on relational infrastructure.
- *Hexastore*[‡] is a well-known memory-resident store.

Postprocessing. As stated, this task involves decompression and indexing in order to make queryable the compressed data set retrieved from the publisher. Table 4.3 also organizes post-processing times for all data sets. It is worth noting that we compare our HDT + lzma against a baseline comprising lzma decompression and RDF3X indexing because it reports the best numbers. Cells containing " >24 h" mean that the process was not finished after 24 h. Thus, indexing the mash-up in our consumer is a very heavy task requiring a lot of computational resources and also wasting a lot of time.

HDT-based postprocessing largely outperforms RDF3X for all original data sets in our setup. HDT performs decompression and indexing from ≈ 25 (DBPedia) to 114 (Freebase) times faster than RDF3X. This situation is due to

---

[*] RDF3X is available at http://www.mpi-inf.mpg.de/~neumann/rdf3x/
[†] Virtuoso is available at http://www.openlinksw.com/
[‡] Hexastore has been kindly provided by the authors.

two main reasons. On the one hand, HDT-encoded data sets are smaller than its counterparts in NTriples and it improves decompression performance. On the other hand, HDT-FoQ generates its additional indexing structures (see section "Querying HDT-Encoded Data sets: HDT-FoQ") over the original HDT encoding, whereas RDF3X first needs parsing the data set and then building their specific indices from scratch. Both features share an important fact: the most expensive processing was already done in the server side and HDT-encoded data sets are clearly better for machine consumption.

Exchange and post-processing times can be analyzed together and because of it the total time than a consumer must wait until the data is able to be efficiently used in any application. Our integrated approach, around HDT encoding and data structures, completes all the tasks 8–43 times faster than the traditional combination of compression and RDF indexing. It means, for instance, that the configured consumer retrieves and makes queryable Freebase in roughly 23 min using HDT, but it needs almost 17 h to complete the same process over the baseline. In addition, we can see that indexing is clearly the heavier task in the baseline, whereas exchange is the longer task for us. However, in any case, we always complete exchange faster due to our achievements in space.

Querying. Once the consumer has made the downloaded data queryable, the infrastructure is ready to build on-top applications issuing SPARQL queries. The data volume emerges again as a key factor because it restricts the ways indices and query optimizers are designed and managed.

On the one hand, RDF3X and Virtuoso rely on disk-based indexes which are selectively loaded into main memory. Although both are efficiently tuned for this purpose, these I/O transfers result in very expensive operations that hinder the final querying performance. On the other hand, Hexastore and HDT-FoQ always hold their indices in memory, avoiding these slow accesses to disk. Whereas HDT-FoQ enables all data sets in the setup to be managed in the consumer configuration, Hexastore is only able to index the smaller one, showing its scalability problems when managing Big Semantic Data.

We obtain two different sets of SPARQL queries to compare HDT-FoQ against the indexing solutions within the state of the art. On the one hand, 5000 queries are randomly generated for each triple pattern. On the other hand, we also generate 350 queries of each type of two-way join, subdivided into two groups depending on whether they have a *small* or *big* amount of intermediate results. All these queries are run over Geonames in order to include both Virtuoso and RDF3X in the experiments. Note that, both classes of queries are resolved without the need of query planning, hence the results are clear evidence of how the different indexing techniques perform.

Figure 4.6 summarizes these querying experiments. The X-axis lists all different queries: the left subgroup lists the triple patterns, and the right ones represent all different join classes. The Y-axis means the number of times that HDT-FoQ is faster than its competitors. For instance, in the pattern (S, V, V) (equivalent to dereference the subject S), HDT-FoQ is more than 3 times

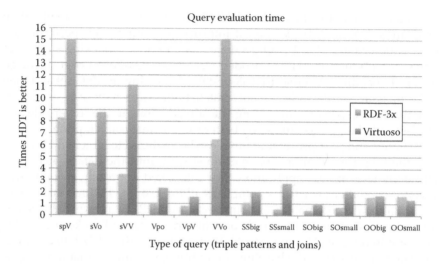

FIGURE 4.6
Comparison on querying performance on Geonames.

faster than RDF3X and more than 11 times faster than Virtuoso. In general, HDT-FoQ always outperforms Virtuoso, whereas RDF3X is slightly faster for (V, P, V), and some join classes. Nevertheless, we remain competitive in all theses cases and our join algorithms are still open for optimization.

Conclusions and Next Steps

This chapter presents basic foundations of Big Semantic Data management. First, we trace a route from the current data deluge, the concept of Big Data, and the need of machine-processable semantics on the WWW. The Resource Description Framework (RDF) and the Web of (Linked) Data naturally emerge in this well-grounded scenario. The former, RDF, is the natural codification language for semantic data, combining the flexibility of semantic networks with a graph data structure that makes it an excellent choice for describing metadata at Web Scale. The latter, the Web of (Linked) Data, provides a set of rules to publish and link Big Semantic Data.

We justify the different and various management problems arising in Big Semantic Data by characterizing their main stakeholders by role (Creators/Publishers/Consumers) and nature (Automatic/Supervised/Human). Then, we define a common workflow Publication-Exchange-Consumption, existing in most applications in the Web of Data. The scalability problems arising to the current state-of-the-art management solutions within this scenario set the basis of our integrated proposal HDT, based on the W3C standard RDF.

HDT is designed as a binary RDF format to fulfill the requirements of portability (from and to other formats), compact ability, parsing efficiency (readiness for postprocessing), and direct access to any piece of data in the data set. We detail the design of HDT and we argue that HDT-encoded data sets can be directly consumed within the presented workflow. We show that lightweight indices can be created once the different components are loaded into the memory hierarchy at the consumer, allowing for more complex operations such as joining basic SPARQL Triple Patterns. Finally, this compact infrastructure, called HDT-FoQ (HDT Focused on Querying) is evaluated toward a traditional combination of universal compression (for exchanging) and RDF indexing (for consumption).

Our experiments show how HDT excels at almost every stage of the publish-exchange-consumption workflow. The publisher spends a bit more time to encode the Big Semantic data set, but in return, the consumer is able to retrieve it twice as fast, and the indexing time is largely reduced to just a few minutes for huge data sets. Therefore, the time since a machine or human client discovers the data set until she is ready to start querying its content is reduced up to 16 times by using HDT instead of the traditional approaches. Furthermore, the query performance is very competitive compared to state-of-the art RDF stores, thanks to the size reduction the machine can keep a vast amount of triples in main memory, avoiding slow I/O transferences.

There are several areas where HDT can be further exploited. We foresee a huge potential of HDT to support many aspects of the workflow Publish-Exchange-Consume. HDT-based technologies can emerge to provide supporting tools for both publishers and consumers. For instance, a very useful tool for a publisher is setting up an SPARQL endpoint on top of an HDT file. As the experiments show, HDT-FoQ is very competitive on queries, but there is still plenty of room for SPARQL optimization, by leveraging efficient resolution of triple patterns, joins, and query planning. Another useful tool for publishers is configuring a dereferenceable URI materialization from a given HDT. Here the experiments also show that performance will be very high because HDT-FoQ is really fast on queries with a fixed RDF subject.

Acknowledgments

This work was partially funded by MICINN (TIN2009-14009-C02-02); Science Foundation Ireland: Grant No. ~ SFI/08/CE/I1380, Lion-II; Fondecyt 1110287 and Fondecyt 1-110066. The first author is granted by Erasmus Mundus, the Regional Government of Castilla y León (Spain) and the European Social Fund. The third author is granted by the University of Valladolid: programme of Mobility Grants for Researchers (2012).

References

Abadi, D., A. Marcus, S. Madden, and K. Hollenbach. 2009. SW-Store: A vertically partitioned DBMS for Semantic Web data management. *The VLDB Journal* 18, 385–406.

Adida, B., I. Herman, M. Sporny, and M. Birbeck (Eds.). 2012. *RDFa 1.1 Primer*. W3C Working Group Note. http://www.w3.org/TR/xhtml-rdfa-primer/.

Akar, Z., T. G. Hala, E. E. Ekinci, and O. Dikenelli. 2012. Querying the Web of Interlinked Datasets using VOID Descriptions. In *Proc. of the Linked Data on the Web Workshop (LDOW)*, Lyon, France, Paper 6.

Alexander, K. 2008. RDF in JSON: A Specification for serialising RDF in JSON. In *Proc. of the 4th Workshop on Scripting for the Semantic Web (SFSW)*, Tenerife, Spain.

Alexander, K., R. Cyganiak, M. Hausenblas, and J. Zhao. 2009. Describing linked datasets-on the design and usage of voiD, the "vocabulary of interlinked data-sets". In *Proc. of the Linked Data on the Web Workshop (LDOW)*, Madrid, Spain, Paper 20.

Álvarez-García, S., N. Brisaboa, J. Fernández, and M. Martínez-Prieto. 2011. Compressed k^2-triples for full-in-memory RDF engines. In *Proc. 17th Americas Conference on Information Systems (AMCIS)*, Detroit, Mich, Paper 350.

Arenas, M., A. Bertails, E. Prud'hommeaux, and J. Sequeda (Eds.). 2012. *A Direct Mapping of Relational Data to RDF*. W3C Recommendation. http://www.w3.org/TR/rdb-direct-mapping/.

Arias, M., J. D. Fernández, and M. A. Martínez-Prieto. 2011. An empirical study of real-world SPARQL queries. In *Proc. of 1st Workshop on Usage Analyss and the Web of Data (USEWOD)*, Hyderabad, India. http://arxiv.org/abs/1103.5043.

Atemezing, G., O. Corcho, D. Garijo, J. Mora, M. Poveda-Villalón, P. Rozas, D. Vila-Suero, and B. Villazón-Terrazas. 2013. Transforming meteorological data into linked data. *Semantic Web Journal* 4(3), 285–290.

Atre, M., V. Chaoji, M. Zaki, and J. Hendler. 2010. Matrix "Bit" loaded: A scalable lightweight join query processor for RDF data. In *Proc. of the 19th World Wide Web Conference (WWW)*, Raleigh, NC, pp. 41–50.

Auer, S., C. Bizer, G. Kobilarov, J. Lehmann, and Z. Ives. 2007. Dbpedia: A nucleus for a web of open data. In *Proc. of the 6th International Semantic Web Conference (ISWC)*, Busan, Korea, pp. 11–15.

Baeza-Yates, R. and B. A. Ribeiro-Neto. 2011. *Modern Information Retrieval—the Concepts and Technology Behind Search* (2nd edn.). Pearson Education Ltd.

Beckett, D. (Ed.) 2004. *RDF/XML Syntax Specification (Revised)*. W3C Recommendation. http://www.w3.org/TR/rdf-syntax-grammar/.

Beckett, D. and T. Berners-Lee. 2008. *Turtle—Terse RDF Triple Language*. W3C Team Submission. http://www.w3.org/TeamSubmission/turtle/.

Berners-Lee, T. 1998. *Notation3*. W3C Design Issues. http://www.w3.org/DesignIssues/Notation3.

Berners-Lee, T. 2002. Linked Open Data. What is the idea? http://www.thenational-dialogue.org/ideas/linked-open-data (accessed October 8, 2012).

Berners-Lee, T. 2006. Linked Data: Design Issues. http://www.w3.org/DesignIssues/LinkedData.html (accessed October 8, 2012).

Bizer, C., T. Heath, and T. Berners-Lee. 2009. Linked data—the story so far. *International Journal on Semantic Web and Information Systems* 5, 1–22.

Brickley, D. 2004. *RDF Vocabulary Description Language 1.0: RDF Schema.* W3C Recommendation. http://www.w3.org/TR/rdf-schema/.

Brisaboa, N., R. Cánovas, F. Claude, M. Martínez-Prieto, and G. Navarro. 2011. Compressed string dictionaries. In *Proc. of 10th International Symposium on Experimental Algorithms (SEA)*, Chania, Greece, pp. 136–147.

Cukier, K. 2010. Data, data everywhere. *The Economist* (February, 25). http://www.economist.com/opinion/displaystory.cfm?story_id=15557443 (accessed October 8, 2012).

Cyganiak, R., H. Stenzhorn, R. Delbru, S. Decker, and G. Tummarello. 2008. Semantic sitemaps: Efficient and flexible access to datasets on the semantic web. In *Proc. of the 5th European Semantic Web Conference (ESWC)*, Tenerife, Spain, pp. 690–704.

De, S., T. Elsaleh, P. M. Barnaghi, and S. Meissner. 2012. An internet of things platform for real-world and digital objects. *Scalable Computing: Practice and Experience* 13(1), 45–57.

Dijcks, J.-P. 2012. Big Data for the Enterprise. *Oracle (white paper)* (January). http://www.oracle.com/us/products/database/big-data-for-enterprise-519135.pdf (accessed October 8, 2012).

Dumbill, E. 2012a. *Planning for Big Data*. O'Reilly Media, Sebastopol, CA.

Dumbill, E. 2012b. What is big data? *Strata* (January, 11). http://strata.oreilly.com/2012/01/what-is-big-data.html (accessed October 8, 2012).

Fernández, J. D., M. A. Martínez-Prieto, and C. Gutiérrez. 2010. Compact representation of large RDF data sets for publishing and exchange. In *Proc. of the 9th International Semantic Web Conference (ISWC)*, Shangai, China, pp. 193–208.

Fernández, J. D., M. A. Martínez-Prieto, C. Gutiérrez, and A. Polleres. 2011. *Binary RDF Representation for Publication and Exchange (HDT)*. W3C Member Submission. http://www.w3.org/Submission/2011/03/.

Foulonneau, M. 2011. Smart semantic content for the future internet. In *Metadata and Semantic Research*, Volume 240 of *Communications in Computer and Information Science*, pp. 145–154. Springer, Berlin, Heidelberg.

García-Silva, A., O. Corcho, H. Alani, and A. Gómez-Pérez. 2012. Review of the state of the art: Discovering and associating semantics to tags in folksonomies. *The Knowledge Engineering Review* 27(01), 57–85.

González, R., S. Grabowski, V. Mäkinen, and G. Navarro. 2005. Practical implementation of rank and select queries. In *Proc. of 4th International Workshop Experimental and Efficient Algorithms (WEA)*, Santorini Island, Greece, pp. 27–38.

Grossi, R., A. Gupta, and J. Vitter. 2003. High-order entropy-compressed text indexes. In *Proc. of 9th Annual ACM-SIAM Symposium on Discrete Algorithms (SODA)*, Baltimore, MD, pp. 841–850.

Haas, K., P. Mika, P. Tarjan, and R. Blanco. 2011. Enhanced results for web search. In *Proc. of the 34th International Conference on Research and Development in Information Retrieval (SIGIR)*, Beijing, China, pp. 725–734.

Halfon, A. 2012. Handling big data variety. http://www.finextra.com/community/fullblog. aspx?blogid = 6129 (accessed October 8, 2012).

Hausenblas, M. and M. Karnstedt. 2010. Understanding linked open data as a web-scale database. In *Proc. of the 1st International Conference on Advances in Databases (DBKDA)*, 56–61.

Heath, T. and C. Bizer. 2011. *Linked Data: Evolving the Web into a Global Data Space.* Synthesis Lectures on the Semantic Web: Theory and Technology, Morgan & Claypool.

Hey, T., S. Tansley, and K. M. Tolle. 2009. Jim Gray on eScience: A transformed scientific method. In *The Fourth Paradigm.* Microsoft Research.

Hogan, A., A. Harth, J. Umbrich, S. Kinsella, A. Polleres, and S. Decker. 2011. Searching and browsing linked data with SWSE: The semantic web search engine. *Journal of Web Semantics* 9(4), 365–401.

Hogan, A., J. Umbrich, A. Harth, R. Cyganiak, A. Polleres, and S. Decker. 2012. An empirical survey of linked data conformance. *Web Semantics: Science, Services and Agents on the World Wide Web* 14(0), 14–44.

Huang, J., D. Abadi, and K. Ren. 2011. Scalable SPARQL querying of large RDF graphs. *Proceedings of the VLDB Endowment* 4(11), 1123–1134.

Knoblock, C. A., P. Szekely, J. L. Ambite, S. Gupta, A. Goel, M. Muslea, K. Lerman, and P. Mallick. 2012. Semi-Automatically Mapping Structured Sources into the Semantic Web. In *Proc. of the 9th Extended Semantic Web Conference (ESWC),* Heraklion, Greece, pp. 375–390.

Le-Phuoc, D., J. X. Parreira, V. Reynolds, and M. Hauswirth. 2010. RDF On the Go: An RDF Storage and Query Processor for Mobile Devices. In *Proc. of the 9th International Semantic Web Conference (ISWC),* Shangai, China. http://ceur-ws.org/Vol-658/paper503.pdf.

Lohr, S. 2012. The age of big data. *The New York Times* (February, 11). http://www.nytimes.com/2012/02/12/sunday-review/big-datas-impact-in-the-world.html (accessed October 8, 2012).

Loukides, M. 2012. *What is Data Science?* O'Reilly Media.

Manola, F. and E. Miller (Eds.). 2004. *RDF Primer.* W3C Recommendation. www.w3.org/TR/rdf-primer/.

Martínez-Prieto, M., M. Arias, and J. Fernández. 2012a. Exchange and consumption of huge RDF data. In *Proc. of the 9th Extended Semantic Web Conference (ESWC),* Heraklion, Greece, pp. 437–452.

Martínez-Prieto, M., J. Fernández, and R. Cánovas. 2012b. Querying RDF dictionaries in compressed space. *ACM SIGAPP Applied Computing Reviews* 12(2), 64–77.

Marz, N. and J. Warren. 2013. *Big Data: Principles and Best Practices of Scalable Realtime Data Systems.* Manning Publications.

McGuinness, D. L. and F. van Harmelen (Eds.). 2004. *OWL Web Ontology Language Overview.* W3C Recommendation. http://www.w3.org/TR/owl-features/.

Neumann, T. and G. Weikum. 2010. The RDF-3X engine for scalable management of RDF data. *The VLDB Journal* 19(1), 91–113.

Prud'hommeaux, E. and A. Seaborne (Eds.). 2008. *SPARQL Query Language for RDF.* http://www.w3.org/TR/rdf-sparql-query/. W3C Recommendation.

Quesada, J. 2008. Human similarity theories for the semantic web. In *Proceedings of the First International Workshop on Nature Inspired Reasoning for the Semantic Web,* Karlsruhe, Germany.

Ramakrishnan, R. and J. Gehrke. 2000. *Database Management Systems.* Osborne/McGraw-Hill.

Schmidt, M., M. Meier, and G. Lausen. 2010. Foundations of SPARQL query optimization. In *Proc. of the 13th International Conference on Database Theory (ICDT),* Lausanne, Switzerland, pp. 4–33.

Schneider, J. and T. Kamiya (Eds.). 2011. *Efficient XML Interchange (EXI) Format 1.0.* W3C Recommendation. http://www.w3.org/TR/exi/.

Schwarte, A., P. Haase, K. Hose, R. Schenkel, and M. Schmidt. 2011. FedX: Optimization techniques for federated query processing on linked data. In *Proc. of the 10th International Conference on the Semantic Web (ISWC)*, Bonn, Germany, pp. 601–616.

Selg, E. 2012. The next Big Step—Big Data. *GFT Technologies AG (technical report).* http://www.gft.com/etc/medialib/2009/downloads/techreports/2012. Par.0001.File. tmp/gft_techreport_big_data.pdf (accessed October 8, 2012).

Sidirourgos, L., R. Goncalves, M. Kersten, N. Nes, and S. Manegold. 2008. Column-store Support for RDF Data Management: not All Swans are White. *Proc. of the VLDB Endowment* 1(2), 1553–1563.

Taheriyan, M., C. A. Knoblock, P. Szekely, and J. L. Ambite. 2012. Rapidly integrating services into the linked data cloud. In *Proc. of the 11th International Semantic Web Conference (ISWC)*, Boston, MA, pp. 559–574.

Tran, T., G. Ladwig, and S. Rudolph. 2012. Rdf data partitioning and query processing using structure indexes. *IEEE Transactions on Knowledge and Data Engineering* 99. Doi: ieeecomputersociety.org/10.1109/TKDE.2012.134

Tummarello, G., R. Cyganiak, M. Catasta, S. Danielczyk, R. Delbru, and S. Decker. 2010. Sig.ma: Live views on the web of data. *Web Semantics: Science, Services and Agents on the World Wide Web* 8(4), 355–364.

Urbani, J., J. Maassen, and H. Bal. 2010. Massive semantic web data compression with MapReduce. In *Proc. of the 19th International Symposium on High Performance Distributed Computing (HPDC) 2010*, Chicago, IL, pp. 795–802.

Volz, J., C. Bizer, M. Gaedke, and G. Kobilarov. 2009. Discovering and maintaining links on the web of data. In *Proc. of the 9th International Semantic Web Conference (ISWC)*, Shanghai, China, pp. 650–665.

Weiss, C., P. Karras, and A. Bernstein. 2008. Hexastore: Sextuple indexing for semantic web data management. *Proc. of the VLDB Endowment* 1(1), 1008–1019.

Witten, I. H., A. Moffat, and T. C. Bell. 1999. *Managing Gigabytes: Compressing and Indexing Documents and Images.* San Francisco, CA, Morgan Kaufmann.

5

Linked Data in Enterprise Integration

Sören Auer, Axel-Cyrille Ngonga Ngomo, Philipp Frischmuth, and Jakub Klimek

CONTENTS

Introduction

Data integration in large enterprises is a crucial but at the same time a costly, long-lasting, and challenging problem. While business-critical information is often already gathered in integrated information systems such as ERP, CRM, and SCM systems, the integration of these systems themselves as well as the integration with the abundance of other information sources is still a major challenge. Large companies often operate hundreds or even thousands of different information systems and databases. This is especially true for large OEMs. For example, it is estimated that at Volkswagen there are approximately 5000 different information systems deployed. At Daimler—even after a decade of consolidation efforts—the number of independent IT systems still reaches 3000.

After the arrival and proliferation of IT in large enterprises, various approaches, techniques, and methods have been introduced in order to solve the data integration challenge. In the last decade, the prevalent data integration approaches were primarily based on XML, Web Services, and *Service-Oriented Architectures* (SOA) [9]. XML defines a standard syntax for data representation, Web Services provide data exchange protocols, and SOA is a holistic approach for distributed systems architecture and communication. However, we become increasingly aware that these technologies are not sufficient to ultimately solve the data integration challenge in large enterprises. In particular, the overheads associated with SOA are still too high for rapid and flexible data integration, which are a prerequisite in the dynamic world of today's large enterprises.

We argue that classic SOA architectures are well suited for transaction processing, but more efficient technologies are available that can be deployed for solving the data integration challenge. Recent approaches, for example, consider ontology-based data integration, where ontologies are used to describe data, queries, and mappings between them [33]. The problems of ontology-based data integration are the required skills to develop the ontologies and the difficulty to model and capture the dynamics of the enterprise. A related, but slightly different approach is the use of the Linked Data paradigm for integrating enterprise data. Similarly, as the data web emerged complementing the document web, data intranets can complement the intranets and SOA landscapes currently found in large enterprises.

The acquisition of Freebase by Google and Powerset by Microsoft are the first indicators that large enterprises will not only use the Linked Data paradigm for the integration of their thousands of distributed information systems, but they will also aim at establishing Enterprise Knowledge Bases (EKB; similar to what Freebase now is for Google) as hubs and crystallization points for the vast amounts of structured data and knowledge distributed in their data intranets.

Examples of public LOD data sources being highly relevant for large enterprises are *OpenCorporates** (a knowledge base containing information about more than 50,000 corporations worldwide), *LinkedGeoData* [1] (a spatial knowledge base derived from OpenStreetMap containing precise information about all kinds of spatial features and entities) or *Product Ontology*[†]

---

* http://opencorporates.com/
† http://www.productontology.org/

(which comprises detailed classifications and information about more than 1 million products). For enterprises, tapping this vast, crowd-sourced knowledge that is freely available on the web is an amazing opportunity. However, it is crucial to assess the quality of such freely available knowledge, to complement and contrast it with additional nonpublic information being available to the enterprise (e.g., enterprise taxonomies, domain databases, etc.) and to actively manage the life cycle of both—the public and private data—being integrated and made available in an Enterprises data intranet.

In order to make large enterprises ready for the service economy, their IT infrastructure landscapes have to be made dramatically more flexible. Information and data have to be integrated with substantially reduced costs and in extremely short-time intervals. Mergers and acquisitions further accelerate the need for making IT systems more interoperable, adaptive, and flexible. Employing the Linked Data approach for establishing enterprise data intranets and knowledge bases will facilitate the digital innovation capabilities of large enterprises.

In this chapter, we explore the challenges large enterprises are still facing with regard to data integration. These include, but are not limited to, the development, management, and interlinking of enterprise taxonomies, domain databases, wikis, and other enterprise information sources (cf. "Challenges in Data Integration for Large Enterprises"). Employing the Linked Data paradigm to address these challenges might result in the emergence of enterprise Big Data intranets, where thousands of databases and information systems are connected and interlinked. Only a small part of the data sources in such an emerging Big Data intranet will actually be the Big Data itself. Many of them are rather small- or medium-sized data and knowledge bases. However, due to the large number of such sources, they will jointly reach a critical mass (volume). Also, we will observe on a data intranet a large semantic heterogeneity involving various schemas, vocabularies, ontologies, and taxonomies (variety). Finally, since Linked Data means directly publishing RDF from the original data representations, changes in source databases and information systems will be immediately visible on the data intranet and thus result in a constant evolution (velocity). Of particular importance in such a Big Data intranet setting is the creation of links between distributed data and knowledge bases within an enterprise's Big Data intranet. Consequently, we also discuss the requirements for linking and transforming enterprise data in depth (cf. "Linked Data Paradigm for Integrating Enterprise Data"). Owing to the number of linking targets to be considered and their size, the time efficiency of linking is a key issue in Big Data intranets. We thus present and study the complexity of the first reduction-ratio-optimal algorithm for link discovery (cf. "Runtime Complexity"). Moreover, we present an approach for reducing the discrepancy (i.e., improving the coherence) of data across knowledge bases (cf. "Discrepancy").

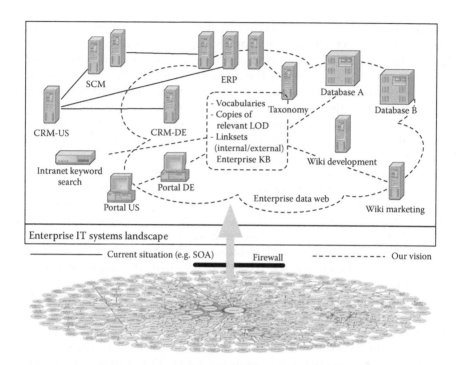

FIGURE 5.1
Our vision of an Enterprise Data Web (EDW). The solid lines show how IT systems may be
currently connected in a typical scenario. The dotted lines visualize how IT systems could be
interlinked employing an internal data cloud. The EDW also comprises an EKB, which consists
of vocabulary definitions, copies of relevant Linked Open Data, as well as internal and external
link sets between data sets. Data from the LOD cloud may be reused inside the enterprise, but
internal data are secured from external access just like in usual intranets.

The introductory section depicts our vision of an *Enterprise Data Web* and
the resulting semantically interlinked enterprise IT systems landscape (see
Figure 5.1). We expect existing enterprise taxonomies to be the nucleus of
linking and integration hubs in large enterprises, since these taxonomies
already reflect a large part of the domain terminology and corporate and
organizational culture. In order to transform enterprise taxonomies into
comprehensive EKBs, additional relevant data sets from the Linked Open
Data Web have to be integrated and linked with the internal taxonomies and
knowledge structures. Subsequently, the emerging EKB can be used (1) for
interlinking and annotating content in enterprise wikis, content management
systems, and portals; (2) as a stable set of reusable concepts and identifiers;
and (3) as the background knowledge for intranet, extranet, and site-search
applications. As a result, we expect the current document-oriented intranets
in large enterprises to be complemented with a data intranet, which facilitates the lightweight, semantic integration of the plethora of information systems and databases in large enterprises.

Challenges in Data Integration for Large Enterprises

We identified six crucial areas (Table 5.1) where data integration challenges arise in large enterprises. Figure 5.2 shows the Linked Data life cycle in conjunction with the aforementioned challenges. Each challenge may be related to a single or to multiple steps in the Linked Data life cycle.

Enterprise Taxonomies. Nowadays, almost every large enterprise uses taxonomies to provide a shared linguistic model aiming at structuring the large quantities of documents, emails, product descriptions, enterprise directives, etc. which are produced on a daily basis. Currently, terminology in large enterprises is managed in a centralized manner mostly by a dedicated and independently acting department (often referred to as *Corporate Language Management (CLM)*). CLM is in charge of standardizing all corporate terms both for internal and external uses. As a result, they create multiple dictionaries for different scopes that are not interconnected. An employee who aims at looking up a certain term needs to know which dictionary to use in that very context, as well as where to retrieve the currently approved version of it. The latter may not always be the case, especially for new employees. The former applies to all employees, since it might be unclear, which dictionary should be used, resulting in a complicated look-up procedure or worse the

TABLE 5.1

Overview of Data Integration Challenges Occurring in Large Enterprises

Information Integration Domain	Current State	Linked Data Benefit
Enterprise Taxonomies	Proprietary, centralized, no relationships between terms, multiple independent terminologies (dictionaries)	Open standards (e.g., SKOS), distributed, hierarchical, multilingual, reusable in other scenarios
XML Schema Governance	Multitude of XML schemas, no integrated documentation	Relationships between entities from different schemas, tracking/documentation of XML schema evolution
Wikis	Text-based wikis for teams or internal-use encyclopedias	Reuse of (structured) information via data wikis (by other applications), interlinking with other data sources, for example, taxonomies
Web Portal and Intranet Search	Keyword search over textual content	Sophisticated search mechanisms employing implicit knowledge from different data sources
Database Integration	Data warehouses, schema mediation, query federation	Lightweight data integration through RDF layer
Enterprise Single Sign-On	Consolidated user credentials, centralized SSO	No passwords, more sophisticated access control mechanisms (arbitrary metadata attached to identities)

FIGURE 5.2
Linked data life cycle supports four crucial data integration challenges arising in enterprise environments. Each of the challenges can relate to more than one lifecycle stage.

abandonment of a search at all. As a result, the main challenge in the area of enterprise taxonomies is defragmentation of term definitions without centralization of taxonomy management. We propose to represent enterprise taxonomies in RDF employing the standardized and widely used *SKOS* [17] vocabulary as well as publishing term definitions via the Linked Data principles.

XML Schema Governance. The majority of enterprises to date use XML for message exchange, data integration, publishing, and storage, often in a form of Web Services and XML databases. To be able to process XML documents efficiently, it need to be known what kind of data can be expected to find them. For this purpose, XML schemas should be presented for each XML format used. XML schemas describe the allowed structure of an XML document. Currently, there are four widespread languages for describing XML schemas: the oldest and the simplest DTD [3], the popular XML Schema [31], the increasingly used Relax NG [4], and the rule-based Schematron [12]. In a typical enterprise, there are hundreds or even thousands of XML schemas in use, each possibly written in a different XML schema language. Moreover, as the enterprise and its surrounding environment evolve, the schemas need to adapt. Therefore, new versions of schemas are created, resulting in a proliferation of XML schemas. *XML schema governance* now is the process of bringing order into the large number of XML schemas being generated and used within large organizations. The sheer number of IT systems deployed in large enterprises that make use of the XML technology bear a challenge in *bootstrapping and maintaining an XML schema repository*. In order to create such a repository, a bridge between XML schemata and RDF needs to be established. This requires in the first place the identification of XML schema resources and the respective entities that are defined by them. Some useful information can be extracted automatically from XML schema definitions that are available in a machine-readable format, such as XML schemas and DTDs. While this is probably given for systems that employ XML for information exchange, it may not always be the case in proprietary software systems that employ XML only for data storage. In the latter case as well as for maintaining additional metadata (such as responsible department, deployed IT systems, etc.), a substantial amount of manual work is required. In a second step, the identified schema metadata needs to be represented in RDF on a fine-grained level. The challenge here is the development of an ontology, which not only allows for the annotation of XML schemas, but also enables domain experts to establish *semantic relationships* between schemas. Another important challenge is to develop methods for capturing and describing the evolution of XML schemata, since IT systems change over time and those revisions need to be aligned with the remaining schemas.

Wikis. These have become increasingly common through the last years reaching from small personal wikis to the largest Internet encyclopedia Wikipedia. The same applies for the use of wikis in enterprises [16] too. In addition to traditional wikis, there is another category of wikis, which are called semantic wikis. These can again be divided into two categories: semantic text wikis and semantic data wikis. Wikis of this kind are not yet commonly used in enterprises, but crucial for enterprise data integration since they make (at least some of) the information contained in a wiki machine-accessible. Text-based semantic wikis are conventional wikis (where text is still the main content type), which allow users to add some semantic annotations to the texts (e.g., typed links). The semantically enriched content can then be used within the wiki itself (e.g., for dynamically created wiki pages) or can be queried, when the structured data are stored in a separate data store. An example is Semantic MediaWiki [14] and its enterprise counterpart SMW+ [25]. Since wikis in large enterprises are still a quite new phenomenon, the deployment of data wikis instead of or in addition to text wikis will relatively be easy to tackle. A challenge, however, is to train the users of such wikis to actually create semantically enriched information. For example, the value of a fact can either be represented as a plain literal or as a relation to another information resource. In the latter case, the target of the relation can be identified either by a newly generated URI or one that was introduced before (eventually already attached with some metadata). The more the users are urged to reuse information wherever appropriate, the more all the participants can benefit from the data. It should be part of the design of the wiki application (especially the user interface), to make it easy for users to build quality knowledge bases (e.g., through autosuggestion of URIs within authoring widgets). Data in RDF are represented in the form of simple statements, information that naturally is intended to be stored in conjunction (e.g., geographical coordinates) is not visible as such *per se*. The same applies for information which users are accustomed to edit in a certain order (e.g., address data). A nonrational editing workflow, where the end-users are confronted with a random list of property values, may result in invalid or incomplete information. The challenge here is to develop a *choreography of authoring widgets* in order to provide users with a more logical editing workflow. Another defiance to tackle is to make the deployed wiki systems available to as many stakeholders as possible (i.e., cross department boundaries) to allow for an improved information reuse. Once Linked Data resources and potentially attached information are reused (e.g., by importing such data), it becomes crucial to keep them in synchronization with the original source. Therefore, mechanisms for *syndication* (i.e., propagation of changes) and *synchronization* need to be developed, both for intra- and extranet semantic wiki resources. Finally, it is also necessary to consider access control in this context. Semantic representations contain implicit information, which can be revealed by inferencing and reasoning. A challenge is to develop and deploy scalable access control mechanisms, which are aligned with existing access control policies in the enterprise and which are safe with regard to the hijacking of ontologies [10].

Web Portal and Intranet Search. The biggest problem with enterprise intranets today is the huge difference in user experience when compared to the Internet [18]. When using the Internet, the user is spoiled by modern technologies from, for example, Google or Facebook, which provide very comfortable environments, precise search results, auto-complete text boxes, etc. These technologies are made possible through large amounts of resources invested in providing comfort for the millions of users, customers, beta testers, and by their large development team and also by the huge number of documents available, which increases the chances that a user will find what he is looking for. In contrast, in most enterprises, the intranet experience is often poor because the intranet uses technologies from the previous millennium. In order to implement search systems that are based on a Linked Data approach and that provide a substantial benefit in comparison with traditional search applications, the challenge of *bootstrapping an initial set of high-quality RDF datasources* needs to be tackled first. For example, as a prerequisite for linking documents to terms a hierarchical taxonomy should be created (see "Challenges in Data Integration for Large Enterprises"). Mechanisms then need to be established to automatically create high-quality links between documents and an initial set of terms (e.g., by crawling), since it is not feasible to manually link the massive amount of available documents. Furthermore, the process of semi-automatic linking of (a) terms that occur in documents but are not part of the taxonomy yet (as well as their placement in the taxonomy) and (b) terms that do not occur in documents but are related and thus useful in a search needs to be investigated and suitable tools should be developed to support responsible employees. To provide results beyond those that can be obtained from text-based documents directly, other data sets need to be transformed to RDF and queried. Finally, although a search engine that queries RDF data directly works, it results in suboptimal performance. The challenge here is to develop methods for improving performance to match traditional search engines, while keeping the advantages of using SPARQL directly. In an enterprise there exist at least two distinct areas where search technology needs to be applied. On the one hand, there is corporate internal search, which enables employees to find relevant information required for their work. On the other hand, all large enterprises need at least simple search capabilities on their public web portal(s), since otherwise the huge amounts of information provided may not be reachable for potential customers. Some dedicated companies (e.g., automotive companies) would actually have a need for more sophisticated query capabilities, since the complexity of offered products is very high. Nevertheless, in reality, search, both internal and external, is often solely based on keyword matching. We argue that by employing the Linked Data paradigm in enterprises the classical keyword-based search can be enhanced. Additionally, more sophisticated search mechanisms can be easily realized since more information is available in a uniform and machine-processable format.

Database Integration. Relational Database Management Systems (RDBMS) are the predominant mode of data storage in the enterprise context. RDBMS are used practically everywhere in the enterprise, serving, for example, in computer-aided manufacturing, enterprise resource planning, supply chain management, and content management systems. We, therefore, deem the integration of relation data into Linked Data a crucial Enterprise Data Integration technique. A primary concern when integrating relational data is the *scalability and query performance*. With our R2RML-based tool *SparqlMap*,* we show that an efficient query translation is possible, thus avoiding the higher deployment costs associated with the data duplication inherent in ETL approaches. The challenge of closing the gap between triple stores and relational databases is also present in SPARQL-to-SQL mappers and drives research. A second challenge for mapping relational data into RDF is a current lack of best practices

---

* http://aksw.org/Projects/SparqlMap

and *tool support for mapping creation*. The standardization of the *RDB to RDF Mapping Language* (R2RML) by the W3C RDB2RDF Working Group establishes a common ground for an interoperable ecosystem of tools. However, there is a lack of mature tools for the creation and application of R2RML mappings. The challenge lies in the creation of user-friendly interfaces and in the establishment of best practices for creating, integrating, and maintaining those mappings. Finally, for a *read–write integration* updates on the mapped data need to be propagated back into the underlying RDBMS. An initial solution is presented in [5]. In the context of enterprise data, an integration with *granular access control* mechanisms is of vital importance. Consequently, semantic wikis, query federation tools, and interlinking tools can work with the data of relation databases. The usage of SPARQL 1.1 query federation [26] allows relational databases to be integrated into query federation systems with queries spanning over multiple databases. This federation allows, for example, portals, which in combination with an EKB provide an integrated view on enterprise data.

Enterprise Single Sign-On. As a result of the large number of deployed software applications in large enterprises, which are increasingly web-based, *single sign-on* (SSO) solutions are of crucial importance. A Linked Data-based approach aimed at tackling the SSO problem is WebID [30]. In order to deploy a WebID-based SSO solution in large enterprises, a first challenge is to *transfer user identities* to the Enterprise Data Web. Those Linked Data identities need to be enriched and interlinked with further background knowledge, while maintaining privacy. Thus, mechanisms need to be developed to assure that only such information is publicly (i.e., public inside the corporation) available, that is required for the authentication protocol. Another challenge that arises is related to *user management*. With WebID a distributed management of identities is feasible (e.g., on department level), while those identities could still be used throughout the company. Though this reduces the likeliness of a single point of failure, it would require the introduction of mechanisms to ensure that company-wide policies are enforced. Distributed group management and authorization is already a research topic (e.g., *dgFOAF* [27]) in the area of social networks. However, requirements that are gathered from distributed social network use-cases differ from those captured from enterprise use-cases. Thus, social network solutions need a critical inspection in the enterprise context.

Linked Data Paradigm for Integrating Enterprise Data

Addressing the challenges from the previous section leads to the creation of a number of knowledge bases that populate a data intranet. Still, for this intranet to abide by the vision of Linked Data while serving the purpose of companies, we need to increase its coherence and establish links between the data sets. Complex applications that rely on several sources of knowledge usually integrate them into a unified view by the means of the extract-trans-form-load (ETL) paradigm [13]. For example, IBM's DeepQA framework [8] combines knowledge from DBpedia,* Freebase,† and several other knowledge bases to determine the answer to questions with a speed superior to that of human champions. A similar view to data integration can be taken within the Linked Data paradigm with the main difference that the load step can be discarded when the knowledge bases are not meant to be fused, which is mostly the case. While the extraction was addressed above, the transfor-mation remains a complex challenge and has currently not yet been much addressed in the enterprise context. The specification of this integration pro-cesses for Linked Data is rendered tedious by several factors, including

1. A great number of knowledge bases (*scalability*) as well as
2. The Schema mismatches and heterogeneous conventions for prop-erty values across knowledge bases (*discrepancy*)

Similar issues are found in the Linked Open Data (LOD) Cloud, which con-sists of more than 30 billion triples‡ distributed across more than 250 knowl-edge bases. In the following, we will use the Linked Open Data Cloud as reference implementation of the Linked Data principles and present semi-automatic means that aim to ensure high-quality Linked Data Integration.

The scalability of Linked Data Integration has been addressed in manifold previous works on link discovery. Especially, Link Discovery frameworks such as LIMES [21–23] as well as time-efficient algorithms such as PPJoin+ [34] have been designed to address this challenge. Yet, none of these manifold approaches provides theoretical guarantees with respect to their performance. Thus, so far, it was impossible to predict how Link Discovery frameworks would perform with respect to time or space requirements. Consequently, the deployment of techniques such as customized memory management [2] or time-optimization strategies [32] (e.g., automated scaling for cloud computing when provided with very complex linking tasks) was rendered very demanding if not impossible. A novel approach that addresses these drawbacks is the $\mathcal{HR}^3$ algorithm [20]. Similar to the HYPPO algorithm [22] (on whose formalism it is based), $\mathcal{HR}^3$ assumes that the property values that are to be compared are expressed in an affine space with a Minkowski distance. Consequently, it can be most naturally used to process the portion of link specifications that compare numeric values (e.g., temperatures, elevations, populations, etc.). $\mathcal{HR}^3$ goes beyond the state of the art by being able to carry out Link Discovery tasks with *any achievable reduc-tion ratio* [6]. This theoretical guarantee is of practical importance, as it does not only allow our approach to be more time-efficient than the state of the art

---

* http://dbpedia.org
† http://www.freebase.com
‡ http://www4.wiwiss.fu-berlin.de/lodcloud/state/

but also lays the foundation for the implementation of customized memory management and time-optimization strategies for Link Discovery.

The difficulties behind the integration of Linked Data are not only caused by the mere growth of the data sets in the Linked Data Web, but also by large number of discrepancies across these data sets. In particular, ontology mismatches [7] affect mostly the extraction step of the ETL process. They occur when different classes or properties are used in the source knowledge bases to express equivalent knowledge (with respect to the extraction process at hand). For example, while Sider* uses the class `sider:side_effects` to represent diseases that can occur as a side effect of the intake of certain medication, the more generic knowledge base DBpedia uses `dbpedia:Disease`. Such a mismatch can lead to a knowledge base that integrates DBpedia and Sider containing duplicate classes. The same type of mismatch also occurs at the property level. For example, while Eunis[†] uses the property `eunis:binomialName` to represent the labels of species, DBpedia uses `rdfs:label`. Thus, even if the extraction problem was resolved at class level, integrating Eunis and DBpedia would still lead to the undesirable constellation of an integrated knowledge base where instances of species would have two properties that serve as labels. The second category of common mismatches mostly affects the transformation step of ETL and lies in the different conventions used for equivalent property values. For example, the labels of films in DBpedia differ from the labels of films in LinkedMDB[‡] in three ways: First, they contain a language tag. Second, the extension "(film)" if another entity with the same label exists. Third, if another film with the same label exists, the production year of the film is added. Consequently, the film `Liberty` from 1929 has the label "Liberty (1929 film)@en" in DBpedia, while the same film bears the label "Liberty" in LinkedMDB. A similar discrepancy in naming persons holds for film directors (e.g., `John Frankenheimer` (DBpedia: John Frankenheimer@ en, LinkedMDB: John Frankenheimer (Director)) and `John Ford` (DBpedia: John Ford@en, LinkedMDB: John Ford (Director))) and actors. Finding a conform representation of the labels of movies that maps the LinkedMDB representation would require knowing the rules replace("@en", ε) and replace("(*film)", ε), where ε stands for the empty string.

Runtime Complexity

The development of scalable algorithms for link discovery is of crucial importance to address for the Big Data problems that enterprises are increasingly faced with. While the variety of the data is addressed by the extraction

---

* http://sideeffects.embl.de/

† http://eunis.eea.europa.eu/

‡ http://linkedmdb.org/

processes presented in the sections above, the mere volume of the data makes it necessary to have single linking tasks carried out as efficiently as possible. Moreover, the velocity of the data requires that link discovery is carried out on a regular basis. These requirements were the basis for the development of $\mathcal{HR}^3$ [20], the first reduction-ratio-optimal link discovery algorithm. In the following, we present and evaluate this approach.

Preliminaries

In this section, we present the preliminaries necessary to understand the subsequent parts of this section. In particular, we define the problem of Link Discovery, the reduction ratio, and the relative reduction ratio formally as well as give an overview of space tiling for Link Discovery. The subsequent description of $\mathcal{HR}^3$ relies partly on the notation presented in this section.

Link Discovery. The goal of Link Discovery is to compute the set of pair of instances $(s, t) \in S \times T$ that are related by a relation R, where S and T are two not necessarily distinct sets of instances. One way of automating this discovery is to compare $s \in S$ and $t \in T$ based on their properties using a distance measure. Two entities are then considered to be linked via R if their distance is less or equal to a threshold θ [23].

Definition 1: Link Discovery on Distances

Given two sets S and T of instances, a distance measure δ over the properties of $s \in S$ and $t \in T$ and a distance threshold $\theta \in [0, \infty[$, *the goal of Link Discovery is to compute the set $M = \{(s, t, \delta(s, t)): s \in S \land t \in T \land \delta(s, t) \leq \theta\}$*

Note that in this paper, we are only interested in lossless solutions, that is, solutions that are able to find all pairs that abide by the definition given above.

Reduction Ratio. A brute-force approach to Link Discovery would execute a Link Discovery task on S and T by carrying out $|S \| T|$ comparisons. One of the key ideas behind time-efficient Link Discovery algorithms $\mathcal{A}$ is to reduce the number of comparisons that are effectively carried out to a number $C(\mathcal{A}) < |S \| T|$ [29]. The reduction ratio RR of an algorithm $\mathcal{A}$ is given by

$$RR(\mathcal{A}) = 1 - \frac{C(\mathcal{A})}{|S \| T|}. \tag{5.1}$$

$RR(\mathcal{A})$ captures how much of the Cartesian product $|S \| T|$ was not explored before the output of $\mathcal{A}$ was reached. It is obvious that even an optimal lossless solution which performs only the necessary comparisons cannot achieve an RR of 1. Let C_{min} be the minimal number of comparisons necessary to complete the Link Discovery task without losing recall, that is, $C_{min} = |\mathcal{M}|$. We define the relative reduction ratio $RRR(\mathcal{A})$ as the proportion of the minimal number of comparisons that was carried out by the algorithm $\mathcal{A}$ before it terminated. Formally,

$$RRR(\mathcal{A}) = \frac{1-(C_{min}/\mid S \parallel T \mid)}{1-(C(\mathcal{A})/\mid S \parallel T \mid)} = \frac{\mid S \parallel T \mid -C_{min}}{\mid S \parallel T \mid -C(\mathcal{A})}. \qquad (5.2)$$

$RRR(\mathcal{A})$ indicates how close $\mathcal{A}$ is to the optimal solution with respect to the number of candidates it tests. Given that $C(\mathcal{A}) \geq C_{min}$, $RRR(\mathcal{A}) \geq 1$. Note that the larger the value of $RRR(\mathcal{A})$, the poorer the performance of $\mathcal{A}$ with respect to the task at hand.

The main observation that led to this work is that while most algorithms aim to optimize their RR (and consequently their RRR), current approaches to Link Discovery do not provide any guarantee with respect to the RR (and consequently the RRR) that they can achieve. In this work, we present an approach to Link Discovery in metric spaces whose RRR is guaranteed to converge to 1.

Space Tiling for Link Discovery. Our approach, $\mathcal{HR}^3$, builds upon the same formalism on which the HYPPO algorithm relies, that is, space tiling. HYPPO addresses the problem of efficiently mapping instance pairs $(s, t) \in S \times T$ described by using exclusively numeric values in an n-dimensional metric space and has been shown to outperform the state of the art in the previous work [22]. The observation behind space tiling is that in spaces (Ω, δ) with orthogonal (i.e., uncorrelated) dimensions,* common metrics for Link Discovery can be decomposed into the combination of functions $\phi_{i,i\in\{1...n\}}$, which operate on exactly one dimension of Ω: $\delta = f(\phi_1,...,\phi_n)$. For Minkowski distances of order p, $\phi_i(x, \omega) = \mid x_i - \omega_i \mid$ for all values of i and

$$\delta(x,\omega) = \sqrt[p]{\sum_{i=1}^{n} \phi_i^p(x,\omega)^p} \;.$$

A direct consequence of this observation is the inequality $\phi_i(x,\omega) \leq \delta$ (x, ω). The basic insight into this observation is that the hypersphere $H(\omega, \theta) = \{x \in \Omega : \delta(x, \omega) \leq \theta\}$ is a subset of the hypercube V defined as $V(\omega, \theta) = \{x \in \Omega : \forall i \in \{1...n\}, \phi_i(x_i, \omega_i) \leq \theta\}$. Consequently, one can reduce the number of comparisons necessary to detect all elements of $H(\omega, \theta)$ by discarding all elements that are not in $V(\omega, \theta)$ as nonmatches. Let $\Delta = \theta/\alpha$, where $\alpha \in \mathbb{N}$ is the *granularity parameter* that controls how fine-grained the space tiling should be (see Figure 5.3 for an example). We first tile Ω into the adjacent hypercubes (short: cubes) C that contain all the points ω such that

$$\forall i \in \{1...n\}, c_i \Delta \leq \omega_i < (c_i + 1)\Delta \quad \text{with } (c_1,...,c_n) \in \mathbb{N}^n. \qquad (5.3)$$

We call the vector $(c_1, ..., c_n)$ the coordinates of the cube C. Each point $\omega \in \Omega$ lies in the cube $C(\omega)$ with coordinates $(\lfloor \omega_i/\Delta \rfloor)_{i=1...n}$. Given such a space

---

* Note that in all cases, a space transformation exists that can map a space with correlated dimensions to a space with uncorrelated dimensions.

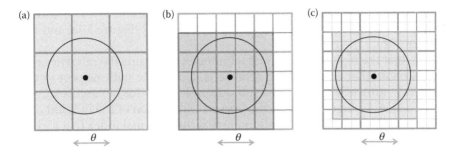

FIGURE 5.3
Space tiling for different values of α. The colored squares show the set of elements that must be compared with the instance located at the black dot. The points within the circle lie within the distance θ of the black dot. Note that higher values of α lead to a better approximation of the hypersphere but also to more hypercubes.

tiling, it is obvious that $V(\omega,\theta)$ consists of the union of the cubes such that $\forall i \in \{1,\ldots,n\} : |c_i - c(\omega)_i| \le \alpha$.

Like most of the current algorithms for Link Discovery, space tiling does not provide optimal performance guarantees. The main goal of this paper is to build upon the tiling idea so as to develop an algorithm that can achieve any possible RR. In the following, we present such an algorithm, $\mathcal{HR}^3$.

The $\mathcal{HR}^3$ Algorithm

The goal of the $\mathcal{HR}^3$ algorithm is to efficiently map instance pairs $(s, t) \in S \times T$ that are described by using exclusively numeric values in an n-dimensional metric space where the distances are measured by using any Minkowski distance of order $p \ge 2$. To achieve this goal, $\mathcal{HR}^3$ relies on a *novel indexing scheme* that allows achieving any RRR greater than or equal to than 1. In the following, we first present our new indexing scheme and show that we can discard more hypercubes than simple space tiling for all granularities α such that $n(\alpha - 1)^p > \alpha^p$. We then prove that by these means, our approach can achieve any RRR greater than 1, therewith proving the *optimality of our indexing scheme* with respect to RRR.

Indexing Scheme

Let $\omega \in \Omega = S \cup T$ be an arbitrary reference point. Furthermore, let δ be the Minkowski distance of order p. We define the *index* function as follows:

$$\text{index}(C,\omega) = \begin{cases} 0 & \text{if } \exists i : |c_i - c(\omega)_i| \le 1 \quad \text{with } i \in \{1,\ldots,n\}, \\ \displaystyle\sum_{i=1}^{n} (|c_i - c(\omega)_i| - 1)^p & \text{else,} \end{cases}$$

$$(5.4)$$

where C is a hypercube resulting from a space tiling and $\omega \in \Omega$. Figure 5.4 shows an example of such indices for $p = 2$ with $\alpha = 2$ (Figure 5.4a) and $\alpha = 4$ (Figure 5.4b).

Note that the highlighted square with index 0 contains the reference point ω. Also note that our indexing scheme is symmetric with respect to $C(\omega)$. Thus, it is sufficient to prove the subsequent lemmas for hypercubes C such that $c_i > c(\omega)_i$. In Figure 5.4, it is the upper right portion of the indexed space with the gray background. Finally, note that the maximal index that a hypercube can achieve is $n(\alpha - 1)^p$ as $\max |c_i - c_i(\omega)| = \alpha$ per construction of $H(\omega, \theta)$.

The indexing scheme proposed above guarantees the following:

Lemma 1

$Index(C, \omega) = x \rightarrow \forall s \in C(\omega), \forall t \in C, \delta^p(s,t) > x\Delta^p.$

Proof

This lemma is a direct implication of the construction of the index. $Index(C, \omega) = x$ implies that

$$\sum_{i=1}^{n} (c_i - c(\omega)_i - 1)^p = x.$$

Now given the definition of the coordinates of a cube (Equation (5.3)), the following holds:

$$\forall s \in C(\omega), \forall t \in C, \quad |s_i - t_i| \geq (|c_i - c(\omega)_i| - 1)\Delta.$$

Consequently,

$$\forall s \in C(\omega), \forall t \in C, \quad \sum_{i=1}^{n} |s_i - t_i|^p \geq \sum_{i=1}^{n} (|c_i - c(\omega)_i| - 1)^p \Delta^p.$$

By applying the definition of the Minkowski distance of the index function, we finally obtained $\forall s \in C(\omega), \forall t \in C, \delta^p(s,t) > x\Delta^p$

Note that given that $\omega \in C(\omega)$, the following also holds:

$$index(C, \omega) = x \rightarrow \forall t \in C : \delta^p(\omega, t) > x\Delta^p. \tag{5.5}$$

Approach

The main insight behind $\mathcal{HR}^3$ is that in spaces with Minkowski distances, the indexing scheme proposed above allows one to safely (i.e., without

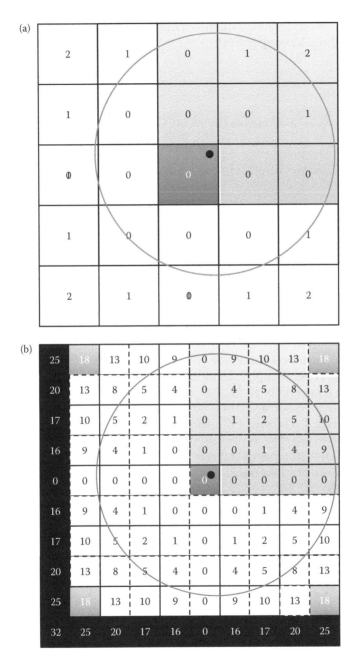

FIGURE 5.4
Space tiling and resulting index for a two-dimensional example. Note that the index in both subfigures was generated for exactly the same portion of space. The black dot stands for the position of ω.

dismissing correct matches) discard more hypercubes than when using simple space tiling. More specifically,

Lemma 2

$\forall s \in S : index(C,s) > \alpha^p$ implies that all $t \in C$ are nonmatches.

Proof

This lemma follows directly from Lemma 1 as

$$index(C,s) > \alpha^p \rightarrow \forall t \in C, \delta^p(s,t) > \Delta^p \alpha^p = \theta^p. \tag{5.6}$$

For the purpose of illustration, let us consider the example of $\alpha = 4$ and $p = 2$ in the two-dimensional case displayed in Figure 5.4b. Lemma 2 implies that any point contained in a hypercube C_{18} with index 18 cannot contain any element t such that $\delta(s, t) \leq \theta$. While space tiling would discard all black cubes in Figure 5.4b but include the elements of C_{18} as candidates, $\mathcal{HR}^3$ discards them and still computes exactly the same results, yet with a better (i.e., smaller) RRR.

One of the direct consequences of Lemma 2 is that $n(\alpha - 1)^p > \alpha^p$ is a necessary and sufficient condition for $\mathcal{HR}^3$ to achieve a better RRR than simple space tiling. This is simply due to the fact that the largest index that can be assigned to a hypercube is $\sum_{i=1}^{n}(\alpha - 1)^p = n(\alpha - 1)^p$. Now, if $n(\alpha - 1)^p > \alpha^p$, then this cube can be discarded. For $p = 2$ and $n = 2$, for example, this condition is satisfied for $\alpha \geq 4$. Knowing this inequality is of great importance when deciding on when to use $\mathcal{HR}^3$ as discussed in the "Evaluation" section.

Let $\mathcal{H}(\alpha,\omega) = \{C : index(C,\omega) \leq \alpha^p\}$. $\mathcal{H}(\alpha, \omega)$ is the approximation of the hypersphere $H(\omega) = \{\omega':\delta(\omega,\omega') \leq \theta\}$ generated by $\mathcal{HR}^3$. We define the volume of $\mathcal{H}(\alpha, \omega)$ as

$$V(\mathcal{H}(\alpha,\omega)) = |\mathcal{H}(\alpha,\omega)| \Delta^p. \tag{5.7}$$

To show that given any $r > 1$, the approximation $\mathcal{H}(\alpha, \omega)$ can always achieve an RRR($\mathcal{HR}^3$) $\leq r$, we need to show the following.

Lemma 3

$\lim_{\alpha \to \infty} RRR(\mathcal{HR}^3, \alpha) = 1.$

Proof

The cubes that are not discarded by $\mathcal{HR}^3(\alpha)$ are those for which $(|c_i - c_i(\omega)| - 1)$ $^p \leq \alpha^p$. When $\alpha \to \infty$, Δ becomes infinitesimally small, leading to the cubes being single points. Each cube C thus contains a single point x with coordinates $x_i = c_i \Delta$. Especially, $c_i(\omega) = \omega$. Consequently,

$$\sum_{i=1}^{n} (|c_i - c_i(\omega)| - 1)^p \leq \alpha^p \leftrightarrow \sum_{i=1}^{n} \left(\frac{|x_i - \omega_i| - \Delta}{\Delta} \right)^p \leq \alpha^p. \tag{5.8}$$

Given that $\theta = \Delta\alpha$, we obtain

$$\sum_{i=1}^{n} \left(\frac{|x_i - \omega_i| - \Delta}{\Delta} \right)^p \leq \alpha^p \leftrightarrow \sum_{i=1}^{n} (|x_i - \omega_i| - \Delta)^p \leq \theta^p. \tag{5.9}$$

Finally, $\Delta \to 0$ when $\alpha \to \infty$ leads to

$$\sum_{i=1}^{n} (|x_i - \omega_i| - \Delta)^p \leq \theta^p \wedge \alpha \to \infty \to \sum_{i=1}^{n} |x_i - \omega_i|^p \leq \theta^p. \tag{5.10}$$

This is exactly the condition for linking specified in Definition 1 applied to Minkowski distances of order p. Consequently, $\mathcal{H}(\omega,\infty)$ is exactly $H(\omega, \theta)$ for any θ. Thus, the number of comparisons carried out by $\mathcal{HR}^3$ (α) when $\alpha \to \infty$ is exactly C_{min}, which leads to the conclusion $\lim_{\alpha \to \infty} RRR(\mathcal{HR}^3, \alpha) = 1$.

Our conclusion is illustrated in Figure 5.5, which shows the approximations computed by $\mathcal{HR}^3$ for different values of α with $p = 2$ and $n = 2$. The higher the α, the closer the approximation is to a circle. Note that these results allow one to conclude that for any RRR-value r larger than 1, there is a setting of $\mathcal{HR}^3$ that can compute links with a RRR smaller or equal to r.

Evaluation

In this section, we present the data and hardware we used to evaluate our approach. Thereafter, we present and discuss our results.

Experimental Setup

We carried out four experiments to compare $\mathcal{HR}^3$ with LIMES 0.5's HYPPO and SILK 2.5.1. In the first and second experiments, we aimed to deduplicate DBpedia places by comparing their names (`rdfs:label`), minimum elevation, elevation, and maximum elevation. We retrieved 2988 entities that possessed all four properties. We use the Euclidean metric on the last three values with the thresholds 49 and 99 m for the first and second experiments, respectively. The third and fourth experiments aimed to discover links between Geonames and LinkedGeoData. Here, we compared the labels (`rdfs:label`), longitude,

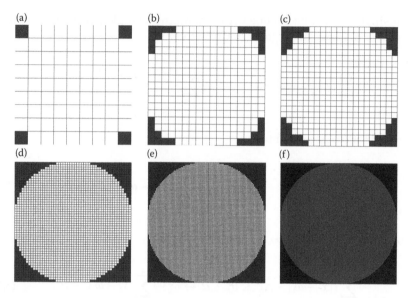

FIGURE 5.5

Approximation generated by $\mathcal{HR}^3$ for different values of α. The white squares are selected, whilst the colored ones are discarded. (a) $\alpha = 4$, (b) $\alpha = 8$, (c) $\alpha = 10$, (d) $\alpha = 25$, (e) $\alpha = 50$, and (f) $\alpha = 100$.

and latitude of the instances. This experiment was of considerably larger scale than the first one, as we compared 74,458 entities in Geonames with 50,031 entities from LinkedGeoData. Again, we measured the runtime necessary to compare the numeric values when comparing them by using the Euclidean metric. We set the distance thresholds to 1 and 9° in experiments 3 and 4, respectively. We ran all experiments on the same Windows 7 Enterprise 64-bit computer with a 2.8 GHz i7 processor with 8 GB RAM. The JVM was allocated 7 GB RAM to ensure that the runtimes were not influenced by swapping. Only one of the kernels of the processors was used. Furthermore, we ran each of the experiments three times and report the best runtimes in the following.

Results

We first measured the number of comparisons required by HYPPO and $\mathcal{HR}^3$ to complete the tasks at hand (see Figure 5.6). Note that we could not carry out this section of evaluation for SILK 2.5.1 as it would have required altering the code of the framework. In the experiments 1, 3, and 4, $\mathcal{HR}^3$ can reduce the overhead in comparisons (i.e., the number of unnecessary comparisons divided by the number of necessary comparisons) from approximately 24% for HYPPO to approximately 6% (granularity = 32). In experiment 2, the overhead is reduced from 4.1 to 2%. This difference in overhead reduction is mainly due to the data clustering around certain values and the clusters having a radius between 49 and 99 m. Thus, running the algorithms with a threshold of 99 m led to only a small *a priori* overhead and HYPPO performing remarkably well. Still, even on such data distributions, $\mathcal{HR}^3$ was able to discard even more data and to reduce the number of unnecessary computations by more than 50% relative. In the best case (experiment 4, $\alpha = 32$, see Figure 5.6d), $\mathcal{HR}^3$ required approximately 4.13×10^6 less comparisons than HYPPO for $\alpha = 32$. Even for the smallest setting (experiment 1, see Figure 5.6a), $\mathcal{HR}^3$ still required 0.64×10^6 less comparisons.

We also measured the runtimes of SILK, HYPPO, and $\mathcal{HR}^3$. The best runtimes of the three algorithms for each of the tasks is reported in Figure 5.7. Note that SILK's runtimes were measured without the indexing time, as the data fetching and indexing are merged to one process in SILK. Also note that in the second experiment, SILK did not terminate due to higher memory requirements. We approximated SILK's runtime by extrapolating approximately 11 min it required for 8.6% of the computation before the RAM was filled. Again, we did not consider the indexing time.

Because of the considerable difference in runtime (approximately two orders of magnitude) between HYPPO and SILK, we report solely HYPPO and $\mathcal{HR}^3$'s runtimes in the detailed runtimes Figures 5.8a,b. Overall, $\mathcal{HR}^3$ outperformed the other two approaches in all experiments, especially for $\alpha = 4$. It is important to note that the improvement in runtime increases with the complexity of the experiment. For example, while $\mathcal{HR}^3$ outperforms HYPPO by 3% in the second experiment, the difference grows to more than 7% in the fourth experiment. In addition, the improvement in runtime augments with the threshold. This can be seen in the third and fourth experiments. While $\mathcal{HR}^3$ is less than 2% faster in the third experiment, it is more than 7% faster when $\theta = 4$ in the fourth experiment. As expected, $\mathcal{HR}^3$ is slower than HYPPO for $\alpha < 4$ as it carries out exactly the same comparisons but still has the overhead of computing the index. Yet, given that we know that $\mathcal{HR}^3$ is only better when $n(\alpha - 1)^p > \alpha^p$, our implementation only carries out the indexing when this inequality holds. By these means, we can ensure that $\mathcal{HR}^3$ is only used when it is able to discard hypercubes that HYPPO would not discard, therewith reaching superior runtimes both with small and large values α. Note that the difference between the improvement of the number of comparisons necessitated by $\mathcal{HR}^3$ and the improvement in runtime over all experiments is due to the supplementary indexing step required by $\mathcal{HR}^3$.

Finally, we measured the RRR of both $\mathcal{HR}^3$ and HYPPO (see Figures 5.8c and d). In the two-dimensional experiments 3 and 4, HYPPO achieves an RRR close to 1. Yet, it is still outperformed by $\mathcal{HR}^3$ as expected. A larger difference between the RRR of $\mathcal{HR}^3$ and HYPPO can be seen in the three-dimensional experiments, where the RRR of both algorithms diverge significantly. Note that the RRR difference grows not only with the number of dimensions, but also with the size of the problem. The difference in RRR between HYPPO and $\mathcal{HR}^3$ does not always reflect the difference in runtime due to the indexing overhead of $\mathcal{HR}^3$. Still, for $\alpha = 4$, $\mathcal{HR}^3$ generates a sufficient balance of

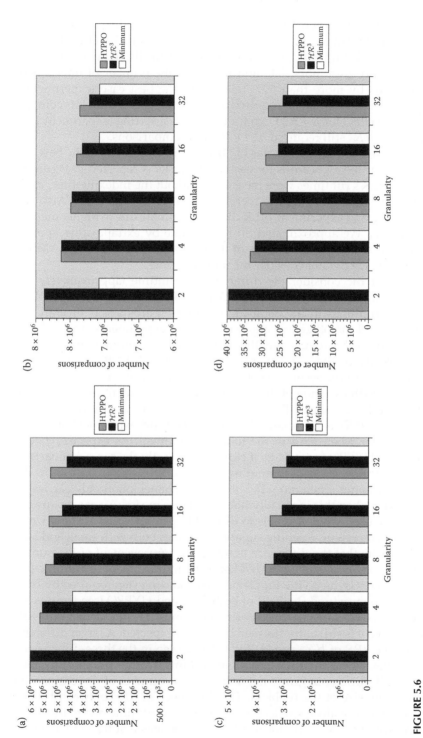

FIGURE 5.6
Number of comparisons for $\mathcal{HR}^3$ and HYPPO.

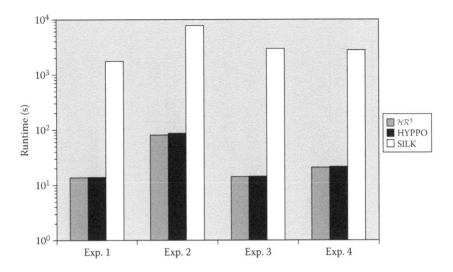

FIGURE 5.7
Comparison of the runtimes of $\mathcal{HR}^3$, HYPPO, and SILK 2.5.1.

indexing runtime and comparison runtime (i.e., RRR) to outperform HYPPO in all experiments.

Discrepancy

In this section, we address the lack of coherence that comes about when integrating data from several knowledge data and using them within one application. Here, we present CaRLA, the *Canonical Representation Learning Algorithm* [19]. This approach addresses the discrepancy problem by learning canonical (also called conform) representation of data-type property values. To achieve this goal, CaRLA implements a simple, time-efficient, and accurate learning approach. We present two versions of CaRLA: a batch learning and an active learning version. The batch learning approach relies on a training data set to derive rules that can be used to generate conform representations of property values. The active version of CaRLA (aCarLa) extends CaRLA by computing unsure rules and retrieving highly informative candidates for annotation that allow one to validate or negate these candidates. One of the main advantages of CaRLA is that it can be configured to learn transformations at character, *n*-gram, or even word level. By these means, it can be used to improve integration and link discovery processes based on string similarity/distance measures ranging from character-based (edit distance) and *n*-gram-based (*q*-grams) to word-based (Jaccard similarity) approaches.

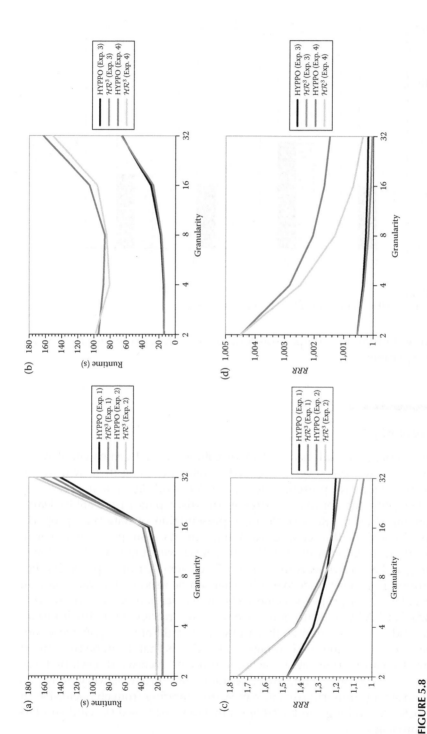

FIGURE 5.8
Comparison of runtimes and RRR of $\mathcal{HR}^3$ and HYPPO. (a) Runtimes for experiments 1 and 2, (b) runtimes for experiments 3 and 4, (c) RRR for experiments 1 and 2, and (d) RRR for experiments 3 and 4.

Preliminaries

In the following, we define terms and notation necessary to formalize the approach implemented by CaRLA. Let $s \in \Sigma^*$ be a string from an alphabet Σ. We define a tokenization function as follows:

Definition 2: Tokenization Function

Given an alphabet A of tokens, a tokenization function token: $\Sigma^* \to 2^A$ maps any string $s \in \Sigma^*$ to a subset of the token alphabet A.

Note that string similarity and distance measures rely on a large number of different tokenization approaches. For example, the Levenshtein similarity [15] relies on a tokenization at character level, while the Jaccard similarity [11] relies on a tokenization at word level.

Definition 3: Transformation Rule

A transformation rule is a function $r: A \to A$ that maps a token from the alphabet A to another token of A.

In the following, we will denote transform rules by using an arrow notation. For example, the mapping of the token "Alan" to "A." will be denoted by <"Alan" → "A." >. For any rule $r = <x \to y>$, we call x the *premise* and y the *consequence* of r. We call a transformation rule *trivial* when it is of the form $<x \to x>$ with $x \in A$. We call two transformation rules r and r' *inverse* to each other when $r = <x \to y>$ and $r' = <y \to x>$. Throughout this work, we will assume that the characters that make up the tokens of A belong to $\Sigma \cup \{\varepsilon\}$, where ε stands for the empty character. Note that we will consequently denote deletions by rules of the form $<x \to \varepsilon>$, where $x \in A$.

Definition 4: Weighted Transformation Rule

Let Γ be the set of all rules. Given a weight function $w: \Gamma \to \mathbb{R}$, a weighted transformation rule is the pair $(r, w(r))$, where $r \in \Gamma$ is a transformation rule.

Definition 5: Transformation Function

Given a set R of (weighted) transformation rules and a string s, we call the function $\varphi_R: \Sigma^* \to \Sigma^* \cup \{\varepsilon\}$ a transformation function when it maps s to a string $\varphi_R(s)$ by applying all rules $r_i \in R$ to every token of token(s) in an arbitrary order.

For example, the set $R = \{<\text{"Alan"} \to \text{"A."}>\}$ of transformation rules would lead to φ_R ("James Alan Hetfield") = "James A. Hetfield".

CaRLA

The goal of CaRLA is two-fold: First, it aims to compute rules that allow to derive conform representations of property values. As entities can have several values for the same property, CaRLA also aims to detect a condition under which two property values should be merged during the integration process. In the following, we will assume that two source knowledge bases are to be integrated to one. Note that our approach can be used for any number of source knowledge bases.

Formally, CaRLA addresses the problem of finding the required transformation rules by computing an equivalence relation ε between pairs of property values (p_1, p_2), that is, such that $\varepsilon(p_1, p_2)$ holds when p_1 and p_2 should be mapped to the same *canonical representation p*. CaRLA computes ε by generating two sets of weighted transformation function rules R_1 and R_2 such that for a given similarity function $\sigma \varepsilon(p_1, p_2) \rightarrow \sigma(\varphi_{R_1}(p_1), \varphi_{R_2}(p_2)) \geq \theta$, where θ is a similarity threshold. The canonical representation p is then set to $\varphi_{R_1}(p_1)$. The similarity condition $\sigma(\varphi_{R_1}(p_{R_1}), \varphi_{R_2}(p_2)) \geq \theta$ is used to distinguish between the pairs of properties values that should be merged.

To detect R_1 and R_2, CaRLA assumes two training data sets P and N, of which N can be empty. The set P of positive training examples is composed of pairs of property value pairs (p_1, p_2) such that $\varepsilon(p_1, p_2)$ holds. The set N of negative training examples consists of pairs (p_1, p_2) such that $\varepsilon(p_1, p_2)$ does not hold. In addition, CaRLA assumes being given a similarity function σ and a corresponding tokenization function *token*. Given this input, CaRLA implements a simple three-step approach: It begins by computing the two sets R_1 and R_2 of plausible transformation rules based on the positive examples at hand (Step 1). Then it merges inverse rules across R_1 and R_2 and discards rules with a low weight during the rule merging and filtering step. From the resulting set of rules, CaRLA derives the similarity condition $\varepsilon(p_1, p_2) \rightarrow \sigma(\varphi_{R_1}(p_1), \varphi_{R_2}(p_2)) \geq \theta$. It then applies these rules to the negative examples in N and tests whether the similarity condition also holds for the negative examples. If this is the case, then it discards rules until it reaches a local minimum of its error function. The retrieved set of rules and the novel value of θ constitute the output of CaRLA and can be used to generate the canonical representation of the properties in the source knowledge bases.

In the following, we explain each of the three steps in more detail. Throughout the explanation, we use the toy example shown in Table 5.2. In addition, we will assume a word-level tokenization function and the Jaccard similarity.

Rule Generation

The goal of the rule generation set is to compute two sets of rules R_1 and R_2 that will underlie the transformation φ_{R_1} and φ_{R_2}, respectively. We begin by tokenizing all positive property values p_i and p_j such that $(p_i, p_j) \in P$. We call T_1

TABLE 5.2

Toy Example Data Set

Type	Property Value 1	Property Value 2
⊕	"Jean van Damne"	"Jean Van Damne (actor)"
⊕	"Thomas T. van Nguyen"	"Thomas Van Nguyen (actor)"
⊕	"Alain Delon"	"Alain Delon (actor)"
⊕	"Alain Delon Jr."	"Alain Delon Jr. (actor)"
⊖	"Claude T. Francois"	"Claude Francois (actor)"

Note: The positive examples are of type ⊕ and the negative of type ⊖.

the set of all tokens p_i such that $(p_i, p_j) \in P$, while T_2 stands for the set of all p_j. We begin the computation of R_1 by extending the set of tokens of each $p_j \in T_2$ by adding ε to it. Thereafter, we compute the following rule score function *score*:

$$score(<x \rightarrow y>) = |\{(p_i, p_j) \in P : x \in token(p_i) \wedge y \in token(p_j)\}| . \quad (5.11)$$

score computes the number of co-occurrences of the tokens x and y across P.

All tokens, $x \in T_1$, always have a maximal co-occurrence with ε as it occurs in all tokens of T_2. To ensure that we do not compute only deletions, we decrease the score of rules $<x \rightarrow \varepsilon>$ by a factor $\kappa \in [0, 1]$. Moreover, in the case of a tie, we assume the rule $<x \rightarrow y>$ to be more natural than $<x \rightarrow y'>$ if $\sigma(x, y) > \sigma(x, y')$. Given that σ is bound between 0 and 1, it is sufficient to add a fraction of $\sigma(x, y)$ to each rule $<x \rightarrow y>$ to ensure that the better rule is chosen. Our final score function is thus given by

$$score_{final}(<x \rightarrow y>) = \begin{cases} score(<x \rightarrow y>) + \sigma(x,y)/2, & \text{if } y \neq \epsilon, \\ \kappa \times score(<x \rightarrow y>) & \text{else.} \end{cases} \quad (5.12)$$

Finally, for each token $x \in T_1$, we add the rule $r = <x \rightarrow y>$ to R_1 iff $x \neq y$ (i.e., r is not trivial) and $y = \text{argmax}_{y' \in T_2} score_{final}(<x \rightarrow y'>)$. To compute R_2, we simply swap T_1 and T_2, invert P (i.e., compute the set $\{(p_j, p_i): (p_i, p_j) \in P\}$) and run through the procedure described above.

For the set P in our example, we obtain the following sets of rules: $R_1 = \{(<\text{"van"} \rightarrow \text{"Van"}>, 2.08), (<\text{"T."} \rightarrow \varepsilon>, 2)\}$ and $R_2 = \{(<\text{"Van"} \rightarrow \text{"van"}>, 2.08), (<\text{"(actor)"} \rightarrow \varepsilon>, 2)\}$.

Rule Merging and Filtering

The computation of R_1 and R_2 can lead to a large number of inverse or improbable rules. In our example, R_1 contains the rule $<\text{"van"} \rightarrow \text{"Van"}>$ while R_2 contains $<\text{"Van"} \rightarrow \text{"van"}>$. Applying these rules to the data would consequently not improve the convergence of their representations. To ensure that the transformation rules lead to similar canonical forms, the rule merging step first discards all rules $<x \to y> \in R_2$ such that $<y \to x> \in R_1$ (i.e., rules in R_2 that are inverse to rules in R_1). Then, low-weight rules are discarded. The idea here is that if there is not enough evidence for a rule, it might just be a random event. The initial similarity threshold θ for the similarity condition is finally set to

$$\theta = \min_{(p_1, p_2) \in P} \sigma(\varphi_{R_1}(p_1), \varphi_{R_2}(p_2)). \tag{5.13}$$

In our example, CaRLA would discard $<$"van" $\to$ "Van"$>$ from R_2. When assuming a threshold of 10% of P's size (i.e., 0.4), no rule would be filtered out. The output of this step would consequently be $R_1 = \{(<$"van" $\to$ "Van"$>$, 2.08), $(<$"T." $\to \varepsilon>$, 2)$\}$ and $R_2 = \{(<$"(actor)" $\to \varepsilon>$, 2)$\}$.

Rule Falsification

The aim of the rule falsification step is to detect a set of transformations that lead to a minimal number of elements of N having a similarity superior to θ via σ. To achieve this goal, we follow a greedy approach that aims to minimize the magnitude of the set

$$E = \left\{ (p_1, p_2) \in N : \sigma(\varphi_{R_1}(p_1), \varphi_{R_2}(p_2)) \geq \theta = \min_{(p_1, p_2) \in P} \sigma(\varphi_{R_1}(p_1), \varphi_{R_2}(p_2)) \right\}. \tag{5.14}$$

Our approach simply tries to discard all rules that apply to elements of E by ascending score. If E is empty, then the approach terminates. If E does not get smaller, then the change is rolled back and the next rule is tried. Else, the rule is discarded from the set of final rules. Note that discarding a rule can alter the value of θ and thus E. Once the set E has been computed, CaRLA concludes its computation by generating a final value of the threshold θ.

In our example, two rules apply to the element of N. After discarding the rule $<$"T." $\to \varepsilon>$, the set E becomes empty, leading to the termination of the rule falsification step. The final set of rules are thus $R_1 = \{<$"van" $\to$ "Van"$>\}$ and $R_2 = \{<$"(actor)" $\to \varepsilon>\}$. The value of θ is computed to be 0.75. Table 5.3 shows the canonical property values for our toy example. Note that this threshold allows to discard the elements of N as being equivalent property values.

It is noteworthy that by learning transformation rules, we also found an initial threshold θ for determining the similarity of property values using σ as similarity function. In combination with the canonical forms computed by CaRLA, the configuration (σ, θ) can be used as an initial configuration for Link Discovery frameworks such as LIMES. For example, the

TABLE 5.3

Canonical Property Values for Our Example Data Set

Property Value 1	Property Value 2	Canonical Value
"Jean van Damne"	"Jean Van Damne (actor)"	"Jean Van Damne"
"Thomas T. van Nguyen"	"Thomas Van Nguyen (actor)"	"Thomas T. Van Nguyen"
"Alain Delon"	"Alain Delon (actor)"	"Alain Delon"
"Alain Delon Jr."	"Alain Delon Jr. (actor)"	"Alain Delon Jr."
"Claude T. Francois"		"Claude T. Francois"
	"Claude Francois (actor)"	"Claude Francois"

smallest Jaccard similarity for the pair of property values for our example lies by 1/3, leading to a precision of 0.71 for a recall of 1 (*F*-measure: 0.83). Yet, after the computation of the transformation rules, we reach an *F*-measure of 1 with a threshold of 1. Consequently, the pair (σ, θ) can be used for determining an initial classifier for approaches such as the RAVEN algorithm [24].

Extension to Active Learning

One of the drawbacks of batch learning approaches is that they often require a large number of examples to generate good models. As our evaluation shows (see the "Evaluation" section), this drawback also holds for the batch version of CaRLA, as it can easily detect very common rules but sometimes fails to detect rules that apply to less pairs of property values. In the following, we present how this problem can be addressed by extending CaRLA to aCARLA using active learning [28].

The basic idea here is to begin with small training sets P_0 and N_0. In each iteration, all the available training data are used by the batch version of CaRLA to update the set of rules. The algorithm then tries to refute or validate rules with a score below the score threshold s_{min} (i.e., unsure rules). For this purpose, it picks the most unsure rule r that has not been shown to be erroneous in a previous iteration (i.e., that is not an element of the set of banned rules B). It then fetches a set Ex of property values that map the left side (i.e., the premise) of r. Should there be no unsure rule, then Ex is set to the q property values that are most dissimilar to the already known property values. Annotations consisting of the corresponding values for the elements of Ex in the other source knowledge bases are requested by the user and written in the set P. Property values with no corresponding values are written in N. Finally, the sets of positive and negative examples are updated and the triple (R_1, R_2, θ) is learned anew until a stopping condition such as a maximal number of questions is reached. As our evaluation shows, this simple extension of the CaRLA algorithm allows it to detect efficiently the pairs of annotations that might lead to a larger set of high-quality rules.

Evaluation

Experimental Setup

In the experiments reported in this section, we evaluated CaRLA by two means: First, we aimed to measure how well CaRLA could compute transformations created by experts. To achieve this goal, we retrieved transformation rules from four link specifications defined manually by experts within the LATC project.* An overview of these specifications is given in Table 5.4. Each link specification aimed to compute owl:sameAs links between entities across two knowledge bases by first transforming their property values and by then computing the similarity of the entities based on the similarity of their property values. For example, the computation of links between films in DBpedia and LinkedMDB was carried out by first applying the set of $R_1 = \{<(film) \rightarrow \varepsilon>\}$ to the labels of films in DBpedia and $R_2 = \{<(director) \rightarrow \varepsilon>\}$ to the labels of their directors. We ran both CaRLA and aCaRLA on the property values of the interlinked entities and measured how fast CaRLA was able to reconstruct the set of rules that were used during the Link Discovery process.

In addition, we quantified the quality of the rules learned by CaRLA. In each experiment, we computed the boost in the precision of the mapping of property pairs with and without the rules derived by CaRLA. The initial precision was computed as $|P|/|M|$, where $M = \{(p_i, p_j) : \sigma(p_i, p_j) \geq \min_{(p_1, p_2) \in P} \sigma(p_1, p_2)\}$. The precision after applying CaRLA's results was computed as $|P|/|M'|$, where $M' = \{(p_i, p_j) : \sigma(\varphi_{R_1}(p_i), \varphi_{R_2}(p_j)) \geq \min_{(p_1, p_2) \in P} \sigma(\varphi_{R_1}(p_1), \varphi_{R_2}(p_2))\}$. Note that in both cases, the recall was 1 given that $\forall (p_i, p_j) \in P : \sigma(p_i, p_j) \geq \min_{(p_1, p_2) \in P} \sigma(p_1, p_2)$. In all experiments, we used the Jaccard similarity metric and a word tokenizer with $\kappa = 0.8$. All runs were carried on a notebook running Windows 7 Enterprise with 3 GB RAM and an Intel Dual Core 2.2 GHz processor. Each of the algorithms was ran five times. We report the rules that were discovered by the algorithms and the number of experiments within which they were found.

TABLE 5.4

Overview of the Data Sets

Experiment	Source	Target	Source Property	Target Property	Size
Actors	DBpedia	LinkedMDB	rdfs:label	rdfs:label	1172
Directors	DBpedia	LinkedMDB	rdfs:label	rdfs:label	7353
Movies	DBpedia	LinkedMDB	rdfs:label	rdfs:label	9859
Producers	DBpedia	LinkedMDB	rdfs:label	rdfs:label	1540

* http://latc-project.eu

Results and Discussion

Table 5.5 shows the union of the rules learned by the batch version of CaRLA in all five runs. Note that the computation of a rule set lasted under 0.5 s even for the largest data set, that is, Movies. The columns P_n give the probability of finding a rule for a training set of size n in our experiments. R_2 is not reported because it remained empty in all setups. Our results show that in all cases, CaRLA converges quickly and learns rules that are equivalent to those utilized by the LATC experts with a sample set of 5 pairs. Note that for each rule of the form <"@en" → y> with $y \neq \varepsilon$ that we learned, the experts used the rule <$y \to \varepsilon$> while the linking platform automatically removed the language tag. We experimented with the same data sets without language tags and computed exactly the same rules as those devised by the experts. In some experiments (such as Directors), CaRLA was even able detect rules that where not included in the set of rules generated by human experts. For example, the rule <"(filmmaker)" → "(director)"> is not very frequent and was thus overlooked by the experts. In Table 5.5, we marked such rules with an asterix. The Director and the Movies data sets contained a large number of typographic errors of different sort (incl. misplaced hyphens, character repetitions such as in the token "Neilll", etc.), which led to poor precision scores in our experiments. We cleaned the first 250 entries of these data sets from these errors and obtained the results in the rows labels Directors_clean and Movies_clean. The results of CaRLA on these data sets are also shown in Table 5.5. We also measured the improvement in precision that resulted from applying CaRLA to the data sets at hand (see Figure 5.9). For that the precision remained constant across the different data set sizes. In the best case (cleaned Directors data set), we are able to improve the precision of the property mapping by 12.16%. Note that we

TABLE 5.5

Overview of Batch Learning Results

Experiment	R_1	P_5	P_{10}	P_{20}	P_{50}	P_{100}
Actors	<"@en" → "(actor)">	1	1	1	1	1
Directors	<"@en" → "(director)">	1	1	1	1	1
	<"(filmmaker)" → "(director)">*	0	0	0	0	0.2
Directors_clean	<"@en" → "(director)">	1	1	1	1	1
Movies	<"@en" → ε>	1	1	1	1	1
	<"(film)" → ε>	1	1	1	1	1
	<"film)" → ε>*	0	0	0	0	0.6
Movies_clean	<"@en" → ε>	1	1	1	1	1
	<"(film)" → ε>	0	0.8	1	1	1
	<"film)" → ε>*	0	0	0	0	1
Producers	<"@en" → (producer)>	1	1	1	1	1

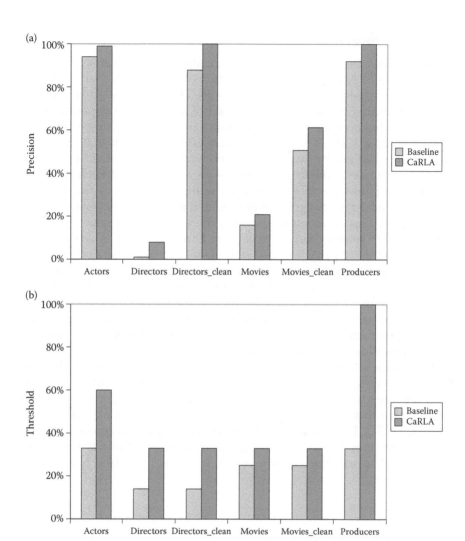

FIGURE 5.9
Comparison of the precision and thresholds with and without CaRLA. (a) Comparison of the precision with and without CaRLA. (b) Comparison of the thresholds with and without CaRLA.

can improve the precision of the mapping of property values even on the noisy data sets.

Interestingly, when used on the Movies data set with a training data set size of 100, our framework learned low-confidence rules such as <"(1999" → ε>, which were yet discarded due to a too low score. These are the cases where aCaRLA displayed its superiority. Thanks to its ability to ask for annotation when faced with unsure rules, aCaRLA is able to validate or negate unsure rules. As the results on the Movies example show,

TABLE 5.6

Overview of Active Learning Results

Experiment	R_1	P_5	P_{10}	P_{20}	P_{50}	P_{100}
Actors	<"@en" → "(actor)">	1	1	1	1	1
Directors	<"@en" → "(director)">	1	1	1	1	1
	<"(actor)" → "(director)">*	0	0	0	0	1
Directors_clean	<"@en" → "(director)">	1	1	1	1	1
Movies	<"@en" → ε>	1	1	1	1	1
	<"(film)" → ε>	1	1	1	1	1
	<"(film)" → ε>*	0	0	0	0	1
	<"(2006" → ε>*	0	0	0	0	1
	<"(199" → ε>*	0	0	0	0	1
Movies_clean	<"@en" → ε>	1	1	1	1	1
	<"(film)" → ε>	0	1	1	1	1
	<"(film)" → ε>*	0	0	0	0	1
Producers	<"@en" → (producer)>	1	1	1	1	1

aCaRLA is able to detect several supplementary rules that were overlooked by human experts. Especially, it clearly shows that deleting the year of creation of a movie can improve the conformation process. aCaRLA is also able to generate a significantly larger number of candidate rules for the user's convenience. For example, it detects a large set of low-confidence rules such as <"(actress)" → "(director)">, <"(actor)" → "(director)"> and <"(actor/director)" → "(director)"> on the Directors data set. Note that in one case aCARLA misses the rule <"(filmmaker)" → "(director)" > that is discovered by CaRLA with a low probability. This is due to the active learning process being less random. The results achieved by aCaRLA on the same data sets are shown in Table 5.6. Note that the runtime of aCaRLA lied between 50 ms per iteration (cleaned data sets) and 30 s per iteration (largest data set, Movies). The most time-expensive operation was the search for the property values that were least similar to the already known ones.

Conclusion

In this chapter, we introduced a number of challenges arising in the context of Linked Data in Enterprise Integration. A crucial prerequisite for addressing these challenges is to establish efficient and effective link discovery and data integration techniques, which scale to large-scale data scenarios found in the enterprise. We addressed the transformation and linking steps of the Linked Data Integration by presenting two algorithms, $\mathcal{HR}^3$ and CaRLA. We proved that $\mathcal{HR}^3$ is optimal with respect to its reduction ratio by showing that its RRR converges toward 1 when α converges toward ∞. $\mathcal{HR}^3$ aims to be the first of a novel type of Link Discovery approaches, that is, approaches that can guarantee theoretical optimality, while also being empirically usable. In the future work, more such approaches will enable superior memory and space management. CaRLA uses batch and active learning approach to discover a large number of transformation rules efficiently and was shown to increase the precision of property mapping by up to 12% when the recall is set to 1. In addition, CaRLA was shown to be able to detect rules that escaped experts while devising specifications for link discovery.

References

1. S. Auer, J. Lehmann, and S. Hellmann. LinkedGeoData: Adding a spatial dimension to the Web of Data. *The Semantic Web-ISWC 2009*, pp. 731–746, 2009.
2. F. C. Botelho and N. Ziviani. External perfect hashing for very large key sets. In *CIKM*, pp. 653–662, 2007.
3. T. Bray, J. Paoli, C. M. Sperberg-McQueen, E. Maler, and F. Yergeau. *Extensible Markup Language (XML) 1.0* (Fifth Edition). W3C, 2008.
4. J. Clark and M. Makoto. *RELAX NG Specification*. Oasis, December 2001. http://www.oasis-open.org/committees/relax-ng/spec-20011203.html.
5. V. Eisenberg and Y. Kanza. D2RQ/update: Updating relational data via virtual RDF. In *WWW (Companion Volume)*, pp. 497–498, 2012.
6. M. G. Elfeky, A. K. Elmagarmid, and V. S. Verykios. Tailor: A record linkage tool box. In *ICDE*, pp. 17–28, 2002.
7. J. Euzenat and P. Shvaiko. *Ontology Matching*. Springer-Verlag, Heidelberg, 2007.
8. D. A. Ferrucci, E. W. Brown, J. Chu-Carroll, J. Fan, D. Gondek, A. Kalyanpur, A. Lally et al. Building Watson: An overview of the deepQA project. *AI Magazine*, 31(3):59–79, 2010.
9. A. Halevy, A. Rajaraman, and J. Ordille. Data integration: The teenage years. In *Proceedings of the 32nd International Conference on Very Large Data Bases (VLDB'06)*, pp. 9–16. VLDB Endowment, 2006.
10. A. Hogan, A. Harth, and A. Polleres. Scalable authoritative OWL reasoning for the web. *International Journal on Semantic Web and Information Systems (IJSWIS)*, 5(2):49–90, 2009.
11. P. Jaccard. Étude comparative de la distribution florale dans une portion des Alpes et des Jura. *Bulletin del la Société Vaudoise des Sciences Naturelles*, 37:547–579, 1901.
12. R. Jelliffe. *The Schematron—An XML Structure Validation Language using Patterns in Trees*. ISO/IEC 19757, 2001.
13. R. Kimball and J. Caserta. *The Data Warehouse ETL Toolkit: Practical Techniques for Extracting, Cleaning, Conforming, and Delivering Data*. Wiley, Hoboken, NJ, 2004.
14. M. Krötzsch, D. Vrandečić, and M. Völkel. Semantic Media Wiki. *The Semantic Web-ISWC 2006*, pp. 935–942, 2006.

15. V. I. Levenshtein. Binary codes capable of correcting deletions, insertions, and reversals. Technical Report 8, 1966.

16. A. Majchrzak, C. Wagner, and D. Yates. Corporate wiki users: Results of a survey. In *WikiSym'06: Proceedings of the 2006 International Symposium on Wikis,* Odense, Denmark. ACM, August 2006.

17. A. Miles and S. Bechhofer. SKOS Simple Knowledge Organization System Reference. *W3C Recommendation,* 2008. http://www.w3.org/TR/skos-reference/.

18. R. Mukherjee and J. Mao. Enterprise search: Tough stuff. *Queue,* 2(2):36, 2004.

19. A.-C. Ngonga Ngomo. Learning conformation rules for linked data integration. In *International Workshop on Ontology Matching,* Boston, USA, 2012.

20. A.-C. Ngonga Ngomo. Link discovery with guaranteed reduction ratio in affine spaces with Minkowski measures. In *International Semantic Web Conference (1),* Boston, USA, pp. 378–393, 2012.

21. A.-C. Ngonga Ngomo. On link discovery using a hybrid approach. *J. Data Semantics,* 1(4):203–217, 2012.

22. A.-C. Ngonga Ngomo. A time-efficient hybrid approach to link discovery. In *Sixth International Ontology Matching Workshop,* Bonn, Germany, 2011.

23. A.-C. Ngonga Ngomo and S. Auer. LIMES—A time-efficient approach for large-scale link discovery on the web of data. In *Proceedings of IJCAI,* Barcelona, Catalonia, Spain, 2011.

24. A.-C. Ngonga Ngomo, J. Lehmann, S. Auer, and K. Höffner. RAVEN—Active learning of link specifications. In *Proceedings of OM@ISWC,* Bonn, Germany, 2011.

25. ontoprise. SMW + —Semantic Enterprise Wiki, 2012. http://www.smwplus.com.

26. E. Prud'hommeaux. SPARQL 1.1 Federation Extensions, November 2011. http://www.w3.org/TR/sparql11-federated-query/.

27. F. Schwagereit, A. Scherp, and S. Staab. Representing distributed groups with dgFOAF. *The Semantic Web: Research and Applications,* pp. 181–195, 2010.

28. B. Settles. Active learning literature survey. Technical Report 1648, University of Wisconsin-Madison, 2009.

29. D. Song and J. Heflin. Automatically generating data linkages using a domain-independent candidate selection approach. In *ISWC,* Boston, USA, pp. 649–664, 2011.

30. M. Sporny, T. Inkster, H. Story, B. Harbulot, and R. Bachmann-Gmür. WebID 1.0: Web identification and Discovery. W3C Editors Draft, December 2011. http://www.w3.org/2005/Incubator/webid/spec/.

31. H. S. Thompson, D. Beech, M. Maloney, and N. Mendelsohn. *XML Schema Part 1: Structures* (Second Edition). W3C, 2004.

32. L. M. Vaquero, L. Rodero-Merino, and R. Buyya. Dynamically scaling applications in the cloud. *SIGCOMM Comput. Commun. Rev.,* 41:45–52.

33. H. Wache, T. Voegele, U. Visser, H. Stuckenschmidt, G. Schuster, H. Neumann, and S. Hübner. Ontology-based integration of information—A survey of existing approaches. *IJCAI-01 Workshop: Ontologies and Information Sharing,* 2001:108–117, 2001.

34. C. Xiao, W. Wang, X. Lin, and J. X. Yu. Efficient similarity joins for near duplicate detection. In *WWW,* Beijing, China, pp. 131–140, 2008.

6

Scalable End-User Access to Big Data

**Martin Giese, Diego Calvanese, Peter Haase, Ian Horrocks,
Yannis Ioannidis, Herald Kllapi, Manolis Koubarakis, Maurizio Lenzerini,
Ralf Möller, Mariano Rodriguez Muro, Özgür Özçep, Riccardo Rosati,
Rudolf Schlatte, Michael Schmidt, Ahmet Soylu, and Arild Waaler**

CONTENTS

This chapter proposes steps toward the solution to the *data access problem* that end-users typically face when dealing with Big Data:

- They need to pose *ad-hoc* queries to a collection of data sources, possibly including streaming sources.

- They are unable to query these sources on their own, but are dependent on assistance from IT experts.

- The turnaround time for information requests is in the range of days, possibly weeks, due to the involvement of the IT personnel.

- The volume, complexity, variety, and velocity of the underlying data sources put very high demands on the scalability of the solution.

We propose to approach this problem using *ontology-based data access* (OBDA), the idea being to capture end-user conceptualizations in an ontology and use declarative mappings to connect the ontology to the underlying data sources. End-user queries posed are in terms of concepts of ontology and are then rewritten as queries against the sources.

The chapter is structured as follows. First, in the "The Data Access Problem of Big Data" section, we situate the problem within the more general discussion about Big Data. Then, in section "Ontology-Based Data Access," we review the state of the art in OBDA, explain why we believe OBDA is a superior approach to the data access challenge posed by Big Data, and also explain why the field of OBDA is currently not yet sufficiently mature to deal satisfactory with these problems. The rest of the chapter contains concepts for raising OBDA to a level where it can be successfully deployed to Big Data.

The ideas proposed in this chapter are investigated and implemented in the FP7 Integrated Project *Optique—Scalable End-user Access to Big Data*, which runs until the end of year 2016. The *Optique* solutions are evaluated on two comprehensive use cases from the energy sector with a variety of data access challenges related to Big Data.*

Data Access Problem of Big Data

The situation in knowledge- and data-intensive enterprises is typically as follows. Massive amounts of data, accumulated in real time and over decades, are spread over a wide variety of formats and sources. End-users operate on these collections of data using specialized applications, the operation of which requires expert skills and domain knowledge. Relevant data are extracted from the data sources using predefined queries that are built into the applications. Moreover, these queries typically access just some specific sources with identical structure. The situation can be illustrated like this:

In these situations, the turnaround time, by which we mean the time from when the end-user delivers an information need until the data are there, will typically be in the range of minutes, maybe even seconds, and Big Data technologies can be deployed to dramatically reduce the execution time for queries.

Situations where users need to explore the data using *ad hoc* queries are considerably more challenging, since accessing relevant parts of the data typically requires in-depth knowledge of the domain *and* of the organization of data repositories. It is very rare that the end-users possess such skills themselves. The situation is rather that the end-user needs to collaborate

---

* See http://www.optique-project.eu/

with an IT-skilled person in order to jointly develop the query that solves the problem at hand, illustrated in the figure below:

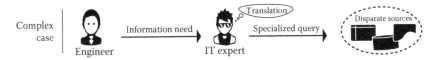

The turnaround time is then mostly dependent on human factors and is in the range of days, if not worse. Note that the typical Big Data technologies are of limited help in this case, as they do not in themselves eliminate the need for the IT expert.

The problem of end-user data access is ultimately about being able to put the enterprise data in the hands of the expert end-users. Important aspects of the problem are volume, variety, velocity, and complexity (Beyer et al., 2011), where by volume we mean the complete size of the data, by variety we mean the number of different data types and data sources, by velocity we mean the rate at which data streams in and how fast it needs to be processed, and by complexity we mean factors such as standards, domain rules, and size of database schemas that in normal circumstances are manageable, but quickly complicate data access considerably when they escalate.

Factors such as variety, velocity, and complexity can make data access challenging even with fairly small amounts of data. When, in addition to these factors, data volumes are extreme, the problem becomes seemingly intractable; one must then not only deal with large data sets, but at the same time also has to cope with dimensions that to some extent are complementary. In Big Data scenarios, one or more of these dimensions go to the extreme, at the same time interacting with other dimensions.

Based on the ideas presented in this chapter, the *Optique* project implements a solution to the data access problem for Big Data in which all the above-mentioned dimensions of the problem are addressed. The goal is to enable expert end-users access the data themselves, without the help of the IT experts, as illustrated in this figure.

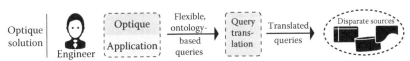

Ontology-Based Data Access

We have observed that, in end-user access to Big Data, there exists a bottleneck in the process of translating end-users' information needs into

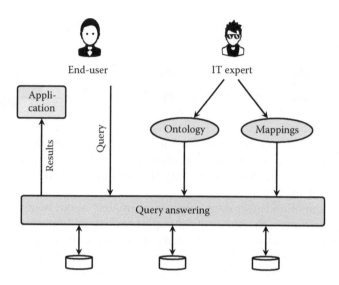

FIGURE 6.1
The basic setup for OBDA.

executable and optimized queries over data sources. An approach known as "ontology-based data access" (OBDA) has the potential to avoid this bottleneck by automating this query translation process. Figure 6.1 shows the essential components in an OBDA setup.

The main idea is to use an *ontology*, or domain model, that is a formalization of the vocabulary employed by the end-users to talk about the problem domain. This ontology is constructed entirely independent of how the data are actually stored. End-users can formulate queries using the terms defined by the ontology, using some formal query language. In other words, queries are formulated according to the end-users' view of the problem domain.

To execute such queries, a set of *mappings* is maintained which describe the relationship between the terms in the ontology and their representation(s) in the data sources. This set of mappings is typically produced by the IT expert, who previously translated end-users' queries manually.

It is now possible to give an algorithm that takes an end-user query, the ontology, and a set of mappings as inputs, and computes a query that can be executed over the data sources, which produces the set of results expected for the end-user query. As Figure 6.1 illustrates, the result set can then be fed into some existing domain-specific visualization or browsing application which presents it to the end-user.

In the next section, we will see an example of such a query translation process, which illustrates the point that including additional information about the problem domain in the ontology can be very useful for end-users. In general, this process of query translation becomes much more complex than just substituting pieces of queries using the mappings. The generated query can also, in some cases, become dramatically larger than the original ontology-based query formulated by the end-user.

The theoretical foundations of OBDA have been thoroughly investigated in recent years (Möller et al., 2006; Calvanese et al., 2007a,b; Poggi et al., 2008). There is a very good understanding of the basic mechanisms for query rewriting, and the extent to which expressivity of ontologies can be increased, while maintaining the same theoretical complexity as is exhibited by standard relational database systems.

Also, prototypical implementations exist (Acciarri et al., 2005; Calvanese et al., 2011), which have been applied to minor industrial case studies (e.g., Amoroso et al., 2008). They have demonstrated the conceptual viability of the OBDA approach for industrial purposes.

There are several features of a successful OBDA implementation that lead us to believe that it is the right basic approach to the challenges of end-user access to Big Data:

- It is declarative, that is, there is no need for end-users, nor for IT experts, to write special-purpose program code.
- Data can be left in existing relational databases. In many cases, moving large and complex data sets is impractical, even if the data owners were to allow it. Moreover, for scalability it is essential to exploit existing optimized data structures (tables), and to avoid increasing query complexity by fragmenting data. This is in contrast to, for example, data warehousing approaches that copy data: OBDA is more flexible and offers an infrastructure which is simpler to set up and maintain.
- It provides a flexible query language that corresponds to the end-user conceptualization of the data.
- The ontology can be used to hide details and introduce abstractions. This is significant in cases where there is a source schema which is too complex for the end-user.
- The relationship between the ontology concepts and the relational data is made explicit in the mappings. This provides a means for the DB experts to make their knowledge available to the end-user independent of specific queries.

Example

We will now present a (highly) simplified example that illustrates some of the benefits of OBDA and explains how the technique works. Imagine that an engineer working in the power generation industry wants to retrieve data about generators that have a turbine fault. The engineer is able to formalize this information need, possibly with the aid of a suitable tool, as a query of the form:

$$Q1(g) \leftarrow \text{Generator}(g) \wedge \text{hasFault}(g,f) \wedge \text{TurbineFault}(f)$$

TABLE 6.1

Example Ontology and Data for Turbine Faults

Human Readable	Logic
Ontology	
Condenser is a CoolingDevice that is part of a Turbine	Condenser ⊑ Cooling Device ⊓ ∃isPartOf.Turbine
Condenser Fault is a Fault that affects a Condenser	Condenser Fault ≡ Fault ⊓ ∃affects.Condenser
Turbine Fault is a Fault that affects part of a Turbine	TurbineFault ≡ Fault ⊓ ∃affects.(∃isPartOf. Turbine)
Data	
$g1$ is a Generator	Generator($g1$)
$g1$ has fault $f1$	hasFault($g1$,f1)
$f1$ is a CondenserFault	CondenserFault($f1$)

which can be read as "return all g such that g is a generator, g has a fault f, and f is a turbine fault."

Now consider a database that includes the tuples given in the lower part of Table 6.1. If Q1 is evaluated over these data, then $g1$ is not returned in the answer, because $f1$ is a condenser fault, but not a turbine fault. However, this is not what the engineer would want or expect, because the engineer knows that the condenser is a part of the turbine and that a condenser fault is thus a kind of turbine fault.

The problem is caused by the fact that the query answering system is not able to use the engineer's expert knowledge of the domain. In an OBDA system, (some of) this knowledge is captured in an *ontology*, which can then be exploited in order to answer queries "more intelligently." The ontology provides a conceptual model that is more intuitive for users: it introduces familiar vocabulary terms and captures declaratively the relationships between terms.

In our running example, the ontology might include the declarative statements shown in the upper part of Table 6.1. These introduce relevant vocabulary, such as condenser, cooling device, affects, etc. and establish relationships between terms. The first axiom, for example, states that "every condenser is a cooling device that is part of a turbine." If we formalize these statements as axioms in a suitable logic, as shown in the right hand side of Table 6.1, we can then use automated reasoning techniques to derive facts that must hold, but are not explicitly given by the data, such as *TurbineFault($g1$)*. This in turn means that $g1$ is recognized as a correct answer to the example query. Using an ontology and automated reasoning techniques, query answering can relate to the whole set of implied information, instead of only that which is explicitly stated.

Automated reasoning can, in general, be computationally very expensive. Moreover, most standard reasoning techniques would need to interleave operations on the ontology and the data, which may not be practically feasible if the data are stored in a relational database. OBDA addresses both these issues by answering queries using a two-stage process, first using the ontology to rewrite the query and then evaluating the rewritten query over the data (without any reference to the ontology). The rewriting step generates additional queries, each of which can produce extra answers that follow from a combination of existing data and statements in the ontology. Ensuring that this is possible for all possible combinations of data, and ontology statements require some restrictions on the kinds of statement that can be included in the ontology. The OWL 2 QL ontology language profile has been designed as a maximal subset of OWL 2 that enjoys this property.

Coming back to our example, we can easily derive from the ontology that a condenser fault is a kind of turbine fault, and we can use this to rewrite the query as

$$Q2(g) \leftarrow \text{Generator}(g) \wedge \text{hasFault}(g,f) \wedge \text{CondenserFault}(f)$$

Note that there are many other possible rewritings, including, for example,

$$Q3(g) \leftarrow \text{Generator}(g) \wedge \text{hasFault}(g,f) \wedge \text{Fault}(f) \wedge \text{affects}(f,c) \wedge \text{Condenser}(c)$$

all of which need to be considered if we want to guarantee that the answer to the query will be complete for any data set, and this can result in the rewritten query becoming very large (in the worst case, exponential in the size of the input ontology and query).

One final issue that needs to be considered is how these queries will be evaluated if the data are stored in a data store such as a relational database. So far, we have assumed that the data are just a set of ground tuples that use the same vocabulary as the ontology. In practice, however, we want to access data in some kind of data store, typically a relational database management system (RDBMS), and typically one whose schema vocabulary does not correspond with the ontology vocabulary. In OBDA, we use *mappings* to declaratively capture the relationships between ontology vocabulary and database queries. A mapping typically takes the form of a single ontology vocabulary term (e.g., `Generator`) and a query over the data sources that retrieves the instances of this term (e.g., "SELECT id FROM Generator"). Technically, this kind of mapping is known as global as view (GAV).

In our example, the data might be stored in an RDBMS using tables for generators and faults, and using a hasFault table to capture the one-to-many relationship between generators and faults, as shown in Table 6.2. Mappings from the ontology vocabulary to RDBMS queries can then be defined as follows:

```
Generator         ↦    SELECT id FROM Generator
CondenserFault    ↦    SELECT id FROM Fault WHERE type = 'C'
TurbineFault      ↦    SELECT id FROM Fault WHERE type = 'T'
hasFault          ↦    SELECT g-id,f-id FROM hasFault
```

TABLE 6.2

Database Tables

Generator		Fault		hasFault	
id	Serial	id	Type	g-id	f-id
g1	1234	f1	C	g1	f1
g2	5678	f2	T	g2	f2
⋮	⋮	⋮	⋮	⋮	⋮

When combined with $Q2$, these mappings produce the following query over the RDBMS:

```
SELECT Generator.id FROM Generator, Fault, hasFault
WHERE Generator.id = g-id AND f-id = Fault.id AND
   type = 'C'
```

The answer to this query will include $g1$. However, in order to ensure that all valid answers are returned, we also need to include the results of $Q1$ (the original query) and all other possible rewritings. In an SQL setting, this leads to a UNION query of the form:

```
SELECT Generator.id FROM Generator, Fault, hasFault
WHERE Generator.id = g-id AND f-id = Fault.id AND
   type = 'T'
UNION
SELECT Generator.id FROM Generator, Fault, hasFault
WHERE Generator.id = g-id AND f-id = Fault.id AND
type = 'C'
UNION
...
```

Limitations of the State of the Art in OBDA

As mentioned above, OBDA has been successfully applied to first industrial case studies. Still, realistic applications, where nontechnical end-users require access to large corporate data stores, lie beyond the reach of current technology in several respects:

1. The *usability* is hampered by the need to use a formal query language that makes it difficult for end-users to formulate queries, even if the vocabulary is familiar.
2. The *prerequisites* of OBDA, namely ontology and mappings, are in practice expensive to obtain.
3. The *scope* of existing systems is too narrow: they lack many features that are vital for applications.
4. The *efficiency* of both the translation process and the execution of the resulting queries is too low.

In the remainder of this chapter, we discuss possible approaches to overcome these shortcomings and how the state of the art will have to be advanced in order to realize them. Figure 6.2 shows a proposed architecture supporting this approach. In short terms, the ideas are as follows.

End-user acceptance depends on the *usability* for nontechnical users, for example, by providing a user-friendly *Query Formulation* front-end (see Figure 6.2) that lets the end-user navigate the vocabulary and presents a menu of possible refinements of a query (see section "Query Formulation Support"). Advanced users must have the possibility to switch back and forth as required between the navigational view and a more technical view where the query can be edited directly. This will make it possible for a non-technical user to author large parts of a query, but receive help from a technical expert when required.

The second problem that needs to be addressed is providing and maintaining the *prerequisites*: ontology and mappings. In practice, these will have to be treated as evolving, dynamic entities which are updated as required for formalizing end-users' information requirements. An industrial-scale front-end needs to support both the semiautomatic derivation of an initial ontology and mappings in new deployments, and the extension of the ontology during query formulation, for example, by adding new technical terms or relationships that were not previously captured. In the architecture of Figure 6.2, this is accomplished by the *Query Formulation* and *Ontology and Mapping Management* front-end components. This mechanism

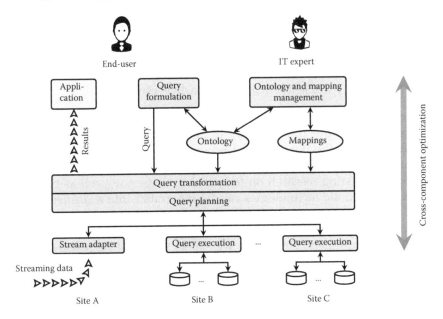

FIGURE 6.2
Platform architecture for scalable OBDA.

of bootstrapping and query-driven ontology construction can enable the creation of an ontology that fits the end-users' needs at a moderate cost. The same *Ontology and Mapping Management* component can then also support the IT expert in maintaining a set of mappings that is consistent with the evolving ontology. The sections on "Query Formulation" (see section "Query Formulation Support") and "Ontology and Mapping Management" (see section "Ontology and Mapping Management") expand on the requirements for such a management component.

Providing a robust answer to the *scope* problem is difficult, because there is a trade-off between expressivity and efficiency: very expressive mechanisms in the ontology and mapping languages, which would guarantee applicability to virtually any problem that might occur in industrial applications, are known to preclude efficient query rewriting and execution (Brachman and Levesque, 1984; Artale et al., 2009; Calvanese et al., 2012). To ensure efficiency, a restricted set of features must be carefully chosen for ontology and mapping languages, with the aim of covering as many potential applications as possible.

Still, concrete applications will come with their own specific difficulties that cannot be covered by a general-purpose tool. This expressivity problem needs to be resolved by plugging application-specific modules into the query answering engine. These domain-specific plug-ins must take care of query translation and optimization in those cases where a generic declarative mechanism is not powerful enough for an application. A wide range of special-purpose vocabulary and reasoning could be covered by such domain-specific modules, such as, to name just a few,

- Geological vocabulary in a petroleum industry application
- Protein interactions and pathways in molecular biology
- Elementary particle interactions for particle physics

On the other hand, important features that occur in many applications need to be built into the core of any OBDA system. Notably, temporal aspects and the possibility of progressively processing data as it is generated (stream processing) are vital to many industrial applications. Fortunately, existing research on temporal databases, as well as time and streams in semantic technologies can be integrated into a unified OBDA framework (see section "Time and Streams"). Another important domain that occurs in many applications is that of geospatial information, spatial proximity, containment, etc. Again, we expect that existing research about geospatial data storage, querying, and semantics can be integrated into the OBDA framework.

Other examples are aggregation (summation, averaging, etc.) and epistemic negation (questions about missing data) that have received little theoretical or practical attention, but which are important in many practical applications.

To address *efficiency*, we propose to decompose the "Query Answering" component into several layers, as shown in Figure 6.2:

1. *Query Transformation* using the ontology and mappings
2. *Query Planning* to distribute queries to individual servers
3. *Query Execution* using existing scalable data stores, or a massively parallelized (cloud) architecture

The implementation of the query transformation layer can take recent theoretical advances in query rewriting into account, which can lead to significantly improved performance (see section "Query Transformation"). The same holds for query execution, which can take advantage of research on massive parallelization of query execution, with the possibility of scaling orders of magnitude beyond a conventional RDBMS architecture (see section "Distributed Query Execution").

We surmise, however, that to gain a *real* impact on efficiency, a holistic, cross-component view on query answering is needed: current OBDA implementations leave query planning and execution to off-the-shelf database products, often leading to suboptimal performance on the kinds of queries produced by a rewriting component. The complete query answering stack needs to be optimized as a whole, so that the rewritten queries can capitalize on the strengths of the query execution machinery, and the query execution machinery is optimized for the queries produced by the rewriting component.

In the following sections, we give a detailed discussion of the state of the art in the mentioned aspects, and the necessary expansions for an industrial-scale OBDA tool.

Query Formulation Support

Traditional database query languages, such as SQL, require some technical skills and knowledge about language syntax and domain schema. More precisely, they require users to recall relevant domain concepts and syntax elements and communicate their information need in a programmatic way. Such an approach makes information systems almost, if not completely, inaccessible to the end-users. Direct manipulation (Schneiderman, 1983) languages, which employ recognition (rather than recall) and direct manipulation objects (rather than a command language syntax), have emerged as a response to provide easy to use and intuitive interactive systems. In the database domain, *Visual Query Systems* (Catarci et al., 1997) follow the direct manipulation approach in which the domain of interest and the information need are represented by visual elements. Various interaction mechanisms and visualization paradigms—such as diagrams, forms, etc.—have been employed (Epstein, 1991; Catarci et al., 1997) to enable end-users to easily formulate and construct their query requests. However, early approaches mostly missed a key notion, that is, usability (Catarci, 2000), whose concern is the quality of the interaction between the user and the software system rather than the functionality or the technology of the software product. Increasing awareness of the usability in database domain is visible through a growing amount of research addressing end-user database access (e.g., Uren et al., 2007; Barzdins et al., 2008; Popov et al., 2011).

One of the key points for the success of a system, from the usability perspective, is its ability to clearly communicate the provided affordances for user interaction and the domain information that the user is expected to operate on. This concerns the representation and interaction paradigm employed by the system and the organization of the underlying domain knowledge. Concerning the former, researchers mostly try to identify the correlation between task (e.g., simple, complex, etc.) and user type (e.g., novice, expert, etc.) and the visual representation and interaction paradigm used (Catarci et al., 1997; Catarci, 2000; Popov et al., 2011). Regarding the latter, ontologies are considered a key paradigm for capturing and communicating domain knowledge with the end-users (Uren et al., 2007; Barzdins et al., 2008; Tran et al., 2011).

A key feature of any OBDA system is that the ontology needs to provide a user-oriented conceptual model of the domain against which queries can be posed. This allows the user to formulate "natural" queries using familiar terms and without having to understand the structure of the underlying data sources. However, in order to provide the necessary power and flexibility, the underlying query language will inevitably be rather complex. It would be unrealistic to expect all domain experts to formulate queries directly in such a query language, and even expert users may benefit from tool support that exploits the ontology in order to help them to formulate coherent queries. Moreover, the ontology may not include all the vocabulary expected or needed by a given user. Ideally, it should be possible for users with differing levels of expertise to cooperate *on the same query*, by allowing them to switch between more or less technical representations as required, and to extend the ontology *on the fly* as needed for the query being formulated.

Many existing applications today use navigation of simple taxonomic ontologies in order to search for information; a user of eBay, for example, can navigate from "electronics" to "cameras & photography" to "camcorders" in order to find items of interest. In some cases, additional attributes may also be specified; in the above example, attributes such as "brand," "model," and "price" can also be specified. This is sometimes called *faceted search* (Schneiderman, 1983; Suominen et al., 2007; Lim et al., 2009; Tunkelang, 2009), but the structure of the ontology is very simple, as is the form of the query— effectively just retrieving the instances of a given concept/class. The faceted search is based on series of orthogonal categories that can be applied in combination to filter the information space. Facets are derived from the properties of the information elements. In an ontology-based system, identification of these properties is straightforward. An important benefit of faceted search is that it frees users from the burden of dealing with complex form-based interfaces and from the possibility of reaching empty result sets. This faceted search approach, however, in its most common form breaks down as soon as a "join" between information about several objects is required. Consider, for example, searching for camcorders available from sellers who also have a digital camera with ≥12 MP resolution on offer.

Similarly, ontology development tools such as Protégé may allow for the formulation of query concepts using terms from the ontology, but the query is again restricted to a single concept term. Specialized applications have sometimes used GUIs or form-based interfaces for concept formulation, for example, the Pen & Pad data entry tool developed in the GALEN project (Nowlan et al., 1990), but if used for querying this would again provide only for concept/class instance retrieval queries.

An essential part of any practically usable system must be an interface that supports technically less advanced users by some kind of "query by navigation" interface, where the user gradually refines the query by selecting more specific concepts and adding relationships to other concepts, with the ontology being used to suggest relevant refinements and relationships (Nowlan et al., 1990; Catarci et al., 2004). Work on ontology-supported faceted search (Suominen et al., 2007; Lim et al., 2009) is also relevant in this context. Owing to the rising familiarity of users with faceted search interfaces, a promising direction seems to be to extend faceted search with, among others,

- The ability to select several pieces of information for output (querying instead of search)
- A possibility for adding restrictions on several objects connected through roles, in order to allow joins
- A possibility to specify aggregation, like summation or averaging
- A possibility to specify the absence of information (e.g., that a vendor has no negative reviews)

The amalgamation of faceted search and navigational search, so-called *query by navigation* (ter Hofstede et al., 1996), is of significance for the realization of the aforementioned objectives. The navigational approach exploits the graph-based organization of the information to allow users to browse the information space by iteratively narrowing the scope. Stratified hypermedia (Bruza and van der Weide, 1992), a well-known example of the navigational approach, is an architecture in which information is organized via several layers of abstraction. The base layer contains the actual information, while other layers contain the abstraction of this information and enable access to the base layer. In a document retrieval system, the abstraction layer is composed of hierarchically organized keywords. An indexing process is required to characterize the documents and to construct the abstraction layer. However, the characterization of information instances in an ontology-based system is simple and provided by the reference ontology (ter Hofstede et al., 1996). The query by navigation approach is particularly supportive at the exploration phase of the query formulation (Marchionini and White, 2007). Recent applications of query by navigation are available in the Semantic Web domain in the form of textual semantic data browsers (e.g., Popov et al., 2011; Soylu et al., 2012).

A particular approach that combines faceted search and a diagrammatic form of query by navigation is presented in Heim and Ziegler (2011). The approach is based on the hierarchical organization of facets, and hence allows joins between several information collections. The main problem with such diagrammatic approaches and with textual data browsers is that they do not support dealing with large complex ontologies and schemata well, mainly lacking balance between overview and focus. For instance, a diagrammatic approach is good at providing an overview of the domain; however, it has its limits in terms of information visualization and users' cognitive bandwidths. A textual navigation approach is good at splitting the task into several steps; however, it can easily cause users to lose the overview. Therefore, it is not enough to provide navigation along the taxonomy and relations captured in the ontology. In many cases, it turns out that accessing data is difficult even for end-users who are very knowledgeable in their domain, for two reasons: (a) not only because of the complexity of the data model—which can be hidden using an ontology and mappings, but also (b) because of the complexity of an accurate description of the domain. Often an ontology that accurately describes all relevant details of the domain will be more complicated than even experienced domain experts usually think about it in their daily work. This means that they approach the task of query construction without having complete knowledge of all the details of the domain model. It is therefore necessary to develop novel techniques to support users in formulating coherent queries that correctly capture their requirements. In addition to navigation, a query formulation tool should allow searching by name for properties and concepts the expert knows must be available in the ontology. The system should help users understand the ontology by showing how the concepts and properties relevant for a query are interconnected.

For instance, assume that the user would like to list all digital cameras with ≥12 MP resolution. This sounds like a reasonable question that should have a unique interpretation. But the ontology might not actually assign a "resolution" to a camera. Rather, it might say that a camera has at least one image sensor, possibly several,* each of which has an effective and a total resolution. The camera also may or may not support a variety of video resolutions, independent of sensor's resolution. The system should let the users search for "resolution,"

---

* For instance, front-facing and rear-facing on a mobile phone, two sensors in a 3D camcorder, etc.

help them find chains of properties from "Camera" to the different notions of "Resolution," and help them find out whether all sensors need to have ≥12 MP, or at least one of them, etc., and which kind of resolution is meant.

For complex queries, any intuitive user interface for nontechnical users will eventually reach its limits. It is therefore important to also provide a textual query interface for technically versed users, which allows direct editing of a query using a formal syntax such as the W3C SPARQL language. Ideally, both interfaces provide views on an underlying partially constructed query, and users can switch between views at will. Even in the textual interface, there should be more support than present-day interfaces provide, in the form of context-sensitive completion (taking account of the ontology), navigation support, etc. (as is done, e.g., in the input fields of the Protégé ontology editor; Knublauch et al., 2005).

Finally, no ontology can be expected to cover a domain's vocabulary completely. The vocabulary is to a certain extent specific to individuals, projects, departments, etc. and subject to change. To adapt to changing vocabularies, cater for omissions in the ontology, and to allow a light-weight process for ontology development, the query formulation component should also support "on the fly" extension of the ontology during query formulation. This can be achieved by adapting techniques from ontology learning (Cimiano et al., 2005; Cimiano, 2006) in order to identify relevant concepts and relations, and adapting techniques from ontology alignment (aka matching) in order to relate this new vocabulary to existing ontology terms. In case such on-the-fly extensions are insufficient, users should also have access to the range of advanced tools and methodologies discussed in the "Ontology and Mapping Management" section, although they may require assistance from an IT expert in order to use such tools.

Ontology and Mapping Management

The OBDA architecture proposed in this chapter depends crucially on the existence of suitable ontologies and mappings. In this context, the ontology provides a user-oriented conceptual model of the domain that makes it easier for users to formulate queries and understand answers. At the same time, the ontology acts as a "global schema" onto which the schemas of various data sources can be mapped.

Developing suitable ontologies from scratch is likely to be expensive. A more cost-effective approach is to develop tools and methodologies for semiautomatically "bootstrapping" the system with a suitable initial ontology and for extending the ontology "on the fly" as needed by a given application. This means that in this scenario, ontologies are dynamic entities that evolve (i) to incorporate new vocabulary required in user queries and (ii) to accommodate new data sources. In both cases, some way is needed to ensure that vocabulary and axioms are added to the ontology in a coherent way.

Regarding the ontology/data-source mappings, many of these will, like the ontology, be generated automatically from either database schemata and other available metadata or formal installation models. However, these initial mappings are unlikely to be sufficient in all cases, and they will certainly need to evolve along with the ontology. Moreover, new data sources may be added, and this again requires extension and adjustment of the mappings. The management of large, evolving sets of mappings must be seen as an engineering problem on the same level as that of ontology management.

Apart from an initial translation from structured sources like, for example, a relational database schema, present-day ontology management amounts to using interactive ontology editors like Protégé, NeOn, or TopBraid Composer.* These tools support the construction and maintenance of complex ontologies, but they offer little support for the kind of ontology evolution described above.

The issue of representing and reasoning about schema mappings has been widely investigated in recent years. In particular, a large body of work has been devoted to studying operators on schema mappings relevant to model management, notably, composition, merge, and inverse (Madhavan and Halevy, 2003; Fagin et al., 2005c, 2008b, 2009b; Kolaitis, 2005; Bernstein and Ho, 2007; Fagin, 2007; Arenas et al., 2009, 2010a,b; Arocena et al., 2010). In Fagin et al. (2005a,b), Arenas et al. (2004), Fuxman et al. (2005), and Libkin and Sirangelo (2008), the emphasis is on providing foundations for data interoperability systems based on schema mappings. Other works deal with answering queries posed to the target schema on the basis of both the data at the sources, and a set of source-to-target mapping assertions (e.g., Abiteboul and Duschka, 1998; Arenas et al., 2004; Calì et al., 2004) and the surveys (e.g., Ullman, 1997; Halevy, 2001; Halevy et al., 2006).

Another active area of research is principles and tools for comparing both schema mapping languages, and schema mappings expressed in a certain language. Comparing schema mapping languages aim at characterizing such languages in terms of both expressive power and complexity of mapping-based computational tasks (ten Cate and Kolaitis, 2009; Alexe et al., 2010). In particular, ten Cate and Kolaitis (2009) studied various relational schema mapping languages with the goal of characterizing them in terms of structural properties possessed by the schema mappings specified in these languages. Methods for comparing schema mappings have been proposed in Fagin et al. (2008a, 2009b), Gottlob et al. (2009), and Arenas et al. (2010a), especially in the light of the need of a theory of schema mapping optimization. In Fagin et al. (2009b) and Arenas et al. (2010a), schema mappings are compared with respect to their ability to transfer source data and avoid redundancy in the target databases, as well as their ability to cover target data. In Fagin et al. (2008a), three notions of equivalence are introduced. The first one is the

---

* http://protege.stanford.edu/, http://neon-toolkit.org/, and http://www.topbraidcomposer.com/

usual notion based on logic: two schema mappings are logically equivalent if they are indistinguishable by the semantics, that is, if they are satisfied by the same set of database pairs. The other two notions, called data exchange and conjunctive query equivalence, respectively, are relaxations of logical equivalence, capturing indistinguishability for different purposes.

Most of the research mentioned above aim at methods and techniques for analyzing schema mappings. However, mapping management is a broader area, which includes methods for supporting the development of schema mappings, debugging such mappings, or maintaining schema mappings when some part of the specification (e.g., one of the schemas) changes. Although some tools are already available (e.g., CLIO; Fagin et al., 2009a), and some recent papers propose interesting approaches (e.g., Glavic et al., 2010), this problem is largely unexplored, especially in the realm of OBDA. Specifically, the following problems are so far unsolved in the area, but are crucial in dealing with complex scenarios:

1. Once a set of mappings has been defined, the designer often needs to analyze them, in order to verify interesting properties (e.g., minimality).

2. Mappings in OBDA systems relate the elements of the ontology to the data structures of the underlying sources. When the ontology changes, some of the mappings may become obsolete. Similarly, when the sources change, either because new sources are added, or because they undergo modifications of various types, the mappings may become obsolete.

3. Different types of mappings (LAV, GAV, etc.) have been studied in the literature. It is well known that the different types have different properties from the point of view of expressive power of the mapping language and computational complexity of mapping-based tasks. The ideal situation would be to use rich mapping languages during the design phase and then transforming the mappings in such a way that efficient query answering is possible with them. This kind of transformation is called *mapping simplification*. Given a set of mappings M, the goal of simplification is to come up with a set of mappings that are expressed in a tractable class C, and approximate at best M, that is, such that no set M' of mappings in C exists which is "closer" to M than M'.

Regarding ontologies, the required management and evolution described above could be reached by a combination of different techniques, including ontology alignment (Shvaiko and Euzenat, 2005; Jiménez-Ruiz et al., 2009) and ontology approximation (Brandt et al., 2001; Pan and Thomas, 2007). Both the addition of user-defined vocabulary from a query formulation process and the incorporation of the domain model for a new data source are instances of an ontology alignment problem. The results of aligning new user-requested vocabulary or new knowledge coming from new data sources, with the existing ontology do not necessarily fall within the constrained fragments required for efficient OBDA (such as OWL 2 QL; Calvanese et al., 2007b). This problem can be dealt with by an *approximation* approach, that is, transforming the ontology into one that is as expressive as possible while still falling within the required profile. In general, finding an optimal approximation may be costly or even undecidable, but effective techniques are known for producing good approximations (Brandt et al., 2001; Pan and Thomas, 2007).

Concerning mapping management, in order to be able to freely analyze schema mappings, one possibility is to define a specific language for querying schema mappings. The goal of the language is to support queries of the following types: return all mappings that map concepts that are subsets of concept C; or, return all mappings that access table T in the data source S. The basic step is to define a formal meta-model for mapping specification, so that queries over schema mappings will be expressions over this meta-model. A query language can thus be defined over such a meta-model: the general idea is to design the language in such a way that important properties (e.g., scalability of query answering) will be satisfied.

Based on this meta-model, reasoning techniques could be designed that support the evolution of schema mappings. The meta-model could also be used in order to address the issue of monitoring changes and reacting to them. Indeed, every change to the elements involved in the schema mappings may be represented as specific updates on the instance level of the meta-level. The goal of such a reasoning system is to specify the actions to perform, or the actions to suggest to the designer, when these update operations change the instances of the meta-model.

Query Transformation

The OBDA architecture proposed in this chapter relies heavily on query rewriting techniques. The motivation for this is the ability of such techniques to separate ontology reasoning from data reasoning, which can be very costly in the presence of Big Data. However, although these techniques have been studied for several years, applying this technology to Big Data introduces performance requirements that go far beyond what can be obtained with simple approaches. In particular, emphasis must be put both on the performance of the rewriting process and on the performance of the evaluation of the queries generated by it. At the same time, meeting these performance requirements can be achieved by building on top of the experiences in the area of OBDA optimization which we now briefly mention.

In the context of query rewriting with respect to the ontology only (i.e., mappings and query execution aside), recent results (Rosati and Almatelli,

2010; Kikot et al., 2011) have shown that performing query rewriting by means of succinct query expressions, for example, nonrecursive Datalog programs, can be orders of magnitude faster than the approaches that produce UCQs (unions of conjunctive queries) *a priori* (Calvanese et al., 2007b; Pérez-Urbina et al., 2008; Calì et al., 2009; Chortaras et al., 2011). Moreover, these succinct query representations are, in general, cheaper to deal with during optimization, since the structure that needs to be optimized is smaller. Complementary to these results are optimization results for OBDA systems in which the data are in control of the query answering engine, where dramatic improvements can be achieved when load-time precomputation of inferences is allowed. In particular, it has been shown in Rodríguez-Muro and Calvanese (2011) that full materialization of inferences is not always necessary to obtain these benefits, that it is possible to capture most of the semantics of DL-Lite ontologies by means of simple and inexpensive indexing structures in the data-storage layer of the query answering system. These precomputations allow one to further optimize the rewriting process and the queries returned by this process.

In the context of query rewriting in the presence of mappings and where the data sources cannot be modified by the query answering system, a point of departure are recent approaches that focus on the analysis of the data sources and the mappings of the OBDA system (Rodríguez-Muro, 2010). Existing approaches (Rodríguez-Muro and Calvanese, 2011) focus on detecting the state of completeness of the sources with respect to the semantics of the ontology. The result of this analysis can be used for at least two types of optimization, namely: (i) optimization of the ontology and mappings used during query rewriting (offline optimization) and (ii) optimization of the rewritten queries (online optimization). For the former, initial work can be found in the semantic preserving transformations explored in Rodríguez-Muro and Calvanese (2011). For the latter, early experiences (Pérez-Urbina et al., 2008; Rodríguez-Muro, 2010; Calvanese et al., 2011; Rodríguez-Muro and Calvanese, 2012) suggest that traditional theory of Semantic Query Optimization (SQO; Grant et al., 1997) can be applied in the OBDA context as long as the chosen rewriting techniques generate queries that are cheap to optimize using SQO techniques (e.g., Rosati and Almatelli, 2010; Kikot et al., 2011). Complementarily, a first-order logics-based approach to SQO in the context of semantic data formats and reasoning has been proposed in Schmidt et al. (2010). Finally, previous experiences also suggest that in the context of query rewriting into SQL, obtaining high performance is not guaranteed by using an optimized DBMS system; instead, it has been shown (Rodríguez-Muro, 2010) that the form of the SQL query (e.g., use of subqueries, views, nested expressions, etc.) plays a critical role and that even in commercial DBMS engines, care must be taken to guarantee that the SQL queries are in a form that the DBMS can plan and execute efficiently.

Regarding systems, a lot of experience has been accumulated in the past years and can be used to build the next-generation OBDA systems.

In particular, most of the aforementioned rewriting techniques, as well as optimization techniques, have been accompanied by prototypes that were used to benchmark and study the applicability of these techniques empirically. The first example of these systems is QuOnto (Acciarri et al., 2005), a system that implements the core algorithms presented in Calvanese et al. (2007b) and that seeded the idea of query answering through query rewriting in the context of Description Logic (DL) ontologies. QuOnto has also served as a platform for the implementation of the epistemic-query answering techniques proposed in Calvanese et al. (2007a) and served as a basis for the Mastro system (Calvanese et al., 2011), which implements OBDA-specific functionality. While these systems allowed for query answering over actual databases, initially they put little attention to the performance issue. Because of this, following prototypes focused strongly on the performance of the query rewriting algorithms; examples are Requiem (Pérez-Urbina et al., 2010), which implemented the resolution-based query rewriting techniques from Pérez-Urbina et al. (2008), and Presto (Rosati and Almatelli, 2010), which implemented a succinct query translation based on nonrecursive Datalog programs. Finally, the latest generation OBDA systems such as Quest (Rodríguez-Muro and Calvanese, 2012) and Prexto (Rosati, 2012) have focused on the exploitation of efficient rewriting techniques, SQO optimization, as well as the generation of efficient SQL queries.

At the same time, while these initial steps toward performance are promising, there are many challenges that arise in the context of industrial applications and Big Data that are not covered by current techniques. For example, optimizations of query rewriting techniques have only been studied in the context of rather inexpressive ontology and query languages such as OWL 2 QL/DL-Lite and UCQs; however, empirical evidence indicates that none of these languages is enough to satisfy industrial needs. Also, current proposals for optimization using constraints have considered only the use of few classes of constraints, in particular, only simple inclusion dependencies, and little attention has been given to the use of functional dependencies and other forms of constraints that allow one to represent important features of the sources and that are relevant for query answering optimization.

Likewise, optimization of OBDA systems has so far only been considered either in a pure "on-the-fly" query rewriting context, in which sources are out of the scope of the query answering system, or in a context in which the data has been removed from the original source and transformed into an ABox. However, the experience that has been obtained experimenting with the current technology indicates, that in practice, a middle ground could give rise to a higher degree of optimization of the query answering process. It also appears that in the context of Big Data and the complex analytical queries that are often used in this context, good performance cannot be achieved otherwise and these hybrid approaches might be the only viable alternative. It has also become clear that declarative OBDA might not be the best choice to handle all tasks over Big Data. In some cases, domain-specific procedures

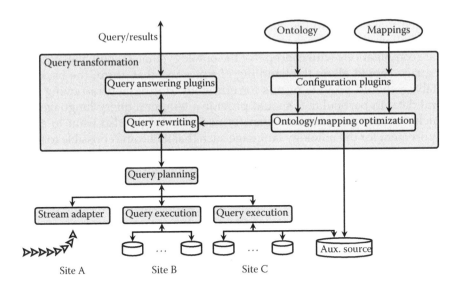

FIGURE 6.3
Fine structure of the query transformation component.

can be more efficient, and hence an OBDA system should provide the means to define such procedures (e.g., by means of domain-specific plug-ins).

To conclude, an optimal system for query answering through query rewriting in the context of Big Data must be approached in an integral way, including modules that handle and optimize each of the aspects of the query answering process, while trying to maximize the benefits that are obtained by separating reasoning with respect to the ontology vs. reasoning with respect to the data. The resulting architecture of such a system may look like the one proposed in this chapter and is depicted in Figure 6.3, where all optimization techniques previously mentioned are combined into a single framework that is expressive enough to capture industrial requirements, can understand the data sources (in the formal sense), and is able to identify the best way to achieve performance, being able to go from pure on-the-fly query answering to (partially) materialized query answering as needed.

Time and Streams

Time plays an important role in many industrial applications. Hence, OBDA-based solutions for such applications have to provide means for efficiently storing and querying timed-stamped data. If we recast these user requirements to technical ones on the OBDA components involved in the life cycle of a query, we come to the conclusion that, first, the user query language should allow the reference to time (instances, intervals) and allow for adequate combinations with concepts of the ontology; that, second, the mapping language should allow the handling of time; and that, third, the back-end database should provide means for efficiently storing and retrieving temporal data, in particular, it should provide a temporal query language into which the user query will be transformed. One might also want to add a requirement for the ontology language such that it becomes possible to build temporal-thematic concepts in the user ontology; but regarding well-known unfeasibility results on temporal description logics (Artale et al., 2010), we will refrain from discussing any aspect concerning temporal constructors for ontology languages and rather focus on temporal query languages and temporal DBs.

While SQL provides built-in data types for times and dates, which can be used, for instance, for representing birthday data, representing validity of facts using, say, two attributes *Start* and *End* imposes severe problems for formulating queries in SQL. For instance, in a Big Data scenario involving possibly mobile sensors of one or more power plants, measurement values might be stored in a table *Sensor* with schema

$$Sensor(ID, Location, Value, Start, End),$$

and it might happen that the location changes while the value remains the same.

ID	Location	Value	Start	End
...	...	...	...	...
S_42	Loc_1	16	15	20
S_42	Loc_1	17	20	25
S_42	Loc_2	17	25	30
S_42	Loc_2	18	30	35
...	...	...	...	...

Now, querying for the (maximum) duration of a measurement with a particular value 17 (and neglecting the location of the sensor) should return a relation

$$\{(S\_42, 17, 20, 30)\}.$$

Although in principle one could specify an SQL query that maximizes the interval length to be specified in result tuples (see, e.g., Zaniolo et al. 1997 for pointers to the original literature in which solutions were developed), the query is very complex (Zaniolo et al., 1997, p. 104) and will hardly be optimized appropriately by standard SQL query engines. Even worse, if only (irregular) time points are stored for measurements, one has to find the next measurement of a particular sensor and time point by a minimization query, and the problem of maximizing validity intervals in output relations as described above remains. In addition, an attribute *Timepoint* might also refer to the insertion time (transaction time) of the tuple rather than to the valid time as we have assumed in the discussion above.

In order to support users in formulating simpler queries for accessing temporal information appropriately, extensions to relational database technology and query languages such as SQL have been developed (e.g., TSQL2; see Zaniolo et al., 1997 for an overview). The time ontology usually is defined by a linear time structure, a discrete representation of the real-time line, and proposals for language standards as well as implementations provide data types for intervals or timestamps. A useful distinction adapted from constraint databases (Kuper et al., 2000) is the one between abstract and concrete temporal databases (Chomicki and Toman, 2005). The representation-independent definitions of temporal databases relying on the infinite structures of the time ontology are called abstract temporal databases; these are the objects relevant for describing the intended semantics for query answering. Finite representations of abstract temporal databases are termed concrete temporal databases (Chomicki and Toman, 2005); these rely on compact representations by (time) intervals.

Temporal databases provide for means of distinguishing between valid time and transaction time. Valid time captures the idea of denoting the time period during which a fact is considered to be true (or to hold with respect to the real world). With transaction time, the time point (or time period) during which a fact is stored in the database is denoted. It might be the case that valid time is to be derived from transaction time (due to a sampling interval). In the case of a transaction time point often valid time is to be derived by retrieving the "next" entry, assuming an assertion is valid until the next one appears. It might also be the case that both types of time aspects are stored in the database leading to the so-called bitemporal databases (Jensen et al., 1993). Using a temporal database, a query for checking which values the sensors indicate between time units should be as easy as in the following example:

```
SELECT ID, Value FROM Sensor WHERE Start >= 23 and End <= 27;
```

with the intended result being a single tuple

$$\{(S\_42,17)\}.$$

The reason for expecting this result can be explained by the abstract vs. concrete distinction. The table with the mobile sensor from the beginning of this section is considered to be part of a concrete temporal database that represents an abstract temporal database. The abstract temporal database holds relations of the form

Sensor(ID,Location,Value,T)

meaning that sensor *ID*, located in *Location*, has a value *Value* measured/valid in time *T* for all *T* such that there is an entry in the concrete temporal database with *Start* and *End* values in between which *T* lies.

Note that the resulting answer to the last query above is the empty set if the mobile sensor data are understood as being part of a pure (nontemporal) SQL DB.

One could extend the simple SQL query from above to a temporal SQL query that also retrieves the locations of the sensors.

```
SELECT ID, Location, Value FROM Sensor WHERE Start >= 20 and
    End <= 27;
```

The expected result with respect to the semantics of abstract temporal databases is

{(*S_42,Loc_1,17*),(*S_42,Loc_2,17*)}.

Again note that the resulting answer set would have been different for nontemporal SQL, namely

{(*S_42,Loc_1,17*)}.

A third example of querying a temporal database is given by the following query, which retrieves start and end times of sensor readings. For the query

```
SELECT ID, Value, Start, End FROM Sensor WHERE Start <= 23 and
    End >= 27;
```

the expected result is

{(*S_42,17,20,30*)}.

Index structures for supporting these kinds of queries have been developed, and add-ons to commercial products offering secondary-memory query answering services such as those sketched above are on the market. Despite the fact that standards have been proposed (e.g., ATSQL), no agreement has been achieved yet, however. Open source implementations for mapping ATSQL to SQL have been provided as well (e.g., TimeDB; Steiner, 1997; Tang et al., 2003).

For many application scenarios, however, only small "windows" of data are required, and thus, storing temporal data in a database (and in external memory) as shown above might cause a lot of unnecessary overhead in some application scenarios. This insight gave rise to the idea of stream-based query answering. In addition to window-based temporal data access, stream-based query answering adopts the view that multiple queries are registered and assumed to be answered "continuously." For this kind of continuous query answering, appropriate index structures and join algorithms have been developed in the database community (see, e.g., Cammert et al. 2003, 2005 for an overview). Data might be supplied incrementally by multiple sources. Combining these sources defines a fused stream of data over which a set of registered queries is continuously answered. In stream-based query answering scenarios, an algebraically specified query (over multiple combined streams set up for a specific application) might be implemented by several query plans that are optimized with respect to all registered queries. An expressive software library for setting up stream-based processing scenarios is described in Cammert et al. (2003).

Rather than by accessing the whole stream, continuous queries refer to only a subset of all assertions, which is defined by a sliding time window. Interestingly, the semantics of sliding windows for continuous queries over data streams is not easily defined appropriately, and multiple proposals exist in the literature (e.g., Zhang et al., 2001; Krämer and Seeger, 2009).

For event recognition, temporal aggregation operators are useful extensions to query languages, and range predicates have to be supported in a special way to compute temporal aggregates (Zhang et al., 2001). In addition, expectation on trajectories helps one to answer continuous queries in a faster way (Schmiegelt and Seeger, 2010). Moreover, it is apparent that the "best" query plan might depend on the data rates of various sources, and dynamic replanning might be required to achieve best performance over time (Krämer et al., 2006; Heinz et al., 2008).

While temporal query answering and stream-based processing have been discussed for a long time in the database community (e.g., Law et al., 2004), recently NOSQL data representation formats and query answering languages have become more and more popular. Besides XML, for example, the Resource Description Format (RDF) has been investigated in temporal or stream-based application contexts. Various extensions to the RDF query language SPARQL have been proposed for stream-based access scenarios in the RDF context (Bolles et al., 2008; Barbieri et al., 2010b; Calbimonte et al., 2010). With the advent of SPARQL 1.1, aggregate functions are investigated in this context as well.

Streaming SPARQL (Bolles et al., 2008) was one of the first approaches based on a specific algebra for streaming data. However, data must be provided "manually" in RDF in this approach. On the other hand, mappings for relating source data to RDF ontologies in an automated way have been investigated in stream-based query answering scenarios as well (e.g., Calbimonte et al., 2010). In contrast to OBDA methods, nowadays these approaches require the materialization of structures at the ontology level (RDF) in order to provide the input data for stream-based query systems. For instance, C-SPARQL queries are compiled to SPARQL queries over RDF data that was produced with specific mappings. C-SPARQL deals with entailments for RDFS or OWL 2 RL by relying on incremental materialization (Barbieri et al., 2010a). See also Ren and Pan (2011) for an approach based on EL++.

SPARQLstream (Calbimonte et al., 2010) provides for mappings to ontology notions and translates to stream-based queries to SNEEQL (Brenninkmeijer et al., 2008), which is the query language for SNEE, a query processor for wireless sensor networks. Stream-based continuous query answering is often used in monitoring applications for detecting events, possibly in real time. EP-SPARQL (Anicic et al., 2011a), which is tailored for complex event processing, is translated to ETALIS (Event TrAnsaction Logic Inference System; Anicic et al., 2011b), a Prolog-based real-time event recognition system based on logical inferences.

While translation to SQL, SPARQL, or other languages is attractive with respect to reusing existing components in a black box approach, some information might be lost, and the best query execution plan might not be found. Therefore, direct implementations of stream-based query languages based on RDF are also investigated in the literature. CQELS (Phuoc et al., 2011) is a much faster "native" implementation (and does not rely on transformation to underlying non-stream-based query languages). In addition, in the latter stream-based querying approach, queries can also refer to static RDF data (e.g., linked open data). In addition, a direct implementation of temporal and static reasoning with ontologies has been investigated for media data interpretation in Möller and Neumann (2008) and Peraldi et al. (2011). Event recognition with respect to expressive ontologies has been investigated recently (Wessel et al., 2007, 2009; Luther et al., 2008; Baader et al., 2009).

As we have seen, it is important to distinguish between temporal queries and window-based continuous queries for streams. Often the later are executed in main memory before data are stored in a database, and much work has been carried out for RDF. However, temporal queries are still important in the RDF context as well. T-SPARQL (Grandi, 2010) applies techniques from temporal DBs (TSQL2, SQL/Temporal, TimeDB) to RDF querying (possibly also with mappings to plain SQL) to define a query language for temporal RDF. For data represented using the W3C standard RDF, an approach for temporal query answering has been developed in an industrial project (Motik, 2010). It is shown that ontology-based answering of queries with specific temporal operators can indeed be realized using a translation to SQL.

In summary, it can be concluded that there is no unique semantics for the kind of queries discussed above, that is, neither for temporal nor for stream-based queries. A combination of stream-based (or window-based), temporal (history-based), and static querying is useful in applications, but is not provided at a time by most approaches. Early work on deductive event recognition (Neumann, 1985; Neumann and Novak, 1983, 1986; André et al., 1988; Kockskämper et al., 1994) already contains many ideas of recently published efforts, and in principle a semantically well-founded combination of quantitative temporal reasoning with respect to valid time has been developed. However, scalability was not the design goal of these works.

While database-based temporal querying approaches or RDF-based temporal and stream-querying approaches as discussed above offer fast performance for large data and massive streams with high data rates, query answering with respect to (weakly expressive) ontologies is supported only with brute-force approaches such as materialization. It is very unlikely that this approach results in scalable query answering for large real-world ontologies of the future due to the enormous blowup (be the materialization managed incrementally or not). Furthermore, reasoning support is quite limited, that is, the expressivity of the ontology languages that queries can refer to is quite limited. Fortunately, it has been shown that brute-force approaches involving materialization for ontology-based query answering are not required for efficiently accessing large amounts of data if recently developed OBDA techniques are applied.

A promising idea for scalable stream-based answering of continuous queries is to apply the idea of query transformation with respect to ontologies also for queries with temporal semantics. Using an ontology and mapping rules to the nomenclature used in particular relational database schemas, query formulation is much easier. Scalability can, for example, be achieved by a translation to an SQL engine with temporal extensions and native index structures and processing algorithms (e.g., as offered by Oracle).

As opposed to what current systems offer, stream-based processing of data usually does not give rise to the instantiation of events with absolute certainty. Rather, data acquired (observations) can be seen as cues that have to be aggregated or accumulated in order to be able to safely infer that a certain event has occurred. These events might be made explicit in order to be able to refer to them directly in subsequent queries (rather than recomputing them from scratch all the time). The central idea of Gries et al. (2010) is to use aggregation operators for data interpretation. Note that interpretation is more than mere materialization of the deductive closure: with interpretation, new and relevant data are generated to better focus temporal and stream-based query answering algorithms.

Distributed Query Execution

In the past, OBDA approaches simply assumed centralized query execution using a well-known relational database system, for example, PostgreSQL

(Savo et al., 2010). However, this assumption does not usually hold in the real world where data are distributed over many autonomous, heterogeneous sources. In addition, existing relational database systems, such as PostgreSQL, cannot scale when faced with TBs of data and the kinds of complex queries to be generated by a typical OBDA query translation component (Savo et al., 2010).

Relevant research in this area includes previous work on query processing in parallel, distributed, and federated database systems, which has been studied for a long time by the database community (Sheth, 1991; DeWitt and Gray, 1992; Özsu and Valduriez, 1999; Kossmann, 2000). Based on principles established in these pioneering works, recently also a variety of approaches for federated query processing in the context of semantic data processing have been proposed (see Görlitz and Staab, 2011 for a recent survey). Falling into this category, our own work on FedX (Schwarte et al., 2011) presents a federated query processing engine operating on top of autonomous semantic databases. The FedX engine enables the virtual integration of heterogeneous sources and implements efficient query evaluation strategies, driven by novel join processing and grouping techniques to minimize the number of requests sent to the federation members. These techniques are based on innovative source selection strategies, pursuing the goal to identify minimal sets of federation members that can contribute answers to the respective subqueries. Coming with all these features, FedX can easily be leveraged to OBDA scenarios whenever the source systems scale with the amounts of data and queries to be processed in the concrete ODBA scenario.

For truly large scale, heterogeneous data stores, efficient evaluation of queries produced by the query translation component discussed in section "Query Transformation" requires massively parallel and distributed query execution. To cover such scenarios, cloud computing has attracted much attention in the research community and software industry. Thanks to virtualization, cloud computing has evolved over the years from a paradigm of basic IT infrastructures used for a specific purpose (clusters), to grid computing, and recently to several paradigms of resource provisioning services: depending on the particular needs, infrastructures (IaaS—Infrastructure as a Service), platforms (PaaS—Platform as a Service), and software (SaaS—Software as a Service) can be provided as services (Gonzalez et al., 2009). One of the important advantages of these newest incarnations of cloud computing is the cost model of resources. Clusters represent a fixed capital investment made up-front and a relatively small operational cost paid over time. In contrast, IaaS, PaaS, and SaaS clouds are characterized by elasticity (Kllapi et al., 2011), and offer their users the ability to lease resources only for as long as needed, based on a per quantum pricing scheme, for example, one hour on Amazon EC2.* Together with the lack of any up-front cost, this represents a major benefit of clouds over earlier approaches.

---

* http://aws.amazon.com/ec2

The ability to use computational resources that are available on demand challenges the way that algorithms, systems, and applications are implemented. Thus, new computing paradigms that fit closely the elastic computation model of cloud computing were proposed. The most popular of these paradigms today is MapReduce (Dean and Ghemawat, 2008). The intuitive appeal of MapReduce, and the availability of platforms such as Hadoop (Apache, 2011), has recently fueled the development of Big Data platforms that aim to support the query language SQL on top of MapReduce (e.g., Hive; Thusoo et al. 2010 and HadoopDB; Bajda-Pawlikowski et al. 2011).

Our own work on massively parallel, elastic query execution for Big Data takes place in the framework of the *Athena Distributed Processing* (*ADP*) system (Tsangaris et al., 2009; Kllapi et al., 2011). Massively parallel query execution is the ability to run queries with the maximum amount of parallelism at each stage of execution. Elasticity means that query execution is flexible; the same query can be executed with more or less resources, given the availability of resources for this query and the execution time goals. Making sure that these two properties are satisfied is a very hard problem in a federated data sources environment such as those discussed in this chapter. The current version of ADP, and its extensions planned for the near future, provides a framework with the right high-level abstractions and an efficient implementation for offering these two properties.

ADP utilizes state-of-the-art database techniques: (i) a declarative query language based on data flows, (ii) the use of sophisticated optimization techniques for executing queries efficiently, (iii) operator extensibility to bring domain-specific computations into the database processing, and (iv) execution platform independence to insulate applications from the idiosynchracies of execution environments such as local clusters, private clouds, or public clouds.

Figure 6.4 shows the current architecture of ADP. The queries are expressed in a data flow language allowing complex graphs with operators as nodes and with edges representing producer–consumer relationships.

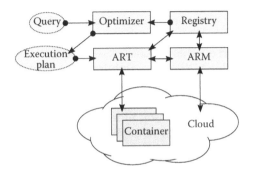

FIGURE 6.4
The architecture of the ADP system.

Queries are optimized and transformed into execution plans that are executed in ART, the ADP Run Time. The resources needed to execute the queries (machines, network, etc.) are reserved or allocated by ARM, the ADP Resource Mediator. Those resources are wrapped into containers. Containers are used to abstract from the details of a physical machine in a cluster or a virtual machine in a cloud. The information about the operators and the state of the system is stored in the Registry. ADP uses state-of-the-art technology and well-proven solutions inspired by years of research in parallel and distributed databases (e.g., parallelism, partitioning, various optimizations, recovery).

Several services that are useful to the OBDA paradigm discussed in this chapter have already been developed on top of ADP: an SQL engine (AdpDB), a MapReduce engine (AdpMR), and a data mining library (AdpDM). Some core research problems have also been studied in depth. For example, in Kllapi et al. (2011), we have studied the problem of scheduling data flows that involve arbitrary data-processing operators in the context of three different optimization problems: (1) minimize completion time given a fixed budget, (2) minimize monetary cost given a deadline, and (3) find trade-offs between completion time and monetary cost without any *a priori* constraints. We formulated these problems and presented an approximate optimization framework to address them that uses resource elasticity in the cloud. To investigate the effectiveness of our approach, we incorporate the devised framework into ADP and instantiate it with several greedy, probabilistic, and exhaustive search algorithms. Finally, through several experiments that we conducted with the prototype elastic optimizer on numerous scientific and synthetic data flows, we identified several interesting general characteristics of the space of alternative schedules as well as the advantages and disadvantages of the various search algorithms. The overall results are very promising and show the effectiveness of our approach.

To maximize the impact of ADP to the OBDA Big Data paradigm discussed in this chapter, ADP will be extended as follows:

- *Tight integration with query transformation modules*: We will develop query planning and execution techniques for queries produced by query translators such as the ones of section "Query Transformation" by integrating the ADP system tightly with Quest (Rodríguez-Muro and Calvanese, 2012). The integration will start by interfacing with SQL using the AdpDB service and continue using lower level data-flow languages and providing hints (e.g., the degree of parallelism) to the ADP engine in order to increase its scalability.

- *Federation*: Building on the input of the query transformation modules, federation will be supported in ADP by scheduling the operators of the query to the different sites so that appropriate cost metrics are minimized. Among others, the techniques include scheduling of operators close to the appropriate data sources and moving data (when possible) to sites with more compute power.

- *Continuous and temporal query support*: Continuous queries such as the ones discussed in section "Time and Streams" will be supported natively by data streaming operators. Similarly, temporal queries will be supported by special operators that can handle temporal semantics.

Conclusion

Giving end-users with limited IT expertise flexible access to large corporate data stores is a major bottleneck in data-intensive industries. Typically, standard domain-specific tools only allow users to access data using a predefined set of queries. Any information need that goes beyond these predefined queries will require the help of a highly skilled IT expert, who knows the data storage intimately and who knows the application domain sufficiently well to communicate with the end-users.

This is costly, not only because such IT experts are a scarce resource, but also because the time of the expert end-users are not free for core tasks. We have argued how OBDA can provide a solution: by capturing the end-users' vocabulary in a formal model (ontology) and maintaining a set of mappings from this vocabulary to the data sources, we can automate the translation work previously done by the IT experts.

OBDA has, in recent years, received a large amount of theoretical attention, and there are also several prototypical implementations. But in order to apply the idea to actual industry data, a number of limitations still need to be overcome. In the "Limitations of the State of the Art in OBDA" section, we have identified the specific problems of usability, prerequisites, scope, and efficiency.

We have argued that these problems can be overcome by a novel combination of techniques, encompassing an end-user oriented query interface, query-driven ontology construction, new ideas for scalable query rewriting, temporal and streaming data processing, and query execution on elastic clouds.

The ideas proposed in this chapter are now investigated and implemented in the FP7 Integrating Project *Optique—Scalable End-user Access to Big Data.*[*]

---

[*] See http://www.optique-project.eu/

References

Abiteboul, S. and O. Duschka. 1998, Complexity of answering queries using materialized views. In *Proc. of the 17th ACM SIGACT SIGMOD SIGART Symp. on Principles of Database Systems (PODS'98)*, Seattle, WA, 254–265.

Acciarri, A., D. Calvanese, G. De Giacomo, D. Lembo, M. Lenzerini, M. Palmieri, and R. Rosati. 2005, QuOnto: Querying ontologies. In *Proc. of the 20th Nat. Conf. on Artificial Intelligence (AAAI 2005)*, Pittsburgh, PA, 1670–1671.

Alexe, B., P. Kolaitis, and W.-C. Tan. 2010, Characterizing schema mappings via data examples. In *Proc. of the 29th ACM SIGACT SIGMOD SIGART Symp. on Principles of Database Systems (PODS 2010)*, Indianapolis, IA, 261–271.

Amoroso, A., G. Esposito, D. Lembo, P. Urbano, and R. Vertucci. 2008, Ontology-based data integration with Mastro-i for configuration and data management at SELEX Sistemi Integrati. In *Proc. of the 16th Ital. Conf. on Database Systems (SEBD 2008)*, Mondello (PA), Italy, 81–92.

André, E., G. Herzog, and T. Rist 1988, On the simultaneous interpretation of real world image sequences and their natural language description: The system Soccer. In *Proc. of the European Conference on Artificial Intelligence (ECAI 1988)*, Munich, Germany, 449–454.

Anicic, D., P. Fodor, S. Rudolph, and N. Stojanovic. 2011a, EP-SPARQL: A unified language for event processing and stream reasoning. In *Proc. of the 20th Int. World Wide Web Conference (WWW 2011)*, Hyderabad, India.

Anicic, D., P. Fodor, S. Rudolph, R. Stühmer, N. Stojanovic, and R. Studer. 2011b, ETALIS: Rule-based reasoning in event processing. In *Reasoning in Event-Based Distributed Systems* (Sven Helmer, Alex Poulovassilis, and Fatos Xhafa, eds.), volume 347 of *Studies in Computational Intelligence*, 99–124, Springer, Berlin/Heidelberg.

Apache. 2011, Apache Hadoop, http://hadoop.apache.org/.

Arenas, M., P. Barcelo, R. Fagin, and L. Libkin. 2004, Locally consistent transformations and query answering in data exchange. In *Proc. of the 23rd ACM SIGACT SIGMOD SIGART Symp. on Principles of Database Systems (PODS 2004)*, Paris, France, 229–240.

Arenas, M., R. Fagin, and A. Nash. 2010a, Composition with target constraints. In *Proc. of the 13th Int. Conf. on Database Theory (ICDT 2010)*, Lausanne, Switzerland, 129–142.

Arenas, M., J. Pérez, J. L. Reutter, and C. Riveros. 2010b, Foundations of schema mapping management. In *Proc. of the 29th ACM SIGACT SIGMOD SIGART Symp. on Principles of Database Systems (PODS 2010)*, Indianapolis, IA, 227–238.

Arenas, M., J. Pérez, and C. Riveros 2009, The recovery of a schema mapping: Bringing exchanged data back. *ACM Trans. on Database Systems*, 34, 22:1–22:48.

Arocena, P. C., A. Fuxman, and R. J. Miller. 2010, Composing local-as-view mappings: Closure and applications. In *Proc. of the 13th Int. Conf. on Database Theory (ICDT 2010)*, Lausanne, Switzerland, 209–218.

Artale, A., D. Calvanese, R. Kontchakov, and M. Zakharyaschev. 2009, The DL-Lite family and relatives. *Journal of Artificial Intelligence Research*, 36, 1–69.

Artale, A., R. Kontchakov, V. Ryzhikov, and M. Zakharyaschev. 2010, Past and future of DL-Lite. In *AAAI Conference on Artificial Intelligence*, Atlanta, GA.

Baader, F., A. Bauer, P. Baumgartner, A. Cregan, A. Gabaldon, K. Ji, K. Lee, D. Rajaratnam, and R. Schwitter. 2009, A novel architecture for situation awareness systems. In *Proc. of the 18th Int. Conf. on Automated Reasoning with Analytic Tableaux and Related Methods (Tableaux 2009)*, Oslo, Norway, volume 5607 of *Lecture Notes in Computer Science*, 77–92, Springer-Verlag.

Bajda-Pawlikowski, K., D. J. Abadi, A. Silberschatz, and E. Paulson. 2011, Efficient processing of data warehousing queries in a split execution environment. In *Proc. of SIGMOD*, Athens, Greece.

Barbieri, D. F., D. Braga, S. Ceri, E. D. Valle, and M. Grossniklaus. 2010a, Incremental reasoning on streams and rich background knowledge. In *Proc. of the 7th Extended Semantic Web Conference (ESWC 2010)*, Heraklion, Greece, volume 1, 1–15.

Barbieri, D. F., D. Braga, S. Ceri, E. D. Valle, and M. Grossniklaus. 2010b, Querying RDF streams with C-SPARQL. *SIGMOD Record*, 39, 20–26.

Barzdins, G., E. Liepins, M. Veilande, and M. Zviedris. 2008, Ontology enabled graphical database query tool for end-users. In *Databases and Information Systems V—Selected Papers from the Eighth International Baltic Conference, DB&IS 2008, June 2–5, 2008, Tallinn, Estonia* (Hele-Mai Haav and Ahto Kalja, eds.), volume 187 of *Frontiers in Artificial Intelligence and Applications*, 105–116, IOS Press, Netherlands.

Bernstein, P. A. and H. Ho. 2007, Model management and schema mappings: Theory and practice. In *Proc. of the 33rd Int. Conf. on Very Large Data Bases (VLDB 2007)*, Vienna, Austria, 1439–1440.

Beyer, M. A., A. Lapkin, N. Gall, D. Feinberg, and V. T. Sribar. 2011, 'Big Data' is only the beginning of extreme information management. Gartner report G00211490.

Bolles, A., M. Grawunder, and J. Jacobi. 2008, Streaming SPARQL—Extending SPARQL to process data streams. In *Proc. of the 5th European Semantic Web Conference (ESWC 2008)*, Tenerife, Canary Islands, Spain, 448–462. http://data.semantic-web.org/conference/eswc/2008/paper/3.

Brachman, R. J. and H. J. Levesque. 1984, The tractability of subsumption in frame-based description languages. In *AAAI*, 34–37, Austin, TX.

Brandt, S., R. Küsters, and A-Y. Turhan. 2001, Approximation in description logics. LTCS-Report 01-06, LuFG Theoretical Computer Science, RWTH Aachen, Germany. Available at http://www-lti.informatik.rwth-aachen.de/Forschung/Reports.html.

Brenninkmeijer, C., I. Galpin, A. Fernandes, and N. Paton. 2008, A semantics for a query language over sensors, streams and relations. In *Sharing Data, Information and Knowledge, 25th British National Conference on Databases (BNCOD 25)*, Cardiff, UK (Alex Gray, Keith Jeffery, and Jianhua Shao, eds.), volume 5071 of *Lecture Notes in Computer Science*, 87–99, Springer, Berlin/Heidelberg.

Bruza, P. D. and T. P. van der Weide. 1992, Stratified hypermedia structures for information disclosure. *Computer Journal*, 35, 208–220.

Calbimonte, J.-P., Ó. Corcho, and A. J. G. Gray. 2010, Enabling ontology-based access to streaming data sources. In *Proc. of the 9th Int. Semantic Web Conf. (ISWC 2010)*, Bonn, Germany, 96–111.

Calì, A., D. Calvanese, G. De Giacomo, and M. Lenzerini. 2004, Data integration under integrity constraints. *Information Systems*, 29, 147–163.

Calì, A., G. Gottlob, and T. Lukasiewicz. 2009, A general datalog-based framework for tractable query answering over ontologies. In *Proc. of the 28th ACM Symposium on Principles of Database Systems (PODS 2009)*, Providence, RI, 77–86.

Calvanese, D., G. De Giacomo, D. Lembo, M. Lenzerini, A. Poggi, M. Rodríguez-Muro, R. Rosati, M. Ruzzi, and D. F. Savo. 2011, The MASTRO system for ontology-based data access. *Semantic Web Journal*, 2, 43–53.

Calvanese, D., G. De Giacomo, D. Lembo, M. Lenzerini, and R. Rosati. 2007a, EQL-Lite: Effective first-order query processing in description logics. In *Proc. of the 20th Int. Joint Conf. on Artificial Intelligence (IJCAI 2007)*, Hyderabad, India, 274–279.

Calvanese, D., G. De Giacomo, D. Lembo, M. Lenzerini, and R. Rosati. 2007b, Tractable reasoning and efficient query answering in description logics: The *DL-Lite* family. *Journal of Automated Reasoning*, 39, 385–429.

Calvanese, D., G. De Giacomo, D. Lembo, M. Lenzerini, and R. Rosati. 2012, Data complexity of query answering in description logics. *Artificial Intelligence*, 195, 335–360.

Cammert, M., C. Heinz, J. Krämer, M. Schneider, and B. Seeger. 2003, A status report on XXL—a software infrastructure for efficient query processing. *IEEE Data Eng. Bull.*, 26, 12–18.

Cammert, M., C. Heinz, J. Krämer, and B. Seeger. 2005, Sortierbasierte Joins über Datenströmen. In *BTW 2005*, volume 65 of *LNI*, Karlsruhe, Germany, 365–384, GI, http://dblp.uni-trier.de/db/conf/btw/btw2005.html#CammertHKS05.

Catarci, T. 2000, What happened when database researchers met usability. *Information Systems*, 25, 177–212. http://www.sciencedirect.com/science/article/pii/S0306437900000156.

Catarci, T., M. F. Costabile, S. Levialdi, and C. Batini. 1997, Visual query systems for databases: A survey. *Journal of Visual Languages & Computing*, 8, 215–260. http://www.sciencedirect.com/science/article/pii/S1045926X97900379.

Catarci, T., P. Dongilli, T. Di Mascio, E. Franconi, G. Santucci, and S. Tessaris. 2004, An ontology based visual tool for query formulation support. In *Proc. of the 16th Eur. Conf. on Artificial Intelligence (ECAI 2004)*, Valencia, Spain (Ramon López de Mántaras and Lorenza Saitta, eds.), 308–312, IOS Press, Netherlands.

Chomicki, J. and D. Toman. 2005, Temporal databases. In *Handbook of Temporal Reasoning in Artificial Intelligence* (Michael Fisher, Dov M. Gabbay, and Lluis Vila, eds.), volume 1, 429–467, Elsevier B.V., Amsterdam, The Netherlands.

Chortaras, A., D. Trivela, and G. B. Stamou. 2011, Optimized query rewriting for OWL 2 QL. In *Proc. of the 23st Int. Conf. on Automated Deduction (CADE 2011)*, Wroclaw, Poland, 192–206.

Cimiano, P. 2006, *Ontology Learning and Population from Text: Algorithms, Evaluation and Applications*. Springer, USA.

Cimiano, P., A. Hotho, and S. Staab. 2005, Learning concept hierarchies from text corpora using formal concept analysis. *Journal of Artificial Intelligence Research*, 24, 305–339.

Dean, J. and S. Ghemawat. 2008, MapReduce: simplified data processing on large clusters. *Communications of the ACM*, 51, 107–113. http://doi.acm.org/10.1145/1327452.1327492.

DeWitt, D. J. and J. Gray. 1992, Parallel database systems: The future of high performance database systems. *Communications of the ACM*, 35, 85–98.

Tunkelang, D. 2009, *Faceted Search*. Morgan and Claypool.

Epstein, R. G. 1991, The tabletalk query language. *Journal of Visual Languages & Computing*, 2, 115–141. http://www.sciencedirect.com/science/article/pii/S1045926X05800266.

Fagin, R. 2007, Inverting schema mappings. *ACM Transactions on Database Systems*, 32, 25:1–25:53.

Fagin, R., L. M. Haas, M. A. Hernández, R. J. Miller, L. Popa, and Y. Velegrakis. 2009a, Clio: Schema mapping creation and data exchange. In *Conceptual*

Modeling: Foundations and Applications—Essays in Honor of John Mylopoulos (A. T. Borgida, V. K. Chaudhri, P. Giorgini, and E. S. Yu), 198–236, Springer, Berlin/Heidelberg.

Fagin, R., P. G. Kolaitis, R. J. Miller, and L. Popa. 2005a, Data exchange: Semantics and query answering. *Theoretical Computer Science*, 336, 89–124.

Fagin, R., P. G. Kolaitis, A. Nash, and L. Popa. 2008a, Towards a theory of schema-mapping optimization. In *Proc. of the 27th ACM SIGACT SIGMOD SIGART Symp. on Principles of Database Systems (PODS 2008)*, Vancouver, Canada, 33–42.

Fagin, R., P. G. Kolaitis, and L. Popa. 2005b, Data exchange: Getting to the core. *ACM Transactions on Database Systems*, 30, 174–210.

Fagin, R., P. G. Kolaitis, L. Popa, and W.-C. Tan. 2005c, Composing schema mappings: Second-order dependencies to the rescue. *ACM Transactions on Database Systems*, 30, 994–1055.

Fagin, R., P. G. Kolaitis, L. Popa, and W.-C. Tan. 2008b, Quasi-inverses of schema mappings. *ACM Transactions on Database Systems*, 33, 1–52.

Fagin, R., P. G. Kolaitis, L. Popa, and W.-C. Tan. 2009b, Reverse data exchange: Coping with nulls. In *Proc. of the 28th ACM SIGACT SIGMOD SIGART Symp. on Principles of Database Systems (PODS 2009)*, Providence, RI, 23–32.

Fuxman, A., P. G. Kolaitis, R. Miller, and W.-C. Tan. 2005, Peer data exchange. In *Proc. of the 24rd ACM SIGACT SIGMOD SIGART Symp. on Principles of Database Systems (PODS 2005)*, Baltimore, MD, 160–171.

Glavic, B., G. Alonso, R. J. Miller, and L. M. Haas. 2010, TRAMP: Understanding the behavior of schema mappings through provenance. *PVLDB*, 3, Singapore, 1314–1325.

Gonzalez, L. M. V., L. Rodero-Merino, J. Caceres, and M. A. Lindner. 2009, A break in the clouds: Towards a cloud definition. *Computer Communication Review*, 39, 50–55.

Görlitz, O. and S. Staab. 2011, Federated data management and query optimization for linked open data. In *New Directions in Web Data Management* (A. Vakali and L. C. Jain), *1*, 109–137, Springer-Verlag, Berlin/Heidelberg.

Gottlob, G., R. Pichler, and V. Savenkov. 2009, Normalization and optimization of schema mappings. *Proceedings of the VLDB Endowment*, Lyon, France, 2, 1102–1113.

Grandi, F. 2010, T-SPARQL: A TSQL2-like temporal query language for RDF. In *Proc. of the ADBIS 2010 Int. Workshop on Querying Graph Structured Data (GraphQ 2010)*, Novi Sad, Serbia, 21–30.

Grant, J., J. Gryz, J. Minker, and L. Raschid. 1997, Semantic query optimization for object databases. In *Proc. of the 13th IEEE Int. Conf. on Data Engineering (ICDE'97)*, Birmingham, UK, 444–453.

Gries, O., R. Möller, A. Nafissi, M. Rosenfeld, K. Sokolski, and M. Wessel. 2010, A probabilistic abduction engine for media interpretation based on ontologies. In *Proc. of the 4th Int. Conf. on Web Reasoning and Rule Systems (RR 2010)*, Bressanone/Brixen, Italy (J. Alferes, P. Hitzler, and Th. Lukasiewicz, eds.) Springer, Berlin/Heidelberg.

Halevy, A. Y. 2001, Answering queries using views: A survey. *Very Large Database Journal*, 10, 270–294.

Halevy, A. Y., A. Rajaraman, and J. Ordille. 2006, Data integration: The teenage years. In *Proc. of the 32nd Int. Conf. on Very Large Data Bases (VLDB 2006)*, VLDB 2006, Seoul, Korea, 9–16.

Heim, P. and J. Ziegler. 2011, Faceted visual exploration of semantic data. In *Proceedings of the Second IFIP WG 13.7 Conference on Human-Computer Interaction and Visualization*, HCIV 2009, co-located with INTERACT 2009, Uppsala, Sweden, 58–75, Springer-Verlag, Berlin, Heidelberg. http://dl.acm.org/citation.cfm?id=1987029.1987035.

Heinz, C., J. Krämer, T. Riemenschneider, and B. Seeger. 2008, Toward simulation-based optimization in data stream management systems. In *Proc. of the 24th Int. Conf. on Data Engineering (ICDE 2008)*, Cancun, Mexico, 1580–1583.

Jensen, C. S., M. D. Soo, and R. T. Snodgrass. 1993, Unification of temporal data models. In *Proceedings of IEEE International Conference on Data Engineering, (ICDE 1993)*, Vienna, Austria, 262–271.

Jiménez-Ruiz, E., B. C. Grau, I. Horrocks, and R. B. Llavori. 2009, Logic-based ontology integration using ContentMap. In *Proc. of XIV Jornadas de Ingeniería del Software y Bases de Datos (JISBD 2009)*, San Sebastián, Spain (Antonio Vallecillo and Goiuria Sagardui, eds.), 316–319, Los autores. download/2009/JCHB09c.pdf.

Kikot, S., R. Kontchakov, and M. Zakharyaschev. 2011, On (in)tractability of OBDA with OWL 2 QL. In *Proc. of the 24th Int. Workshop on Description Logic (DL 2011)*, Barcelona, Spain.

Kllapi, H., E. Sitaridi, M. M. Tsangaris, and Y. E. Ioannidis. 2011, Schedule optimization for data processing flows on the cloud. In *Proc. of SIGMOD* (SIGMOD 2011), Athens, Greece, 289–300.

Knublauch, H., M. Horridge, M. A. Musen, A. L. Rector, R. Stevens, N. Drummond, P. W. Lord, N. F. Noy, J. Seidenberg, and H. Wang. 2005, The Protégé OWL experience. In *Proc. of the OWL: Experience and Directions Workshop (OWLED 2005)*, Galway, Ireland, volume 188 of *CEUR* (http://ceur-ws.org/).

Kockskämper, S., B. Neumann, and M. Schick. 1994, Extending process monitoring by event recognition. In *Proc. of the 2nd Int. Conf. on Intelligent System Engineering (ISE'94)*, Hamburg-Harburg, Germany, 455–460.

Kolaitis, P. G. 2005, Schema mappings, data exchange, and metadata management. In *Proc. of the 24rd ACM SIGACT SIGMOD SIGART Symp. on Principles of Database Systems (PODS 2005)*, Baltimore, MD, 61–75.

Kossmann, D. 2000, The state of the art in distributed query processing. *ACM Computing Surveys*, 32, 422–469.

Krämer, J. and B. Seeger. 2009, Semantics and implementation of continuous sliding window queries over data streams. *ACM Transactions on Database Systems*, 34, 4:1–4:49.

Krämer, J., Y. Yang, M. Cammert, B. Seeger, and D. Papadias. 2006, Dynamic plan migration for snapshot-equivalent continuous queries in data stream systems. In *Proc. of EDBT 2006 Workshops* (EDBT 2006), Munich, Germany, volume 4254 of *Lecture Notes in Computer Science*, 497–516, Springer, Berlin/Heidelberg.

Kuper, G. M., L. Libkin, and J. Paredaens, eds. 2000, *Constraint Databases*. Springer, Berlin Heidelberg.

Law, Y.-N., H. Wang, and C. Zaniolo. 2004, Query languages and data models for database sequences and data streams. In *Proc. of the 30th Int. Conf. on Very Large Data Bases (VLDB 2004)*, Toronto, Canada, 492–503, VLDB Endowment. http://dl.acm.org/citation.cfm?id=1316689.1316733.

Libkin, L. and C. Sirangelo. 2008, Data exchange and schema mappings in open and closed worlds. In *Proc. of the 27th ACM SIGACT SIGMOD SIGART Symp. on Principles of Database Systems (PODS 2008)*, Vancouver, Canada, 139–148.

Lim, S. C. J., Y. Liu, and W. B. Lee. 2009, Faceted search and retrieval based on semantically annotated product family ontology. In *Proc. of the WSDM 2009 Workshop on Exploiting Semantic Annotations in Information Retrieval (ESAIR 2009)*, Barcelona, Spain, 15–24. http://doi.acm.org/10.1145/1506250.1506254.

Luther, M., Y. Fukazawa, M. Wagner, and S. Kurakake. 2008, Situational reasoning for task-oriented mobile service recommendation. *Knowledge Engineering Review*, 23, 7–19. http://dl.acm.org/citation.cfm?id=1362078.1362080.

Madhavan, J. and A. Y. Halevy. 2003, Composing mappings among data sources. In *Proc. of the 29th Int. Conf. on Very Large Data Bases (VLDB 2003)*, Berlin, Germany, 572–583.

Marchionini, G. and R. White. 2007, Find what you need, understand what you find. *International Journal of Human-Computer Interaction*, 23, 205–237.

Möller, R. and B. Neumann. 2008, Ontology-based reasoning techniques for multimedia interpretation and retrieval. In *Semantic Multimedia and Ontologies: Theory and Applications* (Yiannis Kompatsiaris and Paola Hobson, eds.), Springer-Verlag, London.

Möller, R., V. Haarslev, and M. Wessel. 2006, On the scalability of description logic instance retrieval. In *29. Deutsche Jahrestagung für Künstliche Intelligenz* (C. Freksa and M. Kohlhase, eds.), Bremen, Germany, Lecture Notes in Artificial Intelligence. Springer, Netherlands.

Motik, B. 2010, Representing and querying validity time in RDF and OWL: A logic-based approach. In *Proc. of the 9th Int. Semantic Web Conf. (ISWC 2010)*, Bonn, Germany, volume 1, 550–565.

Neumann, B. 1985, Retrieving events from geometrical descriptions of time-varying scenes. In *Foundations of Knowledge Base Management—Contributions from Logic, Databases, and Artificial Intelligence* (J. W. Schmidt and Costantino Thanos, eds.), 443, Springer Verlag, Berling/Heidelberg.

Neumann, B. and H.-J. Novak. 1986, NAOS: Ein System zur natürlichsprachlichen Beschreibung zeitveränderlicher Szenen. *Informatik Forschung und Entwicklung*, 1, 83–92.

Neumann, B. and H.-J. Novak. 1983, Event models for recognition and natural language description of events in real-world image sequences. In *Proc. of the 8th Int. Joint Conference on Artificial Intelligence (IJCAI'83)*, Karlsruhe, Germany, 724–726.

Nowlan, W. A., A. L. Rector, S. Kay, C. A. Goble, B. Horan, T. J. Howkins, and A. Wilson. 1990, PEN&PAD: A doctors' workstation with intelligent data entry and summaries. In *Proceedings of the 14th Annual Symposium on Computer Applications in Medical Care (SCAMC'90)*, Washington, DC (R. A. Miller, ed.), 941–942. IEEE Computer Society Press, Los Alamitos, California.

Özsu, M. T. and P. Valduriez. 1999, *Principles of Distributed Database Systems*, 2nd edition. Prentice-Hall.

Pan, J. Z. and E. Thomas. 2007, Approximating OWL-DL ontologies. In *Proc. of the 22nd Nat. Conf. on Artificial Intelligence (AAAI-07)*, Vancouver, British Columbia, Canada, 1434–1439.

Peraldi, I. S. E., A. Kaya, and R. Möller 2011, Logical formalization of multimedia interpretation. In *Knowledge-Driven Multimedia Information Extraction and Ontology Evolution*, volume 6050 of *Lecture Notes in Computer Science*, 110–133, Springer, Berlin/Heidelberg.

Pérez-Urbina, H., B. Motik, and I. Horrocks. 2008, Rewriting conjunctive queries over description logic knowledge bases. In *Revised Selected Papers of the 3rd Int. Workshop on Semantics in Data and Knowledge Bases (SDKB 2008)*, Nantes, France,

(K.-D. Schewe and B. Thalheim, eds.), volume 4925 of *Lecture Notes in Computer Science*, 199–214, Springer, Berlin/Heidelberg.

Pérez-Urbina, H., B. Motik, and I. Horrocks. 2010, Tractable query answering and rewriting under description logic constraints. *Journal of Applied Logic*, 8, 186–209.

Phuoc, D. L., M. Dao-Tran, J. X. Parreira, and M. Hauswirth. 2011, A native and adaptive approach for unified processing of linked streams and linked data. In *Proc. of the 10th Int. Semantic Web Conf. (ISWC 2011)*, Boston, MA, 1, 370–388.

Poggi, A., D. Lembo, D. Calvanese, G. De Giacomo, M. Lenzerini, and R. Rosati. 2008, Linking data to ontologies. *Journal on Data Semantics*, X, 133–173.

Popov, I. O., M. C. Schraefel, W. Hall, and N. Shadbolt. 2011, Connecting the dots: a multi-pivot approach to data exploration. In *Proceedings of the 10th International Conference on The Semantic web—Volume Part I*, ISWC'11, Boston, MA, 553–568. Springer-Verlag, Berlin, Heidelberg. http://dl.acm.org/citation.cfm?id=2063016.2063052.

Ren, Y. and J. Z. Pan 2011, Optimising ontology stream reasoning with truth maintenance system. In *Proc. of the ACM Conference on Information and Knowledge Management (CIKM 2011)*, Glasgow, Scotland.

Rodríguez-Muro, M. 2010, *Tools and Techniques for Ontology Based Data Access in Lightweight Description Logics*. Ph.D. thesis, KRDB Research Centre for Knowledge and Data, Free University of Bozen-Bolzano.

Rodríguez-Muro, M. and D. Calvanese. 2011, Dependencies to optimize ontology based data access. In *Proc. of the 24th Int. Workshop on Description Logic (DL 2011)*, Barcelona, Spain, volume 745 of *CEUR* (http://ceur-ws.org/).

Rodríguez-Muro, M. and D. Calvanese 2012, Quest, an owl 2 ql reasoner for ontology-based data access. In *Proc. of the 9th Int. Workshop on OWL: Experiences and Directions (OWLED 2012)*, Heraklion, Crete, volume 849 of *CEUR Electronic Workshop Proceedings*. http://ceur-ws.org/.

Rosati, R. 2012, Prexto: Query rewriting under extensional constraints in dl-lite. In *Proc. of the 9th Extended Semantic Web Conference (ESWC 2012)*, Heraklion, Crete, volume 7295 of *LNCS*, 360–374, Springer, Berlin/Heidelberg.

Rosati, R. and A. Almatelli. 2010, Improving query answering over *DL-Lite* ontologies. In *Proc. of the 12th Int. Conf. on the Principles of Knowledge Representation and Reasoning (KR 2010)*, Toronto, Canada, 290–300.

Savo, D. F., D. Lembo, M. Lenzerini, A. Poggi, M. Rodríguez-Muro, V. Romagnoli, M. Ruzzi, and G. Stella. 2010, Mastro at work: Experiences on ontology-based data access. In *Proc. of the 23rd Int. Workshop on Description Logic (DL 2010)*, Waterloo, Canada, volume 573 of *CEUR* (http://ceur-ws.org/), 20–31.

Schmidt, M., M. Meier, and G. Lausen. 2010, Foundations of sparql query optimization. In *ICDT 2010*, Lausanne, Switzerland, 4–33.

Schmiegelt, P. and B. Seeger. 2010, Querying the future of spatio-temporal objects. In *Proc. of the 18th SIGSPATIAL Int. Conf. on Advances in Geographic Information Systems (GIS 2010)*, San Jose, CA, 486–489, ACM. http://doi.acm.org/10.1145/1869790.1869868.

Schneiderman, B. 1983, Direct manipulation: A step beyond programming languages. *Computer*, 16, 57–69.

Schwarte, A., P. Haase, K. Hose, R. Schenkel, and M. Schmidt. 2011, Fedx: Optimization techniques for federated query processing on linked data. In *International Semantic Web Conference (ISWC 2011)*, Boston, MA, 601–616.

Sheth, A. P. 1991, Federated database systems for managing distributed, heterogeneous, and autonomous databases. In *VLDB*, Barcelona, Spain, 489.

Shvaiko, P. and J. Euzenat. 2005, A survey of schema-based matching approaches. *Journal on Data Semantics*, IV, 146–171.

Soylu, A., F. Modritscher, and P. De Causmaecker. 2012, Ubiquitous web navigation through harvesting embedded semantic data: A mobile scenario. *Integrated Computer-Aided Engineering*, 19, 93–109.

Steiner, A. 1997, *A Generalisation Approach to Temporal Data Models and their Implementations*. Ph.D. thesis, Departement Informatik, ETH Zurich, Switzerland.

Suominen, O., K. Viljanen, and E. Hyvänen. 2007, User-centric faceted search for semantic portals. In *Proc. of the 4th European Semantic Web Conf. (ESWC 2007)*, Innsbruck, Austria, 356–370. http://dx.doi.org/10.1007/978-3-540-72667-8_26.

Tang, Y., L. Liang, R. Huang, and Y. Yu. 2003, Bitemporal extensions to non-temporal RDBMS in distributed environment. In *Proc. of the 8th Int. Conf. on Computer Supported Cooperative Work in Design*, Xiamen, China, 370-374. DOI: 10.1109/CACWD.2004.1349216.

ten Cate, B. and P. G. Kolaitis. 2009, Structural characterizations of schema-mapping languages. In *Proc. of the 12th Int. Conf. on Database Theory (ICDT 2009)*, Saint-Petersburg, Russia, 63–72.

ter Hofstede, A. H. M., H. A. Proper, and Th. P. van der Weide. 1996, Query formulation as an information retrieval problem. *The Computer Journal*, 39, 255–274. http://comjnl.oxfordjournals.org/content/39/4/255.abstract.

Thusoo, A., J. Sen Sarma, N. Jain, Z. Shao, P. Chakka, N. Zhang, S. Anthony, H. Liu, and R. Murthy. 2010, Hive—a petabyte scale data warehouse using Hadoop. In *Proc. of the 26th IEEE Int. Conf. on Data Engineering (ICDE 2010)*, Long Beach, CA, 996–1005.

Tran, T., D. M. Herzig, and G. Ladwig. 2011, Semsearchpro—using semantics throughout the search process. *Web Semantics: Science, Services and Agents on the World Wide Web*, 9, 349–364. http://www.sciencedirect.com/science/article/pii/S15708268110 00758. JWS special issue on Semantic Search.

Tsangaris, M. M., G. Kakaletris, H. Kllapi, G. Papanikos, F. Pentaris, P. Polydoras, E. Sitaridi, V. Stoumpos, and Y. E. Ioannidis. 2009, Dataflow processing and optimization on grid and cloud infrastructures. *IEEE Data Eng. Bull.*, 32, 67–74.

Ullman, J. D. 1997, Information integration using logical views. In *Proc. of the 6th Int. Conf. on Database Theory (ICDT'97)*, volume 1186 of *Lecture Notes in Computer Science*, Delphi, Greece, 19–40. Springer, London.

Uren, V., Y. Lei, V. Lopez, H. Liu, E. Motta, and M. Giordanino. 2007, The usability of semantic search tools: A review. *Knowl. Eng. Rev.*, 22, 361–377. http://dx.doi.org/10.1017/S0269888907001233.

Wessel, M., M. Luther, and R. Möller. 2009, What happened to Bob? Semantic data mining of context histories. In *Proc. of the 2009 Int. Workshop on Description Logics (DL 2009)*, Oxford, UK. CEUR Workshop Proceedings, Vol. 477.

Wessel, M., M. Luther, and M. Wagner. 2007, The difference a day makes—Recognizing important events in daily context logs. In *Proc. of the Int. Workshop on Contexts and Ontologies: Representation and Reasoning C&O:RR 2007*, collocated with CONTEXT 2007, Roskilde, Denmark. CEUR Workshop Proceedings, Vol. 298.

Zaniolo, C., S. Ceri, Chr. Faloutsos, R. T. Snodgrass, V. S. Subrahmanian, and R. Zicari. 1997, *Advanced Database Systems*, chapter Overview of Temporal Databases. Morgan Kaufmann, USA.

Zhang, D., A. Markowetz, V. J. Tsotras, D. Gunopulos, and B. Seeger. 2001, Efficient computation of temporal aggregates with range predicates. In *Proceedings of the Twentieth ACM SIGACT-SIGMOD-SIGART Symposium on Principles of Database Systems (PODS 2001)* (Peter Buneman, ed.), May 21–23, 2001, Santa Barbara, CA. ACM 2001, ISBN 1-58113-361-8.

7

Semantic Data Interoperability: The Key Problem of Big Data

Hele-Mai Haav and Peep Küngas

CONTENTS

Introduction

Data-intensive applications (social media sites, e-commerce, e-government, e-health, e-science, etc.) are common in our society. They utilize and generate huge volumes of data of different kinds. For example, according to the

245

recent report on Big Data by McKinsey Global Institute, enterprises world-wide stored more than 7 exabytes and consumers stored more than 6 exa-bytes of new data in 2010 (Manyika et al. 2011). The report also refers to the fact that volume of data created globally is expected to grow exponentially in forthcoming years. As a consequence, the "Big Data" problem has emerged.

Currently, the term "Big Data" does not have a well-defined and com-monly accepted meaning. Therefore, many researchers and practitioners use the term rather freely. However, there is a common understanding regarding the three characteristics of Big Data, which are as follows: volume, veloc-ity, and variety (Gartner 2012). Volume usually indicates large volumes (e.g., petabytes or more) of data of different types. Taking into account the com-plexity of data, volumes of data may be smaller for highly complex data sets compared to the simple ones. For example, taking into account the complex-ity dimension of data, 30 billion of RDF[*] triples can be viewed as Big Data. Volume is also dependent on what sizes of data sets are common in a par-ticular field. It is difficult to draw a certain boundary over what all data sets can be considered as Big Data. Velocity characterizes time sensitiveness of data for applications like fraud or trade event detection, where near real-time analysis of large volumes of data is needed. Variety refers to different types of data that need to be integrated and analyzed together. As a rule, these data are originated from various data sources (e.g., SQL/NoSQL databases, textual and XML[†] documents, web sites, audio/video streams, etc.). In many cases, volumes of data are not that big issue as meaningful interoperability of relevant data extracted from disparate sources.

Data interoperability as a term might be confused with notions of data integration and data exchange well known from database management field. In this chapter, we define semantic data interoperability as the ability of sys-tems to automatically and accurately interpret meaning of the exchanged data. Semantic interoperability in its broad sense covers data and process interoperability. Data interoperability is a precondition for process interop-erability. In this chapter, we consider only semantic data interoperability (see also Stuckenschmidt 2012). For achieving semantic data interoperability, systems need not only to exchange their data, but also exchange or agree to explicit models of these data (Harmelen 2008). These shared explicit models are known as ontologies that formally represent knowledge used to interpret the data to be exchanged. Using stronger ontology representation languages increases the semantic interoperability among systems. For example, RDF enables less semantic interoperability than OWL DL[‡] as it is less expressive knowledge representation language.

In the context of Big Data, achieving meaningful (semantic) interoper-ability of data from heterogeneous sources is a challenging problem. This

---

[*] RDF; http://www.w3.org/RDF/
[†] XML; http://www.w3.org/XML/
[‡] OWL DL; www.w3.org/TR/owl-guide

mainly addresses the variety of characteristic of Big Data. Practical solutions to this problem are important for enterprises and public sector.

There is not a single technology that could solve the data heterogeneity issue of Big Data, but combining different technologies may provide a solution. One possible way is to consider semantic data interoperability problem of Big Data as a semantic data interoperability problem of large-scale distributed systems providing data or data analytics services. According to this approach, semantic technologies are combined with Web services technologies that are used to handle the complexity of networking systems. Semantic technologies allow adding meaning (semantics) to data and linking data provisioning services. The meaning is provided to data through semantic enrichment of data. This means linking each data element to a shared ontology component. Ontologies are used in this context to give a common interpretation of terminology of different data sources. They are represented in a formal language (e.g., OWL DL), enabling machine readability and automatic reasoning. OWL DL representations of different modular ontologies can be linked together and when a set of linked ontologies grows, it can by itself become complex Big Data.

One advantage of this approach is that such semantic enrichment of data provides meta-data that is machine-interpretable and linked to the data independent of any system that uses the data. This is in contrast to current Hadoop/MapReduce Big Data solutions that mostly embed meta-data into the code (Marshall 2012) and thus render data integration more complex.

In this chapter, we consider semantic enrichment of data combined with linked data and web services technology in order to build infrastructure for semantic data interoperability of Big Data. We show how large-scale semantic data interoperability problems can be solved in the domain of public sector administration by using a combination of SQL database technology, linked data, semantic technology, and Web services. In this book, we discuss several semantic data interoperability issues and share our personal experience derived from design and implementation of the Estonian semantic interoperability framework of state information systems and related data interoperability solutions.

Data Interoperability Framework for Estonian e-Government

We base our discussion in this chapter on the real case study from the field of information systems of public administration that covers different emerging semantic data interoperability issues. The case study is about long-term development of Estonian e-government infrastructure and efforts to cope with data interchange between wide varieties of disparate data sources being independently designed and managed by different governmental agencies. The case study presents Big Data challenges as a network of distributed heterogeneous state information systems data sources (about 600 data sources including more than 20,000 different data fields) by showing a need for semantic data interoperability.

Before providing infrastructure for data sharing, the Estonian government faced common problems of disparity of data sources that could be characterized as follows: wide variety in data types and semantics; varying access and security policies; low degree of interoperability and reuse of information; unclear ownership of data. In order to overcome these problems, the Estonian government decided to build a distributed secure data exchange framework based on Web services approach that allows implementation of platform neutral data services to be accessed via standard Internet protocols. Since Web services can be used as wrappers around existing state information systems (mostly legacy systems), it is possible to connect distributed disparate information systems to the network while hiding its complexity. In 2001, the first version of the middleware platform X-Road (Kalja 2009) started to provide secure data transfer between governmental IS data sources and between individuals and governmental institutions.

Nowadays, X-road platform is based on SOAP[*] standard for data transfer, its data service descriptions are presented in WSDL[†] language and registered in UDDI[‡] register (X-road 2011). X-road services differ from ordinary Web services in that data are transferred through standardized security gateways (servers) and service providers need to implement a custom component called adapter server in order to connect to X-road. The role of adapter servers is to convert an X-road query to the query acceptable by data server of a particular information system (e.g., based on SQL, SOAP, etc. protocols) and transform the results back into services responses. In order to guarantee secure data transfer, all complex security processes (e.g., authenticity, integrity, confidentiality of the exchanged data, etc.) are performed by security gateways that are needed for each of the information systems connected to X-road (X-road 5.0. 2011).

Currently, about 1500 e-government data services are registered and run on X-road. Data sources of more than about 600 organizations are connected via X-road middleware (X-road 2011, X-road 5.0. 2011). X-road services are operable 24/7 and some of them are accessible via dedicated e-government portals by any Estonian citizen. According to the statistics provided regularly by the Administration System for the State Information System (RIHA 2009), the estimated number of requests was 226 million in 2010 and 240 million in 2011.

In X-road approach, data interoperability between disparate data sources is achieved by data services that reduce effort needed for custom-coding. In this case, provided secure data services form an abstract layer between data

---

[*] SOAP; http//www.w3.org/TR/soap12-part1/#intro
[†] WSDL; http://www.w3.org/TR/wsdl
[‡] UDDI; http://uddi.xml.org/

sources of state information systems and consumers of that data as shown in Figure 7.1. Services layer hides complexity of accessing data sources and reduces a need for knowledge about the underlying data structures.

For example, population register has published among others the most widely used data service that given national ID code of a citizen, returns detailed data about the citizen like first name, last name, date of birth, etc. This service in turn is used by other more complex data services that run queries over different heterogeneous databases by combining different data services. For example, one can have an application that provides an opportunity to ask a national ID code of the owner of a car given a vehicle's registration number. In this case, data services provided by population register and vehicle registration database are combined into one service. This web service composition is custom-coded by application/service providers and published in the X-road service register for further use. However, as we see in the following sections, there are attempts to automate service composition process by using semantic technologies.

Although X-road approach provides means for data interoperability, it does not solve semantic data interoperability problems. Data semantics is hard coded into data services (i.e., X-road services). Currently, state information systems provide data services and corresponding WSDL descriptions that do not contain or refer to the meaning of data used. It is sufficient for a person if a data object has, besides a label, a textual description in a natural language they can understand, but a software agent (e.g., a web service, a search engine, a service matchmaker, etc.) requires some formal description of data object to interpret its label. For both humans and software agents to interpret the meaning of data objects in the same way, descriptions of data objects must be enriched with semantic descriptions, that is, references to the concepts used in a given ontology. The X-road data services use data objects as input–output parameters of services. Enriching descriptions of X-road data services with

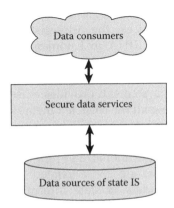

FIGURE 7.1
Data interoperability approach used by X-road middleware.

semantic references to the components of the ontology of the relevant domain makes it possible to use software agents for maintaining X-road data services and facilitating semantic data and service interoperability.

Semantic Data Interoperability Architecture for Estonian e-Government

X-road middleware does not support semantic data interoperability. Therefore, the strategic document on semantic interoperability of state information technology (RISO 2007, Vallner 2006) was issued by Estonian Ministry of Economic Affairs in 2005. Following this visionary document, the semantic interoperability architecture for Estonian state information systems was proposed by Haav et al. (2009). It is designed as the semantic layer on top of X-road infrastructure providing general principles for semantically describing objects of state information systems. Central components of this architecture are domain ontologies related to state information systems databases. OWL DL was chosen as an ontology description language. It is W3C recommendation and a commonly used standard. The architecture concentrates on two types of objects; data objects and input/output parameters of operations of data services that are to be semantically described by using domain ontologies. Semantic descriptions are seen as semantic enrichments of descriptions of data by providing a link to the meaning of the data elements in domain ontology. Currently, data services of state information systems are described in WSDL and data structures of state databases are presented among other formats by their XMI[*] data model descriptions. SAWSDL[†] has been chosen for semantic enrichment of these descriptions, as it provides mechanisms for semantic annotations of WSDL and XMI descriptions.

As a repository of domain ontologies and semantic descriptions of data services (semantic data services), the Administration System for the State Information System (called RIHA in Estonian) is used. As explained by Parmakson and Vegmann (2009), RIHA is a secure web-based database that stores systematic and reliable meta-data, including semantic meta-data, about public information systems. It provides a user-friendly web interface for searching and browsing all the collected meta-data.

In addition, the semantic interoperability architecture suggests that ontology creation, as well as semantic enrichment, is supported by corresponding policies, guidelines, tools, educational, and promotional activities.

The architecture was set up by a related legislation in Estonia in 2009 demanding from holders of state information systems creation of

---

[*] XMI; http://www.omg.org/spec/XMI/
[†] SAWSDL; http://www.w3.org/TR/sawsdl/

corresponding domain ontologies in OWL and semantic annotations of Web services in SAWSDL (RIHA 2009).

After that, the process of collecting semantic descriptions of domain ontologies and data services to RIHA has started. However, in 2012, only 13 domain ontologies were published in RIHA. There are several reasons for that. First of all, there is a lack of knowledge about semantic technologies and ontology engineering in Estonia. Therefore, a number of training courses were provided to approximately 200 domain experts responsible for ontology creation in their respective domains. In 2010–2011, special hands-on training courses were offered to smaller groups of domain experts in order to develop ontology descriptions of their respective domain. This activity resulted in 22 new ontologies. The main problem was that not all ontologies were completed after the courses and were not published in RIHA repository. Some of them did not meet quality requirements set to ontologies to be stored in RIHA and needed redesign. However, it was decided at the beginning of the ontology development that four critical ontologies that captured semantics of 80% of data elements used by governmental data services will have high priority. These are ontologies of population, business, and address registers as well as Estonian topographic database. By now, three of these ontologies have been completed and the population register ontology is under development. These four basic ontologies can be and are reused by many other domain ontologies making further ontology development processes easier and faster. However, still a lot of ontology engineering work is to be done in order to support full semantic enrichment of data elements of state information systems data sources.

On the other hand, feedback from training courses has shown that general existing ontology engineering methodologies like METHONTOLOGY (Gómez-Pérez et al. 2004) are too technically demanding for domain experts creating a need for more practical and domain-expert centric approaches. In reality, public administration agencies do not have a large number of ontology engineers or knowledge engineers available for converting domain knowledge to a formal ontology. In view of this situation, a practical methodology for developing domain ontologies was created by Haav (2010a, 2011) and guidelines for semantic enrichment of data services with domain ontologies were developed by Küngas (2010). We introduce these in the following sections of this chapter.

Ontology Development

Ontology Network

Domain ontologies of state information systems are not isolated ontologies, but they form a network of interlinked ontologies. Modular ontologies are easier to develop, reuse, and maintain. As we planned that domain experts do ontology engineering of their respective fields, then creation of modular and simple ontologies was our intention from the very beginning. Each of the domain ontologies is not large and of high complexity. As a rule, state information systems domain ontologies contain only descriptions of primitive classes. These are classes that do not have any sets of necessary and sufficient conditions; they only may have necessary conditions (Horrige 2011). A typical description of state information systems domain ontology includes about 60 descriptions of classes, 25 object properties, and 100 data-type properties. Its Description Logics (DL) complexity is ALCQ(D) (Baader et al. 2003).

As mentioned above, state information systems in Estonia have over 20,000 data entity attributes that should be semantically enriched using corresponding ontology components (i.e., data-type properties). Consequently, the ontology network should contain in the worst case approximately the same number of data-type properties in addition to the number of concepts and object properties. By now, we are in the initial stage of development of ontology network of state information systems in Estonia.

Besides domain ontologies, the semantic interoperability framework has foreseen creation of Estonian Top Ontology. This ontology is a linguistic ontology that has been developed by converting EuroWordNet Estonian (EuroWordNet Estonian 1999) to the corresponding machine readable OWL representation. Estonian Top Ontology is available (not publicly) and it can be used for linking domain ontology concepts to corresponding linguistic concepts.

Domain Expert Centric Ontology Development Methodology

Overview

One of the main reasons why domain ontologies and semantic data services are not developed and completed in time is the complexity of ontology development and the process of semantic enrichment. Generally, most of well-known ontology development methodologies (Staab et al. 2001, Gómez-Pérez et al. 2004, Haase et al. 2006) are technically demanding and are not easy to learn by employees of governmental agencies. They are domain experts rather than knowledge engineers. Therefore, it was important to reduce the complexity of ontology development by providing an easy to learn domain expert centric ontology development methodology. The idea was to disable the roles of mediators (i.e., knowledge and ontology engineers) from the chain of ontology engineering provided by most of current ontology development methodologies (Gómez-Pérez et al. 2004, Haase et al. 2006, Lavbiĉ and Krisper 2010) and delegate activities of these roles to a domain expert as an actual knowledge holder. A new ontology engineering methodology was provided and presented by Haav (2011) aimed at development of lightweight domain ontologies in OWL by domain experts without any profound knowledge of semantic technologies. The main goal of the methodology is to make ontology development process easier for domain experts by providing processes and guidelines that they could learn and use. Ontologies to be developed according to the methodology are intended to be used for semantic enrichment of data and data services of the state information systems. In meta-level, the methodology takes into account some of the proposals of widely accepted ontology development methodologies like METHONTOLOGY (Gómez-Pérez et al. 2004) and NeOn (Haase et al. 2006).

The domain expert centric ontology development methodology defines ontology development process as a sequence of ontology development activities, their inputs, and outputs. In more detail, the methodology is presented by Haav (2011). However, in this chapter, we briefly discuss some of its practical aspects and show its novel features.

As an input to the ontology development process, different reuseable knowledge resources including ontological and nonontological resources that are available in governmental agencies are used. Reuse of these resources speeds up ontology development process. For example, nonontological resources are conceptual schemas of databases, vocabularies, thesauri, regulatory documents of a state information systems, databases, data service descriptions, etc. Ontological resources are primarily domain ontologies of state information systems collected to RIHA repository, but may also be ontologies available in other repositories.

The methodology defines main activities of ontology development process for specification, conceptualization, and implementation phases of ontology. Management and support activities are defined as in METHONTOLOGY methodology.

For a lifecycle model, two levels of ontology development are identified and the corresponding lifecycle model was developed as follows:

- *Domain ontology level.* An iterative lifecycle model is used for creation of ontology modules corresponding to domain ontologies of state information systems. During each of the iterations, domain ontologies are improved until all the requirements are met.
- *Ontology network level.* A method of evolutionary prototyping is proposed for development of entire ontology network. In the beginning, a partial network of state information systems domain ontologies meeting already known requirements is developed as a prototype. This is assessed by different applications and after that the requirements are refined based on feedback from the application developers.

Ontology Development Process

Ontology development process of the proposed methodology was made as simple as possible for domain experts. This was achieved by merging together ontology conceptualization and implementation phases and

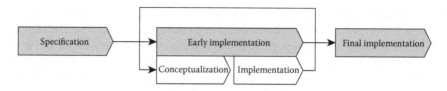

FIGURE 7.2
Main activities of ontology development process.

applying iterative lifecycle model to this merged process called early implementation as shown in Figure 7.2. Early implementation phase is composed of the following steps:

- *Conceptualization.* The middle out conceptualization strategy is chosen as the most appropriate for domain experts. They can easily identify central concepts of a domain and move from there toward more general or more specific concepts, if necessary. In contrast, top-down approach (from legislation terminology to data fields) creates too many concept hierarchy levels of ontology and bottom-up method (from data fields to domain concepts) makes generalization hard as differentiation of concepts and attributes is not easy. Conceptualization activity starts with identification of 7–10 central concepts (classes) of a domain and generalization and specification of these concepts one level up or down in concept hierarchy. After that, main relationships (object properties) between these central concepts are defined.

- *Implementation.* At the first iteration, conceptualization in the scope of basic (central) domain concepts is implemented as ontology represented in OWL. During each of the next iterations, new concepts and relationships are added and implemented.

Early implementation enables one to detect logical errors of ontology description at early stage of its implementation as well as to evaluate how well it meets the requirements.

Attributes of individuals of concepts are added in the final implementation stage. After that ontology is evaluated according to the requirements, for example, are all input/output parameters of Web services covered by corresponding components of respective domain ontology? Or are all data objects covered by data type properties? If not, then missing components are added. Ontology editing tool Protégé* was used for ontology implementation process. This tool enables usage of DL reasoners (e.g., Pellet,† Fact++,‡ etc.) in

---

* Protégé; http://protege.stanford.edu
† Pellet; http://www.clarkparsia.com/pellet
‡ Fact++; http://owl.man.ac.uk/factplusplus

order to automatically find inconsistencies in ontology description presented in OWL. This activity was highly recommended to ontology developers as a part of ontology implementation process.

During the process of implementation, ontologies are commented in Estonian and English languages in order to provide also human understandable ontology descriptions.

Evaluation

The provided methodology has been iteratively developed and evaluated during 2010–2011. The methodology was widely used in numerous training courses on ontology engineering provided for domain experts of state information systems. By now, the methodology is accepted as the ontology development methodology of creation of domain ontologies of state information systems in Estonia and made publicly available in RIHA (Haav 2010a). In addition, guidelines and requirements for creation of domain ontologies of state information systems have been developed by Haav (2010b) in order to assure quality of ontology descriptions loaded to RIHA repository.

However, applying the methodology shows that its implementation activity is sometimes still too complex for domain experts even if using simple ontology editors. Therefore, in the future this ontology development methodology will be improved by introducing simple intermediate representations of domain conceptualizations that could be automatically translated to corresponding OWL ontology. In this case, implementation activity of the methodology may be automatic or at least semiautomatic.

Semantic Enrichment of Data and Services

Although ontologies facilitate explicit description of domain knowledge, which can be effectively used in applications, in order to exploit the knowledge automatically, a binding must be created between the application, data, and ontology elements. Depending on the application and its architecture, such bindings may include application-specific details, which aim to simplify the usage of ontologies in particular applications. In the case of Estonian semantic interoperability framework, the complete set of applications has not been finally determined since involved parties have low expectations with respect to semantic technologies. Anyway, the initial applications are artifact indexing and discovery, automated Web service composition, linking open data, and redundancy detection in Web services.

In fact, it has been indicated (Ventrone and Heiler 1994) that about 80% of data are redundant in large information systems leading to high maintenance costs from both technical and organization perspectives. Systematic indexing of software artifacts, that is, descriptions of Web services and database schemata in XML form, leverages the exploration of dependencies between them through which they can be optimized. Service composition is relevant in the Estonian context since the state information system is based on individual services and the overall intuition is that new value-added services can be formed by skillfully combining the existing ones. Finally, integration of heterogeneous data is recognized as an issue since many decisions are currently made based on data collected by individual organizations solely for their own purposes. This, however, has limited the quality of decision-making, since a lot of decisions are based on partial or insufficient data.

Finally, it is important to note that the choice for linking meta-data to artifacts themselves is preferred to make the sources as self-explanatory as possible.

On the basis of these applications, we have set the following requirements to annotations:

- Minimal effort should be required to annotate artifacts.
- The annotation schemata should facilitate specification of the semantics as specifically as possible.
- The annotations should facilitate matching the artifacts and exposing dependencies between them explicit.
- Annotations should allow namespaces and it should be possible to attach to them additional descriptions (i.e., links to the Web resources).

We scoped annotation to Web services descriptions and realization-level data models and used the cost-effective schema annotation methodology described by Küngas and Dumas (2009) and inspired by UPON (Nicola et al. 2009).

Semantic Descriptions in SAWSDL

There are several languages for describing semantic Web services like OWL-S,[*] WSMO[†] and SAWSDL. In the context of the Estonian e-government case study, the semantics of Web services are presented in SAWSDL since it provides mechanisms for embedding semantic annotations to existing WSDL and XSD descriptions of services. For expressing the semantics of schema elements, SAWSDL defines an extension to XSD and WSDL in terms of three attributes: *modelReference*, *liftingSchemaMapping*, and *loweringSchemaMapping*. Model reference attributes are used mainly for linking schema elements with any meta-model (in our case, an ontology), while schema mapping attributes are to support schema transformations.

---

[*] OWL-S; http://www.w3.org/Submission/OWL-S/
[†] WSMO; http://www.wsmo.org/

However, SAWSDL itself is far from being perfect for schema annotations. Namely, SAWSDL is very general and too flexible concerning style and meaning of semantic annotations as well as the type of concepts that are used for annotations. These issues are also recognized in the works devoted to SAWSDL-based semantic service matchmaking (Klusch et al. 2009, Schulte et al. 2010). Therefore, for the Estonian e-government case study, the following constraints have been imposed on the usage of SAWSDL:

- It is required that the semantic concepts are to be formally defined in OWL DL ontology language—the SAWSDL specification, in general, allows heterogeneity in ontologies and ontology languages. The only constraint of the SAWSDL specification is that the resources (in our case, ontology elements), semantically describing WSDL elements, should be identifiable via URI references. In general, this may create a problem with respect to automatic interpretation of these concepts.

- References to multiple ontologies to describe the semantics of the same WSDL element are allowed but their usage is strictly regulated— elements from different ontologies are allowed in two cases. First, if alternative semantics are described due to the usage of the semantics in a specific context. And second, when an annotation is refined by following the RDF graph of an ontology, which imports other ontologies.

- Bottom-level annotations are recommended—the SAWSDL specification does not set any restrictions to the style of annotations: both top- and bottom-level annotations are supported. The top-level annotation means that a complex type or element definition of a message parameter is described by a model reference as a whole. A bottom-level annotation enhances the parts of the definition of a complex type or element. In the Estonian semantic interoperability framework, a set of bottom-level annotation rules for the SAWSDL service descriptions is provided by Küngas (2010) and applied. These rules specify that only leaf nodes of data structures of message parts of service operations are annotated and give bottom-level schemas (patterns) for annotation of different XSD types.

An example of bottom-level annotations, where WSDL elements "county" and "street" are enriched with data-type properties *countyName* and *streetName* from the *land* ontology using SAWSDL model reference statements is presented as follows:

<wsdl:types >
...
<complexType name = "aadress1" >
  <sequence >
    <element name = "county" type = "xsd:string" **sawsdl:model
        Reference = "http://www.riik.ee/onto/land/countyName"**/ >

```
<element name = "street" type = "xsd:string" sawsdl:model
   Reference = "http://www.riik.ee/onto/land/streetName"/ >
...
</sequence >
</complexType >
...
</wsdl:types >
```

Annotation Patterns for Semantic Enrichment of Schemas

We do not distinguish services and data definitions from annotation point of view. In fact, our main concern in services is their data semantics. This allows us to use the same annotation approach to both data and services.

We have defined four reification patterns for presenting semantics of data attributes. In general, the patterns define a path in the RDF graph, which encodes the semantics of a particular data attribute. In the following, we write URIdtp, URIop, and URIc, respectively, to denote URI-s of OWL data-type properties, object properties, and classes. The four basic patterns are usually sufficient for describing the semantics of well-structured data structures. Other constructs might be needed mostly in cases where data structures are either too generic, originate from legacy systems, or their usage has changed in time. Since such cases mostly originate from ignorance with respect to best practices in data model design, we assume that the data models will be aligned with the best practices before annotation.

Pattern 1—URIdtp

In case a schema element is used to encode a data attribute for a wide range of settings, that is, its domain is not restricted, a reference to data-type property in an ontology would be sufficient for annotation. In the following example, a data-type property *nationalIdCode*, defined in namespace http://ws.soatrader.com/ontology/BaseOntology.owl, is used to refer to an attribute, which can encode a national code of citizens from any country:

```
<element xmlns:sawsdl = "http://www.w3.org/ns/sawsdl" sawsdl:model
Reference = "http://www.soatrader.com/ontology/Base Ontology.owl/
nationalIdCode" name = "national_idcode" type = "string"/ >
```

While writing such one-element annotations, one should bear in mind that the subject of a particular attribute should comply with the domain of the data-type property. For instance, if, in the preceding example, the national identification code attribute is used only for presenting the national identification codes of notaries in a data set and the domain of the national identification code is not the notary, then this pattern is not applicable. In this case, pattern 2 is needed for semantic annotations.

To summarize, this pattern should only be applied in cases where there is no need to distinguish classes in ontologies—either the semantics of a data type is general enough or the attribute, to be annotated, is domain-specific and appears only in very specific data sets and contexts.

Pattern 2—URIc URIdtp

In order to explicitly state semantics of data entity attributes more precisely, one should combine the elements of developed ontologies. For instance, in ontology http://www.soatrader.com/ontology/BaseOntology.owl, we have class *Notary* to encode the concept of a notary and a datatype property for referring to the semantics of any national identification code (*nationalIdCode*). By applying pattern "URIc URIdtp," we can represent the semantics for a national identification code of a notary given that class *Notary* is allowed to be used as a domain of the datatype property. The preceding is demonstrated in the following annotation:

<element xmlns:sawsdl = "http://www.w3.org/ns/sawsdl" sawsdl:model Reference = "**http://www.soatrader.com/ontology/BaseOntology.owl/ Notary http://www.soatrader.com/ontology/BaseOntology.owl/nationalId Code**" name = "notary_idcode" type = "string"/>

By applying this pattern, we are able to semantically describe majority of data attributes when the number of ontologies for the state information system is relatively small and their modularity is low.

Pattern 3—URIop URIc URIdtp

In the case of ontologies of higher degree of modularity, such as the ones where property clumps (an ontology design anomaly) are resolved under specific classes, there is a need for richer patterns than the previously introduced ones. In the following example, we show how to specify semantics of an e-mail address of an arbitrary person after resolution of property clumps has been applied. In ontology, http://www.soatrader.com/ontology/BaseOntology.owl, we have defined a class for representing contact information (*ContactInfo*). This class is a domain for data-type properties encoding the semantics of contact info attributes such as e-mail addresses, street names, postal codes, etc. In the current case, there is a data-type property *e-mailAddress* for encoding the semantics of an e-mail address of an arbitrary entity. In order to bind the contact information to a specific subject, the ontology contains object property *hasContactInfo*, which encodes the semantics of having contact information. By applying pattern "URIop URIc URIdtp" to these three ontology elements, we can express the semantics of an e-mail address belonging to contact information of an arbitrary subject.

<element xmlns:sawsdl = "http://www.w3.org/ns/sawsdl"
sawsdl:modelReference = "**http://www.soatrader.com/ontology/
BaseOntology.owl/hasContactInfo http://www.soatrader.com/ontology/
BaseOntology.owl/ContactInfo http://www.soatrader.com/ontology/
BaseOntology.owl/e-mailAddress**" name = "e-mail" type = "string"/ >

Since such semantic description pattern does not state explicitly the subject (of contact info in particular case) it suits for annotating data attributes, which are not scoped to a particular subject type.

Pattern 4—URIc URIop URIc URIdtp

In the case of ontologies with higher degree of modularity, there is a need to describe relations between subjects and relevant data objects. In such case, it is not enough to apply pattern 3. In the following example, we exemplify the usage of pattern 4 in conjunction with expressing explicitly subject–object relation within an annotation.

In ontology, http://www.soatrader.com/ontology/BaseOntology.owl, we have defined classes *Notary* and *ContactInfo*. Class *ContactInfo* is a domain for data-type properties encoding semantics of contact information details of organizations and individuals. One of such properties is *e-mailAddress* for representing semantics of any e-mail address. In order to bind the contact information to a specific subject, the ontology contains object property *hasContactInfo*, which encodes the semantics of having contact information. By applying pattern 4 to these ontology elements, we are able to express in the following example the semantics of an e-mail address within notary contact information.

<element xmlns:sawsdl = "http://www.w3.org/ns/sawsdl"
sawsdl:modelReference = "**http://www.soatrader.com/ontology/
BaseOntology.owl/Notary http://www.soatrader.com/ontology/
BaseOntology.owl/hasContactInfo
http://www.soatrader.com/ontology/BaseOntology.owl/ContactInfo
http://www.soatrader.com/ontology/BaseOntology.owl/e-mailAddress**"
name = "notary_e-mail" type = "string"/ >

Common Faults in Semantic Annotation

Throughout our case study, we have experienced common faults, which appear in annotations. Here, we list the most prevalent ones as follows:

1. Precision of semantic annotation—people tend to think in terms of their own field and do not often see relations to other fields. Thus,

they often provide annotations by considering its applicability within a particular application of their own domain. In practice, it means that mostly pattern 1 is used in annotations. In such cases, in addition to incomplete semantic descriptions, there is also a risk that, even if an ontology is initially constructed for a single domain, in time it gets linked to others and this implies that the semantic scope of annotations will change, if not explicitly constrained.

2. Class vs Data-type property in semantic annotations—people without proper training in knowledge engineering tend to mix the meanings/intentions of datatype properties and classes in ontologies.

3. Encoding vs meaning—people tend to get confused by the representation of data and often extend domain ontologies with encoding details. Therefore, we encourage them to design the data models and interfaces in such a way that the semantic descriptions will be kept simple.

Applications of Semantics

We have built several applications that use semantically enriched data and services. In this section, we introduce applications that exploit semantic annotations for semantic data analysis as well as for interoperability of data and services.

Semantic Data Analysis: Redundancy Detection

We have used the developed annotations for analyzing redundancy (Küngas and Dumas 2010) in WSDL descriptions of information system interfaces (services). The intuition here is that redundancy in interfaces leads to redundancy in data management. However, since developers use different naming conventions and structuring styles in interface descriptions, we used semantic annotations first to identify links between the interfaces and then applied the developed metrics for redundancy detection. In Figure 7.3, cluster map layout is used for visualizing an overlap in entity attributes (i.e., leaf nodes of data structures) from different information systems. The dots represent entity attributes with specific semantics, while the clusters visualize the information systems. An entity attribute appears in a cluster if it appears in interface descriptions of the corresponding information system. One can see that there is a significant overlap in entity attributes of different information systems.

In the Estonian state information systems case study, we were able to automatically detect the redundancy with relatively high precision and recall (Küngas and Dumas 2010). Furthermore, the proposed framework allowed

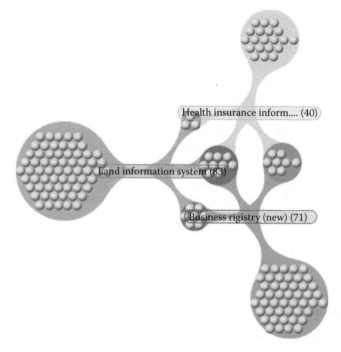

FIGURE 7.3
Cluster map representation of redundant entity attributes.

identification of the primary location (an individual information system in the federated information system) of redundant attributes. This finding suggests that in future while developing new information systems we have the capability of suggesting in which information systems new types of data should be managed and how to rearrange the data models and services of existing systems with respect to new ones.

This case study unveiled that, although individual information systems might not have a lot of data redundancy, there can be considerable redundancy in federated state information system as a whole. More specifically, we found that 79% of data items are redundant, which is consistent with findings of Ventrone and Heiler (1994), who point to several cases where data model overlap in large federated information systems was up to 80%.

Data Interoperability with Semantic Data Services

One of the most studied applications of semantics of Web services is matchmaking of services (Klusch et al. 2009, Küngas and Dumas 2009, Schulte et al. 2010) and their (automated) composition (Rao et al. 2006, Maigre et al. 2013). Although there are tools available for facilitating automated composition, they are mostly exploited in scientific environments (Stevens et al. 2003, Wassermann and Emmerich 2006, Villegas et al. 2010) where new workflows for scientific computation can be composed from existing Web services. There are some approaches (Haav et al. 2007, Maigre et al. 2013) to automate semantic web service composition taking into account the requirements of the Estonian e-government case study. However, these methods are not implemented within some practical service composition tools.

Major benefits of using automated Web services composition include the following: (1) complex components can be managed by different organizations and still used collectively allowing to share the IT management costs and (2) data-intensive computations can be performed close to the data reducing the network bottlenecks and increasing performance of computations.

Such benefits are not well recognized in the context of the Estonian state information systems, where public sector service providers do not timely enrich their data services with semantic annotations.

Therefore, in order to demonstrate the capabilities of semantic annotations of services, we developed a prototype solution, which, instead of public sector services, uses the services publicly available in the Web. Furthermore, one of the aims of building the prototype solution was to demonstrate how the semantics of services can be used for automated service composition in end-user applications. Therefore, one of the objectives was to hide the complexities related to composition and semantic annotations from the user.

As a result, we developed a framework, where we fused natural language processing, ontology reasoning, service annotation, discovery, composition and execution, Web technologies, Web widgets, and on-the-fly semantic data aggregation into a deep web search engine. Flowchart of the framework platform is illustrated in Figure 7.4. The idea of the prototype was simple—after a user has entered a search query, a simple Web application

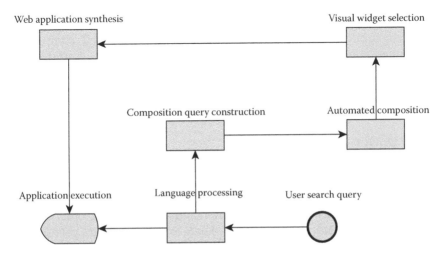

FIGURE 7.4
The flowchart illustrating the prototype implementation.

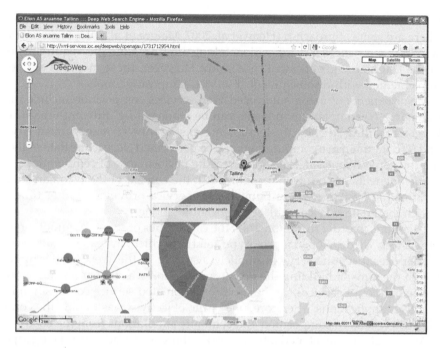

FIGURE 7.5
An instance of a synthesized Web application.

is synthesized, which will answer user's query, when executed. For doing this, language technology is used to process the query and transform it to semantic service composition task. This task is used to initiate composition and services selection. After the set of relevant services has been identified, suitable visual widgets with matching interfaces are selected. Finally, the Web application will be synthesized from discovered components and named entities in the original search query are used to initialize and execute the application. The latter will visualize search results to the user. A sample application synthesized for a company background check query is presented in Figure 7.5.

Linked Open Government Data

Open data initiatives have been expected to positively impact the economy, increase openness of societies, accelerate democracy, and other aspects, which are important from political point of view and are of concern to decision-makers. Here, Estonia is no exception and a thread of the open data initiative is managed at the national level. There are no guidelines yet on which level the openly provided governmental data should comply with respect to the five star scale proposed by Tim Berners-Lee at his Bag of Chips talk at the Gov 2.0 Expo in 2010 (Berners-Lee 2010). In this scale, one star means that data are available in any format and five stars means that data are available in RDF format and are linked with other data sets.

To understand the benefits, in 2011 a competition was launched in Estonia where four private sector service providers were granted funding for developing demonstrators for exposing and using open data. One of the demonstrators, which is currently under development took the linked data approach. The main motivators for this choice were scalability and reduction in the number of technologies for using the data set with other data sets. While model-based data integration, which can be bound easily to linked data, provides scalability from data integration point of view, simplified reuse is leveraged through reduced number of different technologies to be used for data processing when it comes to its usage.

Although ontologies are not a prerequisite for linked data, they provide extended possibilities for querying data sets with languages such as SPARQL* or SERQL† Ontologies in such case provide a sort of view of the data and impose the domain-specific constraints and rules for automated inference. The latter simplifies usage of linked data in the sense that you do not need to encode extensive domain knowledge into your applications.

The linked data demonstrator uses data provisioning services from the Estonian Register of Buildings to first download the records of all buildings (database consists of about 900 k records). Then these data are linked to the data from Address Data System to bind addresses to the buildings. The addresses of companies are then linked to the data set as well to facilitate linking buildings with companies. Finally, the data set in a structural database is transformed into RDF triples (about 200M triples are expected for this dataset) and stored into an RDF data store where it can be either downloaded or queried directly. More specifically, OpenLink Virtuoso Open Source Edition is used to store and expose the linked data from the Register of Buildings through its SPARQL endpoint. Besides RDF, JSON‡ and other data formats are also supported by the platform.

For updating the data set, an existing data service is regularly invoked to retrieve and store the updates. This approach has set additional requirements to services engineering—for such an open linked data creation and update mechanism, we need two kinds of services—services for retrieving changes or identifiers of changed records and services for retrieving complete data records or changes. Furthermore, there is a need for a specific service for retrieving data records, which exposes only public data. Currently, the majority of services return both confidential and public data since the main service consumers have been traditionally public sector authorities and organizations.

---

* SPARQL; http://www.w3.org/TR/rdf-sparql-query/

† SERQL; http://www.w3.org/2001/sw/wiki/SeRQL

‡ JSON; http://www.json.org/

Although for this solution mappings from structured data to RDF format are provided currently manually, we see great potential in using the semantic annotations of data provisioning services in construction of such mappings automatically.

Conclusion and Future Work

We have discussed some practical semantic interoperability problems of data in the domain of public sector administration on the basis of the Estonian case study. We have provided e-government solutions that benefit from semantic technologies used together with Web services and open data technologies.

According to our experience, meta-data creation and semantic enrichment of data and services are hard problems to solve before successful semantic data interoperability solutions can be developed and deployed. For existing legacy systems as in the Estonian case study, it is very hard. For new information systems, it can be included to the system development life cycle as a part of system analysis and implementation activities.

In order to make semantic technologies practically applicable, we have created the domain expert centric agile method for ontology development and the set of rules for semantic enrichment of data and services using OWL ontologies.

We have considered application of semantics in detection of data redundancy of information systems, in achieving semantic data interoperability with semantic data services using automatic service composition and in linking open government data. Although the case of the Estonian Register of Buildings, with an estimated number of 200M RDF triples, does not classify yet as a Big Data case, further activities in the context of the open data initiative are expected to grow this linked data set to the reasonable size in the following few years. Furthermore, we have learned that enhancing linked data by ontological structures makes data integration easier and provides benefits to (open) data publishing.

We are working on improving our ontology development methodology. We intend to provide (semi)automatic generation of machine readable meta-data (e.g., domain ontologies).

We continue our work on automatic composition of data provisioning services based on semantic annotations of service parameters. We also foresee that the semantic annotations of data provisioning services can be used for automatically constructing mappings from structured data to RDF to be used in the context of linked data.

According to our experience, manual creation of domain ontologies and semantic enrichment of data and data services is too resource-consuming to be widely used for solving semantic data interoperability problems of Big

Data (possible coming from distributed heterogeneous sources). By considering our experience with linked data and services, we suggest that some of the future challenges of large-scale semantic data interoperability are related to (semi)automatic generation of machine readable meta-data, ontology matching and (semi)automatic semantic enrichment of data and data services. Solutions in these fields will facilitate building an infrastructure for meaningful interoperability of heterogeneous data sources and on-demand flexible integration of data.

Acknowledgments

This research was supported by the target-financed theme no. SF0140007s12 of the Estonian Ministry of Education and Research, and by the European Regional Development Fund (ERDF) through the project no 3.2.1201.13-0026 and EXCS.

References

Baader, F., D. Calvanese, D. McGuiness, D. Nardi, and P. Patel-Schneider. 2003. *The Description Logic Handbook: Theory, Implementation and Applications.* Cambridge University Press, Cambridge, UK.

Berners-Lee, T. 2010. Open, Linked Data for a Global Community. http://www.youtube.com/watch?v = ga1aSJXCFe0 (accessed January 17, 2013).

EuroWordNet Estonian. 1999. OLAC record of EuroWordNet Estonian. http://www.language-archives.org/item/oai:catalogue.elra.info:ELRA-M0022 (accessed October 1, 2012).

Gartner. 2012. Gartner Says Solving 'Big Data' Challenge Involves More Than Just Managing Volumes of Data. http://www.gartner.com/it/page.jsp?id = 1731916 (accessed October 1, 2012).

Gómez-Pérez, A., M. Fernández-López, and O. Corcho. 2004. *Ontological Engineering with Examples from the Areas of Knowledge Management, e-Commerce and the Semantic Web.* Springer, Heidelberg.

Haase, P., S. Rudolph, Y. Wang et al. 2006. NeOn Deliverable D1.1.1: Networked Ontology Model. http://www.neon-project.org (accessed March 12, 2012).

Haav, H.-M. 2010a. Nõuded RIHA ontoloogiatele. http://www.ria.ee/public/RIHA/nouded_riha_ontoloogiatele_r26.PDF (accessed October 3, 2012) (in Estonian).

Haav, H.-M. 2010b. Ontoloogiate loomise metoodika. http://www.ria.ee/public/RIHA/ontoloogiate_loomise_metoodika_v4.PDF (accessed October 3, 2012) (in Estonian).

Haav, H.-M. 2011. A practical methodology for development of a network of e-government domain ontologies. In *Building the e-World Ecosystem: 11th IFIP WG 6.11*

Conference on e-Business, e-Services, and e-Society, I3E 2011, Revised Selected Papers, eds. T. Skersys, R. Butleris, L. Nemuraite, and R. Suomi, pp. 1–13, Springer, Heidelberg.

Haav, H.-M., T. Tammet, V. Kadarpik, K. Kindel et al. 2007. A semantic-based web service composition framework. In *Advances in Information Systems Development: New Methods and Practice for the Networked Society [Proc. of 15th Int. Conf. on Information Systems Development, ISD 2006* (Budapest, Aug./Sept. 2006)], eds. G. Magyar et al., (1), pp. 379–391, Springer, New York.

Haav, H.-M., A. Kalja, P. Küngas, and M. Luts. 2009. Ensuring large-scale semantic interoperability: The Estonian public sector's case study. In *Databases and Information Systems V*, eds. H.-M. Haav and A. Kalja, pp. 117–129, IOS Press, Amsterdam, the Netherlands.

Harmelen, F. van. 2008. Semantic web technologies as the foundation for the information infrastructure. In *Creating Spatial Information Infrastructures*, ed. P. van Ooster, Wiley, New York.

Horrige, M. 2011. A Practical Guide to Building OWL Ontologies Using Protégé 4 and CO-ODE Tools. http://owl.cs.manchester.ac.uk/tutorials/protegeowltutorial (accessed January 9, 2013).

Kalja, A. 2009. New version of the x-road. In *Information Society Yearbook 2009*. Ministry of Economic Affairs and Communications of Estonia, Department of State Information Systems (RISO). http://www.riso.ee/en/pub/2009it/#p = 2-1-4 (accessed August 3, 2012).

Klusch, M., P. Kapahnke, and I. Zinnikus. 2009. SAWSDL-MX2: A machine-learning approach for integrating semantic web service matchmaking variants. In *Proceedings of the 2009 IEEE International Conference on Web Services (ICWS)*, Los Angeles, CA, pp. 335–342, IEEE Computer Society.

Küngas, P. 2010. Semantilise kirjeldamise juhis v0.4. http://ftp.ria.ee/pub/riha/Semantilise_kirjeldamise_juhis_v04.pdf (accessed October 1, 2012) (in Estonian).

Küngas, P. and M. Dumas. 2009. Cost-effective semantic annotation of XML schemas and web service interfaces. In *Proceedings of the IEEE International Conference on Services Computing (SCC 2009)*, Bangalore, India, pp. 372–379, IEEE Computer Society Press.

Küngas, P. and M. Dumas. 2010. Redundancy detection in service-oriented systems. In *Proceedings of the 19th International Conference on World Wide Web (WWW'10)*, eds. M. Rappa, P. Jones, J. Freire, and S. Chakrabarti, pp. 581–590, ACM, New York.

Lavbiĉ, D. and M. Krisper. 2010. Rapid ontology development, In *Proceedings of the 19th Conference on Information Modelling and Knowledge Bases XXI*, Maribor, Slovenia, eds. T. Welzer Družovec, H. Jaakkola, Y. Kiyoki, T. Tokuda, and N. Yoshida, pp. 283–290, IOS Press.

Maigre, R., P. Grigorenko, H.-M. Haav, and A. Kalja. 2013. A semantic method of automatic composition of e-government services. In *Databases and Information Systems VII: Selected Papers from 10th Int. Baltic Conf. on Databases and Information Systems, Baltic DB&IS 2012*, Frontiers of Artificial Intelligence and Applications, eds. A. Caplinskas, G. Dzemyda, A. Lupeikene, and O. Vasilecas, (249):204–217, IOS Press, Amsterdam, the Netherlands.

Manyika, J., M. Chui, B. Brown, et al. 2011. Big data: The next frontier for innovation, competition, and productivity. McKinsey Global Institute. http://www.

mckinsey.com/insights/mgi/research/technology_and_innovation/big_data_ the_next_frontier_for_innovation (accessed September 15, 2012).

Marshall, P. 2012. What you need to know about big data. Government Computer News, February 7. http://gcn.com/articles/2012/02/06/feature-1-future-of-big-data.aspx (accessed October 1, 2012).

Nicola, A., M. Missikoff, and R. Navigli. 2009. A software engineering approach to ontology building. *Information Systems* 34(2):258–275.

Parmakson, P. and E. Vegmann. 2009. The administration system of the state information system (RIHA). In *Information Society Yearbook 2009*. Ministry of Economic Affairs and Communications of Estonia, Department of State Information Systems (RISO). http://www.riso.ee/en/pub/2009it/#p = 2-1-6 (accessed August 3, 2012).

Rao, J., P. Küngas, and M. Matskin. 2006. Composition of semantic web services using linear logic theorem proving. *Information Systems* 31(4–5):340–360.

RIHA. 2009. Riigi infosüsteemi haldussüsteem. https://www.riigiteataja.ee/akt/12933746?leiaKehtiv (accessed October 3, 2012) (in Estonian).

RISO. 2007. Riigi infosüsteemide semantilise koosvõime raamistik. http://www.riso.ee/et/files/RISsemantikaV07-loplik.pdf. Versioon 0.7 (01.08.2007) (accessed October 1, 2012) (in Estonian).

Schulte, S., U. Lampe, J. Eckert, and R. Steinmetz. 2010. LOG4SWS.KOM: Self-adapting semantic web service discovery for SAWSDL. In *Proceedings of the 2010 IEEE 6th World Congress on Services (SERVICES-1)*, Miami, FL, pp. 511–518, IEEE Computer Society.

Staab, S., H.P. Schnurr, R. Studer, and Y. Sure. 2001. Knowledge processes and ontologies. *IEEE Intelligent Systems* 16(1):26–34.

Stevens, R.D., A.J. Robinson, and C.A. Goble. 2003. MyGrid: Personalised bioinformatics on the information grid. *Bioinformatics* 19:i302–i304.

Stuckenschmidt, H. 2012. Data semantics on the web. *Journal of Data Semantics* 1:1–9.

Vallner, U. 2006. Nationwide components of Estonia's state information system. *Baltic IT&T Review* 3(42):34–38.

Ventrone, V. and S. Heiler. 1994. Some advice for dealing with semantic heterogeneity in federated database systems. In *Proceedings of the Database Colloquium*, San Diego, CA, August 1994, Armed Forces Communications and Electronics Assc (AFCEA).

Villegas, M., N. Bel, S. Bel, and V. Rodríguez. 2010. A case study on interoperability for language resources and applications. In *Proceedings of the Seventh conference on International Language Resources and Evaluation (LREC'10)*, ed. N. Calzolari et al., pp. 3512–3519, European Language Resources Association (ELRA), Paris, France.

Wassermann, B. and W. Emmerich. 2006. Reliable scientific service compositions. In *Proceedings of the 4th International Conference on Service-oriented Computing (ICSOC'06)*, eds. D. Georgakopoulos, N. Ritter, B. Benatallah et al., 14–25, Springer-Verlag, Berlin, Heidelberg.

X-road 5.0. 2011. Turvaserveri kasutusjuhend. Redaktsioon 5.05 (29.04.2011). http://ee.x-rd.net/docs/est/turvaserveri_kasutusjuhend.pdf (accessed October 1, 2012) (in Estonian).

X-road. 2011. Nõuded infosüsteemidele ja adapterserveritele. Versioon 8.0 (04.05.2011). http://ee.x-rd.net/docs/est/nouded_infosusteemidele_ja_adapterserveritele.pdf (accessed October 1, 2012) (in Estonian).

Section III

Big Data Processing

8

Big Data Exploration

Stratos Idreos

CONTENTS

Introduction

The Big Data Era

We are now entering the era of data deluge, where the amount of data outgrows the capabilities of query processing technology. Many emerging applications, from social networks to scientific experiments, are representative examples of this deluge, where the rate at which data are produced exceeds any past experience. For example, scientific analysis such as astronomy is soon expected to collect multiple terabytes of data on a daily basis, while already web-based businesses such as social networks or web log analysis are confronted with a growing stream of large data inputs. Therefore, there is a clear need for efficient Big Data query processing to enable the evolution of businesses and sciences to the new era of data deluge.

In this chapter, we focus on a new direction of query processing for Big Data where data exploration becomes a first-class citizen. Data exploration is necessary when new big chunks of data arrive rapidly and we want to react quickly, that is, with little time to spare for tuning and set-up. In particular, our discussion focuses on database systems technology, which for several decades has been the predominant data processing tool.

In this chapter, we introduce the concept of data exploration and discuss a series of early techniques from the database community toward the direction of building database systems which are tailored for Big Data exploration, that is, adaptive indexing, adaptive loading, and sampling-based query processing. These directions focus on reconsidering fundamental assumptions and on designing next-generation database architectures for the Big Data era.

In Need for Big Data Query Processing

Let us first discuss the need for efficient query processing techniques over Big Data. We briefly discuss the impact of Big Data both in businesses and in sciences.

Big Data in Businesses

For businesses, fast Big Data analysis translates to better customer satisfaction, better services, and in turn it may happen to be the catalyst in creating and maintaining a successful business. Examples of businesses in need for analyzing Big Data include any kind of web- and data-based IT business, ranging from social networks to e-commerce, news, emerging mobile data businesses, etc. The most typical example in this case is the need to quickly understand user behavior and data trends; this is necessary in order to dynamically adapt services to the user needs.

Businesses continuously monitor and collect data with regard to the way users interact with their systems, for example, in an e-commerce web site, in a social network, or in a GPS navigation system, etc. and these data need to be analyzed quickly in order to discover interesting trends. Speed here is of essence as these businesses get multiple terabytes of data on a daily basis and the kinds of trends observed might change from day to day or from hour to hour. For example, social networks and mobile data applications observe rapid changes on user interests, for example, every single minute there are 700,000 status updates on Facebook and 700,000 queries on Google. This results in staggering amounts of data that businesses need to analyze as soon as possible and while it is still relevant.

Big Data in Sciences

For sciences, fast Big Data analysis can push scientific discovery forward. All sciences nowadays struggle with data management, for example, astronomy, biology, etc. At the same time, the expectation is that in the near future sciences will increase their ability to collect data even more. For example, the Large Synoptic Survey Telescope project in the USA expects a daily collection of 20 terabytes, while the Large Hadron Collider in CERN in Europe already creates an even bigger amount of data. With multiple terabytes of data on a daily basis, data exploration becomes essential in order to allow scientists to quickly focus on data parts where there is a good probability of finding interesting observations.

Big Data Challenges for Query Processing

We continue the discussion by focusing on the challenges that Big Data bring for state-of-the-art data management systems.

Existing Technology

Data management technology has a tremendous and important history of achievements and numerous tools and algorithms to deal with scalable data processing. Notable recent examples include column-store database systems (Boncz et al. 2005; Stonebraker et al. 2005) and MapReduce systems (Dean and Ghemawat 2004) as well as recent hybrids that take advantage of both the structured database technology and the massively scalable MapReduce technology (Abouzeid et al. 2009; Hadapt 2012; Platfora 2012). All small and major organizations rely on data management technology to store and analyze their data. Sciences, on the other hand, rely on a mix of data management technologies and proprietary tools that accommodate the specialized query processing needs in a scientific environment.

Big Data Challenges

Regardless of the kind of technology used, the fundamental problem nowadays is that we cannot consume and make sense of all these data fast enough. This is a direct side effect of some of the assumptions that are inherent in modern data management systems.

First, state-of-the-art database systems assume that there is always enough workload knowledge and idle time to tune the system with the proper indices, with the proper statistics, and with any other data structure that is expected to speed up data access. With Big Data arriving quickly, unpredictably, and with the need to react fast, we do not have the luxury to spend considerable amounts of time in tuning anymore. Second, database systems are designed with the main assumption that we should always consume all data in an effort to provide a correct and complete answer. As the data grow bigger, this becomes a significantly more expensive task.

Overall, before being able to use a database system for posing queries, we first need to go through a complex and time-consuming installation process to (a) load data inside the database system and (b) to tune the system. These steps require not only a significant amount of time (i.e., in the order of several hours for a decent database size), but also expert knowledge as well as workload knowledge. In other words, we need to know exactly what kind of queries we are going to pose so that we can tune the system accordingly. However, when we are in need to explore a Big Data pile, then we do not necessarily know exactly what kind of queries we would like to pose before the exploration process actually progresses; the answer to one query leads to the formulation of the next query.

Attempts to "throw more silicon" to the problem, that is, with Big Data clusters, can allow for more scalability (until the data grow even bigger), but at the expense of wasted resources when consuming data that is not really necessary for the exploration path. This brings yet another critical side effect of Big Data into the picture, that is, energy consumption. Overall, high-performance computing and exploitation of large clusters are complementary to the approaches described in this chapter; to deal with Big Data, we need innovations at all fronts.

Because More is Different

We cannot use past solutions to solve radically new problems. The main observation is that with more data, the query-processing paradigm also has to change. Processing all data is not possible; in fact, often it is not even necessary. For example, a scientist in the astronomy domain is interested in studying parts of the sky at a time searching for interesting patterns, maybe even looking for specific properties at a time. This means that the numerous terabytes of data brought every few hours by modern telescopes are not relevant all the time. Why should a scientist spend several hours loading all data in a database? Why should they spend several hours indexing all the data? Which data parts are of importance becomes apparent only after going over parts of the data and at least after partially understudying the trends. To make things worse, in a few hours, several more terabytes of data will arrive, that is, before we make sense of the previous batch of data.

Similarly, in a business analytics setting, changing the processing paradigm can be of critical importance. As it stands, now analysts or tools need to scan all data in search of interesting patterns. Yet in many emerging applications, there is no slack time to waste; answers are needed fast, for example, when trying to figure out user behavior or news trends, when observing traffic behavior or network monitoring for fraud detection.

Data Exploration

With such overwhelming amounts of data, *data exploration* is becoming a new and necessary paradigm of query processing, that is, when we are in search for interesting patterns often not knowing *a priori* exactly what we are looking for. For example, an astronomer wants to browse parts of the sky to look for interesting effects, while a data analyst of an IT business browses daily data of monitoring streams to figure out user behavior patterns. What both cases have in common is a daily stream of Big Data, that is, in the order of multiple terabytes and the need to observe "something interesting and useful."

Next-generation database systems should interpret queries by their intent, rather than as a contract carved in stone for complete and correct answers. The result in a user query should aid the user in understanding the database's content and provides guidance to continue the data exploration journey. Data analysts should be able to stepwise explore deeper and deeper the database, and stop when the result content and quality reaches their satisfaction point. At the same time, response times should be close to instant such that they allow users to interact with the system and explore the data in a contextualized way as soon as data become available.

With systems that support data exploration, we can immediately discard the main bottleneck that stops us from consuming Big Data today; instead of considering a Big Data set in one go with a slow process, exploration-based systems can incrementally and adaptively guide users toward the path that their queries and the result lead. This helps us avoid major inherent costs, which are directly affected by the amount of data input and thus are showstoppers nowadays. These costs include numerous procedures, steps, and algorithms spread throughout the whole design of modern data management systems.

Key Goals: Fast, Interactive, and Adaptive

For efficient data exploration to work, there are few essential goals.

First, the system should be fast to the degree that it feels interactive, that is, the user poses a question and a few seconds later an answer appears. Any data that we load do not have to be complete. Any data structure that we build does not have to represent all data or all value ranges. The answer itself does not have to represent a correct and complete result but rather a hint of how the data look like and how to proceed further, that is, what the next query should be. This is essential in order to engage data analysts in a seamless way; the system is not the bottleneck anymore.

Second, the system and the whole query-processing procedure should be adaptive in the sense that it adapts to the user requests; it proceeds with actions that speed up the search toward eventually getting the full answer the user is looking for. This is crucial in order to be able to finally satisfy the user needs after having sufficiently explored the data.

Metaphor Example

The observations to be made about the data in this case resemble an initially empty picture; the user sees one pixel at a time with every query they pose to the system. The system makes sure it remembers all pixels in order to guide the user toward areas of the picture where interesting shapes start to appear. Not all the pictures have to be completed for interesting effects to be seen from a high-level point of view, while again not all the pictures are needed for certain areas to be completed and seen in more detail.

Data Exploration Techniques

In the rest of this chapter, we discuss a string of novel data exploration techniques that aim to rethink database architectures with Big Data in mind. We discuss (a) adaptive indexing to build indices on-the-fly as opposed to *a priori*, (b) adaptive loading to allow for direct access on raw data without *a priori* loading steps, and (c) database architectures for approximate query processing to work over dynamic samples of data.

Adaptive Indexing

In this section, we present adaptive indexing. We discuss the motivation for adaptive indexing in dynamic Big Data environments as well as the main bottlenecks of traditional indexing approaches. This section gives a broad description of the state of the art in adaptive indexing, including topics such as updates, concurrency control, and robustness.

Indexing

Good performance in state-of-the-art database systems relies largely on proper tuning and physical design, that is, creating the proper accelerator structures, called indices. Indices are exploited at query-processing time to provide fast data access. Choosing the proper indices is a major performance parameter in database systems; a query may be several orders of magnitude faster if the proper index is available and is used properly. The main problem is that the set of potential indices is too large to be covered by default. As such, we need to choose a subset of the possible indices and implement only those.

In the past, the choice of the proper index collection was assigned to database administrators (DBAs). However, as applications became more and more complex, index selection too became complex for human administration alone. Today, all modern database systems ship with tuning advisor tools. Essentially, these tools provide suggestions regarding which indices should be created. A human DBA is then responsible of making and implementing the final choices.

Offline Indexing

The predominant approach is offline indexing. With offline indexing, all tuning choices happen up front, assuming sufficient workload knowledge and idle time. Workload knowledge is necessary in order to determine the appropriate tuning actions, that is, to decide which indices should be created, while idle time is required in order to actually perform those actions. In other words, we need to know what kind of queries we are going to ask and we need to have enough time to prepare the system for those queries.

Big Data Indexing Problems

However, in dynamic environments with Big Data, workload knowledge and idle time are scarce resources. For example, in scientific databases, new data arrive on a daily or even hourly basis, while query patterns follow an exploratory path as the scientists try to interpret the data and understand the patterns observed; there is no time and knowledge to analyze and prepare a different physical design every hour or even every day; even a single index may take several hours to create.

Traditional indexing presents three fundamental weaknesses in such cases: (a) the workload may have changed by the time we finish tuning; (b) there may be no time to finish tuning properly; and (c) there is no indexing support during tuning.

Database Cracking

Recently, a new approach, called database cracking, was introduced to the physical design problem. Cracking introduces the notion of continuous, incremental, partial, and on-demand adaptive indexing. Thereby, indices are incrementally built and refined during query processing. The net effect is that there is no need for any upfront tuning steps. In turn, there is no need for any workload knowledge and idle time to set up the database system. Instead, the system autonomously builds indices during query processing, adjusting fully to the needs of the users. For example, as scientists start exploring a Big Data set, query after query, the system follows the exploration path of the scientist, incrementally building and refining indices only for the data areas that seem interesting for the exploration path. After a few queries, performance adaptively improves to the level of a fully tuned system. From a technical point of view, cracking relies on continuously physically reorganizing data as users pose more and more queries.

Every query is treated as a hint on how data should be stored.

Column Stores

Before we discuss cracking in more detail, we give a short introduction to column-store databases. Database cracking was primarily designed for modern column stores and thus it relies on a number of modern column-store characteristics. Column-stores store data one column at a time in fixed-width dense arrays. This representation is the same both for disk and for main memory. The net effect compared to traditional row stores is that during query processing, a column store may access only the referenced data/columns. Similarly, column stores rely on bulk and vector-wised processing. Thus, a select operator typically processes a single column in one go or in a few steps, instead of consuming full tuples one at a time. Specifically for database cracking, the column-store design allows for efficient physical reorganization of arrays. In effect, cracking performs all physical reorganization actions efficiently in one go over a single column; it does not have to touch other columns.

Selection Cracking Example

We now briefly recap the first adaptive indexing technique, selection cracking, as it was introduced in Idreos et al. (2007a). The main innovation is that the physical data store is continuously changing with each incoming query q, using q as a hint on how data should be stored. Assume an attribute A stored as a fixed-width dense array in a column store. Say a query requests all values where A < 10. In response, a cracking DBMS clusters all tuples of A with A < 10 at the beginning of the respective column C, while pushing all tuples with A ≥ 10 to the end. In other words, it partitions on-the-fly and in-place column C using the predicate of the query as a pivot. A subsequent query requesting A ≥ v1, where v1 ≥ 10, has to search and crack only the last part of C, where values A ≥ 10 reside. Likewise, a query that requests A < v2, where v2 < 10, searches and cracks only the first part of C. All crack actions happen as part of the query operators, requiring no external administration.

The terminology "cracking" reflects the fact that the database is partitioned (cracked) into smaller and manageable pieces.

Data Structures

The cracked data for each attribute of a relational table are stored in a normal column (array). The very first query on a column copies the base column to an auxiliary column where all cracking happens. This step is used such that we can always retrieve the base data in its original form and order. In addition, cracking uses an AVL-tree to maintain partitioning information such as which pieces have been created, which values have been used as pivots, etc.

Continuous Adaptation

The cracking actions continue with every query. In this way, the system reacts to every single query, trying to adjust the physical storage, continuously reorganizing columns to fit the workload patterns. As we process more queries, the more performance improves. In essence, more queries introduce more partitioning, while pieces become smaller and smaller. Every range query or more precisely every range select operator needs to touch at most two pieces of a column, that is, those pieces that appear at the boundaries of the needed value range. With smaller pieces, future queries need less effort to perform the cracking steps and as such performance gradually improves.

To avoid the extreme status where a column is completely sorted, cracking poses a threshold where it stops cracking a column for pieces which are smaller than L1 cache. There are two reasons for this choice. First, the AVL-tree, which maintains the partitioning information, grows significantly, and causes random access when searching. Secondly, the benefit brought by cracking pieces that are already rather small is minimal. As such, if during a query, a piece smaller than L1 is indicated for cracking, the system completely sorts this piece with an in-memory quick sort. The fact that this piece is sorted is marked in the AVL-tree. This way, if a future query needs to search within a piece p which happens to be fully sorted, then it simply performs a binary search on this piece as opposed to physically reorganizing it.

Performance Examples

In experiments with the Skyserver real query and data logs, a database system with cracking enabled, finished answering 160,000 queries, while a traditional system was still half way creating the proper indices and without having answered a single query (Halim et al. 2012). Similarly, in experiments with the business standard TPC-H benchmark, perfectly preparing a system with all the proper indices took ~3 h, while a cracking database system could answer all queries in a matter of a few seconds with zero preparation, while still reaching optimal performance, similar to that of the fully indexed system (Idreos et al. 2009).

Being able to provide this instant access to data, that is, without any tuning, while at the same time being able to quickly, adaptively, and incrementally approach optimal performance levels in terms of response times, is exactly the property that creates a promising path for data exploration. The rest of the chapter discusses several database architecture challenges that arise when trying to design database kernels where adaptive indexing becomes a first-class citizen.

Sideways Cracking

Column-store systems access one column at a time. They rely on the fact that all columns of the same table are aligned. This means that for each column, the value in the first position belongs in the first tuple, the one in the second position belongs to the second tuple, and so on. This allows for efficient query processing for queries that request multiple columns of the same table, that is, for efficient tuple reconstruction.

When cracking physically reorganizes one column, the rest of the columns of the same table remain intact; they are separate physical arrays. As a result, with cracking, columns of the same table are not aligned anymore. Thus, when a future query needs to touch more than one columns of the same table, then the system is forced to perform random access in order to reconstruct tuples on-the-fly. For example, assume a selection on a column A, followed by a projection on another column B of the same table. If column A has been cracked in the past, then the tuple IDs, which is the intermediate result out of the select operator on A, are in a random order and lead to an expensive access to fetch the qualifying values from column B.

One approach could be that every time we crack one column, we also crack in the same way all columns of the same table. However, this defeats the purpose of exploiting column stores; it would mean that every single query would have to touch all attributes of the referenced table as opposed to only touching the attributes which are truly necessary for the current query.

Sideways cracking solves this problem by working on pairs of columns at a time (Idreos et al. 2009) and by adaptively forwarding cracking actions across the columns of the same table. That is for a pair of columns A and B, during the cracking steps on A, the B values follow this reorganization. The values of A and B are stored together in a binary column format, making the physical reorganization efficient. Attribute A is the head of this column pair, while attribute B is the tail. When more than two columns are used in a query, sideways cracking uses bit vectors to filter intermediate results, while working across multiple column-pairs of the same head. For example, in order to do a selection on attribute A and two aggregations, one on attribute B and one attribute C, sideways cracking uses pairs AB and AC. Once both pairs are cracked in the same way using the predicates on A, then they are fully aligned and they can be used in the same plans without tuple reconstruction actions.

Essentially, sideways cracking performs tuple reconstructions via incremental cracking and alignment actions as opposed to joins. For each pair, there is a log to maintain the cracking actions that have taken place in this pair as well as in other pairs that use the same head attribute. Two column-pairs of the same head are aligned when they have exactly the same history, that is, they have been cracked for the same bounds and exactly in the same order.

Partial Cracking

The pairs of columns created by sideways cracking can result in a large set of auxiliary cracking data. With Big Data, this is an important concern. Cracking creates those column pairs dynamically, that is, only what is needed is created and only when it is needed. Still though, the storage overhead may be significant. Partial cracking solves this problem by introducing partial cracking columns (Idreos et al. 2009). With partial cracking, we do not need to materialize complete columns; only the values needed by the current hot workload set are materialized in cracking columns. If missing values are requested by future queries, then the missing values are fetched from the base columns the first time they are requested.

With partial cracking, a single cracking column becomes a logical view of numerous smaller physical columns. In turn, each one of the small columns is cracked and accessed in the same way as described for the original database cracking technique, that is, it is continuously physically reorganized as we pose queries.

Users may pose a storage budget and cracking makes sure it will stay within the budget by continuously monitoring the access patterns of the various materialized cracking columns. Each small physical column of a single logical column is completely independent and can be thrown away and recreated at any time. For each column, cracking knows how many times it has been accessed by queries and it uses an LRU policy to throw away columns when space for a new one is needed.

Updates

Updates pose a challenge since they cause physical changes to the data which in combination with the physical changes caused by cracking may lead to significant complexity. The solution proposed in Idreos et al. (2007b) deals with updates by deferring update actions for when relevant queries arrive. In the same spirit as with the rest of the cracking techniques, cracking updates do not do any work until it is unavoidable, that is, until a query, which is affected by a pending update, arrives. In this way, when an update comes, it is simply put aside. For each column, there is an auxiliary delete column where all pending deletes are placed and an auxiliary insertions column where all pending inserts are placed. Actual updates are a combination of a delete and then an insert action.

Each query needs to check the pending deletes and inserts for pending actions that may affect it. If there are any, then those qualifying pending insertions and deletions are merged with the cracking columns on-the-fly. The algorithm for merging pending updates into cracking columns takes advantage of the fact that there is no strict order within a cracking column. For example, each piece in a cracking column contains values within a given value range but once we know that a new insertion, for example, should go within this piece, then we can place it in any position of the piece; within each cracking piece, there is no strict requirement for maintaining any order.

Adaptive Merging

Cracking can be seen as an incremental quicksort where the pivots are defined by the query predicates. Adaptive merging was introduced as a complementary technique, which can be seen as an incremental merge sort where the merging actions are defined by the query predicates (Graefe and Kuno 2010). The motivation is mainly toward disk-based environments and toward providing fast convergence to optimal performance.

The main design point of adaptive merging is that data are horizontally partitioned into runs. Each run is sorted in memory with a quicksort action. This preparation step is done with the first query and results in an initial column that contains the various runs. From there on, as more queries arrive data are moved from the initial column to a results column where the final index is shaped. Every query merges into the results column only data that are defined by its selection predicates and those that are missing from the results column. If a query is covered fully by the results column, then it does not need touch the initial runs. Data that are merged are immediately sorted in place in the results column; once all data are merged, the results column is actually a fully sorted column. With data pieces being sorted both in the initial column and in the results column, queries can exploit binary search both during merging and accessing only the results column.

Hybrids

Adaptive merging improves over plain cracking when it comes to convergence speed, that is, the number of queries needed to reach performance levels similar to that of a full index is significantly reduced. This behavior is mainly due to the aggressive sorting actions during the initial phase of adaptive merging; it allows future queries to access data faster. However, these sorting actions put a sizeable overhead on the initial phase of a workload, causing the very first query to be significantly slower. Cracking, on the other hand, has a much more smooth behavior, making it more lightweight to individual queries. However, cracking takes much longer to reach the optimal index status (unless there is significant skew in the workload).

The study in Idreos et al. (2011a,b) presents these issues and proposes a series of techniques that blend the best properties of adaptive merging with the best properties of database cracking. A series of hybrid algorithms are proposed where one can tune how much initialization overhead and how much convergence speed is needed. For example, the crack–crack hybrid (HCC) uses the same overall architecture as adaptive merging, that is, using an initial column and a results column where data are merged based on query predicates. However, the initial runs are now not sorted; instead, they are cracked based on query predicates. As a result, the first query is not penalized as with adaptive merging. At the same time, the data placed in the results column are not sorted in place. Several combinations are proposed where one can crack, sort, or radix cluster the initial column and the result column. The crack–sort hybrid, which cracks the initial column, while it sorts the pieces in the result column, brings the best overall balance between initialization and converge costs (Idreos et al. 2011a,b).

Robustness

Since cracking reacts to queries, its adaptation speed and patterns depend on the kind of queries that arrive. In fact, cracking performance crucially depends on the arrival order of queries. That is, we may run exactly the set of queries twice in slightly different order and the result may be significantly different in terms of response times even though exactly the same cracking index will be created. To make this point more clear, consider the following example. Assume a column of 100 unique integers in [0, 99]. Assume a first query that asks for all values v where $v < 1$. As a result, cracking partitions the column into two pieces. In piece P1, we have all values in [0, 1) and in piece P2 we have all values in [1, 99]. The net effect is that the second piece still contains 99 values, meaning that the partitioning achieved by the first query is not so useful; any query falling within the second piece still has to analyze almost all values of the column. Now assume that the second query requests all values v, where $v < 2$. Then, the third query requests all values v, where $v < 3$, and so on. This sequence results in cracking having to continuously analyze large portions of the column as it always leaves back big pieces. The net effect is that convergence speed is too slow and in the worst case cracking degrades to a performance similar to that of a plain scan for several queries, resulting in a performance which is not robust (Halim et al. 2012).

To solve the above problem, Halim et al. (2012) propose stochastic cracking. The main intuition is that stochastic cracking plugs in stochastic cracking actions during the normal cracking actions that happen during processing. For example, when cracking a piece of a column for a pivot X, stochastic cracking adds an additional cracking step where this piece is also cracked for a pivot which is randomly chosen. As a result, the chances of leaving back big uncracked pieces become significantly smaller.

Concurrency Control

Cracking is based on continuous physical reorganization of the data. Every single query might have side effects. This is in strong contrast with what normally happens in database systems where plain queries do not have side effects on the data. Not having any side effects means that read queries may be scheduled to run in parallel. Database systems heavily rely on this parallelism to provide good performance when multiple users access the system simultaneously. On the other hand, with cracking, every query might change the way data are organized and as a result it is not safe to have multiple queries working and changing the same data in parallel.

However, we would like to have both the adaptive behavior of database cracking, while still allowing multiple users to query Big Data simultaneously. The main trick to achieve this is to allow concurrent access on the various pieces of each cracking column; two different queries may be physically reorganizing the same column as long as they do not touch the exact same piece simultaneously (Graefe et al. 2012). In this way, each query may lock a single piece of a cracking column at a time, while other queries may be working on the other pieces. As we create more and more pieces, there are more opportunities to increase the ability for multiple queries to work in parallel. This bonds well with the adaptive behavior of database cracking; if a data area becomes hot, then more queries will arrive to crack it into multiple pieces and subsequently more queries will be able to run in parallel because more pieces exist.

Contrary to concurrency control for typical database updates, with adaptive indexing during read queries, we change only the data organization; the data contents remain intact. For this reason, all concurrency mechanisms for adaptive indexing may rely on latching as opposed to full-fledged database locks, resulting in a very lightweight design (Graefe et al. 2012).

Summary

Overall, database cracking opens an exciting path towards database systems that inherently support adaptive indexing. As we do not require any workload knowledge and any tuning steps, we can significantly reduce the time it takes to query newly arrived data, assisting data exploration.

Adaptive Loading

The previous section described the idea of building database kernels that inherently provide adaptive indexing capabilities. Indexing is one of the major bottlenecks when setting up a database system, but it is not the only one. In this section, we focus on another crucial bottleneck, that is, data loading. We discuss the novel direction of adaptive loading to enable database systems to bypass the loading overhead and immediately be able to query data before even being loaded in a database.

The Loading Bottleneck

Data loading is a necessary step when setting up a database system. Essentially, data loading copies all data inside the database system. From this point on, the database fully controls the data; it stores data in its own format and uses its own algorithms to update and access the data. Users cannot control the data anymore directly, but only through the database system. The reason to perform the loading step is to enable good performance during query processing; by having full control on the data, the database system can optimize and prepare for future data accesses. However, the cost of copying and transforming all data are significant; it may take several hours to load a decent data size even with parallel loading.

As a result, in order to use the sophisticated features of a database system, users have to wait until their data are loaded (and then tuned). However, with Big Data arriving at high rates, it is not feasible anymore to reserve several hours for data loading as it creates a big gap between data creation and data exploitation.

External Files

One feature that almost all open source and commercial database products provide is external tables. External files are typically in the form of raw text-based files in CSV format (comma-separated values). With the external tables functionality, one can simply attach a raw file to a database without loading the respective data. When a query arrives for this file, the database system automatically goes back to the raw file to access and fetch the data on-the-fly. This is a useful feature in order to delay data loading actions but unfortunately it is not a functionality that can be used for query processing. The reason is that it is too expensive to query raw files; there are several additional costs involved. In particular, parsing and tokenizing costs dominate the total query processing costs. Parsing and tokenizing are necessary in order to distinguish the attribute values inside raw files and to transform them into binary form. For this reason, the external tables functionality is not being used for query processing.

Adaptive Loading

The NoDB project recently proposed the adaptive loading direction (Alagiannis et al. 2012; Idreos et al. 2011a,b); the main idea is that loading actions happen adaptively and incrementally during query processing and driven by the actual query needs. Initially, no loading actions take place; this means that there is no loading cost and that users can immediately query their data. With every query, the system adaptively fetches any needed data from the raw data files. At any given time, only data needed by the queries are loaded. The main challenge of the adaptive loading direction is to minimize the cost to touch the raw data files during query processing, that is, to eliminate the reason that makes the external tables fuctionality unusable for querying.

The main idea is that as we process more and more queries, NoDB can collect knowledge about the raw files and significantly reduce the data access costs. For example, it learns about how data reside on raw files in order to better look for it, if needed, in the future.

Selective Parsing

NoDB pushes selections down to the raw files in order to minimize the parsing costs. Assume a query that needs to have several filtering conditions checked for every single row of a data file. In a typical external files process, the system tokenizes and parses all attributes in each row of the file. Then, it feeds the data to the typical data flow inside the database system to process the query. This incurs a maximum parsing and tokenizing cost. NoDB removes this overhead by performing parsing and tokenizing selectively on a row-by-row basis, while applying the filtering predicates directly on the raw file. The net benefit is that as soon as any of the filtering predicates fails, then NoDB can abandon the current row and continue with the next one, effectively avoiding significant parsing and tokenizing costs. To achieve all these steps, NoDB overloads the scan operator with the ability to access raw file in addition to loaded data.

Indexing

In addition, during parsing, NoDB creates and maintains an index to mark positions on top of the raw file. This index is called positional map and its functionality is to provide future queries with direct access to a location of the file that is close to what they need. For example, if for a given row we know the position of the fifth attribute and the current query needs to analyze the seventh attribute, then the query only needs to start parsing as of the attribute on the fifth position of the file. Of course, given that we cannot realistically assume fixed length attributes, the positional map needs to maintain information on a row-by-row basis. Still though, the cost is kept low, as only a small portion of a raw file needs to be indexed. For example, experiments in Alagiannis et al. (2012) indicate that once 15% of a raw file is indexed, then performance reaches optimal levels.

Caching

The data fetched from the raw file are adaptively cached and reused if similar queries arrive in the future. This allows the hot workload set to always be cached and the need to fetch raw data appears only during workload shifts. The policy used for cache replacement is LRU in combination with adaptive loading specific parameters. For example, integer attributes have a priority over string attributes in the cache; fetching string attributes back from the raw file during future queries is significantly less expensive than fetching integer attributes. This is because the parsing costs for string attributes are very low compared to those for integer values.

Statistics

In addition, NoDB creates statistics on-the-fly during parsing. Without proper statistics, optimizers cannot make good choices about query plans. With adaptive loading, the system is initiated without statistics as no data is loaded up front. To avoid bad plans and to guarantee robustness, NoDB immediately calculates statistics the very first time an attribute of a given raw file is requested by a query. This puts a small overhead at query time, but it allows us to avoid bad optimization choices.

Splitting Files

When accessing raw files, we are limited in exploiting the format of the raw files. Typically, data are stored in CSV files where each row represents an entry in a relational table and each file represents all data in a single relational table. As a result, every single query that needs to fetch data from raw files has to touch all data. Even with selective parsing and indexing, at the low level the system still needs to touch almost all the raw file. If the data were *a priori* loaded and stored in a column-store format, then a query would need to touch only the data columns it really needs. NoDB proposed the idea of text cracking, where during parsing the raw file is separated into multiple files and each file may contain one or more of the attributes of the original raw file (Idreos et al. 2011a,b). This process works recursively and as a result future queries on the raw file, can significantly reduce the amount of data they need to touch by having to work only on smaller raw files.

Data Vaults

One area where adaptive loading can have a major impact is sciences. In the case of scientific data management, several specialized formats already exist and are in use for several decades. These formats store data in a binary form and often provide indexing information, for example, in the form of clustering data based on the date of creation. In order to exploit database systems for scientific data management, we would need to transform data from the scientific format into the database format, incurring a significant cost. The data vaults project provides a two-level architecture that allows exploiting the metadata in scientific data formats for adaptive loading operations (Ivanova et al. 2012). Given that the scientific data are already in a binary format, there are no considerations regarding parsing and tokenizing costs. During the initialization phase, data vaults load only the metadata information, resulting in a minimal set-up cost. During query processing time, the system uses the metadata to guide the queries to the proper files and to transform only the needed data on-the-fly. This way, without performing any *a priori* transformation of the scientific data, we can pose queries through the database system directly and selectively.

Summary

Loading represents a significant bottleneck; it raises a wall between users and Big Data. Adaptive loading directions provide a promising research path towards systems that can be usable immediately as soon as data arrive by removing loading costs.

Sampling-Based Query Processing

Loading and indexing are the two essential bottlenecks when setting up a database system. However, even after all installation steps are performed, there are more bottlenecks to deal with; this time bottlenecks appear during query processing. In particular, the requirements for correctness and completeness raise a significant overhead; every single query is treated by a database system as a request to find all possible and correct answers.

This inherent requirement for correctness and completeness has its roots in the early applications of database systems, that is, mainly in critical sectors such as in banking and financial applications where errors cannot be tolerated. However, with modern Big Data applications and with the need to explore data, we can afford to sacrifice correctness and completeness in favor of improved response times. A query session that may consist of several exploratory queries can lead to exactly the same result, regardless of whether the full answer is returned every time; in an exploratory session, users are mainly looking for hints on what the next query should be and a partial answer may already be informative enough.

In this section, we discuss a number of recent approaches to create database systems that are tailored for querying with partial answers, sacrificing correctness, and completeness for improved response times.

Sciborg

Sciborg proposed the idea of working over data that is organized in a hierarchy of samples (Sidirourgos et al. 2011). The main idea is that queries can be performed over a sample of the data providing a quick response time. Subsequently, the user may choose to ask for more detail and to query more samples. Essentially, this is a promising research path to enable interactive query processing. The main innovation in Sciborg is that samples of data are not simply random samples; instead, Sciborg creates weighted samples driven by past query-processing actions and based on the properties of the data. In this way, it can better follow the needs of the users by collecting relevant data together such as users can infer interesting patterns using only a small number of samples.

Blink

Another recent project, Blink, proposes a system where data are also organized in multiple samples (Agarwal et al. 2012). The characteristic of Blink is its seamless integration with cloud technology, being able to scale to massive amounts of data and processing nodes.

Both the Blink and the Sciborg projects represent a vision to create database kernels where the system inherently supports query processing over samples. For example, the user does not have to create a sample explicitly and then query it, followed by the creation of a different sample, while repeating this process multiple times. In a database architecture that supports samples at its core, this whole process is transparent to the user and has the potential to be much more effective. For example, with tailored database kernels (a) the samples are created with minimal storage overhead, (b) they adapt continuously, and (c) query results over multiple samples can be merged dynamically by the system.

One-Minute DB Kernels

Another vision in the direction of exploration-based database kernels is the one-minute database kernels idea (Kersten et al. 2011). Similar to Sciborg and Blink, the main notion is that correctness and completeness are sacrificed in favor of performance; however, contrary to past approaches, this happens at a very low level, that is, at the level of database operators. Every decision in the design of database algorithms can be reconsidered to avoid expensive actions by sacrificing correctness. For example, a join operator may choose to drop data from the inner join input as soon as the size of the hash table exceeds the size of the main memory or even the size of CPU cache. A smaller hash table is much faster to create and it is also much faster to probe, avoiding cache misses. Similar decisions can be made across the whole design of database kernels.

Essentially, the one-minute database kernels approach is equivalent to the sample-based ideas. The difference is that it pushes the problem at a much lower level where possibly we may have better control of parameters that affect performance. One of the main challenges is to be able to provide quality guarantees for the query results.

dbTouch

One significant bottleneck when querying database systems is the need to be an expert user; one needs to be aware of the database schema and needs to be fluent in SQL. When it comes to Big Data exploration, we would like to render data accessible to more people and to make the whole process of discovering interesting patterns as easy as possible. dbTouch extends the vision of sample-based processing with the notion of creating database kernels which are tailored for touch-based exploration (Idreos and Liarou 2013). Data appear in a touch device in a visual form, while users can simply touch the data to query. For example, a relational table may be represented as a table shape and a user may slide a finger over the table to run a number of aggregations. dbTouch is not about formulating queries; instead, it proposes a new database kernel design which reacts instantly to touch. Users do not pose queries as in normal systems; in dbTouch, users point to interesting data and the system continuously reacts to every touch. Every touch corresponds to analyzing a single tuple (or at most a few tuples), while a slide gesture can be seen as multiple single touches and can be used to explore a given data area. As such, only a sample of the data is processed every time, while now the user has full control regarding which data are processed and when; by changing the direction or the speed of a slide gesture, users can control the exploration process, while observing running results as they are visualized by dbTouch.

The main challenge with dbTouch is in designing database kernels that can react instantly to every touch and to provide quick response times even though the database does not control anymore the order and the kind of data processed for every query session.

Summary

Overall, correctness and completeness pose a significant bottleneck during query time; with Big Data, this problem becomes a major showstopper as it becomes extremely expensive to consume big piles of data. The novel research directions described in this chapter make a first step towards a new era of database kernels where performance becomes more important than correctness and where exploration is the main query-processing paradigm.

In the presence of Big Data, query processing is facing significant new challenges. A particular aspect of those challenges has to do with the fact that there is not enough time and workload knowledge to properly prepare and tune database management systems. In addition, producing correct and complete answers by consuming all data within reasonable time bounds is becoming harder and harder. In this chapter, we discussed the research direction of data exploration where adaptive and incremental processing become first-class citizens in database architectures.

Adaptive indexing, adaptive loading, and sampling-based database kernels provide a promising path towards creating dedicated exploration systems. It represents a widely open research area as we need to reconsider every single aspect of database design established in the past.

References

Abouzeid, A., K. Bajda-Pawlikowski, D. J. Abadi, A. Rasin, and A. Silberschatz. HadoopDB: An architectural hybrid of MapReduce and DBMS technologies for analytical workloads. *Proceedings of the Very Large Databases Endowment (PVLDB)* 2(1), 2009: 922–933.

Agarwal, S., A. Panda, B. Mozafari, A. P. Iyer, S. Madden, and I. Stoica. Blink and it's done: Interactive queries on very large data. *Proceedings of the Very Large Databases Endowment (PVLDB)* 5(6), 2012: 1902–1905.

Alagiannis, I., R. Borovica, M. Branco, S. Idreos, and A. Ailamaki. NoDB: Efficient query execution on raw data files. *ACM SIGMOD International Conference on Management of Data*, Scottsdale, AZ, 2012.

Boncz, P. A., M. Zukowski, and N. Nes. MonetDB/X100: Hyper-pipelining query execution. *Biennial Conference on Innovative Data Systems Research (CIDR)*, Asilomar, CA, 2005. pp. 225–237.

Dean, J. and S. Ghemawat. MapReduce: Simplified data processing on large clusters. *USENIX Symposium on Operating Systems Design and Implementation (OSDI)*, San Francisco, CA, 2004. pp. 137–150.

Graefe, G., F. Halim, S. Idreos, S. Manegold, and H. A. Kuno. Concurrency control for adaptive indexing. *Proceedings of the Very Large Databases Endowment (PVLDB)* 5(7), 2012: 656–667.

Graefe, G. and H. A. Kuno. Self-selecting, self-tuning, incrementally optimized indexes. *International Conference on Extending Database Technology (EDBT)*, Lausanne, Switzerland, 2010.

Hadapt. 2012. http://www.hadapt.com/

Halim, F., S. Idreos, P. Karras, and R. H. C. Yap. Stochastic database cracking: Towards robust adaptive indexing in main-memory column-stores. *Proceedings of the Very Large Databases Endowment (PVLDB)* 5(6), 2012: 502–513.

Idreos, S., and E. Liarou. dbTouch: Analytics at your Fingetips. *International Conference on Innovative Data Systems Research (CIDR)*, Asilomar, CA, 2013.

Idreos, S., I. Alagiannis, R. Johnson, and A. Ailamaki. Here are my Data Files. Here are my Queries. Where are my results? *International Conference on Innovative Data Systems Research (CIDR)*, Asilomar, CA, 2011a.

Idreos, S., M. Kersten, and S. Manegold. Database cracking. *International Conference on Innovative Data Systems Research (CIDR)*, Asilomar, CA, 2007a.

Idreos, S., M. Kersten, and S. Manegold. Self-organizing tuple reconstruction in column-stores. *ACM SIGMOD International Conference on Management of Data*, Providence, RI, 2009.

Idreos, S., M. Kersten, and S. Manegold. Updating a cracked database. *ACM SIGMOD International Conference on Management of Data*, Beijing, China, 2007b.

Idreos, S., S. Manegold, H. Kuno, and G. Graefe. Merging what's cracked, cracking what's merged: Adaptive indexing in main-memory column-stores. *Proceedings of the Very Large Databases Endowment (PVLDB)* 4(9), 2011b: 585–597.

Ivanova, M., M. L. Kersten, and S. Manegold. Data vaults: A symbiosis between database technology and scientific file repositories. *International Conference on Scientific and Statistical Database Management (SSDBM)*, Chania, Crete, Greece, 2012.

Kersten, M., S. Idreos, S. Manegold, and E. Liarou. The researcher's guide to the data deluge: Querying a scientific database in just a few seconds. *Proceedings of the Very Large Databases Endowment (PVLDB)* 4(12), 2011: 174–177.

Platfora. 2012. http://www.platfora.com/

Sidirourgos, L., M. L. Kersten, and P. A. Boncz. SciBORQ: Scientific data management with bounds on runtime and quality. *International Conference on Innovative Data systems Research (CIDR)*, Asilomar, CA, 2011.

Stonebraker, M. et al. C-Store: A column-oriented DBMS. *International Conference on Very Large Databases (VLDB)*, Trondheim, Norway, 2005, pp. 553–564.

9

Big Data Processing with MapReduce

Jordà Polo

CONTENTS

Introduction

Current trends in computer science drive users toward more service-oriented architectures such as the so-called cloud platforms. The cloud allows provisioning of computing and storage, converting physical central-ized resources into virtual shared resources. The ideas behind it are not that different from previous efforts such as utility or grid computing, but

thanks to the development of technologies, it is becoming much more efficient: cost-, maintenance-, and energy-wise.

At the same time, more business are becoming aware of the relevance of
the data they are able to gather: from social websites to log files, there is a
lot of *hidden* information ready to be processed and mined. Not so long ago,
it was relatively difficult to work with large amounts of data, and so most
of it was usually discarded. The problem was not with hard drive capacity,
which has increased a lot over the years, but that with access speed, which is
improving only at a much lower pace. However, new tools, most of which are
originally designed and built around web-related technologies, are making
things easier. Developers are finally getting used to the idea of dealing with
large data sets.

Both of these changes are not coincidental and respond to certain needs.
On the one hand, nowadays it is much easier for companies to become global,
target a larger number of clients, and consequently deal with more data. On
the other hand, there is a limit to the initial expenses that they are willing
to spend. Another issue that these new trends help one to address is that
benefits may only arrive when dealing with sufficiently large data, but the
upfront cost and the maintenance of the large clusters required to process
such data sets is usually a hindrance compared to the benefits.

Despite the availability of new tools and the shift to service-oriented computing, there is still room for improvement, especially with regard to the
integration of the two sides of cloud computing: the applications that provide services and the systems that run these applications.

Developers still need to think about the requirements of the applications
in terms of resources (CPU, memory, etc.) and will inevitably end up either
under- or over-provisioning. In a cloud environment, it is easier to update
the provisioning as needed, but for many applications this process is still
manual and requires human intervention.

Moving away from the old style of managing resources is one of the major
challenges of cloud computing. In a way, it can be thought of as the equivalent of the revolution that the introduction of time-sharing supposed in the
era of batch processing. Time-sharing allowed everyone to interact with
computers as if they were the owners of the system. Likewise, freeing users
from thinking about provisioning is the definite step in creating the illusion
of the cloud as an unlimited source of computing resources.

The main obstacle, though, is that the cloud is not actually an infinite and
free source of computing: maintaining it is not trivial, resources are limited,
and providers need some way to prioritize services. If users are freed of the
task of provisioning, then there must be some other mechanism to make
both, sharing and accounting, possible.

On the other hand, some parts of these systems seem to be ready for this
shift, especially the lower level components and the middleware. But the
applications that run the services on top of cloud platforms seem to be lag-
ging behind. The cloud is still a relatively young development platform, so

it is to be expected that not all applications are fully integrated. But it seems clear that these applications represent the next and most obvious target in order to consolidate cloud platforms. One example of this kind of application is the MapReduce programming framework. The MapReduce model allows developers to write massively parallel applications without much effort and is becoming an essential tool in the software stack of many companies that need to deal with large data sets. MapReduce fits well with the idea of dynamic provisioning, as it may run on a large number of machines and is already widely used in cloud environments.

MapReduce Model

MapReduce [5] is a programming model used to develop massively parallel applications that process and generate large amounts of data. It was first introduced by Google in 2004 and has since become an important tool for distributed computing. It is especially suited to operate on large data sets on clusters of computers, as it is designed to tolerate machine failures.

Essentially, MapReduce divides the work into small computations in two major steps, *map* and *reduce*, which are inspired by similar primitives that can be found in LISP and other functional programming languages. The input is formed by a set of key-value pairs, which are processed using the user-defined map function to generate a second set of intermediate key-value pairs. Intermediate results are then processed by the reduce function, which merges values by key.

While MapReduce is not something entirely new nor a revolutionary concept, it has helped us to standardize parallel applications. And even though its interface is simple, it has proved to be powerful enough to solve a wide-range of real-world problems: from web indexing to image analysis to clustering algorithms.

MapReduce provides high scalability and reliability, thanks to the division of the work into smaller units. Jobs are submitted to a master node, which is in charge of managing the execution of applications in the cluster. After submitting a job, the master initializes the desired number of smaller tasks or units of work and puts them to run on worker nodes. First, during the map phase, nodes read and apply the map function to a subset of the input data. The map's partial output is stored locally on each node and served to worker nodes executing the reduce function.

Input and output files are usually stored in a distributed file system, but in order to ensure scalability, the master tries to assign *local* work, meaning the input data are available locally. On the other hand, if a worker node fails to deliver the unit of work it has been assigned to complete, the master node is always able to send the work to some other node.

Comparison with Other Systems

Analyzing and performing computations on massive data sets is not something new, but it is not easy to compare MapReduce to other systems since it is often used to do things in a way that simply was not possible before using standardized tools. But besides creating a new *market*, MapReduce is also drawing the attention of developers, who use it for a wide range of purposes. The following comparison describes some of the technologies that share some kind of functionality with MapReduce.

RDBMS

Relational Database Management Systems are the dominant choice for transactional and analytical applications, and they have traditionally been a well-balanced and good enough solution for most applications. Yet its design has some limitations that make it difficult to keep the compatibility and provide optimized solution when some aspects such as scalability are the top priority.

There is only a partial overlap of functionality between RDBMSs and MapReduce: relational databases are suited to do things for which MapReduce will never be the optimal solution, and vice versa. For instance, MapReduce tends to involve processing most of the data set, or at least a large part of it, while RDBMS queries may be more fine-grained. On the other hand, MapReduce works fine with semistructured data since it is interpreted while it is being processed, unlike RDBMSs, where well-structured and normalized data are the key to ensure integrity and improve performance. Finally, traditional RDBMSs are more suitable for interactive access, but MapReduce is able to scale linearly and handle larger data sets. If the data are large enough, doubling the size of the cluster will also make running jobs twice as fast, something that is not necessarily true of relational databases.

Another factor that is also driving the move toward other kind of storage solutions are disks. Improvements in hard drives seem to be relegated to capacity and transfer rate only. But data access in an RDBMS is usually dominated by seek times, which have not changed significantly for some years. Solid-state drives may prove to be a good solution in the medium to long term [10], but they are still far from affordable compared to HDD, and besides, databases still need to be optimized for them.

MapReduce has been criticized by some RDBMS proponents due to its low-level abstraction and lack of structure. But taking into account the different features and goals of relational databases and MapReduce, they can be seen as complementary rather than opposite models. So the most valid criticism is probably not related to the technical merits of MapReduce, but with the hype generated around it, which is pushing its use to solve problems for which it may not be the best solution.

Distributed Key-Value and Column-Oriented DBMS

Alternative database models such as Distributed Key-Value and Column-oriented DBMS are becoming more widely used for similar reasons as MapReduce. These two different approaches are largely inspired by Amazon's Dynamo [6] and Google's BigTable [3]. Key-value storage systems have properties of databases and distributed hash tables, while column-oriented databases serialize data by column, making it more suitable for analytical processing.

Both models depart from the idea of a fixed schema-based structure and try to combine the best of both worlds: distribution and scalability of systems like MapReduce with a higher and more database-oriented level of abstraction. In fact, some of the most popular data stores actually use or implement some sort of MapReduce. Google's BigTable, for instance, uses Google MapReduce to process data stored in the system, and other column-oriented DBMS such as CouchDB use their own implementations of MapReduce internally.

This kind of databases also mark a new trend and make it clear that the differences between traditional databases and MapReduce systems are blurring as developers try to get the best of both worlds.

Grid Computing

Like MapReduce, Grid computing services are also focused on performing computations to solve a single problem by distributing the work across several computers. But these kinds of platforms often built on a cluster with a shared file system, which are good for CPU-bound jobs, but not good enough for data-intensive jobs. And that is precisely one of the key differences between these kind of systems: Grid computing does not emphasize as much as MapReduce on data, especially on doing the computation near the data.

Another distinction between MapReduce and Grid computing is the interface it provides to the programmer. In MapReduce, the programmer is able to focus on the problem that needs to be solved since only the map and reduce functions need to be implemented, and the framework takes care of the distribution, communication, fault-tolerance, etc. In contrast, in Grid computing the programmer has to deal with lower-level mechanisms to control the data flow, checkpoint, etc. which makes it more powerful, but also more error-prone and difficult to write.

Shared-Memory Parallel Programming

Traditionally, many large-scale parallel applications have been programmed in shared-memory environments such as OpenMP. Compared to MapReduce, this kind of programming interfaces are much more generic and provide solutions for a wider variety of problems. One of the typical use cases of these systems is parallel applications that require some kind of synchronization (e.g., critical sections).

However, this comes at a cost: they may be more flexible, but the interfaces are also significantly more low level and difficult to understand. Another difference between MapReduce and this model is the hardware for which each of these platforms has been designed. MapReduce is supposed to work on commodity hardware, while interfaces such as OpenMP are only efficient in shared-memory multiprocessor platforms.

Examples and Uses of MapReduce

MapReduce is currently being used for many different kinds of applications, from very simple helper tools that are part of a larger environment, to more complete and complex programs that may involve multiple, chained MapReduce executions.

This section includes a description of a typical MapReduce application, and what needs to be done to make it work, following the steps from the input to the final result. After the initial description, you will find a list of some of the problems MapReduce is able to solve, briefly explained. And finally, a more detailed study of how it is currently being used in production.

Word Count: MapReduce's "Hello World!"

The goal of a word count application is to get the frequency of words in a very large collection of documents. Word count was the problem that exemplified MapReduce in the original paper [5] and has since become the canonical example to introduce how MapReduce works.

To compute the frequency of words, a sequential program would be needed to read all the documents, keeping a list of ⟨word, count⟩ pairs, incrementing the appropriate count value every time a word is found.

As you will see below, MapReduce's approach is slightly different. First of all, the problem is divided into two stages known as *map* and *reduce*, named after the functions that are applied while they are in progress. The map() function is applied to every single element of the input, and since there is no need to do so in any particular order, it effectively makes it possible to parallelize all the work. For each element, map() emits key-value pairs to be worked on later during the reduce stage. The generated key-value pairs are grouped and processed by keys, so for every key there will be a list of values. The reduce() function is applied to these lists of values produced during the map stage and provides the final result.

Listings 9.1 and 9.2 show how these functions are implemented in an application such as word count. The map() is simple: it takes a line of the input, splits it into words, and for each word emits a ⟨word, count⟩ key-value pair, where count is the partial count and thus always 1. Note that in this example the input is split into lines, but it could have been split into some other identifiable unit (e.g., paragraphs, documents, etc.).

Listing 9.1: Word count: `map()` function

```
//i: ignored in this example
//line: line contents
void map(string i, string line):
        for word in line:
                print word, 1
```

The `reduce` function takes ⟨key, list(values)⟩ pairs and goes through all the values to get the aggregated result for that particular key.

Listing 9.2: Word count: `reduce()` function

```
//word: the key
//partial_counts: a list of partial count values
void reduce(string word, list partial_counts):
        total = 0
        for c in partial_counts:
                total += c
        print word, total
```

A good exercise to understand how data are processed by MapReduce is to follow step by step how a small input evolves into the final output. For instance, imagine that the input of the word count program is as follows:

```
Hello World
Hello MapReduce
```

Since, in this example, the `map()` function is applied to every line and the input has two lines, it is possible to run two `map()` functions simultaneously. Each function will produce a different output, but the format will be similar: ⟨word, 1⟩ pairs for each word. For instance, the `map()` reading the first line will emit the following partial output:

```
Hello, 1
World, 1
```

During the reduce stage, the intermediate output is *merged* grouping outputs by keys. This results in new pairs formed by key and lists of values: ⟨Hello, (1, 1)⟩, ⟨World, (1)⟩, and ⟨MapReduce, (1)⟩. These pairs are then processed by the `reduce()` function, which aggregates the lists and produces the final output:

```
Hello, 2
World, 1
MapReduce, 1
```

Word count is an interesting example because it is simple, and the logic behind the map() and reduce() functions is easy to understand. As can be seen in the following examples, MapReduce is able to compute a lot more than a simple word count, but even though it is possible to make these functions more complex, it is recommended to keep them as simple as possible to help distribute the computation. If need be, it is always possible to chain multiple executions, using the output of one application as the input of the next one.

On the other hand, MapReduce may seem a bit overkill for a problem like word counting. For one thing, it generates huge amounts of intermediate key-value pairs, so it may not be entirely efficient for small inputs. But it is designed with scalability in mind, so it begins to make sense as soon as the input is large enough. Besides, most MapReduce programs also require some level of tweaking on both the application itself and on the server side (block size, memory, etc.). Some of these refinements are not always obvious, and it is usually after a few iterations that applications are ready to be run on production.

It should also be noted that this example is focused on the MapReduce computation, and some steps such as input distribution, splitting, and reduce partitioning are intentionally omitted, but will be described in more detail later.

Use Cases

MapReduce is especially well suited to solve *embarrassingly* parallel problems, that is, problems with no dependencies or communication requirements in which it is easy to achieve a speedup proportional to the size of the problem when it is parallelized.

Below is the description of some of the main problems (not necessarily embarrassingly parallel) and areas where MapReduce is currently used.

Distributed Search and Sort

Besides the aforementioned word frequency counting application, searching and sorting are some of the most commonly used examples to describe the MapReduce model. All these problems also share the fact that they are helper tools, thought to be integrated into larger environments with other applications, very much like their pipeline-based UNIX-like equivalent tools: wc, grep, sort, etc. Moreover, knowing how these problems are implemented in MapReduce can be of great help to understand it, as they use different techniques.

A distributed version of grep is especially straightforward to implement using MapReduce. Reading line by line, maps only emit the current line if it matches the given pattern. And since the map's intermediate output can be used as the final output, there is no need to implement the reduce() function.

Sorting is different from searching in that the map stage only reads the input and emits everything (identity map). If there is more than one reducer and the output is supposed to be sorted globally, the important part is how to get the appropriate key and partition the input so that all keys for a particular reducer N come before all the keys for the next reducer $N + 1$. This way the output of the reducers can be numbered and concatenated after they are all finished.

Inverted Indexing and Search Engines

When Google's original MapReduce implementation was completed, it was used to regenerate the index of their search engine. Keeping indices up to date is one of the top priorities of Internet search engines, but web pages are created and updated every day, so a scalable solution is a must.

Inverted indices are one of the typical data structures used for information retrieval. Basically, an inverted index contains a list of references to documents for each word. To implement an inverted index with MapReduce, the map reads the input and for each words emits the document ID. MapReduce then reads it and outputs words along with the list of documents in which they appear.

Other than Google, other major search engines such as Yahoo! are also based on MapReduce. The need to improve the scalability of the Free, open-source software search engine Nutch also promoted the foundation of Hadoop, one of the most widely used MapReduce implementations to date.

Log Analysis

Nowadays service providers generate large amounts of logs from all kinds of services, and the benefits of analyzing them are to be found when processing them *en masse*. For instance, if a provider is interested in tracking the behavior of a client during long periods of time, reconstructing user sessions, it is much more convenient to operate over all the logs.

Logs are a perfect fit for MapReduce for other reasons too. First, logs usually follow a certain pattern, but they are not entirely structured, so it is not trivial to use an RDBMS to handle them and may require changes to the structure of the database to compute something new. Secondly, logs represent a use case where scalability not only matters, but is also a key to keep the system sustainable. As services grow, so does the amount of logs and the need of getting something out of them.

Companies such as Facebook and Rackspace [8] use MapReduce to examine log files on a daily basis and generate statistics and on-demand analysis.

Graph Problems

MapReduce is not perfectly fit for all graph problems, as some of them require walking through the vertices, which will not be possible if the mappers receive only a part of the graph, and it is not practical to receive the whole graph as it would be way too big to handle and require a lot of bandwidth to transfer. But there are ways to work around these issues [4] such as using multiple maps and reduce iterations, along with custom optimized graph representations such as sparse adjacency matrices.

A good example of an Internet-scale graph problem solved using MapReduce is PageRank, an algorithm that ranks interlinked elements. PageRank can be implemented as a chained MapReduce application that at each step iterates over all the elements calculating its PageRank value until converging.

MapReduce Implementations

Google MapReduce

MapReduce is both, the name of the programming model and the original framework, designed and implemented by Jeff Dean and Sanjay Ghemawat at Google [5]. Even though it is only used internally at Google and its code is not freely available, it is known to be written in C + +, with interfaces in Python and Java.

Google MapReduce is used in some of the largest MapReduce clusters to date. According to an interview with Jeff Dean, "The MapReduce software is increasing use within Google. It ran 29,000 jobs in August 2004 and 2.2 million in September 2007. Over that period, the average time to complete a job has dropped from 634 seconds to 395 seconds, while the output of MapReduce tasks has risen from 193 terabytes to 14,018 terabytes. On any given day, Google runs about 100,000 MapReduce jobs; each occupies about 400 servers and takes about 5 to 10 minutes to finish."

In November 2008, Google reported that their MapReduce implementation was able to sort 1 TB of data on 1000 computers in 68 seconds, breaking the previous record of 209 seconds on 910 computers.

Hadoop

Hadoop is a popular and widely used open source MapReduce implementation. It has a large community base and is also backed and used by companies such as Yahoo!, IBM, Amazon, Facebook, etc.

Hadoop was originally developed by Doug Cutting to support distribution for the Nutch search engine. The first working version was available by the end of 2005, and soon after that, in early 2006, Doug Cutting joined Yahoo! to work on it full-time with a dedicated team of developers. In February 2008, Yahoo! announced that they were using a 10,000-core Hadoop cluster in production to generate their search index.

In April 2008, Hadoop was able to sort a terabyte of data on a 910-node cluster in 209 seconds [12]. That same year in November, Google managed to break that record by a wide margin with a time of 68 seconds on a 1000-node cluster. But in May 2009, Yahoo! reclaimed the record with a time of 62 seconds on a cluster with 1460 nodes running Hadoop [13].

Hadoop is now a top-level Apache project and hosts a number of subprojects such as HDFS, Pig, HBase, ZooKeeper, etc. For a more detailed description of how the Hadoop project is organized, see section "Open-Source Implementation: Hadoop."

Disco

Disco is another open source implementation of the MapReduce programming model, developed at Nokia Research Center as a lightweight framework for rapid scripting of distributed data processing.

The Disco core is written in Erlang, a functional language that is designed for building robust fault-tolerant distributed applications. MapReduce programs are typically written in Python, though, which lowers the entry barrier and makes it possible to write data-processing code in only a few lines of code.

Unlike Hadoop, Disco is only a minimal MapReduce implementation, and does not include a customized file system. Instead, Disco supports POSIX-compatible distributed file systems such as GlusterFS.

Skynet

Skynet is an open source implementation of the MapReduce framework created at Geni. It is written in Ruby, and MapReduce programs are also written in the same language. It has gained some popularity, especially in the Ruby community, since it can be easily integrated into web development frameworks such as Rails.

As expected, Skynet claims to be fault-tolerant, but unlike other implementations, its administration is fully distributed and does not have a single point of failure such as the *master* servers that can be found in Google MapReduce and Hadoop. It uses a *peer recovery* system in which workers watch out for each other. If a node dies or fails for any reason, another worker will notice and pick up that task.

Dryad

Dryad is an ongoing research project and Microsoft's response to MapReduce. Dryad intends to be a more general-purpose environment to execute data parallel applications [9]. It is not exactly a new MapReduce implementation, but it subsumes other computation frameworks, including MapReduce. Instead of simply dividing applications into map and reduce, Dryad programs are expressed as directed acyclic graphs in which vertices are computations and edges are communication channels.

Dryad has been deployed at Microsoft since 2006, where it runs on various clusters of more than 3000 nodes and is used by more than 100 developers to process 10 PB of data on a daily basis. The current implementation is written in C++, but there are interfaces that make it possible to use higher-level languages.

Open-Source Implementation: Hadoop

Since its first releases, Hadoop has been the standard Free software MapReduce implementation.* Even though there are other open source MapReduce implementations, they are not as complete and usually lack some component of the full platform (e.g., a storage solution). It is more difficult to compare to proprietary solutions, as most of them are not freely available, but judging from the results of the Terasort benchmark [12,13], Hadoop is able to compete even with the original Google MapReduce.

This section describes how MapReduce is implemented in Hadoop and provides an overview of its architecture.

Project and Subprojects

Hadoop is currently a top-level project of the Apache Software Foundation, a nonprofit corporation that supports a number of other well-known projects such as the Apache HTTP Server.

Hadoop is mostly known for its MapReduce implementation, which is in fact a Hadoop subproject, but there are also other subprojects that provide the required infrastructure or additional components. The core of Hadoop upon which most of the other components are built is formed by the following subprojects:

Common The common utilities and interfaces that support the other Hadoop subprojects (configuration, serialization, RPC, etc.).

MapReduce Software framework for distributed processing of large data sets on compute clusters of commodity hardware.

HDFS Distributed file system that runs on large clusters and provides high throughput access to application data.

The remaining subprojects are simply additional components that are usually used on top of the core subprojects to provide additional features. Some of the most noteworthy are:

Pig High-level data-flow language and execution framework for parallel computation [11]. Programs written in the high-level language are translated into sequences of MapReduce programs.

HBase Distributed, column-oriented database modeled after Bigtable [3] that supports structured data storage for large tables. It is built on top of HDFS and supports MapReduce computations.

---

* Hadoop is licensed under the Apache License 2.0, a free software license that allows developers to modify the code and redistribute it. It is not a copyleft license, though, so distribution of modified versions is not required.

Hive Data warehouse infrastructure that provides data summarization and *ad-hoc* querying and analysis of large files. It uses a language similar to SQL, which is automatically converted to MapReduce jobs.

Chukwa Data collection and monitoring system for managing large distributed systems [2]. It stores system metrics as well as log files into HDFS, and uses MapReduce to generate reports.

Cluster Overview

A typical Hadoop MapReduce cluster is formed by a single master, also known as the *jobtracker*, and a number of slave nodes, also known as *tasktrackers*. The jobtracker is in charge of processing the user's requests, and distributing and scheduling the work on the tasktrackers, which are in turn supposed to execute the work they have been handed and regularly send status reports back to the jobtracker.

In the MapReduce context, a *job* is the unit of work that users submit to the jobtracker (Figure 9.1) and involves the input data as well as the map() and reduce() functions and its configuration. Jobs are divided into two different kinds of *tasks*, *map tasks* and *reduce tasks*, depending on the operation they execute. Tasktrackers control the execution environment of tasks and are configured to run up to a certain amount of *slots* of each kind. It defaults to two slots for map tasks and two slots for reduce tasks, but it can vary significantly depending on the hardware and the kind of jobs that are run in the cluster.

Before assigning the first map tasks to the tasktrackers, the jobtracker divides the input data depending on its format, creating a number of virtual *splits*. The jobtracker then prepares as many map tasks as splits, and as soon

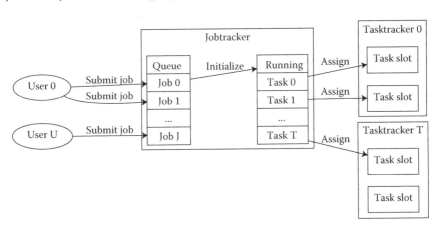

FIGURE 9.1
Job submission.

as a tasktracker reports a free map slot, it is assigned one of the map tasks (along with its input split).

The master continues to keep track of all the map tasks, and once all of them have been completed it is able to schedule the reduce tasks. Except for this dependency, for the jobtracker there is no real difference between kinds of tasks, so map and reduce tasks are treated similarly as the smallest scheduling unit.

Other than scheduling, the jobtracker must also make sure that the system is tolerant to faults. If a node fails or times out, the jobs the tasktracker was executing can be rescheduled by the jobtracker. Additionally, if some tasks make no apparent progress, it is also able to re-launch them as speculative tasks on different tasktrackers.

Note that Hadoop's master is not distributed and represents a single point of failure, but since it is aware of the status of the whole cluster, it also allows for some optimizations and reducing the complexity of the system.*

Storage with HDFS

Hadooop MapReduce is designed to process large amounts of data, but it does so in a way that does not necessarily integrate perfectly well with previous tools, including file systems. One of the characteristics of MapReduce is that it moves computation to the data and not the other way around. In other words, instead of using an independent, dedicated storage, the same low-cost machines are used for both computation and storage. This means that the storage requirements are not exactly the same as for regular, general purpose file systems.

The Hadoop Distributed File System [1] (HDFS) is designed to fulfill Hadoop's storage needs, and like the MapReduce implementation, it was inspired by a Google paper that described their file system [7]. HDFS shares many features with other distributed file systems, but it is specifically conceived to be deployed on commodity hardware and thus even more fault-tolerant.

Another feature that makes it different from other file systems is its emphasis on streaming data and achieving high throughput rather than low latency access. POSIX semantics impose many requirements that are not needed for Hadoop applications, so in order to achieve its goals, HDFS relaxes some of the standard file system interfaces. Similarly, HDFS's coherency model is intentionally simple in order to perform as fast as possible, but everything comes at a cost: for instance, once a file is created, it is not possible to change it.

Like MapReduce, HDFS is also based on a client-server architecture. It consists of a single master node, also known as the *namenode*, and a number of slaves or clients known as *datanodes*. The namenode keeps all the metadata associated with the file system (permissions, file locations, etc.) and

---

* Initial versions of Google's File system and MapReduce are also known to have in masters their single point of failure to simplify the design, but more recent versions are reported to use multiple masters [14] in order to be more fault-tolerant.

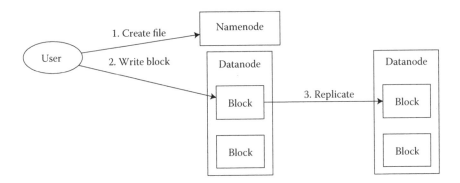

FIGURE 9.2
HDFS file creation.

coordinates operations such as opening, closing, or renaming. Datanodes are spread throughout the cluster and are responsible of storing the data, allowing read and write requests.

As in other general-purpose file systems, files in HDFS are split into one or more *blocks*, which is the minimum unit used to store files on datanodes and to carry out internal operations. Note that just like HDFS is designed to read and write very large files, its block size is likewise larger than the block size of other file systems, defaulting to 64 MB. Also, to ensure fault tolerance, files have a replication factor, which is used to enforce the number of copies of each block available in the cluster.

In order to create a new file, the client first requests it to the namenode, but upon approval it writes directly to the datanodes (Figure 9.2). This process is handled by the client and is transparent for the user. Similarly, replication is coordinated by the namenode, but data are directly transferred between datanodes. If a datanode fails or times out, the namenode goes through all the blocks that were stored in that datanode, issuing replication requests for all the blocks that have fallen behind the desired replication ratio.

Dataflow

The previous sections introduced how MapReduce and the file system work, but one of the keys to understanding Hadoop is to know how both systems are combined and how data flow from the initial input to the processing and final output.

Note that although the MapReduce model assumes that data are available in a distributed fashion, it does not directly deal with pushing and maintaining files across the cluster, which is the file system's job. A direct advantage of this distinction is that Hadoop's MapReduce supports a number of file systems with different features. In this description, though, as well as in the remaining chapters of this document, the cluster is assumed to be running HDFS (described in section "Storage with HDFS"), which is the most widely used file system.

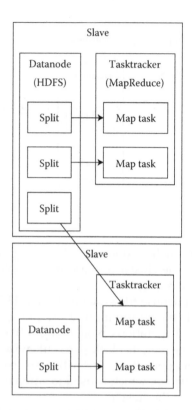

FIGURE 9.3
Local and remote reads from HDFS to MapReduce.

MapReduce is able to start running jobs as soon as the required data are available in the file system. First of all, jobs are initialized by creating a series of map and reduce tasks. The number of map tasks is usually determined by the number of splits into which the input data are divided. Splitting the input is what makes it possible to parallelize the map phase and can have a great impact on the performance, so splits can also be thought of as the first level of granularity of the system, and it also shows how the file system and MapReduce are integrated. For instance, if the input consists of a single 6.25 GB file in an HDFS file system, using a block size (dfs.block.size) of 64 MB and the default input format, the job will be divided into 1000 map tasks, one for each split.

Map tasks read its share of the input directly from the distributed file system, meaning they can read either locally if the data are available, or remotely from another host if they are not (Figure 9.3). While reading and processing the input, the partial output is continuously written to a circular memory buffer. As can be observed in Figure 9.4, as soon as the buffer reaches a certain threshold (defined by io.sort.spill.percent,

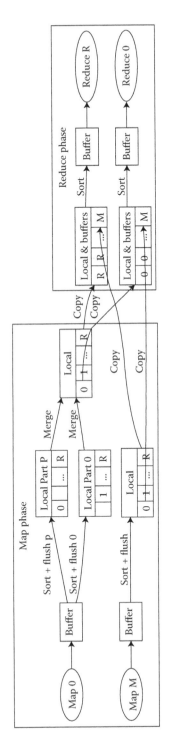

FIGURE 9.4
Hadoop dataflow.

defaults to 80%), its contents are sorted and flushed to a temporary file in the local disk. After reading the input, if there is more than one temporary file, the map task will merge them and write the merged result again to disk. Optionally, if the number of spills is large enough, Hadoop will also perform the combined operation at this point in order to make the output smaller and reduce bandwidth usage.

Note that in the end it is always necessary to write the map's result to disk even if the buffer is not completely filled: map tasks run on its own JVM instance and are supposed to finish as soon as possible and not wait indefinitely for the reducers. So after writing to disk, the map's partial output is ready to be served to other nodes via HTTP.

The number of reduce tasks is determined by the user and the job's needs. For example, if a job requires global sorting, a single reducer may be needed.* Otherwise, any number of reduces may be used: using a larger number of reducers increases the overhead of the framework, but can also help it to improve the load balancing of the cluster.

Reduce tasks are comprised of three phases: copy, sort, and reduce. Even though reduce tasks cannot be completed until all map tasks are, it is possible to run the first phase of reduce tasks at the same time as map tasks. During the copy phase (also known as shuffle), reduce tasks request their partitions of data to the nodes where map tasks have already been executed, via HTTP. As soon as data are copied and sorted in each reducer, they are passed to the reduce() function, and its output is directly written to the distributed file system.

Summary

This chapter presented the MapReduce model and how it is currently used to process massive amounts of data. The simplicity of this model, which splits the work into two smaller steps, map and reduce, has become a standard for parallel data processing. MapReduce makes data processing easier for developers, but it is still powerful enough to solve a wide range of problems, from indexing to log analysis. At the same time, its scalability and reliability ensure its affinity with the goals of Big Data.

While there are a number of MapReduce implementations, this chapter focused on the architecture of Hadoop, a free and open source software version that has become one of the most widely used MapReduce frameworks and is now a basic component of the Big Data toolset.

---

* For some kind of problems, there may be more efficient options such as chaining multiple jobs, using the output of one job as the input for the next one.

References

1. HDFS Architecture, 2009. http://hadoop.apache.org/core/docs/current/hdfs_design.html

2. J. Boulon, A. Konwinski, R. Qi, A. Rabkin, E. Yang, and M. Y. Chukwa. A large-scale monitoring system. In *Cloud Computing and Its Applications (CCA 08)*, pp. 1–5, Chicago, IL, 10/2008 2008.

3. F. Chang, J. Dean, S. Ghemawat, W. C. Hsieh, D. A. Wallach, M. Burrows, T. Chandra, A. Fikes, and R. E. Gruber. Bigtable: A distributed storage system for structured data. In *OSDI'06: Proceedings of the 7th USENIX Symposium on Operating Systems Design and Implementation*, p. 15, Berkeley, CA, USA, USENIX Association, 2006.

4. J. Cohen. Graph twiddling in a MapReduce world. *Computing in Science and Engineering*, 11(4):29–41, 2009.

5. J. Dean and S. Ghemawat. MapReduce: Simplified data processing on large clusters. In *OSDI'04: Sixth Symposium on Operating System Design and Implementation*, pp. 137–150, San Francisco, CA, December 2004.

6. G. DeCandia, D. Hastorun, M. Jampani, G. Kakulapati, A. Lakshman, A. Pilchin, S. Sivasubramanian, P. Vosshall, and W. Vogels. Dynamo: Amazon's highly available key-value store. *SIGOPS Oper. Syst. Rev.*, 41(6):205–220, 2007.

7. S. Ghemawat, H. Gobioff, and S.-T. Leung. The Google file system. *SIGOPS Oper. Syst. Rev.*, 37(5):29–43, 2003.

8. S. Hood: MapReduce at Rackspace, January 23, 2008. http://blog.racklabs.com/?p=66 15.

9. M. Isard, M. Budiu, Y. Yu, A. Birrell, and D. Fetterly. Dryad: distributed data-parallel programs from sequential building blocks. *SIGOPS Oper. Syst. Rev.*, 41(3):59–72, 2007.

10. S.-W. Lee, B. Moon, C. Park, J.-M. Kim, and S.-W. Kim. A case for flash memory SSD in enterprise database applications. In *SIGMOD'08: Proceedings of the 2008 ACM SIGMOD International Conference on Management of Data*, pp. 1075–1086, New York, NY, USA, ACM, 2008.

11. C. Olston, B. Reed, U. Srivastava, R. Kumar, and A. Tomkins. Pig latin: A not-so-foreign language for data processing. In *SIGMOD'08: Proceedings of the 2008 ACM SIGMOD International Conference on Management of Data*, pp. 1099–1110, New York, NY, USA, ACM, 2008.

12. O. O'Malley. Terabyte sort on Apache Hadoop, 2008. http://sortbenchmark.org/YahooHadoop.pdf.

13. O. O'Malley, and A. Murthy. Winning a 60 second dash with a yellow elephant, 2009.

14. S. Quinlan and M. K. McKusick, GFS: Evolution on fast-forward. *Queue*, 7(7):10–20, 2009.

15. T. White. *Hadoop: The Definitive Guide*. 2nd edition, O'Reilly and Yahoo! Press, New York, 2009.

10

Efficient Processing of Stream Data over Persistent Data

M. Asif Naeem, Gillian Dobbie, and Gerald Weber

CONTENTS

Introduction

A data stream is a continuous sequence of items produced in real time. A stream can be considered to be a relational table of infinite size [1]. It is therefore considered impossible to maintain an order of the items in the stream with respect to an arbitrary attribute. Likewise, it is impossible to store the entire stream in memory. However, results of operations are expected to be produced as soon as possible. As a consequence, standard relational query processing cannot be straightforwardly applied, and online stream processing has become a new field of research in the area of data management. A number of common examples where online stream processing is important are network traffic monitoring [2–6], sensor data [7], web log analysis [8,9], online auctions [10], inventory and supply-chain analysis [11–13], as well as real-time data integration [14,15].

Data Stream Processing

Conventional Database Management Systems (DBMSs) are designed using the concept of persistent and interrelated data sets. These DBMSs are stored in reliable repositories, which are updated and queried frequently. But there are some modern application domains where data are generated in the form of a stream, and Data Stream Management Systems (DSMSs) are required to process the stream data continuously. A variety of stream processing engines have been described in the literature [1,16].

The basic difference between a traditional DBMS and a DSMS is the nature of query execution. In DBMSs, data are stored on disk and queries are performed over persistent data [17,18]. In DSMSs, in contrast, data items arrive online and stay in the memory for short intervals of time. DSMSs need to work in nonblocking mode while executing a sequence of operations over the data stream [16,19–21]. The eight important requirements for processing real-time stream data are described by Stonebraker et al. [22]. To accommodate the execution of a sequence of operations, DSMSs often use the concept of a window. A window is basically a snapshot taken at a certain point in time and it contains a finite set of data items. When there are multiple operators, each operator executes and stores its output in a buffer, which is further used as an input for some other operator. Each operator needs to manage the contents of the buffer before it is overwritten.

Common operations performed by most DSMSs are filtering, aggregation, enrichment, and information processing. A stream-based join is required to perform these operations.

Stream-Based Joins

A stream-based join is an operation that combines information coming from multiple data sources. These sources may be in the form of streams or they may be disk-based. Stream-based joins are important components in modern system architectures, where just-in-time delivery of data is expected. There are a number of important examples that can be interpreted as stream joins, even if they might often be implemented with different methods. For example, in the field of networking, two streams of data packets can be joined using their packet *id*s to synchronize the flow of packets through routers [6]. Another example is an online auction system which generates two streams, one stream for opening an auction, while the other stream consists of bids on that auction [23,24]. A stream-based join can relate the bids with the corresponding opened auction in a single operation.

In this chapter, we consider a particular class of stream-based joins, namely a join of a single stream with a traditional relational table. This table is given in advance and considered to be so slowly changing, that it can be considered constant for the discussion of the algorithm. The application scenario most widely considered in the literature is near-real-time data warehousing [14,15,25–28], as outlined in the following.

Application Scenario

In traditional data warehousing, the update tuples are buffered and joined when resources become available [29,30]. In contrast to this, in real-time data warehousing, these update tuples are joined when they are generated in the data sources.

In this application, the slowly changing table is typically a master data table. Incoming real-time sales data may comprise the stream. The stream-based join can be used, for example, to enrich the stream data with master data. The most natural type of join in this scenario would be an equijoin, performed, for example, on a foreign key in the stream data. In near-real-time data warehousing, stream-based joins can be used in the ETL (extract-transform-load) layer. Typical applications would be the detection of duplicate tuples, identification of newly inserted tuples, and the enriching of some new attribute values from master data. One common transformation is the key transformation. The key used in the data source may be different from that in the data warehouse and therefore needs to be transformed into the required value for the warehouse key. This transformation can be obtained by implementing a join operation between the update tuples and a lookup table. The lookup table contains the mapping between the source keys and the warehouse keys. Figure 10.1 shows a graphical interpretation of such a transformation. In the figure, the attributes with column name *id* in both data sources DS_1 and DS_2 contain the source data keys and the attribute with name *warehouse key* in the lookup table contains the warehouse key value corresponding to these data source keys. Before loading each transaction into the data warehouse, each source key is replaced by the warehouse key with the help of a join operator.

One important factor related to the join is that both inputs of the join come from different sources with different arrival rates. The input from the data

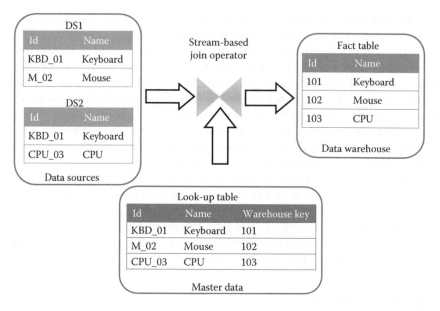

FIGURE 10.1
An example of stream-based join.

sources is in the form of an update stream which is fast, while the access rate of the lookup table is comparatively slow due to disk I/O cost. This creates a bottleneck in the join execution and the research challenge is to minimize this bottleneck by amortizing the disk I/O cost on the fast update stream.

Existing Approaches and Problem Definition

A novel stream-based equijoin algorithm, MESHJOIN (Mesh Join) [14,15], was described by Polyzotis et al. in 2008. MESHJOIN was designed to support streaming updates over persistent data in the field of real-time data warehousing. The MESHJOIN algorithm is in principle a hash join, where the stream serves as the build input and the disk-based relation serves as the probe input. The main contribution is a staggered execution of the hash table build and an optimization of the disk buffer for the disk-based relation. The algorithm reads the disk-based relation sequentially in segments. Once the last segment is read, it again starts from the first segment. The algorithm contains a buffer, called the disk buffer, to store each segment in memory one at a time, and has a number of memory partitions, equal in size, to store the stream tuples. These memory partitions behave like a queue and are differentiated with respect to the loading time. The number of partitions is equal to the number of segments on the disk, while the size of each segment on the disk is equal to the size of the disk buffer. In each iteration, the algorithm reads one disk segment into the disk buffer and loads a chunk of stream tuples into the memory partition. After loading the disk segment into memory, it joins each tuple from that segment with all stream tuples available in different partitions. Before the next iteration, the oldest stream tuples are expired from the join memory and all chunks of the stream are advanced by one step. In the next iteration, the algorithm replaces the current disk segment with the next one, loads a chunk of stream tuples into the memory partition, and repeats the above procedure. An overview of MESHJOIN is presented in Figure 10.2, where we consider only three partitions in the queue, with the same number of pages on disk. For simplicity, we do not consider the hash table at this point and assume that the join is performed directly with the queue.

The crux of the algorithm is that the total number of partitions in the stream queue must be equal to the total number of partitions on the disk and that number can be determined by dividing the size of the disk-based relation R by the size of disk buffer b (i.e., $k = N_R/b$). This constraint ensures that a stream tuple that enters into the queue is matched against the entire disk relation before it expires.

As shown in the figure, for each iteration, the algorithm reads a partition of stream tuples, w_i, into the queue and one disk page p_j into the disk buffer. At any time t, for example, when the page p_3 is in memory the status of the stream tuples in the queue can be explained. The w_1 tuples have already joined with the disk pages p_1 and p_2 and therefore after joining with the page p_3 they will be expired. The w_2 tuples have joined only with the page p_2 and

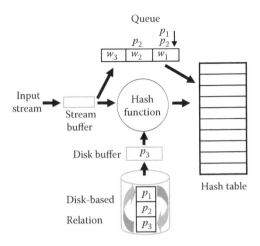

FIGURE 10.2
Interpretation of MESHJOIN when disk page p_3 is in memory.

therefore, after joining with page p_3 they will advance one step in the queue. Finally, the tuples w_3 have not joined with any disk pages and they will also advance by one step in the queue after joining with page p_3. Once the algorithm completes the cycle of R, it again starts loading sequentially from the first page.

The MESHJOIN algorithm successfully amortizes the fast arrival rate of the incoming stream by executing the join of disk pages with a large number of stream tuples. However, there are still some further issues that exist in the algorithm. Firstly, due to the sequential access of R, the algorithm reads the unused or less used pages of R into memory with equal frequency, which increases the *processing time* for every stream tuple in the queue due to extra disk I/O(s). *Processing time* is the time that every stream tuple spends in the join window from loading to matching without including any delay due to the low arrival rate of the stream. The average *processing time* in the case of MESHJOIN can be estimated using the given formula.

$$\text{Average } \textit{processing time}(s) = \frac{1}{2}(\textit{seek time} + \textit{access time}) \text{ for the whole of } R$$

To determine the access rate of disk pages of R, we performed an experiment using a benchmark that is based on real market economics. The detail is available in the "Tests with Locality of Disk Access" section. In this experiment, we assumed that R is sorted in an ascending order with respect to the join attribute value and we measure the rate of use for the same size of segments (each segment contains 20 pages) at different locations of R. From the results shown in Figure 10.3, it is observed that the rate of page use decreases towards the end of R. The MESHJOIN algorithm does not consider this factor and reads all disk pages with the same frequency.

Secondly, MESHJOIN cannot deal with bursty input streams effectively. In MESHJOIN, a disk invocation occurs when the number of tuples in the stream buffer is equal to or greater than the stream input size w. In the case of intermittent or low arrival rate (λ) of the input stream, the tuples already in the queue need to wait longer due to a disk invocation delay. This *waiting time* negatively affects the performance. The average *waiting time* can be calculated using the given formula

$$\text{Average } \textit{waiting time} (s) = \frac{w}{\lambda}$$

Index nested loop join (INLJ) is another join operator that can be used to join an input stream S with the disk-based relation R, using an index on the join attribute. In INLJ for each iteration, the algorithm reads one tuple from S and accesses R randomly with the help of the index. Although in this approach both of the issues presented in MESHJOIN can be handled, the

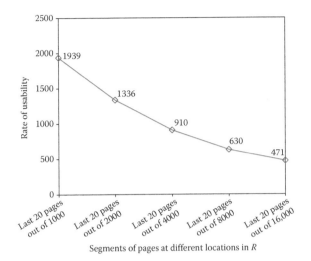

FIGURE 10.3
Measured rate of page use at different locations of R while the size of total R is 16,000 pages.

access of R for each tuple of S makes the disk I/O cost dominant. This factor affects the ability of the algorithm to cope with the fast arrival stream of updates and eventually decreases the performance significantly.

In summary, the problems that we consider in this chapter are: (a) the minimization of the *processing time* and *waiting time* for the stream tuples by accessing the disk-based relation efficiently and (b) dealing with the true nature of skewed and bursty stream data.

Proposed Solution

In the previous section, we explained our observations related to the MESHJOIN and INLJ algorithms. As a solution to the stated problems, we propose a robust stream-based join algorithm called Hybrid Join (HYBRIDJOIN). In this section, we describe the architecture, pseudo-code, and run-time analysis of our proposed algorithm. We also present the cost model that is used for estimating the cost of our algorithm and for tuning the algorithm.

Execution Architecture

The schematic execution architecture for HYBRIDJOIN is shown in Figure 10.4. The key components of HYBRIDJOIN are the disk buffer, hash table, queue, and stream buffer. The disk-based relation R and stream S are the

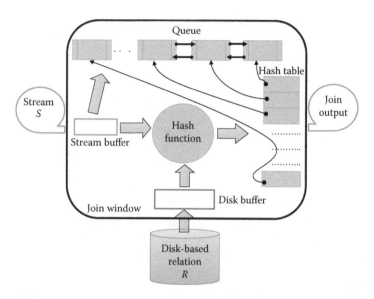

FIGURE 10.4
Architecture of HYBRIDJOIN.

inputs. In our algorithm, we assume that R is sorted and has an index on the join attribute. The disk page of size v_p from relation R is loaded into the disk buffer in memory. The component queue, based on a double linked list, is used to store the values for join attributes, and each node in the queue also contains the addresses of its one-step neighbor nodes. Contrary to the queue in MESHJOIN, we implement an extra feature of random deletion in our HYBRIDJOIN queue. The hash table is an important component that stores the stream tuples and the addresses of the nodes in the queue corresponding to the tuples. The key benefit of this is when the disk page is loaded into memory using the join attribute value from the queue as an index, instead of only matching one tuple as in INLJ, the algorithm matches the disk page with all the matching tuples in the queue. This helps one to amortize the fast arrival stream. In the case where there is a match, the algorithm generates that tuple as an output and deletes it from the hash table along with the corresponding node from the queue, while the unmatched tuples in the queue are dealt with in a similar way to the MESHJOIN strategy. The role of the stream buffer is to hold the fast stream if necessary. To deal with the intermittencies in the stream, for each iteration, the algorithm loads a disk page into memory and checks the status of the stream buffer. In the case where no stream tuples are available in the stream buffer, the algorithm will not stop but continues its working until the hash table becomes empty. However, the queue keeps on shrinking continuously and will become empty when all tuples in the hash table are joined. On the other hand, when tuples arrive from the stream, the queue again starts growing.

In MESHJOIN, every disk input is bound to the stream input, while in HYBRIDJOIN we remove this constraint by making each disk invocation independent of the stream input.

Algorithm

Once the memory has been distributed among the join components, HYBRIDJOIN starts its execution, according to the procedure defined in Algorithm 1. Initially since the hash table is empty, h_s is assigned to stream input size w where h_s is the total number of slots in the hash table H (line 1). The algorithm consists of two loops: one is called the outer loop, while the other is called the inner loop. The outer loop, which is an endless loop, is used to build the stream input in the hash table (line 2), while the inner loop is used to probe the disk tuples in the hash table (line 9). In each outer loop iteration, the algorithm examines the availability of stream input in the stream buffer. If stream input is available, the algorithm reads w tuples of the stream and loads them into the hash table while also placing their join attribute values in the queue. Once the stream input is read, the algorithm resets the value of w to zero (lines 3–6). The algorithm then reads the oldest value of a join attribute from the queue and loads a disk partition into the disk buffer, using that join attribute value as an index (lines 7 and 8). After the disk partition has been loaded into memory, the inner loop starts and for each iteration of the inner loop the algorithm reads one disk tuple from the disk buffer and probes it into the hash table. In the case of a match, the algorithm generates the join output. Since the hash table is a multi-hash-map, there may be more than one match against one disk tuple. After generating the join output, the algorithm deletes all matched tuples from the hash table, along with the corresponding nodes from the queue. Finally, the algorithm increases w with the number of vacated slots in the hash table (lines 9–15).

Algorithm 1: HYBRIDJOIN

Input: A master data R with an index on join attribute and a stream of updates S
Output: $S \bowtie R$
Parameters: w tuples of S and a partition of R
Method:

1: $w \leftarrow h_S$
2: **while** (true) **do**
3: **if** (stream available) **then**
4:      READ w tuples from the stream buffer and load them into hash table, H, while enqueuing their join attribute values in queue, Q
5:      $w \leftarrow 0$

6:   **end if**
7:   READ the oldest join attribute value from Q
8:   READ a partition of R into disk buffer using that join attribute value as an index
9:   **for** each tuple r in the chosen partition **do**
10:      **if** $r \in H$ **then**
11:          OUTPUT $r \bowtie H$
12:          DELETE all matched tuples from H along with the related nodes from Q
13:          $w \leftarrow w+$ number of matching tuples found in H
14:      **end if**
15:   **end for**
16: **end while**

Asymptotic Runtime Analysis

We compare the asymptotic runtime of HYBRIDJOIN with that of MESHJOIN and INLJ as throughput, that is, the time needed to process a stream section. The throughput is the inverse of the service rate. Consider the time for a concrete stream prefix s. We denote the time needed to process stream prefix s as MEJ(s) for MESHJOIN, as INLJ(s) for INLJ, and as HYJ(s) for HYBRIDJOIN. Every stream prefix represents a binary sequence, and by viewing this binary sequence as a natural number, we can apply asymptotic complexity classes to the functions above. Note therefore that the following theorems do not use functions on input lengths, but on concrete inputs. The resulting theorems imply analogous asymptotic behavior on input length, but are stronger than statements on input length. We assume that the setup for HYBRIDJOIN and for MESHJOIN is such that they have the same number h_s of stream tuples in the hash table—and in the queue accordingly.

Comparison with MESHJOIN: Theorem 1: HYJ(s) = O(MEJ(s))

Proof

To prove the theorem, we have to prove that HYBRIDJOIN performs no worse than MESHJOIN. The cost of MESHJOIN is dominated by the number of accesses to R. For asymptotic runtime, random access of disk pages is as fast as sequential access (seek time is only a constant factor). For MESHJOIN with its cyclic access pattern for R, every page of R is accessed exactly once after every h_s stream tuples. We have to show that for HYBRIDJOIN no page is accessed more frequently. For that we look at an arbitrary page p of R at the time it is accessed by HYBRIDJOIN. The stream tuple at the front of the queue has some position i in the stream. There are h_s stream tuples currently in the hash table, and the first tuple of the stream that is not yet read into the hash table has position $i + h_s$ in the stream. All stream tuples in the hash table are joined against the disk-based master data tuples on p, and all matching tuples are removed from the queue. We now have to determine the earliest time that p could be loaded again by HYBRIDJOIN. For p to be loaded again, a stream tuple must be at the front of the queue and has to match a master data tuple on p. The first stream tuple that can do so is the aforementioned stream tuple with position $i + h_s$, because all earlier stream tuples that match data on p have been deleted from the queue. This proves the theorem.

Comparison with INLJ: Theorem 2: HYJ(s) = O(INLJ(s))

Proof

INLJ performs a constant number of disk accesses per stream tuple. For the theorem, it suffices to prove that HYBRIDJOIN performs no more than a constant number of disk accesses per stream tuple as well. We consider first those stream tuples that remain in the queue until they reach the front of the queue. For each of these tuples, HYBRIDJOIN loads a part of R and hence makes a constant number of disk accesses. For all other stream tuples, no separate disk access is made. This proves the theorem.

Cost Model

In this section, we derive the general formulas to calculate the cost for our proposed HYBRIDJOIN. We generally calculate the cost in terms of memory and processing time. Equation 10.1 describes the total memory used to implement the algorithm (except the stream buffer). Equation 10.3 calculates the processing cost for w tuples, while the average size for w can be calculated using Equation 10.2. Once the processing cost for w tuples is measured, the service rate μ can be calculated using Equation 10.4. The symbols used to measure the cost are specified in Table 10.1.

Memory Cost

In HYBRIDJOIN, the maximum portion of the total memory is used for the hash table H, while a comparatively smaller amount is used for the disk buffer and the queue. We can easily calculate the size for each of them separately.

Memory reserved for the disk buffer (bytes) = v_P

Memory reserved for the hash table (bytes) = $\alpha (M - v_P)$

Memory reserved for the queue (bytes) = $(1 - \alpha)(M - v_P)$

The total memory used by HYBRIDJOIN can be determined by aggregating all the above.

$$M = v_P + \alpha(M - v_P) + (1 - \alpha)(M - v_P). \tag{10.1}$$

TABLE 10.1

Notations Used in Cost Estimation of HYBRIDJOIN

Parameter Name	Symbol
Total allocated memory (bytes)	M
Stream arrival rate (tuples/s)	λ
Service rate (processed tuples/s)	μ
Average stream input size (tuples)	w
Stream tuple size (bytes)	v_S
Size of disk buffer (bytes) = size of disk page	v_P
Size of disk tuple (bytes)	v_R
Size of disk buffer (tuples)	$d = \dfrac{v_P}{v_R}$
Memory weight for hash table	α
Memory weight for queue	$(1 - \alpha)$
Size of hash table (tuples)	h_s
Size of disk-based relation R (tuples)	R_t
Exponent value for benchmark	e
Cost to read one disk page into disk buffer (ns)	$c_{I/O}(v_P)$
Cost of removing one tuple from the hash table and queue (ns)	c_E
Cost of reading one stream tuple into the stream buffer (ns)	c_S
Cost of appending one tuple into the hash table and queue (ns)	c_A
Cost of probing one tuple into the hash table (ns)	c_H
Cost to generate the output for one tuple (ns)	c_O
Total cost for one loop iteration of HYBRIDJOIN (s)	c_{loop}

Currently, we are not including the memory reserved for the stream buffer due to its small size (0.05 MB was sufficient in all our experiments).

Processing Cost

In this section, we calculate the processing cost for HYBRIDJOIN. To calculate the processing cost, it is necessary to calculate the average stream input size w first.

Calculate average stream input size w: In HYBRIDJOIN the average stream input size w depends on the following four parameters.

- Size of the hash table, h_S (in tuples)
- Size of the disk buffer, d (in tuples)
- Size of the master data, R_t (in tuples)
- The exponent value for the benchmark, e

In our experiments, w is directly proportional to h_S and d (where dv_P/v_R) and inversely proportional to R_t. Further details about these relationships can be found in the "Analysis of w with respect to its Related Components" section. The fourth parameter represents the exponent value for the stream data distribution as explained in section " Tests with Locality of Disk Access," and using an exponent value equal to 1 the 80/20 Rule [31] can be formulated approximately for market sales. Therefore, the formula for w is:

$$w \propto \frac{h_S \cdot d}{R_t},$$

$$w = k \frac{h_S \cdot d}{R_t},$$

(10.2)

where k is a constant influenced by system parameters. The value of k has been obtained from measurements. In this setup, it is 1.36.

On the basis of w, the processing cost can be calculated for one loop iteration. In order to calculate the cost for one loop iteration, the major components are:

Cost to read one disk partition $= c_{I/O}(v_P)$

Cost to probe one disk partition into the hash table$=(v_P/v_R)c_H$

Cost to generate the output for w matching tuples $= w \cdot c_O$

Cost to delete w tuples from the hash table and the queue $= w \cdot c_E$

Cost to read w tuples from the stream $S = w \cdot c_S$

Cost to append w tuples into the hash table and the queue $= w \cdot c_A$

By aggregation, the total cost for one loop iteration is:

$$C_{loop} = 10^{-9} \left[c_{I/O}(v_P) + \frac{v_P}{v_R} c_H + w \cdot c_O + w \cdot c_E + w \cdot c_S + w \cdot c_A \right]. \quad (10.3)$$

Since the algorithm processes w tuples of the stream S in c_{loop} seconds, the service rate μ can be calculated by dividing w by the cost for one loop iteration:

$$\mu = \frac{w}{C_{loop}} \quad (10.4)$$

Analysis of w with Respect to its Related Components

This section presents details of the experiments that have been conducted to observe the individual effects of each component on w.

Effect of the Size of the Master Data on w

An experiment has been conducted to observe the effect of the size of the master data, denoted by R_t, on w. In this experiment, the value of R_t has been increased exponentially while keeping the values for other parameters, h_s and d, fixed. The results of this experiment are shown in Figure 10.5a. It is clear that the increase in R_t affects w negatively. This can be explained as follows: increasing R_t decreases the probability of matching the stream tuples for the disk buffer. Therefore, the relationship of R_t with w is inversely proportional, represented mathematically as $w \propto 1/R_t$.

Effect of the Hash Table Size on w

This experiment has been conducted to examine the effect of hash table size hs on w. In order for us to observe the individual effect of hs on w, the values for other parameters, R_t and d, have been assumed to be fixed. The value of h_s

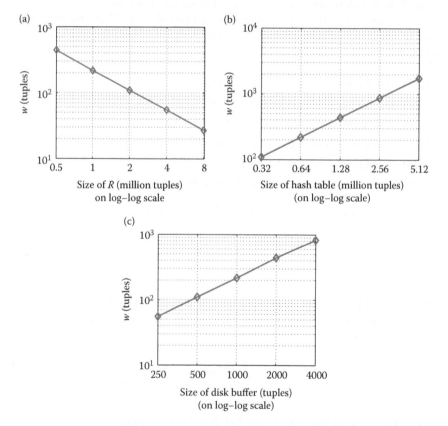

FIGURE 10.5
Analysis of w while varying the size of necessary components. (a) Effect of size of R on w; (b) effect of size of hash table on w; (c) effect of size of disk buffer on w.

has been increased exponentially and w has been measured for each setting. The results of the experiment are shown in Figure 10.5b. It can be observed that w increases at an equal rate while increasing h_s. The reason for this is that with an increase in h_s more stream tuples can be accommodated in memory. Therefore, the matching probability for the tuples in the disk buffer with the stream tuples increases and that causes w to increase. Hence, w is directly proportional to h_s which can be described mathematically as $w \propto h_s$.

Effect of the Disk Buffer Size on w

Another experiment has been conducted to analyze the effect of the disk buffer size d on w. Again the effect of only d on w can be observed, and the values for other parameters, R_t and h_s, have been considered to be fixed. The size of the disk buffer has been increased exponentially and w has been measured against each setting. Figure 10.5c presents the results of this experiment. It is clear that increasing d results in w increasing at the same rate. The reason for this behavior is that, when d increases, more disk tuples can be loaded into the disk buffer. This increases the probability of matching for stream tuples with the tuples in the disk buffer and eventually w increases. The relationship of w with d is directly proportional, that is, $w \propto d$.

Tuning

Tuning of the join components is important to make efficient use of available resources. In HYBRIDJOIN, the disk buffer is the key component to tune to amortize the disk I/O cost on fast input data streams. From Equation (10.4), the service rate depends on w and the cost c_{loop}, required to process these w tuples. In HYBRIDJOIN for a particular setting ($M = 50$ MB) assuming the size of R and the exponent value are fixed ($R_t = 2$ million tuples and $e = 1$), from Equation (10.2) w then depends on the size of hash table and the size of disk buffer. Furthermore, the size of the hash table is also dependent on the size of the disk buffer as shown in Equation (10.1). Therefore, using Equations (10.2)–(10.4), the service rate μ can be specified as a function of v_P and the value for v_P at which the service rate is maximum can be determined by applying standard calculus rules.

In order to explain it experimentally, Figure 10.6 shows the relationship between the I/O cost and service rate. From the figure, it can be observed that in the beginning, for a small disk buffer size, the service rate is also small because there are fewer matching tuples in the queue. In other words, we can say w is also small. However, the service rate increases with an increase in the size of the disk buffer due to more matching tuples in the queue. After reaching a particular value of the disk buffer size, the trend changes and performance decreases with further increments in the size of the disk buffer. The plausible reason behind this decrease is the rapid increment in the disk I/O cost.

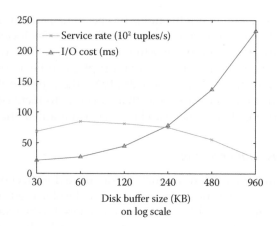

FIGURE 10.6
Tuning of the disk buffer.

Tests with Locality of Disk Access

A crucial factor for the performance of HYBRIDJOIN is the distribution of master data foreign keys in the stream. If the distribution is uniform, then HYBRIDJOIN may perform worse than MESHJOIN, but by a constant factor, in line with the theoretical analysis. Note, however, that HYBRIDJOIN still has the advantage of being efficient for intermittent streams, while the original MESHJOIN would pause in intermittent streams, and leave tuples unprocessed for an open-ended period.

It is also obvious that HYBRIDJOIN has advantages if R contains unused data, for example, if there are old product records that are currently accessed very rarely, that are clustered in R. HYBRIDJOIN would not access these areas of R, while MESHJOIN accesses the whole of R.

More interesting, however, is whether HYBRIDJOIN can also benefit from more general locality. Therefore, the question arises whether we can demonstrate a natural distribution where HYBRIDJOIN measurably improves over a uniform distribution, because of locality.

The popular types of distributions are Zipfian distributions, which exhibit a power law similar to Zipf's law. Zipfian distributions are discussed as at least plausible models for sales [31], where some products are sold frequently while most are sold rarely. This kind of distribution can be modeled using Zipf's law.

A generator for synthetic data has been designed that models a Zipfian distribution, and it has been used to demonstrate that HYBRIDJOIN performance increases through locality and that HYBRIDJOIN outperforms MESHJOIN.

In order to simplify the model, it has been assumed that the product keys are sorted in the master data table according to their frequency in the stream. This is a simplifying assumption that would not automatically hold in typical warehouse catalogues, but it provides a plausible locality behavior and makes the degree of locality very transparent.

Finally, in order to demonstrate the behavior of the algorithm under intermittence, a stream generator has been implemented that produces stream tuples with a timing that is self-similar.

This bursty generation of tuples models a flow of sales transactions which depends upon fluctuations over several time periods, such as market hours, weekly rhythms, and seasons. The pseudo-code for the generation of the benchmark used here is shown in Algorithm 2. In the figure, $S_{TREAM}G_{ENERATOR}$ is the main procedure, while $G_{ET}D_{ISTRIBUTION}V_{ALUE}$ and $S_{WAP}S_{TATUS}$ are the subprocedures that are called from the main procedure. According to the main procedure, a number of virtual stream objects (in this case 10), each representing the same distribution value obtained from the $G_{ET}D_{ISTRIBUTION}V_{ALUE}$ procedure, are inserted into a priority queue, which always keeps sorting these objects into ascending order (lines 5–7). Once all the virtual stream objects have been inserted into the priority queue, the top most stream object is taken out (line 8). A loop is executed to generate an infinite stream (lines 9–18). In each iteration of the loop, the algorithm waits for a while (which depends upon the value of variable *oneStep*) and then checks whether the current time is more than the time when that particular object was inserted. If the condition is true, the algorithm dequeues the next object from the priority queue and calls the $S_{WAP}S_{TATUS}$ procedure (lines 11–14). The $S_{WAP}S_{TATUS}$ procedure enqueues the current dequeued stream object by updating its time interval and bandwidth (lines 19–27). Once the value of the variable *totalCurrentBandwidth* has been updated, the main procedure generates the final stream tuple values as an output, using the procedure $G_{ET}D_{ISTRIBUTION}V_{ALUE}$ (lines 15–17). For each call of the procedure $G_{ET}D_{ISTRIBUTION}V_{ALUE}$, it returns a value based on Zipf's law (lines 28–31).

Algorithm 2: $S_{TREAM}G_{ENERATOR}$

1: *totalCurrentBandwidth* ← 0
2: *timeInChosenUnit* ← 0
3: *on* ← *false*
4: *d* ← $G_{ET}D_{ISTRIBUTION}V_{ALUE}$()
5: **for** *i* ← 1 to N **do**
6:    PriorityQueue.enqueue(*d; bandwidth* ← Math.power(2,*i*), *timeInChosen Unit* ← currentTime())
7: **end for**
8: *current* ← PriorityQueue.dequeue()
9: **while** (*true*) **do**
10:    wait(*oneStep*)
11:    if (currentTime() > *current:timeInChosenUnit*) **then**

12:      *current* ← PriorityQueue.dequeue()
13:      $S_{WAP}S_{TATUS}(current)$
14:   **end if**
15:   **for** j ← 1 to *totalCurrentBandwidth* **do**
16:         OUTPUT $G_{ET}D_{ISTRIBUTION}V_{ALUE}()$
17:   **end for**
18: **end while**
procedure $S_{WAP}S_{TATUS}$(current)
19: *timeInChosenUnit* ← (*current:timeInChosenUnit* + getNextRandom()
   × *oneStep* × *currentBandwidth*)
20: **if** *on* **then**
21:      *totalCurrentBandwidth* ← *totalCurrentBandwidth* - *current:bandwidth*
22:      *on* ← *false*
23: **else**
24:      *totalCurrentBandwidth* ← *totalCurrentBandwidth* + *current.bandwidth*
25:      *on* ← *true*
26: **end if**
27: PriorityQueue.enqueue(*current*)
end procedure
procedure $G_{ET}D_{ISTRIBUTION}V_{ALUE}()$

28: $sumOfFrequency \leftarrow \int \frac{1}{x} dx\ _{at\ x=max} - \int \frac{1}{x} dx\ _{at\ x=min}$
29: *random* ← getNextRandom()
30: *distributionValue* ← inverseIntegralOf (*random* × *sumOfFrequency* +
$\int \frac{1}{x} dx\ _{at\ x=min}$)
31: RETURN [*distributionValue*]
end procedure

The experimental representation of the benchmark is shown in Figures 10.7 and 10.8, while the environment in which the experiments have been conducted is described in the "Experimental Arrangement" section. As described previously in this section, the benchmark is based on two characteristics: one is the frequency of sales of each product, while the other is the flow of these sales transactions. Figure 10.7 validates the first characteristic, that is, Zipfian distribution for market sales. In the figure, the *x*-axis represents the variety of products, while the *y*-axis represents the sales. It can be observed that only a limited number of products (20%) are sold frequently, while the rest of the products are sold rarely.

The HYBRIDJOIN algorithm is adapted to these kinds of benchmarks in which only a small portion of *R* is accessed again and again, while the rest of *R* is accessed rarely.

Figure 10.8 represents the flow of transactions, which is the second characteristic of the benchmark. It is clear that the flow of transactions varies with time and the stream is bursty rather than input appearing at a regular rate.

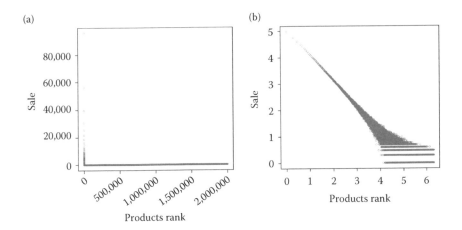

FIGURE 10.7
A long tail distribution using Zipf's law that implements 80/20 Rule. (a) On plain scale; (b) on log-log scale.

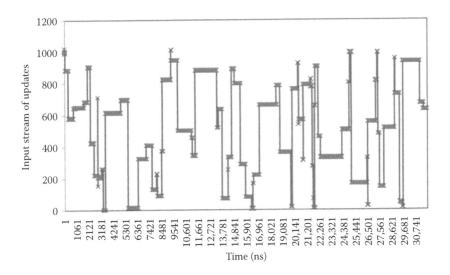

FIGURE 10.8
An input stream having bursty and self-similarity type of characteristics.

Experiments

We performed an extensive experimental evaluation of HYBRIDJOIN, proposed in the "Proposed Solution" section, on the basis of synthetic data sets. In this section, we describe the environment of our experiments and analyze the results that we obtained using different scenarios.

Experimental Arrangement

In order to implement the prototypes of existing MESHJOIN, INLJ, and our proposed HYBRIDJOIN algorithms, we used the following hardware and data specifications.

Hardware Specifications

We carried out our experimentation on a *Pentium—IV* 2 × 2.13 GHz machine with 4 GB main memory. We implemented the experiments in *Java* using the *Eclipse IDE*. We also used built-in plugins, provided by *Apache*, and *nano-Time()*, provided by the *Java API*, to measure the memory and processing time, respectively.

Data Specifications

We analyzed the performance of each of the algorithms using synthetic data. The relation *R* is stored on disk using a *MySQL* database, while the bursty type of stream data is generated at run time using our own benchmark algorithm.

In transformation, a join is normally performed between the *primary key* (key in lookup table) and the *foreign key* (key in stream tuple) and therefore our HYBRIDJOIN supports join for both one-to-one and one-to-many relationships. In order to implement the join for one-to-many relationships, it needs to store multiple values in the hash table against one key value. However, the hash table provided by the *Java API* does not support this feature and therefore we used *Multi-Hash-Map*, provided by *Apache*, as the hash table in our experiments. The detailed specification of the data set that we used for analysis is shown in Table 10.2.

Measurement Strategy

The performance or service rate of the join is measured by calculating the number of tuples processed in a unit second. In each experiment, the algorithm runs for 1 h and we start our measurements after 20 min and continue it for 20 min. For more accuracy, we calculate confidence intervals for every result by considering 95% accuracy. Moreover, during the execution of the algorithm, no other application is assumed to run in parallel.

Experimental Results

We conducted our experiments in two dimensions. In the first dimension, we compare the performance of all three approaches and in the second dimension we validate the cost by comparing it with the predicted cost.

TABLE 10.2

Data Specification

Parameter	Value
Disk-Based Data	
Size of disk-based relation R	0.5 million to 08 millions tuples
Size of each tuple	120 bytes
Stream Data	
Size of each tuple	20 bytes
Size of each node in queue	12 bytes
Stream arrival rate, λ	125–2000 tuples/s

Performance Comparison

As the source for MESHJOIN is not openly available, we implemented the MESHJOIN algorithm ourselves. In our experiments, we compare the performance in two different ways. First, we compare HYBRIDJOIN with MESHJOIN with respect to the time, both *processing time* and *waiting time*. Second, we compare the performance in terms of service rate with the other two algorithms.

Performance Comparisons with Respect to Time

In order to test the performance with respect to time, two different types of experiments have been conducted. The experiment, shown in Figure 10.9a, presents the comparisons with respect to the *processing time*, while Figure 10.9b depicts the comparisons with respect to *waiting time*. The terms *processing time* and *waiting time* have already been defined in the "Proposed Solution" section. According to Figure 10.9a, the *processing time* in the case of HYBRIDJOIN is significantly smaller than that of MESHJOIN. The reason behind this is that in HYBRIDJOIN a different strategy has been used to access R. The MESHJOIN algorithm accesses all disk partitions with the same frequency without considering the rate of use of each partition on the disk. In HYBRIDJOIN, an index-based approach that never reads unused disk partitions has been implemented to access R. The experiment has not reflected the *processing time* for INLJ because it was constant even when the size of R changes.

In the experiment shown in Figure 10.9b, the time that each algorithm waits has been compared. In the case of INLJ, since the algorithm works at tuple level, the algorithm does not need to wait, but this delay then appears in the form of a stream backlog that occurs due to a faster incoming stream rate than the processing rate. The amount of this delay increases further when the stream arrival rate increases. Turning to the other two approaches, from the figure the ratio of *waiting time* in MESHJOIN is greater than in HYBRIDJOIN.

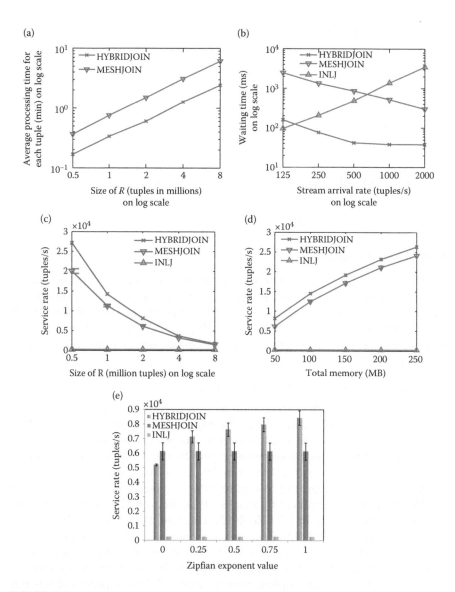

FIGURE 10.9
Experimental results. (a) Processing time; (b) waiting time; (c) performance comparison: *R* varies; (d) performance comparison: *M* varies; (e) performance comparison: *e* varies.

In HYBRIDJOIN, since there is no constraint to match each stream tuple with the whole of *R*, each disk invocation is not synchronized with the stream input. However, for stream arrival rates of less than 150 tuples/s, the waiting time in HYBRIDJOIN is greater than that in INLJ. A plausible reason for this is the greater I/O cost in the case of HYBRIDJOIN when the size of the input stream has been assumed to be equal in both algorithms.

Performance Comparisons with Respect to Service Rate

In this category of experiments, the performance of HYBRIDJOIN has been compared with that of the other two join algorithms in terms of the service rate by varying both the total memory budget and the size of R with a bursty stream. In the experiment shown in Figure 10.9c, the total allocated memory for the join is assumed fixed (50 MB), while the size of R varies exponentially. It can be observed that for all sizes of R, the performance of HYBRIDJOIN is significantly better than the other join approaches.

In the second experiment of this category, the performance of HYBRIDJOIN has been analyzed using different memory budgets, while the size of R is fixed (2 million tuples). Figure 10.9d depicts the comparisons of all three approaches. From the figure, it is clear that for all memory budgets the performance of HYBRIDJOIN is better than the other two algorithms.

Finally, the performance of HYBRIDJOIN has been evaluated by varying the skew in the input stream S. The value of the Zipfian exponent e is varied in order to vary the skew. In these experiments, it was allowed to range from 0 to 1. At 0 the input stream S is uniform and the skew increases as e increases. Figure 10.9e presents the results of the experiment. It is clear from Figure 10.9e that under all values of e except 0, HYBRIDJOIN performs considerably

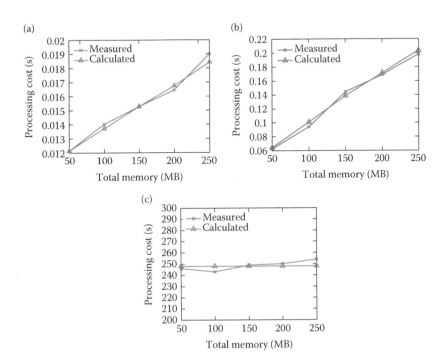

FIGURE 10.10
Cost validation. (a) HYBRIDJOIN; (b) MESHJOIN; (c) INLJ.

better than MESHJOIN and INLJ. Also this improvement increases with an increase in *e*. The plausible reason for this better performance in the case of HYBRIDJOIN is that the algorithm does not read unused parts of *R* into memory and this saves unnecessary I/O cost. Moreover, when the value of *e* increases the input stream *S* becomes more skewed and, consequently, the I/O cost decreases due to an increase in the size of the unused part of *R*. However, in a particular scenario, when *e* is equal to 0, HYBRIDJOIN performs worse than MESHJOIN but worse only by a constant factor.

Cost Validation

In this experiment, we validate the cost model for all three approaches by comparing the predicted cost with the measured cost. Figure 10.10 presents the comparisons of both costs. In the figure, it is demonstrated that the predicted cost closely resembles the measured cost in every approach which also reassures us that the implementations are accurate.

Summary

In the context of real-time data warehousing, a join operator is required to perform a continuous join between the fast stream and the disk-based relation within limited resources. In this chapter, we investigated two available stream-based join algorithms and presented a robust join algorithm, HYBRIDJOIN. Our main objectives in HYBRIDJOIN are: (a) to minimize the stay of every stream tuple in the join window by improving the efficiency of the access to the disk-based relation and (b) to deal with the nonuniform nature of update streams. We developed a cost model and tuning methodology in order to achieve the maximum performance within the limited resources. We designed our own benchmark to test the approaches according to current market economics. To validate our arguments, we implemented a prototype of HYBRIDJOIN that demonstrates a significant improvement in service rate under limited memory. We also validate the cost model for our algorithm.

References

1. D. J. Abadi, D. Carney, U. Çetintemel, M. Cherniack, C. Convey, S. Lee, M. Stonebraker, N. Tatbul, S. Zdonik, Aurora: A new model and architecture for data stream management, *The VLDB Journal*, 12(2), 120–139, 2003.
2. A. Arasu, M. Cherniack, E. Galvez, D. Maier, A. S. Maskey, E. Ryvkina, M. Stonebraker, R. Tibbetts, Linear road: A stream data management benchmark,

Proceedings of the Thirtieth International Conference on Very Large Data Bases, Toronto, Canada, 30, 480–491, 2004.

3. C. Cranor, Y. Gao, T. Johnson, V. Shkapenyuk, O. Spatscheck, Gigascope: High performance network monitoring with an SQL interface, *Proceedings of the 2002 ACM SIGMOD International Conference on Management of Data,* Wisconsin, pp. 623–623, 2002.

4. A. C. Gilbert, Y. Kotidis, S. Muthukrishnan, M. J. Strauss, QuickSAND: Quick summary and analysis of network data, *Technical Report 2001-43, DIMA CS,* 2001.

5. S. Madden, M. J. Franklin, Fjording the stream: An architecture for queries over streaming sensor data, *Proceedings of 18th IEEE International Conference on Data Engineering,* San Jose, CA, pp. 555–566, 2002.

6. M. Sullivan, A. Heybey, Tribeca: A system for managing large databases of network traffic, *Proceedings of the Annual Technical Conference on USENIX,* Louisiana, pp. 2–2, 1998.

7. P. Bonnet, J. Gehrke, P. Seshadri, Towards sensor database systems, *Proceedings of the Second International Conference on Mobile Data Management,* Hong Kong, pp. 3–14, 2001.

8. C. Cortes, K. Fisher, D. Pregibon, A. Rogers, F. Smith, Hancock: A language for extracting signatures from data streams, *Proceedings of the Sixth ACM SIGKDD International Conference on Knowledge Discovery and Data Mining,* Boston, MA, pp. 9–17, 2000.

9. A. C. Gilbert, Y. Kotidis, S. Muthukrishnan, M. Strauss, Surfing wavelets on streams: One-pass summaries for approximate aggregate queries, *Proceedings of the 27th International Conference on Very Large Data Bases,* Rome, Italy, pp. 79–88, 2001.

10. A. Arasu, S. Babu, J. Widom, An abstract semantics and concrete language for continuous queries over streams and relations, *Stanford Info Lab,* 2002.

11. M. J. Franklin, S. R. Jeffery, S. Krishnamurthy, F. Reiss, S. Rizvi, E. Wu, O. Cooper, A. Edakkunni, W. Hong, Design considerations for high fan-in systems: The HiFi approach, *Proceedings of Second Biennial Conference on Innovative Data Systems Research (CIDR'05),* California, pp. 290–304, 2005.

12. H. Gonzalez, J. Han, X. Li, D. Klabjan, Warehousing and analyzing massive RFID data sets, *Proceedings of the 22nd IEEE International Conference on Data Engineering,* Georgia, pp. 83–83, 2006.

13. E. Wu, Y. Diao, S. Rizvi, High-performance complex event processing over streams, *Proceedings of the 2006 ACM SIGMOD International Conference on Management of Data,* Illinois, pp. 407–418, 2006.

14. N. Polyzotis, S. Skiadopoulos, P. Vassiliadis, A. Simitsis, N. E. Frantzell, Supporting streaming updates in an active data warehouse, *ICDE 2007: Proceedings of the 23rd International Conference on Data Engineering,* Washington, DC, pp. 476–485, 2007.

15. N. Polyzotis, S. Skiadopoulos, P. Vassiliadis, A. Simitsis, N. E. Frantzell, Meshing streaming updates with persistent data in an active data warehouse, *IEEE Transactions on Knowledge and Data Engineering,* 20(7), 976–991, 2008.

16. A. Arasu, B. Babcock, S. Babu, J. Cieslewicz, M. Datar, K. Ito, R. Motwani, U. Srivastava, J. Widom, STREAM: The Stanford data stream management system, *Concrete,* 2004.

17. P. A. Bernstein, D. W. Chiu, Using semi-joins to solve relational queries, *Journal of transactions of the ACM,* 28(1), 25–40, 1981.

18. A. Gupta, I. S. Mumick, Maintenance of materialized views: Problems, techniques, and applications, *IEEE Data Engineering Bulletin*, 18, 3–18, 1995.
19. A. Arasu, J. Widom, Resource sharing in continuous sliding-window aggregates, *Proceedings of the Thirtieth international conference on Very Large Data Bases*, Toronto, Canada, pp. 336–347, 2004.
20. S. Babu, J. Widom, Continuous queries over data streams, *SIGMOD Rec.*, 30(3), 109–120, 2001.
21. L. Golab, M. T. Özsu, Issues in data stream management, *SIGMOD Rec.*, 32(2), 5–14, 2003.
22. M. Stonebraker, U. Çetintemel, S. Zdonik, The 8 requirements of real-time stream processing, *SIGMOD Rec.*, 34(4), 42–47, 2005.
23. P. A. Tucker, D. Maier, T. Sheard, Applying punctuation schemes to queries over continuous data streams, *IEEE Data Eng. Bull.*, 26(1), 33–40, 2003.
24. Y. Ya-xin, Y. Xing-hua, Y. Ge, W. Shan-shan, An indexed non-equijoin algorithm based on sliding windows over data streams, *Wuhan University Journal of Natural Sciences*, 11(1), 2006.
25. F. Araque, Real-time data warehousing with temporal requirements, *CAiSE Workshops*, Austria, pp 293–297, 2003.
26. L. Golab, T. Johnson, J. S. Seidel, V. Shkapenyuk, Stream warehousing with Data Depot, *SIGMOD'09: Proceedings of the 35th SIGMOD International Conference on Management of Data*, Providence, RI, pp. 847–854, 2009.
27. A. Karakasidis, P. Vassiliadis, E. Pitoura, ETL queues for active data warehousing, *IQIS'05: Proceedings of the 2nd International Workshop on Information Quality in Information Systems*, Baltimore, MD, pp. 28–39, 2005.
28. M. A. Naeem, G. Dobbie, G. Weber, An event-based near real-time data integration architecture, *EDOCW'08: Proceedings of the 2008 12th Enterprise Distributed Object Computing Conference Workshops*, Munich, Germany, pp. 401–404, 2008.
29. A. N. Wilschut, P. M. G. Apers, Dataflow query execution in a parallel main-memory environment, *PDIS'91: Proceedings of the First International Conference on Parallel and Distributed Information Systems*, Florida, pp. 68–77, 1991.
30. L. D. Shapiro, Join processing in database systems with large main memories, *ACM Transactions of Database Systems*, 11(3), 239–264, 1986.
31. C. Anderson, The Long Tail: Why the Future of Business is Selling Less of More, 2006, Hyperion, pp. 125, ISBN: 1401302378.

Section IV

Big Data and Business

11

Economics of Big Data: A Value Perspective on State of the Art and Future Trends

Tassilo Pellegrin

CONTENTS

Introduction

Big Data has emerged as one of the most hyped IT terms of the last few years. It has been heralded as "a game-changing asset" (The Economist 2011) bringing the global economy "to a cusp of a new wave of growth and productivity" (McKinsey 2011, p. 15).

But what is actually the substance behind this relatively fuzzy concept? And what indicators exist that might prove the disruptive business potential of Big Data?

Big Data refers to the notion that with increasing availability of large amounts of data and networked computing facilities, new business opportunities arise from advanced analytics and corresponding knowledge discovery purposes. This will be scrutinized by discussing three issues in the utilization of Big Data: (1) the underlying infrastructure as supportive layer to harness Big Data, (2) the role of semantic interoperability in the exploitation of Big Data, and (3) the need for diversified licensing models to nurture business around Big Data.

Complementary trends such as cloud computing, social computing, and mobile computing contribute to the cost-sensitive domestication of Big Data beyond the scope of large corporations, opening up new opportunities for small and medium enterprises that would normally lack the financial resources and skills to engage in this business area. In this respect, Big Data is closely related to concepts such as virtualization and cloud computing, which lay the basis for service orientation and contribute to the cost-efficient utilization of Big Data for business purposes—be it within open or closed environments.

An additional aspect associated with the emergence of Big Data refers to the changing nature of the Internet as a universal distribution platform for information and communication. Because as the Internet becomes increasingly content-centric (Cisco 2012) providing massive amounts of unstructured data from text and multimedia, data will be stored in various formats and separate locations, generated, owned, and shared by a multitude of organizations and individuals across the globe for the most diverse purposes. Hence, new approaches for integration of heterogeneous data from multiple sources are needed to pave new ways for exploiting existing and continuously generated data with higher accuracy, thus contributing to value creation within organizational settings. Here the concept of Linked Data comes into play, a technological paradigm originating from and incorporating the basic principles of the Semantic Web, which acts as a design catalyst to draw added value from data by making it a networked resource.

And finally new licensing strategies are needed that better suit the attributes of data in highly networked environments. According to a recent report from the World Economic Forum (2012), a diversification of licensing strategies for Big Data is a necessary condition to foster cross-sectoral cooperation and new forms of value creation within collaborative environments.

Defining "Big Data"

"Big Data" is a poorly defined concept. Despite numerous market studies, business surveys, technology white papers, and management briefings on the topic, the concept itself remains fuzzy and hard to grasp. Oracle (2012, p. 4) refers to Big Data as "datasets that are challenging to store, search, share, visualize and analyze." The consulting firm Price Waterhouse Coopers describes Big Data as "data sets that are growing exponentially and that are too large, too raw, or too unstructured for analysis using relational database techniques" (Gruman 2010, p. 6). And McKinsey (2011, p. 1) refers to Big Data as "datasets whose size is beyond the ability of typical database software tools to capture, store, manage and analyze."

Existing definitions are at best epistemic, oscillating between a technology buzz word for marketing purposes—in bringing data technologies and analytics to the masses—and the attempt to frame incremental path dependencies that derive from the massive digitization of society.

So how can we gain a better understanding of what Big Data actually is? An often referenced approach defines "Big Data" by the attributes of volume, variety, and velocity (Russom 2011).

Volume

The attribute volume refers to the quantitative characteristics of "Big Data" especially for analytical purposes. Since the massive adoption of digital technologies in the 1980s, the emergence of the World Wide Web in the mid-1990s, and the increasing appropriation of mobile and sensor technologies in recent years, the available amount of data has exploded and is doubling every 18 months (Cisco 2012). This "data deluge" varies across regions (see Figure 11.1) and is often dramatically illustrated by astronomic numbers and pictorial metaphors.

According to Mitchell and Wilson (2012) by 2015 the globally available amount of digital information will reach 8 zettabytes with an annual growth rate of 6–10. Metaphorically speaking, in the 1920s the available amount of data would have covered the size of Madagascar and in 2020 it will take up to 1700 globes to represent all the data that have been generated till then (Mitchell and Wilson 2012, p. 3), which equals the amount of information stored in 60,000 US Libraries of Congress (McKinsey 2011, p. 15).

At the enterprise level, "Big Data" is usually defined from the perspective of data capacities (from terabytes to petabytes), temporal characteristics, or formats. From this perspective, Big Data can be quantified by measuring bytes, counting records, transactions or files, taking time series into account (i.e., a fiscal period of seven years), or counting the organizational units that generate and share data (Russom 2011).

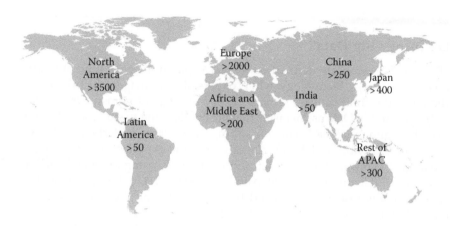

FIGURE 11.1
New data stored by region in 2010 (in petabytes). (Adapted from McKinsey 2011. Big data: The next frontier for innovation, competition and productivity. Research Report. http://www. mckinsey.com/insights/mgi/research/technology_and_innovation/big_data_the_next_frontier_for_innovation (accessed September 14, 2012).)

Variety

The attribute of variety takes account of the fact that Big Data is fuelled by various sources such as data warehouses, document stores, logs, clickstreams, social media, sensors, mobile phones, and many more. These data vary in structure, volume, and format and due to their heterogeneity pose serious challenges to storage, integration, and analytics. Just about 5% of the information that is created everyday is "structured," which means that it comes in a standardized, machine-readable format (The Economist 2010, p. 3). The rest is available as unstructured or semistructured information such as images, videos, or text as a result of the increasing amount of content being transferred electronically.

Taking a more systematic approach, Big Data can be distinguished in terms of structure, volume, and purpose. Table 11.1 gives an overview of relevant data types.

Velocity

A third attribute of Big Data is velocity which circumscribes the speed at which data are generated, circulated, and delivered for analytical purposes. To illustrate this in 2010, an average of 294 billion emails has been sent, approximately 750 million Facebook users generated an average of 90 pieces of content every month, and the retail giant Wal-Mart has fed more than one million transactions every hour into databases comprising more than 2.5 petabytes of data (The Economist 2011, p. 6).

TABLE 11.1

Data Realms Definitions According to Oracle Information Architecture Framework

Data Realm	Structure	Volume	Description	Examples
Master data	Structured	Low	Enterprise-level data entities that are of strategic value to an organization. Typically nonvolatile and nontransactional in nature	Customer, product, supplier, and location/site
Transaction data	Structured and semistructured	Medium–high	Business transactions that are captured during business operations and processes	Purchase records, enquiries, and payments
Reference data	Structured and semistructured	Low–medium	Internally managed or externally sourced facts to support an organization's ability to effectively process transactions, manage master data, and provide decision support capabilities	Geodata, market data, dictionaries, terminologies, encyclopedic data
Metadata	Structured	Low	Defined as "data about the data." Used as an abstraction layer for standardized descriptions and operations, for example, integration, intelligence, services	Data name, data dimensions, units or relations, properties, definition of a data entity, or a calculation formula of metrics
Analytical data	Structured	Medium–high	Derivations of the business operation and transaction data used to satisfy reporting and analytical needs	Data that reside in data warehouses, data marts, and other decision support applications
Documents and content	Unstructured	Medium–high	Documents, digital images, geospatial data, and multimedia files	Claim forms, medical images, maps, video files
Big data	Structured, semistructured, unstructured	High	Large data sets that are challenging to store, search, share, visualize, and analyze	User and machine-generated content through social media, web and software logs, cameras, information-sensing mobile devices, aerial sensory technologies, and genomics

Source: Adapted from Oracle 2012. Oracle Information Architecture: An Architect's Guide to Big Data. White Paper. http://www.oracle.com/technetwork/topics/entarch/articles/oea-big-data-guide-1522052.pdf (accessed September 10, 2012).

TABLE 11.2

Frequency of Data Analytics among 96 US Companies

Frequency	Value (%)
Annually	15
Monthly	35
Weekly	14
Daily	24
Every few hours	5
Hourly	4
Real time	4

Source: Adapted from Russom, P. 2011. Big Data Analytics. TDWI Research Report, 4. Quarter 2011. http://tdwi. org/bdr-rpt.aspx (accessed September 14, 2012).

The growing amount of data sources generates a steady stream of data that are being collected, archived, and increasingly analyzed. But according to a survey by Russom (2011, p. 19), the analytical frequency of generated data varies widely. Table 11.2 illustrates the intervals at which analytical tasked are performed within companies.

While the availability of large quantities of data is not necessarily new, new storage, processing, and visualization technologies allow to explore this data in a cost-effective way, bringing the discipline of data analytics to the masses. It is these analytical capabilities that actually define the business value of Big Data and allow organizations and individuals to draw deeper insights from available data sources.

Value of Big Data

Empirically testing productivity gains through information technology at the macro- and microeconomic level is a complex, ambiguous, and tricky endeavor. Models and estimations are time- and context-dependent, often fuzzy in nature, and sometimes biased or even contradictory. Nevertheless, economic and market research testifies Big Data's tremendous economic potential and goes hand in hand with public policies and entrepreneurial initiatives to stimulate business and markets.

Macroeconomic Perspective: Big Data Policies and Expected Benefits

The McKinsey (2011) estimates that added value derived from Big Data equals $600 billion potential annual consumer surplus, $300 billion savings for the US healthcare system, $250 billion market stimulation in Europe through Open Government Data, and a 60% potential increase in retailer's operating margins.

These numbers are impressive but also highly volatile and subject to negotiation. Nevertheless, the potential impact of Big Data can be estimated by looking at the institutional framework in which Big Data is about to unfold.

In this respect, at the macroeconomic level, Big Data has less to do with technology than policy. Policies are deliberate social actions to create certain conditions that benefit certain groups or foster desired societal arrangements. A well-documented example for a policy-driven action to stimulate market growth is Open Government Data. This policy originated in the United States with the Obama Administration in 2009 and has swept over to the European Union and parts of Asia in the following years (Kundra 2012). Especially in the European Union, where due to historical reasons disclosure policies have been handled more restrictive than in the US Open Government Data has become one of the pillars of the Digital Agenda for Europe to foster the creation of a single European market for digital products and services.[*] In December 2011, Nellie Kroes, Vice President of the European Commission, publicly announced that Open Data available as public sector information already generates €32 billion of economic activity each year, which would at least double with the prospected release of new data as envisioned with running and future activities[†] and reach a level of up to €300 billion till 2020 (McKinsey 2011, p. 61).

A recent macroeconomic survey from the British Centre for Economics and Business Research (Cebr 2012) provides interesting insights into the effects of Big Data on the expected UK gross domestic product in 2017. Within their simulation, the added value is derived from increased business efficiency in the areas customer intelligence, supply chain management, quality management, risk management, performance management, and fraud detection.

While in 2011, the gross equity generated by the utilization of Big Data equaled £25 billion, this value will increase to £216 billion in the period from 2012 to 2017. Table 11.3 illustrates the absolute growth in economic equity generated by Big Data according to the economic stimulators activated by Big Data.

Herein, the operational benefits derived from the utilization of Big Data draw from cost savings and increased revenue opportunities leading to an average growth of 2.2% for the UK economy as a whole till 2017. These findings correlate with research results from Brynjolfsson et al. (2011), who predict a growth effect of 5–6% due to the adoption of data-driven decision support systems.

It is open to debate whether these numbers will be reached in the years to come. But it illustrates the high expectations attached to the Big Data hype. A look at the microeconomic effects of Big Data will point to the business drivers behind the appropriation of Big Data at the enterprise level.

---

[*] See http://ec.europa.eu/digital-agenda/en/our-targets/pillar-i-digital-single-market (accessed October 4, 2012).
[†] See http://europa.eu/rapid/press-release_SPEECH-11-872_en.htm (accessed October 4, 2012).

TABLE 11.3

Estimated Economic Benefit by Economic Stimulators in £ Million

Economic Benefits	Data Equity by 2011	Data Equity by 2017
Business efficiency	17,379	149,471
Business innovation	2865	24,062
Business creation	4843	42,430
Total	25,087	215,964

Source: Adapted from Cebr 1012. Data Equity. Unlocking the Value of Big Data. Research Report. http://www.sas.com/offices/europe/uk/downloads/data-equity-cebr.pdf (accessed September 12, 2012).

Microeconomic Perspective: Big Data and the Value Chain

From a microeconomic perspective, the economic value of Big Data derives from efficiency gains it generates in the process of value creation. The concept of the value chain is rooted in competition theory, where it is used to provide an analytical framework for business management processes and competition strategies. According to this notion, a company's value chain comprises its value activities (as primary and supportive activities) together with the profit margin (as the difference between return on investment and operating costs). The concept of the value chain was first introduced by Porter (1985) and since then been adopted in a variety of ways to describe the structure of sector-specific value creation mechanisms and sequential production logics.[*]

As communication within electronic networks has become increasingly content-centric (Cisco 2012)—in terms of the growing amount of unstructured information that is produced and transmitted electronically[†]—the concept of the value chain has gained popularity in the discipline of information and media economics where it has been used to distinguish the production logic of informational subsectors such as print, broadcasting, telecommunications, software, and online media from each other and illustrate their specificities with respect to information assets and revenue models (Zerdick et al. 1999). Figure 11.2 depicts an adopted version of Porter's model under special consideration of a generic value creation process in the production of content.

The following section will discuss how Big Data contributes to value creation in the support activities of the value chain. The added value derived from Big Data in the primary activities will be discussed in the following section under special consideration of semantic interoperability as a central

---

[*] Although often criticized for its rigid and reductionist abstraction level that does not reflect the dynamic and intertwined nature of contemporary production practices, newer approaches prefer to talk about value or connectivity networks (i.e., Winter 2006). Although these newer approaches are better suited to capture the real-world circumstances of value creation, they also increase the analytical complexity and therefore are difficult to operationalize, which is why the author sticks to the metaphor of the value chain.

[†] Cisco (2012) reports for the time period from 2011 to 2016 an increase of 90% of video content, 76% of gaming content, 36% VoIP, 36% file sharing being transmitted electronically.

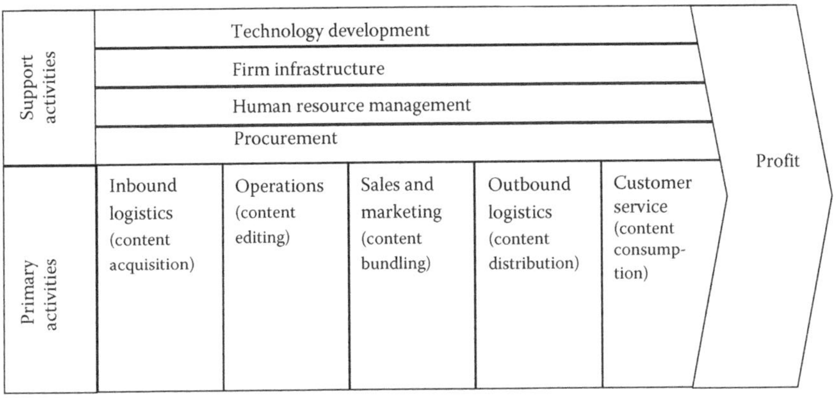

FIGURE 11.2
Porter's model of the value chain. (Adapted from Porter, M. 1985. *Competitive Advantage*. New York, Free Press.)

attribute of next generation Big Data. Although a quantification of economic benefits is difficult to achieve due to structural dependencies and specificities of the various industry sectors, anecdotal evidence shall be applied to carve out the promises and pitfalls of Big Data as an enabler of business opportunities and market growth.

Technology Development

Productivity gains through Big Data highly correlate with the underlying infrastructure necessary to improve existing business processes and leverage savings and new business opportunities. In this respect, the emergence of Big Data coincides with the increasing popularity of cloud computing as cost-effective alternative to conventional IT architectures. Grounding technologies such as Hadoop,[*] MapReduce,[†] related applications such as Cloudera[‡] or Hive[§] and their adoption through large vendors such as IBM, Oracle, or SAS strongly contributed to the rise of Big Data and the broad reception within a wider public.

The cloud computing paradigm[¶] builds on the premise that computational capacity can be consumed on-demand, thus reducing the costs at

---

[*] See http://hadoop.apache.org (accessed October 1, 2012).
[†] See http://research.google.com/archive/mapreduce.html (accessed October 1, 2012).
[‡] See http://www.cloudera.com (accessed October 1, 2012).
[§] See http://hive.apache.org (accessed October 1, 2012).
[¶] According to the National Institute of Standards and Technology (NIST), cloud computing can be defined as a model for enabling convenient, on-demand network access to a shared pool of configurable computing resources (e.g., networks, servers, storage, applications, and services) that can be rapidly provisioned and released with minimal management effort or service provider interaction. See http://csrc.nist.gov/publications/drafts/800-146/Draft-NIST-SP800-146.pdf (accessed September 5, 2012).

the demand side while improving the utilization of resources at the supply side. According to Biocic et al. (2011), virtualization via cloud computing can increase the utilization of computing infrastructures from an average of 15% up to 90% compared to traditional IT environments, thus leading to significant productivity gains over the long run. The expected benefits draw from flexible management of capacities to perform computational tasks without investing in new infrastructure, training of personnel, or licensing of software. This is especially relevant in the area of Big Data where the increasing availability of heterogeneous data requires large amounts of storage capacities and compute-intensive analytics to derive business value from this new kind of resource.

Case studies from market research and business literature suggest that Big Data storage systems based on the principle of cloud computing coincide with massive savings in IT infrastructure and operation. Numbers exist, that is, for Walt Disney, who had set up a Hadoop cluster with annual operating costs of $300,000 to $500,000, roughly a tenth of the amount necessary if the same functional requirements would have been solved with conventional technologies.[*] With this technological approach, Walt Disney lowered the company's IT expense growth from 27 to 3%, while increasing its annual processing growth from 17 to 45% (Gruman 2010, p. 6f).

This anecdotal evidence is further illustrated by a model calculation from AMD (2010) as discussed in the following section.

Excursion: The Costs of Cloud Computing[†]

Consider a hypothetical application designed to retrieve and catalog all of the images on the Internet. As part of the process, the application will convert each image to a 100×100 thumbnail, compute an MD5 hash on each image, extract EXIF data and store when available, and then push the generated catalog to a central location.

Let us estimate the cost per billion images to create an image catalog of all images on the net. For the purposes of this exercise, we will assume that the technologies used include:

- Nutch (an apache open-source search engine based on Hadoop)
- Hadoop
- Amazon EC2
- Amazon Elastic Block Store (a web service for storage but with better performance characteristics than S3)

---

[*] Similar findings are also reported from Savitz (2012).
[†] The following section was adopted from an AMD white paper on the business effects of cloud computing (AMD 2010).

We will use the following cost estimate methodology. We will randomly select approximately 70,000 domain names, crawl the home page of each, and extract all images from the crawled pages. Next, we will randomly select 100,000 images from the gathered set. Then, we will retrieve and process selected images as described above. From the costs determined in this exercise, we can extrapolate the cost per billion.

First, let us look at numbers associated with computing and bandwidth capacity. Low-end EC2 instances can successfully retrieve and process about 100,000 images per hour. Once processed, the resulting image data within the catalog averages to approximately 2 k bytes compressed. Further, we find that it takes about 10,000 h of computing time to retrieve 1 billion images, with a storage requirement of about 2 TB of data per billion.

We therefore find that the server cost per billion images is $850. This is because low-end EC2 instances sell for $0.085 per hour. We also find that the storage cost is $0. This is because the data will not be stored by Amazon.com, but will be pushed to a site owned by the developer.

Next, bandwidth costs inbound are $0, since inbound bandwidth on Amazon.com is currently free. However, we can assume $750 per billion images in the future at current bandwidth prices. Bandwidth outbound costs are about $300 per billion, noting the cost of $15 per GB with 1 billion images yielding 2 TB of data. The resulting total cost, then, is about $1200 per billion images, rising to as much as $2000 per billion if Amazon.com starts charging for inbound bandwidth.

Some additional considerations are that data acquisition at a rate of 1 billion images per month requires about 15 servers. Low-end EC2 instances can push about 30 mbps of bandwidth, which, multiplied by 15 servers, puts us at about 450 mbps of bandwidth consumed to retrieve 1 billion images per month.

What if we had performed this same exercise in 2000? To begin, there was no cloud-computing option, so we would have had to actually purchase and provision 15 rack mounted servers at a cost of about $75,000. Costs associated with a data center infrastructure to support the servers, such as racks, routers, and switches, would have been, conservatively, $250,000. The cost of 450 mbps of bandwidth per month would have run about $300,000.

In short, the costs would have been not only $325,000 up front capital investment, but also some $300,000 per month in ongoing bandwidth costs. This puts the cost at about $500,000 just to retrieve 1 billion images processed.

Firm Infrastructure

Numerous authors have discussed the key advantages of cloud computing compared to conventional architectures (i.e., Zheng and Chen 2010; Rafique et al. 2011) and provided cost models that quantify the effective savings from the application of cloud services (i.e., Niyato et al. 2009; Wu and Gan

2011; Chaisiri et al. 2012; Martens et al. 2012). Summing up the literature, the following cost incentives drive the adoption of Big Data for analytical purposes:

- *Economies of scale:* The shared provision of infrastructures allows savings at the supply side, the demand side, and multitenancy efficiency due to dynamic provision/consumption of infrastructure, lower cost of electricity consumption, infrastructure labor cost distribution, security, and reliability and buying power for negotiations.

- *Reduced upfront costs:* The utilization of existing resources shifts the fixed costs of market entrance to operative costs depending on the size of demand and production (Pay-As-You-Go-Principle). Thus, necessary hardware is immediately available when required and it can be flexibly configured to serve individual purposes either for standard tasks or completely new classes of applications.

- *Lower management and operational costs:* The reduced complexity of IT management due to the layered architecture and APIs coincides with less labor costs in running and maintaining an operational infrastructure.

Human Resource Management

Big Data adoption will incrementally grow as long as existing technologies advance in conjunction with the necessary skills for the utilization of Big Data technologies to solve complex tasks.

In other words, it is not primarily the technology that creates a bottleneck to economic growth but the analytical competence in terms of data-savvy personnel needed to derive effective value from it. Hence, inadequate staffing or skills for Big Data analytics is perceived as one of the major bottlenecks in the adoption of Big Data technologies (Russom 2011, p. 12; The Economist 2011, p. 19; Evans 2012). As Bollier (2010) points out, the sheer volume of data might be completely senseless without the necessary scientific and statistical understanding to derive valid and reliable subsets from Big Data sets for analytical purposes. It is this kind of expertise that will prevent analysts confusing correlations of causalities and vice versa that often lead to faulty decisions despite an abundance of data.

According to McKinsey (2011, p. 105), the US market will demand 4 million experts in the area of Big Data analytics by 2018 from which just 2.5 million can be covered by new graduates. The rest has to be filled by retraining existing workforce and importing talent from abroad. The unserved demand will in turn generate a new area of business and job opportunities. The British Centre for Economics and Business Research (Cebr 2012) expects a cross-sectoral leverage effect of 36,000 new start ups and 60,000 new jobs in the area of Big Data analytics in the UK till 2017 increasing the adoption rate of Big Data analytics among the UK industry from an average of 34% by the year 2011 to an estimated 54% by 2017.*

Procurement

Procurement—in the widest sense—will be one of those economic areas where Big Data analytics will play an important role. This coincides with the increasing role of Business Intelligence applications in areas such as enterprise resource planning, R&D, and marketing to leverage operational efficiency, competitive advantages, and risk reduction. This is especially relevant to the retail area where better consumer targeting, faster fraud detection, more accurate predictions, and customer segmentation play an important role. These are also the areas where most of the added value from Big Data analytics is to be expected (i.e., Russom 2011, p. 11; The Economist 2011, p. 11).

McKinsey (2011, p. 67) provides a heuristic overview of relevant retail levers associated with Big Data (Table 11.4).

TABLE 11.4

Big Data Levers in the Retail Industry

Function	Big Data Lever
Marketing	Cross-selling
	Location-based marketing
	In-store behavior analysis
	Customer microsegmentation
	Sentiment analysis
	Enhancing the multichannel consumer experience
Merchandising	Assortment optimization
	Pricing optimization
	Placement and design optimization
Operations	Performance transparency
	Labor inputs optimization
Supply chain	Inventory management
	Distribution and logistics optimization
	Informing supplier negotiations
New business models	Price comparison services
	Web-based markets

Source: Adapted from McKinsey 2011. Big Data. The next frontier for innovation, competition and productivity. Research Report. http://www.mckinsey.com/insights/mgi/research/technology_and_innovation/big_data_the_next_frontier_for_innovation (accessed September 14, 2012).)

---

* This adoption rate coincides with results from an independent survey conducted by Russom (2011, p. 10) who report that approximately 34% of the respondents utilize Big Data analytics within their organization.

Why Linking Big Data?: The Added Value of Semantic Interoperability in the Primary Activities of the Value Chain

Enabling and managing interoperability at the data and the service level is probably one of the strategic key issues in networked environments and a growing issue in the effective management of Big Data (Mitchell and Wilson 2012). Without interoperability, silos of data and systems are being created that prohibit the ecosystem to nurture network effects and positive feedback loops around its assets. This is especially relevant for data-driven businesses that rely on fast and flexible data analytics from federated sources to generate content for decision support purposes. Here, interoperability is a precondition to enable the cost-effective transaction and integration of data and provide adequate tools for its consumption (Cranford 2009).

The following sections will focus on the added value of semantic interoperability in the primary activities of the value chain as enabled by the so-called Linked Data principles for the effective integration and reutilization of data on top of semantic metadata.

Metadata as an Economic Asset

A key concept in the creation of interoperability for Big Data is metadata. Metadata has become a key enabler in the creation of controllable and exploitable information ecosystems under highly networked circumstances (The Economist 2010). This coincides with findings from Saumure and Shiri (2008) who revealed that with the emergence of the World Wide Web as a universal platform for the creation and distribution of information the nature and importance of metadata has changed significantly. To illustrate this, they conducted a survey on research topics in the Library and Information Sciences by analyzing publications from the LISTA Database (Library, Information Science, and Technology Abstracts)* with the year 1993 as a demarcation line of a pre-web and a post-web era. Table 11.5 shows their research results.

The survey illustrates three trends: (1) the spectrum of research areas has broadened significantly from originally complex and labor-intensive methodologies to more light-weight, application-oriented approaches; (2) while certain areas have kept their status over the years (i.e., Cataloging and Classification or Machine Assisted Knowledge Organization), new areas of research have gained importance (i.e., Metadata Applications and Uses, Classifying Web Information, Interoperability Issues), and others have declined or dissolved into other areas; and (3) metadata issues have significantly increased in popularity in terms of the quantity of papers that is explicitly and implicitly dealing with corresponding issues.

---

* See http://www.ebscohost.com/academic/library-information-science-technology-abstracts-lista, as of April 4, 2012.

TABLE 11.5

Research Areas in Library and Information Science

Research Area	Pre-Web (%)	Post-Web (%)
Metadata applications/uses	—	16
Cataloging/classification	14	15
Classifying web information	—	14
Interoperability	—	13
Machine-assisted knowledge organization	14	12
Education	7	7
Digital preservation/libraries	—	7
Thesauri initiatives	7	5
Indexing/abstracting	29	4
Organizing corporate or business information	—	4
Librarians as knowledge organizers of the web	—	2
Cognitive models	29	1

Source: Adapted from Saumure, K., Shiri, A. 2008. *Journal of Information Science,* 34/5, 651–666.

These findings coincide with results from an econometric survey of various information growth patterns by Haase (2004), who points to the fact that from a certain point in time the economic value of metadata is rising faster than the actual instance data that is being managed by it. In other words, a sustainable metadata strategy is a necessary means to preserve and leverage the value of data for purposes such as aggregation, processing, and consumption of information. And the retail giant Wal-Mart illustrated that these theoretical assumptions have a real economic impact. They recently announced that improved semantic interoperability in their e-commerce system has increased sales up to 15% since its deployment in 2012.[*]

Semantic Interoperability and the Benefits of Linked Data

From the large amount of information produced every day, just about 5% is "structured" (The Economist 2010, p. 3). But 92% of all analytical activities are exercised on top of structured data (Russom 2011, p. 18). The remaining data are currently hardly utilized or discarded as a whole. Hence, new approaches are being developed to improve the machine-processability of available data ideally by not just creating more structured data but also by applying structural principles that support interoperability. One of these approaches is called Linked Data.

Since 2009, the Linked Data paradigm has emerged as a light-weight approach to improve data portability among systems. According to this

---

[*] See http://www.computerworld.com/s/article/9230801/Walmart_rolls_out_semantic_search_engine_sees_business_boost (accessed September 10, 2012).

approach, the web is being perceived as "an immense database that can be mined to link to data, rather than document-based resources" (Mitchell and Wilson 2012, p. 11). This is especially relevant in environments that are characterized by heterogeneous data formats and sources that are spread among various locations and time zones. By building on Semantic Web standards, the Linked Data approach offers significant benefits compared to conventional data integration approaches. These are according to Auer (2011):

- *De-referencability.* IRIs are not just used for identifying entities, but since they can be used in the same way as URLs, they also enable locating and retrieving resources describing and representing these entities on the Web.

- *Coherence.* When an RDF triple contains IRIs from different namespaces in subject and object position, this triple basically establishes a link between the entity identified by the subject (and described in the source dataset using namespace A) with the entity identified by the object (described in the target data set using namespace B). Through these typed RDF links, data items are effectively interlinked.

- *Integrability.* Since all Linked Data sources share the RDF data model, which is based on a single mechanism for representing information, it is very easy to attain a syntactic and simple semantic integration of different Linked Data sets. A higher-level semantic integration can be achieved by employing schema and instance matching techniques and expressing found matches again as alignments of RDF vocabularies and ontologies in terms of additional triple facts.

- *Timeliness.* Publishing and updating Linked Data is relatively simple, thus facilitating a timely availability. In addition, once a Linked Data source is updated, it is straightforward to access and use the updated data source, as this is time-consuming and error-prone extraction, transformation, and loading are not required.

On top of these technological principles, Linked Data promises to lower the costs of data integration (Cranford 2009), thereby improving the reusability and richness of information (in terms of depth and broadness). According to Mitchell and Wilson (2012, p. 14), Linked Data provides an efficient means for "brokering, mapping, interconnecting, indexing and feeding real-time information from a variety of sources. [It allows to] infer relationships from big data analysis that might otherwise have been discarded."

Along this line of argument, the following section will elaborate on how these characteristics contribute to the primary activities of the content value chain.

Added Value of Linked Data in the Content Value Chain

With reference to Zerdick et al. (1999), we now refer to a modified view of the value chain that takes account of the specificities of content creation. Herein the content production process consists of five sequential steps: (1) content acquisition, (2) content editing, (3) content bundling, (4) content distribution, and (5) content consumption. As illustrated in Figure 11.3, Linked Data can contribute to each step by supporting the associated intrinsic production function. The following sections will discuss achievements and challenges in the application of Linked Data to the management of unstructured and semistructured content.

Content Acquisition

Content acquisition is mainly concerned with the collection, storage, and integration of relevant information necessary to produce a content item. In the course of this process, information is being pooled from internal or external sources for further processing.

At the time of writing, limited attention is being paid to issues of data pooling for business purposes from a content-perspective. While "immature integration capabilities" have already been subject to criticism several years ago (i.e., Goth 2006), modest approaches do exist that address the topic of data acquisition from a general perspective (i.e., Hausenblas 2009; Graube et al. 2011; Heino et al. 2011) and multimedia content (i.e., Kobilarov et al. 2009; Messina et al. 2011; Schandl et al. 2011).

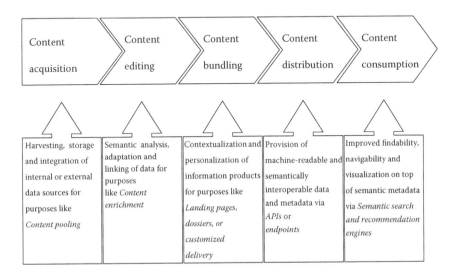

FIGURE 11.3
Linked Data in the content value chain. (Adapted from Pellegrini, T. 2012. *Proceeding of the 16th International Academic MindTrek Conference* 2012. ACM SIGMM, pp. 125–133.)

Most work dealing with syndication, acquisition, and integration issues of Linked Data concentrates on the technological feasibility, but none of them addresses aspects of data quality such as provenance, reliability, validity, or completeness of data sources. But data quality as well as the explorative and narrative value of data sources within the triangle of "objectivity vs. selectivity vs. validity" are crucial factors in the content production process and should be targeted carefully when integration issues for analytical purposes are concerned. Hence, more research is needed to develop machine-readable quality metrics for linked data sets with respect to their syntactic and semantic attributes.

Content Editing

The editing process entails all necessary steps that deal with the semantic adaptation, interlinking, and enrichment of data. Adaptation can be understood as a process in which acquired data are provided in a way that it can be reused within editorial processes. Interlinking and enrichment are often performed via processes such as annotation and/or referencing to enrich documents either by disambiguating existing concepts or by providing background knowledge for deeper insights.

Especially, the enrichment of documents in the editorial workflow has been subject to numerous works and is probably the most elaborated area in the utilization of semantic metadata. Earlier work (i.e., Kosch et al. 2005; Ohtsuki et al. 2006; Smith and Schirling 2006) provides design principles for a metadata lifecycle management and demonstrates the value of well-structured metadata for indexing and compiling unstructured content across various modalities such as text, speech, and video. Hu et al. (2009) present an ontology-based reasoning system that supports the automated analysis and aggregation of content items from very large corpora. Their system is capable of extracting names, terms, temporals (i.e., time stamps and durations), and locations incorporating metadata from third party sources (such as OpenCyc* and IPTC†) and reason over these elements to detect semantic similarities between content items. Kim et al. (2008) discuss the benefits of domain ontologies as integration layers for tagging purposes in collaborative environments. They demonstrate that shared knowledge models can help one to improve the reuse of descriptors from various systems and increase flexibility in the editorial process without disrupting it. Yu et al. (2010) describe a system that uses a two-stage SOA-based approach for semantically annotating and brokering TV-related services in Electronic Program Guides. By utilizing the light-weight semantics available from Linked Data, they were

---

* See http://www.opencyc.org/doc (accessed October 10, 2012).
† The IPTC (International Press & Telecommunications Codes) NewsCodes consist of the following subsets: EventsML-G2, NewsML-G2, SportsML-G2, rNews, IIM, NewsML 1, IPTC 7901, NITF. See: http://www.iptc.org/site/Home/ (accessed April 4, 2012).

able to significantly lower the integration complexity of external data and improve the maintenance of the system for developers. And Mannens et al. (2009) propose a system for automated metadata enrichment and indexing to improve customized delivery of news items based on the IPTC NewsML-G2 standard. They enrich the IPTC news model with extracted entities from DBpedia[*] and generate facets that help the user to fuzzily browse a knowledge base thus improving content discovery.

As content editing is a highly time- and cost-intensive task, the work discussed in this section is of high importance in editorial processes. Unfortunately, most research is not taking account of the technological preconditions (infrastructure, skills) in organizations and structural constraints in editorial workflows (i.e., time constraints, underdeveloped metadata culture). The work discussed above builds on the premise that a sufficient amount of quality approved metadata is already available. As this is rarely the case, further research is necessary on the (semi-)automatic generation of high-quality metadata, on the one hand, and its reuse for the semantic adaptation, interlinking, and enrichment of documents, on the other hand.

Content Bundling

The bundling process is mainly concerned with the contextualization and personalization of information products. It can be used to provide customized access to information and services, that is, by using metadata for the device-sensitive delivery of content or to compile thematically relevant material into Landing Pages or Dossiers thus improving the navigability, findability, and reuse of information.

In the area of content bundling, we find a large amount of work that is dealing with the role of semantic metadata in the development of new products and delivery services. In 2001, Jokela et al. (2001) have proposed a system called "SmartPush" that adapts to personal preferences of users by linking user feedback to the well-structured set of metadata used to annotate news items. They applied a Mixed-Initiative-Approach, which has outperformed purely algorithmic recommendation services but suffers from a cold-start problem. A similar approach has been proposed by Bomhardt (2004), Zhou et al. (2007), and Gao et al. (2009) who utilize behavioral data (i.e., browsing history) to match personal reading preferences with structural similarities between content items. And Knauf et al. (2011) present a system that uses a rich set of metadata derived from manual and automated video annotations to discover semantic links and similarities between multimedia files and use this for personalized delivery especially on mobile devices.

But excessive collection and reuse of behavioral data poses threats to user privacy and can cause adverse effects among the targeted users (McKinsey 2011; Cebr 2012). As an alternative to approaches that match content items to

---

[*] See http://dbpedia.org/About (accessed September 20, 2012).

user profiles, Liu et al. (2007), Bouras and Tsogkas (2009), and Schouten et al. (2010) illustrate how the extraction of metadata from documents can be used to calculate similarities between files and thus improve the relevance of automated content selection and recommendation services. They achieve this by combining rule-based natural language processing techniques with domain ontologies, thus providing fuzzy-search mechanisms to explore document stores. This approach is also followed by Ijntema et al. (2010) who propose a framework to build content personalization services by combining domain ontologies with text analytics from GATE and WordNet. This work is extended by Goosen et al. (2011) who use a Concept Frequency—Inverse Document Frequency algorithm for personalized content services on top of the same framework.

What the latter approaches have in common is that they utilize domain ontologies to organize metadata and pull reasonable information from linked vocabularies. This allows new forms of knowledge discovery and delivery services that go beyond the established search and retrieval paradigms and provide the users with a richer interaction experience without necessarily intruding their privacy. But the availability and costs of qualitatively sufficient ontologies are a significant barrier to the deployment of Linked Data techniques in this area. In addition, the quality of recommendations is difficult to evaluate and can be accompanied by reactance effects on the user side.

Content Distribution

In a Linked Data environment, the process of content distribution mainly deals with the provision of machine-readable and semantically interoperable (meta)data via Application Programming Interfaces (APIs) or SPARQL Endpoints (Zimmermann 2011). These can be designed either to serve internal purposes so that data can be reused within controlled environments (i.e., within or between organizational units) or for external purposes so that data can be shared between anonymous users (i.e., as open SPARQL Endpoints on the Web).

Over the past years, we have seen several examples where (mainly media) companies have started to offer news-relevant data as Linked Data. Since 2009, BBC is offering public SPARQL Endpoints for their program, music, and sports data (i.e., Kobilarov et al. 2009; Smethurst 2009; Rayfield 2012) and in the same year the New York Times has started to offer large amounts of subjects headings as SKOS[*] via their Article Search API[†] (Larson and Sandhaus 2009). The Reuters Open Calais API[‡] supports SOAP, REST, and

---

[*] SKOS (Simple Knowledge Organization System) is a set of specifications and standards to support the use of knowledge organization systems (KOS) such as thesauri, classification schemes, subject heading systems, and taxonomies within the framework of the Semantic Web. See http://www.w3.org/2004/02/skos/ (accessed October 3, 2012).

[†] See http://developer.nytimes.com/docs (accessed September 20, 2012).

[‡] See http://www.opencalais.com/documentation/calais-web-service-api (accessed September 20, 2012).

HTTP requests providing data in RDF. And The Guardian is offering an MP Data SPARQL Editor* from which data about British politicians can be retrieved in RDF.

Despite these encouraging examples, companies have not yet embraced the logic and culture of open publishing, especially when data assets are concerned. Here, we face a typical chicken-and-egg-problem where the willingness of opening up data sources heavily depends on the quantifiable added value that can be derived from such a strategy. Economic gains derived from an open data strategy heavily vary by industry sector and structural factors such as revenue portfolio, licensing constraints, and competition strategy. Nevertheless—as the following section on Big Data Licensing will argue—a diversification of the licensing strategy might also foster new business and revenue opportunities within networked environments.

Content Consumption

The last step in the content value chain is dealing with content consumption. This entails any means that enable a human user to search for and interact with content items in a pleasant und purposeful way. So according to this view, this step mainly deals with end-user applications that make use of Linked Data to provide access to content items (i.e., via search or recommendation engines) and generate deeper insights (i.e., by providing reasonable visualizations).

While most of the methodologies for contextualization and personalization and corresponding applications such as search and recommendation services described in the previous section (Content Bundling) serve the purpose of content consumption, increasing attention has also been paid to visualization and interaction issues associated with Linked Data although most of it is still in an experimental phase. A comprehensive overview is given by Paulheim (2011) who developed a tool called Semantic Data Explorer. And Freitas et al. (2012) discuss recent challenges, approaches, and trends in querying and visualizing heterogeneous data sets on the Linked Data web. Böhm et al. (2010) present a tool called GovWild that integrates and cleanses open government data at a large scale, thus providing easy access to linked government data via a simple search interface. A similar approach is followed by Hoxha et al. (2011) who provide a research tool to visualize Albanian Government Data using the Google Visualization API to process RDF data retrieved via an easy to use SPARQL endpoint.

Research on the improvement of interface design for the handling of semantic data services will be one of the crucial success factors in the broad adaptation of Linked Data for Big Data analytics. Tools and functionalities need to be designed to meet the requirements and skills of technology laypersons. Technology should be harbored from them as good as possible, but accessible, documented, and transparent for personal scrutiny. This is important

---

* See http://api.talis.com/stores/guardian (accessed September 20, 2012).

as filtering mechanisms deprive users of their informational autonomy and consumers of sovereignty. Hence, the "tyranny of the algorithms" and the "technological unconscious" might outweigh expected benefits due to reactance as an effect of insufficient functional and editorial transparency.

Licensing Big Data

New technology has never been a sufficient precondition for the transformation of business practices but has always been accompanied and influenced by nontechnological modes of cultural change (Ghosch 2005). In the case of Big Data, one of these nontechnological modes is the changing notion of ownership in digital products and the corresponding emergence of alternative legal instruments (i.e., commons-based approaches) and licensing practices. These allow the owner of intellectual property rights to design ownership models that better suite the attributes and specificities of the digital asset in networked products and services. According to a recent report from the World Economic Forum (2012), a diversification of licensing strategies for Big Data is a necessary condition to foster cross-sectoral cooperation and new forms of value creation within collaborative environments.

Traditional IPR Instruments

Semantic metadata is a fairly new kind of intellectual asset that is still subject to debate concerning the adequate protection instruments (Sonntag 2006). Table 11.6 gives an overview over the applicability of various IPR instruments to various asset types.

TABLE 11.6

IPR Instruments for Semantic Metadata

	Copyright	Database Right	Unfair Practice	Patents
Documents	YES	YES	YES	NO
Base data	NO	NO	PARTLY	NO
Description	YES	NO	YES	NO
Identifier	NO	YES	NO	NO
Name space	YES	YES	YES	NO
Vocabulary	PARTLY	YES	YES	NO
Classification	PARTLY	PARTLY	PARTLY	NO
Ontology	PARTLY	YES	YES	PARTLY
Rules	PARTLY	YES	YES	PARTLY

Source: Adapted from Pellegrini, T. 2012. *Proceeding of the 16th International Academic MindTrek Conference 2012.* ACM SIGMM, pp. 125–133.

- *Copyright* basically protects the creative and original nature of a literary work and gives its holder the exclusive legal right to reproduce, publish, sell, or distribute the matter and form of the work. Hence, any literary work that can claim a sufficient degree of originality can be protected by copyright.

- *Database Right* protects a collection of independent works, data, or other materials which are arranged in a systematic or methodological way and are individually accessible by electronic or other means. Databases are also protected as literary works and need to have a sufficient degree of originality that requires a substantial amount of investment.

- An *Unfair Practices Act* protects rights holders against certain trade practices, which are considered unfair in terms of misappropriation, advertising, sales pricing, or damages to reputation. Especially, the first aspect is relevant to semantic metadata, which actually occurs, when data are being reused without appropriate compensation, that is, in terms of attribution or financial return.

- *Patenting* does not directly impact the protection of semantic metadata as—at least in Europe—patents can just be acquired for hardware-related inventions. But as soon as semantic metadata becomes indispensable subject of a methodology that generates physical effects, has a sufficient level of inventiveness, and can be exploited commercially, these components can be protected under Patent Law.

Table 11.6 illustrates the complex nature of semantic metadata as intellectual property. Various instruments can be applied to various assets, while copyright, database right, and competition right are the most relevant ones.

But traditional IPR approaches pose the problem of "over-protection," which means that inadequate rights management stifles economic and cultural development, especially under collaborative working conditions. Hence, complementary approaches have emerged over the past few years that allow complementary and flexible alternatives to traditional licensing regimes.

Commons-Based Approaches

The open and nonproprietary nature of Linked Data design principles allow one to easily share and reuse these data for collaborative purposes. This also offers new opportunities to content publishers to diversify their assets and nurture new forms of value creation (i.e., by extending the production environment to open or closed collaborative settings) or unlock new revenue channels (i.e., by establishing highly customizable data syndication services on top of fine granular accounting services based on SPARQL).

To meet these requirements, commons-based licensing approaches such as Creative Commons* or Open Data Commons† have gained popularity over the last years, allowing a high degree of reusability while at the same time providing a legal framework for protection against unfair usage practices and rights infringements. Nevertheless to meet the requirements of the various asset types a Linked Data licensing strategy should make a deliberate distinction between the database and the content stored in it. This is necessary as content and databases are distinct subjects of protection in intellectual property law and therefore require different treatment and protection instruments. An appropriate commons-based protection strategy for a data provider could look as follows:

- The *contents* of a linked data set, which are comprised of the terms, definitions, and its ontological structure, are protected by a CC-License,‡ which allows the commercial and/or noncommercial reuse of any published artifact.

- The underlying *database*, which comprises all independent elements and works that are arranged in a systematic or methodological way and are accessible by electronic or other means, are protected by a ODC-License,§ which also allows for the commercial and/or noncommercial reuse of any published artifact.

- In addition to these two aspects, the licensing strategy should also incorporate a *Linking Policy Community Norm*, which explicitly defines the expectations of the rights holder towards good conduct when links are made to the various artifacts provided in the dataset.¶ This norm should provide administrative information (i.e., creator, publisher, license, and rights), structural information about the data set (i.e., version number, quantity of attributes, types of relations), and recommendations for interlinking (i.e., preferred vocabulary to secure semantic consistency).

All in all, the three elements of a commons-based licensing policy—the CC-License, the ODC-License, and the Community Norm—provide a secure and resilient judicial framework to protect against the unfair appropriation of open data sets. In combination with traditional IPR instruments as part of a dual licensing strategy, the defined framework can be the basis for new business models and revenue streams.

---

* See http://creativecommons.org/ (accessed September 22, 2012).
† See http://opendatacommons.org/ (accessed September 22, 2012).
‡ See http://creativecommons.org/licenses/, (accessed September 22, 2012).
§ See http://opendatacommons.org/ (accessed September 22, 2012).
¶ See, for example, the community norm provided by the Leibniz Information Center for Economics: http://zbw.eu/stw/versions/8.08/mapping/gnd/ (accessed September 22, 2012).

Conclusion

This chapter discussed the economic value of Big Data from macro- and a microeconomic perspectives. It illustrated how technology and new skills can nurture opportunities to derive benefits from large, constantly growing, dispersed data sets and how semantic interoperability and new licensing strategies will contribute to the uptake of Big Data as a business enabler and source of value creation. There is no doubt that Big Data is a possible lever for economic growth and well being, but it also touches upon societal issues such as copyright, security, and privacy go beyond the simplistic desire for competitive advantage and profit. A detailed discussion of the ethical implications of Big Data would have gone beyond the scope of this paper, but it is obvious that the massive availability of data and the increasing desire to link it for gaining better analytical insights might be accompanied by deep cultural disruptions. Balancing the promises and perils of Big Data will therefore be one of many critical factors to its success.

Nevertheless, the business adoption of Big Data is still in its infancy. Time will tell whether the concept of Big Data is here to stay.

References

AMD 2010. Big Data. The Software and Compelling Economics of Big Data Computing. White Paper. http://sites.amd.com/us/Documents/Big_Data_Whitepaper.pdf (accessed October 3, 2012).

Auer, S. 2011. Creating knowledge out of interlinked data. In: *Proceedings of WIMS'11*, May 25–27, 2011, New York: ACM, pp. 1–8.

Biocic, B., Tomic, D., Ogrizovic, D. 2011. Economics of cloud computing. In: *Proceedings of MIPRO 2011*, Opatija, Croatia, May 23–27, pp. 1438–1442.

Böhm, C., Naumann, F., Freitag, M. 2010. Linking open government data: What journalists wish they had known. In: *Proceedings of the 6th International Conference on Semantic Systems*, Graz, Austria, ACM, pp. 1–4.

Bollier, D. 2010. The Promise and Peril of Big Data. Research Report by The Aspen Institute, Washington. http://www.thinkbiganalytics.com/uploads/Aspen-Big_Data.pdf (accessed October 10, 2012).

Bomhardt, C. 2004. NewsRec, a SVM-driven personal recommendation system for news websites. In: *IEEE/WIC/ACM International Conference on Web Intelligence*, 20–24 Sept. 2004, pp. 545–548.

Bouras, C., Tsogkas, V. 2009. Personalization mechanism for delivering news articles on the user's desktop. In: *Fourth International Conference on Internet and Web Applications and Services*, Venice, Italy, 24–28 May 2009, pp. 157–162.

Brynjolfsson, E., Hitt, L. M., Kim, H. H. 2011. Strength in Numbers: How Does Data-Driven Decisionmaking Affect Firm Performance? In: SSRN, Working Paper,

April 2011. http://papers.ssrn.com/sol3/papers.cfm?abstract_id=1819486 (accessed September 25, 2012).

Cebr 1012. Data Equity. Unlocking the Value of Big Data. Research Report. http://www.sas.com/offices/europe/uk/downloads/data-equity-cebr.pdf (accessed September 12, 2012).

Chaisiri, S., Lee, B.-S., Niyato, D. 2012. Optimization of resource provisioning cost on cloud computing. *IEEE Transactions on Services Computing*, 5/2, 164–177.

Cisco 2012. Cisco Visual Networking Index: Forecast and Methodology, 2011–2016, http://www.cisco.com/en/US/solutions/collateral/ns341/ns525/ns537/ns705/ns827/white_paper_c11–481360_ns827_Networking_Solutions_White_Paper.html (accessed September 30, 2012).

Cranford, S. 2009. Spinning a data web. In: *Price Waterhouse Coopers* (Ed.). Technology Forecast, Spring. http://www.pwc.com/us/en/technology-forecast/spring2009/index.jhtml (accessed September 20, 2012).

Evans, B. 2012. The Deadly Cost of Ignoring Big Data: $71.2 Million per Year. Forbes, September 20, 2012. https://blogs.oracle.com/TheInnovationAdvantage/entry/the_deadly_cost_of_ignoring (accessed October 10, 2012).

Freitas, A., Curry, E., Oliveira, J. G., O'Riain, S. 2012. Querying heterogeneous data-sets on the linked data web. Challenges, approaches, and trends. *IEEE Internet Computing*, 16/1, 24–33.

Gao, F., Yuhong L., Li, H., Jian, M. 2009. InfoSlim: An ontology-content based per-sonalized mobile news recommendation system. In: *5th International Conference on Wireless Communications, Networking and Mobile Computing*, New York, USA, 24–26 Sept. 2009, pp. 1–4.

Ghosch, R. A. 2005. *CODE. Collaborative Ownership in the Digital Economy*. Cambridge: MIT Press.

Goosen, F., Ijntema, W., Frasincar, F., Hogenboom, F., Kaymak, U. 2011. News person-alization using the CF-IDF semantic recommender. In: *Proceedings of WIMS'11*, New York, USA, May 25–27, 2011, pp. 1–12.

Goth, G. 2006. Data-driven enterprise. Slouching toward the semantic web. *IEEE Distributed Systems Online*, 7/3, 1–5.

Graube, M., Pfeffer, J., Ziegler, J., Urbas, L. 2011. Linked data as integrating technology for industrial data. In: *2011 International Conference on Network-Based Information Systems*, Tirana, Albania, 7–9 Sept. 2011, pp. 162–167.

Gruman, G. 2010. Tapping into the power of Big Data. In: *Price Waterhouse Coopers Technology Forecast. Making Sense of Big Data*. 3/2010, pp. 4–13. http://www.pwc.com/us/en/technology-forecast/2010/issue3/index.jhtml (accessed September 14, 2012).

Haase, K. 2004. *Context for Semantic Metadata*. In: MM'04, October 10–16, 2004, New York, USA: ACM.

Hausenblas, M. 2009. Exploiting linked data to build web applications. *IEEE Internet Computing*, 13/4, 68–73.

Heino, N., Tramp, S., Auer, S. 2011. Managing Web Content using Linked Data Principles—Combining semantic structure with dynamic content syndication. In: *35th IEEE Annual Computer Software and Applications Conference*, Munich, Germany, 18–22 July 2011, pp. 245–250.

Hoxha, J., Brahaj, A., Vrandecic, D. 2011. open.data.al—Increasing the utilization of government data in Albania. In: *Proceedings of the 7th International Conference on Semantic Systems*, Graz, Austria, ACM, pp. 237–240.

Hu, B., Wang, J., Zhou, Y. 2009. Ontology Design for Online News Analysis. In: *WRI Global Congress on Intelligent Systems*, Xiamen, China, 19–21 May 2009, pp. 202–206.

Ijntema, W., Goossen, F., Frasincar, F., Hogenboom, F. 2010. Ontology-based news recommendation. In: *EDBT'10 Proceedings of the 2010 EDBT/ICDT Workshops*, New York, USA, 22–26 March 2010, pp. 1–6.

Jokela, S., Turpeinen, M., Kurki, T., Savia, E., Sulonen, R. 2001. The role of structured content in a personalized news service. In: *System Sciences, 2001. Proceedings of the 34th Annual Hawaii International Conference*, Hawaii, USA. pp. 1–10.

Kim, H. L., Passant, A., Breslin, J. G., Scerri, S., Decker, S. 2008. Review and alignment of tag ontologies for semantically-linked data in collaborative tagging spaces. In: *IEEE International Conference on Semantic Computing*, Santa Clara, USA, 4–7 Aug. 2008, pp. 315–322.

Knauf, R., Kürsten, J., Kurze, A., Ritter, M., Berger, A., Heinich, S., Eibl, M. 2011. Produce. annotate. archive. repurpose: Accelerating the composition and metadata accumulation of tv content. In: *Proceedings of the 2011 ACM International Workshop on Automated Media Analysis and Production for Novel TV Services*, New York, USA, 1 December 2011, pp. 31–36.

Kobilarov, G., Scott, T., Raimond, Y., Oliver, S., Sizemore, C., Smethurst, M., Bizer, C., Lee, R. 2009. Media meets Semantic Web—How the BBC uses DBpedia and Linked Data to make Connections. In: *Proceedings of ESWC 2009, the 6th European Semantic Web Conference*. New York: Springer LNCS, pp. 723–747.

Kosch, H., Boszormenyi, L., Doller, M., Libsie, M., Schojer, P., Kofler, A. 2005. The life cycle of multimedia metadata. *Multimedia, IEEE*, 12(1), 80–86.

Kundra, V. 2012. Digital Fuel of the 21st Century: Innovation through Open Data and the Network Effect. Harvard: Joan Shorenstein Center on the Press, Politics and Public Policy. Discussion Paper.

Larson, R., Sandhaus, E. 2009. NYT to release thesaurus and enter linked data cloud. http://open.blogs.nytimes.com/2009/06/26/nyt-to-release-thesaurus-and-enter-linked-data-cloud/ (last accessed April 20, 2012).

Liu, Y., Wang, Q. X., Guo, L., Yao, Q., Lv, N., Wang, Q. 2007. The optimization in news search engine using formal concept analysis. In: *4th International Conference on Fuzzy Systems and Knowledge Discovery*, Haikou, China, 24–27 Aug. 2007, pp. 45–49.

Martens, B., Walterbusch, M., Teuteberg, F. 2012. Costing of cloud computing services: A total cost of ownership approach. In: *Proceedings of the 45*th Hawaii International Conference on System Sciences, Hawaii, USA, pp. 1563–1572.

Mannens, E., Troncy, R., Braeckman, K., Van Deursen, D., Van Lancker, W., De Sutter, R., Van de Walle, R. 2009. Automatic metadata enrichment in news production. In: *10th Workshop on Image Analysis for Multimedia Interactive Services*, London, England, 6–8 May 2009, pp. 61–64.

McKinsey 2011. Big data: The next frontier for innovation, competition and productivity. Research Report. http://www.mckinsey.com/insights/mgi/research/technology_and_innovation/big_data_the_next_frontier_for_innovation (accessed September 14, 2012).

Messina, A., Montagnuolo, M., Di Massa, R., Elia, A. 2011. The hyper media news system for multimodal and personalised fruition of informative content. In: *Proceedings of ICMR'11*, New York, USA, April 17–20, 2011, pp. 1–2.

Mitchell, I., Wilson, M., 2012. Linked Data. Connecting and exploiting big data. Fujitsu White Paper, March 2012. http://www.fujitsu.com/uk/Images/

Linked-data-connecting-and-exploiting-big-data-%28v1.0%29.pdf (accessed September 12, 2012).

Niyato, D., Chaisiri, S., Lee, B.-S. 2009. Economic analysis of resource market in cloud computing environment. In: _Proceedings of 2009 IEEE Asia-Pacific Services Computing Conference_, Singapore, pp. 156–162.

Ohtsuki, K., Katsuji, B., Yoshihiro, M., Shoichi, M., Yoshihiko, H. 2006. Automatic multimedia indexing: combining audio, speech, and visual information to index broadcast news. _Signal Processing Magazine, IEEE_, 23(2), 69–78.

Oracle 2012. Oracle Information Architecture: An Architect's Guide to Big Data. White Paper. http://www.oracle.com/technetwork/topics/entarch/articles/oea-big-data-guide-1522052.pdf (accessed September 10, 2012).

Paulheim, H. 2011. Improving the usability of integrated applications by using interactive visualizations of linked data. In: _Proceedings of the International Conference on Web Intelligence, Mining and Semantics WIMS'11_, New York, USA, ACM, pp. 1–12.

Pellegrini, T. 2012. Semantic metadata in the news production process. Achievements and challenges. In: Lugmayr, A., Franssila, H., Paavilainen, J., Kärkkäinen, H. (Eds). _Proceeding of the 16th International Academic MindTrek Conference 2012_, Tampere, Finland. ACM SIGMM, pp. 125–133.

Porter, M. 1985. _Competitive Advantage_. New York: Free Press.

Rafique, K., Tareen, A. W., Saeed, M., Wu, J., Qureshi, S. S. 2011. Cloud computing economics—Opportunities and challenges. In: _Proceedings of IEEE IC-BNMT2011_, Shenzhen, China, pp. 401–406.

Rayfield, J. 2012. Sports refresh: Dynamic semantic publishing. In: http://www.bbc.co.uk/blogs/bbcinternet/2012/04/sports_dynamic_semantic.html (last accessed April 20, 2012).

Russom, P. 2011. Big Data Analytics. TDWI Research Report, 4. Quarter 2011. http://tdwi.org/bdr-rpt.aspx (accessed September 14, 2012).

Saumure, K., Shiri, A. 2008. Knowledge organization trends in library and information studies: A preliminary comparison of pre- and post-web eras. _Journal of Information Science_, 34/5, 651–666.

Savitz, E. 2012. The Big Cost of Big Data. Forbes, April 16, 2012. http://www.forbes.com/sites/ciocentral/2012/04/16/the-big-cost-of-big-data/ (accessed October 10, 2012).

Schandl, B., Haslhofer, B., Bürger, T., Langegger, A., Halb, W. 2011. Linked Data and multimedia: The state of affairs. In: _Multimedia Tools and Applications_, Online First, pp. 1–34.

Schouten, K., Ruijgrok, P., Borsje, J., Frasincar, F., Levering, L., Hogenboom, F. 2010. A semantic web-based approach for personalizing news. In: _SAC'10 Proceedings of the 2010 ACM Symposium on Applied Computing_, Sierre, Switzerland, 22–26 March 2010, pp. 854–861.

Smethurst, M. 2009. BBC Backstage SPARQL endpoint for programmes and music. http://www.bbc.co.uk/blogs/radiolabs/2009/06/bbc_backstage_sparql_endpoint.shtml (accessed April 20, 2012).

Smith, J. R., Schirling, P. 2006. Metadata standards roundup. _IEEE Multimedia_, 13/2, 84–88.

Sonntag, M. 2006. Rechtsschutz für ontologien. In: Schweighofer, E., Liebwald, D., Drachsler, M., Geist, A. (Eds.). _e-Staat und e-Wirtschaft aus Rechtlicher Sicht_. Stuttgart: Richard Boorberg Verlag, pp. 418–425.

The Economist 2010. Data, data everywhere. A special report on managing information. http://www.emc.com/collateral/analyst-reports/ar-the-economist-data-data-everywhere.pdf (accessed September 30, 2012).

The Economist 2011. Big Data. Harnessing a game-changing asset. A report by the Economist Intelligence Unit. http://lp.pervasive.com/rs/pervasive/images/Big-Data-Strategy-EconomistReport.pdf (accessed September 18, 2012).

Winter, C. 2006. TIME-Konvergenz als Herausforderung für Management und Medienentwicklung. In: Karmasin, M. Winter, C. (Eds.). *Konvergenzmanagement und Medienwirtschaft*. Munich: Wilhelm Fink Verlag, pp. 13–54.

World Economic Forum 2012. Big Data, Big Impact: New Possibilities for International Development. White Paper. http://www.weforum.org/reports/big-data-big-impact-new-possibilities-international-development (accessed October 5, 2012).

Wu, Z., Gan, A. 2011. Qualitative and quantitative analysis of the value of cloud computing. In: *Proceedings of the 2011 International Conference on Information Management, Innovation Management and Industrial Engineering*, Shenzhen, China, pp. 518–521.

Yu, H. Q., Benn, N., Dietze, S., Pedrinaci, C., Liu, D., Domingue, J., Siebes, R. 2010. Two-staged approach for semantically annotating and brokering TV-related services. In: *IEEE International Conference on Web Services*, Miami, Florida, 5–10 July 2010, pp. 497–503.

Zerdick, A., Picot, A., Schrape, K., Artope, A., Golhammer, K., Lange, U., Vierkant, E., Lopez-Escobar, E., Silverstone, R. 1999. *E-Conomics. Strategies for the Digital Market Place*. New York: Springer.

Zheng, J.-W., Chen, L. 2010. The evolution process and economic analysis of cloud computing. In: *Proceedings of the 2010 International Conference on Challenges in Environmental Science and Computer Engineering*, Wuhan, China, pp. 361–364.

Zhou, Y.-Q., Hu, Y.-F., He, H.-C. 2007. Learning user profile in the personalization news service. In: *International Conference on Natural Language Processing and Knowledge Engineering*, 2007, Beijing, China, pp. 485–490.

Zimmermann, A. 2011. Leveraging the linked data principles for electronic communications. In: *IEEE/WIC/ACM International Conferences on Web Intelligence and Intelligent Agent Technology*, Lyon, France, 22–27 Aug. 2011, pp. 385–388.

12

Advanced Data Analytics for Business

Rajendra Akerkar

CONTENTS

Introduction

Every individual on amazon.com undergoes a personalized experience, based on the actions they venture on the site. For decades, credit card firms have been analyzing our purchasing patterns to sense hazardous behavior or illegal use. These examples reflect the growing power of data analytics in how we purchase, sell, serve—and occasionally even design or refine what we offer. The next wave of innovation promises us to have an even more pervasive impact on our life. It also holds better opportunities for enterprises to create differentiating value for those they serve. Primarily business data analytics tap information within the closed system in which a company operates. Amazon, for example, captures an increasingly rich profile of each site visitor and customer's habits by studying their data trails while on the site. Many businesses enlarge their understanding of customers by buying that data from each other. They more efficiently connect with their customers' needs by tracking purchasing histories, demographics, and how customers engage with them.

Yet they are limited by the restricted data drawn from the closed or proprietary mechanisms they use. The data are considerable yet they are not social. They lack a broader context about the relationships and behaviors of the people creating them. That context can be gathered from what is stored and shared openly on the Internet, or can be captured via mobile and tablet usage. Smart companies are observing and analyzing our *social* choices, especially from what can be observed in social interactions, such as co-creating, sharing, liking, and following. These behaviors are often more accurate than surveys, for instance, that ask consumers, what they believe, want and will do.

Even without the social capacity, this data deluge has enabled firms to predict prices, reconfigure supply chains, and shape consumer behavior. This *Big Data* flood of information refers to the digital wave of emails, voicemails, images, video files, and many more. This enormous information is being crunched to reveal patterns and to predict individual and collective behavior. The rapidly growing volume of such electronic data is staggering.

Nowadays, the exceptional value of Big Data is driving creation of new tools and systems to facilitate *intelligence* in consumer behavior, economic forecasting, and capital markets. Market domination may be driven by which companies absorb and use the best data fastest. Understanding the *social* context of individuals' and organizations' actions means a company can track, not just what their customers do, but get much closer to learning why they do what they do.

The chapter is divided into five sections. Section "Classification of Analytics Landscape" presents an overall classification of analytics landscape. Next, section "Big Data Analytics" describes Big Data management technologies and approaches to data analytics. Section "Learning from Data" deals with concept of learning and machine learning techniques. Various cases of analytic technologies are presented in the "Examples of Analytic Technologies" section. Finally, conclusion is given in the "Conclusion" section.

Classification of Analytics Landscape

Business intelligence (BI) is not a new concept. Davenport and Harris (2007) define BI as "a set of technologies and processes that use data to understand and analyze business performance." They also define analytics as "the extensive use of data, statistical and quantitative analysis, explanatory and predictive models, and fact-based management to drive decisions and actions."

Nowadays, a tremendous amount of data is available in the form of structured data (from sensors) and unstructured data (from cameras, social media, and sentiment from the social network). The main factor behind the growth of business analytics is the availability of enormous amounts of data.

Business analytics is being used within the information technology industry to refer to the use of computing to gain insights from data. The data may be obtained from a company's internal sources, such as its enterprise resource planning application, data warehouses/marts, from a third-party data provider, or from public sources. Enterprises seek to leverage the digitized data from transaction systems and automated business processes to support "fact-based" decision-making. Thus, business analytics is a category of computing rather than a specific method, application, or product.

In today's challenging economic world, "acceptable" is no longer satisfactory. For instance, in any scam analysis knowing what happened yesterday and stopping the same thing from happening in the future is only the first step. By using advanced analytics, organizations now have the capability of identifying fraud before they write a check, refund money, or settle a claim. Organizations with good enterprise data management practices, processes, and infrastructures that were built for old-fashioned BI reporting are not always positioned to successfully address the complex requirements and unpredictable workloads of operational analytics. However, the question often asked is how to use current production platforms and maintain predictable performance without restricting the ability of analysts to explore, transform, and develop data and models in an off-the-cuff way. No doubt, advanced analytics requires a demand-driven, forward-looking, flexible, exploratory process. Any attempt to limit these dimensions will inhibit the effectiveness of the analyst.

Application Areas

Numerous functions within a business can benefit from analytics. The most common functional categories include:

1. *Customer analytics*: This category includes applications to marketing (customer profiling, segmentation, social network analysis, brand reputation analysis, marketing mix optimization) and customer experience.

2. *Supply chain analytics (SCA)*: This includes demand forecasting and optimization of inventory, pricing, scheduling, transportation, and storage, while mitigating and risk. A branch of SCA, *human capital analytics* aka *workforce analytics,* relates to service industries where human resources are the foremost means of production.

3. *Analytics in public domain*: Driven by natural resource constraints, governments are using analytics for tasks such as detecting water leakages in distribution systems, making energy grids and traffic systems smarter, and improving public safety.

4. *Fraud and risk analytics*: This includes assessment of various types of risk (market, operational, credit) mostly in the financial sector.

Degree of Complexity

Complexity of analytics can be broken down into three layers: descriptive analytics, predictive analytics, and prescriptive analytics. To be specific, business analytics center around five key themes of customer needs, as given below:

- *Information access*: This fragment is foundational to business analytics. It is all about fostering informed or collaborative decision-making across the organization—safeguarding that decision-makers can understand how their area of the business is performing, so they can make informed decisions.

- *Insight*: Gaining a deeper understanding of why things are happening, for instance, gaining a thorough view of your customer (transaction history, segmentation, sentiment and opinion, etc.) to make better decisions and enable profitable growth.

- *Foresight*: Leveraging the past to predict potential future outcomes so that actions and decisions are computed in order to meet the objectives and requirements of the organization.

- *Business agility*: Driving real-time decision optimization in both people-centric process and automated-centric processes.

- *Strategic alignment*: This fragment of the market is about tactically aligning everyone in the organization—from strategy to execution. It deals with recording the preferences, priorities, objectives, and requirements that drive decision-making.

Organizations that undertake a voyage into the applications of business analytics must begin with an information management agenda that treats data and information as a strategic asset. Once information is treated as an asset, then descriptive, predictive, and prescriptive analytics can be applied. Every organization begins this voyage by examining the data generated from its automation systems: enterprise resource planning, customer relationship management, time and attendance, e-commerce, warranty management, and the like. Data warehouses, data mining, and database technologies have existed in various forms for years. *Big Data* as a term might be new, but many IT professionals have worked with large amounts of data in various industries for years. However, now Big Data is not just about large amounts of data. Digging and analyzing semistructured and unstructured data is new. A decade ago, we did not analyze email messages, PDF files, or videos. The Internet was just a new trend; distributed computing was not created yesterday, but being able to distribute and scale out a system in a flash is new. Similarly, wanting to predict the future is not a new concept, but being able to access and store all the data that are created is new.

Many enterprises have multiple databases and multiple database vendors, with terabytes or even petabytes of data. Some of these systems accumulated data over several years. Many enterprises build entire data warehouse and analytic platforms off this old data. For data to be useful to users, they must integrate customers with finance and sales data, with product data, with marketing data, with social media, with demographic data, with competitors' data, and more.

After decades of channelizing data collection, structures, storage, access, and retrieval, a value chain has emerged. The value chain connects Big Data and Analytics through the convergence of complexity and diversity shown in Figure 12.1.

Descriptive Analytics

Several businesses start with descriptive analytics to analyze business performance. Descriptive analytics analyze historical data and identifies

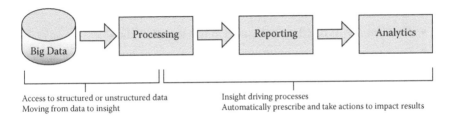

FIGURE 12.1
The analytics value chain.

patterns from samples for reporting of trends. Techniques such as data modeling, visualization, and regression analysis are most common in this analytics.

Descriptive analytics can be classified into following tasks:

- *Usual reporting and dashboards*: What took place? How does it relate to our blueprint?
- *Ad hoc reporting*: How many? Where?
- *Analysis/query*: What exactly is the challenge? Why is this happening?

Descriptive analytics are the commonly used and well-understood type of analytics. It basically categorizes, characterizes, consolidates, and classifies data. Tools for descriptive analytics may provide mechanisms for interfacing to enterprise data sources. They contain report generation, distribution capability, and data visualization facilities. Descriptive analytic techniques are mostly applied to structured data, although there have been attempts to extend to unstructured data, through the creation of structured metadata and indices. Descriptive analytics help us provide an understanding of the past as well as events occurring in real-time.

In general, organizations that effectively use descriptive analytics typically have a single view of the past and can focus their attention on the present, rather than on reconciling different views of the past.

Predictive Analytics

Predictive analytics use data to find out what could happen in the future. It is a more refined and higher level usage of analytics. It predicts future probabilities and trends and finds relationships in data not instantly apparent with traditional analysis. Data mining and predictive modeling tools and techniques are being used in this kind of analytics.

Predictive analytics are applied both in real-time to affect the operational process or in batch. The predictions are made by examining data about the past, detecting patterns, or relationships in these data, and then inferring these relationships forward in time.

Predictive analytics can be classified into six tasks:

- *Data mining*: What data are correlated with other data?
- *Forecasting*: What revenue will we close our annual balance sheet with?
- *Root cause analysis*: Why did it occur?
- *Pattern recognition*: When should we alter a process?
- *Monte-Carlo simulation*: What could emerge?
- *Predictive modeling*: What will happen then?

As descriptive analytics reach the stage where they support anticipatory action, a threshold is passed into the domain of predictive analytics. Predictive analysis applies sophisticated techniques to investigate scenarios and helps one to detect hidden patterns in large quantities of data in order to project forthcoming events. It uses techniques that segment and group data into comprehensible sets in order to predict behavior and detect trends. It utilizes clustering, rules, decision trees, and even neural network tools and techniques.

From a broader perspective, data are pooled from descriptive data (attributes, demographics), behavior data (orders, transaction), interaction data (e-mail, Web click-streams), and attitudinal data (opinions, preferences). At this juncture, customers can achieve superior performance and significant outcomes.

Beyond acquiring the data, accessing trusted and social data inside and outside of the organization, and modeling and applying predictive algorithms, deployment of the model is just as crucial in order to maximize the impact of analytics in real-time operations.

Prescriptive Analytics

Once the past is understood and predictions can be made about what might happen in the future, one need to know what the best action will be, given the limited resources of the enterprise. This is the area of prescriptive analytics. Prescriptive analytics use data to propose the best course of action to increase the chances of realizing the finest outcome. Optimization and simulation techniques are being used for this kind of analytics. Prescriptive analytics are based on the concept of optimization, which can be divided into two areas:

- *Optimization*: How can we achieve the best results?
- *Stochastic optimization*: How can we achieve the best result and tackle improbability in the data to make better decisions?

A perfect example of prescriptive analytics is the use of product recommendation engines such as Amazon and NetFlix. Usually, internal workflow of such engine is fully automated, for instance: data are collected, models are built and updated, and their final recommendations are pushed back to their users. While data scientists monitor high-level model results, no one is in charge for ensuring that your recommendations are updated on the website. The analytic results, associated content, and delivery of said content are all controlled through an automated workflow.

Big Data, combined with Prescriptive Analytics, is how we would make the Big Data trend productive.

Scale and Interactive Analysis

Some business applications need to process huge amounts of data on a real-time streaming basis (e.g., analysis of stock market, mining of financial transactions to detect fraud, stemming from sensors, search engine logs, etc.) using special-purpose computing hardware and software. The value of Big Data obviously lies in the patterns hidden inside them. In order to detect these patterns, analyzing Big Data sets is essential. As we are moving from the terabyte to peta and exabyte scale, the conventional techniques, even MapReduce, seem to have limited power. A general comparison of the Big Data processing systems is shown in Figure 12.2.

Some other applications require interactivity (e.g., an application that guides a staff in a business process outsourcing (BPO) firm as the conversation with the customer unfolds). On the contrary to what existing data processing solutions provide in batch type, the necessity for interactive analysis increases.

Many organizations depend on MapReduce to handle their large-scale data processing needs. As companies across diverse industries adopt MapReduce alongside parallel databases, new MapReduce workloads have emerged that feature many small, short, and increasingly interactive jobs. These workloads depart from the original MapReduce use case targeting purely batch computations and share semantic similarities with large-scale interactive query processing, an area of expertise of the RDBMS community. Consequently, recently query-like programming extensions for MapReduce and applying query optimization techniques to MapReduce brought considerable benefit. However, integrating these ideas into business-critical systems requires configuration tuning and performance benchmarking against real-life production MapReduce workloads. Knowledge of such workloads is currently limited to a handful of technology companies.

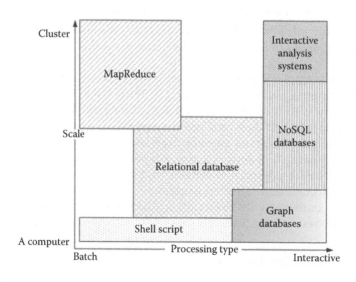

FIGURE 12.2
A comparison of Big Data processing systems.

Big Data Analytics

Data analytics refer to the business intelligent technologies that are grounded mostly in data mining and statistical analysis. Most of these techniques rely on the mature commercial technologies of relational DBMS, data warehousing, ETL, OLAP, and BPM. Since the late 1980s, various data mining algorithms have been developed by researchers from the artificial intelligence, algorithm, and database communities (Akerkar and Lingras, 2007). There are many data mining algorithms covering classification, clustering, regression, association analysis, and network analysis—such as C4.5, k-means, SVM (support vector machine), Apriori, EM (expectation maximization), PageRank, AdaBoost, k-NN (k-nearest neighbors), Naive Bayes, and CART. Most of these popular data mining algorithms have been incorporated in commercial and open source data mining systems (Witten et al., 2011). Other advances such as neural networks for classification/prediction and clustering and genetic algorithms for optimization and machine learning have all contributed to the success of data mining in different applications.

Two other data analytic approaches commonly taught in business school are also critical for business analytics. Grounded in statistical theories and models, multivariate statistical analysis covers analytical techniques such as regression, factor analysis, clustering, and discriminant analysis that have been used successfully in various business applications. Developed in the management science community, optimization techniques, and heuristic search are also suitable for selected business analytic problems such as database feature selection and web crawling.

Owing to the success achieved collectively by the data mining and statistical analysis community, data analytics continue to be an active area of research. Statistical machine learning often based on well-grounded mathematical models and powerful algorithms; techniques such as Bayesian networks, Hidden Markov models, support vector machine, reinforcement learning, and ensemble models have been applied to data, text, and web analytic applications. Other new data analytic techniques explore and leverage unique data characteristics, from sequential/temporal mining and spatial mining, to data mining for high-speed data streams and sensor data.

There are obviously several privacy issues in e-commerce, e-government, and healthcare applications and thus privacy preserving data mining has become an emerging area of Research. Many of these methods are data-driven, relying on various anonymization techniques, while others are process-driven, defining how data can be accessed and used (Gelfand, 2011/2012). Over the past decade, process mining has also emerged as a new research field that focuses on the analysis of processes using event data. Process mining has become possible due to the availability of event logs in various businesses (e.g., healthcare, supply chains) and new process discovery and conformance checking techniques (van der Aalst, 2012).

In addition to active academic research on data analytics, business research and development has also generated much interest, notably with respect to Big Data analytics for semistructured content. Unlike the structured data that can be handled repeatedly through a RDBMS, semistructured data may call for *ad hoc* and one-time extraction, parsing, processing, indexing, and analytics in a scalable and distributed MapReduce or Hadoop environment. MapReduce has been hailed as a revolutionary new platform for large-scale, massively parallel data access (Patterson, 2008).

Inspired in part by MapReduce, Hadoop provides a Java-based software framework for distributed processing of data-intensive transformation and analytics. The open source Apache Hadoop has also gained significant traction for business analytics, including Chukwa for data collection, HBase for distributed data storage, Hive for data summarization and *ad hoc* querying, and Mahout for data mining (Henschen, 2011). Stonebraker et al. (2012) compared MapReduce with the parallel DBMS. The commercial parallel DBMS showed clear advantages in efficient query processing and high-level query language and interface, whereas MapReduce excelled in ETL and analytics for "read only" semistructured data sets (Chaudhuri et al., 2011). New Hadoop- and MapReduce-based systems have become another viable option for Big Data analytics in addition to the commercial systems developed for RDBMS, column-based DBMS, in-memory DBMS, and parallel DBMS.

Big Data Management Technologies

Big Data represents data management and analytic solutions that could not previously be supported because of technology performance limitations, the high costs involved, or limited information. Big Data solutions allow organizations to build optimized systems that improve performance, reduce costs, and allow new types of data to be captured for analysis. Big Data involves two important data management technologies:

- *Analytic relational systems* that are optimized for supporting complex analytic processing against both structured and multistructured data. These systems are evolving to support not only relational data, but also other types of data structures. These systems may be offered as software-only solutions or as custom hardware/software appliances.
- *Non-relational systems* that are well suited to the processing of large amounts of multistructured data. There are many different types of nonrelational systems, including distributed file systems, document management systems, and database and analytic systems for handling complex data such as graph data.

When combined, these Big Data technologies can support the management and analysis of the many types of electronic data that exist in organizations, regardless of volume, variety, or volatility. They are used in concurrence with four advances in business analytics:

1. Latest and improved analytic techniques and algorithms that increase the sophistication of existing analytic models and results and allow the creation of new types of analytic applications.
2. Value-added data visualization techniques that make large volumes of data easier to explore and understand.
3. Analytics-powered business processes that enhance the pace of decision-making and enable close to real-time business agility.
4. Stream processing systems that filter and analyze data in action as it flows through IT systems and across IT networks.

These developments in business analytics enable users to make more precise and speedy decisions and also answer questions that were not earlier possible for economical or technology reasons. They also empower data scientists to investigate Big Data to look for new data patterns and identify new business opportunities. This investigation work is done using an independent investigative computing platform. The results from exploratory computing may lead to novel and enhanced analytic models and analyses, or innovative built-for-purpose analytic applications and systems.

Approaches to Big Data Analysis

MapReduce

MapReduce is a distributed computing engine inspired by concepts of functional languages and has become a ubiquitous tool for massive data processing. The MapReduce program consists only of two functions, called Map and Reduce that are written by a user to process key/value data pairs. The input data set is stored in a collection of partitions in a distributed file system deployed on each node in the cluster. The program is then injected into a distributed processing framework and executed in a manner to be described. The Map function reads a set of "records" from an input file, does any desired filtering or transformations, and then outputs a set of intermediate records in the form of new key/value pairs. As the Map function produces these output records, a "split" function partitions the records into R disjoint buckets by applying a function to the key of each output record. This split function is typically a hash function, though any deterministic function will suffice. Each map bucket is written to the processing node's local disk. The Map function terminates having produced R output files, one for each bucket. In general, there are multiple instances of the Map function running on different nodes of a compute cluster. We use the term instance to mean a unique running invocation of either the Map or Reduce function. Each Map instance is assigned a distinct portion of the input file by the MapReduce scheduler to process. If there are M such distinct portions of the input file, then there are R files on disk storage for each of the M Map tasks, for a total of $M \times R$ files; $F_{ij}, 1 \leq i \leq M, 1 \leq j \leq R$.

The key observation is that all Map instances use the same hash function; thus, all output records with the same hash value are stored in the same output file. The second phase of a MapReduce program executes R instances of the Reduce program, where R is typically the number of nodes. The input for each Reduce instance R_j consists of the files $F_{ij}, 1 \leq i \leq M$. These files are transferred over the network from the Map nodes' local disks. At this point, all output records from the Map phase with the same hash value are consumed by the same Reduce instance, regardless of which Map instance produced the data. Each Reduce processes or combines the records assigned to it in some way, and then writes records to an output file (in the distributed file system), which forms part of the computation's final output. The input data set exists as a collection of one or more partitions in the distributed file system. It is the job of the MapReduce scheduler to decide how many Map instances to run and how to allocate them to available nodes. Likewise, the scheduler must also decide on the number and location of nodes running Reduce instances. The MapReduce main controller is responsible for coordinating the system activities on each node. A MapReduce program finishes execution once the final result is written as new files in the distributed file system.

The typical MapReduce implementation of PageRank is quite popular. The graph is serialized as adjacency lists for each vertex, along with the current PageRank value. Mappers process all the vertices in parallel. For each vertex on the adjacency list, the mapper releases a transitional key–value pair with the destination vertex as the key and the partial PageRank contribution as the value. The shuffle stage performs a large "group by," gathering all key–value pairs with the same destination vertex, and each reducer sums up the partial PageRank contributions. Each iteration of PageRank corresponds to a MapReduce task. Running PageRank to convergence requires lots of iterations. This is handled by a control program that sets up the MapReduce task, waits for it to complete, and then checks for convergence by reading in the updated PageRank vector, and comparing it with the previous. The cycle repeats until convergence. Interestingly, the primitive structure of this algorithm can be applied to a large class of "message-passing" graph algorithms.

The key advantages of MapReduce are: the ability to horizontally scale to petabytes of data on thousands of servers, unfussy programming semantics, and a high degree of fault tolerance.

Parallel DBMSs

Database systems support standard relational tables and SQL, and thus the fact that the data are stored on multiple machines is transparent to the end-user. The two crucial aspects that enable parallel execution are that most tables are partitioned over the nodes in a cluster and that the system uses an optimizer that translates SQL commands into a query plan whose execution is divided among multiple nodes. Because programmers only need to specify their goal in a high-level language, they are not burdened by the underlying storage details, such as indexing options and join strategies.

Let us consider a SQL command to filter the records in a table T_1 based on a predicate, along with a join to a second table T_2 with an aggregate computed on the result of the join. A primary idea of how this command is processed in a parallel DBMS contains three stages. Since the database will have already stored T_1 on some collection of the nodes partitioned on some attribute, the filter subquery is first performed in parallel at these sites similar to the filtering performed in a Map function. Following this step, one of the two common parallel join algorithms is employed based on the size of data tables. Suppose, if the number of records in T_2 is small, then the DBMS could replicate it on all nodes when the data are first loaded. This allows the join to execute in parallel at all nodes. So, each node then computes the aggregate using its portion of the answer to the join. A final step is required to compute the final answer from these partial aggregates.

If the size of the data in T_2 is large, then T_2's contents will be distributed across multiple nodes. If these tables are partitioned on different attributes than those used in the join, the system will have to hash both T_2 and the filtered version of T_1 on the join attribute using a common hash function. The redistribution of both T_2 and the filtered version of T_1 to the nodes is similar to the processing that occurs between the Map and the Reduce functions. Once each node has the necessary data, it then performs a hash join and calculates the preliminary aggregate function. Again, a roll-up computation must be performed as a last step to produce the final answer.

Many complex analytical problems require the capabilities provided by both systems. This requirement motivates the need for interfaces between MapReduce systems and DBMSs that allow each system to do what it is good at. The result is a much more efficient overall system than if one tries to do the entire application in either system.

Learning from Data

The concept of learning can be termed as "to gain knowledge, or understanding, by study, instruction, or experience." Trying to understand how humans learn, researchers attempt to develop methods for accomplishing the acquisition and application of knowledge algorithmically, naming this *machine learning*. According to Mitchell's definition, "machine learning is concerned with the question how to construct computer program that automatically improve with experience" (Mitchell, 1995).

Learning can be divided into four types: rote learning (that is memorization by repetition), learning by being told, learning from examples, and learning by analogy. Learning by examples is employing *inductive inference*, in the sense that general concepts are resulting from particular examples. Inductive inference is used as a common mechanism in knowledge discovery, data mining, machine learning, statistics, etc., namely in disciplines that concern learning from data. These disciplines are not mutually exclusive, as emerges from the following well-known definitions.

Learning from data is the nontrivial process of identifying valid, novel, potentially useful, and ultimately understandable patterns in data. It can be viewed as a multidisciplinary activity that exploits artificial intelligence (machine learning, pattern recognition, knowledge-based systems, knowledge acquisition) and mathematics disciplines (statistics, theory of information, and uncertainty processing).

The *verification* of the user's hypothesis and the *discovery* of the new patterns are two goals of the learning from data process. The *Discovery* goal can further be divided into *Prediction*, where new patterns are found for the purpose of predicting the future behavior of some entities and *Description*, where patterns can be found for the purpose of presenting them to a user in an understandable form.

In the paradigm of learning from examples, one possible representation is a vector of *attributes* (features, variables) describing *examples* (instances, objects). One of the basic machine learning tasks is *classification:* to map examples into predefined groups or *classes*. This task is often referred to as *supervised* learning, because the classes are determined before examining the data. Given a training set of data and correct classes, the computational model successively applies each entry in the training set. Based on its ability to handle each of these entries correctly, the model is changed to ensure that it works better with this entry if it were applied again. Given enough input values, the model will learn the correct behavior for any potential entry. Machine learning algorithms such as decision trees, neural networks, and genetic algorithms are examples of supervised learning algorithms (Akerkar and Sajja, 2012).

In the *unsupervised* learning approach, models are built from data without predefined classes. The goal is to organize or to reduce dimensionality of the unlabelled data to obtain insights about internal data structure. Data instances are grouped together using a certain similarity metric. With the help of some evaluation methods, a decision can be made about the meaning of the formed clusters. Examples of unsupervised learning algorithms are k-means clustering and self-organizing maps.

Machine learning can also accomplish tasks that would be difficult to program explicitly due to data complexity and difficult-to-enumerate processing procedures. Big Data can come from sensors and sources of almost any and all types, from text to video, raw or organized, and many challenges associated with mining such complex aggregations of data are well suited to machine learning. The kinds of undirected association and classification tasks we want to perform to extract knowledge and meaning from the flood of Big Data are strengths of machine learning algorithms.

Decision Trees

Decision tree learning is one of the most used methods for inductive inference. It is a classification method that approximates a discrete-valued target function (Akerkar and Lingras, 2007).

Decision trees are constructed using only those attributes best able to differentiate the concepts to be learned. The selection of the attribute to be used for splitting is determined by measures as *information gain* or *gain ratio*. They measure how well a given attribute separates the training examples according to the target classification. A decision tree is built by initially selecting a subset of instances from a training set. This subset is then used by the algorithm to construct a decision tree. The remaining training set instances test the accuracy of the constructed tree. If the decision tree classifies the instances correctly, the procedure terminates. If an instance is incorrectly classified, the instance is added to the selected subset of training instances and a new tree is constructed. This process continues until a tree that correctly classifies all nonselected instances is created or the decision tree is built from the entire training set.

To improve the readability, the learned trees can be converted into sets of if-then rules. ID3 and C4.5 are among the most well-known decision-tree algorithms. The improved version of ID3, C4.5 (and its commercial version C5.0) includes methods for dealing with numeric attributes, missing values, noisy data, and generating rules from trees.

Recently, Revolution R* Enterprise 6.1 software includes "rxDTree" function, an approximate decision tree algorithm with horizontal data parallelism, that is a powerful tool for fitting classification and regression trees, which are among the most frequently used algorithms for data analysis and data mining. The implementation provided in Revolution Analytics' RevoScaleR package is parallelized, scalable, and designed with Big Data in mind. The Big Data decision trees are parallelized in different ways to enable large-scale learning. Data parallelism partitions the data either horizontally or vertically so that different processors see different observations or variables and task parallelism builds different tree nodes on different processors. With this function, one can control the balance between time complexity and prediction accuracy by specifying the maximum number of bins for the histogram. The algorithm builds the histogram with roughly equal number of observations in each bin and takes the boundaries of the bins as the candidate splits for the terminal tree nodes. Since only a limited number of split locations are examined, it is possible that a suboptimal split point is chosen causing the entire tree to be different from the one constructed by a classical algorithm.

---

* http://www.revolutionanalytics.com

Rule Induction

If-then rules are human readable representations of induced models. They may sometimes be preferable to decision trees, which can result in very complex and difficult trees. One way to obtain a more readable representation is first to learn a decision tree and second to translate the tree into a set of rules (e.g., C4.5 rules). Another alternative is to employ algorithms that directly learn sets of rules. One approach for rule induction is the *covering* approach, which at each stage identifies a rule that "covers" some of the instances. The covering approach considers each class and seeks a way of covering all instances in it, at the same time excluding instances not in the class. Algorithms for rule induction provide rules in propositional representation, or allow for more expressive rules, for example, learn rule-sets of first-order rules that contain variables.

Clustering

Clustering is considered as a method of unsupervised learning. Unlike classification, the groups are not predefined. The grouping is performed by finding similarities between data. A basic issue in clustering is to define the similarity metric for the considered data. Subsequently, clusters can be defined as follows:

- Set of alike elements. Elements from different clusters are not alike.
- The distance between points in a cluster is smaller than the distance between a point in the cluster and any point outside it.

k-means is a core algorithm for many clustering strategies that operates by calculating the Euclidean distance (in multidimensional "feature space") from every instance to each of k cluster centroids and associating the instances with the centroid to which they are nearest. Initially, the number of clusters to be sought (k) is chosen by the user (or sometimes algorithmically, when k-means is part of a more complex organizing algorithm) and the initial placement of the k centroids in feature space is chosen at random. In every iteration, after associating all instances to the closest centroid, k-means calculates a new position for the centroid based on the mean "location" of the associated instances in feature space. In due course, cluster membership and the locations of the centroids stabilize, and the iteration is complete. k-means is sensitive to initial choices of "seed" locations of the centroids and can easily settle into local minima. Finding universally optimal clusters may be very difficult. To increase the odds of success, it is common to run the algorithm multiple times with different seeds and choose the results with the least total squared distance of the instances to the centroids. Used skillfully, k-means is a powerful mechanism for exposing order in unlabelled data sets.

Figure 12.3 shows an example of k-means clustering on an artificial two-dimensional data set. The data come from two different normal distributions, one centered at (0, 0) and the other at (1, 1).

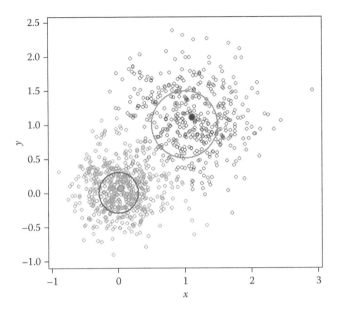

FIGURE 12.3
k-means clustering iterations.

Clustering algorithms can be categorized as hierarchical or partitional. In hierarchical clustering, a nested set of clusters is created and the number of clusters is not fixed beforehand. Hierarchical algorithms can be further categorized as agglomerative, that is, clusters are created in a bottom-up fashion, and divisive algorithms work in a top-down fashion. Hierarchical algorithms differ in the way they compute the distance between items. Well-known hierarchical algorithms are single link, complete link, and average link. Partitional clustering results into just one set of clusters, containing a fixed number of clusters.

While using *k*-means on Big Data, one has to run the algorithm several times. The RevoScaleR* package inversion4.3 has a *k*-means function called, rxKmeans, implemented as an external memory algorithm that works on a portion of data at a time. Since the *k*-means algorithm is absurdly parallel, rxKmeans reads portions of data at a time and iterates the algorithm on each portion (in parallel if multiple processors are available). Once all of the portions have been processed, the means are updated one last time to produce the final result.

Logistic Regression

Logistic regression was invented in the late 1930s by statisticians Ronald Fisher and Frank Yates. Binomial (or binary) logistic regression is a form of regression which is used when the dependent is a dichotomy and the

---

* http://www.revolutionanalytics.com/products/revolution-enterprise.php

independents are of any type. Logistic regression is a discriminative probabilistic classification model that operates over real-valued vector inputs. The dimensions of the input vectors being classified are called "features" and there is no constraint against them being correlated. Logistic regression is a popular probabilistic classifier, measured in both log loss and first-best classification accuracy across a number of tasks. Logistic regression models provide multicategory classification in cases where the categories are exhaustive and mutually exclusive. Inputs are coded as real-valued vectors of a fixed dimensionality. The dimensions are called features. There is no prerequisite that they are independent, and with regularization, they may be linearly correlated. The model comprises of parameter vectors for categories of the dimensionality of inputs. The last category does not get a parameter vector; or equivalently, it gets a constant 0 parameter vector.

If the inputs are of dimension d and there are k categories, the model consists of $k - 1$ vectors $\beta[0]$, ..., $\beta[k - 2]$. Then for a given input vector x of dimensionality k, the conditional probability of a category given the input is defined to be:

$$p(0 \mid x) \propto \exp(\beta[0]^*x)$$

$$p(1 \mid x) \propto \exp(\beta[1]^*x)$$

$$\cdots$$

$$p(k - 2 \mid x) \exp(\beta[k - 2]^*x)$$

$$p(k - 1 \mid x) \exp(0^*x)$$

Generated the probability estimates:

$$p(0 \mid x) = \exp(\beta[0]^*x)/(\exp(\beta[0]^*x) + \ldots + \exp(\beta[k - 2]^*x) + \exp(0^*x))$$

$$p(1 \mid x) = \exp(\beta[1]^*x)/(\exp(\beta[0]^*x) + \ldots + \exp(\beta[k - 2]^*x) + \exp(0^*x))$$

$$\cdots$$

$$p(k - 2 \mid x) = \exp(\beta[k - 2]^*x)/(\exp(\beta[0]^*x) + \ldots + \exp(\beta[k - 2]^*x) + \exp(0^*x))$$

$$p(k - 1 \mid x) = \exp(0^*x)/(\exp(\beta[0]^*x) + \ldots + \exp(\beta[k - 2]^*x) + \exp(0^*x))$$

Thus, for $c < k - 1$:

$$p(c \mid x) = \exp(\beta[c]^*x)/(1 + \Sigma i < k - 1 \exp(\beta[i]^*x))$$

and for $c = k - 1$:

$$p(k - 1 \mid x) = 1/(1 + \Sigma i < k - 1 \; \exp(\beta[i]^*x))$$

Logistic regression has many analogies to the linear regression; however, it does not assume linearity of relationship between the independent variables and the dependent, does not require normally distributed variables, does not assume homoscedasticity, and in general has less stringent requirements. The success of the logistic regression can be assessed by looking at the classification table, showing correct and incorrect classifications of the dependent variable. Also, goodness-of-fit tests are available as indicators of model appropriateness to test the significance of individual independent variables.

Optimization and Control

A set of methods based on constructing an optimal training set (Settles, 2011). The methods are mostly trained on an initial training set, evaluated on the unlabelled set, resulting instances with high model uncertainty are then labeled by humans, and the process is restarted. When learning feedback operators for social media, the active learner selects the set of control inputs with high model uncertainty. The controller then manipulates the inputs to the system and additional input/output data is gathered. The problem of modeling dynamic systems for learning and optimizing feedback operators for social media involves two basic design choices: choosing how to represent dynamic processes and designing experiments to estimate them. This may encompass nonlinear dynamics, delayed effects, and making decisions under uncertainty. These settings present a challenge for classical control theory that is concerned with the existence of solutions and their characteristics under specific assumptions that may not be general enough. Recently, some alternative machine learning approaches have been proposed. Some of the most prominent state-of-the-art approaches are discussed below.

Reinforcement learning is an area of machine learning that focuses on agents making actions in order to maximize cumulative reward. The methodology naturally lends itself to learning the feedback operators: the exploration corresponds to testing different feedback operators and studying their effects and exploitation corresponds to selecting optimal actions that satisfy the given constraints.

There are three important areas of study of any control system: *stability, system identification,* and *optimal control. Stability* is the study of the behavior of a system under a control scheme, to ensure it remains well-behaved. Delays in the control systems usually make a system less stable, an extensively studied area of research. *System identification* relates to understanding the effect that inputs have on the output and therefore serves as a guide to how a controller should behave in order to achieve a desired state. Gaussian processes present a rich and flexible family of stochastic processes capable of modeling highly nonlinear dynamics. Using the Bayesian *optimal control* framework, the processes also model uncertainty. Uncertainty estimates facilitate a principled way of designing experiments (e.g., selecting which feedback operators to apply). The methodology presents a new research direction in social engineering mainly in selecting sensible model priors for the problem domain.

However, there is a need to enhance available methods by modeling a nonlinear control system for analyzing and influencing social and mainstream media, incorporating delayed feedback into the system, and proposing and developing a learning framework (e.g., based on constrained reinforcement learning) with delays.

Feature Construction and Data Reduction

The role of representation has been recognized as a crucial issue in artificial intelligence and machine learning. In the paradigm of learning from examples and attribute-value representation of input data, the original representation is a vector of attributes (features, variables) describing examples (instances, objects). The transformation process of input attributes, used in feature construction, can be formulated as follows: given the original vector of features and the training set, construct a derived representation that is better given some criteria (i.e., predictive accuracy, size of representation). The new transformed attributes either replace the original attributes or can be added to the description of the examples. Examples of attribute transformations are counting, grouping, interval construction/discretization, scaling, flattening, normalization (of numerical values), clustering, principal component analysis, etc. Many transformations are possible, by applying all kinds of mathematical formulas, but in practice, only a limited number of transformations are really effective.

Machine learning is a powerful and essential class of tools for understanding Big Data: discovery of relationships and patterns in the data, predicting new outcomes based on dynamic analysis of time-series records, classifying information and inferring when a set of patterns constitutes a particular opportunity, situation, or diagnosis, adaptively learning from a "warehouse-free" real-time stream of data to almost instantly forecast future trends and detect anomalies, and more.

Examples of Analytic Technologies

Smart Cities

Cities of today are confronting massive urbanization challenges that can threaten long-term sustainability. These challenges can affect the city's economy, businesses, and people and can encompass core infrastructures such as traffic, water, energy, and communication. A "smart city" makes optimal use of all interconnected information available today to better understand and control its operations and optimize the use of limited resources. At this point, we highlight some key domains that play an important role in a city.

The basic conflict between population increase and availability of fresh water leads to increasing concerns over water quality, failing water infrastructures, and overall water management complexity. IT and analytics can help deliver solutions to numerous water-related issues that are currently handled inadequately by inefficient and often manual processes. For example, noninvasive leakage detection is possible using optimization algorithms at the network level, by detecting anomalies between modeled performance and actual sensor readings.

The idea here is to achieve desired levels of citizen protection in an urbanizing world that is becoming more interconnected, fast paced, and unpredictable. There needs to be a fundamental shift from responding to events to anticipating and preventing them when possible. These technology advances include autonomic sense and respond capabilities, analytics, visualization, and computational modeling. Data warehouses can stitch together millions of criminal complaints and national crime records along with billions of public records. Information can be visualized quickly and acted upon by those people who need it.

Congested transportation systems deter economic activity, waste energy, and emit significant amounts of carbon into the atmosphere. Traditional approaches that increase the size of the underlying infrastructure are beginning to hit a wall because it is economically and environmentally unsustainable. Smarter traffic systems take advantage of technology and collect physical data about urban traffic and mobility patterns. These data can help traffic management centers analyze and make better decisions regarding road network management, toll road practices, and public transit services.

Smart cities and Big Data are the important themes, but the insinuations of how the city is being connected, how it is generating new data, how this data might force new theories and models relevant to our understanding, how we might use our strategic models and intelligence to plan the city, building on this new understanding these are all crucial questions to be explored. For sure, Big Data is not just a passing craze or marketing hype, but it is definitely a phenomenon that has a direct impact on the quality of life for those of us that choose to live in a town or city.

Analysis of Structured and Unstructured Data to Generate Business Insights

Market demand for analytics software and integration/consulting solutions is rapidly growing. There is a strong need to handle unstructured data in segments such as Operational/Service Analytics and Marketing/Customer Analytics in domains such as Customer Relationship Management—Business Process Outsourcing (CRM BPO). Customer analytics is an analytics service to capture data from a wide variety of data sources in the enterprise, structured as well as unstructured (such as call logs and conversation transcripts). It enables business analysts to find actionable business insights in a comprehensive and time-efficient manner. The analyst analyzes various heterogeneous data sources enabled by advanced analytical capabilities such as data linking, text clustering, text annotation, sentiment mining, and predictive modeling, to come up with actionable insights regarding customer churn, first call resolution, key customer satisfaction, and dissatisfaction drivers.

The main research challenge addressed in customer analytics involves assisting the analyst in discovering and tracking various concepts and issues mentioned in the text, and detecting which concepts are key drivers of customer sentiments. For concept discovery, customer analytics provide the analyst with sophisticated text clustering algorithms that perform both word and document clustering so that no important concepts are overlooked, and a Synonym-Finder tool that helps in concept expansion by automatically suggesting synonyms from the data, making it robust with respect to noise. An ontology of concepts is maintained for future reuse and bootstrapping new analytics engagements. Concept discovery is backed up by a SentimentMiner tool that automatically segregates the discovered concepts according to sentiment, and a CorrelationMiner tool that efficiently searches the large space of textual concepts and structured dimensions to discover hidden patterns with critical business dimensions. The important concepts so identified are then used by the analyst for predictive modeling/reporting purposes. Usage of unstructured data adds significant value to business insights due to the richness of information available in such sources. The customer analytics tool minimizes the effort required by the human data miner by maximizing the quality of the data analytics workflow output.

Extracting Actionable Insights in Real Time from Massive Amounts of Data

Digital data in enterprises is growing at an unprecedented rate. Most of these data include operational cues (for instance, customer behavior, market trends, etc.) that can be a source of valuable insights for running the business more effectively and efficiently. The challenge most enterprises face is in managing and extracting such insights in a timely manner from the massive amount of accumulated historical data, coupled with the deluge of new data arriving at a high rate.

This massive scale is beyond what most database systems can handle, which has led to the development of a new breed of products that can efficiently handle high volumes of data, both at rest and in motion. IBM

Infosphere BigInsights relies on Apache Hadoop for scalability and provides a programming language and a suite of enterprise grade libraries for processing semistructured and unstructured (text) data. IBM Infosphere Streams processes data in motion, enabling sophisticated real-time analytics of the streaming data through a highly expressive programming language. Significant value can be achieved by deploying such systems at tandem—for instance, the telecommunications company can use BigInsights to analyze the historical data to learn predictive models on user behavior, which can be used to generate promotions in real time by Streams as it analyzes the streaming call records.

Even with the availability of such sophisticated analytics platforms, several challenges remain. For instance, building analytic solutions remains notoriously hard, requiring expertise in machine learning, data management, graph theory, algorithms, systems and parallel processing (for parallel/multicore deployment), which IT staff in most organizations lack. To enable adoption, rapid experimentation, and innovation, there is a need to significantly reduce the entry barrier for creating analytics applications. A promising line of future research, therefore, would be to develop declarative platforms that provide prepackaged high-level primitives that can be assembled together easily.

Social Media Analytics

Many enterprises anxious about managing their public image find that social media are these days a strong force, however one where they are no longer in control of their marketing message. Carrying out reputation management requires Big Data scales of in-depth analysis over heterogeneous streams of social media content and correlated news media, as well as real-time support with deciding upon the extremely suitable course of action and executing it within economic, resource, scheduling, and capability constraints. In order to accomplish reputation management in the social media space, strategic decisions need to be made on a real time: which social media channels are relevant to achieve a given desired effect; which comments have influence based on social network, and when should a response be made; how to customize content toward a specific social media channel; when should a new message be released to best effect and when to initiate public engagement within social media. These decisions depend on the availability of analytic insights over very large amounts of content—such as blogs, microblogs, social networks, newsgroups, discussion forums, media sharing platforms, and product review sites—that is produced and consumed at speed, in heterogeneous formats and across different sites, uses different natural languages, and is of varying quality. To offer truly valuable decision support in questions of marketing and reputation social media management solutions need to turn this complex information space into knowledge.

Recommendation Engine

Machine learning algorithms are at the heart of recommendation engines for online or mobile application companies. These companies use ratings and history of viewed items by a subscriber to learn their tastes and make recommendations. For example, by offering new movies (i.e., new means not earlier viewed by this user) that were highly rated by other users with similar tastes, the application improves the likelihood a recommended video will entertain the user. Part of the recommendation is a prediction of the rating the user will give the movie, should they choose to watch it. Usually 70–75% of the videos watched by an average user are chosen from the recommendations produced and presented by such engine. This is no doubt a strong indicator of its effectiveness.

Foursquare,[*] the mobile location-sharing app has an exceptional recommendation system. Based on your latest check-ins, places your friends found popular, and even the time of day, Foursquare will recommend a best place for eating tikka masala, or the best place to buy sofa.

Interestingly, the real test is to see whether the recommendations produced by new solution are better than those of the legacy system.

Conclusion

Integrating BI and Big Data analytics is no easy task. The goal for any data or analytical system is to make the data useful and available to as many users as possible. In order to do so, we need too powerful platforms providing both highly scalable and low cost data storage tightly integrated with scalable processing. So that businesses will be able to tackle increasingly complex problems by unlocking the power of their data. The capability to understand and act upon their data will open the door to a richer and more robust Big Data ecosystem. This requires time, patience, and innovation.

References

Akerkar, R. and Lingras, P. 2007. *Building an Intelligent Web: Theory and Practice*, Jones & Bartlett Publishers, Sudbury.

Akerkar, R. and Sajja, P. 2012. *Intelligent Technologies for Web Applications*, Taylor & Francis, USA.

---

[*] https://foursquare.com/

Chaudhuri, S., Dayal, U., and Narasayya, V. 2011. An overview of business intelligence technology, *Communications of the ACM* (54:8), 88–98.

Davenport, T. H. and Harris, J. G. 2007, *Competing on Analytics: The New Science of Winning*, Harvard Business School, Boston, MA.

Gelfand, A. 2011/2012. Privacy and biomedical research: Building a trust infrastructure—an exploration of data-driven and process-driven approaches to data privacy, *Biomedical Computation Review*, Winter, 23–28.

Henschen, D. 2011. "Why All the Hadoopla?" Information Week, November 14, pp. 19–26.

Mitchell, T. M. 1995. *Machine Learning*. McGraw-Hill, New York.

Patterson, D. A. 2008. Technical perspective: The data center is the computer, *Communications of the ACM* (51:1), 105.

Settles, B. 2011. Algorithms for active learning. In B. Krishnapuram, S. Yu, and R.B. Rao (Eds.), *Cost-Sensitive Machine Learning*. Chapman & Hall, Boca Raton, FL.

Stonebraker, M., Abadi, D., DeWitt, D. J., Madden, S., Pavlo, A., and Rasin, A. 2012. MapReduce and parallel DBMSs: Friends or foes, *Communications of the ACM* (53:1), 64–71.

van der Aalst, W. 2012. Process mining: Overview and opportunities, *ACM Transactions on Management Information Systems* (3:2), 7:1–7:17.

Witten, I. H., Frank, E., and Hall, M. 2011. *Data Mining: Practical Machine Learning Tools and Techniques*, 3rd ed., Morgan Kaufmann, San Francisco, CA.

Section V

Big Data Applications

13

Big Social Data Analysis

Erik Cambria, Dheeraj Rajagopal, Daniel Olsher, and Dipankar Das

CONTENTS

From Small to Big Social Data Analysis

As the Web rapidly evolves, Web users too are evolving with it. In an era of social connectedness, people are becoming increasingly enthusiastic about interacting, sharing, and collaborating through social networks, online communities, blogs, Wikis, and other online collaborative media. In recent years, this collective intelligence has spread to many different areas, with particular focus on fields related to everyday life such as commerce, tourism, education, and health, causing the size of the social Web to expand exponentially. The distillation of knowledge from such a large amount of unstructured information, however, is an extremely difficult task, as the contents of today's Web are perfectly suitable for human consumption, but remain hardly accessible to machines. Big social data analysis grows out of this need and it includes disciplines such as social network analysis, multimedia management, social media analytics, trend discovery, and opinion mining. The opportunity to capture the opinions of the general public about social events, political movements, company strategies, marketing campaigns, and product preferences, in particular, has raised growing interest both within the scientific community, leading to many exciting open challenges, as well as in the business world, due to the remarkable benefits to be had from marketing and financial market prediction. This has led to the emerging fields of opinion mining and sentiment analysis, which deal with information retrieval and knowledge discovery from text using data mining and natural language processing (NLP) techniques to distill knowledge and opinions from the huge amount of information on the World Wide Web. Opinion mining and sentiment analysis are branches of the broad field of text data mining [21] and refer generally to the process of extracting interesting and nontrivial patterns or knowledge from unstructured text documents. They can be viewed as an extension of data mining or knowledge discovery from (structured) databases [12,36]. As the most natural form of storing information is text, opinion mining is believed to have a commercial potential higher than that of data mining. Opinion mining, however, is also a much more complex task, as it involves dealing with text data that are inherently big, unstructured, and fuzzy.

Most of the existing approaches to opinion mining rely on the extraction of a vector representing the most salient and important text features, which is later used for classification purposes. Some of the most commonly used features are term frequency [42] and presence [33]. The latter is a binary-valued feature vectors in which the entries merely indicate whether a term occurs (value 1) or not (value 0) formed a more effective basis for reviewing polarity classification. This is indicative of an interesting difference between typical topic-based text categorization and polarity classification. While a topic is more likely to be emphasized by frequent occurrences of certain keywords, overall sentiment may not usually be highlighted through repeated use of the same terms. Other term-based features are often added to the features vector. Position is one of these, in consideration of how the position of a token in a text unit can affect the way in which the token affects the sentiment of the text. Also presence of n-grams, typically bi-grams and tri-grams, is often taken into account as useful features.

Some methods also rely on the distance between terms. Part of speech (POS) information (nouns, adjectives, adverbs, verbs, etc.) are also commonly exploited in general textual analysis as a basic form of word sense disambiguation [41]. Certain adjectives, in particular, have been proved to be good indicators of sentiment and sometimes have been used to guide feature selection for sentiment classification. In other works, eventually, the detection of sentiments was performed through selected phrases, which were chosen via a number of prespecified POS patterns, most including an adjective or an adverb [39]. All such approaches mainly rely on parts of text in which opinions and sentiments are explicitly expressed, for example, polarity terms, affect words, and their co-occurrence frequencies. Opinions and sentiments, however, are often conveyed implicitly through context- and domain-dependent concepts, which make purely syntactical approaches ineffective. To this end, novel approaches that go beyond mere word-level sentiment analysis are needed. Such approaches should employ new techniques capable of better grasping the conceptual rules that govern sentiment and the clues that can convey these concepts from realization to verbalization in the human mind. Next-generation opinion mining systems need broader and deeper common-sense knowledge bases and more cognitive and affective inspired reasoning methods, in order to better understand natural language opinions and sentiments and, hence, more efficiently bridge the gap between (unstructured) textual information and (structured) machine-processable data.

Large-Scale Sentiment Analysis and Tracking

Sentiment analysis research at large scale has mainly been performed through syntactical approaches. Godbole et al. [16] proposed a system for large-scale analysis of news and blogs built on *Lydia* [32]. Their approach involves the identification of sentiments and the subsequent assignment of orientation to them. Seven sentiment dimensions were chosen, namely *general, health, crime, sports, business, politics,* and *media*. An initial seed of sentiments is expanded using the synonym and antonym queries in two steps. During the first iteration, a preliminary score for each word is calculated using a WordNet-based depth function. During the second iteration, the number of *flips,* or apparent alternations, of words is calculated. The words that qualify above the 5-hop threshold are classified as valid sentiment words. The extracted sentiments were assigned both a polarity and a subjectivity score, which were exploited for the classification of news and blogs.

Kucuktunc et al. [24] showed that human factors affect sentiments extracted from big data. They analyzed the Yahoo! Answers Corpus, a large-scale online question and answering system, where people ask questions and the community provides relevant answers. Users can choose a category for the question and vote on answers. Corpus contained 412 M sentences with about 34 M questions and 132 M answers. Several features that affected the sentiment of answers were analyzed: textual features, for example, question length (a general observation was that negative sentiments were dominant in the longer questions), punctuation (after 3–4 question marks, the attitude and sentimentality of the sentence shows a decreasing trend), and starting words; topical and temporal features; demographical features, for example, gender (women show a general positive attitude in their answers, whereas men are mostly neutral), age (a general trend is that the sentimentality decreases with increasing age), and education level (an increased sentimentality level is observed with increasing education level).

A large-scale distributed system for Twitter sentiment analysis was built by Khuc et al. [23]. Twitter is a huge source of text data but the character limit of 140 makes it difficult to mine the sentiment data effectively. Twitter data, in fact, do not comply well with the existing NLP engines because of the increased use of nonlexical words and smileys to indicate sentiments. The primary advantage of Khuc et al.'s system is the identification of sentiments of nontrivial sentiment words such as abbreviations and extended words, for example, *lol* and *veeerrryyy goooodddd,* and emoticons. After a lexicon builder normalizes the incoming tweets, a co-occurrence matrix is created through bi-gram phrases using the MapReduce framework. The cosine similarity between words is then computed and the edges with low cosine score are removed. Finally, a sentiment score propagation algorithm is implemented and the sentiment scores are calculated. Brew et al. [2] use a crowdsourced approach to label sentiments. They ask volunteers to manually annotate RSS feeds and use these for training on a daily basis, in order to create a sentiment tag cloud. Although the approach presents very good accuracy, the scope of the work is very narrow.

The major issue with using machine-learning techniques is that a model that works well for sentiments in one domain might not work well for another. To overcome such an issue, Glorot et al. [14] proposed a deep learning approach that trains a classifier in one domain and successfully applies it to another. This method is called *domain adaptation*. The intuition behind using the intermediate concepts is that these better guide the semantic and affective transfer among domains. The approach works at two levels. Firstly, an unsupervised classifier learns higher-level features from Amazon reviews in all available domains. Secondly, a linear SVM with squared hinge loss is used for the training phase on the labeled data from the source domain and tested on the target domain.

A task that immediately derives from large-scale sentiment analysis is big sentiment data tracking, that is, the aggregation of all the scattered emotional information related to a specific topic through the delivery of an at-a-glance presentation of the main sentiment topics or a graphical visualization of how sentiment changes from time to time over multiple events. To this end, related sentiment components need to be gathered and associated in a structured way, so that the affective information is tractable with respect to user, topic/event, sentiment, and time. In many applications, analysts and other users are interested in tracking changes in sentiment about a product, political candidate, company, or other issues, over time.

Early work proposed to detect and track events from text archives [40]. Such events were extracted from different newspaper texts, stories, and other important documents, where occurrence time of events, temporal location, and ordering of the events were specified. The event–sentiment association highlights the fact that, though events and sentiments are closely coupled with each other from social, psychological, and commercial perspectives, there has been very little attention regarding their detection. The identification of the temporal relations between two events by taking the sentiment feature into account is also crucial in analyzing and tracking human sentiments. This is also important in a wide range of other NLP applications that include temporal question answering, document summarization, current information retrieval systems, etc.

Later studies focused on temporal sentiment identification from social events. Fukuhara et al. [13] analyzed the temporal trends of sentiments and topics from a text archive that provided timestamps in weblogs and news

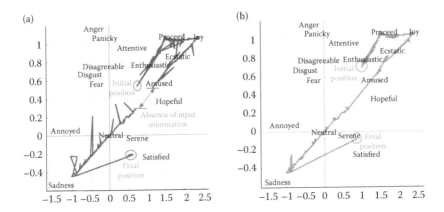

FIGURE 13.1

Ensemble sentiment streams obtained when fusing natural language data and facial expressions, without (a) and with (b) Kalman filtering.

articles. The system produces two kinds of graphs: topic graph, which shows the temporal change of topics associated with a sentiment, and sentiment graph, which shows temporal change of sentiments associated with a topic. Mishne and de Rijke [28] proposed MoodViews, a system for the analysis of sentiment temporal changes based on LiveJournal mood tags. Similarly, Havre et al. [20] proposed ThemeRiver, a tool for visualizing thematic flows along with a timeline.

In the context of multimodal sentiment analysis, finally, Cambria et al. [3] proposed a scalable methodology for fusing multiple cognitive and affective recognition modules in real time. Such a methodology is able to fuse any number of unimodal categorical modules, with very different time-scales and output labels. This is possible thanks to the use of a multidimensional vector space that provides the system with mathematical capabilities to deal with temporal issues. The proposed methodology outputs a continuous multidimensional stream that represents the user's cognitive and affective progress over time in a novel and efficient way (Figure 13.1). A Kalman filtering technique controls the ensemble stream in real time to ensure temporal consistency and robustness. In particular, the methodology has been shown effective to fuse two different modalities: natural language data and facial expressions. In general, evaluation issues are largely solved for categorical recognition approaches. Unimodal categorical modules can be exhaustively evaluated, thanks to the use of large well-annotated databases and well-known measures and methodologies (such as percentage of correctly classified instances, cross-validation, etc.). The evaluation of the performance of dimensional approaches is, however, an open and difficult issue to be solved. To this end, future works are expected to focus in depth on evaluation issues applicable to dimensional approaches and multimodality.

Toward the Concept-Level Analysis of Big Sentiment Data

Standard approaches to opinion mining can be classified into three main categories: keyword spotting, lexical affinity, and statistical methods. All such approaches mainly rely on specific affect words that need to be explicitly used in the opinionated text. Hence, when emotions are conveyed implicitly, standard approaches are unable to correctly mine opinions and sentiments. More recent approaches to sentiment analysis, for example, the energy-based knowledge representation formalism [30] and sentic computing [4], in turn, work at concept-level in which they exploit semantic networks that allow one to take into account the conceptual and affective information implicitly conveyed by natural language concepts.

Although scientific research in the area of emotion stretches back to the nineteenth century when Charles Darwin and William James proposed theories of emotion that continue to influence thinking today [8,22], the injection of affect into computer technologies is much more recent. During most of the last century, research on emotions was conducted by philosophers and psychologists, whose work was based on a small set of emotion theories that continue to underpin research in this area. The first researchers to try linking text to emotions were actually social psychologists and anthropologists who tried to find similarities on how people from different cultures communicate [31]. This research was also triggered by dissatisfaction with the dominant cognitive view centered around humans as 'information processors' [26]. Later on, in the 1980s, researchers such as Turkle [38] began to speculate about how computers might be used to study emotions. Systematic research programs in this front began to emerge in the early 1990s. For example, Scherer [35] implemented a computational model of emotion as an expert system. A few years later, Picard's landmark book affective computing [34] prompted a wave of interest among computer scientists and engineers looking for ways to improve human–computer interfaces by coordinating emotions and cognition with task constraints and demands.

Affect detection is critical because an affect-sensitive interface can never respond to users' affective states if it cannot sense their affective states. Affect detection need not be perfect but must be approximately on target. Affect detection is, however, a very challenging problem because emotions are constructs (i.e., conceptual quantities that cannot be directly measured) with fuzzy boundaries and with substantial individual difference variations in expression and experience. To overcome such an issue, sentic computing[*] builds upon a brain-inspired and psychologically motivated affective categorization model [5] that can potentially describe the full range of emotional experiences in terms of four independent but concomitant dimensions, whose different levels of activation make up the total emotional state of the mind

---

[*] http://sentic.net/sentics

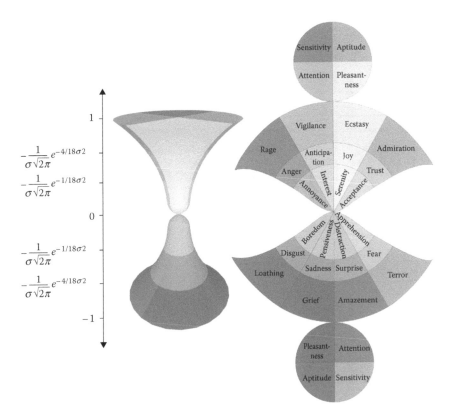

FIGURE 13.2
The hourglass of emotions.

(Figure 13.2). In sentic computing, whose term derives from the Latin *sentire* (root of words such as sentiment and sentience) and *sensus* (intended both as capability of feeling and as common-sense), the analysis of natural language is based on affective ontologies and common-sense reasoning tools, which enable the analysis of text not only at document-, page-, or paragraph-level, but also at sentence- and clause-level. In particular, sentic computing involves the use of AI and Semantic Web techniques, for knowledge representation and inference; mathematics, for carrying out tasks such as graph mining and multi-dimensionality reduction; linguistics, for discourse analysis and pragmatics; psychology, for cognitive and affective modeling; sociology, for understanding social network dynamics and social influence; finally ethics, for understanding related issues about the nature of mind and the creation of emotional machines.

In order to effectively mine and analyze opinions and sentiments, it is necessary to bridge the gap between unstructured natural language data and structured machine-processable data. To this end, an intelligent software engine has been proposed, within the umbrella of sentic computing, to

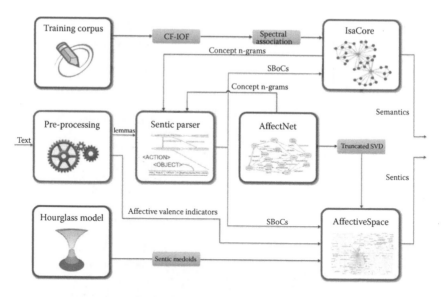

FIGURE 13.3
Opinion mining engine block diagram. After performing a first skim of the input text, the engine extracts concepts from it and, hence, infers related semantics and sentics.

extract the semantics and sentics (i.e., the conceptual and affective information) associated with natural language text, in a way that the opinions and sentiments in it contained can be more easily aggregated and interpreted. The engine exploits graph mining and multi-dimensionality reduction techniques on IsaCore [7] and AffectNet [4], respectively (Figure 13.3). Several other affect recognition and sentiment analysis systems [1,9–11,25,27,37] are based on different emotion categorization models, which generally comprise a relatively small set of categories (Table 13.1). The Hourglass of Emotions, in turn, allows the opinion-mining engine to classify affective information both in a categorical way (according to a wider number of emotion categories) and in a dimensional format (which facilitates comparison and aggregation).

The opinion-mining engine consists of four main components: a preprocessing module, which performs a first skim of the opinion; the sentic parser, whose aim is to extract concepts from the opinionated text; the IsaCore module, for inferring the semantics associated with the given concepts; the AffectiveSpace module, for the extraction of sentics.

The pre-processing module first exploits linguistic dictionaries to interpret all the affective valence indicators usually contained in opinionated text, for example, special punctuation, complete upper-case words, cross-linguistic onomatopoeias, exclamation words, degree adverbs, and emoticons. Second, the module detects negation and spreads it in such a way that it can be accordingly associated to concepts during the parsing phase. Handling

TABLE 13.1

An Overview of Recent Model-Based Sentiment Analysis Systems

Study	Techniques	Model	Corpora	Knowledge Base
[25]	NB, SVM	2 categories	Political articles	None
[10]	LSA, MLP, NB, KNN	3 categories	Dialog turns	ITS interaction
[11]	Cohesion indices	4 categories	Dialog logs	ITS interaction
[9]	VSM, NB, SVM	5 categories	ISEAR	ConceptNet
[37]	WN presence, LSA	6 categories	News stories	WNA
[27]	WN presence	6 categories	Chat logs	WNA
[1]	Winnow linear, C4.5	7 categories	Children stories	None
[15]	VSM, *k*-means	24 categories	YouTube, LiveJournal	ConceptNet, WNA, HEO
[6]	VSM, neural networks	24 categories	PatientOpinion	ConceptNet, WNA
[7]	VSM, *k*-medoids, LDA	24 categories	Twitter, LiveJournal, PatientOpinion	ConceptNet, Probase

Note: Studies are divided by techniques applied, number of categories of the model adopted, corpora, and knowledge base used.

negation is an important concern in opinion- and sentiment-related analysis, as it can reverse the meaning of a statement. Such task, however, is not trivial as not all appearances of explicit negation terms reverse the polarity of the enclosing sentence and that negation can often be expressed in rather subtle ways, for example, sarcasm and irony, which are quite difficult to detect. Lastly, the module converts text to lower-case and, after lemmatizing it, splits the opinion into single clauses according to grammatical conjunctions and punctuation.

For parsing text, a modified version of COGPARSE [29] is exploited for quickly identifying meaningful stretches of text without requiring time-consuming phrase structure analysis. The use of *constructions*, defined as "stored pairings of form and function" [17], makes it possible to link distributed linguistic components to one another, easing extraction of semantics from linguistic structures. Constructions are composed of fixed lexical items and category-based *slots*, or "spaces" that are filled in by lexical items during text processing. An interesting example from the relevant literature would be the construction [<ACTION> <OBJECT> <DIRECTION> <OBJECT>], instances of which include "sneeze the napkin across the table" or "hit the ball over the fence." Constructions help us understand not only how various lexical items work together to create overall meanings, but also give the parser a sense of what categories of words are used together and thus which words to expect where. The sentic parser uses this knowledge to determine which constructions are matched by which lexical items and how good each match is. Each sentic parser's construction contributes its own unique semantics and carries a unique name. The sentic parser uses knowledge about the lexical items found in text to choose the best possible construction for each span of text. Specifically, the parser looks each lexical item up in AffectNet and IsaCore, obtaining information about the basic category membership of that word. It then efficiently compares these potential memberships with the categories specified for each construction in the Corpus, finding the best matches so that, for example, the parser can extract a concept such as "buy christmas present" from a sentence such as "today I bought a lot of very nice Christmas bells." Constructions are typically *nested* within one another: the sentic parser is capable of finding only those construction overlaps that are semantically sensible based on the overall semantics of constructions and construction slot categories, thus greatly reducing the time taken to process large numbers of texts. In the Big Data environment, a key benefit of construction-based parsing is that only small regions of correct text are required in order to extract meaning; word category information, and the generally small size of constructions mean that use can still be made of error-filled or otherwise normally unparseable texts. Texts do not have to have correct sentence-wide phrase structure in order to be parsed.

Additionally, the sentic parser provides, for each retrieved concept, its relative frequency, valence, and status, that is, the concept's occurrence in the text, its positive or negative connotation, and the degree of intensity with which the concept is expressed, respectively. For each clause, the module outputs a small bag of concepts (SBoC), which is later on analyzed separately by the IsaCore and AffectiveSpace modules to infer the conceptual and affective information associated with the input text, respectively. In case any of the detected concepts is found more than once in the vector space (i.e., any of the concepts has multiple senses), all the SBoC concepts are exploited for a context-dependent coarse sense disambiguation. In particular, to represent the expected semantic value of the clause as a whole, the vectors corresponding to all concepts in the clause (in their ambiguous form) can be averaged together. The resulting vector does not represent a single meaning but the *"ad hoc* category" of meanings that are similar to the various possible meanings of concepts in the clause [19]. Then, to assign the correct sense to the ambiguous concept, the concept sense with the highest dot product (and thus the strongest similarity) with the clause vector is searched.

Once natural language text is deconstructed into concepts, these are given as input to both the Isacore and the AffectiveSpace modules. While the former exploits the graph representation of the common and common-sense knowledge base to detect semantics, the latter exploits the vector space representation of AffectNet to infer sentics. In particular, the IsaCore module applies spectral association for assigning activation to key nodes of the semantic network, which are used as seeds or centroids for classification. Such seeds can simply be the concepts corresponding to the class labels of interest plus their available synonyms and antonyms, if any. Seeds can also be found by applying CF-IOF [4] on a training corpus (when available), in order to perform a classification that is more relevant to the data under analysis. After seed concepts are identified, the module spreads their values across the IsaCore graph. This operation, an approximation of many steps of spreading activation, transfers the most activation to concepts that are connected to the seed concepts by short paths or many different paths in affective common-sense knowledge. Therefore, the concepts of each SBoC provided by the sentic parser are projected on the matrix resulting from spectral association in order to calculate their semantic relatedness to each seed concept and, hence, their degree of belonging to each different class. Such classification measure is directly proportional to the degree of connectivity between the nodes representing the retrieved concepts and the seed concepts in the IsaCore graph.

The concepts retrieved by the sentic parser are also given as input to the AffectiveSpace module, which, in turn, exploits dimensionality reduction techniques to infer the affective information associated with them. To this end, the concepts of each SBoC are projected into AffectiveSpace and, according to their position in the vector space representation of affective common-sense knowledge, they are assigned to an affective class defined through the sentic medoids technique [3]. As well as in the IsaCore module, the categorization does not consist in simply labeling each concept, but also in assigning a confidence score to each emotional label, which is directly proportional to the degree of belonging to a specific affective cluster (dot product between the given concept and the relative sentic medoid). Such affective information can also be exploited to calculate a polarity value associated with each SBoC provided by the sentic parser, as well as to detect the overall polarity associated with the opinionated text.

In order for the engine to perform fast real-time opinion mining, the sentic vector associated with each AffectNet concept can be calculated *a priori* and saved in an SQL database. At runtime, then, the sentic vectors relative to each of the concepts composing the SBoC can be retrieved from such a database and aggregated to compute the overall affective information associated with the specific SBoC. This allows the sentic extraction process to be faster than directly applying the AffectiveSpace process. Similarly, spectral association can be computed *a priori* on IsaCore and the semantic classification of each concept (i.e., a set of different topic labels and the confidence associated with these) can be stored in an SQL database. On average, in fact, while the processing of a 100-word opinion is in the order of tens of seconds when directly applying the AffectiveSpace and IsaCore processes, the extraction of semantics and sentics is in the order of seconds when using the corresponding SQL databases. Both resources are in the order of hundreds of megabytes and, hence, easily exportable and embeddable into bigger systems for the development of applications in fields such as social media marketing, human–computer interaction, and e-health [4].

Conclusion

As society evolves at the same pace of the Web, online social data are becoming increasingly important for both individuals and businesses. The Web 2.0, however, has unleashed an era of online participation that is causing user-generated contents to grow exponentially and, hence, to become continuously larger and more complex. In order to reduce such complexity, we need to adopt a multidisciplinary approach to big social data analysis, which combines different perspectives by means of social media analytics, trend discovery, multimedia management, social network analysis, opinion mining, and more. Specifically, in order to translate mere collected intelligence into true collective intelligence [18], we need to aim for a concept-level analysis of online social data that can enable the aggregation of the semantics and sentics associated with text. Next-generation opinion mining systems, thus, need broader and deeper affective commonsense knowledge bases, coupled with more brain-inspired and psychologically motivated reasoning models, in order to better understand natural language opinions through more efficiently bridging the gap between (unstructured) human-processable information and (structured) machine-processable data.

References

1. C. Alm, D. Roth, and R. Sproat. Emotions from text: Machine learning for text-based emotion prediction. In *HLT/EMNLP*, pp. 347–354, Vancouver, 2005.
2. A. Brew, D. Greene, and P. Cunningham. Using crowdsourcing and active learning to track sentiment in online media. In *ECAI*, pp. 145–150, Lisbon, 2010.
3. E. Cambria, N. Howard, J. Hsu, and A. Hussain. Sentic blending: Scalable multimodal fusion for the continuous interpretation of semantics and sentics. In *IEEE SSCI*, pp. 108–117, Singapore, 2013.
4. E. Cambria and A. Hussain. *Sentic Computing: Techniques, Tools, and Applications*. Springer, Dordrecht, the Netherlands, 2012.
5. E. Cambria, A. Livingstone, and A. Hussain. The hourglass of emotions. In A. Esposito, A. Vinciarelli, R. Hoffmann, and V. Muller, editors, *Cognitive Behavioral Systems*, volume 7403 of *Lecture Notes in Computer Science*, pp. 144–157. Springer, Berlin, 2012.
6. E. Cambria, T. Mazzocco, and A. Hussain. Application of multi-dimensional scaling and artificial neural networks for biologically inspired opinion mining. *Biologically Inspired Cognitive Architectures*, 4:41–53, 2013
7. E. Cambria, Y. Song, H. Wang, and N. Howard. Semantic multi-dimensional scaling for open-domain sentiment analysis. *IEEE Intelligent Systems*, DOI 10.1109/MIS.2012.118, 2013.

8. C. Darwin. *The Expression of the Emotions in Man and Animals.* John Murray, London, 1872.

9. T. Danisman and A. Alpkocak. Feeler: Emotion classification of text using vector space model. In *AISB*, Aberdeen, 2008.

10. S. D'Mello, S. Craig, J. Sullins, and A. Graesser. Predicting affective states expressed through an emote-aloud procedure from autotutor's mixed-initiative dialogue. *International Journal of Artificial Intelligence in Education*, 16:3–28, 2006.

11. S. D'Mello, N. Dowell, and A. Graesser. Cohesion relationships in tutorial dialogue as predictors of affective states. In *Conf. Artificial Intelligence in Education*, pp. 9–16, Brighton, 2009.

12. U. Fayyad, G. Piatetsky, and P. Smyth. From data mining to knowledge discovery: An overview. In *Advances in Knowledge Discovery and Data Mining*, U. Fayyad, G. Piatetsky-Shapiro, P. Smyth, and R. Uthurusamy, eds. pp. 1–36. MIT Press, Cambridge, 1996.

13. T. Fukuhara, H. Nakagawa, and T. Nishida. Understanding sentiment of people from news articles: Temporal sentiment analysis of social events. In *ICWSM*, Boulder, 2007.

14. X. Glorot, A. Bordes, and Y. Bengio. Domain adaptation for large-scale sentiment classification: A deep learning approach. In *ICML*, Bellevue, 2011.

15. M. Grassi, E. Cambria, A. Hussain, and F. Piazza. Sentic web: A new paradigm for managing social media affective information. *Cognitive Computation*, 3(3):480–489, 2011.

16. N. Godbole, M. Srinivasaiah, and S. Skiena. Large-scale sentiment analysis for news and blogs. In *ICWSM*, Boulder, 2007.

17. A. Goldberg. Constructions: A new theoretical approach to language. *Trends in Cognitive Sciences*, 7(5):219–224, 2003.

18. T. Gruber. Collective knowledge systems: Where the social web meets the semantic web. *Web Semantics: Science, Services and Agents on the World Wide Web*, 6(1):4–13, 2007.

19. C. Havasi, R. Speer, and J. Pustejovsky. Coarse word-sense disambiguation using common sense. In *AAAI CSK*, Arlington, 2010.

20. S. Havre, E. Hetzler, P. Whitney, and L. Nowell. Themeriver: Visualizing thematic changes in large document collections. *IEEE Transactions on Visualization and Computer Graphics*, 8(1):9–20, 2002.

21. M. Hearst. Text data mining: Issues, techniques, and the relationship to information access. In *UW/MS Workshop on Data Mining*, Berkeley, 1997.

22. W. James. What is an emotion? *Mind*, 34:188–205, 1884.

23. V. Khuc, C. Shivade, R. Ramnath, and J. Ramanathan. Towards building large-scale distributed systems for twitter sentiment analysis. In *ACM Symposium on Applied Computing*, pp. 459–464, Riva del Garda, 2012.

24. O. Kucuktunc, B. Cambazoglu, I. Weber, and H. Ferhatosmanoglu. A large-scale sentiment analysis for Yahoo! answers. In *ACM International Conference on Web Search and Data Mining*, pp. 633–642, Seattle, 2012.

25. W. Lin, T. Wilson, J. Wiebe, and A. Hauptmann. Which side are you on? Identifying perspectives at the document and sentence levels. In *Conference on Natural Language Learning*, pp. 109–116, Boston, 2006.

26. C. Lutz and G. White. The anthropology of emotions. *Annual Review of Anthropology*, 15:405–436, 1986.

27. C. Ma, A. Osherenko, H. Prendinger, and M. Ishizuka. A chat system based on emotion estimation from text and embodied conversational messengers. In *International Conference on Active Media Technology*, pp. 546–548, Kagawa, 2005.

28. G. Mishne and M. de Rijke. Capturing global mood levels using blog posts. In *AAAI*, pp. 145–152, Boston, 2006.

29. D. Olsher. COGPARSE: Brain-inspired knowledge-driven full semantics parsing. In *Advances in Brain Inspired Cognitive Systems, Volume of 7366 Lecture Notes in Computer Science*, pp. 1–11, 2012.

30. D. Olsher. Full spectrum opinion mining: Integrating domain, syntactic and lexical knowledge. In *ICDM*, Brussels, 2012.

31. C. Osgood, W. May, and M. Miron. *Cross-Cultural Universals of Affective Meaning*. University of Illinois Press, Brussels, pp. 693–700, 1975.

32. B. Pang and L. Lee. Opinion mining and sentiment analysis. *Foundations and Trends in Information Retrieval*, 2:1–135, 2008.

33. B. Pang, L. Lee, and S. Vaithyanathan. Thumbs up? Sentiment classification using machine learning techniques. In *EMNLP*, pp. 79–86, Philadelphia, 2002.

34. R. Picard. *Affective Computing*. The MIT Press, Boston, 1997.

35. K. Scherer. Studying the emotion-antecedent appraisal process: An expert system approach. *Cognition and Emotion*, 7:325–355, 1993.

36. E. Simoudis. Reality check for data mining. *IEEE Expert*, 11(5), 1996.

37. C. Strapparava and R. Mihalcea. Learning to identify emotions in text. In *ACM Symp. Applied Computing*, pp. 1556–1560, Fortaleza, 2008.

38. S. Turkle. *The Second Self: Computers and the Human Spirit*. Simon & Schuster, New York, 1984.

39. P. Turney. Thumbs up or thumbs down? Semantic orientation applied to unsupervised classification of reviews. In *ACL*, pp. 417–424, Philadelphia, 2002.

40. C. Wayne. Multilingual topic detection and tracking: Successful research enabled by corpora and evaluation. In *LREC*, pp. 1487–1494, Athens, 2000.

41. Y. Wilks and M. Stevenson. The grammar of sense: Using part-of-speech tags as a first step in semantic disambiguation. *Journal of Natural Language Engineering*, 4(2):135–143, 1998.

42. H. Wu, R. Luk, K. Wong, and K. Kwok. Interpreting TF-IDF term weights as making relevance decisions. *ACM Transactions on Information Systems*, 26(3), Article 13, 2008.

14

Real-Time Big Data Processing for Domain Experts: An Application to Smart Buildings

Dario Bonino, Fulvio Corno, and Luigi De Russis

CONTENTS

After nearly 10 years of Ambient Intelligence research (see [8] for an overview), smart environments, and, in particular, smart buildings are slowly becoming a reality, with installations starting to spread all around the world. Smart offices, smart factories, and smart housing, especially social housing, are nowadays giving a new impulse to AmI research, with new needs and issues to tackle. Among the several problematics stemming from such a wide deployment of these technologies, Big Data issues are currently gaining a new momentum: while installations grow and start covering large-scale settings with hundreds or thousands of installed sensors and actuators, data granularity, frequency, scalability, and cardinality issues are increasingly attracting research efforts. In prototypical environments, these issues were usually neglected or tackled with custom data sampling and representation. In real-world large settings, instead, standard, fast, and effective solutions shall be designed, enabling modularity, reusability, and easy adaptation to the different installation features.

Big Data research is already facing similar issues, aiming at effectively handling, processing, and delivering high-cardinality and/or high-through-put streams of data stemming from several sources, be they blogs, tweets, Internet sensors, or measures extracted from a smart building. Smart build-ings, in effect, are a highly demanding test environment for Big Data tech-nologies as almost all of the most important issues are present. In a smart building, say a smart factory, data are typically delivered at high rates, with single event delivery at intervals often much lower than a second. Data gran-ularity is diverse, as sensors on the field operate on different time frames, for example, process control sensors work on milliseconds time scales, whereas energy metering usually operates on a minute or hour scale. On the one hand, such diversity shall be preserved, as fine-grained events are needed to identify anomalous situations or to perform short-term adaptation and/or forecasting. On the other hand, this great amount of data is seldom of inter-est for the high-level processes driving smart-building operations, and effec-tive data aggregation and summarization shall be performed, accounting for the inherently temporal nature of involved events. Finally, data cardinality is usually high as building, office, or factory-level automation (or "smartness") involves hundreds or thousands of sensors deployed in possibly different locations, ranging from multiple buildings to distributed factories.

These issues can actually be addressed by exploiting some of the current Big Data solutions, in particular, by exploiting the so-called complex event processing (CEP) theory [1,10,12,15] and the related solutions. Initially studied and developed in the context of Business Process Management and Operations Research [14,23], CEP offers reliable, fast, and cost-effective solutions for handling high-throughput and high-granularity data streams. Nowadays engines [9,17], in fact, can effectively handle data at rates ranging from 1000 to over 100,000 events per second, by relying on a number of techniques involv-ing event-pattern detection, event abstraction, event hierarchies, etc.

CEP application in the smart-building domain, however, is still confined to a niche of stream-processing experts as quite in-depth knowledge of the inner processing mechanisms and engines (see [13,22] to get a glimpse of required skills) is required to effectively set-up usable monitoring and pro-cessing functions.

While easily responding to data elaboration issues, at multiple granular-ity levels (single event and aggregation), current CEP engines are difficult to adopt in smart buildings, as AmI designers, process engineers, asset, and energy managers, the technical staff who continuously monitor and tune-up the environment performance, are usually not able to directly use CEP syntaxes for defining data aggregation and delivery. Moreover, direct writing of customized CEP queries (e.g., in STREAM [12]) is seldom suited for industrial or large-scale settings where the ability to reuse validated processes is a key factor to cost reduction.

This chapter summarizes and contextualizes around 1 year of research activities [3,4] in this field, by introducing the *spChains* Big Data elaboration framework and by discussing its applicability and effectiveness in the smart-building application domain. *spChains* is specifically designed to tackle two main data-processing issues emerging from the smart-building domain: (a) decoupling low-level CEP query writing from high-level definition of monitoring processes, which shall be accessible to teams having reduced knowledge of CEP systems; (b) providing a modular approach to query definition, reducing the efforts needed to write common, often reused, processing functions while maintaining almost unchanged the event processing performance typical of direct CEP operation.

To satisfy these apparently contrasting goals, *spChains* represents monitoring (and alerting) tasks in form of reusable and modular *processing chains* built atop of a set of standard, and extensible, *stream processing blocks*. Each block encapsulates a single (parametrized and optimized) stream query, for example, windowed average or threshold checking, and can be cascaded to other blocks to obtain complex elaboration chains, using a pipes-and-filter [11] composition pattern. Stream processing blocks are defined in an extensible library and designed to be application-independent; the library components cover a relevant set of elaborations emerging from typical smart-building applications, with a particular focus on energy monitoring. They can readily be reused in almost any processing task. On the converse, chains (i.e., Direct Acyclic Graphs of processing blocks) must be designed according to the specific monitoring needs, composing the available blocks, and extending the base block library when needed.

Basic Principles and Terminology

For the sake of clarity, we report a short overview of basic principles and domain-specific terminology used throughout the chapter. Experienced readers may directly refer to section "Block-Based Stream Processing" for gaining insights into the framework approach to Big Data issues.

Pipes-and-Filters Pattern

Pipes and filters is a widely adopted design pattern involving the application of a set of transformations to a stream of data. Firstly described in [6], it divides

FIGURE 14.1
The pipes-and-filter design pattern.

a large processing task into a sequence of smaller, independent processing steps (filters) connected by channels (pipes). Each filter exposes a very simple interface: it receives messages on the inbound pipes, processes the message, and publishes the results to the outbound pipes (Figure 14.1). The pipe connects two filters sending messages from one filter output to the next filter input. Because all filters use the same external interface, they can be composed into different solutions by connecting the filter components to different pipes. A well-known implementation of this pattern is the Unix operating system's support for the pipe operator "|" which connects processes that read data from the standard input stream and write results to the standard output stream.

Complex Event Processing

According to Luckham [15], CEP is a set of tools and techniques for analyzing and controlling the complex series of interrelated events that drive modern distributed information systems. CEP consists of a mix of old and new techniques: rule-based systems, tracking causal histories of events in large distributed computer systems, use of patterns of events, and event relationships, to recognize the presence of complex events from hundreds or thousands of simpler events.

Events, Queries, and Time Windows

CEP typically deals with *event stream* processing. An event stream is a possibly infinite temporal sequence of discrete events. Events can be raw measures or complex objects carrying contextual information identifying the data origin, its unit of measure, and other information useful to discriminate and further process the event data. In the *spChains* framework, events are defined as data structures (objects) carrying a simple numeric payload, either a real number with a unit of measure expressed according to the "Unified Code for Units of Measure" (UCUM) [20], or a Boolean value, and they are marked with a time stamp value reporting the time instant during which they have been generated (Figure 14.2).

The CEP system applies complex computations, for example, event-pattern matching, time-dependent operators, etc., on the live feed of events and produces new event streams, usually by aggregating low-level data into more meaningful/usable information. CEP operators, that is, queries (Figure 14.3), can either involve single events, by applying numerical transformations

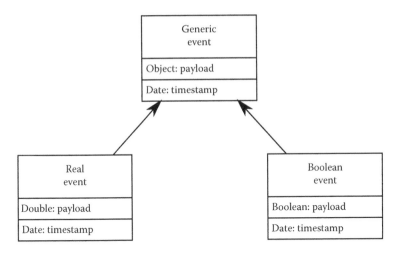

FIGURE 14.2
Basic structure of the *spChains* events.

(e.g., scaling or thresholding), or multiple events gathered in the so-called time windows.

Each time window is an interval that starts with the occurrence of an event that satisfies some predicates and terminates with an occurrence of another event that satisfies a predicate, or when a given period has elapsed [10]. Following paragraphs better detail the two most important variants of time windows: *sliding* or *moving* windows and *batch* windows.

```
Over ConsumptionQuery: Samples data from a given power meter M1 averaging measures over
one hour and compares it to a reference value, e.g. 1kW. If the computed average execeeds the
given threshold, a new (Boolean) event is generated, signalling a possible alert condition.

insert into RealEvent(src, streamName, value,unitOfMeasure)
select ''Average'', ''Average-out'', avg(value) as value,
unitOfMeasure
from realEvent (streamName=''M1'').win:time\_batch(''1h'')
group by src, streamName, unitOfMeasure;

insert into BooleanEvent(src, streamName, booleanValue)
select ''Threshold'', ''Threshold-out'' as streamName, true as value
from pattern
[every (oldSample=RealEvent(streamName=''Average-out'',
MeasureEventComparator.compareToMeasure(oldSample,''1kW'',
EventComparisonEnum.LESS_THAN_OR_EQUAL))
->
newSample=RealEvent(streamName=oldSample.streamName,
MeasureEventComparator.compareToMeasure(newSample,''1kW'',
EventComparisonEnum.GREATER_THAN)))
].win:length(2);
```

FIGURE 14.3
A sample CEP query (in EPL).

Moving Window

A *moving window* (or *sliding window*) is a time period that stretches back in time from the present. For instance, a moving window of two minutes includes any events that have occurred in the past two minutes. Moving windows enable to limit the number of events considered by a processing block, usually with the purpose of aggregating event information or detecting specific event patterns. Figure 14.4 illustrates the typical behavior of a moving window.

The diagram starts at a given time t and displays the contents of the window at $t + 4$ and $t + 5$ s and so on. The activity as illustrated by the diagram is as follows:

1. At time $t + 4$ s, an event W1 arrives and enters the moving window.
2. At time $t + 5$ s, an event W2 arrives and enters the moving window.
3. At time $t + 6.5$ s, an event W3 arrives and enters the moving window.
4. At time $t + 8$ s, the event W1 leaves the time window.

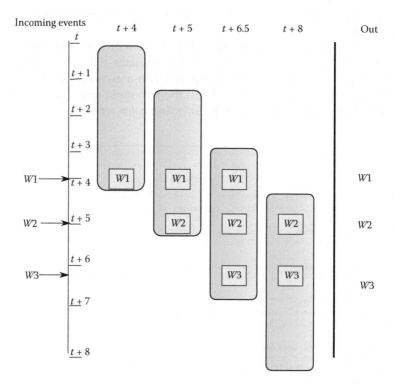

FIGURE 14.4
Sliding window.

Batch Window

The *batch window* buffers events and releases them every specified time interval in one update. Batch windows are opened at regular intervals. These windows are not tied to a particular time of the day; instead, each window is opened at a specified time after its predecessor. Each window has a fixed size, specified either as a time interval or a count of event instances [10]. Figure 14.5 illustrates the typical behavior of a batch window.

The diagram starts at a given time t and displays the contents of the time window at $t + 3$ and $t + 4$ s and onwards. The activity as illustrated by the diagram is as follows:

1. At time $t + 1$ s, an event W1 arrives and enters the batch.
2. At time $t + 3$ s, an event W2 arrives and enters the batch.
3. At time $t + 4$ s, the batch window ends and a new batch is started.
4. At time $t + 6.5$ s, an event W3 arrives and enters the batch.
5. At time $t + 8$ s, the batch window ends and a new batch is started.

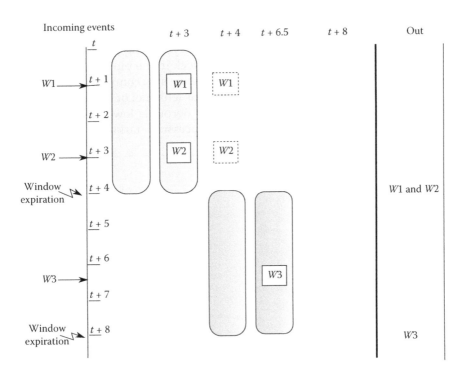

FIGURE 14.5
Batch window.

Block-Based Stream Processing

Typical CEP queries manipulate information packed into *event streams*: whatever operator is applied, be it simple aggregation (e.g., a temporal average), pattern matching (e.g., selecting all the events that are preceded by a sequence of three events with ascending values), or complex stream join, input and output are both represented as streams. When queries involve more than one CEP operator, many intermediate streams might be generated, as such queries are usually organized into subqueries, each applying a partial elaboration on the original stream data (or on partially elaborated streams) and generating a new event stream processed by subsequent subqueries. Figures 14.6 through 14.8 report the *Source Monitoring Query* defined in the ATLaS example pages[*] (adopted to check the 10-min exponentially decaying average of the number of packets from a set of source hosts, on a per-minute basis), respectively, using the ATLaS, CQL, and EPL query languages, and highlights the different subqueries using a double-dash (–) notation.

In all the previous cases (Figures 14.6 through 14.8), subquery organization of complex CEP processing is evident, and it actually results in a shared feature between most of the currently available stream processing engines and languages. This supports the hypothesis of using subquery organization as a suitable base for abstracting the CEP query-writing process. Moreover, each involved subquery clearly reminds a block in the pipes-and-filters pattern: it is, in fact, a small, independent processing step connected to the other process subqueries by means of event streams (channel or pipe).

spChains exploits this query structure, to decouple low-level CEP query writing from high-level definition of processing tasks, using a block

```
stream summary(srcIP, num):
aggregate ExpDecAvg(iNum):(exp):
insert into summary

-- sub-query 1

select srcIP, count(srcIP)
over (range 60 slide 60)
from Packets
group by srcIP:

-- sub-query 2

select srcIP, ExpDecAvg(num)
over (range 10*60 slide 60)
from summary
group by srcIP:
```

FIGURE 14.6
Sample query in ATLaS.

---

[*] http://wis.cs.ucla.edu/wis/atlas/examples/netmon.html

```
-- sub-query 1

Q1: Select    Rstream(srcIP, Count(*) as num)
     From      Packets [Range 1 Minute
                        Slide 1 Minute]
     Group By srcIP

-- sub-query 2

Q2: Select    Rstream(srcIP, ExpDecAvg(num))
     From      Q1 [Range 10 Minute
                   Slide 1 Minute]
     Group By srcIP
```

FIGURE 14.7
Sample query in CQL.

```
-- sub-query 1

insert into Q1 select srcIp, count(*) as num
from Packets.win:time(60 seconds)

-- sub-query 2

insert into Q2 select srcIp, ExpDecAvg(num)
from Q1.win:time(10 minutes) output last every 60 seconds
```

FIGURE 14.8
Sample query in EPL.

composition approach, in some aspects very similar to well-known block-based programming paradigms such as in Scratch [16] or in well-established processing tools, for example, LabView,* Simulink,† etc. In such a way, complex CEP query writing is mapped to simpler block interconnection (see Figure 14.9), while keeping the processing efficiency almost unchanged.

Stream Processing Blocks

We define a *stream processing block* as a (software) component taking one or more event streams in input and generating one or more event streams as output. The output and input streams are correlated by means of a processing function (i.e., a CEP query), which, in general, is not linear (e.g., threshold) and/or with memory (e.g., a moving average). A block is

- *Transparent* if the block filters out a subset of its entering events, only, depending on some block parameter. On the contrary, it is called *opaque* if it computes/generates new event values.

---

* http://www.ni.com/labview/i/
† http://www.mathworks.it/products/simulink/

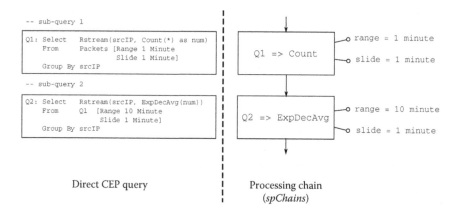

```
-- sub-query 1

Q1: Select    Rstream(srcIP, Count(*) as num)
    From      Packets [Range 1 Minute
                       Slide 1 Minute]
    Group By srcIP

-- sub-query 2

Q2: Select    Rstream(srcIP, ExpDecAvg(num))
    From      Q1  [Range 10 Minute
                   Slide 1 Minute]
    Group By srcIP
```

Q1 => Count   range = 1 minute
                     slide = 1 minute

Q2 => ExpDecAvg   range = 10 minute
                     slide = 1 minute

Direct CEP query   Processing chain
                                    (*spChains*)

FIGURE 14.9
Direct CEP query mapped on processing blocks.

- *Linear* if the processing function only applies linear operators to the input stream, while it is *nonlinear* otherwise.
- *With memory* if the computation made for generating the output stream depends on past events, while it is *without memory* if the processing function only depends on the last event.

Figure 14.10 shows the general structure of a stream processing block. A stream processing block has a set of input ports, and a set of output ports, identified by unique port identifiers. Every port can only handle a specific type of event, that is, it has an associated data type, either real-valued or Boolean, that shall match the type of events received (generated) in input (output). A set of constant parameters can be defined to affect/tune the inner block functionality (i.e., the generated CEP query), for example, values, window lengths, operating modes (see the example given in Figure 14.11). Temporal computations performed by blocks can be based on moving or

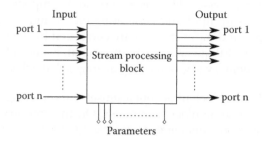

Input   Output

port 1 ──────▶   ──────▶ port 1

            Stream processing
                 block

port n ──────▶   ──────▶ port n

              Parameters

FIGURE 14.10
Generic stream processing block.

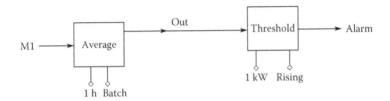

FIGURE 14.11
A sample chain (hourly average).

batch windows. The base library is composed of 14 blocks whose functionalities and features are briefly summarized in Table 14.1. More complex blocks can be easily designed and integrated.

Blocks are instantiated by data-centric applications through a simple XML-based notation, called spXML (see the example given in Figure 14.12).

Chains, Drains, and Sources

spChains elaboration pipelines (i.e., CEP queries), or *chains*, are composed by connecting together several block instances, depending on the specific application need. Interblock connection rules permit only to connect blocks with compatible input/output ports (e.g., Boolean event streams cannot be connected with real-valued inputs) and prevent cycles in connections: a chain is therefore a directed acyclic graph of stream processing blocks (Figure 14.11).

Real-valued events are automatically handled as physical quantities, that is, as numbers with a unit of measure (defined according to the UCUM standard) and computations involving different units and scales are automatically handled performing the needed conversions. Every chain consumes data from one or more *event sources* and produces data for one or more *event drains*. Drains and sources are simple interfaces defining a standard way of pushing/extracting events in/from the *spChains* framework.

spXML

According to the design goal of decoupling CEP query writing from processing task definition, *spChains* blocks and chains are defined using a language neutral (with respect to the adopted CEP engine) representation based on an XML notation: *spXML*. This allows, on the one hand, to widen the accessibility of the representation to all stakeholders somewhat exposed to the XML syntax and rules. On the other hand, it provides an intermediate representation easy to exploit by user-level graphic applications, thus enabling in the long-term support for fully fledged CEP development environments for domain experts, for example, for energy managers, with specific libraries of processing blocks.

TABLE 14.1

The *spChains* Stream Processing Blocks

Block Name	Type	Description	#I/#O/#P
Last	Transparent, linear, with memory	Given the time window w, whenever w expires, this block provides as output the last received event within the window. Every time a filtering window expires, events in the window are dropped and a new batch filtering is started	1/2/1
Average	Opaque, nonlinear, with memory	It computes the average of all (real-valued) events received in a given time window w. It can either operate in *batch* or *moving* mode	1/2/2
Sum	Opaque, linear, with memory	The Sum block is an opaque block computing the sum of all events received in a given time window w. It can either operate in *batch* or *moving* mode	1/2/2
Threshold	Opaque, nonlinear, with memory	Generates a stream of Boolean events by monitoring one real-valued event stream for specific threshold passing. The threshold block can work in 3 different threshold checking modes	1/1/2
Hysteresis threshold	Opaque, nonlinear, with memory	The Hysteresis threshold block acts almost like the threshold block except for the threshold traversal detection, which exploits a tunable hysteresis parameter to smooth frequent near-threshold triggers that might make the output signal too unstable	1/1/3
Time Guard	Opaque, nonlinear	Generates a Boolean event stream by monitoring a stream of Boolean or real-valued events for time limit/frequency compliance. It has two operating modes: *missing* and *present*	1/1/3
Range	Opaque, nonlinear, with memory	The Range block is an opaque, nonlinear block that checks real-valued input events against a range of accepted values (either in-range or out-range checking is supported)	1/1/4

Name	Properties	Description	
Time Filter	Transparent, linear	The Time Filter is a linear, transparent block which acts as a time-based switch, allowing incoming events to pass through depending on the current time	1/1/1
And	Opaque, nonlinear, without memory	The And block is a nonlinear and opaque block which acts as a multiport time guard. Given a time window t_w usually short (around few seconds or less) the block provides one output event (Boolean) *iff* all input ports have received at least one event in t_w	n/1/1
Join	Transparent, linear, without memory	The Join block is a linear, transparent block that multiplexes input events on different channels into a single output channel. It works with an event-based paradigm: whenever an event arrives on any input port, it is automatically forwarded to the output port	n/1/0
Delta	Opaque, linear, with memory	The Delta block is a linear, opaque block that computes the difference between pairs of consecutive events arriving on the block real-valued input port. Events participating in the difference are discarded one at time, that is, the block works with a moving sampling window having a width of 2 samples	1/1/0
Scale	Opaque, linear, without memory	The Scale block is a linear, opaque block that scales the value of input events by a given multiplying factor s defined as block parameter	1/1/1
Abs	Opaque, nonlinear, without memory	The Abs block is an opaque block that provides as output (real-valued, positive) the absolute value of incoming real-valued events	1/1/1
Difference	Opaque, linear, without memory	The Difference block is an opaque block that provides as output (real-valued) the difference of last real-valued events arriving on the 2 input ports in the given t_w (usually very short)	2/1/1

Hourly average: If the hourly average of a given event stream, e.g., consumed energy, exceeds a given threshold generate an alarm event.

```
<spConfig:streamProcessingConfiguration>

<!-- SECTION 1: CHAINS DEFINITION -->

 <spConfig:chains>
  <spXML:chain id="usecase1">
   <spXML:blocks>
    <spXML:block id="Avg1" function="AVERAGE">
     <spXML:param name="window" value="1" unitOfMeasure="h" />
     <spXML:param name="mode" value="batch" />
    </spXML:block>
    <spXML:block id="Th1" function="THRESHOLD">
     <spXML:param name="threshold" value="1" unitOfMeasure="kW" />
    </spXML:block>
   </spXML:blocks>
   <spXML:connections>
    <spXML:connection>
     <spXML:from blockId="Avg1" port="out" />
     <spXML:to blockId="Th1" port="in" />
    </spXML:connection>
   </spXML:connections>
   <spXML:input blockId="Avg1" port="in" id="in" />
   <spXML:output blockId="Th1" port="out" id="out" />
  </spXML:chain>
 </spConfig:chains>

<!-- SECTION 2: SOURCES and DRAINS -->

 <spConfig:eventSources>
  <spConfig:eventStream id="M1" type="REAL"/>
 </spConfig:eventSources>
 <spConfig:eventDrains>
  <spConfig:eventStream id="Alarm" type="BOOLEAN"/>
 </spConfig:eventDrains>

<!-- SECTION 3: CONNECTIONS -->

 <spConfig:connections>
  <spConfig:connection>
   <spConfig:fromSource chainId="usecase1" inputId="in" source="M1" />
   <spConfig:toDrain chainId="usecase1" drain="Alarm" outputId="out" />
  </spConfig:connection>
 </spConfig:connections>
</spConfig:streamProcessingConfiguration>
```

FIGURE 14.12
A processing task in spXML.

An *spXML* representation of a set of stream processing tasks is organized in three main sections (Figure 14.12): the first defines the chain instances needed to perform a specific set of computations (at least one chain must be specified); the second identifies the available sources of events and the registered drains (consumers) of processed events; and finally, the third defines the connections between sources and chains, and between chains and drains.

Every elaboration chain is defined in a chain section (Figure 14.13) and is assigned a unique id, possibly mnemonic, to recall the actual goal of the chain itself. It may be composed by a variable number of processing blocks (minimum cardinality 1) connected to form a direct acyclic graph.

Similar to the overall *spXML* file structure, the chain section also is organized into three main parts: (a) block instance definition, (b) description of block interconnections, and (c) identification of the chain inputs and outputs (i.e., of the chain boundary blocks).

Blocks are identified by a unique id (mnemonic) and by a function attribute assuming a value between those defined in the adopted *spChains* block library (the base library allows for 14 different function values corresponding to the 14 available blocks). Depending on the block function, zero or more parameters can be specified for tuning the block functionality to the desired behavior, that is, to set the free parameters of the precompiled CEP query represented by the stream processing block. Each parameter can either be a pure number or a real-valued measure for which a unit must be specified.

```
. . .

  <spXML:chain id="usecase1">

<!-- PART 1: BLOCK DEFINITION -->

   <spXML:blocks>
    <spXML:block id="Avg1" function="AVERAGE">
     <spXML:param name="window" value="1" unitOfMeasure="h" />
     <spXML:param name="mode" value="batch" />
    </spXML:block>
    <spXML:block id="Th1" function="THRESHOLD">
     <spXML:param name="threshold" value="1" unitOfMeasure="kW" />
    </spXML:block>
   </spXML:blocks>

<!-- PART 2: BLOCK INTERCONNECTION -->

   <spXML:connections>
    <spXML:connection>
     <spXML:from blockId="Avg1" port="out" />
     <spXML:to blockId="Th1" port="in" />
    </spXML:connection>
   </spXML:connections>

<!-- PART 3: INPUT AND OUTPUT IDENTIFICATION -->

   <spXML:input blockId="Avg1" port="in" id="in" />
   <spXML:output blockId="Th1" port="out" id="out" />
  </spXML:chain>

. . .
```

FIGURE 14.13
Chain definition in spXML.

Interconnection between blocks is obtained by specifying the block port (block id + port id) from which the connection starts and by selecting the specific block port in which the connection ends. The input and output ports of a chain are assigned a unique id (mnemonic) and mapped to the input and output ports of selected blocks, identified by their ids.

Architecture

The *spChains* logic architecture is deployed along three main tiers (see Figure 14.14): (a) the field-data sources, for example, energy meters, item counters, pressure, position sensors, etc.; (b) the *spChains* processing framework; and (c) the data-centric applications exploiting higher-level data streams generated by *spChains*.

Field data sources generate high-throughput and/or high-cardinality event streams with different temporal behaviors. Events can be delivered either periodically (constant data sampling) or in a sporadic manner (e.g., for wireless sensor networks), and delivery rates vary from few events per minute to hundreds of events per second, depending on the application context. The number of streams to monitor (and elaborate) is rather variable, ranging from few event streams in small deployments (e.g., small offices or small enterprises) to hundreds or thousands of streams for deployment in large companies, possibly extending across multiple sites.

Applications, on the other side of the three-tiered architecture, consume high-level event streams generated by *spChains* at a much lower rate (in the order of few events per second, as they are typically delivered to people such as asset or energy managers) and instruct *spChains* to perform the elaborations required to transform low-level data into meaningful information, for example, into asset-related information in enterprise resource planning (ERP) systems.

spChains

spChains is the middle tier, providing single-event granularity, high-throughput, aggregation, and computation capabilities for monitoring and alerting. It is organized into two main parts dealing with configuration handling (i.e., query generation) and with runtime processing (see Figure 14.15).

Configuration Handling

Given a processing task specification, in *spXML*, the configuration subsystem generates one (or more) instance(s) of stream processor to be employed in runtime elaboration of data streams. Generation is independent of actual

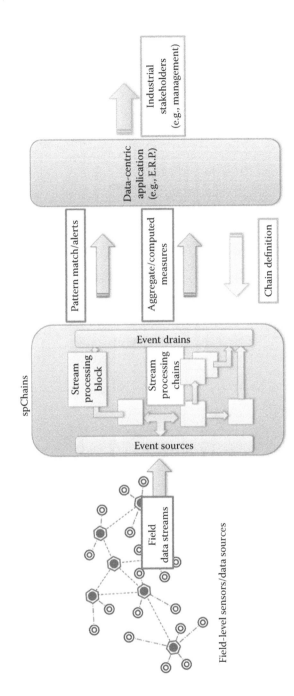

FIGURE 14.14

The *spChains* framework logic architecture.

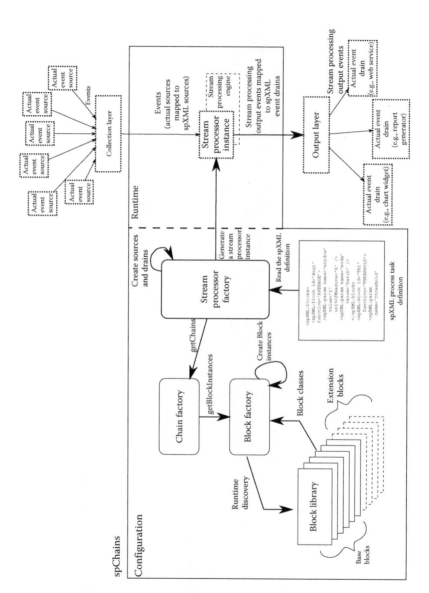

FIGURE 14.15

The inner *spChains* architecture.

block implementations and exploits runtime discovery of available block libraries to locate and correctly instantiate the processing elements defined in the *spXML* specification.

It is deployed along three main stages: block discovery and instantiation, chain creation, and source/drain definition and connection (see Figure 14.16).

In the first stage (Figure 14.17), for each block used by the chains defined in the *spXML* specification, a suitable block class is dynamically discovered, be it part of the core library or of any additional library of blocks accessible to the configuration subsystem (this is accomplished by adopting the Java services pattern [19]).

If a block implementation is found, the processing block is instantiated (resulting in one distinct instance of block for each occurrence in the *spXML* description) and the corresponding CEP query is customized using the block parameters defined in *spXML*. Every block encapsulates a manually tuned, precompiled CEP query and therefore no translation process is actually carried and the parameter customization only acts on the free parameters defined in the precompiled query (Figure 14.18).

This design choice supports development-time query optimization while staged composition of queries, typical of CEP, grants a nearly global optimization of processing chains, as they simply compose the needed subqueries together (see "Section Block-Based Stream Processing").

Block discovery and instantiation is followed by the chain instantiation process (Figure 14.19), which basically deals with block connection, that is, with query composition. Block-generated subqueries are composed together by matching the corresponding event streams, following the typical CEP query composition pattern. Moreover, streams are generated, at the CEP engine level, to host the chain input (source) and output (drain) events.

```
// stream processor factory pseudo code

StreamProcessor processor = createEmptyStreamProcessor();

foreach chainSpXML in processorSpXML
{
    // ----- STAGE 1 & 2 ------
        processor.addChain(ChainFactory.getChain(chainSpXML));
}

//------ STAGE 3 -----
fillDrainList(drainsInSpXML, processor);

fillSourceList(sourcesInSpXML, processor);

connectDrainsAndSources();
```

FIGURE 14.16
Stream processor instantiation and configuration, in pseudo-code.

```
//---------    STAGE 1 -------------

// block factory pseudo code

function getStreamProcessingBlock(spXMLBlock block)
{
  ...

  //search all the stream processing block classes
  //accessible by the current class loader
  foreach blockClass extending StreamProcessingBlock
  {
    if(blockClass.type == block.type)
    {
      //get a block instance
      StreamProcessingBlock currentBlock = blockClass.getInstance();

      //customize block parameters
      currentBlock.setParameters(block.getBlockParametersFromSpXML());

      //class found no more search is needed
      break;
    }
  }
}
```

FIGURE 14.17
Block instantiation and configuration, in pseudo-code.

Finally, the third stage generates stubs to: (a) convey external events to the corresponding *spXML* sources (event consumers) and (b) deliver process results to the actual event consumers associated with *spXML* drains (event publishers). This stage provides as final result a runnable instance of stream processor, implementing the *spXML*-defined processing tasks, ready to be executed at runtime.

```
// create the query template, Abs works only on Real streams
this.queryTemplate = "insert into RealEvent(src, streamName, "
  + "value, unitOfMeasure) select \""
  + this.id
  + "\", \""
  + this.getStreamName(oPort)
  + "\" as streamName, (event1.value-event2.value) as value,"
  + "event1.unitOfMeasure from pattern"
  + "[every( (event1=GenericEvent(streamName=?) and "
  + "event2=GenericEvent(streamName=?))"
  + "where timer:within("
  + windowValue + " " + unitOfMeasure + ") )]\n";

// prepare the statement
this.queryStmt = this.eProcessingEngine.
  prepareStatement(this.queryTemplate);
```

FIGURE 14.18
A sample precompiled query extracted from the Esper-based difference block (core library).

```
//--------- STAGE 2 ------------

// chain factory pseudo code

function getChain(spXMLChain chain)
{
  . . .

  foreach blockSpXML in chain
  {
    BlockFactory.getStreamProcessingBlock(blockSpXML);
  }

  connectBlocks();

  . . .
}
```

FIGURE 14.19
Chain instantiation and configuration, in pseudo-code.

Runtime Stream Processing

At runtime, that is, immediately after the configuration phase, the processing tasks defined in *spXML* are encoded into a suitable stream processor instance, ready to perform the needed computations. In such a phase, on-line processing can start provided that actual event producers and consumers have been "connected" to the processor sources and drains. This is typically done through a collection (on the input side) and an output layer, dealing with event capture/delivery logic. Depending on the application domain, the collection layer can either be a web service client, a complete sampling system or an interface to a smart building management system. In a similar way, the actual output layer implementation depends on the application scope, for example, it can be a web service client, a GUI, etc. Both layers are not part of the *spChains* framework, decoupling the framework from the application domain, for example, ERP versus energy management.

On-line processing starts with the so-called *plug* operation, which triggers the injection of queries into the underlying stream processing engine. Different block and chain implementations can rely on different engines, thus decoupling the framework from the engine implementation, for example, STREAM, Esper, etc. Mixed use of different processing engines or even of custom-built (hardcoded) blocks is allowed, at the cost of a lower performance. Once plugged, the stream processor starts processing incoming events and generating output events.

At any time, the stream processor instance can be *unplugged*, that is, disconnected from input and output events. Such an operation actually removes the corresponding queries from the underlying processing engine, safely supporting changes in the processor configuration.

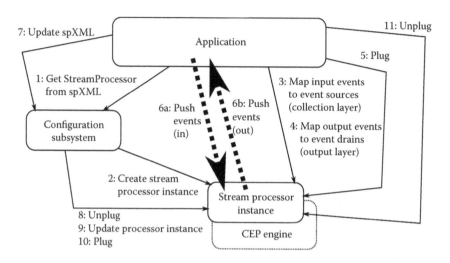

FIGURE 14.20
spChains runtime interactions.

Plugging and unplugging can also work at the single chain level, thus enabling runtime modification of single processing queries. The current implementation of *spChains* (see "Implementation" section) uses this feature to support automatic detection of changes in the *spXML* task definition and to trigger the corresponding chain updates with virtually no downtimes (except for the updated chains); Figure 14.20 shows the runtime interaction diagram.

Implementation

The *spChains* framework is implemented as an open-source Java library, distributed under the Apache v2.0 license.* It provides an abstract implementation of the logical modules of the architecture (Figure 14.21 reports the corresponding class diagram) together with all the utilities needed to automatically verify and establish block connections as well as source-to-chain and chain-to-drain communications.

It is currently composed of 80 Java classes organized in several packages, each dealing with a specific aspect of the spChain architecture. In particular, the abstract implementations for modules shown in Figure 14.21, and discussed in the "Architecture" section, are grouped in the so-called core package. The core is then extended to support specific block implementation,

---

* http://elite.polito.it/spchains

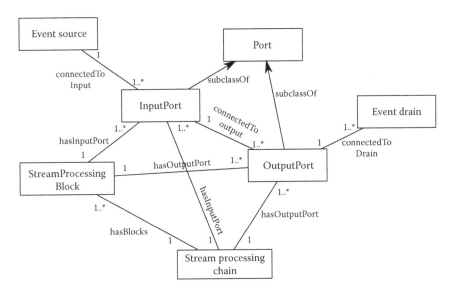

FIGURE 14.21
The abstract *spChains* modules.

based on well-defined CEP engines. Currently, a complete implementation of the base block library (14 blocks) is provided, by exploiting a state-of-the-art CEP engine called Esper [17].

The framework distribution also includes a set of test tools enabling easier development of new blocks, either based on Esper or on other processing engines. A sample visual tool shows how to integrate the framework into existing applications, with advanced features such as dynamic detection of configuration changes and runtime update of processing chains. Figure 14.22 reports a screenshot of such a tool where two sources are feeding events, at 25 Hz frequency to 29 different processing chains (small displays on the right).

Experimental Results

The *spChains* framework underwent a two-level testing process aimed at assessing its applicability in possibly large real-world scenarios. To perform this assessment, two separate test phases have been deployed: a first in-laboratory performance test aimed at assessing the performance of each block, in terms of achieved throughput and memory occupation, and a second real-world deployment of the *spChains* framework in three applications developed by third parties in the smart-building domain and focused on energy monitoring.

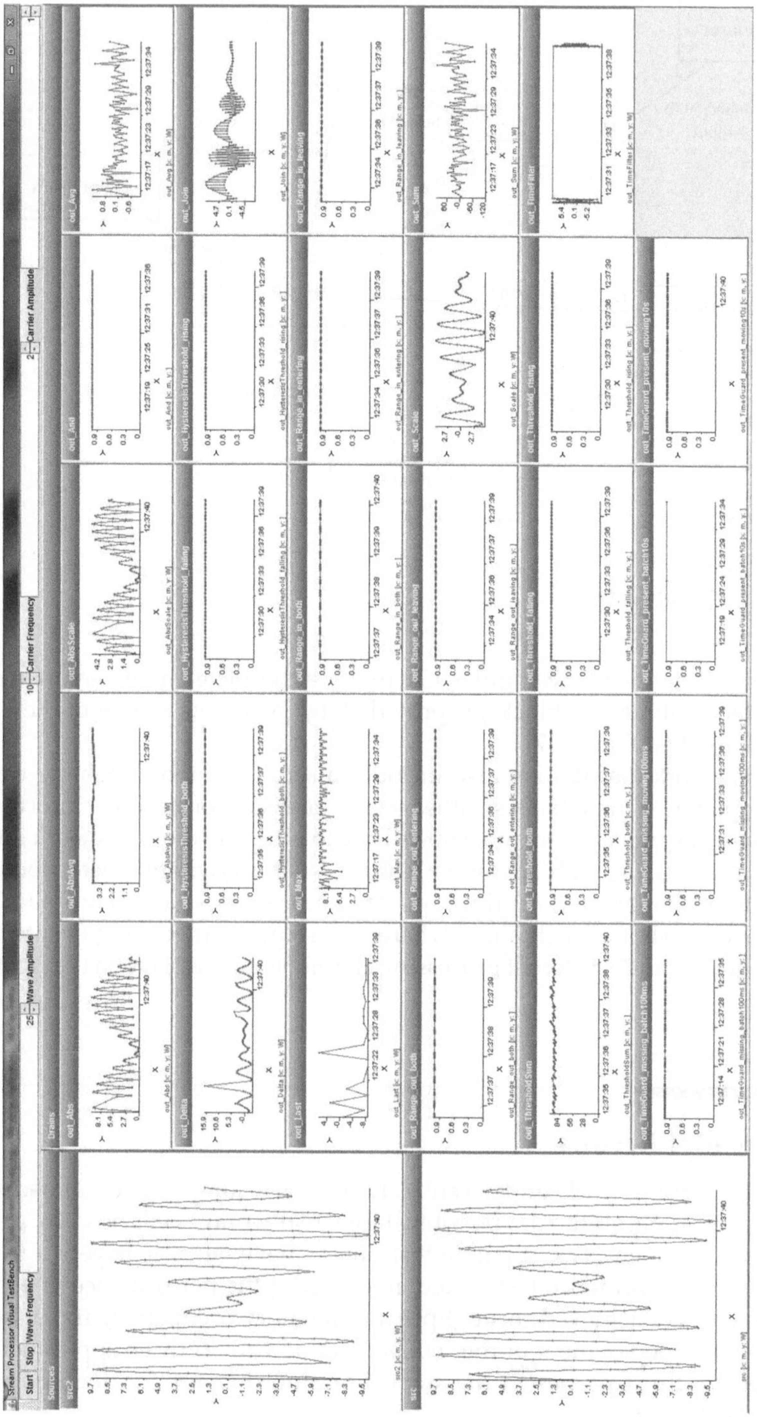

FIGURE 14.22
The *spChains* test tool showing 2 sources and 29 drains (i.e., processing chains).

Performance Characterization

The first test aimed at characterizing the achievable throughput and memory occupation of each block given an event stream with increasing event delivery frequency. The test set-up involves two distinct components, running on the same machine: a random event generator and *spChains*. The event generator uses a fast generation algorithm, which overcomes the current Java virtual machine timing limit of around 1 ms, and reaches an open-loop performance of nearly 700 k events per second on a desktop PC equipped with an Intel Core i5 processor at 2.67 GHz and 4 GB of memory (see Table 14.2). This performance depends on the current machine load and, in the presented tests, degrades to 170 k/200 k events/s due to the concurrent execution of the *spChains* framework (Figure 14.23). Alternative test settings involving more machines connected via a local area network, which might appear more suited for performance profiling, shall be carefully designed as the event delivery rates are near, or over, the capacity of typical 100 MBit/s Ethernet connections.

The 14 blocks composing the *spChains* base library have been tested, with a particular focus on the *Abs*, *And*, *Avg*, *Delta*, *Join*, *Last*, *Scale*, *Max*, and *Difference* blocks. Every block has been connected with the random event generator with an event delivery rate increasing from 100 events per second up to the maximum achievable rate (≈170 k events/s), with an increase factor of 2 (i.e., doubling the event generation rate at each step). Adopted metrics include the achieved throughput (in healthy work conditions, i.e., without losing events in output), compared to the theoretical one, and the corresponding memory occupation. Both have been averaged over 10 trials, for each of the adopted generation rates.

Three different block groups have been identified, on the basis of the above-defined metrics, and analyzed separately: aggregation blocks, blocks without memory, and pattern-based blocks.

Aggregation blocks, for example, *avg*, *max*, show a typically constant throughput (much lower than the corresponding input throughput) and are characterized in terms of memory occupation. Figure 14.24 reports the performance analysis of the *Avg*, *Max*, *Last*, and *Sum* blocks, configured to operate on a 1-s batch time window. As expected, the output rate is almost constant and equal

TABLE 14.2

Event Generation Performance (Averaged on 10 runs)

Events/s (k)	Processor(s)	Clock (GHz)	RAM (GB)	Description
38.6	Intel Atom N330 (4 cores)	1.6	2	Atom-based mini-ITX fanless nettop
748	Intel Core i5-750 (4 cores)	2.67	4	Core I5 consumer desktop PC
648	Intel Core i5-2410M (4 cores)	2.3	6	Acer TimelineX laptop
736	Intel Core i7 (4 cores)	3.4	8	Core I7 high-end desktop PC
432	Intel Xeon X5450 (8 cores)	3.0	8	HP workstation

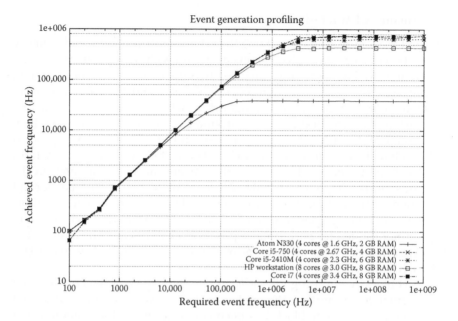

FIGURE 14.23
Event generation performance profiling results.

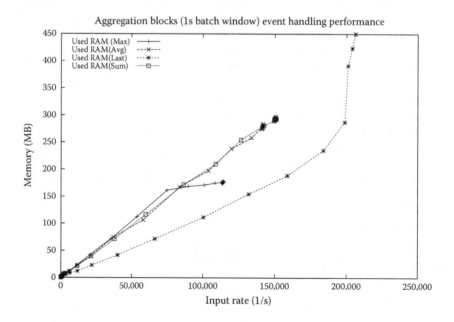

FIGURE 14.24
Aggregation block performance analysis.

to the time window, with a constant delay of 0.05 s due to the chain latency. As can easily be noticed, memory occupation grows almost linearly with respect to the rate of input events. This reflects the fact that, given a fixed size window, an increase in the input delivery rate corresponds to an increase in the amount of events included in the time window. Limit conditions can be detected when the occupied memory stops growing linearly, as in the *Last* case, highlighting a critical condition of the *spChains* framework. Whether such a condition depends on the *spChains* implementation or on the underlying Esper library remains to be investigated. Overall, memory occupation is reasonable, with an average of 1.6 KB per event (in the worst case shown by the *Avg* block). It must be noticed that such an average figure accounts for the memory load due to the block instantiation, connection, and messaging infrastructure as well as for the Esper engine memory occupation. This evidence, together with the results reported in the following paragraphs, suggests one to use *spChains* aggregation blocks as first, highly efficient, elaboration layer able to decimate huge data streams for further elaboration.

Blocks without memory: they typically involve single event operations such as *Abs* or *Scale*, without event pattern matching. They are analyzed in terms of achieved output throughput with respect to the theoretical output rate expected for the blocks, in terms of memory occupation and in terms of maximum achieved throughput (Figure 14.25). Since these blocks operate on single events, they are more sensitive to the computation performance of the implemented CEP queries. In particular, as reported in Figure 14.25, all

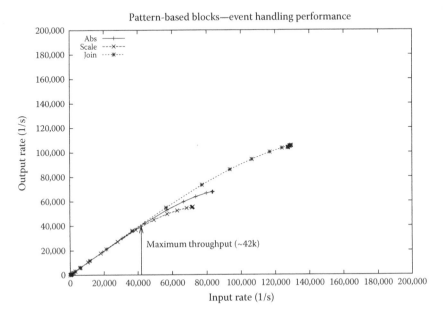

FIGURE 14.25
Single-event block performance analysis.

the tested blocks, that is, *Abs*, *Scale*, and *Join*, show a maximum throughput point of around 40 k events per second, after which the achieved throughput degrades, and input events start to be discarded. Memory occupation, on the other hand, is almost constant (around 32 MB, 64 MB for the Join block) as the number of handled events is fixed and typically equal to 1 (2 in *Join*).

Although the achieved performance is lower than the one achieved by aggregation blocks, it still permits one to effectively handle huge data streams in input. In typical industrial settings, for example, event delivery rates seldom exceed 1 event per second; however, data stream cardinality (i.e., the number of monitored sensors) can be relevant. In such a typical case, a maximum throughput of 40 k events per second permits handling of up to 40 k sensors, much farther than typical amount of installed sensors: the Politecnico di Torino monitoring network, for example, employs around 300 sensors distributed over three different sites.

Pattern-based blocks: they implement computations based on pattern matching, for example, the *And*, *Delta*, and *Difference* blocks. As reported in Figure 14.26, they offer the worst performance of the 3 block groups, achieving a maximum throughput of only 6 k events per second. While being acceptable in most industrial settings, these blocks require further analysis to investigate whether the performance gap with respect to single-event blocks is due to the pattern matching process or if it originates from a poor query optimization, possibly requiring improvements to the current block implementations.

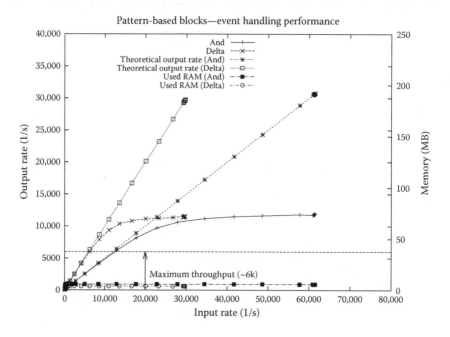

FIGURE 14.26
Pattern-based block performance analysis.

Real-World Deployment

spChains has been tested for real-world applicability in two technology trans-fer projects involving Italian companies[*,†] located in Turin and Milan, respec-tively. In both cases, *spChains* has been integrated into energy monitoring applications for smart buildings: an Enterprise Resource Planning[‡] software in the former case (one installed instance) and energy managers' dashboards in the latter (two installed instances). Events generated by field sensors, 38 in the first case and 47 in the second installation, have been monitored 24/7 with a sampling period of one event per second (per sensor) and with a typ-ical chain delivery time of 15 min (aggregated measures use 15-min win-dows, typically). A formal assessment of *spChains* reliability has not yet been devised; however, preliminary, qualitative feedback has been gathered from the two companies and shows a rather high rating of the system in terms of performance and up-time. Results are summarized in Table 14.3 and they represent the system status at the time of writing: up-time and failures are subject to change as these systems are real-world commercial installations currently deployed at customers' sites.

According to both companies, chain definition by energy managers is sim-ple, even if a visual editing framework is considered a must, especially for large settings, with hundreds of sensors involved in the processing. In both cases, the learning process has been fast and effective as the support requests for chain definition were very few (totally 3) and the adopted processing chains mostly involved blocks for which no sample instantiations were pro-vided (we just provided the block functionality descriptions).

Related Works

Effective data handling and management is attracting an increasing interest due to the constantly growing amount of distributed sensors and devices contributing to production processes or participating in pervasive environ-ments. As the order of magnitude of involved data streams grows, new and more effective data-processing techniques are required to off-load low-level data handling from applications to dedicated middleware [5,21], having the required computational capabilities.

The Solar system [7] provides a data-centric infrastructure to support context-aware applications, exploiting the previously cited filter-and-pipe patterns [11]. Similar to the proposed *spChains*, Solar treats sensors as data stream publishers and applications as data stream consumers. Application

---

[*] Proxima Centauri s.r.l., http://http://www.proxima-centauri.it
[†] Eudata, http://www.eudata.biz/
[‡] http://www.oratio-project.org/

TABLE 14.3

Qualitative Assessment of *spChains* Deployment

Location	Company	Up-Time/#Failures	#Sensors	Sampling	#Chains	Smart Building Size	Feedback
Turin, Italy	Proxima Centauri	7 months/0 failures	38	1 event/s	38	Small enterprise (office), data center	Very positive feedback, no relevant issues were reported, the base library was sufficient to support all required computationsitive feedback
Milan, Italy	Eudata	8 months/0 failures	19	1 event/s	9	Small enterprise (office), data center	Very positive feedback, 3 custom blocks were developed by the company
Northern Italy	Customer of Eudata	8 months/0 failures	28	1 event/s	30	Medium enterprise (unknown)	Very positive feedback

developers explicitly compose desired sensor streams and transform low-level data into more meaningful context using operators (comparable to the *spChains* Stream Processing Blocks). Solar defines operators as custom-developed solutions ranging from simple logic AND to complex supervised machine learning, whereas *spChains* exploits highly efficient stream processing engines, such as Esper, while also permitting nonstream solutions as the ones envisioned in Solar. Moreover, while Solar defines the infrastructure, leaving developers free to design and implement the needed processing operators, *spChains* aims at providing a standard, yet extensible, set of basic processing blocks ensuring reusability of the approach across different application domains.

Obweger et al., in their "CEP off the Shelf" paper [18], tackle this issue by proposing solution templates based on the SARI event-processing framework. Solution templates offer well-proven, standardized event-processing logic for common business needs with an underlying rationale pretty similar to the *spChains* motivations. Similar to *spChains*, solution templates can be assembled from predefined, easy-to-use building blocks, in a way that abstracts from the underlying complexity. However, compared with *spChains*, templates are defined in terms of if-then-else rules, somewhat less expressive than the block composition offered by *spChains*.

In the Jeffery et al. [13] approach, CEP techniques are exploited for building sensor data cleaning infrastructures for pervasive applications. In the extensible sensor stream processing (ESP) framework, they propose, sensor data are cleaned by means of a pipeline defined through declarative mechanisms based on spatial and temporal data features. Two main differences and shortcomings can be identified with respect to *spChains*. First, processing components are defined as CQL [2] queries (supported by the STREAM [12] processing engine), which are difficult to compose and deploy for people without a deep knowledge of stream-processing languages and that are difficult to reuse by being optimized for specific purposes, only. Second, the domain of application is much more restricted than the one targeted by *spChains*: while ESP is focused on data cleaning, *spChains* defines a general framework and a set of standard blocks that can be easily reused and composed into application-specific processing chains.

Conclusions

This chapter introduced the *spChains* framework, a modular approach to support mastering of CEP queries in a simplified, yet effective, manner based on stream processing block composition. The approach aims at unleashing the power of CEP systems for teams having reduced insights into CEP systems. In this context, the *spChains* provides a small, but easy to extend, set of processing block that can be composed, in a "Lego-like" approach enabling effective data-centric processing of huge data flows.

While trading off global query optimization with modular composition, the *spChains* framework is able to handle high-cardinality/high-throughput data flows, with peak processing performance at around 170 k events per second. Performance analysis suggest a general strategy of first instantiating aggregation blocks, as such an operation allows to reach very high elaboration throughputs, of over 100 k events per second, while blocks based on single-event elaboration or on pattern detection are more suited for processing streams at lower rates.

Exploitation in real-world smart buildings is sustainable, as shown by the two commercial applications (in three different installations) reported in the "Experimental Results" section. Currently, we are collaborating with the energy managers of the Politecnico di Torino to deploy a university-wise monitoring network comprising over 300 sensors. Future work will involve further optimization/integration of the base block library, the development of chain definition interfaces (standalone and web-based), and integration of chain/block hot-plugging functionalities, to better support the data processing life cycle in industrial environments.

References

1. D. J. Abadi, D. Carney, U. Çetintemel, M. Cherniack, C. Convey, S. Lee, M. Stonebraker, N. Tatbul, and S. Zdonik. Aurora: A new model and architecture for data stream management. *The VLDB Journal*, 12:120–139, 2003.
2. A. Arasu, S. Babu, and J. Widom. Cql: A language for continuous queries over streams and relations. In G. Lausen and D. Suciu, editors, *Database Programming Languages*, volume 2921 of *Lecture Notes in Computer Science*, pp 123–124. Springer, Berlin, Heidelberg, 2004.
3. D. Bonino and F. Corno. spchains: A declarative framework for data stream processing in pervasive applications. *Procedia Computer Science*, 10(0):316–323, 2012.
4. D. Bonino and L. De Russis. Mastering real-time big data with stream processing chains. *XRDS*, 19(1):83–86, 2012.
5. B. Bony, M. Harnischfeger, and F. Jammes. Convergence of OPC UA and DPWS with a cross-domain data model. In *2011 9th IEEE International Conference on Industrial Informatics (INDIN)*, 26–29 July, Caparica, Lisbon, pp. 187–192, 2011.
6. F. Buschmann, R. Meunier, H. Rohnert, P. Sommerlad, and M. Stal. *Patterns Oriented Software Architecture*. John Wiley & Sons, Chichester, UK, 1996.
7. G. Chen, M. Li, and D. Kotz. Data-centric middleware for context-aware pervasive computing. *Pervasive and Mobile Computing*, 4(2008):216–253, 2007.
8. D. J. Cook, J. C. Augusto, and V. R. Jakkula. Review: Ambient intelligence: Technologies, applications, and opportunities. *Pervasive and Mobile Computing*, 5(4):277–298, 2009.

9. N. Dindar, B. Güç, P. Lau, A. Ozal, M. Soner, and N. Tatbul. Dejavu: Declarative pattern matching over live and archived streams of events. In *Proceedings of the 35th SIGMOD international conference on Management of data (SIGMOD'09)*, pp. 1023–1026, ACM, New York, USA, 2009.

10. O. Etzion and P. Niblett. *Event Processing in Action*. Manning Publications and Co., Stamford, CT, 2010.

11. D. Garlan and M. Shaw. An Introduction to Software Architectures. Technical Report CMU-CS-94-166, Carnegie Mellon University, January 1994.

12. The STREAM Group. STREAM: The Stanford Stream Data Manager. Technical Report 2003-21, Stanford InfoLab, 2003.

13. S. R. Jeffery, G. Alonso, M. J. Franklin, W. Hong, and J. Widom. Declarative support for sensor data cleaning. In *Proceedings of the 4th International Conference on Pervasive Computing (PERVASIVE'06)*, pp. 83–100, Springer-Verlag, Berlin, Heidelberg, 2006.

14. I. Kellner and L. Fiege. Viewpoints in complex event processing: Industrial experience report. In *Proceedings of the Third ACM International Conference on Distributed Event-Based Systems (DEBS'09)*, pp. 9:1–9:8, ACM, New York, USA, 2009.

15. D. C. Luckham. *The Power of Events: An Introduction to Complex Event Processing in Distributed Enterprise Systems*. Addison-Wesley Longman Publishing Co., Inc., Boston, MA, USA, 2001.

16. J. Maloney, M. Resnick, N. Rusk, B. Silverman, and E. Eastmond. The scratch programming language and environment. *ACM Transactions on Computing Education*, 10(4):16:1–16:15, 2010.

17. S. Oberoi. Esper complex event processing engine. *Embedded System Engineering*, 16(2):28–29, 2011.

18. H. Obweger, J. Schiefer, M. Suntinger, F. Breier, and R. Thullner. Complex event processing off the shelf—rapid development of event-driven applications with solution templates. In *2011 19th Mediterranean Conference on Control Automation (MED)*, 20–23 June, Aquis Corfu Holiday Palace, Corfu, pp. 631–638, 2011.

19. J. O'Conner. Creating Extensible Applications With the Java Platform. Technical report, Oracle, Java, 2007.

20. G. Schadow and C. J. McDonald. The unified code for units of measure. Technical report, Regenstrief Institute, Inc. and the UCUM Organization, 2009.

21. H. Schweppe, A. Zimmermann, and D. Grill. Flexible on-board stream processing for automotive sensor data. *IEEE Transactions on Industrial Informatics*, 6(1):81–92, 2010.

22. W. Wang, J. Sung, and D. Kim. Complex event processing in EPC sensor network middleware for both RFID and WSN. In *2008 11th IEEE International Symposium on Object Oriented Real-Time Distributed Computing (ISORC)*, 5–7 May, Orlando, FL, pp. 165–169, 2008.

23. C. Zang and Y. Fan. Complex event processing in enterprise information systems based on RFID. *Enterprise Information Systems*, 1(1):3–23, 2007.

15

Big Data Application: Analyzing Real-Time Electric Meter Data

Mikhail Simonov, Giuseppe Caragnano, Lorenzo Mossucca, Pietro Ruiu, and Olivier Terzo

CONTENTS

Introduction

New electricity metering devices operating within the distribution networks originate data flows. Metering data are created at remote locations and processed somewhere else. The term "Data" denotes a substance, almost all useful data are "given" to us either by nature, as a reward for careful observation of physical processes, or by other people, usually inadvertently. By the term "Big Data," we mean the enormous volume, velocity, and type of data that come from different application fields and have the potential to be turned into business value. More and more companies store great amounts of data and its volume is expanding at a terrifying rate in today's hyperconnected world where people and businesses are creating more and more data every day. For example, very frequent metering—up to subsecond sampling—depicts the true picture about the energy dynamics in power system. Big Data issue concerns: (a) complexity within the data set; (b) amount of value that can be derived from optimized and not analysis techniques; and (c) support data for the analysis. One could describe "big" in terms of the number of useful permutations of sources making useful querying difficult (such as the sensors in an aircraft) and complex interrelationships making cleaning data difficult. We can consider two primary attributes. However, the term "Big" refers to big complexity rather than big volume. Usually relevant and complex data sets of this sort tend to grow rapidly and so Big Data quickly becomes truly astronomical.

Data Sources

According to the known art [1], we can imagine the volume of digital content in the world will grow to 2.7 zettabytes in 2012, up 48% from 2011, and will reach 8 ZB by 2015.

Big Data challenges to understand the origins of the data and extract it into useful information that human brains can use. Not only can the data come from corporate databases, from Internet (web pages, blogs), social networking messages (Facebook, Twitter, MySpace), but also there are many digital sensors worldwide in industrial equipment, electric cars, electricity meters, and so on. They measure and communicate not only *location, movement, quantities* (vibration, temperature, humidity, voltages, currents, power, energy), but also *changes/variations*. Cars, trains, planes, and power stations have increasing numbers of sensors constantly collecting masses of data. It is common to talk of having hundreds of thousands or even millions of sensors that collect *information about* simulation, performance, and activities of a machine or a system along the time. Let us think about one hour of flight monitored through a hundred thousand sensors covering everything from the speed of air over every part of the air frame through to the amount of carbon dioxide in each section of the cabin. Each sensor could act as an *independent device* or *part of a system*. The real interest is usually in combinations of sensor readings.

Also, there are an increasing number of systems that generate very large quantities of very simple data. For instance, media streaming is generating very large volumes with increasing amounts of structured metadata. Similarly, telecommunication companies have to track vast volumes of calls, internet connections, and mobile devices. Let us think about one electricity grid with 20–30 millions of nodes being observed by digital meters supplying readings in real time. Even if these two activities are combined, and petabytes of data are produced, the content is extremely structured. With so many sensors, the combinations are incredibly complex and vary with the error tolerance and characteristics of individual devices. The difficulty is not only storage, but also *processing* that in some cases becomes very costly both in terms of cost and computation.

Methodologies

There are many techniques that draw on fields such as bioinformatics, simulation, and computer science that can be used to analyze data sets. One of the main challenges of working with Big Data is to collect it, assemble it, prepare it for analysis, and store it. Different systems store data in different formats, even within the same company. In this domain, a central challenge is to assemble, to standardize, and to clean data without scrubbing it from the information that makes it valuable. Report [1] states that several kinds of techniques are applicable to Big Data across a range of fields, such as the following.

Data fusion and data integration. A set of techniques to integrate and analyze data from multiple sources in order to develop insights into ways that are more efficient and potentially more accurate than if they were developed by analyzing a single source of data. One application example is IoT sensor data being combined to develop an integrated perspective on the performance of a complex distributed system such as an oil refinery.

Data mining. Means to extract patterns from large data sets by combining methods from statistics and machine learning with database management. They include association rule learning, cluster analysis, classification, and regression. Applications include mining customer data to define segments most likely to respond to an offer, mining human resources data to identify characteristics of most successful employees, or market basket analysis to model the purchase behavior of customers.

Genetic algorithms. Optimization tools inspired by the process of natural evolution or "survival of the fittest." For instance, potential solutions are encoded as "chromosomes" that can combine and mutate. These individual chromosomes are selected for survival within a modeled "environment" that determines the fitness or performance of each individual in the population. Often described as a type of "evolutionary algorithm," these algorithms are well suited for solving nonlinear problems.

Neural networks. Computational models, inspired by the structure and workings of biological neural networks, which find patterns in data. Neural networks are well suited for finding nonlinear patterns. They can be used for pattern recognition and optimization. Some neural network applications involve supervised learning and others involve unsupervised learning.

Network analysis. Toolkit adopted to characterize relationships among discrete nodes in a graph or a network. In social network analysis, connections between individuals in a community are analyzed, for example, how information travels, or who has the most influence over whom.

Signal processing. Methods coming from electrical engineering and applied mathematics originally developed to analyze discrete and continuous signals, that is, representations of analog physical quantities such as radio signals, sounds, and images. This category includes techniques from signal detection theory, which quantifies the ability to discern between signal and noise.

Spatial analysis. A set of techniques, some applied from statistics, which analyze the topological, geometric, or geographical properties encoded in a data set. Often the data for spatial analysis come from Geographic Information Systems that capture data including location information, for example, addresses or latitude/longitude coordinates.

Statistics. The science of the collection, organization, and interpretation of data, including the design of surveys and experiments. Statistical techniques make judgments about what relationships between variables could have occurred by chance (the "null hypothesis"), and what relationships between variables likely result from some kind of underlying causal links.

Simulation. Modeling the behavior of complex systems for forecasting, predicting, and scenario planning. For example, Monte Carlo simulations rely on repeated random sampling, that is, running thousands of simulations, each based on different assumptions.

Big Data Issues

The existence of many data in a distributed manner raises the problem of the network. The data on geographically distributed servers require a strong and efficient network infrastructure. When it comes to Big Data, you think only the issues related to storage of information, and network-related aspects are considered unimportant. The transfer can occur between data center or from a data center to a peripheral location. The existing network infrastructures, especially in Europe, are promising a significant technological improvement in a short time. This means that it will take a lot of work to plan important investments that will create networks able to allow for the exchange of large amounts of data from one location to another. There is also an improvement of applications for cloud computing, virtualized networks that use software to optimize the flow of information in order to have the potential to reach speeds up to 250 times faster than today's Internet. Many US cities participate in the program with dozens of new applications in strategic sectors such as health care, clean energy production, and transportation [2]. With an infrastructure of high-capacity network, stakeholders can perform remote diagnostics, big-crunch data, predict the next hurricane and move people to safety faster, and so on.

Data Transfer Bottleneck

There are several reasons why the Big Data issue can be addressed with the cloud technology. The aim is to make it attractive to keep data in the cloud, for once data is in the cloud for any reason, it may no longer be a bottleneck and may enable new services that could drive the purchase of Cloud Computing cycles. Amazon recently began hosting large public data sets for free on S3; since there is no charge to transfer data between S3 and EC2, these data sets might "attract" EC2 cycles. Another example considers backup services. Since cloud hosting companies send much more data than they receive, the cost of ingress bandwidth could be much less. Therefore, for example, if weekly full backups are moved by compressed daily incremental backups are sent over the network, Cloud Computing might be able to offer an affordable off-premise backup service. Once archived data are conveyed in the cloud, new services become possible. More Cloud Computing cycles could be sold, such as creating searchable indices of all your archival data or performing image analysis on all your archived data to group them according to a specific model. There is also the opportunity to reduce the cost of WAN bandwidth more quickly. Researchers are exploring simpler routers built from commodity components with centralized control as a low-cost alternative to the high-end distributed routers [3]. If such technology were adopted, WAN costs could drop more quickly than they have historically. Therefore, intra-cloud networking technology may be a performance bottleneck as well. Today inside the data center, typically 20–80 processing nodes within a rack are connected via a top-of-rack switch to a second-level aggregation switch. These in turn are connected via routers to storage area networks and wide-area connectivity, such as the Internet or inter-data center WANs. Low-cost 1 Gigabit Ethernet (1GbE) is deployed at the lower levels of aggregation. This bandwidth is considered as a bottleneck for inter-node processing. Another set of batch applications that need higher bandwidth is high-performance computing applications; lack of bandwidth is one reason few scientists using Cloud Computing. It is currently too expensive to deploy a 10 GB Ethernet. However, as the cost per 10 GbE server connections is expected to drop to less than $200 in next years, it will gain widespread deployment inside the cloud since it has the effect of reducing network contention and data transfer latencies. It enables more cores and virtual machines per physical server node by scaling up the network.

Big Database

When you are dealing with activities concerning the management of large amounts of data, one of the preliminary activities that are done at the design stage is the definition of a database, its property, and its features. But "Big data" is defined as data sets whose size is beyond the ability of typical database software tools to capture, store, manage, and analyze [1]. According to this definition, Big Data is not denied in terms of being larger than a certain number of terabytes, but as technology advances over time, the size of data sets that qualify as Big Data will also increase.

There are several solutions to both commercial and noncommercial release of various forms of open source license. Despite being a highly professional, very common in industry, it has difficulty in analyzing the stored data, not in storing it. The database can easily manage billion records; presumably there would have been no difficulty storing the entire billions-row, 10-column table. The big truth about Big Data in traditional databases is that it is easier to get the data in than out. Most DBMSs are designed for an efficient transaction processing: adding, updating, searching for, and retrieving small amounts of information in a large database. Data are typically acquired in a transactional fashion: imagine a user logging into a retail web site (account data are retrieved; session information is added to a log), searching for products (product data are searched for and retrieved; more session information is acquired), and making a purchase (details are inserted in an order database; user information is updated). A fair amount of data has been added effortlessly to a database that, if it is a large site that has been in operation for a while, probably already constitutes "Big Data." In recent years, the context in which decision-makers are working within companies has become increasingly complex. The market environment in which companies are working to change speeds that were unthinkable a few years ago, requiring an increasing amount of information in ever more stringent. At the same time, an increase in count of the number and complexity of systems management at the farms, that if one side makes more information available, the other lengthens the time required to extract and create a potential multiplicity of definitions, resulting overloaded IT departments.

The data warehouse is a solution (a) turning data into information, (b) giving information at the right time to the right people, (c) integrating heterogeneous data sources, (d) offering in-depth historical and independence from source systems, (e) cleansing and certifying data at all levels, and (f) doing business process management by exception.

Today, the prevailing database model is the relational database, and this model explicitly ignores the ordering of rows in tables. Database implementations that follow this model, eschewing the idea of an inherent order on tables, will inevitably end up retrieving data in a nonsequential fashion once it grows large enough that it no longer fits in memory. As the total amount of data stored in the database grows, the problem becomes more significant. To achieve acceptable performance for highly order-dependent queries on truly large data, one must be willing to consider abandoning the purely relational database model for one that recognizes the concept of inherent ordering of data down to the implementation level. Not only in databases, but also in application programming, in general, Big Data greatly magnifies the performance impact of suboptimal access patterns. As data set sizes grow, it becomes increasingly important to choose algorithms that exploit the efficiency of sequential access as much as possible at all stages of processing. Actual trends enable data storage management and analysis in ways that were not possible before with more costly traditional technologies, such as traditional RDBMS. Relational databases were not designed to handle and to work well with "big data" applications. Most of the Internet companies (e.g., Google, Yahoo, Facebook) do not rely on RDBMS technology for this reason. An increasingly important part of Big Data trends is NoSQL. Contrary to misconceptions caused by its name, NoSQL does not prohibit structured query language (SQL). While it is true that some NoSQL systems are entirely nonrelational, others simply avoid selected relational functionality. It can be not only an SQL-based or simply not an SQL-based relational database management system. NoSQL databases form a broad class of nonrelational database management systems that are evolving rapidly, and several solutions are emerging with highly variable feature sets and few standards.

Big Data Tools

Companies and technologies are emerging to solve the Big Data challenges in order to satisfy the increasing demand of novel methods related to discovering, storage, elaboration, and aggregation data to make it manageable.

MapReduce [4] is a programming model for processing large data sets implemented by Google. Usually, MapReduce is used in distributed computing on clusters of computers. The model is inspired by the "map and reduce" functions commonly used in functional programming. Computational processing can occur on data stored either in unstructured file system or in a structure database (also distributed DB). Algorithm is composed of two steps: the first step is Map that consists of dividing tasks into smaller subproblems and distributes them to worker nodes. A worker node may do this again in turn, leading to a multilevel tree structure. The worker node processes the smaller problems and passes the answer back to its master node. Reduce step: consists of collecting the answers to all the subproblems received from worker nodes and combines them in some way to make the output. MapReduce allows for distributed processing of the map and reduction operations. Main features are that each mapping operation must be independent of the others, so all maps can run in parallel way.

Hadoop is an open-source software framework derived from Google's Map Reduce and Google File System (GFS) for reliable, scalable, distributed computing of huge data amounts. It is designed to scale up from single servers to thousands of machines, each offering local computation and storage. Rather than relying on hardware to deliver high-availability, the library itself is designed to detect and handle failures at the application layer, so delivering a highly available service on top of a cluster of computers, each of which may be prone to failures. Hadoop allows splitting them into smaller subtasks, before reducing the results into one master calculation. This technique is not new, it was born with the grid computing that has a new life in the age of cloud computing. Hadoop has been very successful and had seen widespread adoption in both industry and academia alike.

Apache Cassandra is a free open-source, distributed storage system designed to manage large amounts of structured data. It differs from traditional relational database management systems in some significant ways. Cassandra allows scaling to a very large size across many commodity servers, with no single point of failure, and provides a simple schema-optional data model designed to allow maximum power and performance at scale. It was originally developed at Facebook and is now managed as a project of the Apache Software foundation.

HBase is a free open-source, distributed, nonrelational, Hadoop database modeled on Google's Big Table. It is conceived as a distributed, scalable, and Big Data store. HBase is a type of "NoSQL" database. "NoSQL" is a general term meaning that the database is not an RDBMS which supports SQL as its primary access language, but there are many types of NoSQL databases (BerkeleyDB). HBase is more a "Data Store" than "Data Base" because it lacks many of the RDBMS features, such as typed columns, secondary indices, triggers, and advanced query languages. HBase has many features which supports both linear and modular scaling. RDBMS can scale well, but only up to a point—specifically, the size of a single database server—and for the best performance requires specialized hardware and storage devices [5].

Hadoop Distributed File System (HDFS) is designed to store very large data sets reliably and to stream those data sets at high bandwidth to user applications. In a large cluster, thousands of servers both host directly attached to storage and execute user application tasks. By distributing storage and computation across many servers, the resources can grow with demand while remaining economical at every size [6].

R is a free open-source programming language and an integrated environment with software facilities for data manipulation, calculation, and graphical display. The R language has become a de facto standard among statisticians for developing statistical software and is widely used for data analysis. It provides a wide variety of statistical (linear and nonlinear modeling, classical statistical tests, time-series analysis, classification, clustering) and graphical techniques, and is highly extensible. One of R's strengths is the ease with which well-designed publication-quality plots can be produced, including mathematical symbols and formulae where needed.

Clouds of Big Data

As cloud computing is a technological growing trend and more and more enterprises are shifting their information systems into the cloud, it can be assumed that also the migration of Big Data service will be a constant for next years. This shift [7] is also explained by the dropping cost of storage,

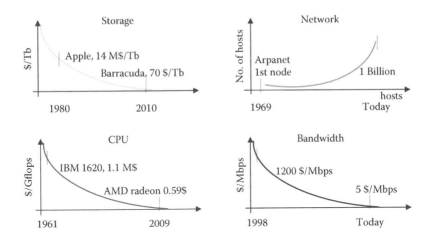

FIGURE 15.1
Cost factors.

CPU, and bandwidth and the exponential increasing of network access over the past decades (see Figure 15.1).

Thus, classes of data that were previously economically unviable to store and mine now can be processed at low cost with cloud services and represent prospects for profit. Cloud and Big Data are not linked only by economic aspects: a strong relationship from the computing point of view can be pointed out. Big data needs performing computing infrastructures for processing huge amount of information and cloud computing is the best and modern way to provide resources in an efficient and dynamic way. Cloud computing in its Infrastructure as a Service (IaaS) model provides computing resources that can be consumed in a pay-per-use way. Typically, it is necessary to build your system manually, to rent virtualized servers and to install your own software. Major providers are Rackspace Cloud, Amazon EC2, Google compute, and Microsoft Azure. It can also be possible to create a Big Data infrastructure in its own data center. In this case should be installed a cloud platform to easily manage computational resources. Some open-source examples are Open Nebula, Open Stack, and Eucalyptus. These platforms exhibit APIs that support also public cloud interaction allowing building hybrid infrastructures. In both cases (public or private cloud), the deployment of clusters for Big Data processing must not be handled manually, but by solutions for automated management of resources and installation of software stacks. Recently, more and more cloud providers offer ready to use Big Data services. Cloud-based Big Data services offer considerable advantages in removing the overhead of configuring and tuning your own clusters, and in ensuring you pay only for what you use. Data locality remains the main issue as it is slow and expensive to transfer data into the cloud, and therefore attention must be given to those solutions where the data are also collected in the cloud. However, cloud services and Big Data are still at an early stage, and in the near future there will be a rapid grow of these technologies, thanks to increasing standardization and innovation.

Renewable Energy Sources

Industrial processes of energy production and distribution occur in nation-wide grid infrastructures. They supply huge quantities of electrical measurements and other data related to the above processes being controlled by Supervisory Control and Data Acquisition (SCADA) systems. To do so, SCADA takes high-frequency measurements and process them in real time. The only small part of the *observational data* could be treated by existing automation algorithms, which are becoming obsolete. Therefore, the true challenge is represented by Big Data management techniques being applied to smart grid and its management. Higher penetration levels of renewable energy sources (RES) in actual energy grid determines the need to manage the unpredictability of the aforementioned RES in real time. Consequently, the Intelligent Distributed Data Processing (IDDP) becomes a new frontier and one valid challenge to solve the above issues by applying the Big Data management. An example is a continuous growing energy production coming from photovoltaic (PV) and other renewable sources that operate independently. In current scenario (Figure 15.2), the cooperative behavior of PV plants is still limited to the *simultaneous injection of the energy flows in the grid,* mainly because the sophisticated optimization techniques would operate with enormous data

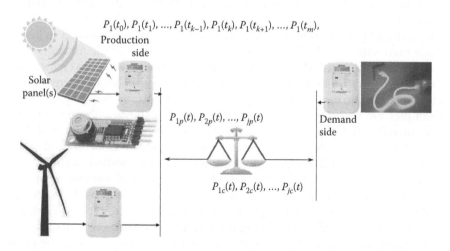

FIGURE 15.2
Abstraction of the power system with photovoltaic and wind electricity plants.

sets from within the very short time frame. Their commitment in generation terms is expressed in a time scale that comes from hours to several days to enable operators to change system parameters to follow the load.

The huge amount of real-time information available from various sensors in the grid is one of the challenges to address with a modernization effort known as the smart grid. Growing data rates in electricity domain is a known fact, so the industry slowly makes the transition toward smart grid, but there is one peculiarity: an increase in data is of multiple orders of magnitude, not simply a doubling or tripling of the amount of data they will be getting.

Installing smart meters at energy production and consumption sites and upgrading utility networks, it provides far more information than the existing processing facilities can elaborate. Once intelligent data-processing systems have fine-grained information about power use, both the supply of power and the demand for it can be managed more efficiently. However, the utilities need to prepare for an onslaught of data before extending them on widespread basis.

Photovoltaic Systems Monitoring

To operate reliably and offer maximum yield, any photovoltaic electric plant requires monitoring and control functions. Most importantly, inverter and grid-related parameter values, for example, PV array voltage V_{DC} (V), grid voltage V_{AC} (V), PV array current I_{DC} (A), grid current I_{AC} (A), PV array power P_{DC} (W), AC grid power P_{AC} (W), and some others are usually available locally being typically stored in an inverter's memory or external data logger for certain time (obviously depending on the data rate) for monitoring purposes. The above items are data logged locally. The *simplest* monitoring can be performed by reading the aforementioned values of almost each grid-connected inverter. The local control might be wired (RS232, RS485), wireless (Bluetooth and Wi-Fi), and powerline interconnecting inverters. The easiest monitoring scheme starts at local PC connected to an inverter (control unit). On a small topology up to 1 km², the neighborhood of PV plants can be monitored at the same time. Remote control and communication between a chain of several dozens of inverters can be realized through an RS485 interface, with a Bluetooth or Wi-Fi wireless connection, or via a powerline grid connection. Wider topologies are typically served by Ethernet, Internet, GSM, UMTS, 4G, and other networking means to reach network-wide control centers. To balance energy production and demand, the gathered and transmitted data have to be analyzed in real time to take control decisions and actuate them timely. From electric viewpoint, photovoltaic production unit has hierarchical structure containing a number of small PV cells assembled in PV modules, PV panels, and PV strings. A number of PV strings originate the electricity production (flow). Since PV production is poorly predictable because it is affected by weather variabilities and many other factors,

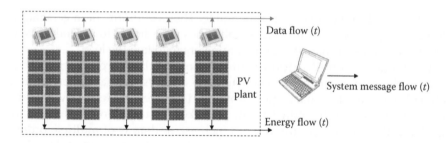

FIGURE 15.3
Abstraction of photovoltaic electricity plant.

more sophisticated monitoring and control schemes require environmental data such as module temperature T_{MOD} (°C), ambient temperature T_{AMB} (°C), global solar irradiance G (W/m²), global solar radiation H (J/m²), wind speed v (m/s), and so on. From ICT viewpoint, photovoltaic energy plant operating from within smart grid context can be abstracted as data provider $D(t)$, physical and digitized energy provider $E(t)$ and $E'(t)$, respectively (Figure 15.3).

Alerts and triggers are elaborated by artificial cognitive systems embodied in software originating system message flow $M(t)$. A growing number of PV plants tending to become ubiquitous/pervasive and very frequent data sampling bring the digital flows accompanying the physical electricity into Big Data problem area. PV plants could store some energy in battery banks. Since continuous overcharging of the batteries would boil their electrolytes, a charge controller is used. Charge controllers used in PV plants monitor the battery voltage. When the battery reaches the full charge, it shorts the PV panel leads. This way some power being generated will be lost, but the operation is harmless for PV panels.

In the context of smart power system, PV plant is an entity originating data volumes going to flow into the grid. Depending on the number of monitored parameters and the frequency of data sampling, the data volumes might vary significantly.

Wind Systems Monitoring

Wind power plants use wind turbines to produce optimized power output corresponding to the most probable wind speeds. Since wind turbines cannot operate at improbable wind speeds, the power output in high wind conditions should be limited to avoid failures of overloaded electrical generators. The yaw position control is used to orient wind turbine rotor perpendicular to the wind stream. Therefore, any wind electric plant requires specific monitoring and control functions. The power control protects the integrity of wind turbine stopping it when the extreme conditions occur. Larger wind turbines (more than 1 kW) could be equipped with active power controls using the combined stall-pitch regulation. Depending on wind speeds, the pitch angle is adjusted continuously to maintain the maximum power specified. In smaller wind (1 kW or less), the whole rotor mechanism could be rotated out of the wind to decrease its rotational speed and power output. Sometimes small wind power plants use the storage. When the wind flow is too low, the wind plant releases the power stored in the batteries. Similarly, the overcharging of the battery bank is managed by charge controllers, but those used in PV plants are unsuitable for wind power applications. Shorting the wind generator output at high-speed spinning, it generates harmful large current spikes. Detaching the generator from the battery with no load on it, it leads to over-speed with a risk of self-destruction. An optimal wind power application charges the battery bank until fully charged and switch to an alternate load then. To do so, the controller constantly monitors the battery charge. When the battery voltage being monitored falls below a given threshold, for example, 0.5 V below the float voltage, the dump load goes offline and the battery charging process starts again. The stored energy is better predictable and it complements the wind production. In this scenario, an intelligent demand-side application can use the additional energy quantities for any useful purpose, such as heating and cooling or anything else, but it calls for real-time energy management schemes. To enable DSM functionalities, system messages could release to the network the status of the batteries being charging.

Wind plant is also an entity originating certain data volumes and data traffic, depending on the data sampling in the way identical to PV plants.

Metering

Electric energy production from *any source* originates a physical energy flow. The energy is flowing across the distribution grid until it reaches the consumers. Observing physical flows, the electric energy digitization process occurs inside electronic meters capable of supplying the instantaneous and cumulative values. Electricity metering is a process that measures the amount of electric energy produced or consumed during a certain timeline, supplying the relevant information about the behavior of the power system in the recent past. In a typical electricity meter, a processor sequentially and endless processes digitized samples coming from the voltage and current inputs performing calculations to measure the power components. The output comes to the peripheral devices for further information processing and knowledge elicitation. The elaborated data are then injected into the powerline communication network. Thus, a digital electricity meter takes the instantaneous electric values (analogic voltages and currents), finding their products to give instantaneous powers first. It integrates them in time dimension to obtain the energy quantities (kW h) and then supplies them to the relevant stakeholders. The collection of daily metering data is frequently displayed as load shape and used in analytics. Automatic meter reading and management (AMM/AMR) is a process automatically collecting and exchanging series of digital data between metering devices and other grid's stakeholders, interpreting the above data and undertaking controlling actions, if any. It originates *data volumes* and *data traffic* (rates) at a smart grid level. In the digital world, AMR is a producer of time (data) series.

Time-driven electricity metering (TDM) is a process that measures the amount of electric energy produced or consumed during a certain period of time, supplying the relevant information about the behavior of the power system in the recent past. AMM automates and makes less expensive operations in smart grids. Operating frequent TDM, near real-time consumption data might replace the estimated/forecasted values. Timely information, broadband connectivity channels (wired/wireless, mobile/handheld, powerline and similar), and automated analytic tools make substantial difference between the Legacy and smart grids providing better process control.

Non-intrusive load monitoring (NILM) is a process for analyzing changes in the electrical quantities such as voltages and/or currents deducing what electric appliances are used in the households and attempting to approximate their individual energy consumption [8]. It detects behavioral patterns of appliances: it models them as finite state machines. Meters with NILM might be used to survey specific uses of electric power in different settings. Although NILM presents privacy concerns [9], it is considered a cheap alternative to intelligent plugs and individual monitors attached on each appliance.

Phasor measurement is a real-time process obtaining representations of the magnitude and phase angle of the electrical waves [10]. The above wave's attributes help one to assess multiple remote points of the electricity grid in stability terms using a common synchronized time source. The increased power quality, prevention of power outages, and demand response automation rely on the use of phasors. The necessary equipment—PMU/PDC units—is rather expensive. This process requires significant data volumes being exchanged in real-time.

The consumption and production are constantly balanced in time dimension. The aim of load management is to ensure the optimum Consumption(t) $\approx$ Production(t) for any t. To manage the production and consumption flows, the electrical quantities should be measured in real time at remote nodes and exchanged at the grid level with grid operators and/or other stakeholders. The electricity metering at remote nodes is the main source of the electricity web data. Small-scale PV plants are usually equipped by time-driven meters characterizing the energy flows several times per day (Figure 15.4) at regular intervals and providing the above information to the grid stakeholders. Using TDM, *a posteriori* analysis detects one power drop occurred between 9.30 and 10.00. The above information supports billing, but it is not timely for controlling purposes because it describes only what had happened in the past.

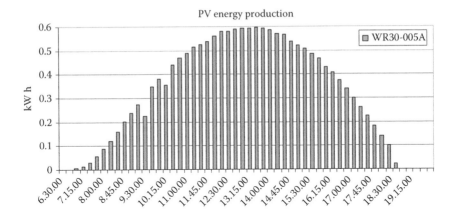

FIGURE 15.4
Energy production on 10 kW h PV plant measured at 15 min time interval daily.

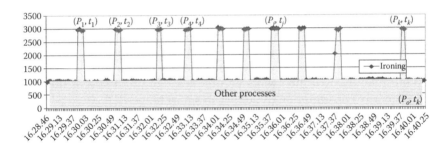

FIGURE 15.5
Very frequent time-driven metering scheme shows ironing process.

To support demand side management (DSM) operations, the variations of the electricity flow should be captured while occurring. To do so, the sampling frequency should be dramatically increased up to subsecond levels. Operating at high temporal resolution, the processes become visible. In the example (Figure 15.5), the consumption dynamics caused by ironing process becomes visible. Similarly, the example (Figure 15.6) shows the variability of photovoltaic production caused by different meteorological conditions (clouds).

Data Volumes and Rates by Metering

In electricity domain, the automated control applications are common and widely used. Meters communicate electricity quantities at regular time

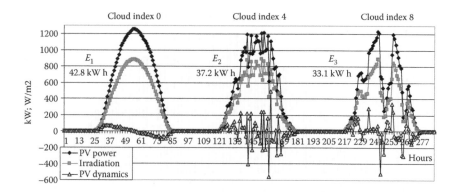

FIGURE 15.6

Frequent measurements of solar radiation (W/m²) and produced power P^{PV} (kW) in 1.6 MW plant shows dynamics in different meteorological conditions.

intervals sending the data to the energy utility company. In the smart grid, the broadband communication channel is fully available, but it is used at certain time intervals only. For instance, having been supplied metering data every 15 min, the communication channel is used 96 times per day to exchange data samples/packets. Table 15.1 compares the information exchange between meters occurring hourly, every minute, or less. At certain sampling rate, the real-life events become tractable, and specifically those causing energy consumption dynamics in smart homes [11].

In general, metering data packets contain attributes describing the power (active and reactive) and/or the energy, the identification of remote nodes, the timestamps, and any further information. In theory, the metering data might be exchanged in raw format. In practice, the industrial protocols add security, interoperability, and other features increasing the payload. Operating sub-second sampling, TDM originates too many data. In the current state of the art of the networking technologies, the grid cannot scale the same increase in

TABLE 15.1

Scalability, Data Volumes Expressed in Tbytes Generated at Different Rates

Nodes	Period	Samples/ Day	Packets	Data Size (raw, Tb)	Data Size (packets, Tb)	Data Rate (Tbps)
30,000,000	Hourly	24	720,000	0.01	0.74	0.01
30,000,000	15 min	96	2,880,000	0.03	2.95	0.03
30,000,000	1 min	1440	43,200,000	0.43	44.24	0.51
30,000,000	1 s	86,400	2,592,000,000	25.92	2,654.21	30.72
30,000,000	0.2 s	432,000	12,960,000,000	129.60	13,271.04	153.60
30,000,000	0.02 s	4,320,000	129,600,000,000	1296.00	132,710.40	1536.00

the sampling rate. In electricity distribution grid with 30 millions of nodes, the data streaming process supplying measurements every 1 s or so will likely produce more than 2 petabytes of data grid-wide (Table 15.1). In saturated grids alimented by significant portion of poorly predictable renewable energies, the real-time load management and control would require higher frequency of data, giving the data volumes expressed in petabytes, and data rates requiring the bandwidth expressed in Pbps, which is unmanageable in the known art. Indeed, metering events traveling every 20 ms grid-wide over 30 million of nodes would become a crowd. Similar to metering operating with power quantities, the control applications observing the remote nodes of the grid operate with Big Data sets. Considering the scalability limits of existing ICT systems, the solution of this Big Data issue would be relevant.

Operating with Metering Data

Smart metering plays an important role in real-time load balancing of power systems using RES. This task uses observational data acquired from within the grid [12]. The algorithms operate both demand's and supply's time series at the grid level. In the context of traditional energy plants, legacy energy plants ensure the stable levels of the energy production. The poor predictability of the photovoltaic and wind energy production—both depending on variable/changing weather conditions—brings an additional difficulty in load balancing. To decide about the appropriate grid control actions, the algorithms operate in time dimension checking constantly and endless the match/mismatch between the energy production and consumption. The non-real-time assessment of load profiles is explained in [13], while the real-time case giving the precise picture of what is happening in the system is discussed in [14]. The Energy Web relies on the cooperation [15] enabled by metering.

Compared with the equipment used in Phasor measurements, the meters are less expensive. Several and different data management techniques could be applied to the data originated by electricity meters in the smart grid. One intuitive option is the use in the control schemes of smart devices calculating *locally* the *indicators* replacing the measurement data to reduce data volumes. Another option derives from the consideration of the hierarchical *structure* of the electricity grid, accounting for the specificity of the distribution processes. The multilayered approach balances the nodes in isolated partitions first and upgrading the broadcast schemes then could be a further option. The third valuable option could be the exploration of *knowledge sharing*. Finally, the anticipatory process knowledge about the natural *processes being translating* between the nodes could give another key to solve Big Data issues.

Making observable low voltage (LV) segments of the smart grid at reasonable cost and keeping the information flow under the flooding thresholds have industrial value. Let us analyze the aforementioned techniques and compare the possible benefits in optimization terms (data volumes and data rates) they could offer.

Event-Driven Metering

The energy delivered into a load is an integral $E(t) = \int_0^t V(t)I(t)dt$ calculated using voltages $V(t)$ and currents $I(t)$. In discrete time–space, the sum $E_t = \Sigma V(t_i)I(t_i)\Delta t$ for $i = [0, t]$ gives steadily growing metering components E_t based on sampled $V(t_i)$ and $I(t_i)$ instead of $E(t)$. Each E_t corresponds to time interval $[0, t]$. The TDM scheme supplies E_t—each $E_t \approx E(t)$ approximately—in discrete time–space with $\Delta t_i = \text{const}$. TDM meter simply delivers computed *electrical values* without any reasoning over time series. For these reasons, very frequent TDM data items supply several repetitive values $E^{TDM}(t_k) \approx E^{TDM}(t_j)$ (Figure 15.7).

Calculating *energy* integrals numerically for short time frames $\Delta t_i = [t_i, t_{i-1}]$, one gets another endless rapid sequences of values $E_{i,i-1} = E(t_i) - E(t_{i-1})$. Because of the relationship $E(t_i) = E(t_{i-1}) + E_{i,i-1}$, the energy variations $E_{i,i-1}$ might be used to filter identical values and to estimate the next expected value. Thus, the event-driven metering (EDM) proposed by Simonov [16] reduces dramatically the data volumes that are being exchanged. The new method eliminates the repetitive/same data being broadcasted in the current metering schemes concentrating on the energy variations only. It sends the data as frequently as the energy dynamics occur.

Since energy flows are not constant with time, $E'(t) \neq 0$ for many t. The factor t (t_i in discrete time–space) sets the trade-off between visibility of electrical processes in their details and the data volume exchanged over the network. The author uses instant t_k in which $E'(t_k) \neq 0$ to modify the dialog between the AMM counterparts obtaining one new metering method. Defining an *event* as a change in the state of one of the metering process elements that influences the AMM/AMR outcomes, the smart meter becomes an *event source* supplying events. Energy utility becomes one of *event recipients*. Thus, *event-driven* approach offering several advantages [17] could be used for metering

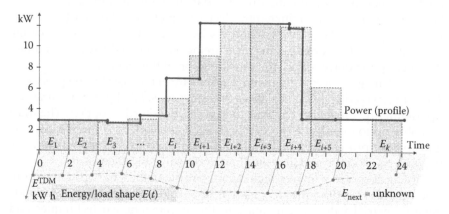

FIGURE 15.7
Time-driven metering.

in smart grids. It changes the way of doing business [18]. The author calculates $E_{1,0}, \cdots E_{i,i-1}$. Until the energy flow is almost constant with time, the author omits grid-wide broadcast of almost identical $E_{i,i-1} = E_{t-1,t-2}$. Instead, the author sends events when $|E(t)'|$ exceeds certain δE value. The plurality of differently programmed smart meters cooperating with intelligent server(s) relates to a novel method of managing electric energy consumption and/or production dynamics and a device therefore described in [16].

Although energy variations are visible in the instant samples of voltage $V(t)$, current $I(t)$, and powers, the method described in [16] operates with integral sums $E_{i,j-k}$ adopting irregular time slicing to match the energy cycles caused by real-life processes. To compare adjacent *integrals* of $E(t)$, it calculates cyclically the speed of variations $E_i' = E_{i,i-1}/\Delta t = (E_i - E_{i-1})/\Delta t$. To detect relevant events, it looks at any (a) *big variation* occurring quickly $E_i' > \delta E$ and (b) series of *small variations* $(E_i' + E_{i-1}' + \cdots) > \delta E$, but for all $\Delta E_i < \delta E$: those accumulating one meaningful change slowly. The first condition is similar to event detection in NILM (variation could be accompanied by semantic labels). The second condition is essential to make observable the grid in stability terms: too many small events could have destabilizing impact on the whole. When the condition (a) or (b) occurs, the meter sends *events* to the network using communication channel. Typically, meters limit the maximal energy using static thresholds. Depending on the contractual conditions of residential/ SOHO users, it could be 3–6 or 20–50 kW h, respectively. For example, δE could be set using 10% of the said threshold.

EDM supplies data series with different timing (Figure 15.8). It originates data when energy variations occur. The server side computers perform intelligent event processing then. The new timing puts online transitions between the stable energy levels. Compared with frequent TDM, the EDM

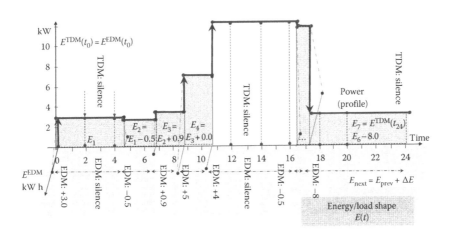

FIGURE 15.8
Load shape with events.

approach reduces data volumes because it omits identical data packets while *streaming EDM data in communication component of the smart grid*. It changes the metering functionality, offering new features; it also adds information, knowledge, and metadata about the variability of energy flows *caused by* real-life processes [19].

In TDM, the factor t sets the trade-off between visibility of electrical processes in their details and the data volume exchanged over the network. In EDM, the events are dispatched when those occur. Thus, the EDM data are time–space variant and should be processed accounting properly the time compression factors. When the transient between two steady states is completed and there is a reasonable certainty that the power system will persist in the above steady state for a certain time-frame (let us think about fridge events happening in night time when other human actors are sleeping), the next energy values are estimated summing the previous level with the variation being occurred $E_{next} = E_{prev} + \Delta E$.

At subsecond levels at scale, TDM could exhaust any bandwidth and increase the costs. In EDM (Figure 15.9), the communication channel is used in a different way, in which remote nodes send data with different time-stamps, reducing the communication bottlenecks.

To be used in grid control applications, the EDM sequence {Meter$_{ID}$, E_1^{EDM},..., E_j^{EDM},...} should be timely delivered. In the known art, the meters are typically asked to send the data (pulling). The new method sends the data proactively from remote meters, without waiting for any polling request from the grid side. In service-oriented approach, the meter publishes data packets E_j^{EDM} and someone subscribes them. Simonov [16] *pushes* the quick/slow energy dynamics when those are occurring at the remote nodes (Figure 15.10).

Legacy applications, including billing procedures, currently use TDM. The new and more efficient real-time control procedures are enabled by EDM because of reducing the data quantities. To keep the compatibility with the legacy and include the newly enabled applications, the hybrid approach could be used (Figure 15.11). It combines two data flows inheriting infrequent TDM samples with real-time EDM messages that are being interleaved.

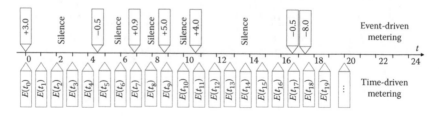

FIGURE 15.9
Time scale in event- and time-driven metering.

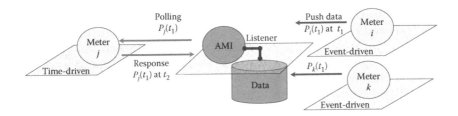

FIGURE 15.10
Grid-side operator pulling remote meters.

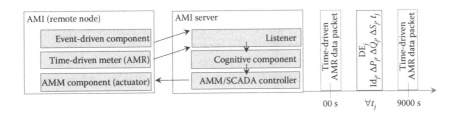

FIGURE 15.11
Time scale in hybrid metering with both events and time-driven components.

Using Event-Driven Metering

Let us compare TDM and EDM series acquired during the same time-frame. Limiting zooming to 900 s (Figure 15.12), the infrequent TDM operated at 15 min time interval in one residential house that supplies values of 337 and 320 W h at 16:30 and 16:45, respectively.

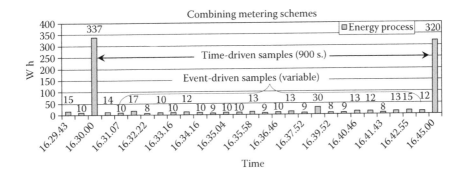

FIGURE 15.12
Hybrid metering scheme with both TDM and EDM components.

The overall energy consumption between 16:30 and 16:45 measured by both TDM and EDM schemes is the same (ca. 320 W h). Using the above *values* and their *timestamps*, the calculation of the superposed (complex) processes in energy terms in new way becomes possible: *event-driven approach* gives analytically energy values for all the subperiods characterized by stable levels and supplied the exact *durations* of each cycle. Thus, EDM supplies additional information about *how* energy processes occur in time dimension. The EDM has the *time-wrapping/compression* property. The EDM data set has the variable time-scale, so it might be analyzed from different perspectives.

The main advantage of EDM is the reduced information flow compared with TDM *at frequent sampling*. In the example, frequent TDM at 1-s sampling gave 900 values, while EDM sequence counts 25 events only. During the same time-frame, 25 EDM samples describe *how* the energy variations are occurred in time dimension. Thus, the new method exchanged fewer events but gave more information about the processes.

Electronic meters are relatively cheap, widely available, and installed at the customer's premises. A good overview of the communication standards used in the commercial metering systems is reported in [20]. Compared with Phasor Measurement Units and Power Quality Analyzers, the above devices represent a low-cost opportunity to trace the footprint of the real-life processes in energy terms. Therefore, the extension of the low-cost device used only for billing purposes to the DSM functionalities appears valuable. The new communication scheme makes unnecessary frequent sampling in metering. It sends metering data for billing purposes at the same time intervals at the same cost as before. The event-driven data exchange brings some additional data and costs, but the additional data traffic is limited to a relatively small number of energy variations occurring at the remote nodes. In turn, it gives the possibility to assess the power system in stability terms and set up the real-time controlling policy over a plurality of the remote nodes equipped by the above devices. The compression ratio offered by EDM could be tuned varying the fuzzy thresholds δE. Because the sensibility of the extended metering system distinguishing between the "meaningful" and "irrelevant" energy dynamics depends on δE, the number of EDM samples being exchanged depends directly on $IF_{fuzzy} (\Delta P_j > \delta P)$ THEN Send_DE_Message().

Cooperative Approach

In the smart grid there are many meters. These might be reprogrammed to supply EDM data in real time (Figure 15.13) telling about the processes and energy dynamics.

Cooperative metering schemes require the presence of *one listener* receiving messages from the network and processing them (Figure 15.14).

Summing the variations occurring in subtopology during the same time frames, some negative dynamics could be compensated by positives ones, giving a chance to obtain new control schemes based on the aforementioned

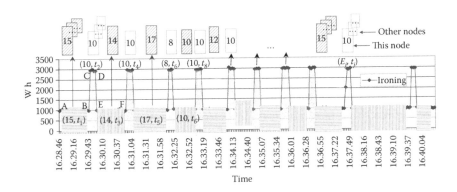

FIGURE 15.13
Visualization of elementary components in hybrid metering.

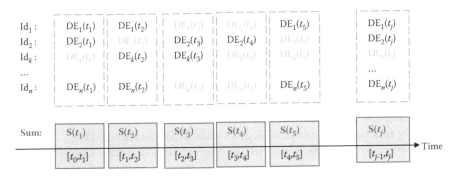

FIGURE 15.14
Server-side aggregation of the energy dynamics.

information. This approach draws from Phasor techniques [10] inheriting their time windowing. For control purposes at the node level, the $E_j(t_k)$ values could be used. In addition, the grid (segments) could be controlled using $S(t_k)$. The grid partitioning could be assessed using $E_j(t_k)$ and $S(t_k)$ series altogether.

The described method enables capturing events. It reduces data volumes and rates.

Use of Explicit Knowledge

Business actors tend to maximize *independently* and *individually* their objectives in energy and economic efficiency terms with no other cooperation forms. They estimate energy quantities using local information related to local conditions and local production dynamics without any knowledge about neighborhood. Several PV plants operating in the same neighborhood are typically affected by the *same* natural phenomena/process slowly migrating over. Once the translation of their effects in time–space becomes tractable, its anticipatory control potential could be used to optimize the energy flows. The almost immediate electronic communication between PV plants lets us share the real-time facts about their energy dynamics. Another method to reduce data volumes relies on the use of process knowledge.

Hyman operate energy flows in time dimension. Energy dynamics are *caused by* some known agents. The processes showing repetitive time series of data are called cyclic or nomothetic. In nomothetic processes, the time series of data are repetitive. Having detected certain patterns or their parts, these could be translated in time–space and reappear again. The simplest example comes from photovoltaic generation *cyclically varying* in the time–space because *depending on* daily Sun path (Figure 15.15). In addition, it is also affected by moving clouds (Figure 15.6) introducing another type of variability being superposed.

The PV energy production originates time series of metering data. Remote nodes in the neighborhood supply daily data sets making large collection of similar load shapes. Using formalized knowledge about ideal PV production shapes and the topology, the dependencies between series might be found and expressed by formulae. Considering the annual Sun path, the calculation of PV production for the next day in the ideal weather conditions becomes possible based on the following functions (Figure 15.16). It gives another key to reduce data.

PV energy production is affected by the rotation of Earth. Consequently, pairs of load shapes from different plants staying in one relatively small neighborhood are dependant (Figure 15.15) *in time dimension*. Sunrise occurring in two—eastern and western—places, but not simultaneous. Therefore, knowing the ideal daily Sun path occurring in one place "A," it becomes

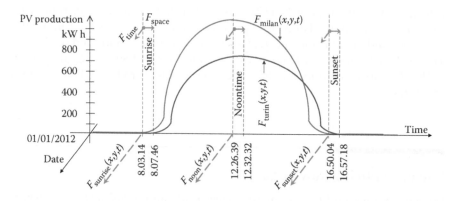

FIGURE 15.15
Cyclic process of photovoltaic generation shows spatial and temporal translations.

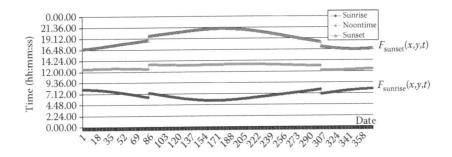

FIGURE 15.16
Annual Sun path. Discontinuity comes from the light-saving time.

possible to calculate the Sun path going to occur in another place "B" nearby "A." The functional link $E_A(t_k) = f(E_B(t_{k-dt}))$ is a method to calculate $E_A(t)$ values when the value of $E_B(t)$ is known. Using this, *repetitive sequences* coming from *different locations* could be reduced. Compared with the speed of electronic communication, the Earth's rotation is much slower. The example is over-simplified to depict the idea, but metering data volumes might be reduced furthermore using the knowledge about *time translation* of effects.

Let us consider two different PV plants j and k supplying load shapes $F_j(t)$ and $F_k(t)$ from the same neighborhood. Because of the Sun path, two observers staying nearby PV_j and PV_k, respectively, will register their *sunrise, noon,* and *sunset* events occurring at different time. The energy variation $E_A(t_k) - E_A(t_{k-1})$ occurring in one place is useful in calculating the expectation of the next $E_B(t_{k+1})$ in the neighborhood. In the experimental setup (Figure 15.17), observers 1 and 5 register power dropouts caused by moving clouds at different time t_j and t_k. The time difference $|t_j - t_k|$ comes from the fraction between spatial distance $|PV_j, PV_k|$ and constant Earth rotation's speed. The spatial distance $|PV_1, PV_2|$ determines the 1-s time difference between $E_1(t)$ and $E_2(t)$. Assuming the same PV production capacity installed at both sites, the $E_B(t_{k+1}) = E_B(t_k) + (E_A(t_k) - E_A(t_{k-1}))$.

Knowing the propagation speed of the phenomenon (Earth's rotation, cloud mobility, etc.) over local topology, the effects caused by the same agent could be calculated in terms of corresponding energy dynamics. In the example (Figure 15.15), the time difference dt between sunset in Milan and Turin— $F_k(t)$ and $F_j(t + dt)$, respectively, on January 1, 2012, is 4 min 32 s, whereas the time difference between the nodes PV_4 and PV_3 depicted in Figure 15.17 is 1 s.

Noncooperative Optimization of PV Plants

The state-of-the-art energy grids use the electronic meters communicat-ing over the ICT networks with central legacy/ERP systems [21]. From the

FIGURE 15.17
Experimental setup used to acquire data in the neighborhood.

ICT viewpoint, the smart grid is an intelligent combination of several roles (e.g., consumer, producer, etc.) operating in real-time with the abstractions of energy flows (data sets). Having been simultaneously exchanged, both energy and information quantities travel across the common grid topology $\mathfrak{R}$ hosting several PV plants PV_i, $i \in [1, n]$, with generation capacities $P^{PV}_i(t)$ expressed in kW h. Let us denote values metered in discrete time–space as $E_i(t_k)$. Electronic meters generate and exchange in the network $\mathfrak{R}$ data series, indicating the amounts of electric energy that have been produced/consumed during given past periods of time $\{(E_1,t_1), (E_2,t_2),..., (E_j,t_j),...\}$.

The renewable energy $E_i(t)$ in $\mathfrak{R}$ depends on several factors, such as geographical coordinates, meteorological effects, installation parameters, age and conditions of PV panels, etc. Predictability is important because the addition of variable PV generation source reduces system stability. Forecasts of expected PV output—let us denote the said believe/expectation by $P_i^*(t)$—and the degree of uncertainty to predict particular *volatile periods* are required for days ahead down to hours ahead. Different methods do exist to forecast solar resources at differing time scales (e.g. [22]). Knowledge about the future production of solar plants $P_i^*(t)$ allows for enhanced planning and management of energy reserve, which leads, as example, to the avoidance of a forced shedding of power supply from renewable energy plants, with a corresponding saving of energy reserve correlated costs [23].

Output of PV plants is considerably variable because of the pluriannual Sun intensity variations, annual Sun path, the degradation of the PV elements, and meteorological events and clouds. Until the forecast is elaborated in advance for each t using any state-of-the-art technique, pairs $P_i^*(t)$ and $P_j^*(t)$ remain *independent*. A single distribution feeder with independent small-scale plants limits the massive RES generation. Operating independent forecasts, the influence of different time dimensions cannot be captured. Modeling *at the same time* influence of large- and small-scale distributed PV plants *in electric terms* of grid voltages and frequencies disturbance is a complex task. Difference between $P_i^{PV}(t)$ and $P_i^*(t)$ might become critical in saturated grids where all reserves $P_i^{PV}(t) - P_i^*(t)$ are already utilized by the existing loads for certain time periods.

PV energy production curve (Figure 15.6) shows power generation profiles of three days with different meteorological conditions: totally sunny day, partial cloud coverage, and rapidly changing cloud coverage. The data set shows that integral sums $E_1 > E_2 > E_3$. E_2 is lower than E_1 *because of* the power drops caused by clouds. The forecast could estimate the expected drop as 13% compared with E_1 *because of* the Sun index, but the known art states nothing about *when* the power drops occur during the day.

To operate with comparable categories, Simonov et al. [22] use the *cloud index* concept partitioning the *conservative* Event Space in numbered similarity clusters from *totally sunny* to *totally cloudy*. The corresponding cloud index values shown in Figure 15.6 are 0, 4, and 8, for totally sunny, partial cloudy, and totally cloudy, respectively, which are in agreement with the values given in [22]. The major forecast errors are mainly concentrated during the days with *cloud index* in the interval 3–7 because the irradiance profile changes sharply due to clouds and their relative movement. Any reduction of negative effect on power quality contributes in better PV integration.

Simonov [16] observes the relationships between power drops (events) attempting to calculate the relevant *timing*. In a massive PV energy distribution, clouds cause diverse changes and ramps in PV output in different parts of the *same* plant or among *different* plants in the same area. The degree of diversity among points/plants can be characterized by the degree of correlation of *simultaneous changes* in the output. The known algorithms remain efficient until $P_j^{PV} = f(P_i^{PV})$ refers to the same t_k. Using EDM scheme, the proposed method captures energy variations. Comparing for a given PV plant j its actual $E_j(t_k)$ with the expected $E_j^*(t_k)$ value supplied by forecast procedures, one data packet should be sent into the network only if $|E_j(t_k) - E_j^*(t_k)|$ exceeds the ΔE threshold. Using this approach, the system populated by a number of *independent agents* remains silent in all the remaining cases, which reduces the data volumes and data rates. Setting $\Delta E = 10\%$ of the nominal power, in the example (Figure 15.6), the number of messages telling about unexpected significant power dropouts was 40 and 35 (cloud index 4 and 8, respectively). The ideal load shape (cloud index 0) acquired by TDM gives 96 messages. Because the method filters all expected values and supplies the only unexpected energy dynamics, it reduces data volumes and rates.

Cooperative Optimization using EDM

Increasing substantially the number of PV sources, system complexity becomes a factor to cope with. Because clouds could cause diverse changes and ramps in PV output among *different* plants in the same area, the calculation of effects caused by clouds locally at one site is statistically relevant to the neighbors because some of them are going to experience *effects of the same cause being translating*. Thus, the elaboration of real-time *metering data* originates a mutual knowledge to *share, exchange*, and *elaborate* using cooperative approach. When the differences between energy dynamics occurring at multiple PV sites are *not simultaneous*, in several cases the *time translation* between similar energy dynamics PV_i and PV_j for different t_k and t_l (Figure 15.18) exists. It could be observed and captured by EDM supplying time series containing certain patterns. Pattern-matching techniques could be used to discover repetitive patterns in time series coming form *different nodes* then.

In one small neighborhood hosting PV plants, meteorological information about the area can help one to *forecast* approaching clouds and predict the impact the atmospheric disturbance will cause on PV output. The time it takes for a passing cloud to shade a PV system depends on the PV plant size, cloud speed, and other factors that can be predicted with some accuracy [22]. However, the independent load forecast becomes inefficient in *saturated* grids with distributed PV generation because it does not consider properly the intraday events.

Simonov [16] *uses* new EDM method in limited 4D areas of *conservative Event Space* to trace and handle the sequence of energy dynamics in real time. One observer—denoted as O_i—takes $E_i(t_k)$ data at each t_k when energy variation happens: $|\Delta E_i(t)| > \delta E$. Using EDM and sharing the data, one *timely* acquires the awareness about sequences of events occurring *in*

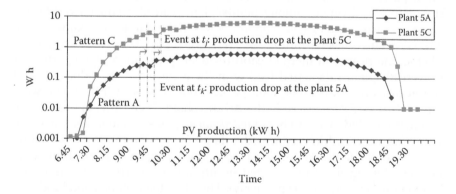

FIGURE 15.18

Two neighbors having different nominal power are linked by one relationship translating effects in time.

different places. O_j has the *simultaneous information* about all effects occurred so far, but O_i knows also what should happen next according to the model and/or formal rules. Thus, one can form the *belief* based on O_i observations and continue waiting until it will be validated positively or negatively at the *right future time*.

The author uses *belief/expectation* expressed by an observer as set of formal rules, expressions, or formulae describing the *expected or calculated* effect going to mature in a certain place at a certain time because of certain process(es) occurring in 4D are being modeled. The belief could be written symbolically as $B_j(P_i, t_k^A, t_{k+dt}^B) = \{R_1, R_2,...,$ because of $P_i\}$, where j characterizes the observer O_j, t^A is the time in the place A, t^B is the time in the place B, P_i is a process originating the effects. In electricity observation by EDM, the belief relates $E(t_k^A) \rightarrow E(t_{k+dt}^B)$ in the time earlier than t_{k+dt}^B. The *conditional probability* $P(B_j|P_i)$ expressed by belief tends to 1 because the *relationship* during short *finite time* $[t_k, t_{k+dt}]$ remains continuous. Unlike the traditional IF SomeCondition(t_k) THEN DoSomething(t_k) clauses calculated at the *same* t_k, belief anticipates the effect $E(t_{k+dt}^B)$ because of P_i, which will become verifiable by IF $E(t_{k+dt}^B)$ later on. The anticipatory discrete systems computing present states as a function of prediction of the model relies on the incursion $x(t_{k+1}) = f[..., x(t_{k-1}), x(t_k), x(t_{k+1}),...]$, where the value of a variable $x(t_{k+1})$ at time t_{k+1} is a function of this variable at past, present, and future times [24]. Operations with the instances of such processes require deeper consideration of time dimension.

This approach enables the *calculation* of the next expected values at one node (k) for which the time–space dependence is given explicitly by one functional, by knowing the observation of energy dynamics occurring at another node (j). The author calculates the expected $E_{B^-}(t_{k+1}) = E_B(t_k) + (E_A(t_k) - E_A(t_{k-1}))$. Until $E_B(t_k)$ and $E_{B^-}(t_k)$ remain identical along the time, there is no need to stream repetitive data grid-wide. In such cases, the knowledge about the function linking $E_B(t)$ and $E_A(t)$ is sufficient to eliminate redundant static samples coming from the second data source. When temporal relationships exist and those could be described explicitly, the new formal knowledge enables anticipatory control schemes. In effect, cause C_1 acting in place A and giving an effect C_1 measured at t_1 is the knowledge anticipating the effect E_2 going to occur—but not yet occurred—in the place B because of the same C_1 in translation from A to B.

The method is valid because daily patterns $\{E_j(t_k), E_j(t_k+1), ...\}$ show effects of the *repetitive* daily processes and events (sunrise, noon, sunset). Occurring in the different points of 4D, the *spatial and temporal distances* could be calculated depending on the Earth's rotation. Mostly eastern observer detects an effect, gains the anticipatory knowledge earlier than the western observers. Using these observations, *any* observer builds his own belief/expectation and remains waiting until the materialization or rejection of said hypothesis. The above calculated shape permits one filtering the unnecessary metering values. In effect, the only unexpected values need to be broadcasted. Because of the temporal distance but instant messaging, the result of the aforementioned computation might be supplied to neighboring observers earlier than the effect of (P_j at PV_j) will occur. Any agent, specifically the eastern ones, can decide appropriate control actions based on the most complete knowledge about the ongoing P_j, effects of P_j occurred elsewhere, and expected effects P_j will have at given premises. In this cooperative way, an anticipatory discrete system with hyper-incursion gains the ability to *compute* the future attributes of electric quantities.

Simonov [16] takes the geographical coordinates of PV plants, calculates the respective *spatial distances* between nodes $d(PV_i, PV_j) = ||x_{ij}, y_{ij}||$, and stores the resulting scalar values in the database. The *temporal distances* $dt^P(PV_i, PV_j)$ between the PV nodes are process-dependant, with the Earth's rotation denoted as P. In northern Italy, the EW component of daily Sun path ($v_{ang}^P = 0.0041 \deg/s$) makes $dt^P \approx 333$ linear meters per second. The result is a function of time–space, but it could be precalculated and represented as a set. In Europe, the morning and afternoon Sun path components are asymmetric. In the example, the $d(PV_3, PV_4) = 609$ m, while the $dt^{Sun\ path}(t, PV_{34})$ gives 1–3 s on the 1st of June. In Figure 15.17, from 2 to 5 s could be available to anticipate the control of PV_1 based on the observation of PV_5. This time is sufficient to control proactively *cyclic processes* occurring at the said nodes based on the dynamics occurring at neighboring ones.

Similarly, the effects of moving clouds could be calculated. The daily events for each PV_i come from EDM observation. The plants in neighborhood could have different nominal production values, for example, $Max(P_j^{PV}(t)) = k_{ij} * Max(P_i^{PV}(t))$. Using coefficients k_{ij} stored in the database, the author makes comparable load shapes $E_i(t)$ and $E_j(t)$ applying $E_i'(t) = E_j(t)/k_{ij}$ and takes the corresponding forecast P', which is produced in advance. Now, the endless EDM flow observation starts. The trigger monitors the difference between the expected and real values. Thus, the formulae $\delta E_i(t) = E_i(t) - E_i^*(t)$ quantifies the difference between the actual and expected values. Since the sequences δE_i and δE_j were made comparable, those might contain patterns being translated in time–space. Pattern matching attempts the detection of the energy dynamics *caused by* the *same agent* acting while moving in 4D. It could make explicit the relationships between some pairs of E_i and E_j, those existing during some time frames. The newly elicited relationship $R^P(E_i, E_j, t)$ linking *neighboring* nodes can be described in mathematical or logical terms. The same cause moving in space *translates* effects *along the time*. Effects of the same causes depend on k_{ij}. If nodes PV_i and PV_j are related by any R, the identical effect occurs when $k_{ij} = 1$. It will be amplified if $k_{ij} > 1$ or reduced if $k_{ij} < 1$.

In the experimental settings (Figure 15.6), two small-scale PV neighbors 5A and 5C have produced load shapes (Figure 15.18) showing the time dependencies between effects: several terms $E_i(t_k)$ and $E_j(t_m)$ were linked by *cause–effect relationship*. Although absolute PV energy dynamics $dE_i(t_k)$ and $dE_j(t_l)$ occurring at the above plants are not yet directly comparable because of k_{ij} (Figure 15.19a), the time-shift becomes visible (Figure 15.19b) operating comparable series.

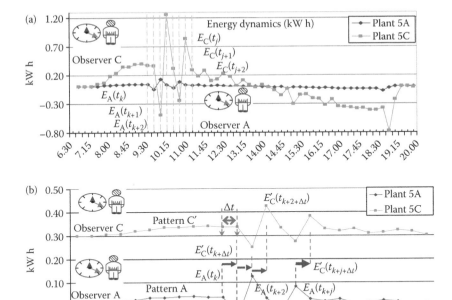

FIGURE 15.19
Energy dynamics on two plants with different nominal power.

Contrary to Sun path dynamics keeping the same time constraints at all nodes, the cloud variability is always limited in time dimension. Once the first pattern match is detected giving $R^P(E_i, E_j, t)$, the validity of R^P needs to be controlled. Using EDM, the author relates at least *three* subsequent patterns to conclude about repetitiveness. The inference on relations is possible because of the transitivity $A(t_k, t_{k+dt}) \to B(t_l, t_{l+dt})$ and $C(t_m, t_{m+dt}) \to D(t_n, t_{n+dt})$ saying that $(A \to C)$ is $(B \to D)$ until $(t_k - t_m)$ and $(t_l - t_n)$ remain the same. Using this approach, the system populated by a number of *cooperative agents* reduces the data volumes and data rates: the only deviations from the corresponding ideal beliefs originate system messages. The system sends no data when actual values are in line with the forecast made for neighbors.

Conclusion

The described methods are useful to *reduce data volumes and data rates* originated by metering in smart grids. The *EDM method* captures energy dynamics in real time making unnecessary very frequent time-driven observations.

Proactive control actions *on a very short time horizon* rely on shared real-time knowledge about energy dynamics going to diverge from the forecasted and/or computed values at any location. Supplying the time series for one plant and the formula to calculate the expected events, the communication of the only unexpected ones reduce data volumes.

Mutual *knowledge* produced by EDM and quickly exchanged with the neighbors anticipates effects of natural phenomena being translated slowly. The relationships between pairs of nodes—even if limited in time—are useful to calculate the time series for neighbors. It reduces the redundant data collections and gives a tool to simplify massive incorporation of RES in saturated grid conditions. Example shows how the new computational method masters real-time cooperation between PV plants during the days with variable cloudiness (cloud index stays in the range 3–7) impacting proportionally on all PV plants in the neighborhood but at different times. When the only predictive model to reduce uncertainty becomes insufficient, the local cooperative approach brings both the collective optimization and anticipatory control. The real-life achievable impact still depends on the capacity to operate efficient decision-making within the relatively short timeframes. The author exploited the information available locally at the grid level transforming the implicit knowledge into benefits in a collective global optimization perspective.

References

1. J. Manyika, M. Chui, B. Brown, J. Bughin, R. Dobbs, C. Roxburgh, A. Hung Byers, Big data: The next frontier for innovation, competition, and productivity, Report. McKinsey Global Institute, USA.
2. Next-generation Internet applications, http://us-ignite.org (accessed January 2013).
3. N. Mckeown, T. Anderson, H. Balakrishnan, G. ParuklarL, L. Peterson, J. Rexford, S. Shenker, J. Turner, OpenFlow: Enabling innovation in campus networks. *ACM SIGCOMM Computer Communication Review* 38, 2 (April 2008).
4. J. Dean, S. Ghemawat, MapReduce: Simplified data processing on large clusters, *Communications of the ACM—50th anniversary issue*: 1958, 51(1), 107–113, 2008.
5. HBASE, http://hbase.apache.org/ (accessed January 2013).
6. HADOOP, hadoop.apache.org/ (accessed January 2013).
7. M. Driscoll, Tutorial: Building Data Startups, Strata On Line Conference, May 2011, http://strataconf.com/strata-may2011/public/schedule/detail/20623
8. G. Hart, E. Kern, F. Schweppe, U.S. Patent 4858141, 1989.
9. T. Nicol, T. Overbye, Toward technological defenses against Load Monitoring techniques, *North American Power Symposium*, NAPS 2010, Arlington, TX, pp. 1–5, 26–28 Sept. 2010.
10. A.G. Phadke, J.S. Thorp, *Synchronized Phasor Measurements and Their Applications*, Springer, New York, 2008.

11. A. Ricci, B. Vinerba, E. Smargiassi, I. De Munari, V. Aisa, P. Ciampolini, Power-Grid Load Balancing by Using Smart Home Appliances, Consumer Electronics, 2008. ICCE 2008, Hoi An City, Vietnam. Digest of Technical Papers. Int. Conf., pp. 1–2, 9–13 Jan. 2008.

12. S. Bruno, S. Lamonaca, S.M. La Scala, G. Rotondo, U. Stecchi, Load control through smart-metering on distribution networks, *PowerTech, 2009 IEEE Bucharest*, pp. 1–8, June 28, 2009–July 2, 2009.

13. D. Gerbec, F. Gubina, Z. Toros, Actual load profiles of consumers without real-time metering, Power Engineering Society General Meeting, 2005. *IEEE*, 3, 2578–2582, 2005.

14. M. Dondo, M. El-Hawary, An approach to implement electricity metering in real-time using artificial neural networks, *IEEE Transactions on Power Delivery*, 18(2), 383–386, 2003.

15. D. Tuan, The Energy Web: Concept and challenges to overcome to make large scale renewable and distributed energy resources a true reality, Industrial Informatics, 2009. INDIN 2009, Cardiff, UK. *7th IEEE Int. Conf.*, pp. 384–389, 2009.

16. M. Simonov, ISMB Patent application PCT/IB2011/055991, 2011.

17. S. Sucic, B. Bony, L. Guise, Standards-compliant event-driven SOA for semantic-enabled smart grid automation: Evaluating IEC 61850 and DPWS integration, *2012 IEEE International Conference on Industrial Technology (ICIT-2012)*, Athens, Greece, pp. 403–408, 2012.

18. C. Edwards, Working the event horizon [Systems Event-Driven SOA], *Information Professional*, 4(6), 30–34, 2007.

19. M. Simonov, R. Zich, M. Mussetta, Information processing in smart grids and consumption dynamics, In A. Soro, E. Vargiu, G. Armano and G. Paddeu (eds), *Information Retrieval and Mining in Distributed Environments, Studies in Computational Intelligence*, 2011, Vol. 324/2011, pp. 267–286, DOI: 10.1007/978-3-642-16089-9_15, Springer, Heidelberg, 2011.

20. K. De Cramer, G. Deconick, Analysis of state-of-the-art smart metering communication standards, *Proc. of YRS-2010 Conf*, Leuven, 2010.

21. J. Fan, S. Borlase, The evolution of distribution, *IEEE Power and Energy Magazine*, 7(2), 63–68, 2009.

22. M. Simonov, M. Mussetta, F. Grimaccia, S. Leva, R. Zich, Artificial Intelligence forecast of PV plant production for integration in smart energy systems, *International Review of Electrical Engineering (IREE)*, 7(1), 3454–3460, 2012.

23. E. Collino, C. Dainese, D. Ronzio, Application of solar radiation forecast for the management of a mixed PV-biomass power plant: A preliminary evaluation, *EMS Annual Meeting Abstracts*, Vol. 8, EMS2011-530-1, 2011, 11th EMS/10th ECAM, September 2011.

24. D. Dubois, Computing Anticipatory Systems with Incursion and Hyperincursion, *1st Int.l Conf. on Computing Anticipatory Systems: CASYS*, The American Institute of Physics, AIP Conference Proceedings, Vol. 437, pp. 3–29, USA, 1998.

16

Scaling of Geographic Space from the Perspective of City and Field Blocks and Using Volunteered Geographic Information[*]

Bin Jiang and Xintao Liu

CONTENTS

Introduction

Scaling of geographic space refers to the fact that for a large geographic area, the small constituents or units are far more common than the large ones (Jiang 2010). For example, there are far more short streets than long ones (Jiang 2007, Kalapala et al. 2006); far more small city blocks than large ones (Lämmer et al. 2006); far more small cities than large ones, a phenomenon referred to as Zipf's law (1949); far more short axial lines than long ones (Jiang

---

[*] This chapter is a reprint, with permission of the publisher, of the original paper: Jiang B. and Liu X. 2012, Scaling of geographic space from the perspective of city and field blocks and using volunteered geographic information. *International Journal of Geographical Information Science*, 26(2), 215–229.

and Liu 2010). This notion of far more small things than large ones is a de facto heavy-tailed distribution that includes power law, exponential, log-normal, stretched exponential, and power law with a cutoff (Clauset et al. 2009). The heavy-tailed distributions have been well studied to characterize many natural and societal phenomena and have received a revival of interest in the Internet age; interested readers can refer to Clauset et al. (2009) and references therein for more details. The heavy-tailed distributions differ fundamentally from a normal distribution. For things that follow a normal distribution, the sizes of the things would not vary much but be centered around a typical value—a mean or an average. In this respect, the standard deviation is used to measure the overall variation between the individual values and the mean. The scaling of geographic space is closely related to, yet fundamentally different from, the conventional concept of spatial heterogeneity, which is usually characterized by a normal distribution (Anselin 2006, Goodchild 2004).

This paper is motivated by the belief that geographic space essentially exhibits a heavy-tailed distribution rather than a normal distribution. We attempt to investigate the scaling of geographic space from the perspective of city and field blocks using street networks involving both cities and countryside of the three largest European countries: France, Germany, and the UK. We take the three-street networks and decompose them into individual blocks, each of which forms a minimum ring or cycle such as city blocks and field blocks. The sizes of the blocks in each country exhibit a log-normal distribution, that is, far more small blocks than large ones. We further find that the mean of the blocks make a clear-cut distinction between small and large blocks and that the blocks with a size below the mean tend to belong to city blocks, while those above the mean belong to field blocks. In contrast to city blocks, field blocks are surrounded by a minimum ring of road segments in countryside. Based on this interesting finding and using the concept of spatial autocorrelation, we develop an approach to defining and identifying cities or city boundaries for countries. We define the border number as the topological distance of blocks far from the outmost borders extracted from the street networks; refer to the "Data and Data Processing" section for more details. We map the border number for individual blocks to identify true center(s) of the countries.

This paper is further motivated by another intriguing issue, that is, how to delineate city boundaries. Delineating city boundaries objectively is essential for many urban studies and urban administrations (Rozenfeld et al. 2008). Researchers and practitioners alike usually rely on the boundaries provided by census or statistical bureaus. These imposed boundaries are considered to be subjective or even arbitrary. Advanced geospatial technologies such as geographic information system (GIS) and remote sensing provide updated data sources for extracting urban boundaries. However, to the best of our knowledge, existing solutions are established on a raster format. For example, detecting urban areas from satellite imagery, in particular, using nightlight imagery (Sutton 2003) and creating city boundaries from density surface of street junctions based on kernel density estimation

(Borruso 2003, Thurstain-Goodwin and Unwin 2000). Jiang and Jia (2011) adopted an approach that clusters street nodes (including intersections and ends) first and then imposes a grid to delineate city boundaries, thus being raster-based in essence. The raster-based solutions, due to the resolution choice, inevitably suffer from the modified areal unit problem—the sizes of map units affect the results of statistical hypothesis tests (Openshaw 1984). Following scaling analysis of city and field block sizes, this paper suggests a vector-based approach to delineating city boundaries. This approach is considered to be a by-product of the scaling analysis, a nice application of the head/tail division derived (cf. section "Lognormal Distribution of Block Sizes and Head/Tail Division Rule" for more details).

The contribution of this paper is three-fold: (1) we find that the mean of block sizes can divide all blocks into city blocks and field blocks; (2) based on this finding, we develop a novel approach to delineating city boundaries from large street networks; and (3) we define border number from a topological perspective to map the centers of a large geographic space. Besides, we provide a set of procedures or algorithms to extract city and field blocks from large street networks using data-intensive geospatial computing.

The remainder of this paper is structured as follows. Section "Data and Data Processing" introduces in a detailed manner data and data processing to extract individual city and field blocks from the large street networks of the three European countries. Section "Lognormal Distribution of Block Sizes and Head/Tail Division Rule" illustrates the log-normal distribution of block sizes, based on which we derive the head/tail division rule to characterize the inbuilt imbalance between a minority of blocks in the head and a majority of those in the tail. Based on the head/tail division rule, in the "Delineating Urban Boundaries or Defining Natural Cities Based on Head/Tail Division Rule" section, we develop an approach to delineating urban boundaries that are naturally defined, termed by natural cities. The sizes of the natural cities follow a power law-like distribution, $P(x) \sim x^{-\alpha}$, one of the heavy-tailed distributions. Section "Mapping the Image of the Country Using the Border Number" adopts the concept of border number to map the center(s) of countries or cities. Before drawing a conclusion to this paper, we elaborate on the implications of the study in the "Discussions on the Study" section, in particular, on how a country, a city, or geographic space, in general, can be compared to a complex organism in terms of the imbalanced structure and the self-organization processes.

Data and Data Processing

Data and data processing constitute a very important part of the research. The data are taken from OpenStreetMap (OSM; www.openstreetmap.org), a wiki-like collaboration or grass roots movement, which aims to create a free editable map of the world using free sources such as GPS traces and digital imagery (Bennett 2010, Haklay and Weber 2008). The OSM data are one of many successful examples of volunteered geographic information contributed by individuals and supported by the Web 2.0 technologies (Goodchild 2007). The quantity and quality of OSM data can be compared to that of data collected by national mapping agencies or commercial companies.

Data Pre-Processing for Building Up Topological Relationships

We adopt the street networks of three largest European countries (France, Germany, and the UK) for computation and experiments. Before the extraction of individual blocks for scaling analysis, we need to build up topological relationships. This is because the original OSM data are without topology, much like digitizing lines without generating coverage—a topology-based vector data format. Through this pre-processing, all line segments will be assigned a direction and become arcs that meet at nodes and have left and right polygons. The original OSM data are too large to load into any existing GIS package for the preprocessing. To solve this problem, we parceled them into several pieces, processed them separately, and merged them again afterward. To have some idea of the data sizes, the numbers of arcs for the individual countries are listed in Table 16.1. As one can see, there are several million arcs for each of the three networks, up to 8 million arcs for the Germany street network. It took several hours for a 64-bit machine (4 cores CPU, 48 GB memory, and 1 TB hard disk) to finish the preprocessing of creating the topological relationships for each of the three networks.

Extraction of City and Field Blocks

Based on the preprocessing, we compute the arc-based networks to extract individual blocks in order to investigate some scaling properties. To introduce the computation, we adopt a fictive street network shown in Figure 16.1, which includes 40 blocks and several dangling arcs that do not constitute any part of the blocks. To extract the individual blocks, we first need to set a minimum bounding box for the network in order to select an outmost

TABLE 16.1

The Number of Arcs, Blocks, and the Maximum Border Number for the Three Street Networks

	France	Germany	UK
Arcs	2,323,980	8,176,518	2,970,534
Blocks	569,739	2,095,388	586,809
MaxBorder#	79	125	73

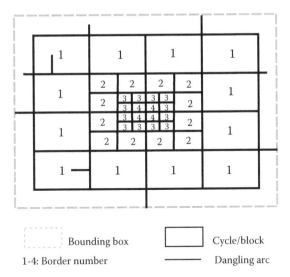

Bounding box   Cycle/block

1-4: Border number   Dangling arc

FIGURE 16.1
Illustration of the minimum cycles (or blocks) and the maximum cycle.

arc to start traversal processes. There are two kinds of traversal processes: left traversal process and right traversal process. The left traversal process means that when it comes to a node with two or more arcs, it always chooses the most left arc. On the other hand, it always chooses the most right arc for the right traversal process. Once the traversal process (starting from the outmost arc) is over, it ends up with one cycle: either a minimum cycle (which is a block) or a maximum cycle that is the outmost border. If the maximum cycle is not generated, then the program chooses a reverse direction for the traversal process until the maximum cycle is detected, and the corresponding arcs are marked with the traversal direction (left or right).

The next step is to choose an arc on the border and begin the traversal process along the opposite direction as previously marked, until all arcs on the border are processed. This way all the blocks on the border are detected and are assigned to border number 1. This process goes recursively for the blocks that are adjacent to the blocks with border number 1. We will get all the blocks with border number 2. The above process continues until all the blocks are exhausted and are assigned to an appropriate border number; refer to Appendix and Figure A.1 for details on the algorithmic procedures. As a note on computation, it takes many hours for the server-like machine to have the process done: France and the UK each about 5 h, and Germany 63 h. Eventually, those dangling arcs are dropped out in the process of extracting the blocks. The border number is a de facto topological distance of a block far from the outmost border. (Note: the border is not necessarily a country border.) Every block has a border number, showing how far it is from the outmost border. The higher the border number, the farther the block is from the border, or reversely the lower the border number, the closer the block is to the border.

We apply the above computing process to the three networks and obtain large numbers of blocks as shown in Table 16.1. We can note that Germany has far more blocks than France and the UK, almost four times as many. Each individual block is assigned a border number to show how far it is to the outmost border. Interestingly, the maximum border number for the farthest block from the border varies from one country to another. Both France and the UK have very similar maximum border numbers at around 70–80, while Germany has the largest maximum border number of 125. We will illustrate that the blocks with the maximum border number tend to be in the deep center of the countries. By center, we mean topological centers rather than geometric ones. This point will be clearer later on when we visualize all the blocks according to their border numbers.

Log-Normal Distribution of Block Sizes and Head/Tail Division Rule

We conduct detailed analysis of the extracted blocks and find that there are far more small blocks than large ones. For example, 90% of blocks are small ones, while 10% are large ones in the UK. This observation is applicable to the other two networks, although the percentages may slightly vary from one to another (Table 16.2). The block sizes for the individual countries follow a log-normal distribution (Figure 16.2), rather than a power-law distribution as claimed in a previous study by Lämmer et al. (2006) that focuses only on city blocks. This finding is very interesting. Even more interesting is the fact that the mean of block sizes can make a clear-cut distinction between small blocks and large blocks. For example, 0.4 km^2 is the mean to distinguish the small blocks and the large blocks for the UK network. This mean varies slightly from one country to another (Table 16.2). Overall, there is a very high percentage of small blocks and a

TABLE 16.2

The Numbers of Blocks in Head and Tail for the Three Networks

	France	Germany	UK
Number of blocks (all)	569,739	2,095,388	586,809
Mean value of block sizes (km^2)	0.9	0.2	0.4
Number of blocks (<mean)	534,800	1,802,924	526,302
Tail (<mean)%	94	86	90
Head (>mean)%	6	14	10

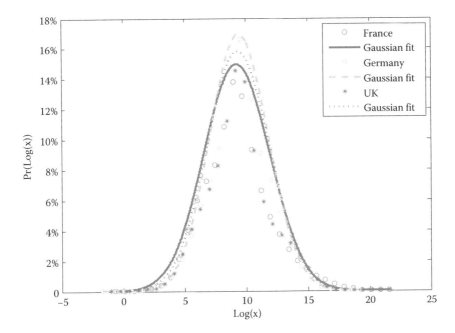

FIGURE 16.2
Log-normal distribution of the block sizes for the three street networks.

very low percentage of large blocks. Put more generally, *given a variable X, if its values x follow a heavy-tailed distribution, then the mean (m) of the values can divide all the values into two parts: a high percentage in the tail, and a low percentage in the head.* For the sake of convenience, we call this regularity the head/tail division rule.

We apply the head/tail division rule into the three networks and find some very interesting results related to the 80/20 principle or the principle of least effort (Zipf 1949). As seen from Table 16.2, about 10% of blocks are larger blocks constituting rural areas, and 90% of blocks are smaller blocks forming urban areas. On the other hand, the 10% of blocks enclose about 90% of the land, and the 90% of the blocks enclose only 10% of the land, which is located in cities. In contrast, the 10% of the land owns 90% of the blocks (which are in cities), and the 90% of the land owns only 10% of the blocks (which are in the countryside). This inbuilt imbalance between the minority (in the head) and the majority (in the tail) is exactly what the 80/20 principle or the principle of least effort illustrates. A further investigation on the areas of the blocks indeed illustrates the above facts as shown in Table 16.3, where all the blocks are divided into the head and the tail in terms of the areas of the blocks rather than the number of blocks. The head/tail division rule constitutes a foundation for delineating cities which is the topic of the next section.

TABLE 16.3

The Areas (km²) of Blocks in the Head and the Tail for the Three Networks

	France	Germany	UK
Area of blocks (all)	528,706	353,706	209,062
Mean of block sizes	0.9	0.2	0.4
Area of blocks (< mean)	27,687	42,669	16,186
Head (< mean)%	5	12	8
Tail (> mean)%	95	88	92

Delineating Urban Boundaries or Defining Natural Cities Based on Head/Tail Division Rule

Because all blocks in one country exhibit a heavy-tailed distribution, we can use the mean to divide all the blocks into smaller ones (smaller than the mean) and larger ones (larger than the mean). We then cluster the smaller blocks into individual groups. This clustering process goes like this. Starting from any smaller block whose neighboring blocks are also smaller ones, we design a program to traverse its adjacent blocks, and cluster those smaller blocks whose adjacent blocks are also smaller ones. This processing continues recursively until all the smaller ones are exhausted. We find that the sizes of the clustered groups demonstrate a heavy-tailed distribution. Because of this, we then rely on the head/tail division rule to divide the groups into smaller ones (smaller than the mean) and larger ones (larger than the mean). The larger groups are de facto cities or natural cities as shown in Figure 16.3.

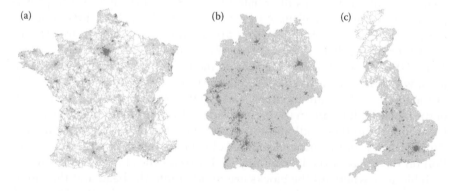

FIGURE 16.3

All natural cities in red identified for the three networks of (a) France, (b) Germany, and (c) the UK. (Note: the gray background shows the extracted blocks.)

The natural cities in this paper are defined as agglomerated smaller blocks (smaller than the mean), whose adjacent blocks are also smaller ones. In the above clustering process, we in fact consider the spatial autocorrelation effect, which helps us to exclude smaller blocks, whose adjacent blocks are larger ones. The spatial autocorrelation can be expressed equivalently by the first law of geography, which reads "everything is related to everything else, but near things are more related than distant things" (Tobler 1970). These smaller blocks, whose adjacent blocks are larger ones, are unlikely to be part of cities. Following this rule has one potential side effect, that is, the smaller blocks that initially form a part of a city edge are mistakenly categorized into the countryside category. However, this side effect is very trivial. This is because the blocks that are mistakenly categorized into countryside are at the city edge, so they are relatively large according to spatial autocorrelation. So categorizing them as countryside is still a reasonable decision given their relatively large sizes.

The above process of delineating city boundaries is quite straightforward. It is mainly the selection based on the head/tail division rule and a clustering process of smaller blocks by considering spatial autocorrelation. The entire process can be summarized as this: all blocks > smaller blocks > clustered groups > cities, where > denotes the processes of the selection or clustering. It is worth noting that only the head part of the clustered groups is considered to be cities, that is, we filtered out smaller groups in the tail. These cities are what we call natural cities, as the boundaries are naturally or automatically obtained. The sizes of the natural cities follow power-law distributions as shown in Figure 16.4. This power-law detection is strictly based on the method suggested by Clauset et al. (2009), but only France and Germany pass the goodness-of-fit test. The reason why the UK did not pass the statistical test is a matter of research. However, we suspect that it may be due to the fact that it is an island country, and the urban growth is constrained by the coastline.

Mapping the Image of the Country Using the Border Number

In this section, we will examine how the defined border number in section "Data and Data Processing" can be used to map the image of the country, a notion with a similar meaning as in *The Image of the City* (Lynch 1960). That is how those distinguished cities (being landmarks) shape the mental image of the country by filtering out the vast majority of redundant or trivial human settlements in the heavy or fat tail. As we have learned, all those blocks on the border has border number 1, those blocks adjacent to the border number 1 have border number 2, and so on. Every block has a unique border number; the more central a block, the higher the border number. The blocks with the highest numbers are within the deep centers of the megacities in the countries.

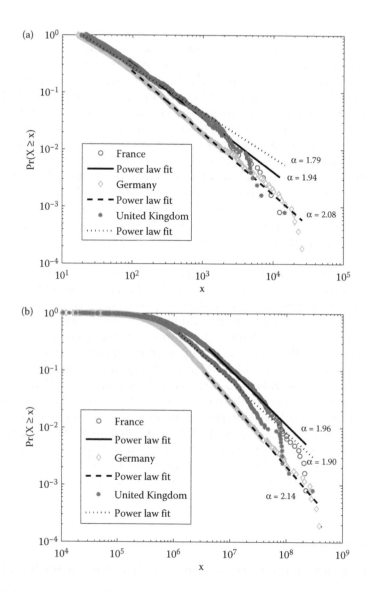

FIGURE 16.4
Power-law distribution of city sizes for the three networks in terms of (a) the number of city blocks and (b) the area or physical extent (m²).

Using a spectral color legend, we map the blocks according to their border numbers (Figure 16.5). The patterns shown in Figure 16.5 reflect the true structure of the countries, for example, the red spots or patches are the true centers of the countries. The sizes of the spots or patches vary from one country to another. This reflects another interesting structure which deserves some further elaboration. We learn from the mapping that the red spots or patches

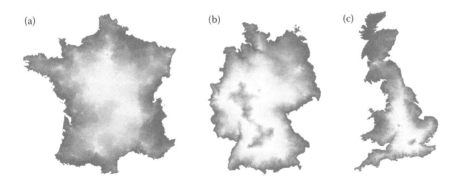

FIGURE 16.5
Mapping the border number using a spectral color legend. (*Note*: the higher the border number, the warmer the color; red and blue represent, respectively, the highest and lowest border numbers. (a) France, (b) Germany, and (c) UK.)

represent the largest cities (in terms of both the number of blocks and physical extent) in the countries. Owing to the use of Jenks' natural breaks (Jenks 1967), which minimize intraclasses variation and maximize interclasses one, it implies that in France there is no other cities in the same group as Paris—the largest city in the country. This is indeed true that Paris has 62,242 city blocks, more than five times bigger than the second largest city. In the case of Germany, this is another extreme that all biggest cities are very similar in size around 20,000–30,000 blocks. This can also be seen from Figure 16.3.

The patterns shown in Figure 16.5 are illustrated from a topological perspective, which is very different from a geometric one. For example, given any country border or shape, we can partition the shape into equal-sized rectangular cells (at a very fine scale, e.g., 1000 × 1000) and then compute the border number for the individual cells. Eventually, we obtain the patterns shown in Figure 16.6. As we can see, the centers of the countries are geometric or gravity centers that are equal distances to the corresponding edges of the borders. Essentially, the country forms or shapes are viewed symmetrically. This is a distorted image of the countries, since the geometric centers are not true centers that the human minds perceive. This geometric view is the fundamental idea behind the concept of medial axis (Blum 1967), which has found a variety of applications in the real world in describing the shape of virtually all kinds of objects from the infinitely large to the infinitely small including biological entities (Leymarie and Kimia 2008). While medial axis is powerful enough in capturing a symmetric structure of a shape, it presents a distorted image of a shape as seen from Figure 16.6. This distortion is particularly true for France, since the true center Paris is far from the geometric or gravity center. We should stress that the point here is not so much about how Figure 16.5 captures the mental image of the country for different people, but rather how the topological perspective (the border number and block perspective) is superior to the geometric view as shown in Figure 16.6,

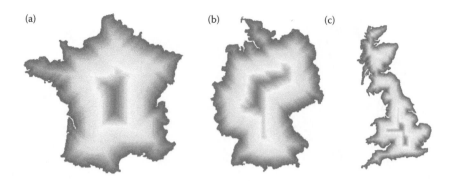

FIGURE 16.6
Distorted images of the country based on the geometric distance far from the outmost boundaries. (a) France, (b) Germany, (c) the UK.

which gives a distorted image. This is the message we want to convey about the image of the country.

The above scaling analysis and insights into the structure can be extended to individual cities to illustrate their internal structure and patterns. Taking London, for example, those blocks with the highest border numbers reflect a true center of the city (Figure 16.7a). We found that the city block sizes of London follow a log-normal distribution as well, one of the heavy-tailed distributions. To some extent, it is consistent with an early study that claims a power-law distribution of city block sizes (Lämmer et al. 2006), since both log-normal and power law are heavy-tailed distributions. The fact that the block sizes follow a log-normal distribution gives us a possibility to distinguish the blocks above the mean and below the mean. Those blocks above the mean constitute individual city core or cores, which match pretty well to the city center (Figure 16.7b).

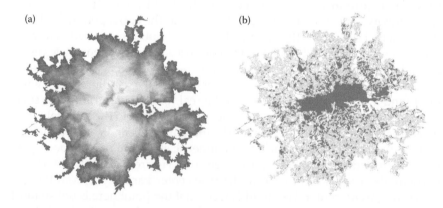

FIGURE 16.7
Scaling patterns illustrated with the case of London (a) city border number, and (b) city cores. (Note: the border is relative to the London city rather than the UK country border.)

Discussions on the Study

This study provides an example of uncovering new knowledge from massive geographic information using ever increasing computing power of personal computers. The increasingly available volunteered geographic information such as the OSM data, GPS traces, and geotagged photos provides an unprecedented data source for the kind of scaling analysis without any particular constraints (Crandall et al. 2009). Nowadays researchers can take the street networks of virtually the entire world for computing and analysis. The computation at the massive data scale can lead to some in-depth insights into structure or patterns of large geographic space. For example, it is surprise to us that the head/tail division rule can be used to delineate city boundaries in such a simple manner. The ever increasing computing power of personal computers makes the data-intensive computing involved in this kind of study possible. As a by-product of the study, we generate two valuable data sets that can be of use for various urban studies: one about blocks and another about natural cities for the three counties. We will release soon the data up to 2 GB for research uses.

The head/tail division rule we derived from the study has some implications to other natural and socioeconomic phenomena that exhibit a power-law distribution or a heavy-tail distribution, in general. For example, the distinction between rich and poor may clearly be defined by the mean of all individuals' wealth in a country or society. This of course warrants a further study for verification. In a previous study (Jiang 2007), we divided streets around the mean connectivity (which is 4) into two categories: well-connected and less connected. In addition, these extremely well connected or extremely few tend to shape part of mental maps about geographic space or cities. Those most connected streets in a city tend to stay in the human mind, just as most people tend to remember those richest people in the world.

We believe that the perspective of city and field blocks has a certain implication to understanding morphology of organism as well. This perspective of city and field blocks is in fact a topological perspective rather than a geometric one. This can be seen from the difference of pattern or structure illustrated by Figures 16.5 and 16.6: the former being the topological perspective, while the latter being the geometric one. Given a biological entity like a human body, the medial axis can indeed help one to derive bone structure or skeleton which is symmetric in essence, just like the one illustrated in Figure 16.6. However, it is hard or impossible for medial axis to derive true centers of human bodies: the brains and the hearts. Consequently, we believe that the idea of the border number can be extended to some complex organisms. We know that cells are the basic constituents of biological organisms. For example, human beings have about 100 trillion or 10^{14} cells, and the cell sizes range from 4 to 135 μm. We believe, based on the high ratio of the biggest cell to the smallest cell 135/4, that the human body's cell sizes follow a heavy-tailed distribution. Also the highly complex organisms such as the brains and the hearts tend to have smaller cells. This is much like the smaller city blocks in a capital city or other megacities in a country. Thus, mapping the border number for all the human body cells that make up the solid tissues including muscle and skeletal cells would illustrate true centers of the human body, that is, two red spots representing the heart and the mind as one can imagine following the patterns shown in Figures 16.5 and 16.7. Note that the cells we discussed and compared here could be unknown units, which are equivalent to the blocks in geographic space. This speculation is not yet supported by scientific references. We also believe that for the cells or the unknown units of the brains and hearts, they have similar heavy-tailed distributions of sizes as the cells in the human bodies.

Following the analog between geographic space and complex organisms, we tend to believe that geographic spaces or cities, in particular, are self-organized. There has been an increasing awareness that a city needs to be better understood as a biological entity in terms of its form and how it functions. For example, theoretical physicist Geoffrey West and his co-workers (1999) have studied a set of scaling laws originated in biology and found that the laws hold true remarkably precise for cities. The scaling laws state a nonlinear relationship, for example, the bigger the city, the less infrastructure per capital. This economy of scale indicates that various infrastructures such as utilities networks, street networks, and buildings needed to sustain a big city are far less than the amount one would expect. This is much along the line of research on allometry—the study on the growth of part of an organism in relation to that of the entire organism. Some studies on how cities can be compared to organisms have been carried out (Batty et al. 2008, Samaniego and Moses 2008, Steadman 2006). We can foresee more studies coming up in the near future due to the availability of massive geographic information.

Conclusion

Geographic space is essentially very large and very complex. There is no average place that can represent any other places. The scaling of geographic space can characterize this inherent "spatial heterogeneity" by a heavy-tailed distribution. In this paper, we examined the scaling of geographic space from the perspective of city and field blocks. We found that block sizes at both country and city levels exhibit a log-normal distribution and that the mean size can divide all the blocks into a low percentage at the head and a high percentage in the tail. This head/tail division rule has been used to differentiate urban and rural areas. Thus, we developed a simple solution to delineating urban boundaries from large street networks. The perspective of blocks is unique in the sense that it can capture underlying structure and patterns of geographic space. In this regard, the defined border number is particularly of use in detecting the centers of a country or a city.

This study further adds some implications to understanding the morphology of organisms. The city and field blocks can be compared to the cells of complex organisms. We believe that this kind of scaling analysis of geographic space can be applied to complex organisms and we consequently conjecture that a similar scaling structure is appeared in complex organisms such as human bodies or human brains. This would reinforce our belief that cities, or geographic space, in general, can be compared to a biological entity in terms of their structure and their self-organized nature in their evolution. Our future work will concentrate on the further verification of the findings and applications of the head/tail division rule.

Acknowledgments

We thank the OSM community for providing the impressive data of street networks. We also thank Tao Jia for his assistance in creating Figure 16.2, and Marc Barthelemy for his insightful comments on the head/tail division rule. All source codes and produced data are put online for free access at http://fromto.hig.se/~bjg/scalingdata/.

References

Anselin L. 2006, Spatial heterogeneity, In: Warff B. (ed.), *Encyclopedia of Human Geography*, Sage Publications: Thousand Oaks, CA, 452–453.

Batty M., Carvalho R., Hudson-Smith A., Milton R., Smith D. and Steadman P. 2008, Scaling and allometry in the building geometries of Greater London, *European Physical Journal B*, 63, 303–318.

Bennett J. 2010, *OpenStreetMap: Be Your Own Cartographer*, PCKT: Birmingham, UK.

Blum H. 1967, A transformation for extracting new descriptors of form, In: Whaten-Dunn W. (ed.), *Models for the Perception of Speech and Visual Form*, MIT Press: Cambridge, MA, 362–380.

Borruso G. 2003, Network density and the delimitation of urban areas, *Transactions in GIS*, 7(2), 177–191.

Clauset A., Shalizi C. R., and Newman M. E. J. 2009, Power-law distributions in empirical data, *SIAM Review*, 51, 661–703.

Crandall D., Backstrom L., Huttenlocher D., and Kleinberg J. 2009, Mapping the world's photos, *18th International World Wide Web Conference*, Madrid, April 20–24, 2009.

Goodchild M. F. 2004, The validity and usefulness of laws in geographic information science and geography, *Annals of the Association of American Geographers*, 94(2), 300–303.

Goodchild M. F. 2007, Citizens as sensors: The world of volunteered geography, *GeoJournal*, 69(4), 211–221.

Haklay M. and Weber P. 2008, OpenStreetMap: User-generated street maps, *IEEE Pervasive Computing*, 7(4), 12–18.

Jenks G. F. 1967, The data model concept in statistical mapping, *International Yearbook of Cartography*, 7, 186–190.

Jiang B. 2007, A topological pattern of urban street networks: Universality and peculiarity, *Physica A: Statistical Mechanics and Its Applications*, 384, 647–655.

Jiang B. 2010, Scaling of geographic space and its implications, A position paper presented at *Las Navas 20th Anniversary Meeting on Cognitive and Linguistic Aspects of Geographic Space*, Las Navas del Marques, Avila, Spain, July 5–9, 2010.

Jiang B. and Jia T. 2011, Zipf's law for all the natural cities in the United States: A geospatial perspective, *International Journal of Geographical Information Science*, 25(8), 1269–1281.

Jiang, B. and Liu X. 2010, Automatic generation of the axial lines of urban environments to capture what we perceive. *International Journal of Geographical Information Science*, 24(4), 545–558.

Kalapala V., Sanwalani V., Clauset A., and Moore C. 2006, Scale invariance in road networks, *Physical Review E*, 73, 026130.

Lämmer S., Gehlsen B., and Helbing D. 2006, Scaling laws in the spatial structure of urban road networks, *Physica A*, 363(1), 89–95.

Leymarie F. F. and Kimia B. B. 2008, From the infinitely large to the infinitely small: Applications of medial symmetry representations of shape, In: Siddiqi K. and Pizer S. M. (eds), *Medial Representations: Mathematics, Algorithms and Applications*, Springer: Berlin.

Lynch K. 1960, *The Image of the City*, The MIT Press: Cambridge, MA.

Openshaw S. 1984, *The Modifiable Areal Unit Problem*, Norwich: Geo Books.

Rozenfeld H. D., Rybski D., Andrade J. S. Jr., Batty M., Stanley H. E., and Makse H. A. 2008, Laws of population growth, *Proceedings of the National Academy of Sciences*, 105, 18702–18707.

Samaniego H. and Moses M. E. 2008, Cities as organisms: Allometric scaling of urban road networks, *Journal of Transport and Land Use*, 1:1, 21–39.

Steadman P. 2006, Allometry and built form: Revisiting Ranko Bon's work with the Harvard philomorphs, *Construction Management and Economics*, 24, 755–765.

Sutton P. 2003, A scale-adjusted measure of urban sprawl using nighttime satellite imagery, *Remote Sensing of Environment*, 86, 370–384.

Thurstain-Goodwin M. and Unwin D. 2000, Defining and delineating the central areas of towns for statistical monitoring using continuous surface representations, *Transactions in GIS*, 4(4), 305–317.

Tobler W. R. 1970, A computer movie simulating urban growth in the Detroit region, *Economic Geography*, 46, 234–240.

West G. B., Brown J. H. and Enquist B. J. 1999, The fourth dimension of life: Fractal geometry and the allometric scaling of organisms, *Science*, 284, 1677–1679.

Zipf G. K. 1949, *Human Behaviour and the Principles of Least Effort*, Addison Wesley: Cambridge, MA.

Appendix: Algorithmic Functions and Flow Chart for Computing Individual Blocks and the Border Numbers

This appendix is to supplement the description of the data processing introduced in the "Data and Data Processing" section. The algorithmic functions and flow chart (Figure A.1) provide a very detailed description about the computational processes. Interested readers are encouraged to contact us for access of the source codes.

```
Input: a set of arcs with calculated deflection angles
Output: block set
Function BlockDetection ()
    Select the rightmost (leftmost, uppermost or downmost) one in arcs as the start arc
    Let maximum block = MaximumBlock (start arc)
    Let border number of maximum block = 0
    Let new block list = null
    For each arc in maximum block
        Let current block = BlockTracking (current arc, the traversal strategy)
        Let border number of current block = 1
        Add current block to new block list
    While (the number of blocks in new block list > 0)
        Let base block = the first block in new block list
        Add base block to block set
        For each arc in base block
            Let current block = BlockTracking (current arc, the opposite traversal strategy)
            Let border number of current block = border number of base block + 1
            Add current bock to new block list
        Remove the first block in new block list
    Return block set
Function MaximumBlock (start arc)
    Let left block = BlockTracking (start arc, left)
    Let right block = BlockTracking (start arc, right)
    Let maximum block = null
    If (left block contains more of the arcs)
        Let maximum block = left block
        Let traversal strategy of maximum block = left
    If (right block contains more of the arcs)
        Let maximum block = right block
        Let traversal strategy of maximum block = right
    Return maximum block
Function BlockTracking (start arc, traversal strategy)
    Let next arc = null
    Let current arc = start arc
    While (next arc != start arc)
        If (traversal strategy is right)
            Select rightmost connected one in arcs connected with current arc as next arc
        Else
            Select leftmost connected one in arcs connected with current arc as next arc
        Add current arc to current block
        Let current arc = next arc
    Return current block
```

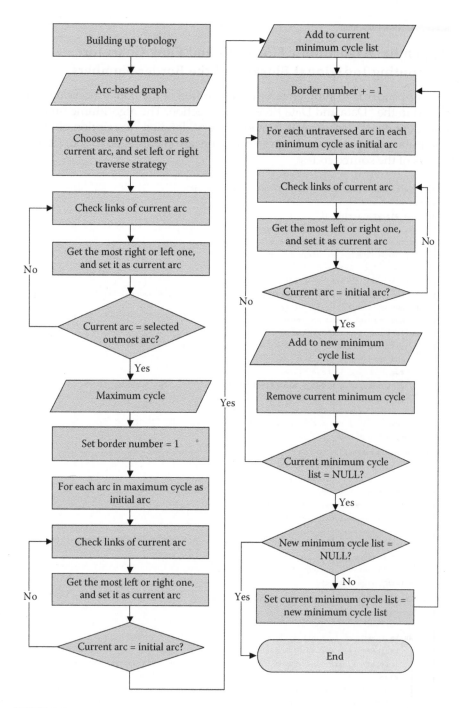

FIGURE A.1
Flow chart of the data processing for computing individual blocks and their border numbers.

17

Big Textual Data Analytics and Knowledge Management

Marcus Spies and Monika Jungemann-Dorner

CONTENTS

Big Data Analytics from Texts

According to a recent publication on challenges and approaches to Big Data (Zikopoulos et al., 2013), it is not sufficient to consider this just a buzzword for the undoubted increase in the size of data in the public, private, and any combined domains. Instead, there are four key dimensions characterizing "Big Data"—volume, velocity, variety/variability, and veracity. On all these dimensions, textual data appearing in the world wide web have significant scores:

1. The volume of textual data can be estimated, for example, from the year 2012 figure of 30+ PB of user data managed by the Facebook social network.

2. The velocity (rate of change over time) of textual data, given the "social web" with its massive posting, chatting, and commenting capabilities, is immense also. For example, the estimated frequency of textual posts on Twitter can be estimated from the current (as of late 2012) 12 TB/day to be roughly 1 million per second. The velocity dimension makes document-based trend analysis a new and important realm within content management.

3. The variety of textual data is rooted in the variety of topics discussed on the web. We also observe a variety of text types being used (like research papers, short reports, blogs); however, the possible text types are much fewer than the dynamic and, to some degree, even unpredictable variety of topics (considering also topics coming up in the context of events in politics, weather, scientific discovery, etc.). While variety and variability are sometimes confused in discussions on Big Data, for textual data variability is quite different from variety. Variability of textual data comes from multilinguality and specific vocabularies (in technology, for instance). Variability is one of the key causes why semantic modeling of complex domains is so difficult. Combining velocity and variety leads to another interesting category of content visualizations, namely dynamically created topic landscapes (not identical to the ISO topic map standard, see below).

4. *Veracity.* A key problem with the content of textual data is the degree to which it is reliable, based on sound analysis, appropriate data, etc. There are many examples of purposeful misinformation, fraudulent, or manipulating content in textual data. A key task of Big Data analytics regarding veracity is to discern reliable from unreliable sources and even to automatically detect fraudulent or manipulating content.

To sum up, even without taking into account a wider range of online resources comprising multimedia, textual data by itself present all the problems which research on Big Data is addressing. Regarding this research, this paper focuses on an approach using knowledge life cycles. Knowledge life cycles allow us to focus on the added value provided by Big Data technologies for enterprises or public purposes. The approach is described in the section "Knowledge Life Cycles" below.

As an example of research on Big Data analytics, we refer to the EU project FIRST. To account for the volume and velocity dimensions, FIRST has developed a data acquisition pipeline building on current no-SQL technology with open source components (Gsell et al., 2012). Regarding the velocity dimension, Twitter posts are scanned with sentiment analysis tools and then visualized (Grcar et al., 2010). This works in the financial domain, but the FIRST team recently showcased the capabilities of real-time sentiment analysis in a preelection TV discussion between presidential candidates by monitoring tweets during the public broadcast in the national TV.

The dimension of variety is taken up in FIRST by providing innovative real-time visualizations of millions of texts on the basis of extracted information on topics. Topic spaces are quite common already in innovation and patent research, where they are used to build a low-dimensional representation of a topic-neighborhood space computed from textual data by sophisticated similarity analysis and the self-organizing map technology (Kohonen et al., 2000). FIRST research has a new approach to computing topic landscapes (see Grcar et al., 2012). We will discuss other recent approaches in the "Topic Modeling" section.

Regarding veracity, many fraud-detection applications can be significantly enhanced if massive amount of textual material can be integrated into the analysis. Well-known examples comprise predictions of political unrest or even terrorist activities from written or spoken text monitoring.

As we will argue, all these research results have immediate benefits as drivers of knowledge life cycles. In fact, one of the reasons of the high awareness for Big Data in the industry is not so much the challenging aspect to database and data management technologies, but rather the business challenges.

In the technology and application parts of the present paper, we elaborate on the variety dimension of Big Data. In the present chapter, we elaborate on the question of how topic structures can be identified from big textual data.

More specifically, we discuss technologies for automated detection of key concepts or topics from large sets of documents. Then, using a sample application based on information extraction, we examine their impact of technologies addressing big textual data on some knowledge life cycles in financial decision-making.

Knowledge Life Cycles and the Processing of Unstructured Information

In this section, we discuss the relationship between knowledge management and processing of unstructured information. We will argue that recent advances in unstructured information processing enable a more effective management of knowledge life cycles.

Introduction to Unstructured Information Processing

Information is called unstructured if it is not provided as a list of attribute-value pairs for attributes with data types defined in a suitable schema. Typically, for data types covering numbers, patterns of numbers and letters, common names, etc., structured information can be provided by a table as an instance of a relation scheme fixing a set of attributes in a relational database. Examples of unstructured data are texts, sound, image, and multimedia data. It should be noted that calling texts unstructured is a particular convention based on this definition of unstructured information. A computer linguist or a language scientist would not call a text unstructured.

The key problem with unstructured data is in fact connected to the variety dimension of Big Data—variety meaning here that the number of variables needed to describe a particular item of unstructured data is extremely high, often not known beforehand. In a common approach to the analysis of texts, the vector space model (more on this below), each possible word corresponds to a variable. For a single language text, without restrictions, this would mean, for English, around 150,000 words, not counting inflection forms. However, many texts, in particular, in science, are not purely single language texts. They comprise multilingual technical terms, acronyms, units of measure, names of persons or entities, etc. that make a much higher reference vocabulary necessary. To give an example, in our recent analysis of a university database with teaching documents, a stemming component (that reduces words to word stems in order to economize on the size of the vocabulary) brought out words like "tology," "ternat," "terpris" which turn out to be improperly parsed words using standard prefixes/suffixes in English). A related problem in computer vision is image preprocessing and image segmentation.

As a consequence, a first problem with unstructured information analytics is variable identification in very high-dimensional spaces. This is true, in particular, also for analyses based on textual data.

Tightly connected to the variety challenge in textual data is the problem of sparse data matrices. Evidently, even large corpora of texts will fail to provide reasonably high counts of any word in a large vocabulary. This problem grows if contexts are taken into account, for example, for a bigram or trigram analysis of word "complexes" as they typically appear in scientific literature, but also in everyday news texts. As the number of possible multiwords grows exponentially with context size, even digitizing the entire literature of humanity would not suffice to resolve the problem with sufficient evidence from data (not taking into account that there is substantial historical change in multiwords and their senses). The problem of smoothing frequency estimates from corpora for unobserved n-grams has been addressed already since some decades in speech technology, where context-based, so-called language models are used to improve the decision of the speech signal decoding component that basically delivers candidate word strings without awareness of any textual context (Jelinek, 1998). Language models in speech recognition typically use smoothing algorithms to give estimates of word sequence probabilities from text corpora also for unseen word sequences.

Consequently, a second issue with analytics based on textual data is parameter smoothing given limited evidence.

The general setting of unstructured information processing from texts can readily be described by comparison to image processing as developed in the field of computer vision.

1. In image processing, one important step is image segmentation— decomposition of an image into parts (e.g., a street and buildings), which is followed by object recognition (e.g., a house).

2. In the next step, relationships between objects can be recognized and output symbolically.

3. A more holistic analysis consists of the discovery of typical object configurations, typical scenes in images. Technically, this is done through cluster analysis applied to results of segmentation or object recognition steps. It is, as we will see in detail below, related to topic analysis from texts.

Segmentation and object recognition are used in two ways. A theme of a segment is recognized (e.g., a landscape, a beach) or specific objects are recognized (e.g., a tree, a shell). Note that segmentation is a prerequisite to further image-processing steps. A special case of object detection is novelty detection (e.g., find an object that does not belong to the theme or scene in question). Novelty detection is of high practical importance in all areas of unstructured information processing.

Object relationships can be of spatial nature only (e.g., a tree on the top of a hill) or they include intentional information (e.g., the hand grasps a cup of coffee).

Image analysis may proceed by single images; it may compare pairs or sequences of images for changes occurring with specific objects or relationships (e.g., in traffic scene analysis).

Both standard machine learning methodology groups, classification (based on supervised learning) and clustering (based on unsupervised learning), can be applied to these processing steps on different levels.

Unstructured Information Processing on Text Data

We now compare equivalent or at least similar methodologies to those explained in the previous section for processing unstructured information in textual documents. We use the common acronym NLP for natural language processing.

Analogous to image segmentation is the decomposition of texts into grammatical units (sentences, etc.) down to specific tokens (words, often irrespective of grammatical forms). This level of analysis is the word level; it is mostly irrelevant to knowledge processing, but it is extensively used in applications such as automatic speech recognition.

Analogous to object recognition is the recognition of a named entity (a company, a person). Named entities may have different names (e.g., IBM, International Business Machines), circumscriptions (the biggest IT services company), etc.

Theme or scene recognition is performed in textual information processing by identifying topics a text is relevant to. This can be learnt in an unsupervised way (e.g., to identify major themes in the texts of an online discussion forum) or in a supervised way (by training the system with texts that are typical for certain topics). Object relationship recognition in the textual domain consists of identifying an instance of a defined relationship between recognized entities (e.g., IBM outsourced the personal computer business to Lenovo).

It should be noted that the development of object and relationship recognition is a comparatively new field in computer linguistics, which is called *information extraction*. Text clustering and text classification are possible without these extraction capabilities if a suitable statistical relationship between text tokens and thematical categories or text groupings can be developed on an empirical basis. This kind of analysis of textual information is often referred to as information *retrieval*. For an encompassing reference on information retrieval, see Manning et al. (2009). *Information extraction*, on the other hand, leads to a specific analysis of text parts that is often provided through annotations. An annotation refers to a span of input text and provides entity or relationship information for this text segment. A widely used application architecture for annotation is the Unstructured Information Management Architecture (UIMA; Apache UIMA Development Community, 2008a,b). Note that annotation can also be used on nontextual unstructured data if the segmentation is suitably coded.

A common aspect to information retrieval and information extraction is reliance on "shallow" NLP with a focus on counting tokens in documents. Preprocessing of tokens can comprise removal of stop words, lemmatization or stemming, and part-of-speech (POS) tagging (Manning et al., 2009). The effectiveness of each of these steps depends on the quality of the component employed and its linguistic background. While removing words like "and, that, is" seems trivial, there are many examples of stop words that are meaningful in certain contexts (like "and" as part of named entity) or indicating language use (used in literary science). So, a stop word remover should usually be configured by a customized word list. Many free text-processing tools have a stemming component, but the reduction of tokens to stems involves assumptions that may be wrong for foreign or technical terms or may introduce ambiguities (flow, flower); therefore, linguists prefer the much more complex morphological processing involved in lemmatization. Finally, POS tagging also is available to some extent in ready-to-go tools, but a professional POS-tagger takes specific grammars and statistical models, for example, the Stanford POS-tagger (Toutanova et al., 2003).

Deep NLP, on the other hand, involves syntactic analysis of the texts being processed and systematically uses lexica for analyzing or identifying features of terms. Deep NLP constructs syntax trees, which has often been considered as impractical for the purposes involved in processing large document corpora for document classification or clustering. For some decades, deep NLP has been mainly used for machine translation and related applications (like multilingual virtual tourist kiosks), but recent research has demonstrated the value of deep NLP for knowledge extraction and knowledge-based question answering. The most prominent result of this research is the IBM Watson[*] system for question answering in Jeopardy![†] games (see Fan et al., 2012; Lally et al., 2012; McCord et al., 2012; Wang et al., 2012). For some time, this system was called DeepQA to stress the reference to deep NLP. Related systems and resources from computer linguistics are presented in Fan et al. (2012).

A key component in Deep NLP systems is a syntactic parser. For the purposes of knowledge extraction or knowledge-based analysis, parsing is performed with a slot grammar (McCord et al., 2012). The slot grammar used in the IBM Watson system builds on a feature-rich lexicon representation of terms (which correspond to terminal symbols in the parse tree) with different syntactic contexts for different senses of the term. Thereby, deep parsing (as it is called in McCord et al., 2012) leads to an analysis of the input text in terms of syntactic structures together with semantic markers. This structure can be transformed to a logical structure involving predicates and arguments (predicate–argument structure, PAS; McCord et al., 2012). This structure can be used by a rule engine downstream the UIMA analysis pipeline for extracting or further processing the knowledge implied in the sentences being analyzed. In the case of DeepQA system, a Prolog engine is used (Lally et al., 2012).

Deep NLP with a focus on knowledge extraction can be used to build "machine readers," components that process large corpora of texts and extract factual knowledge (involving individuals) as well as rule-like knowledge (Fan et al., 2012). One of the key challenges for this analysis is domain independence. In the aforementioned IBM Watson system, a large and extensible type system is used in order to accommodate for the domain independence of the questions to be answered.

One of the key challenges in machine reading is to map the knowledge extracted from texts to common or cultural knowledge. In fact, many linguistic expressions exist even in one language for an entity or a predicate of common knowledge (a usual example for predicates is creation or production of

---

[*] This is a trademark or service mark of International Business Machines Corporation in the United States, or other countries, or both.

[†] This is a trademark or service mark of Jeopardy Productions, Inc., Trustees of Princeton University, or Wikimedia Foundation in the United States, or other countries, or both.

artwork, where terms such as "write," "author," "produce," etc. could appear in a text in verbal, nominalized forms, etc.). Therefore, an additional step for entity or predicate disambiguation is needed. In order to refer to a common type system, relation extraction is needed for appropriate uses of machine reading. Wang et al. (2012) propose a procedure that starts from structured web sources like DBPedia plus machine reading with type matching using public ontologies like Freebase or YAGO (see http://www.mpi-inf.mpg.de/yago-naga/yago/) to generate training data. These data are used to generate a relational topic model, basic mechanisms to do that will be described in the "Latent Dirichlet Allocation" section. This topic model, together with the other training data, is used to train a support vector machine (see, e.g., Hastie et al., 2009) for later document classification. The entire procedure enables relation detection—identifying extracted relations in a given document.

It should be noted that there is another stream of current research addressing machine reading that builds on statistical relational learning (for an overview, see Spies, 2013).

Processing Information and Knowledge from Texts: An Overview

To sum up, we can distinguish knowledge discovery analyses on textual data along several dimensions.

First, with respect to the *scope* of the analysis, we distinguish between document scope (e.g., delivering annotations in the field of information extraction), including inter-document comparisons (e.g., for novelty detection), and corpus scope (descriptor definition and parameter inference for large bodies of textual data). As most text processing involves corpora in the setup phase, the criterion for distinguishing these two scopes is rather the analysis output than the reference to descriptors or parameters that are definable on the corpus level.

Second, with respect to the *modeling level* of the analysis, we distinguish between information retrieval, information extraction, and knowledge extraction. At least for knowledge extraction, deep NLP is needed, while usually the two preceding levels are based on shallow NLP.

For each modeling level, a *subdivision of the modeling focus* makes sense. For information retrieval, we distinguish term from topics focus. The distinction implies that there can be a term-based analysis without explicitly addressing topics. In an analogous way, for the information extraction modeling level, we distinguish entity focus and relationship focus. While named entity recognition has become very common in recent years (e.g., see the Thomson-Reuters powered opencalais service), relationship extraction and recognition are still rather emerging technologies. Finally, for the knowledge extraction field, we have an analogous distinction between fact-based analysis (e.g., find what a text says about the position of Mr X in company Y) and schema or rule focused analysis (like used in the relation extraction component in DeepQA; see above).

Third, with respect to the *machine learning method* approach to the analysis, we distinguish between classification (based on supervised learning) and clustering (unsupervised learning). In practice, the two approaches are often combined in an exploratory phase using clustering for class identification and a detailed modeling phase based on training a classifier on the classes. It is also true that distinction is not sharp—especially in text processing we find methods which would be more appropriately termed semisupervised. In this paper, they are considered to be unsupervised by stipulation.

Table 17.1 summarizes the knowledge discovery procedures possible along these dimensions.

Analysis on a single document scope is used on the information retrieval level with supervised methods either for document classification or for extracting information from a given document (e.g., finding out what company a document is referring to). Document classification can focus on a specific conceptual area of interest. A common usage of document classification is for subject identification. A prominent example of this is found in electronic patent filing (use case European Patent Agency, Inxight 2006, Knowtech Conference Munich, unpublished). Here, documents and reviewers are described according to common taxonomies. Document classification (actually multilabeling) helps assigning reviewers to patent applications based on specific thematic areas covered. The granularity of the assigned labels is much finer than the keywords provided by patent authors, thereby permits near to 80% automatic assignments of reviewers to patent applications.

Document-based information extraction allows us to uncover specific items of information according to a predefined information structure, typically referred to as an information type (and usually modeled by model elements of an XML schema, in some applications also by domain ontologies using the web ontology language OWL; Motik et al., 2006). A common example of information extraction is named entity recognition (NER), whereby an entity like a company can be recognized from different names in different documents, and additional information about the entity is recognized using a type-system-based conceptual structure (for a statistical approach, see Bunescu and Mooney, 2007; for an ontology-based approach, see Cunningham et al., 2008).

Document classification can also be based on information extraction. This is exploited, for example, in opinion or sentiment mining. Here, for small documents or single sentences, a degree or graduation of a concept or set of concepts related to opinions are examined using NER and a simple form of relationship recognition. A form of relationship detection is to identify which sentiment a document is expressing *on a given entity.*

Knowledge extraction applied to a document would enable us to detect statements (like source A says James Watt discovered the steaming engine) or fact schemes corresponding to identified relations (like source A contains information on engineers and their inventions). In practice, supervised

TABLE 17.1

Knowledge Discovery from Texts—Overview

Modeling Level		Information Retrieval			Information Extraction			Knowledge Extraction	
	Scope	Term	Topic	Entity	Relationship	Fact	Rule
Supervised methods	Document	Document classification	Topic relevance scoring	Annotation, type detection	Relation detection	Fact detection	Fact schema detection
	Corpus	Controlled vocabulary	Subject classification	Named entity recognition	Relation extraction	Fact type detection	Rule schema detection
Unsupervised methods	Document	Document similarity	Document profiling	—	—	Lexical type grouping	Fact type grouping
	Corpus	LSA-Space analytics	Topic modeling	Entity class mining	Relationship mining	Fact schema extraction	Rule schema extraction

For details, see text.

methods of knowledge extraction are used to populate ontologies on the basis of given fact schemes from documents. The main distinction of such approaches against information extraction is that shifts in the ontology should be accounted for by the extraction methods without a full reprogramming of entity or relationship patterns.

Analysis on a single document scope with unsupervised methods is used on the information retrieval level either for document term profile generation (document vector representation in a term space, as detailed below in section "Document Vector Models") or for a representation of a document in topic space.

Unsupervised methods for information extraction consist of mining corpora for possible entities or relationships. While this kind of analysis underlies some of the extraction technologies on the knowledge level, it does not seem to have an application on the document scope. Most of the setup analyses in machine reading as discussed above for the DeepQA technology consists of partially unsupervised knowledge extraction methods.

Passing from single document scope to multidocument scope on the information retrieval level, we have document similarity analysis, which is commonly based on the cosine similarity measure applied to a vector space representation of documents. Document similarity analysis, in the first place, allows us to cluster documents according to prototypical profiles and thus to identify groups of specific thematic areas in the domain of discourse. Moreover, this kind of analysis allows us to associate individual documents with clusters of documents as identified beforehand. This can be used for practical applications such as collaborative filtering.

A second application area of multidocument analysis is related to the comparison of different levels of an attribute or a property as they occur across a time series of documents of related content or from one homogeneous corpus. An example of this kind of analysis is given by extending opinion mining for a set of entities as described above to a corpus of newspaper articles within a given time span.

On the modeling level of information extraction, the document is not considered just as a bag of words, but as a collection of mentions of entities and their possible relationships to other entities. Such entities can be named entities like companies or products, or humans. Their relationships can be simple ones like those of belonging to or having, or more complex ones reflecting, for example, business relationships. In recent work, information extraction is combined with conceptual analysis on the formal logical level using ontology-based text annotation technology. In this approach, information extraction entities and relationships are classes or associations from an ontology and are defined in an ontology such that individual information entities or relationships correspond to individual statements conforming to the theory implicit in the underlying ontology. Extracted statements can be used to draw inferences which allow more meaningful conclusions from the results of unstructured information processing.

Finally, applying unsupervised methods for *knowledge extraction* on the corpus level, we have the important areas related to *ontology learning*, that is, the inference of plausible ontology concepts and predicates using knowledge discovery from texts. As a general remark, *ontology population vs ontology learning* are distinguished like *facts vs rules focus* in the corresponding knowledge extraction technologies.

Topic Modeling

This section focuses on topic modeling, as this is currently one of the fastest expanding technologies for Big Data. Interestingly, topic modeling originates from information retrieval, but it has recently been found to be an important preprocessing step in knowledge extraction as well (Wang et al., 2012).

According to the topic-oriented view of a document, topics constitute a holistic level of conceptual theme(s) underlying a document. The ISO standard for topic maps captures this intuition (for an introduction, see Pepper, 2006). According to this standard, the topic is characterized by a few key relationships. The first is that a topic may specialize or generalize another topic. Second, a topic may have associations to another topic, such that documents covering one of these topics will probably cover at least a subset of these associated topics. Finally, a topic is characterized by words that are probable occurrences of this topic in a document. It should be mentioned that words appearing as occurrences of a topic do not constitute a semantic analysis of the topic. Rather, occurrences may be words of quite different kinds and quite different provenience, when a certain topic is being addressed in a document. In statistical terminology, occurrences of words can be seen as indicators of a topic, with each word frequency constituting an indicator variable of the latent topic variable.

Document Vector Models

Frequency-based word profiles for documents have become popular in information retrieval for document management and document indexing during the 1990s. According to the vector space model for documents, a document can be considered as a "bag of words" (BOW, as often found in computer linguistic texts), that is, a multiset containing one or more occurrences of elements drawn from a set of words. In computer linguists' parlance, documents are actually composed of occurrences of terms, called tokens. So, according to linguistic terminology, we model a document as a "bag of tokens," which can be understood as a frequency distribution given by the occurrences of terms in the document's tokens.

Considered as being a mere bag of tokens, a document can be described by the frequency profile of its terms. In information retrieval research, it was found out that, instead of raw term frequencies, a combined measure composed of term frequencies and inverted document frequencies should be used, which captures the characteristics of the text both with regard to terms it contains frequently and specifically compared to other texts. So, usually, an entry (i,j) in a term-document matrix is defined is defined from two corpus data components as follows:

1. A number monotonically increasing with the local frequency of term t_i in document d_j. This number is computed from the raw frequency f_{ij} by applying a local weight, which is often referred to as term frequency (TF). A common choice for computing TF is $\log(f_{ij} + 1)$.

2. A number monotonically decreasing with the overall or global commonality of term t_i across the entire corpus. One common choice is the inverse of $\sqrt{\sum_j f_{ij}^2}$. Note this is equivalent to the inverse of the Euclidean norm of the raw frequency vector over all documents considered as dimensions. Therefore, this choice of the communality component is often referred to as normalization. Another common choice (even combinable with normalization) is the inverted document frequency (IDF). The document frequency (DF) df_i of a term t_i is the number of documents in which t_i appears. For a corpus of size N (meaning it contains N documents), the IDF value is then $\log(N/df_i + 1)$.

3. The two components TF and IDF are combined by multiplication to yield the final entry (i, j) in the term-document matrix.

For a discussion of choices for TF and IDF, see Manning et al. (2009). In practice, different weight functions and nonlinear transformations for TF/IDF are in use. In literary science, the use of IDF weights is rather uncommon, since the overall goal of the analysis here is not a terminology with which to characterize each document but rather an account of words in a "discourse" that exists on the corpus level. A very interesting choice for the TF component reported in a Blog on digital humanities (see http://tedunderwood.com/tech-notes/) is a correction of observed TF by expected term frequency (ETF). By ETF, we mean the expectation of f_{ij} based on a uniform distribution of t_i occurrences among all documents in the corpus, that is,

$$E(f_{ij}) = \frac{\sum_k f_{kj}}{\sum_{k,m} f_{km}} \sum_m f_{im}.$$

This corresponds to the observed frequency of t_i in the corpus, multiplied by the quotient of document length (number of tokens) for d_j, and the overall length (number of tokens) of the corpus. Note that, compared to IDF, the document boundaries are not relevant here, as the observed frequencies are summed over documents. This is in line with the scientific focus of literary science and related approaches in the humanities, where a universe of discourse is relevant rather than a collection of specific documents from which a user might wish to retrieve single elements. The final (possibly negative) TF score proposed by Underwood is the difference $f_{ij} - E(f_{ij})$.

Latent Semantic Analysis

The key drawback of frequency-based document profiles is the strong connection to the physically used terminology in a document or a set of documents. To some degree, this can be alleviated by linguistic preprocessing in order to eliminate stop words from a document and focus the analysis on word stems instead of full words. Interestingly, latent semantic analysis (LSA) resolves, to some extent, the classical problems of homonymy (multiple words with one meaning) and synonymy (multiple meanings of one word) automatically. Evaluations (Landauer and Dumais, 1997) have shown that LSA identifies word meanings in feature vectors without human intervention at approximately the quality of a foreign student passing a TOEFL exam.

Therefore, LSA allows us to describe documents in a compact way by terms representing (at least common sense) word meanings instead of raw words.

Analysis on the topics levels is most often oriented towards either individual document classification, or cross-documents topics comparisons, or document versus corpus representativeness descriptions. Individual document classification aims at identifying one or several topics characteristic for an individual document.

Frequency-based document vector profiles can be used beyond the specific method employed in LSA with unsupervised learning for identifying thematic clusters of documents and with supervised learning for training set guided document classification.

We briefly introduce different approaches to document topic analysis, namely LSA or latent semantic indexing, and latent Dirichlet allocation (LDA), abbreviated, respectively, to LSA, LSI, and LDA. All these approaches are based on an analysis of the term by documents matrix. The entries of this matrix are TF-IDF numbers or related frequency weights. In LSA or latent semantic indexing, a term by documents C matrix is decomposed into three different matrices using the singular value decomposition (SVD) technique that basically generalizes principal components analysis (PCA) to nonsquare matrices (see, e.g., Manning et al., 2009):

$$C = U \Lambda V^{\mathrm{T}}$$

First, the term by latent factors matrix U, which relates the raw words found in the document to hypothetical latent concepts. These concepts can be understood like factors in PCA explaining the term covariance across documents. In particular, latent concepts can represent aggregates of raw terms making up a meaningful concept. Formally, this matrix can be used to give a reduced dimensional approximation of the interterm raw covariance matrix—$CC^T = U\Lambda^2 V^T$. Like in PCA, latent concepts can be understood as weighted combinations of terms.

Second, a latent factors weight matrix Λ, which assigns weights to the identified latent concepts for the entire corpus. These weights correspond to the singular values computed in SVD. Usually, again like in PCA, only a small fraction of singular values are taken into account for further analysis. This leads to the dimensionality reduction aspect of LSA. The purpose here is to have a compressed representation of essential concepts only. Various dimension selection strategies have been implemented (see, e.g., the *dimcalc* functions in the LSA library for R; Wild, 2011).

Third, a latent concept by document matrix V^T, which provides a conceptual characterization of each document in terms of the prevalent latent concepts identified. Formally, this matrix can be used to give a reduced dimensional approximation of the interdocument correlation matrix.

Both matrices U and V^T have orthogonal base vectors in the latent conceptual dimensions; however, they are not square unlike the corresponding matrices in PCA. Orthogonality is useful as it ensures independence of the latent conceptual factors.

In order to evaluate an LSA analysis, usually the low-dimensional approximations to the interterm and interdocument covariance matrices are examined. Typically, clusters of terms and clusters of documents are identifiable by inspection of the factorial structure output from the SVD analysis. In practice, the approximation based on a subset of singular values highlights interterm correlations for terms belonging to a "semantic space" similar to a concept association space as captured by the similar-terms relationships in WordNet (WordNet: An Electronic Lexical Database, 1998). This is of course true only for non-technical documents, but similar observations can also be made in the case of technical or research papers.

Recently, in Bradford (2011) massively scalable implementations of SVD have been provided that allow us to use LSA on a scale suitable for Big Data requirements.

While the parameters of a generative model cannot be smoothly updated on the basis of newly observed texts, LSA/LSI allow for a "folding in" method accounting for new data (see details in Wild, 2011).

Latent Dirichlet Allocation

While LSA or latent semantic indexing have been applied successfully in almost all areas relevant to knowledge discovery from weakly structured or textual data, a key limitation of these techniques is that they do not start from a generative model of documents. In general, such a model predicts relative frequencies of specific terms within a document based on an assumption of a topic or a mixture of topics characterizing any particular document in the entire corpus under consideration. The key assumptions of generative approaches to topic modeling are

1. A topic is a probability distribution over terms. Terms can appear in several topics. (Unique terms to a given topic are referred to as anchor terms.)
2. A topic model on the document level is a probability distribution over topics. Thus, a document is essentially modeled as a specific mixture of topics.

An approach based on these considerations is latent Dirichlet analysis (LDA), which has been implemented in several open source software distributions (Blei et al., 2003b; Heinrich, 2008). The merit of LDA is to integrate a topic-based document generation model with Bayesian inference. Specifically, in its original version, LDA makes use of the Bayesian learning relationship between empirical multinomial distributions and Dirichlet distributions as conjugate priors.

LDA specifies the assumed probability distributions as follows:

1. Each topic distribution is multinomial over the set of terms. These distributions are parameterized on the corpus level.
2. A document topic distribution is locally multinomial over the set of topics. The selection of a locally multinomial topic distribution is based on a corpus level prior distribution (the Dirichlet distribution acting as conjugate prior of a multinomial). This implies that the overall number of topics for a given LDA analysis is fixed and must be specified in advance.

In order to set up an LDA analysis for a given corpus of N documents, we continue letting d_j a document from the corpus, and t_i a term from the vocabulary. Now, the following choices are assumed to be made on the corpus level:

1. An overall number m of topics is chosen. Let $k \in \{1, \ldots, m\}$.
2. A base vocabulary of n terms is selected. Let $i \in \{1, \ldots, n\}$.
3. A Dirichlet prior distribution with hyperparameter vector $\alpha = (\alpha_0, \ldots, \alpha_m)$ for generating the document-topic multinomial with parameter vector θ_j for each document d_j.
4. A Dirichlet prior distribution with hyperparameter vector $\beta = (\beta_0, \ldots, \beta_n)$ for generating the corpus level topic-term multinomials with parameter vector φ_i for each term t_i.
5. A set of topic-term multinomials φ_i drawn from β for all terms t_i in the vocabulary, $i \in \{1, \ldots, n\}$.

6. A set of document-topic multinomials θ_j drawn from α for all documents d_j in the corpus, $j \in \{1, \ldots, N\}$.

   Next, the generative model describes the generation of a document as a combination of a stochastic sampling from these distributions (it should be remarked that "generative" here has a quite different meaning from "generative" in the context of formal grammars, as this generation process by sampling has no implications regarding the sequence of tokens!). Essentially, we have a two-step sampling procedure explaining the generation of each token w (for which we do not introduce an extra index variable here for simplicity) in a given document d_j:

7. A topic t_w is sampled according to the document d_j's topic distribution θ_j. (To illustrate, imagine sampling with replacement from an urn with balls of m different colors with frequencies in proportion to the components of θ_j.)

8. A term "explaining" w is sampled from the topic-term multinomial φ_{t_w} (i.e., the topic-term distribution selected in accordance with topic t_w sampled in the preceding step).

These assumed sampling procedures pave the way for data-driven estimation of all model parameters (Blei et al., 2003b; Heinrich, 2008). In theory, statistical inference proceeds by inverting the above sequence of sampling steps on the basis of a tokenized document corpus and adapting the parameters and hyperparameters according to Bayes' rule. In practice, either Gibbs sampling or variational inference methods are used for selecting and aggregating counts efficiently. The interested reader will find the details in Blei et al. (2003b). A graphical illustration of the Gibbs sampling learning process for LDA can be found in Steyvers and Griffiths (2006). The R topic modeling package supports several algorithms (Grün and Hornik, 2011).

The results of LDA can be evaluated in a multitude of ways. By way of a standard approach, a perplexity calculation like in other probability learning models can be reported on the basis of a held-out set from the training corpus. Usually, perplexity is plotted against the number of topics assumed. A sample from an LDA analysis of an e-learning corpus at the university of the first author is given in Figure 17.1.

A second key to evaluate LDA from a domain perspective is the examination of the word lists by topic and the topic lists by document.

1. Words-by-topic distributions often indicate thematic coherence from a domain-specific point of view. While there is no commonly agreed measure of thematic coherence, domain experts usually can judge by inspection whether a topic analysis is overly mixing concepts or overly separating them among topics. This is a useful indication for the selection of appropriate numbers of topics to use.

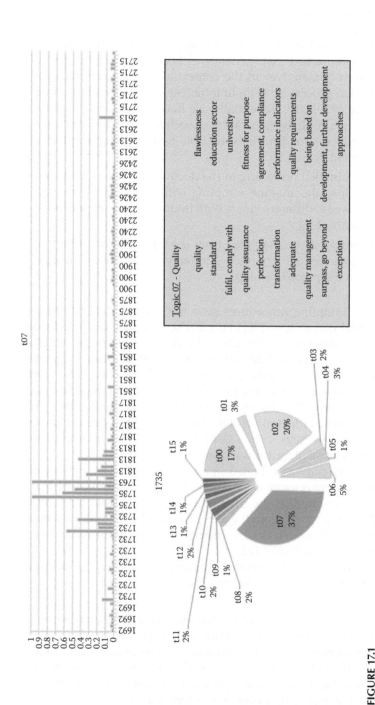

FIGURE 17.1

Example of an LDA analysis taken from e-learning materials at LMU (Trautmann and Suleiman, 2012). The upper diagram shows a scaled likelihood of a given topic (numbered t07) in a set of pdf documents generated from slides of lectures on quality management for the social sciences. This diagram represents the use case of searching documents on a topic basis, such a search would return slide 1735 with high confidence score. The pie diagram illustrates the specific topic distribution on this slide, with 37% going to t07. The topic-term distribution of t07 is visualized as a word list (in two columns, from left to right) in the order of decreasing probability. The topic is named by a human expert. The other highly likely topics on this slide refer to organization theory and organizational learning.

2. Topic-by-document distributions are the basis for classifying documents in thematic search applications. Interestingly, LDA covers multilabel classification by construction, as classes are assigned to documents only up to posterior probabilities, and these distributions can be actually flat over several applicable classes for a given document.

Several successful applications of LDA have been published in Blei (2011, 2012).

In an yet unpublished work at our group at LMU, LDA was applied to scripts and slides from university lectures as presented on an internal online platform to LMU students of different faculties. We could confirm the essential capabilities of LDA to uncover scientific topics "hidden" in the documents. The specific benefit of the analysis from a university point of view is the perspective of a knowledge network comprising learning resources from multiple disciplines integrated by a common topic model viewpoint. It would not be feasible to construct such a network by handcrafted multi-domain ontologies.

Extended Topic Modeling

While LDA in its standard version is sufficient for finding topics in corpora of substantial size, some of the basic assumptions have been replaced either for more generic approaches or for specific modeling requirements. We begin with an overview:

1. The assumption of a fixed number of topics, in practice, leads to explorative approaches in using LDA. As an alternative, an infinite collection of topics from which document-topic distributions are sampled has been proposed.

2. The property of neutrality implicit in the Dirichlet prior both for topic-term and for document-topic distributions is questionable as neutrality prevents correlations between terms viz. topics to be adequately modeled. The correlated topic model (CTM) is an approach to account for these correlations.

3. As a combination of the preceding extensions (flexible number of topics, explicit topic correlations estimated by the model), recently, a new approach based on discrete infinite logistic normal (DILN) distributions has been proposed.

4. An important requirement in topic analysis is hierarchy—in most fields, topics have a hierarchical structure that a statistical analysis should uncover. This requirement has led to several approaches, among which hLDA, the original Pachinko allocation model (PAM), and the more recent hPAM.

The introduction of a flexible number of topics was found to make sense only if new documents can bring in new topics. So, by comparison to clustering methods allowing for an adaptable number of clusters, the specific challenge here is that there is no meaningful distinction of a "training sample" of documents that would provide all the structural information needed for topic analysis. Essentially, topic analysis should always be an open-loop process that allows for new topics coming in at any time. This can be seen from everyday experience, where unexpected political or scientific developments lead to new terms in our vocabulary and new topics (e.g., from recent years include millennium bug, swine flu, high-speed trading, etc.).

Infinitely Many (Possible) Topics

The requirement to account for possibly new topics entering the analysis with each additional document led researchers to extend the LDA approach in a much more general sense than one would need just to have an integrated approach for analyzing, say, a range of possible topics instead of a fixed number. If new topics must be allowed to become introduced with any new document, there is no choice but to allow for a principally infinite number of topics; the issue of infinity also occurs in transformational grammars for natural language (Chomsky, 2006). A countably infinite number of topics correspond, in statistical theory, to a stochastic process with a countable index set. Now, independent of topic modeling research, Bayesian statisticians have defined a stochastic process that exhibits the particular property that any finite partition of the sample space has a Dirichlet distribution (Ferguson, 1973). This so-called Dirichlet process is important as a major approach in nonparametric Bayesian statistics.

As a consequence, a Dirichlet process allows one to define a prior distribution over an infinite set of possible topics, from which a corpus of documents selects a finite subset, corresponding to some partition of the topic space. A technical problem with applying this approach is that several instances of such a process have zero probability of sharing a given topic. So our documents would be lost in a space of infinitely fine-grained topics, as we do not have a neighborhood structure on this space. Therefore, in practice, the Dirichlet process (DP) is used only to model the choice of topics within one document. Then, a generating process is defined on top of this document-specific process that describes how a multitude of documents in a corpus can share topics. This generating process turns out to be another DP. Therefore, the overall construction is named hierarchical Dirichlet process (HDP). A highly attractive feature of HDP is that it readily generalizes to arbitrary many levels. This can be used for modeling topics across several corpora.

It is outside the scope of the present paper to give a full account of HDP, in particular, regarding the learning algorithm (see Teh et al., 2006). However, as we did before for LDA, let us briefly work through the essential steps of document generation. We need extra notation here for the universe of all possible topic-term distributions. Recall that this is actually the universe of all possible topics. For a finite set of m topics, this universe corresponds to a simplex in $m + 1$ space. As the HDP approach can account for infinitely many topics, let us denote the corresponding universe by T.

It is also easier to understand HDP, if we first look at the implied topic modeling within a given document and then generalize to a hierarchical model. So, first, on the level of one document d_j, a DP can be used as follows:

1. On the corpus level, select a prior probability distribution G_0 on the set of topic-term distributions for a given vocabulary. This is usually a "flat" Dirichlet distribution with all parameters equal. Note that each topic-term distribution actually is a definition of a topic in the sense of Bayesian topic modeling.

2. For a given document d_j, sample G_{d_j} from G_0. The result is a distribution of topic-term distributions local to document d_j. Now we introduce a sequential scheme for introducing and reusing topics within d_j. For this, we need a document topic counter c_{d_j}, which initially equals zero. Later, this scheme will be used for inferring the topic distribution in d_j from term occurrence w_{t_i} in d_j. We also need an updatable version of G_{d_j}, g_n. For the nth term occurrence, starting with $n = 1$, $g_1 = G_{d_j}$, do:

   a. With probability $g_{n-1}(T)/(n + g_n - 1 (T))$, select an unused topic according to G_{d_j}. Increment c_{d_j} by 1.

   b. With probability $n/(n + g_{n-1}(T))$, select a topic that was already used, and set $g_n = g_{n-1} + \delta_{\varphi_{cd_j}}$, as explained below.

   c. Go to the next term occurrence.

3. For each term occurrence w_{t_i} in d_j, we sample a topic-term distribution φ_{cd_j} from a normalized version of g_n as constructed in the preceding step.

Note that, if $n = 1$, in step 2 alternative (a) applies with certainty. In the subroutine under step 2, we essentially generalize the fixed-size document-topic distribution per document in conventional LDA. Each of $\delta_{\varphi_{cd_j}}$, a so-called Dirac distribution, gives full probability mass to one out of infinitely many topic-term distributions φ_{cd_j}. Adding $\delta_{\varphi_{cd_j}}$ to g_{n-1} implies that g_n is not normalized for $n > 1$, and this is used to gradually decrease the chance of introducing additional topics as we work through a given document (in step 2(b)).

Second, to this per-document procedure, we now need to add steps for additional documents. It should be stressed that this is a challenge as the stochastic process represented by the sequence of the g_n, $n = 1,...$ is built from a countable sequence of atomic distributions $\delta_{\varphi_{cd_j}}$ which have common elements with probability equal to 0. This implies that without an extra mechanism, documents would never share topics (even if the analysis might identify topics with very similar distributions in several documents). The key to solving this problem is the introduction of a higher-level DP from which the *a priori* per-document topic distributions are sampled. This means that, while an infinite variety of such distributions is possible, with increasing number of documents a reuse of some distributions becomes more likely (as a reuse of topics becomes more likely when sampling repeatedly from the per-document DP). More formally, instead of sampling G_{d_j} from G_0, we take a higher-level DP (G, α_0) from which G_{d_j} is sampled (and then extended in the document generation process according to the description given above).

Simulations have shown that HDP-based topic modeling actually eliminates the need to find out adequate numbers of topics for LDA analyses by experience or examination of the perplexity plot. Another attractive feature of the HDP approach is that it can be extended to multiple corpora. This is particularly interesting if topics across different publication media are to be traced. Recently, a study on the temporal development of topics across multiple corpora has demonstrated the capabilities of this approach in view of the Big Data phenomenon (Zhang et al., 2010).

Correlated Topic Models

CTMs extend LDA by allowing for an explicit representation of topic correlations. Topic correlations are a valuable source of information as different corpora may exhibit different correlation patterns on similar topics. As an example, in the bioinformatics literature, classification and sequence analysis might be highly correlated, while in generic machine learning papers, sequence analysis might be one among several example topics and thus only mildly correlating with classification analysis. Another advantage of a correlation-based approach is that the resulting parameter estimates include correlations which can be interpreted as topic similarities and used for easier generation of tag clouds and navigation interfaces for topic-based end user search applications.

The Dirichlet distribution, since it uses per-topic counts for updating the prior on document-topic distributions, has no parameters for topic correlations. Therefore, a differently constructed prior needs to be used, which implies different learning and inferencing procedures. The most common approach used for CTM builds on a multivariate log-normal prior distribution which has mean vector and covariance matrix like a multivariate Gaussian (Blei and Lafferty, 2007).

Since a transformed multivariate Gaussian still has fixed dimensionality, a challenge to the CTM approach is to extend it to a potentially unlimited number of topics, much like HDP-topic models extend LDA. Recent research has just tackled this problem, by using the DILN approach (Paisley et al., 2012a).

Hierarchical Topic Modeling

Another extension/modification to probabilistic modeling based on LDA is hierarchical topic modeling. Basically, hierarchical topic modeling constructs a tree of topics with more generic topics closer to the root, and more detailed topics closer to the leaves. The challenge is to be able to account for flexible tree structure—the entire hierarchical structure should be inferred using Bayesian statistical inference.

As a side remark, we note that *hierarchical topic modeling* in the sense discussed in this subsection should not be confused with a hierarchical modeling approach. While hierarchical topic modeling constructs end-user visible topic hierarchies, a *hierarchical modeling* approach is concerned with a multilevel hierarchic generation process of documents. This can also be seen from the application of HDP analyses to multiple corpora.

In one approach (hLDA) (Blei et al., 2003a), hierarchies of topics are built for a fixed tree depth with variable tree structure. The topic composition of each document is modeled as a traversal of a possibly infinite branching structure up to the given depth limit. Using a fixed tree depth implies thus a fixed number of topics per document, where topics closer to the root are shared by more documents (all those sharing the particular path from the root to the given node representing one particular topic). All documents share the root node. Therefore, this node usually has a term distribution emphasizing highly common words in a corpus, for example, units of measure, names of institutions hosting document authors, etc.

A related approach is hPAM building on the Pachinko allocation model PAM. PAM was defined from the beginning to account for topic dependencies by a highly flexible structure which does not enforce a fixed hierarchy depth. The original version of PAM (Li and McCallum, 2006) infers a directed acyclic graph (DAG) of topic-like entities; however, only the leaf elements of this DAG are topic-term distributions. So, while PAM generates plausible graphs even for multihierarchical topic structures, the interpretation of nonleaf nodes from an end-user point of view is somewhat difficult. This difficulty has been addressed in an extended model hPAM (Mimno et al., 2007) that estimates topic-term distributions across the entire DAG.

Recently, the hierarchical modeling approach has been combined with hierarchical topic modeling in Paisley et al. (2012b). This paper reports simulations on a very large data set (over 1 million documents).

Practical Considerations

Several tools for building probabilistic topic models are available mainly as standalone code or tool boxes (e.g., for LDA, the original C code on the home page of David Blei, or TMT, the topic modeling toolbox available from U Stanford' NLP web pages), and packaged in libraries for the statistical analysis language/development environment R (Grün and Hornik,

2011). Another integrated modeling toolkit is Mallet (MAchine Learning for LanguagE Toolkit, available on the Computer Science Department home-page of University of Massachusetts).

Regarding LSA, given the fact that it builds on a standard technique from linear algebra, a dedicated tool mainly needs to provide efficient algorithms for processing SVD on sparse matrices. Moreover, it will usually provide utilities for document preprocessing. A commonly used library is the R LSA package (Wild, 2011) which integrates procedures for generating document-term matrices. This nicely integrates with other R tools for text mining, package tm (Feinerer, 2012).

Regarding the volume/velocity dimensions of Big Data, scalability of all topic modeling approaches needs further research. While progress has been reported for LSA for millions of documents and for DILN-extended LDA for over 200 K documents, neither the fast adaptability nor the best method for parameter sharing and updating given a high-speed inflow of documents are clear from the theory. There is also research needed on how to exploit Big-Data specific architectures like Hadoop or Stratosphere and related computational models in statistical inference with large data and parameter sets (Alexandrov et al., 2011).

Latent Factor-Based versus Probabilistic Topic Models

The different approaches underlying LSI/LSA and LDA plus its extensions have been discussed in several perspectives.

A key advantage of LDA over LSA is the two-level model of a text distinguishing a topic mixture layer from a word selection layer. This allows for the same terms appearing with different senses in different topics (e.g., the term "deposit" may occur in the word distribution of both a financial topic and an oil-drilling topic according to the two senses of the word). In LSA, terms as well as documents are represented in a spatial model as points. One space (corresponding to the U matrix) represents topic-like structures as linear combinations of term weights derived from the orthogonalization implicit in SVD. The other space (corresponding to the V^T matrix) represents documents in a low-dimensional orthogonal space computed again from the orthogonalization in SVD. However, these spaces do not share dimensions, and therefore the topics characterizing a document can only be inferred by inspecting the position of the document's term vector in the U-space.

In LDA, on the contrary, the topic mixture composing a document from the generative perspective is an explicit result of the Bayesian learning process.

From the perspective of text analysis in the humanities and literary sciences, there are also advantages of LSA. This is due to the fact that in these sciences, the overall objective is not so much classification of additional texts using the posterior distributions computed by LDA Bayesian parameter learning. Rather, research on inherent conceptual structures in historical corpora can base analyses on document spaces, for example, for following historical trends, while analyses on the term spaces can uncover shifts in terminology. A separation between topic shift and terminology shift is impossible in LDA, and thus, LDA cannot even identify topics across several analyses—which is readily possible with LSA.

Knowledge Life Cycles

In order to examine the impact of unstructured information processing on knowledge management, we introduce the key concepts of a specific approach to knowledge management by Firestone (2003). While many approaches are available, Firestone's work is most closely related to enterprise architecture and enterprise information systems infrastructure. According to this approach, knowledge management is management of enterprise knowledge life cycles. These knowledge life cycles are composed of two essential phases, namely knowledge production and knowledge dissemination. An overview of Firestone's model according to the Object Management Groupy system modeling language (Object Management Group, 2006) is given in Figure 17.2.

Knowledge production comprises all activities related to knowledge generation on an individual, team, or organizational scale. Knowledge production is a problem-solving activity that implies learning or information acquisition activities. Information acquisition consists of integrating information from various sources and applying the results of this research to a specific problem at hand in the daily work of a knowledge worker. A convenient example

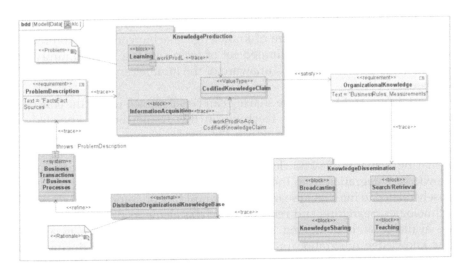

FIGURE 17.2
A SysML model of enterprise knowledge life cycles. For details, see text.

of information acquisition is the application of business intelligence methods to data of relevance to the problem to be solved, for example, market basket data for a decision prioritization problem related to product lifecycle management. Learning, in this framework, is a procedure for generating and testing hypotheses relevant to the problem to be solved. Learning comprises dedicated empirical and even foundational research. Knowledge production by learning is closely related to innovation.

The key task of knowledge production in the overall knowledge life cycle is producing codified knowledge claims. A knowledge claim is not just a hypothesis, whereas it is a specific approach consisting of elements of knowledge supposed to solve the problem that kicked off a particular knowledge lifecycle instance. As an example of a knowledge claim resulting from business intelligence, take a set of association rules derived from mining suitable customer data that suggest a way to address emerging demands with a new product. Codified knowledge claims are passed to a validation process that leads either to the adoption or to the rejection of the claim. An adoption is not merely a confirmation of a hypothesis, but rather means that the knowledge produced is going to be activated in the business transaction space of the organization in question. It means that the validated knowledge claim is now a knowledge asset or part of the organization's intellectual capital.

Activation of a knowledge asset presumes a set of processes that allows one to integrate the related knowledge elements into specific business activities across an organization. These processes are referred to by Firestone as knowledge integration. Knowledge integration comprises all activities related to maintaining and fostering the usage of knowledge that a company or an organization has acquired through knowledge production.

Joseph Firestone distinguishes four key processes of knowledge integration, namely broadcasting, searching or retrieving, teaching, and knowledge sharing. The distinctive feature of knowledge sharing compared to broadcasting is that it addresses a limited set of recipients (e.g., a community of practice), while broadcasting is unaware of the number and composition of recipients.

Broadcasting and knowledge sharing can be subsumed under the concept of knowledge dissemination. Teaching, in this framework, is knowledge sharing with a control loop in which the degree of success of knowledge transfer is monitored and used for adapting the content and even the method of sharing elements of a knowledge domain. Searching and retrieving cover knowledge integration from the demand point of view. These processes are closely related to intelligent search engines building on information retrieval technologies. Searching and retrieving address elements of knowledge that are available without having been supplied without reference to a specific knowledge integration process, for example, government documents, reports, and public domain research reports. Searching and retrieving are also keys to leveraging knowledge captured in organizational document and content repositories.

All knowledge integration activities are focused on, but not confined to the knowledge elements from validated knowledge claims. As an example, consider the adoption of a new go-to market strategy for a product as a result of a knowledge production process. Implementing the new strategy usually affects several existing processes, might require adaptations of roles, etc. The knowledge needed for these implementation specifics is accessed and combined with the newly validated knowledge in knowledge integration.

It should be noted that since the rapid increase of social web functionalities including massive content posting and social bookmarking, knowledge broadcasting has become a widespread everyday activity, even if sometimes on a rather superficial level, contrary to the knowledge management discussions in the 1990s that focused on incentives for fostering knowledge sharing within companies. In addition, Wikipedia and related information resources have considerably reshaped the teaching and the searching/retrieving processes related to knowledge integration. Nevertheless, all four knowledge integration subprocesses take a specific shape when used in a business context of problem solving in the knowledge life cycle. Quality, effectiveness, and reliability of these processes are keys, while the social web realizations of these processes are characterized by spontaneity and large degrees of error tolerance.

Impact of Unstructured Information Processing on Knowledge Management

How can unstructured information processing contribute to knowledge life-cycle processes and their specific implementations?

Considering first the essential phase of the knowledge life cycle, knowledge production, contributions to information acquisition, and even learning processes are possible by either information extraction on the relational level or text clustering in order to identify topics or subjects of interest and estimating their proximity and interrelationships. Information extraction on the relational level is equivalent to formulating meaningful sentences in a given domain related to a specific problem. From a logical point of view, these sentences are individual statements (e.g., "IBM has developed a new software for credit card fraud detection"). Collections of individual statements support accumulation of evidence in favor or against a given hypothesis. Text clustering is a means of identifying topics of interest for knowledge claims. Proximity relationships as revealed by clustering can help formulating specific hypotheses relevant to the knowledge lifecycle instance at hand. As an example, consider the problem to prevent high losses due to system failures at an IT-managed operations provider. Typically, the provider has document collections describing system failures and customer claims data. Through clustering, it is possible to derive significant groupings of system log entries and failure descriptions, on the one hand, and significant groupings of customer claims, on the other hand. Through data merging, it is further possible to use the results from both cluster analyses to derive plausible causation hypotheses for a customer claim given a system failure. A related method of knowledge production has been used in the EU MUSING project for the IT operational risk analysis in the private customers division of a major Italian financial services provider.

Regarding the second essential phase of the knowledge life cycle, knowledge integration, the assignment of unstructured information to distinct information categories by text classification or entity recognition are major supporting technologies for searching and retrieving processes since they allow the integration of much more comprehensive sets of knowledge resources than it would be possible by fixed index terms and predefined document categories. In fact, the first generation of knowledge document repositories in the 1990s was entirely based on author or editor provided document classification terms and search terms under which important facets of documents often went unnoticed. This led to the often described underutilization of such repositories and, finally, to their abandonment in favor of more dynamic socially supported Wikis, etc.

Processing unstructured information is becoming of key importance to further knowledge integration processes as distinguished by Firestone. For teaching, the most promising aspects of applications of unstructured information processing lie in the capabilities of content syndication. Content syndication summarizes the capability to dynamically reorganize textual material with respect to the needs of specific interests of specific user communities or enterprise teams. Finally, with respect to knowledge dissemination, most of the functionalities as supplied by unstructured information processing can provide significant enhancements to today's knowledge-sharing facilities. As an example, in recent years, keyword spotting has become part of many blogsphere platforms, often visualized by word clouds (e.g., see worldle.net). Sophisticated algorithms for information extraction will allow to combine information from different sources in a still more efficient way for information consumers and later information producers.

Enterprise Monitoring: A Case Study

In this part, we describe a pilot application exploiting information extraction from web pages to improve knowledge life cycles for credit information providers and other information service providers regarding business relevant information about companies.

Credit information providers are offering a large variety of services that focus on the sector of company information, such as international company profiles, annual accounts/balance sheets, address data, data of commercial register, etc. The readiness to take a chance and thus fast decision-making are important qualities for successful companies in the fast-moving world of the twenty-first century. Make the right decision and take advantage of Creditreform's reliable business and consumer information. The Creditreform company profiles provide customers with general business information. These profiles help customers to get a short and inexpensive overview of a companies' situation and to add or update the data stored in the own database.

With a monitoring service, customers can even watch single customers or complete customer portfolios in order to notice changes in the address, the financial or corporate structure of a business partners as early as possible.

Updates of information about a company are necessary in the case of change events, which are detected from analyzing the content of web pages or news articles, as soon as a company under monitoring appears in current data sources registered to the application. The underlying events are usually caused by a change of business information, for example, a change in capital, business rating, or address. The list of possible causes that trigger change events has been classified as "a trigger to be monitored by a research analyst."

The monitoring service is based on a MUSING information extraction service that builds the monitoring information by applying natural language processing to the unstructured information resources (web pages, etc.). The overall information flow of the pilot application is depicted in Figure 17.3.

The Creditreform enterprise monitoring service allows users to take into account huge amounts of public data which will speed up the workflow to get the estimation of a company's correct address or the financial situation they can rely on. The interest of customers aims at a high level of transparency of company information and at the collection of details supporting the evaluation of the business conduct of a company.

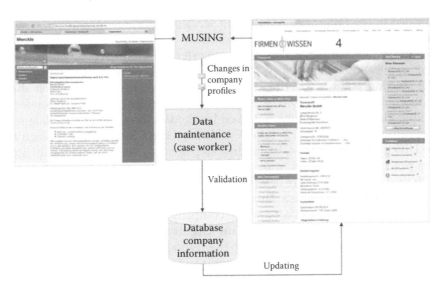

FIGURE 17.3
Enterprise monitoring: overview of the information flow.

The goal of this innovative application is the development of a versatile information extraction service, which is able to aggregate enterprise information from a variety of data sources and is capable of converting it into a predefined format for further processing. Converting the extracted data into a predefined data format is supposed to facilitate a comfortable integration into existing databases of Creditreform in order to have updated information of high quality. Therefore, a final manual checking of the information extracted will be performed by human experts before committing the data to the Creditreform Firmenwissen database.

The application combines thus information extraction and monitoring services and provides the basis for an innovative data maintenance service, which shows the high potential of market relevance in other sectors, for example, address and competitors monitoring.

The use case will start with a researcher of a local branch of Creditreform who needs to update the available information on a company in the central database. Each company information is monitored for a period of time—updates are registered as monitoring events (triggered by a change of business information, e.g., a change in personal, capital or address). These triggers of events have been classified as "reasons to forward a supplement to previously provided information."

In the case of changes of a company website, notifications by e-mail are delivered to the Creditreform analysts and business research experts.

The notifications also identify outdated data in the internal company information database. These alerts facilitate more efficient and time-saving enquiries with respect to company information, for Creditreform's information researchers. Furthermore, they will decide whether the information attached in the Enterprise Monitoring service is of value for customers and should be inserted in the central database.

In the sequel, we explain the processing steps of the enterprise monitoring pilot application as developed in the EU MUSING project (see Figure 17.4). The starting point is a set of URLs of the company websites, which shall be monitored by the service. Every URL is attributed with a Creditreform unique identifier (UID) which is used by Creditreform to identify data sets of specific companies and to encode additional meta-information. Assigning the UID to each company URL is a first step towards simplifying the integration process. Each extract from a company website can easily be attributed with the UID and therefore be easily associated with the corresponding company profile in the database. This is crucial, since in the further process, comparisons between the extract and the company profile need to be conducted in regular intervals. Furthermore, the UID is important for the automatic distribution of notifications/alerts to the responsible Creditreform branch.

The IE tool analyzes the links on company websites, which can easily be identified by the html tags (⟨a href = "URL"⟩description⟨/a⟩). The links, which include strings that indicate they are directed at an imprint page, are then being selected by the IE tool. The administrator will be informed, in the case

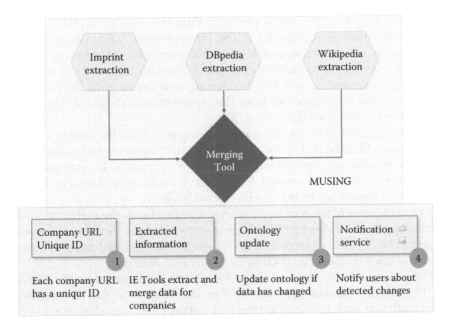

FIGURE 17.4
Enterprise monitoring pilot in MUSING: application workflow.

the imprint page could not be found, so that the imprint URL can be inserted manually if necessary.

After an imprint page has been identified, the extraction process can be executed. The extracted information is aligned with the company profiles by directly mapping it to the FirmenWissen—XML schema. Subsequently, the XML document will be time-stamped automatically in order to keep the time of the extraction stored for later comparisons. This value is important for the monitoring component, because a new extract will always be compared with the last extract to determine whether the provided company information was altered and needs to be analyzed or no further processing is necessary.

There is the eventuality of extracting ballast information while processing the imprint data. Web design agencies often include their contact information on sites they developed for an enterprise. The system must be able to differentiate between that information and the information of the enterprise. By operating on segregated text segments, the IE System is able to avoid these kinds of problems. The system is mainly based on handwritten extraction rules for recognizing patterns. Subsequent to applying the extraction rules, the HTML code of an imprint page is converted into an intermediate format called "WebText." The extraction rules then work with text items, whereby confusions can be minimized. Currently, the manually crafted extraction patterns are being analyzed and utilized to advance in the development of the machine-learning-based IE System.

The link between the online portal of FirmenWissen enterprise profiles and the monitoring component is the FirmenWissen XML Gateway. The comparisons of enterprise profiles and the extracted information, which need to be conducted to identify changes in company information, are realized by the monitoring tool. The monitoring component pulls the company profiles via the XML gateway from the FirmenWissen database. The selection process is based on the given UID.

The normalized extracts can then be compared with the corresponding company profile. The IE Tool extracts information regularly and passes them on to the monitoring component. If the information on the imprint page has changed, an alert will be created. In this case, a monitoring alert is sent to the responsible researcher in the Creditreform Office.

As quality assurance is of high value to Creditreform, the extracted information needs to be checked by a human expert. Information on an imprint page can be obsolete or incorrect, even though it is classified as an administrative offence in countries such as Germany and Austria.

The use case has a large variety of deployment potential as the impact of the enterprise monitoring service may characterize so far. The value of information is high if relevant, true and reliable, and provides impetus for progress in key areas.

The value added of this use case is in enhancing the quality of knowledge work in terms of production efficiency, improvement of performance, and the value of current products and services by allowing the information provider to focus human efforts on more demanding analysis and development phases and generating growth by unearthing revenue opportunities.

A series of validation studies have been carried out on successive versions of a pilot application, implementing the enterprise monitoring service in the framework of the MUSING project. The last validation study (2010) could be performed in direct cooperation with six selected Creditreform branch offices. In the validation phase, 1605 e-mails were generated on the basis of 925 company websites. The functionality of the currently being developed enterprise monitoring service has been validated with regard to the following major items:

- What is the quality of the results delivered by the prototype? This includes questions about the usefulness, completeness, and proper allocation of the extracted information.
- Can the potential time and cost savings as well as the expected improvements in quality, actuality, and degree of filling by using such a monitoring service be estimated?
- Another focus was on the scalability of the prototype at this status.

As a result out of validation, it came out that 84% of the delivered information by the enterprise monitoring application has been useful or partly

useful. There was no problem with the scalability of the service. All valida-
tors confirmed the usefulness of this service as there will be a growing need
for optimized continuous knowledge working instruments on a daily basis.
The classical work of a knowledge worker will change in the upcoming
years. Information must be acquired and processed in a short and efficient
way. However, the goal should be to create automated data synchronization
as a service. The reasons are obvious for that: The monitoring of the whole
or parts of the data is carried out using too much time and person load.
A timely forwarding supporting the current work process would be more
effective. If the application can be effectively adjusted to this requirement,
then this would be a major benefit.

An improvement of the quality of the knowledge or research worker is
achieved by this application. The processing of the internet information base
is part of the daily work. The researcher in the local office receives valuable
input and advice and has not to "pick in the fog." The enterprise monitoring
is an innovative instrument toward intelligent engineering of information.

These results also indicated that the key improvement from knowledge
workers' point of view is not time saving, but rather quality enhancement in
terms of reliability and timeliness of information updates about enterprises.

The value added is in enhancing the quality of reports and reliable
addresses and therefore protecting enterprises from unforeseen risk and
ensuring revenue opportunities.

Conclusion

In the context of knowledge-driven business information gathering, processing, and scoring, MUSING* supports the development in this domain aiming
at enhancing the use of semantic technologies in specific industrial sectors.
With the aid of the semantic technology, information providers or knowledge-driven companies can generate added value through implementation
of business intelligence software. On the other hand, it is clear that knowledge-driven products often purchased based on pressure for modernization
or to higher expectations of the management.

Knowledge life cycles are, in most cases, depending on semi- or unstructured information. From production log sheets that are annotated manually
even in completely automated car manufacturing plants over analyst opinions to customer satisfaction reports—textual information that can initiate
or support knowledge life cycles is abundant. As is well confirmed, the relative amount of unstructured over structured information is increasing fast.
In a standard presentation of its InfoSphere business intelligence suite, IBM

---

* MUlti-industry, Semantic-based next-generation business INtelliGence.

reports an expected four times faster increase in unstructured over structured information in the forthcoming decade (2010 onwards). Many of the texts being produced are not aimed at supporting a given knowledge life cycle; they come from different business contexts. In order to exploit the information residing in these sources, information retrieval and extraction methods are of prime importance.

As our case study has shown, analysis of semistructured (web pages) and unstructured (texts) information for tracing entity descriptions and registering their changes over time is a feasible application of semantic technology. These registered changes can support a knowledge production life cycle quite directly since they amount to codified knowledge claims about an enterprise. They can also deliver back-up arguments for the assessment, rating, or valuation of a company.

On the knowledge integration side, the production of structured information by information extraction methods offers tangible benefits especially for knowledge broadcasting—distributing knowledge to subscribers participating potentially in many different knowledge-related activities. Combined with content syndication mechanisms like RSS or specific publish/subscribe solutions, this step in our case study has enabled a deployment of a research prototype to the desks of many knowledge workers and led to high usability ratings.

The authors of the present paper expect the integration of natural language-processing technologies, notably information extraction, with knowledge lifecycle optimization and knowledge management to continue and to enable a new generation of broadly usable organizational knowledge management support tools.

Acknowledgments

The sections on knowledge life cycles and on enterprise monitoring in the present work have been supported by the European Commission under the umbrella of the MUSING (multi-industry semantics based next generation business intelligence) project, contract number 027097, 2006–2010. The authors wish to thank the editor of the present volume for his continued support.

References

Alexandrov, A., Ewen, S., Heimel, M., Hueske, F., Kao, O., Markl, V., ..., Warneke, D. 2011. MapReduce and PACT—Comparing Data Parallel Programming Models. *Proceedings of the 14th Conference on Database Systems for Business, Technology, and Web (BTW)* (pp. 25–44). Kaiserslautern, Germany: GI.

Apache UIMA Development Community. 2008a. UIMA Overview and SDK Setup (A. S. Foundation, Trans.) (Version 2.2.2 ed.): International Business Machines.

Apache UIMA Development Community. 2008b. UIMA References (A. S. Foundation, Trans.) (Version 2.2.2 ed.): International Business Machines.

Blei, D. M. 2011. *Introduction to Probabilistic Topic Models*. Princeton: Princeton University.

Blei, D. M. 2012. Probabilistic Topic Models. *Communications of the ACM*, 55(4), 77–84.

Blei, D. M. and Lafferty, J. D. 2007. A correlated topic model of Science. *Annals of Applied Statistics*, 1(1), 17–35.

Blei, D. M., Griffiths, T., Jordan, M., and Tenenbaum, J. 2003a. Hierarchical topic models and the nested Chinese restaurant process, *Presented at the Neural Information Processing Systems (NIPS) 2003*, Vancouver, Canada.

Blei, D. M., Ng, A. Y., and Jordan, M. I. 2003b. Latent Dirichlet allocation. *Journal of Machine Learning Research*, 3, 993–1022.

Bradford, R. B. 2011. Implementation techniques for large-scale latent semantic indexing applications. *Proceedings of the 20th ACM International Conference on Information and Knowledge Management* (pp. 339–344). Glasgow, Scotland, UK: ACM.

Bunescu, R. and Mooney, R. 2007. Statistical relational learning for natural language information extraction. In L. Getoor and B. Taskar (Eds.), *Introduction to Statistical Relational Learning* (535-552), Cambridge, MA: MIT Press.

Chomsky, N. 2006. *Language and Mind*, 3rd ed. Cambridge: Cambridge University Press.

Cunningham, H., Maynard, D., Bontcheva, K., Tablan, V., Aswani, N., Roberts, I., Gorrell, G. et al. 2008. *Developing Language Processing Components with GATE (General Architecture for Text Engineering) Version 5—A User Guide*. Sheffield: University of Sheffield.

Fan, J., Kalyanpur, A., Gondek, D. C., and Ferrucci, D. A. 2012. Automatic knowledge extraction from documents. *IBM Journal of Research and Development*, 56(3.4), 5:1–5:10.

Feinerer, I. An introduction to text mining in R. R News, 8(2):19–22, October 2008. R News, now R Journal, is online only.

Ferguson, T. 1973. A Bayesian analysis of some nonparametric problems. *The Annals of Statistics*, 1(2), 209–230.

Firestone, J. M. 2003. *Enterprise Information Portals and Knowledge Management*. Amsterdam, Boston: Butterworth Heinemann.

Grcar, M., Podpecan, V., Jursic, M., and Lavrac, N. 2010. Efficient visualization of document streams. *Lecture Notes in Computer Science*, vol. 6332, 174–188. Berlin: Springer.

Grcar, M., Kralj, P., Smailovic, J., and Rutar, S. 2012. Interactive visualization of textual streams In F. E. p. n. 257928 (Ed.), *Large Scale Information Extraction and Integration Infrastructure for Supporting Financial Decision Making*.

Grün, B. and Hornik, K . 2011. Topicmodels: An R package for fitting topic models. *Journal of Statistical Software*, 40(13), 1–30.

Gsell, M., Razimski, M., Häusser, T., Gredel, L., and Grcar, M. 2012. Specification of the information-integration model. In FIRST EU project no. 257928 (Ed.), *Large Scale Information Extraction and Integration Infrastructure for Supporting Financial Decision Making*. First EU project no. 257928. http://project-first.eu/

Hastie, T., Tibshirani, R., and Friedman, J. 2009. *The Elements of Statistical Learning*. Berlin: Springer.

Heinrich, G. 2008. *Parameter Estimation for Text Analysis*. Leipzig: University of Leipzig.

Jelinek, F. 1998. *Statistical Methods for Speech Recognition*. Cambridge, MA: MIT Press.

Kohonen, T., Kaski, S., Lagus, C., Salojärvi, J., Honkela, J., Paatero, V., and Saarela, A. 2000. Self organization of a massive document collection. *IEEE Transactions on Neural Networks, 11*(3), 574–585. doi: 10.1109/72.846729.

Lally, A., Prager, J. M., McCord, M. C., Boguraev, B. K., Patwardhan, S., Fan, J., Fodor, P., and Chu-Carroll, J. 2012. Question analysis: How Watson reads a clue. *IBM Journal of Research and Development, 56*(3.4), 2:1–2:14.

Landauer, T. K. and Dumais, S. T. 1997. A solution to Plato's problem: The latent semantic analysis theory of acquisition, induction, and representation of knowledge. *Psychological Review, 104*, 211–240.

Li, W. and McCallum, A. 2006. Pachinko allocation: DAG-structured mixture models of topic correlations *ICML*.

Manning, C. D., Raghavan, P., and Schu¨tze, H. 2009. *An Introduction to Information Retrieval*. Retrieved from http://www.informationretrieval.org/.

McCord, M. C., Murdock, J. W., and Boguraev, B. K. 2012. Deep parsing in Watson. *IBM Journal of Research and Development, 56*(3.4), 3:1–3:15.

Mimno, D., Li, W., and McCallum, A. 2007. Mixtures of hierarchical topics with Pachinko allocation. *ICML*.

Motik, B., Patel-Schneider, P., and Horrocks, I. 2006. OWL 1.1 Web Ontology Language Structural Specification and Functional-Style Syntax.

Object Management Group. 2006. OMG Systems Modeling Language (OMG SysML) Specification (Vol. ptc/06-05-04): Object Management Group.

Paisley, J., Wang, C., and Blei, D. M. 2012a. The Discrete Infinite Logistic Normal Distribution. arxiv.org.

Paisley, J., Wang, C., Blei, D. M., and Jordan, M. I. 2012b. Nested Hierarchical Dirichlet Processes. arxiv.org.

Pepper, S. 2006. *The TAO of Topic Maps—Finding the Way in the Age of Infoglut*. Oslo: Ontopia.

Spies, M. 2013. Knowledge discovery from constrained relational data—A tutorial on Markov logic networks. In E. Zimanyi and M.-A. Aufaure (Eds.), *Business Intelligence Second European Summer School, eBISS 2102*. Berlin: Springer.

Steyvers, M. and Griffiths, T. 2006. Probabilistic topic models. In T. Landauer, D. S. McNamara, S. Dennis, and W. Kintsch, (Eds.), *Latent Semantic Analysis: A Road to Meaning*, Hillsdale, NJ: Laurence Erlbaum, 1–15.

Teh, Y. W., Jordan, M. I., Beal, M. J., and Blei, D. M. 2006. Hierarchical Dirichlet processes. *Journal of the American Statistical Association, 101*(476), 1566–1581.

Toutanova, K., Klein, D., Manning, C. D., and Singer, Y. 2003. Feature-rich part-of-speech tagging with a cyclic dependency network. *Paper presented at the Proceedings of the 2003 Conference of the North American Chapter of the Association for Computational Linguistics on Human Language Technology - Volume 1*, Edmonton, Canada.

Trautmann, D. and Suleiman, F. 2012. Topic Analyse auf Grundlage des LDA–Modells. In M. Spies (Ed.), *Knowledge Management Working Papers*. Munich: LMU—University of Munich.

Wang, C., Kalyanpur, A., Fan, J., Boguraev, B. K., and Gondek, D. C. 2012. Relation extraction and scoring in DeepQA. *IBM Journal of Research and Development, 56*(3.4), 9:1–9:12.

Wild, F. 2011. *Latent Semantic Analysis—Package lsa*. CRAN Repository.

WordNet: An Electronic Lexical Database. 1998. Cambridge, MA: MIT Press.

Zhang, J., Song, Y., Zhang, C., and Liu, S. 2010. Evolutionary hierarchical Dirichlet processes for multiple correlated time-varying corpora, Paper presented at the KDD, July 25–28, 2010, Washington, DC.

Zikopoulos, P. C., deRoos, D., Parasuraman, K., Deutsch, T., Corrigan, D., and Giles, J. 2013. *Harness the Power of Big Data: The IBM Big Data Platform*. New York: McGraw-Hill.

Index

T - #0225 - 101024 - C0 - 234/156/30 [32] - CB - 9781466578371 - Gloss Lamination